Shakespeare and Montaigne

In memory of David Bevington, with gratitude

Shakespeare and Montaigne

Edited by Lars Engle, Patrick Gray
and William M. Hamlin

EDINBURGH
University Press

Edinburgh University Press is one of the leading university presses in the UK. We publish academic books and journals in our selected subject areas across the humanities and social sciences, combining cutting-edge scholarship with high editorial and production values to produce academic works of lasting importance. For more information visit our website: edinburghuniversitypress.com

Edinburgh University Press Ltd
The Tun – Holyrood Road, 12(2f) Jackson's Entry, Edinburgh EH8 8PJ

First published in hardback by Edinburgh University Press 2022

Typeset in 11/13 Adobe Sabon by
IDSUK (DataConnection) Ltd, and
printed and bound by CPI Group (UK) Ltd, Croydon, CR0 4YY

A CIP record for this book is available from the British Library

ISBN 978 1 4744 5823 8 (hardback)
ISBN 978 1 4744 5824 5 (paperback)
ISBN 978 1 4744 5825 2 (webready PDF)
ISBN 978 1 4744 5826 9 (epub)

Contents

Acknowledgements   vii

Notes on Contributors   x

Preface: Reading Montaigne by *Colin Burrow*   xv

Introduction: Shakespeare and Montaigne:
A Critical History   1
William M. Hamlin

Introduction: Shakespeare and Montaigne as
Thought-Experiment   28
Lars Engle

1. Of Birds and Bees: Montaigne, Shakespeare and
   the Rhetoric of Imitation   59
   N. Amos Rothschild

2. The Nature of Presence: Facing Violence in Montaigne
   and Shakespeare   78
   Anita Gilman Sherman

3. Narcissism, Epochal Change and 'Public Necessity' in
   Richard II and 'Of Custom, and Not Easily Changing
   an Accepted Law'   90
   William McKenzie

4. Shakespeare, Montaigne and Ricœur: Identity as Narrative   105
   Zorica Bečanović-Nikolić

5. Genre and Gender in Montaigne and Shakespeare   123
   David Schalkwyk

6. Shakespeare, Montaigne and Moral Luck   140
   Maria Devlin McNair

7. Cavell's Tragic Scepticism and the Comedy of the Cuckold:
   Othello and Montaigne Revisited   166
   Cassie M. Miura

8. Feeling Indifference: Flaying Narratives in Montaigne
    and Shakespeare   180
    Alison Calhoun

9. On Belief in Montaigne and Shakespeare   198
    William M. Hamlin

10. Making Sense of 'To be or not to be'   216
    Richard Dillane

11. 'The web of our life is of a mingled yarn': Mixed Worlds
    and Kinds in Montaigne's 'We Taste Nothing Purely' and
    Shakespeare's *All's Well that Ends Well*   233
    Peter G. Platt

12. Radical Neo-Paganism: The Transmission of Discontinuous
    Identity from Plutarch to Montaigne to Shakespeare's
    Antony and Cleopatra   246
    Daniel Vitkus

13. Montaigne, Shakespeare and the Metamorphosis of
    Comedy and Tragedy   263
    Richard Hillman

14. Montaigne's *Essais*, Shakespeare's Trials and Other
    Experiments of Moment   282
    Richard Scholar

15. Montaigne's Shakespeare: *The Tempest* as Test-case   296
    Lars Engle

16. Falstaff's Party: Shakespeare, Montaigne and Their
    Liberal Censors   326
    Patrick Gray

    Afterword: A Philosophical Shakespeare or a
    Dramatic Montaigne?   374
    George Hoffmann

    Afterword: A Philosophical Montaigne and a
    Dramatic Shakespeare?   384
    Katharine Eisaman Maus

Bibliography   392
Index   435

Acknowledgements

Many people have helped to inspire, assemble and refine this collection of essays. Most immediately, the editors would like to thank the contributors for their hard work and compelling insights. We would also like to thank the Commissioning Editor for Literary Studies at Edinburgh University Press, Michelle Houston, for her support, encouragement and good cheer throughout.

Many of the essays published here had their start as lectures, talks and seminar papers: we would like to thank in particular those who participated in the panel 'Scientific and Philosophical Thought in Stuart England: The Influence of Montaigne's *Essays*' at the 61st Annual Meeting of the Renaissance Society of America (RSA) in Berlin, the international conference *Montaigne in Early Modern England and Scotland* at Durham University, and the seminar *Shakespeare and Montaigne* at the 44th Annual Meeting of the Shakespeare Association of America (SAA) in New Orleans. Special thanks go to the Institute of Medieval and Early Modern Studies (IMEMS) at Durham, as well as John O'Brien, Professor Emeritus of French at Durham and Director of the Institute at the time, who served as tutelary genius, for supporting the panel at the RSA and the conference at Durham, in keeping with a research strand at IMEMS, *French Books and Their European Readers, 1500–1700*, sponsored by Durham alumna Joanna Barker. Together with John O'Brien, and in addition to the contributors here, the editors are grateful to several other eminent scholars whose work has informed this collection and who have served as sounding boards for our thoughts on Shakespeare and Montaigne: Warren Boutcher, Philippe Desan, Peter Holbrook and Richard Strier.

Lars Engle would like to thank the members of the English Department of the University of Tulsa for collegial support and a sabbatical leave, the T. U. Research Office for a research grant, organisers and audiences at many conferences and lectures for invitations, responses and questions, and David Bevington, Tom Bishop, Colin Burrow,

Bill Carroll, Tony Dawson, Philippe Desan, Heather Dubrow, Peter Holbrook, Hugh Grady, Holly Laird, Julia Reinhard Lupton, Katharine Maus, Bridget Murnaghan, Lena Orlin, Eric Rasmussen, Bruce Smith, Bob Spoo, Richard Strier, Gordon Turnbull and Paul Yachnin for scholarly encouragement and friendship, often over the *longue durée*. Special thanks to Grady, Laird and Strier (as well as my fellow editors) for detailed commentary on my contributions to this volume.

Patrick Gray would like to thank Rob Carson, Jessica Chiba, John Cox, Derek Dunne, Indira Ghose, Julia Reinhard Lupton, Maria Devlin McNair, John O'Brien, Neema Parvini, Peter Platt and Vidyan Ravinthiran for their friendship, sage advice and good humour over the past several years this collection has been in the making, as well as my colleagues in medieval and early modern studies at Durham. Particular thanks go to the students at Durham who helped me prepare the collection for the press: Orlagh Davies, Fernando Martínez-Periset and Anna-Rose Shack. Thinking back to my own student days, I am especially grateful to Jessica Wolfe, whose undergraduate seminar in Renaissance literature at the University of North Carolina at Chapel Hill introduced me to Montaigne, and who supervised my naive, rough-hewn but enthusiastic senior thesis on Shakespeare and Montaigne. Her erudition, grace, generosity and good sense continue to prove an inspiration. I am also very grateful to friends and interlocutors Ewan Fernie, Peter Holbrook and Jeff Wilson, to whose work I am deeply indebted, even if at times in dissent. As the reader may discover from 'Falstaff's Party', I play the Dover Wilson here to their A. C. Bradley (so to speak), and without enough time and space to do justice to the nuance, originality and scholarly rigour of their arguments. Their essays and books are invaluable and among the first that I would recommend to anyone interested in Shakespeare and ethics.

Will Hamlin extends warm thanks to Trevor Bond, Warren Boutcher, John Cox, Charles Frey, George Hoffmann, Theresa Jordan, Nick Kiessling, Peter Mack, Peter Platt, Donna Potts, Carol Siegel, Tim Steury and the late David Bevington for their encouragement and friendship over many years – not merely during but long before the creation of this book.

For their help seeing *Shakespeare and Montaigne* through to print, in addition to the commissioning editor, Michelle Houston, the editors would like to thank the Assistant Editor for Literary Studies for Edinburgh University Press, Susannah Butler; the two anonymous readers for the Press; the copyeditor, Robert Tuesley

Anderson; the production editors, James Dale and Fiona Conn; and the Covers Design and Production Executive, Caitlin Murphy. We are also grateful to the Fundació Gala-Salvador Dalí for granting us permission to use Dalí's illustration of Montaigne's essay 'Of Custom' as the basis for the cover, one of a series of fascinating illustrations Dalí prepared for a limited edition of a Montaigne's *Essays* published by Doubleday in New York in 1947, comprised of a selection of essays Dalí chose himself from Charles Cotton's 1685–86 English translation (p. 17). Patrick Gray would like to thank his former student at Durham, Fernando Martínez-Periset, for his help negotiating and securing these image rights, as well as Caitlin Murphy for the Press, Mercedes Aznar for the Fundació, and Peter Woronkowicz for the Design and Artists Copyright Society (DACS).

Notes on Contributors

Zorica Bečanović-Nikolić is Associate Professor of Comparative Literature at the University of Belgrade. She is the author of three monographs in Serbian, *U traganju za Šekspirom* [Looking for Shakespeare: An Introduction to Shakespeare's Life and Works] (2013); *Šekspir iza ogledala* [Shakespeare through the Looking Glass: The Conflict of Interpretations in the Reception of Shakespeare's History Plays in the Twentieth Century] (2007); and *Hermeneutika i poetika* [Hermeneutics and Poetics. Paul Ricoeur's Theory of Narrative] (1998), as well as essays in *La construcción estética de Europa*, ed. Victoria Cirlot and Tamara Đermanović (2014), and *Mémoire perdue, mémoire volée*, ed. Brigitte Gautier (2005).

Colin Burrow is Senior Research Fellow at All Souls College, Oxford, and Professor of English and Comparative Literature at the University of Oxford. He is the author of *Imitating Authors: Plato to Futurity* (2019), *Shakespeare and Classical Antiquity* (2013), *Edmund Spenser* (1996) and *Epic Romance: Homer to Milton* (1993), as well as editor of the poems of Ben Jonson (2012), *Metaphysical Poetry* (2006) and *Shakespeare: The Complete Sonnets and Poems* (2002).

Alison Calhoun is Associate Professor of French at Indiana University. Her research focuses on early modern drama, Renaissance philosophy, Montaigne and the history of emotions. In *Montaigne and the Lives of the Philosophers* (2014), she investigates the relationship between philosophy and life writing in Montaigne's *Essays*. In her current book project, *Technologies of the Passions on the French Baroque Stage*, she uses sources in early modern stage engineering to write theatre history back into debates about the human–machine boundary, artificial intelligence and the physiology of emotions.

Richard Dillane is an actor. He studied philosophy at Manchester and has worked in film, television and theatre in the UK and Australia, once playing Hamlet in a small Perth theatre. His uncomfortable failure to understand 'To be' on that occasion – because, of course, an actor must not only mean what he says but seem to be making it up – caused him to think more about it. He was a Visiting Fellow at Sussex University 2014–17.

Lars Engle, Chapman Professor of English at the University of Tulsa, is the author of *Shakespearean Pragmatism* (1993), co-author of *Studying Shakespeare's Contemporaries* (2013) and an editor of *English Renaissance Drama: A Norton Anthology* (2002). He also teaches at the Bread Loaf School of English.

Patrick Gray is Associate Professor of English Studies and Director of Liberal Arts at Durham University. He is the author of *Shakespeare and the Fall of the Roman Republic: Selfhood, Stoicism, and Civil War* (2019), editor of *Shakespeare and the Ethics of War* (2019) and co-editor of *Shakespeare and Renaissance Ethics* (2014). His essays have appeared in *Textual Practice, Shakespeare Survey, Shakespeare Jahrbuch, Skenè, Comparative Drama* and *The Journal of Medieval and Early Modern Studies.*

William M. Hamlin holds the Bornander Distinguished Professorship in the Honors College at Washington State University. He is the author of three monographs, including *Montaigne's English Journey* (2013) and *Tragedy and Scepticism in Shakespeare's England* (2005), and he has been the recipient of research fellowships from the J. S. Guggenheim Foundation, the National Endowment for the Humanities and the British Academy. His most recent book is *Montaigne: A Very Short Introduction* (2020).

Richard Hillman is Professor Emeritus in the Université de Tours (Centre d'Études Supérieures de la Renaissance). His monographs include four books focusing on links between early modern English theatre and France, most recently *The Shakespearean Comic and Tragicomic: French Inflections* (2020). He has also translated and edited a number of early modern French plays, including, recently, Jean Galaut, *Phalante* (c. 1598) and André Mareschal, *The Shepherds' Court* (1638), in *Sidney's Arcadia on the French Stage: Two Renaissance Adaptations* (2018).

George Hoffmann is Professor of French at the University of Michigan. He has published in the history of the book – *Montaigne's Career* (1998) – before turning to social and religious history – *The Reformation of French Culture: Satire, Spiritual Alienation, and*

Connection to Strangers (2018) – both winners of the MLA's Aldo and Jeanne Scaglione Book Prize. He is currently working on religious politics and sixteenth-century Gallicanism. He teaches courses on the French South Pacific, the Algerian War, object theory, post-secular theory and 'What *Westworld* tells us about being human'.

Katharine Eisaman Maus is the author of *Being and Having in Shakespeare* (2012), *Inwardness and Theater in the English Renaissance* (1995) and *Ben Jonson and the Roman Frame of Mind* (1985). She is one of the editors of *The Norton Shakespeare*, *The Norton Anthology of English Literature* and *English Renaissance Drama: A Norton Anthology*. She is currently at work on *The Oxford English Literary History: 1603–1660*.

William McKenzie is Maître de Conférences at the Université Catholique de l'Ouest, Angers, and a member of the research centre there, CHUS ('Centre de recherche Humanités et Sociétés'). He is author of *The Student's Guide to Shakespeare* (2017), also from Edinburgh University Press, and has published articles on early modern narcissism and its afterlife in contemporary theory, Renaissance obscenity, the figure of Echo and changing forms of confession in Renaissance complaint, and French Petrarchism. He is currently working on a monograph on conceptual intersections between narcissism and modernity, as well as an article on the metaphor of the book in plays and poems by Shakespeare.

Maria Devlin McNair received her PhD in English from Harvard University and is the founder of Shakespeare for All, as well as a writer and producer for Lyceum and Ministry of Ideas. Her essays have appeared in *The Spenser Review* and *Spenser Studies*, and she is currently working on a monograph on ethics and early modern comedy.

Cassie M. Miura is Assistant Teaching Professor in the School of Interdisciplinary Arts at the University of Washington Tacoma. She received her doctoral degree in Comparative Literature from the University of Michigan and is currently at work on a monograph titled *The Humor of Skepticism: Therapeutic Laughter from Montaigne to Milton*. She is also co-editor with Cora Fox and Bradley Irish of the volume *Positive Emotions in Early Modern Literature and Culture* (2021).

Peter G. Platt is Ann Whitney Olin Professor and Chair of English at Barnard College. He is the author of *Shakespeare and the Culture of Paradox* (2009) and *Reason Diminished: Shakespeare and* *the Marvelous* (1997), editor of *Wonders, Marvels, and Monsters in Early Modern Culture* (1999), and co-editor of *Shakespeare's Montaigne* (2014). His most recent book is *Shakespeare's Essays: Sampling Montaigne from* Hamlet *to* The Tempest (2020), also from Edinburgh University Press.

N. Amos Rothschild is Associate Professor of English at St. Thomas Aquinas College in Rockland County, New York. He is presently at work on a book project examining representations of learnedness in early modern England.

David Schalkwyk is Professor of Shakespeare Studies and Director of the Centre for Global Shakespeares at Queen Mary University of London. He is the author of *Shakespeare, Love and Language* (2019), *Words in the World: The Bakhtin Circle* (2016), *Hamlet's Dreams: The Robben Island Shakespeare* (2013), *Shakespeare, Love and Service* (2008), *Literature and the Touch of the Real* (2004) and *Speech and Performance in Shakespeare's Sonnets and Plays* (2002), and co-editor of *The Cambridge Companion to Shakespeare and Language* (2019), as well as *The Oxford Handbook of Shakespearean Tragedy* (2018).

Richard Scholar is Professor of French at Durham University. He moved to Durham in 2019 having spent thirteen years as Fellow and Tutor in French at Oriel College, University of Oxford, where from 2015 he was also Professor of French and Comparative Literature. His publications include: *The* Je-Ne-Sais-Quoi *in Early Modern Europe: Encounters with a Certain Something* (2005), *Montaigne and the Art of Free-Thinking* (2010) and, as co-editor with William Poole, *Thinking with Shakespeare: Comparative and Interdisciplinary Essays* (2007).

Anita Gilman Sherman is Professor of Literature at American University in Washington, DC. She is the author of *Skepticism and Memory in Shakespeare and Donne* (2007) and has published essays on Donne, Garcilaso de la Vega, Herbert of Cherbury, Thomas Heywood, Montaigne, W. G. Sebald and Shakespeare in various edited collections and journals. Her most recent book is *Skepticism in Early Modern English Literature: The Problems and Pleasures of Doubt* (2021).

Daniel Vitkus holds the Rebeca Hickel Endowed Chair in Early Modern Literature at the University of California, San Diego. He is the author of *Turning Turk: English Theater and the Multicultural Mediterranean* (2003) and of numerous articles and book chapters on early modern culture. He has edited *Three Turk Plays from Early Modern England* (2000) and *Piracy, Slavery and Redemption: Barbary Captivity Narratives from Early Modern England* (2001). He serves as the editor of *The Journal for Early Modern Cultural Studies*.

Preface: Reading Montaigne

Colin Burrow

For many years I have been a member of group who are reading
Montaigne together, essay by essay, in French.[1] We are now well into
Book 2, and at least the younger members of the group hope to be
alive by the time we finish. During most of these sessions I sit with
Florio's translation on my knee, trying to work out what the French
words mean so that I can translate Florio into English. Meanwhile
my far more learned colleagues explain and expound Montaigne's
sentences in ways that make me realise not only that I do not understand them, but that I am not sure I know what 'understanding' is
any more. Through that very unusual process of reading I get the
scent of something distantly receding from me which is of great interest because it just won't sit still – a lump of Plutarchan solidity meets
a flicker of Lucretius, an anxious turning from profundity follows a
bold statement about values in general or a consciously whimsical
statement of personal preference. Yet another reference is made to
the life of Epaminondas by a 'moi' which is keen to claim it cannot
remember anything. And from that forgetful 'moi' flows an inex-
haustible supply of exempla and quotations from classical history
and literature, not to mention anecdotes about its own life.

Can I quite remember what anyone says about Montaigne at
our meetings? Probably not: certainly not from the sessions held
through the coronavirus lockdown of 2020–21, during which my
fellow readers have been images on a screen, who periodically forget to unmute themselves while they utter what was, no doubt,
the final word about a particular phrase or sentence. Meanwhile
Montaigne glows on another screen in the orange and black and
blue fonts used by the wonderfully useful but cumulatively eye-
dazzling Montaigne Project to indicate different phases of revision
to the *Essays*.[2] Every so often we summon up Montaigne himself
(or rather 'Montaigne himself') in the form of his handwritten notes

on the Exemplaire de Bordeaux, to which readers of the Montaigne Project are given such ready and welcome access, and we muse about why he added a quotation here or changed a word there. I always come away from these exercises in exhaustively slow reading braced, tired and with a sense that if I were a better person I would be carrying away insights, or at least some general grasp of Montaigne's processes of thinking.

This reading experience has a strange affinity with that described Montaigne's essay 'Of Bookes'. Montaigne did not regard texts as just sources of information, or of thoughts, or of historical examples, or of memorable *sententiae*. He declares: 'I am wonderfull curious, to discover and know, the minde, the soule, the genuine disposition, and naturall judgement of my Authors.'[3] Earlier in 'Of Bookes' he describes the essays as 'but my fantasies, by which I endevour not to make things knowen, but myselfe' (236) ('Ce sont icy mes fantasies, par lesquelles je ne tasche point à donner à connoistre les choses, mais moy').[4] Florio's translation of this passage can be read in at least two ways. The primary sense (which is the sense of the French) is 'In them I do not seek to confer knowledge of things but of myself.' The secondary sense is that in the essays he does not seek to make things known, but to make himself. That characteristically discomforting translation does evoke the effect of the essays: they do not make Montaigne an object of knowledge, exactly, but they are performances which appear to make something which looks like a 'moi'. And from time to time they draw attention to the processes by which they and their co-operant 'moi' are made.

The Montaigne who is curious about the mind and 'genuine disposition' of his authors sounds like a solemn and a deedy reader who might be expected to have a 'genuine disposition' of his own. But 'Of Bookes', like many of the essays, simultaneously gestures towards self-revelation and skips away from it. The 'moi' revealed in the essays is what Montaigne calls, in Florio's translation, a 'skipping wit' (236), and the kind of reading Montaigne describes in 'Of Bookes' also skips, in the humdrum sense of leaving out bits of books that seem boring: 'If one booke seeme tedious unto me, I take another, which I follow not with any earnestnes, except it be at such houres as I am idle, or that I am wearie with doing nothing' (236–7). His favoured books, he declares, 'are Plutarke (since he spake French), and Seneca; Both have this excellent commodity for my humour, that the knowledge I seeke in them, is there so scatteringly and loosely handled, that whosoever readeth them is not tied to plod long upon them, whereof I am uncapable' (238: 'plod'

is a word Florio repeatedly uses of over-diligent reading). Of these
two authors, he says, 'fortune brought them both into the world in
one age. Both were Tutors unto two Roman Emperours: Both were
strangers, and came from far Countries' (238). He goes on to offer
a brief 'syncrisis', or comparative analysis, of Plutarch and Seneca,
deploying the rhetorical figure that Plutarch had used in juxtaposing
his lives of Greek and Roman historical figures. In Florio's version
Seneca is 'full-fraught with points and sallies, Plutarke stuft with
matters. The former doth moove and enflame you more; the latter,
content, please, and pay you better' (239). This translation, setting
the 'points and sallies' of Seneca against the 'stuft' Plutarch, suggests that the comparison between the two authors is also a battle
of wits: Seneca's poiniard jabs and stabs at the protective padding of
Plutarch's learning, as a sharp Prince Harry (or indeed a Ned Poins)
fences with a padded Falstaff.[5]

The essay 'Of Bookes' is a microcosm of the way Montaigne operates on his readers: it opens up a fantasy of reading as a means of
experiencing the soul of another, then confesses the messy practical
realities of getting bored, skipping through and getting bogged down
in Cicero. Montaigne concludes the essay by confessing that he often
makes a note at the end of a book he has just read recording 'what
censure or judgement I had of it' so 'it may at least, at another time
represent unto my mind, the aire and generall Idea, I had conceived
of the Author in reading him' (242). He then goes on to transcribe
his notes on Guicciardini and the *Mémoires* of Martin Du Bellay.
These notes are largely a record of disappointment: Guicciardini can
give 'a taste of a kind of scholasticall tedious babling', while of Du
Bellay Montaigne tartly notes 'This is rather a declamation or plead-
ing for King Francis against the Emperour Charles the fifth, then an
Historie' (242). The conclusion of the essay, though, offers a kind of
disappointment which is not quite an anti-climax. The disappointment is that the 'aire and generall Idea' of an author extracted from
Montaigne's reading is not a transcendent insight into the spiritual
essence or 'genuine disposition' promised earlier in the essay, but
a set of notes jotted down to save time when rereading the book,
and which records only what Montaigne happened to think of that
author at the time. But that conclusion to the essay is not quite as
much of a disappointment as it might appear, since by transcribing
the notes he appended to some of his books Montaigne does seem to
invite his readers to sit looking over the shoulder of his 'moi', reading
what he thought while he read. That view over the shoulder of the
artist is the dream of every literary critic.

The intellectual rhythm enacted within 'Of Bookes' is very much the pulse of the *Essays*: it moves from philosophical expansiveness, through intimate self-revelation and confessions of fallibility, to end in a kind of self-diminution ('here are my notes on Guicciardini which I only made because I know I can't remember anything') which is also perhaps a kind of self-aggrandisement ('you will want to know what I thought of these authors'). The essays often promise that a great truth may be about to dawn, before the author darts back into the human darkness of physical pain or forgetfulness, catching his readers in a space between transcendence and contingency. That movement of thought – darting out, shrinking back in 'friskes, skips and jumps' (595) – is, perhaps, something akin to the 'genuine disposition' of Montaigne, provided that 'disposition' is allowed to be a tendency to do more than one single thing, or to pursue a course that is plural and self-contradictory. Montaigne has a disposition to know and grasp all, and a continuing counter-disposition modestly to back down into the messy practices of living, getting bored, jotting, forgetting.

The essay 'Of Bookes' is immediately followed by the essay 'Of Crueltie', which since 1965 has been listed among the texts that get referred to as 'sources' of Shakespeare's *The Tempest* – and which is given thought-provoking attention by Lars Engle and Maria Devlin McNair in this volume.[6] Prospero's statement that 'the rarer action is / In virtue than in vengeance' grows from Montaigne's claim, in Florio's translation, that a naturally mild person who ignores injuries 'should no doubt performe a rare action', but someone who overcomes a 'furiously-blind desire of revenge, and in the end after a great conflict, yeeld himself master over-it, should doubtlesse doe much more' (243). Did Shakespeare read 'Of Bookes' as well as 'Of Crueltie'? Did he read Montaigne in the way Montaigne read his favoured authors, skipping and extracting, while searching for a 'genuine disposition' in what he read? Did he (like many English readers of Florio's massive volume) pay particular attention to passages printed in italic, or, as Lars Engle argues in this volume, to essays which are mentioned in the prefatory matter of the edition of 1603?[7] Maybe these unanswerable questions simply abandon us to the realm of syncrisis, in which we are left comparing Seneca with Plutarch or Shakespeare with Montaigne simply because 'fortune brought them both into the world in one age'.

Maybe – though maybe also one should pause over both 'simply's in the previous sentence. 'Syncrisis' means together-judging, or assessing side by side. Even if literary criticism does not explicitly engage in syncrisis, it is always implicitly comparative. Each member of the large and loose category of texts that get called literary is necessarily understood in relationship to other texts, even if it is understood to be very different from them, and even if the reader does not think that he or she is overtly making acts of comparison. A text is always not another text, and that is a major part of how human beings understand texts. As William Hamlin shows in his expert conspectus of the critical tradition at the start of this volume, the relationship between Shakespeare and Montaigne has raised evidence-based questions which are likely to prove unanswerable: did Shakespeare read Montaigne before the publication of Florio's translation in 1603, or did he simply do things with his rhetorical training which make it look as though he did? Is the vision of a mingled yarn of life in *All's Well That Ends Well* indebted to the italicised phrase '*Man all in all, is but a botching and a party-coloured worke*' from Montaigne's essay 'We taste nothing purely' (2.20; 389), or is it 'simply' analogous to it?

These questions, like the majority of questions that matter in literary criticism, are neither trivial nor answerable. It is perfectly reasonable to argue that Shakespeare before 1600 was (as Richard Scholar suggests below, and as Peter Mack has suggested elsewhere) doing things with his rhetorical training that were uncannily like Montaigne even if they are likely to have predated his reading of or in Florio's translation, or to have had a parallel genesis.[8] There are good reasons to hear what Scholar terms a 'virtual conversation' between Shakespeare and Montaigne: both authors had read many of the same books, and their rhetorical training, although different in degree, was in kind very similar. It is also reasonable to suppose that the moment 'essays' became a fashionable form of writing at the Inns of Court in the later 1590s any playwright who wanted to appeal to that elite and wealthy audience would have wanted to dramatise processes of eclectic reflection and musing, in order to bring onstage the effect of books that were selling well at the cutting edge of literary production. There was, that is, a powerful incentive from the last third of the 1590s onwards to invent or sound like Montaigne even if one had not read him. But the desire to look over Shakespeare's shoulder as he read Montaigne has become so irresistible that someone inserted a forgery of Shakespeare's signature into a copy of Florio in the British Library (C.21.e.17). The forger and the source-hunter are closer kin than probably either would wish to acknowledge: both are driven by the desire for visible evidence that Shakespeare read Montaigne. The critical problem, however, is that even a successful attempt to prove *that* one author read a given text cannot reveal *how* that reading occurred, let alone why (or even if) it mattered. What happens between one text and another is the space of literary criticism, of judgements and comparisons about which reasonable people might disagree, rather than of empirical evidence or certainty.

As I have argued elsewhere, the traditional conception of a 'source' is not well suited to considering the relationship between two texts where the earlier text made the later author think.[9] Reading can be resistant reading, or dialectical reading, or reading with a delight that is qualified by just the occasional sceptical raising of an eyebrow, or reading where one skips and frisks through the dull bits. Several critics have thought that Shakespeare not only read Montaigne but disagreed or 'conferred' with him, in the sense in which Montaigne uses that verb in the essay 'Of the Art of Conferring' (III: 8).[10] 'Of the Art of Conferring' reflects on the value of arguing and disagreeing with another person. It also presents Montaigne himself not as someone to be imitated, but (in Florio's characteristic Frenglish) 'evitated', or avoided: 'My errors are sometimes naturall, incorrigible and remedilesse. But whereas honest men profit the Common-wealth in causing themselves to be imitated. I shall happily benefit the same, in making my selfe to be evitated' (552) ['Mes erreurs sont tantost naturelles et incorrigibles; mais, ce que les honnestes hommes profitent au public en se faisant imiter, je le profiteray à l'avanture à me faire eviter'].[11] Aversive fashioning is still a form of fashioning: 'If I confere with a stubborne wit, and encounter a sturdy wrestler, he toucheth me to the quicke, hits me on the flanks, and pricks me both on the left and right side: his imaginations vanquish and confound mine. Jelousie, glory and contention, drive, cast and raise me above my selfe' (553). Authors can use an earlier text in a way that unsettles its claims (say, the claim that fathers should pass on their children's inheritance while they are still alive) by throwing those principles into new narrative circumstances (by, say, dramatising what happens when an elderly king does give all to his daughters). Shakespeare did this with 'Of the Affections of Fathers to their Children' (2.8) in *King Lear* – and that essay falls within what it is tempting to think of as a particularly 'Shakespearean' cluster of essays in Book 2, including 'Of Bookes' (2.10), 'Of Crueltie' (2.11) and 'An Apologie of *Raymond Sebond*' (2.12). It is probably wrong, or at least too crude, to assume that in these cases Shakespeare 'disagreed' with Montaigne or sought to 'hit him on the flanks', or 'prick him both on the left and right side', though the sparks do sometimes fly from encounters between these two authors, as when Shakespeare (in Lars Engle's words) registers 'ambivalence towards key aspects of Montaigne' by putting speculations drawn from 'Of the Caniballes' into the mouth of Gonzalo in *The Tempest*. The art of conferring is partly an art of making something new and different from what is said before, of undertaking an internal syncrisis with a prior text which shuttles between the claims of the new and of the old. Embodying an abstract argument within a play, unless it is done with a truly plodding flat-footedness, is intrinsically likely to unsettle its certainties, since human actions of any complexity at all are seldom reducible to precepts, and precepts about what it may or may not be good in principle to do are seldom accurate guides to the emotional consequences of any given action once people start arguing about it, or, as humans do, feeling about it. A play can take a precept – give up all to your daughters – and then work out the emotional and societal consequences of that precept in ways that make it look wrong-headed, or disastrous, or emotionally explosive. One of the main things that Shakespearean drama does is to entangle a moral question within a narrative in such a way as to leave it tied up in knots. That was probably not the result of anything so clear as 'an argument' with Montaigne, but was a converging consequence of Shakespeare's representational methods and his 'conference' with Montaigne's essays.

Syncrisis, or judging by comparison, can set spikey Seneca against stuffed Plutarch, or sly Shakespeare against elusive Montaigne. It illuminates by setting texts or people side by side and meditating on the affinities and differences between them, and speculating about the pathways between the two. This can sharpen the gaze (as it notably did for Plutarch), and make features visible on both sides of the comparison that would otherwise have gone unnoticed. There are risks in syncrisis of course, which Shakespeare made comically visible when his Fluellen undertakes a Plutarchan syncrisis of Henry V with 'Alexander the Pig': 'There is a river in Macedon, and there is also moreover a river at Monmouth. It is called Wye at Monmouth, but it is out of my prains what is the name of the other river – but 'tis all one, 'tis alike as my fingers is to my fingers, and there is salmons in both' (*H5* IV, vii, 25–30).

Yet even what may or may not be accidental affinities between authors can be illuminating. So in 'Of Bookes' Montaigne says of Plutarch's Life of Brutus that 'I would rather make choise to know certainly, what talke he had in his Tent with some of his familiar friends, the night fore-going the battell, then the speach he made the morrow after to his Armie: and what he did in his chamber or closet, then what in the Senate or market place' (240). Shakespeare's *Julius Caesar* includes both of these kinds of rhetorical performance, and the direction of Shakespeare's writing after 1599 suggests that he came to share Montaigne's preference for intimate moments of reflection over public declamation. That could have been because Shakespeare read Montaigne and Montaigne influenced the way in which Plutarch influenced him. Or it could just be that, like Montaigne, he was drawn to these moments because he was aware of a wider history of the 'intimate' style, which Kathy Eden has traced with such skill.[12] Or it could have been because Shakespeare was a dramatist and knew that staging an intimate self-colloquy would allow him to get more out of the resources of rhetoric than presenting a public declamation could do. As so often in literary criticism each of these 'ors' is also potentially an 'and', since none of the possibilities is mutually exclusive. A person in private can have the luxury – which Montaigne had by virtue of his social position – of not quite knowing what he thinks, or of trying to work it out as he speaks, but a leader addressing his troops before a battle or a lawyer in front of a court has to know exactly which case he is supporting. A writer of prose meditations and a dramatist both have good generic reasons for favouring modes of stylistic intimacy and interior dialogue which have no predetermined end in view. Even when there just happen to be salmons in both texts which are conjoined through syncrisis, a lot can be learned from watching the different directions in which the fish are swimming in each, and wondering why they might not be following exactly the same course.

Is it possible, indeed, that 'evidence-based' approaches to the relationship between Shakespeare and Montaigne are just another version of salmon spotting? How much is learned, actually, either about Shakespeare or Montaigne, from the Appendix to George Coffin Taylor's *Shakspere's Debt to Montaigne*, which lists 750 words which are supposedly found only on Shakespeare's works after 1603 and which are found also in Florio? Taylor's list includes some words and phrases which it is indeed quite likely Shakespeare took from Florio (such as 'handy dandy'). But it also includes several words which, according to present beliefs about the dating of his works, were used by Shakespeare before 1603 ('petard', 'gaming'), as well as others (to take a random sample from Taylor's list of words beginning with 'g') which had been common in English for well over a century: 'gaged', 'garner', 'glut, vb.', 'gouty', 'gravel', 'generosity' and 'glimpse' – the latter two of which are, according to TCP/EEBO, particularly likely to appear in humanistic translations of a kind which Shakespeare is known to have read. Taylor's list also includes a couple of words beginning with 'g' which in fact Shakespeare did not ever use, 'gladdeth' and 'goatishness', the latter of which is presumably an error for 'goatish', which Shakespeare uses but Florio does not.[13] Do we learn more from this list than that there are words in both? (For the record, there are no 'salmons' in Florio.)

We might legitimately carry away from Taylor's empirical work the suspicion that the 'evidence' invoked by empirical scholarship is sometimes simply false, and that there is more to be gained from thinking about two writers side by side – about their respective attitudes towards cruelty, for example, or about their implied beliefs about moral luck, or about how gender and genre interrelate, or about how argument functions within drama – than from fishing around for verbal parallels. The relationship between Shakespeare and Montaigne was one of the great conferences of minds.

Notes

1. I am extremely grateful to Richard Scholar and Wes Williams for organising these meetings, as well as to the regular attendees, who include Chimene Bateman, Terence Cave, Neil Kenny, Ian Maclean, John O'Brien, Jenny Oliver, Jonathan Patterson, Kirstie Sellevold and Valerie Worth.
2. Montaigne, *Montaigne Project*. Accessed 1 April 2021.
3. Montaigne, *Essays*, trans. Florio, p. 239. Further references to Florio's translation are included parenthetically in the text.
4. Montaigne, *Essais*, ed. Villey and rev. Saulnier, p. 407.
5. Florio adds the stuffing to 'Seneque est plein de pointes et saillies; Plutarque, de choses', Montaigne, *Essais*, ed. Villey and rev. Saulnier, p. 413.
6. Prosser, 'Shakespeare, Montaigne, and the Rarer Action'.
7. William M. Hamlin, *Montaigne's English Journey*, pp. 143–4.
8. Mack, 'Montaigne and Shakespeare'.
9. Burrow, 'Montaignian Moments', p. 245.
10. E.g. Parker, 'Argument', and Salingar, *Dramatic Form*, pp. 107–39.
11. Montaigne, *Essays*, trans. Florio, p. 552; cp. Montaigne, *Essais*, ed. Villey and rev. Saulnier, p. 921. It is tempting to suppose that Shakespeare's sole use of 'evitate' in *The Merry Wives of Windsor* (V, v, 220) derives from Florio, although that play can certainly be dated to 1597. *OED*'s first citation of 'evitate' is from 1588, though the word is actually found at least as early as J. Alday's translation of Pierre Boaistuau's *Theatrum Mundi* (1566), sig. C4r. This indicates the hazards of

seeking 'evidence' of Shakespeare's reading from lexical borrowings: earlier translators from French were just as capable as Florio of borrowing French vocabulary.

12. Eden, *Renaissance Rediscovery*.
13. George Coffin Taylor, *Shakspere's Debt*, pp. 59–66.

Introduction: Shakespeare and Montaigne: A Critical History

William M. Hamlin

One could be forgiven for asking why the question of Shakespeare's relation to Montaigne has ever been seriously entertained. This question never arose during the first century and a half after Shakespeare's death, even though the *Essays* were widely read in England and available in two impressive translations.[1] Montaigne was a French aristocrat, a judicial magistrate, an advisor to kings and twice the mayor of Bordeaux; Shakespeare was a commoner from the English Midlands who made his way to London, became an actor and achieved fame as a playwright for the public stage. Montaigne's wealth and social status freed him from obligatory labour and gave him ready access to solitude and thus to the possibility of sustained introspection. Shakespeare, too, found solitude, but because his profession as a dramatist was by nature collaborative, his day-to-day life was in all likelihood more urgently shaped by temporal restraints and interpersonal obligations than was the life of Montaigne. Indeed, the Frenchman was hugely independent in pursuing his project of essaying himself – of examining his consciousness and shaping a new prose genre as he sought verbal means to represent the movements of his thought.[2] The Englishman's livelihood, meanwhile, depended on appreciative theatrical audiences, and he therefore traded in the narratives, conflicts and exaggerations characteristic of dramatic fiction. He was, moreover, deeply committed to the logic of prevailing generic conventions, despite his remarkable probing of the boundaries of dramatic genre.

In short, the lives of these two men were extraordinarily different, and the forms their writings take are in certain respects almost opposites: unruly, meandering prose versus taut, muscular poetry; intense self-scrutiny versus self-subordination in the interest of creating fictional characters; detached and meditative consideration of ethical questions versus the staging of such questions within the constraints of a popular art form. Despite all this, however, the 'great question' of Shakespeare's relation to Montaigne has been repeatedly raised since the late eighteenth century, and it shows no signs of diminished exigency.[3] Perhaps we suspect that Shakespeare read Montaigne because we see both writers as 'harbingers of modernity'; perhaps we hope to find clues to Shakespeare's genius by tracing ideas, attitudes or habits of contemplation to the work of an earlier writer of astonishing originality.[4] It goes without saying, of course, that we want Shakespeare to have good taste in his reading, just as we do. But it follows from none of this that Shakespeare is any more indebted to Montaigne than Montaigne is to Shakespeare.

Let me turn first to the evidence – and to the more basic question of what counts as evidence in a matter such as this. The scholar Edward Capell observed in 1780 that Gonzalo's commonwealth speech in Act II of *The Tempest* relies heavily on the diction of 'old Montaigne', and specifically on Montaigne's account of native Brazilian customs in 'Des Cannibales'.[5] Capell believed that Shakespeare had read Montaigne in French, but his fellow scholar Edmond Malone soon set him straight, remarking rather ungenerously in 1790 that Capell 'knew so little of his author as to suppose that Shakespeare had the original French before him, though he has almost literally followed [John] Florio's translation'.[6] Malone was right, and no one since his time has doubted that the multiple verbal parallels between Gonzalo's speech and Florio's 1603 rendition of Montaigne constitute indisputable evidence that Shakespeare appropriated this passage from the *Essays*.[7] Some critics have drawn the more extreme conclusion that because Shakespeare lifted phrases from 'Of the Caniballes', he must have read the whole chapter – or indeed the entire 630 pages of Florio's translation. But while this latter supposition may be true, no known form of empirical analysis can prove it. That Shakespeare borrowed language from 'Of the Caniballes' is certain; that the words he borrowed affected his conception of *The Tempest*'s thematic structure is a matter of debate; but that verbal borrowing is, ipso facto, evidence of 'influence' is clearly false.

One of the ironies of source study is that the lexical fragments most easily isolated for discussion are often the least indicative of any significant form of conceptual indebtedness. As Paul Yachnin noted in 2007, the fact that we find so little of Montaigne in Shakespeare could potentially serve as an index of 'the depth of Shakespeare's engagement with Montaigne': the more thoroughly the playwright examines the essayist, the less conspicuously he reveals the traces of that examination.[8] Colin Burrow has recently advanced a similar argument but pressed it considerably further. Observing that 'literary criticism has historically not been well equipped with a vocabulary or a method for writing about relationships between two authors where thinking, rather than direct verbal borrowing, might be involved', Burrow explores several 'Montaignian moments' in which Shakespeare may be supposed to have disassembled various passages from the *Essays* only to reconstitute them in disparate dramatic scenarios.[9] Referring to this process as the 'reactive reading of discursive texts' and showing how Montaignian prose is 'dissolved into dialogue and transformed into different voices', Burrow finds that Shakespeare's encounter with Montaigne leads to 'banter among courtiers [in *The Tempest*], byplay among fools and madmen in *King Lear* . . . and a rich set of connections between the subplots and main plot [of *Measure for Measure*]'.[10] Richard Hillman, meanwhile, has proposed yet another approach to Montaignian dependence, suggesting by way of intertextual theory that deviations from the normative 'grammar' of a given work can indicate the presence of disruptive intertexts with which that work is engaged in tacit, unacknowledged dialogue. Thus Hamlet's enigmatic decision to accept Claudius's wager may constitute an oblique gesture towards Montaigne's use of Pyrrhonian argumentation to disarm the Lutheran critique of Catholicism: both strategies are desperate in so far as successful aggression may entail the annihilation of the aggressor.[11] Hillman's approach, however, still relies on scrupulous attention to the lexical contours of specific works as well as to the broader expectations of contemporary readers and auditors.

Close verbal parallels, then, have always been central to the question of Shakespeare's relation to Montaigne. In 1897 John Robertson amassed many such parallels in support of his view that the *Essays* shaped the mature Shakespeare's mind and that there is thus no doubt regarding Montaigne's 'influence' on the playwright.[12] Five years later, Elizabeth Hooker argued that while Shakespeare is 'no disciple of Montaigne's', he nonetheless treats Florio's translation as a 'store-house of material'; she went on to adduce thirty-four parallel passages which suggest the likelihood of 'a vital connection' between Montaignian source and Shakespearean play.[13] The most comprehensive study of this sort, however, is George Coffin Taylor's 1925 monograph entitled *Shakspere's Debt to Montaigne*. Presenting over a hundred 'close phrasal correspondences' as well as a list of 750 words attested in Florio's Montaigne and used by Shakespeare during and after 1603 (but never before), Taylor attempts to demonstrate that Shakespeare was 'profoundly and extensively influenced by Montaigne: definitely influenced in regard to vocabulary, phrases, short and long passages, and, after a fashion, influenced also in thought'.[14] A corrective response by Frederick Page in 1943 noted that most of Taylor's 750 words had already appeared in English printed books prior to the publication of the *Essayes*, but Taylor's study has nonetheless been received with considerable admiration.[15] T. S. Eliot praised it for its intimation of the extent to which Montaigne's *Essays* might have served as a 'stimulant' to Shakespeare; Kenneth Muir went so far as to call it 'the best treatment' of the question at issue, adding that 'it would be unreasonable to deny that Montaigne had a substantial influence on the thought of *King Lear*'.[16] Muir subsequently offered his own list of ninety-six words – some but not all derived from Taylor – which do not appear in Shakespeare before *Lear*, but which do appear (often for the first time) in Florio's Montaigne; this list includes such memorable terms as 'auricular', 'derogate', 'disnatured', 'goatish', 'marble-hearted', 'sectary', 'sophisticated' and 'sterility'.[17] Muir's assumption of substantial Montaignian influence on the 'thought' of *Lear* may be overconfident, but there seems no doubt that Shakespeare had an extraordinary memory for unusual words and that he recalled these words with ease when doing so suited his purposes. Florio's Montaigne, however, is only one of many books from which he could have developed his immense vocabulary.[18]

It is precisely this too quick leap from evidence of rare-word borrowing to claims of intellectual obligation that has generated scepticism from some of the most astute contributors to the Montaigne–Shakespeare debate. Responding to Robertson and Hooker as well as to other champions of Montaignian influence such as G. F. Stedefeld and Jacob Feis, the great Montaigniste Pierre Villey noted dryly in 1917 that 'one might desire less enthusiasm for the glory of Montaigne – and a bit more proof'.[19] For Villey, such proof required evidence beyond the mere compilation of similitudes and borrowings, although he was willing to acknowledge the persuasive potential of the latter.[20] He accepted Capell's claim as modified by Malone, but rejected the notion of cumulative persuasion as conveyed by multiple instances of possible indebtedness: 'One hundred additional zeros still add up to zero.'[21] And, like Alice Harmon a quarter century later, he rightly stressed that countless commonplaces could be cited on which both Montaigne and Shakespeare might have drawn as they composed their works.[22] Harmon published the decisive formulation of this claim in 1942, arguing that to build an elaborate theory of literary 'influence' upon the evidence of parallel passages alone is unsound, unless coincidences in idea and wording are unmistakable, and unless such agreements in thought and phraseology are not to be found in other accessible sources than the supposed 'influencing' author.[23]

Citing dozens of printed commonplace books and anthologies of classical aphorisms that were available in sixteenth-century Europe, Harmon excoriated the practice of 'influence-grafting' and sharply raised the standard of proof for all future assertions of Shakespearean indebtedness to Montaigne.[24] In testament to the force of her argument, Margaret Hodgen published an article ten years later which explored the possibility that Shakespeare might have found the substance of Gonzalo's commonwealth speech in sources other than 'Of the Caniballes'. Noting the formulaic quality of the rhetoric, the repeated use of negation (e.g., 'no kind of traffic', 'no name of magistrate') and the ubiquity of such descriptions of utopian 'barbarism' in writers ranging from Hesiod and Strabo to André Thevet and Samuel Purchas, Hodgen concluded that 'had the French essayist's work never fallen into the hands of the English dramatist, Gonzalo's speech might well have been written in the same vein'.[25] It is a vein, I might add, whose relentless mining in earlier centuries has rendered suspect any allegation of originality or meaningful indebtedness with respect to textual fragments exhibiting its key features.

The sceptics held sway for several decades during the mid-twentieth century, and it was not until a trio of exceptional essays appeared between 1965 and 1983 that the critical colloquy on Montaigne and Shakespeare gathered new momentum. The first of these, a brief note by Eleanor Prosser, argued that *The Tempest* draws not only on 'Of the Caniballes' but also on a passage from 'Of Crueltie', specifically the section where Montaigne contrasts two hypothetical men: one who forgoes revenge because he is gentle by nature and another who struggles with a passion for vengeance but manages, ultimately, to subdue it. The former would 'no doubt perform a rare action', but the latter, after 'being toucht & stung to the quicke', would act with genuine virtue should he 'arme himselfe with reason against this furiously-blinde desire of revenge'.[26] Prospero echoes these lines when he tells Ariel that while he has been 'struck to th' quick' by the crimes of Alonso and his accomplices, 'yet with my nobler reason 'gainst my fury / Do I take part. The rarer action is / In virtue than in vengeance'. As Prosser notes, even 'conservative' critics will agree that this parallel is 'incontestable'.[27] It also satisfies Harmon's stipulation that 'coincidences in idea and wording' should be 'unmistakable', and in so doing it may constitute a more significant Montaignian borrowing than that identified by Capell, since it relies on an original and intriguing thought rather than on hackneyed formulae of description.[28] Prosser never says as much, but her discovery provides valuable insight into the way that Shakespeare reads, extracts words and concepts, and redistributes them as he composes.

A decade later, Robert Ellrodt published an article that marks a permanent turning point in the nature of the conversation. While not as sceptical as Villey or Harmon, Ellrodt is cautious in his analysis, finding only half a dozen likely parallels between the *Essays* and *Hamlet*, and in general concerning himself more with potential intellectual consequences of a careful reading of Montaigne than with narrower forms of influence. For Ellrodt, the defining mark of self-consciousness is 'a simultaneous awareness of experience and the experiencing self'; it is this amalgam that he finds so prominently displayed not only in the *Essays* but in the introspective speeches of Hamlet, Troilus, Angelo, and Macbeth – and indeed in the works of 'many late Renaissance writers'.[29] Ellrodt thus relies on a model of historical synchronicity – of the simultaneous cross-cultural emergence of particular modes of awareness – and in this regard he implicitly diminishes the originality of both the essayist and the playwright. But such an anticipation of New Historicist methodology is not merely prescient but salutary inasmuch as it offers an antidote to views which unfairly exaggerate the gaps in talent and sensibility between writers of the greatest prominence and their less highly regarded contemporaries.[30]

The final article in the trio to which I have alluded is Leo Salingar's study of verbal and thematic correspondences between *King Lear* and several of Montaigne's most important essays.[31] Impressed by Muir's list of ninety-six words, Salingar claims that rare-word borrowings 'amount to very strong evidence for Shakespeare's interest in Montaigne', and he proceeds to focus on the Montaignian chapter entitled 'Of the Affections of Fathers to their Children', arguing that Shakespeare could have found in this piece 'a study of the relations between age and youth, parents and children, immeasurably more searching, realistic, and challenging than anything in the versions of the Lear legend'.[32] This chapter had in fact been linked with Shakespeare prior to the time of Salingar, but no one had previously discussed it in such convincing detail.[33]

Salingar's particular contribution is that despite his certainty that Shakespeare's reading of Montaigne exerted enormous influence on the characterisations and thematic complexities of *Lear*, he simultaneously believes that Shakespeare assumes a stance of partial opposition to the

Frenchman's optimism. The 'humanist idealism' of Montaigne is subjected to sceptical scrutiny; Shakespeare explores the dark interiors of the human psyche while the essayist remains too rational and civilised to 'submit to the imaginative pull of evil'.[34] Such an observation, at least at one level, merely underscores a difference in obligation between a contemplative intellectual and a writer of stage plays for public performance. But it also sets the tone for a number of subsequent contributions to the Montaigne/Shakespeare conversation, several of them among the finest in the centuries-long forum.

In claiming that it would have been surprising had Shakespeare not displayed an interest in 'the most richly suggestive explorer of men and manners from the previous generation', Salingar exaggerates the degree to which Montaigne's reputation had taken hold in England during the first few years of the Jacobean period.[35] Nonetheless, evidence exists that Montaigne had achieved a modest English vogue by the turn of the seventeenth century, and this fact has aided those who would argue for significant Montaignian influence in *Hamlet*, a play traditionally dated to 1600 or 1601 (two or three years prior to the publication of the *Essayes*). Stedefeld and Feis are only two of the early scholars who have championed the idea of Montaigne's centrality to this play; others include John Sterling, who suggested in 1838 that Hamlet is 'very nearly a Montaigne' (although 'somewhat more passionate'), and Philarète Chasles, who in 1851 volunteered the extravagant claim that 'once we begin to trace the studies and preferences of Shakespeare, we find Montaigne at every corner: in *Hamlet*, in *Othello*, in *Coriolanus*'.[36]

One problem with claims such as these – and a problem quite distinct from their enthusiasm – is that they depend on one of two assumptions: either that Shakespeare read French extremely well or that an English translation of Montaigne was circulating before the 1603 publication of the *Essayes*. Because it seems improbable that Shakespeare would have read extensively in the French text of Montaigne, the prevailing view has always been that he had access to a copy of Florio's manuscript prior to its appearance in print.[37] Scholars ranging from Hooker, Villey, Ellrodt and Hillman to Peter Mack and Stephen Greenblatt have adopted this assumption, and evidence in its favour may be supplied by Sir William Cornwallis, who notes in one of his essays that while he has never read Montaigne in French,

> yet divers of his peeces I have seen translated – they that understand both languages say very wel done – & I am able to say (if you wil take the word of Ignorance) translated into a stile admitting as few Idle words as our language will endure.[38]

This description, however, is scarcely an indisputable reference to the verbally expansive Florio. Indeed, several passages in Cornwallis's book which purport to be quotations or near-quotations from Montaigne suggest to me, rather, that Cornwallis drew on a separate English translation of the *Essays* which has now been lost. In 'The Instruments of a States-man', for example, we read that 'what ever hee is, yet being a Prince, he is to be reverenced and not be practised against, as a wise authour saith, "Good Princes are to bee desired, but howsoever they are, to be obeyed"'.[39] This corresponds to a passage in Montaigne's chapter 'Of Vanitie' in the 1603 *Essayes*, but Florio's rendering is quite distinct: 'One may bewaile the better times, but not avoide the present: one may desire other magistrates, but notwithstanding he must obey those he hath.'[40] I therefore suspect that Cornwallis had access to one of the other efforts at English translation of the *Essays* to which Florio alludes in his preface.[41] Similarly, if the longstanding hypothesis is true that various ideas and locutions in *Hamlet* are derived from Montaigne, then perhaps Shakespeare also drew on the translation used by Cornwallis – or on one of the others, if others existed. Such a theory would help to explain the comparative obliquity of the verbal parallels normally advanced in this case, for none of the supposed borrowings in *Hamlet* approaches the persuasiveness of the Montaignian parallels in *The Tempest* identified by Capell and Prosser.[42]

Articles proposing *Hamlet*'s indebtedness to Montaigne did indeed diminish during the late decades of the twentieth century, and the most recent Arden editions of the play (2006 and 2016) give less attention to Montaigne than does Harold Jenkins's earlier version (1982), which proffers the following assessment: 'I incline therefore to think that of the ideas which Shakespeare so lavishly bestowed on Hamlet, a few at least were prompted by his recent reading in Florio's Montaigne.'[43] But valuable commentaries on Montaigne and *Hamlet* continue to appear – those, for example, of Hillman, Hugh Grady, John Lee, Géralde Nakam, James Shapiro, Patrick Gray, Saul Frampton and, most recently, Peter Platt – even as we observe a growing consensus that the plays dating from 1603 to the end of Shakespeare's career are those in which assumptions of Montaignian influence are most likely to be operative.[44]

In the wake of the seminal articles by Prosser, Ellrodt and Salingar, most of the contributions to the Montaigne–Shakespeare debate follow one of two basic trajectories. Either they discover significant affinities of thought, attitude or approach between the *Essays* and Shakespeare's plays, or else they isolate important and sometimes profound differences between the outlooks of these writers. In both cases, the ethical views expressed by various characters or implied by various scenarios are occasionally attributed to Shakespeare himself, and in both cases the degree of Montaignian influence is construed in multiple ways, most frequently along a spectrum ranging from complete agnosticism on the matter to an overt assumption of deep and pervasive intellectual impact. In the following paragraphs I speak of 'strong' claims when specific arguments are linked to the idea that Shakespeare relies directly and substantially on Montaignian thought; I speak of 'weak' claims when no such argument is advanced or presumed. The terms 'weak' and 'strong', however, are not tied to any evaluation of the overall merit of the arguments under consideration.

Perhaps the most eloquent proponent of the view that several post-*Hamlet* Shakespearean plays are deeply influenced by Montaigne is Arthur Kirsch, who has focused in particular on *All's Well That Ends Well* and *The Tempest*. As early as 1981 Kirsch published preliminary claims concerning the former play, noting that 'the same combination of attitudes' exhibited by Shakespeare with respect to erotic desire versus marital sexuality can be found in Montaigne's celebrated essay 'Upon some Verses of *Virgill*'. Indeed, Shakespeare's primary concern in *All's Well* is 'the paradoxical nature of erotic energy', and Montaigne offers a profound illumination of 'the texture of experience in Shakespeare's dramatisation'.[45] Janet Adelman agreed with Kirsch, writing in 1992 that she was 'indebted to his account' and characterising Montaigne's essay as a 'source' in which Shakespeare discovered a brilliant exploration of the 'deep incompatibility that separates sexuality from marriage'.[46] Kirsch went on to develop his claims in a 1997 article, suggesting that *All's Well* may 'constitute the most detailed and comprehensive appropriation of Montaigne in Shakespeare's canon'; he argued in particular that

> the perception of the mutual dependence of virtue and vice, and of wisdom and folly, governs the way Montaigne thinks about sexuality and human nature throughout the essay and throughout his works, and the identical perception informs not just isolated homiletic speeches, but the entire action of Shakespeare's play.[47]

In the same year Kirsch published a separate study of *The Tempest*, exploring the implications of Prosser's 1965 argument and finding that Shakespeare's orchestration of events seems 'unusually informed by the kind of working out of ideas' characteristic of Montaigne's thinking: 'inclusive; interrogative rather than programmatic; anti-sentimental but humane; tragicomic rather than

only tragic or comic'.[48] Kirsch concentrates not only on 'Of Crueltie' but also on such chapters as 'Of the force of Imagination' and
'Of Diverting and Diversions', and he presents one of the earliest
instances of the argument that Shakespeare is indebted to Montaigne not merely for concepts but for habits of reflection. Thus,
while *The Tempest*'s focus on imagination, compassion and the
topos of life as a dream 'suggests the particular matrix of ideas
found in Montaigne's essays', it is Montaigne's unique way of
thinking about the collocation of vice and virtue that 'informs the
moral consubstantiality' of the play's action.[49]

Similarly strong claims regarding *The Tempest* have been offered
by other scholars, among them Gail Kern Paster, Philip Hendrick,
Paul Yachnin, Kenji Go and Warren Boutcher. Paster, writing in 1984
and thus anticipating Kirsch's interest in 'Of Diverting and Diversions', argues that Shakespeare had read this essay closely and that
Montaigne's 'juxtaposition of consolation and revenge, of Dido and
hardness of heart, convinces me of his influence upon this moment
of *The Tempest* (II, i, 75–84) and of his usefulness when we seek to
understand it'.[50] Hendrick suggests that when Shakespeare turned to
'Of the Caniballes' for Gonzalo's speech, he was exposed not merely
to the views of Montaigne but to the less subtle attitudes of Florio,
who interpreted the Montaignian text with 'unspoken colonialist
assumptions'.[51] Yachnin, whose article I have mentioned earlier, sees
Shakespeare as a 'literary cannibal': a reader preoccupied with the
'humanist incorporation of Montaigne' and a writer whose engagement with the *Essays* 'deepened his ability to create verisimilitude in
characters like Prospero'.[52] Go has recently argued that Shakespeare
took more material from 'Of the Caniballes' than has conventionally been accepted; even the setting of Shakespeare's play may be
inspired by the island discussed at the outset of Montaigne's chapter.
It thus appears, in Go's opinion, that 'Of the Caniballes' should be
judged 'a far more important literary source' of *The Tempest* than
has heretofore been assumed.[53] Boutcher, relying on Go but pursuing
an original and far-reaching argument in which Montaigne stands
at the centre of a pan-European network concerned with the education and training of the nobility, suggests that the scene where Gonzalo deploys language from Florio's Montaigne dramatises or even
satirises 'the elite household process that mediated the arrival of the
Essays in late Renaissance English culture'. Shakespeare's play, in
other words, reflects one of the principal ways in which Montaigne
was read and received in early modern England, and what is at stake
in *The Tempest* is precisely the value of the nobility's 'institution': the

'kinds of free-ranging, idle lectures and exercises, based on classical and continental sources, with which, as they seek to plot their dynasties' futures, they are advised and entertained'.[54]

Boutcher is likewise concerned with *King Lear*, as are several other recent critics. Agreeing with Salingar that Montaigne 'furnished Lear with the "matter" for his exposure of contradictions at the basis of social life', Boutcher elaborates the ways in which the play's preoccupation with inheritance, parental tyranny and moral counsel resonates with Montaignian concerns in 'Of the Affections of Fathers to their Children' and other chapters.[55] Douglas Trevor discusses similar issues, claiming that 'the degree to which "Of the affection" influences not simply Shakespeare's ideas about the particular challenges posed by the relations between fathers and children in *Lear*, but indeed the concepts of love and anger themselves, has not been adequately addressed.' He concludes that what is finally confirmed both in *Lear* and the *Essays* is a sense of 'the mysterious origins of love and the hideous consequences that spawn from the cruel treatment of one's children'.[56] Jonathan Bate, in 2000, argued that the 'influence' of Montaigne's 'Apologie of *Raymond Sebond*' is the key to Shakespeare's 'critique of Stoicism' in *Lear*, and the following year Philip Collington suggested that *Lear* tests and corroborates Montaigne's 'unconventional wisdom' in the chapter 'Of Solitarinesse': Shakespeare's tragedy becomes a 'negative *exemplum*' of Montaigne's hypothesis, for Lear 'never achieves the kind of liberated serenity and integrity of the self that periodic sessions of 'gregarious solitude' would facilitate'.[57] Finally, Lars Engle has made a brilliant case for the claim that 'cruelty, sovereign power, and commitment to abstract principles are linked in *King Lear*' – and that this link is proposed in the *Essays*. Avoiding assertions of direct influence but believing nonetheless that Shakespeare knew 'Of Crueltie' and other chapters, Engle finds that Montaigne never integrates cruelty into his generally sanguine outlook on human behaviour. Rather, he exclaims against it, and there is thus 'a substantial affinity between Montaigne's analysis of cruelty and Shakespeare's treatment of cruelty in *Lear*'. The blinding of Gloucester emerges as a particularly crucial moment in which Shakespeare's dramatic exposition becomes aligned with Montaigne's meditation: 'an abstract principle unleashes cruelty in those predisposed to it, and an outrageous act of physical cruelty becomes the text against which abstract principles are to be judged.'[58]

Strong claims of a broader sort have been current in literary studies since the mid-1980s. Jonathan Dollimore, whose *Radical Tragedy*

appeared in 1984, argues that Montaigne was 'one of the most important single influences on Jacobean drama' and that he served as an
intellectual precursor of Louis Althusser in so far as he understood
custom as a form of ideology which is 'so powerfully internalised
in consciousness that it results in misrecognition'. Dollimore views
Lear as a play that 'disallows' transcendence, and while he does not
find Montaigne directly responsible for Shakespeare's perspective, he
nonetheless discerns in the Frenchman's writings a model for habits of
ideological demystification and conscious detachment from providential readings of human affairs.[59] Hugh Grady has offered arguments
in the same general vein, invoking Michel Foucault on the circulation of social discourses in an effort to demonstrate that Montaigne
and Shakespeare are linked through an 'indirect connection'. Montaigne, in Grady's view, is a 'Renaissance theorist of resistance' who
poses questions, raises doubt and promotes critical rationality; he and
Shakespeare 'share a common mental framework which we could call
Renaissance scepticism' and which 'puts in question all the received
ideas and traditions which underlie their eras' arrangements of wealth
and power'.[60] Agreeing with Grady that Montaigne can be mobilised
against the style of cultural critique that 'insists upon the subjection of
individual agents to imperiously determining social forces', Peter Holbrook suggests that Montaigne and Shakespeare are 'soulmates' who
exhibit many common tendencies in their writings. Both, for example,
are 'pioneers in the formation of a liberal culture of self-creation',
and Shakespeare's *Sonnets* are 'Montaignesque' inasmuch as they are
'committed to individual authenticity'. Indeed, a 'healthy root of self-
love' sustains the *Sonnets*: they are 'the product of a man who, like
Montaigne, "hunger[s] to make [him]self known"'.[61]

Shakespeare's late Roman tragedies have likewise been linked to
Montaignian thought, though not always with the same strength of
argument concerning influence. Geoffrey Miles, for instance, anticipates Jonathan Bate's concern with Montaigne's sceptical critique of
Stoic ideals, suggesting that in *Antony and Cleopatra* Shakespeare
reads 'Plutarch through Montaigne's eyes, with a sense of the "volu-
bilitie and supplenesse" of human emotions'. Miles finds it plausible
that Montaigne 'focused and shaped [Shakespeare's] interest in the
theme of constancy'. and he believes that the two writers 'responded
in similar ways to their reading'.[62] Rob Carson, meanwhile, has
concentrated on *Coriolanus*, arguing that Shakespeare privileges
'an irreconcilable multiplicity of perspectives' in the play. We therefore recognise that his dramaturgical method bears a strong resemblance to the 'dialogic style' not only of Montaigne but of Ludwig

Wittgenstein, whose *Philosophical Investigations* remind Carson of the Pyrrhonian dimensions of Montaigne's 'Apologie', above all in their 'flexible scepticism', which 'encourages us to inhabit the rich irresolution of a debate, amplifying our beliefs so diversely that no dogmatism will seem adequate to contain them'.[63]

Carson, Miles and most of the other critics whose views I have summarised tend to agree that Shakespeare, like Montaigne, is a thinker in his own right, and not merely a dramatist of remarkable talent who rehearses the views of others. But the image of Shakespeare as a thinker has acquired still greater vigour in recent years, partly through the writings of A. D. Nuttall and certainly in the opinion of Terence Cave, whose essay from 2007 has furnished a fresh perspective on the Montaigne–Shakespeare debate. Ignoring questions of 'influence' and thus operating within the sphere of 'weak' claims as I have defined them above, Cave emphasises that Shakespeare stages dramatic moments in which his characters – and his audience members – are prompted to think through specific questions; these moments resemble Montaignian *essais*, or trials of thought. Cave goes on to concoct a fictional meeting between Montaigne and Shakespeare in late Elizabethan London. After attending a stage play with the genial Bard, Montaigne begins to see that

> the theatre provides its own way of 'essaying' things, presenting complex and problematic instances of human behaviour as material for reflection, and in such a way that the required narrative resolution is not accompanied by a facile resolution at that second-order reflective level.[64]

Richard Scholar has valuably pursued a related line of inquiry, agreeing that Shakespearean dramatic scenarios often mirror the 'process of trial-thinking known as the *essai*' and adding that Montaigne and Shakespeare are 'near-contemporary literary masterminds, connected by a common European cultural tradition and by certain shared preoccupations'. When we read their works side by side, we therefore practise a 'comparative approach' which opens the possibility that these works will 'illuminate one another'.[65] Peter Mack has offered a similar argument in a separate context, claiming that we should treat the questions of when Shakespeare read Montaigne and how much he borrowed from him as essentially 'undecideable'. Rather, we should 'make comparisons between the two authors' with the intention of learning about 'the methods and views of both'. Engaging in such comparisons allows us to discern more about what is distinctive in each author – and in each passage – than does scouring texts for potential source-trajectories that may deceive us into think-ing we have found instances of indebtedness when in fact we have compromised our attention to both writers.[66] I myself proposed a similar outlook in 2006, suggesting that however tempting it may be to posit diachronic vectors of intellectual impact, the weaker thesis of 'synchronic affinity' strikes me as more plausible in any Mon-taigne/Shakespeare juxtaposition.[67] But Mack's view has the merit of outlining a productive means of moving forward from any impasse we might reach in arguments over Shakespeare's debt to Montaigne, and in so doing it remains simultaneously receptive to the claims about 'trial-thinking' advanced by Cave and Scholar.[68]

Several critics who have eschewed source-study tactics have found relatively little in common between Montaigne and Shakespeare, implying thereby that others may have exaggerated the supposed affinities between these writers. John Lee, for instance, has argued that while the soliloquies of Hamlet at times mirror the formal fea-tures of the Montaignian essay, on the whole Montaigne is hostile to the human imagination, and as a consequence Shakespeare's plays are 'inhospitable to Montaigne's thought and habits of thinking'.[69] Lee particularly insists that Montaigne 'distrusts imagination as a way of reaching out to the world, for [it] is part of the subjective nature of his experience, one more distorting medium between himself and the world of God's creation'. Shakespeare, on the other hand, is 'perhaps the greatest example in English literature' of how well one can fail in an attempt to escape subjectivity through imaginative verbal cre-ation.[70] Pursuing a separate line of argument, Anita Gilman Sherman has focused on relations between scepticism and memory, finding that Shakespeare, unlike Montaigne, tends to ascribe 'ulterior motives to faulty remembering even as he occludes the nature of those motives'. Engaging with the complexities of Stanley Cavell's interpretation of sceptical thought in Shakespeare, Sherman proposes that, in the case of Montaigne, scepticism 'is not a tragic affair in part because the exemplarity of his friendship with La Boétie and the pleasures of pastoral rob [it] of its sting'.[71] With Shakespeare, however, the vivid depiction of characters beset by uncertainty is more obviously sus-ceptible to Cavellian analysis, and Sherman offers detailed, illumi-nating discussions of *King Lear* and *Antony and Cleopatra*.

Questioning Miles's view that Montaigne and Shakespeare reacted in largely similar ways to what they read, more than a few scholars have concentrated on divergent habits of response in the two writ-ers. Gisèle Mathieu-Castellani, for example, has examined Plutarch as appropriated by the essayist and the playwright, and while she ultimately suggests that the latter's understanding of Plutarch may have been shaped by the former's portrayal, she also points to distinct differences between these writers' uses of the Greek historian and moralist.[72] John Cox shifts the realm of investigation to the Bible, arguing in impressive detail that

> whereas Shakespeare uses biblical references to suggest the interaction of Christian destiny and moral expectation, [Montaigne] consistently uses them as rhetorical *copia*, in just the same way he uses classical citations and often in tandem with them to emphasise the same point.

The result of this contrast, in Cox's view, is that while 'self-recognition, hope for positive change, and charitable acknowledgment of others' are themes important to both writers, they derive in Shakespeare 'from the narrative of Christian destiny', while in Montaigne they typically emerge from 'rational judgment or even from the need to suspend judgment' in the Pyrrhonian fashion so often displayed in the *Essays*.[73] Peter Mack, following his own advice regarding the merit of comparative evaluation, notes that Montaigne and Shakespeare 'teach their audiences how to think ethically by exploring the implications of opposed positions on issues more than by expounding a particular moral teaching'. Montaigne tends to suggest that we should 'rein back' our emotions, especially those which 'extend our concerns beyond ourselves in the direction of duty to others'. Shakespeare, by contrast, uses the late-play speeches of *King Lear* to 'present compassion as a human obligation', stimulating 'new moral thinking' in his audience by means of Lear's juxtaposition of proverbial wisdom with insights born of madness.[74] Finally, I have recently turned to *Measure for Measure* in an effort to contrast the ways in which Shakespeare and Montaigne examine conscience both as a socio-cultural cognitive faculty and as a mental attribute of potentially transcendent origin. Exploring the idea that in early modern Europe the moral conscience is routinely understood to function as a surrogate form of divine immanence, I trace the differing implications of Montaigne's discussions of conscience in the *Essays* and of Shakespeare's contemplation of its putative presence in Angelo as he is observed and tested by the Duke. My argument is that while Montaigne accepts the objective existence of conscience but condemns judicial torture as a cruel and futile effort to manipulate its workings, Shakespeare, in *Measure for Measure*, exposes us to profound scepticism about the transcendental grounding of conscience even as he suggests that belief in such grounding is conducive to the diminishment of hubristic subjectivity and thus to the moral enrichment of the world.[75]

But strong claims of influence continue to surface in contrastive studies of Montaigne and Shakespeare. Leo Salingar, as I have noted, foreshadows this trend in his 1983 essay on *Lear*, and in the 1990s both Jean-Marie Maguin and Fred Parker present arguments concerned with Shakespearean resistance. Focusing on *The Tempest*, Maguin asks whether Shakespeare's appropriation of Montaigne's 'Of the Caniballes' is undertaken 'solely at the expense of Gonzalo, or also at the expense of Montaigne's philosophy'; he opts for the latter possibility, claiming that Gonzalo is 'a mask from behind which Shakespeare is vigorously teasing Montaigne for his radicalism'.[76] Parker adopts a longer perspective, treating not only *The Tempest* but also *Lear*, *Othello* and *Measure for Measure*. Like Maguin, he finds Shakespeare sceptical in the face of Montaigne's utopian optimism in 'Of the Caniballes', but more generally he suggests that despite evident commonalities of thought between these writers, Shakespeare always exhibits a distinct difference of attitude – above all in failing to share the untroubled acknowledgment of human contradiction that is so fundamental to Montaigne.[77] Shakespeare's 'argument' with the essayist, in Parker's view, is thus a deeply sceptical assessment of Montaigne's confidence in the possibility of serene self-acceptance.

Addressing similar issues but focusing sharply on relations between shame and meditative reflection, Lars Engle suggests that while Shakespeare is 'impressed with and provoked by Montaigne', he is at the same time 'deeply suspicious of the very possibility of a sustained Montaignian stance towards the world – a stance of free reflection largely uninterrupted by the continual pressure of negotiation and thereby largely freed from shame imposed by others'. Engle concentrates on *All's Well* and the *Sonnets*, finding that Paroles is one of 'Shakespeare's most Montaignian characters' and disagreeing with Peter Holbrook on the broad commonalities between Montaigne and the sonnet-speaker: the Shakespearean texts 'register a quite different attitude toward reflective mental life from Montaigne's'. Overall, Engle believes that Montaigne must 'be treated with caution as an analogue or model for Shakespeare's treatment of embodied mental life'. The playwright's response to the essayist should be 'recognised as ambivalent rather than assumed to be celebratory and directly appropriative'.[78] Meanwhile, in an original and provocative discussion of *Hamlet*, Patrick Gray has taken up the question of Shakespeare's familiarity with Epicurean ethics – and especially with the

Epicurean principle of *lathe biōsas*, or withdrawal from the world into private idleness. Following Jonathan Bate's suggestion that Shakespeare's acquaintance with Epicureanism is largely the result of his exposure to Montaigne, Gray argues that while the essayist, particularly in his late writings, 'embraces a policy of Epicurean disengagement', Shakespeare is 'sceptical of this approach to life's concerns, finding it ineffective as a means to happiness, or even peace of mind'.[79] But Gray goes further still: Hamlet, he proposes, may be 'modelled on Montaigne himself'. Both the fictional Dane and the historical Frenchman upbraid themselves for lassitude and dullness; both depict their fathers as successful, politically minded, non-Epicurean figures; and the English word 'assay', inseparably linked to its French cognate *essai*, appears almost twice as often in *Hamlet* as in any other Shakespearean work. Gray thus finds compelling reasons for construing *Hamlet* as 'a critique or "assay" of Montaigne, insofar as Montaigne can be said to be an Epicurean'; the play, on the whole, is 'profoundly critical of Epicureanism'.[80]

Probably the most vehement recent account of Shakespearean resistance is that of Stephen Greenblatt in *Shakespeare's Montaigne*. Attending primarily to *King Lear* and *The Tempest*, Greenblatt claims that Shakespeare made repeated 'forays' into Florio's Montaigne so as 'to seize upon things he thought he could use'. In the case of *Lear*, he used Montaigne's reflections on what Greenblatt calls 'geriatric avarice', fashioning Florio's words from 'Of the Affections of Fathers to their Children' into the letter alleged by Edmund to have been written by Edgar.[81] And in *The Tempest*, Shakespeare mined 'Of the Caniballes' for Gonzalo's commonwealth speech – a speech mocked for its incoherence by Antonio and Sebastian. Indeed these two aristocrats, along with the islander Caliban, function as representatives of an intransigent hostility towards utopian dreaming, and this leads Greenblatt to argue that *The Tempest*'s Montaignian dependence must be construed not as 'homage' but as 'aggression'. The same is true with *Lear*: 'it is as if Shakespeare thought Montaigne had a very inadequately developed sense of depravity and evil.'[82] For Greenblatt, then, Shakespeare's attitude towards Montaigne is significantly combative; it derives in particular from an intuition of Montaignian naïveté, and it takes definitive shape in the utterances of characters who privilege self-interest and realpolitik over compassion, generosity and concern for the greater good.

More recently still, Peter Platt has challenged the resistance readings of Salingar, Parker and Greenblatt. Highlighting Montaignian complexity and ambivalence in 'Of the Caniballes', 'We taste nothing purely' and other relevant chapters, Platt argues not only for the strong 'shaping' influence of Florio's Montaigne on Shakespeare but for Shakespeare's capacious, sensitive accommodation of Montaignian ideas.[83] Thus in *Hamlet*, where Platt believes that the Second Quarto (1604–5) represents an extensive authorial revision of the First (1603), Shakespeare's acquaintance with 'Of Diverting and Diversions' from the newly published *Essayes* guides his conception of the Danish prince's 'diversion' from uncompromising revenge to the more ambitious pursuits of ethical behaviour and accurate appraisal of his own and other human lives. Similarly, in *King Lear* – and despite Salingar's claims about Montaigne's 'humanist idealism' – Platt contends that Shakespeare saw beyond the alleged naïveté in 'Of the Affections of Fathers to their Children'; careful analysis of this essay in fact suggests that it may be 'more a source than a site of critique' for the reprehensible conduct of Goneril, Regan, Edmund and Oswald.[84] Speaking broadly of Shakespeare's post-1603 dramatic output, Platt concludes that the playwright's 'essaying' of Florio's translation

> gave him the material with which to challenge his own, and sometimes Montaigne's, ideas about the very nature of the world he scrutinised on stage. To essay human experience is to continue to learn, probe, and try – to be a life-long apprentice and never to resolve.[85]

In effect, Platt imagines a still-inquisitive mid-career Shakespeare whose discovery of Montaigne stimulates his intelligence to such a degree that his maturing dramaturgy bears frequent witness to the encounter.

Near the close of his introduction to *Shakespeare's Montaigne*, Greenblatt asks one of the basic questions to which we must always return in our discussions of Shakespeare and Montaigne. Did the playwright truly need the essayist to think about consciousness, death, imagination, sexuality, faith and identity?[86] The answer, of course, is no. If we knew beyond doubt that Shakespeare had no more acquaintance with the writings of Montaigne than he had with those of Tolstoy or Lady Murasaki Shikibu, we would remain unsurprised by the attitudes he shares with his French contemporary – and by the ways he seems to disagree with him. Major writers will always exhibit occasional convergences of thought, feeling and judgement, and Montaigne and Shakespeare are major writers who lived in similar cultures at the same historical moment. Nonetheless, as we have seen, Shakespeare in fact relies on Montaigne for words, phrases, ideas and modes of reflection. As Elizabeth Hooker put it long ago, the *Essays* serve as a 'store-house' from which he sometimes draws material. But whether he displays any consistent perspective toward the thought of Montaigne is a matter on which we are unlikely to reach consensus. Similarity is not necessarily agreement, nor is difference necessarily resistance. Shakespeare uses Montaigne when he feels a need to do so, but we cannot indisputably show that he has pronounced tendencies to agree or disagree with him; what we can say is that multiple verbal constellations of potentially Montaignian inspiration emerge from within highly specific dramatic scenarios. It would indeed be astonishing if Shakespeare – or anyone else in England at the outset of the seventeenth century – had formed a firm set of opinions about a writer so new to English readers as was Montaigne, particularly given the spectacular range and multi-dimensionality of the *Essays*. In the end, since it is such a tempting matter to overestimate the degree to which the writings of Montaigne shaped or affected those of Shakespeare, we are wise to work upwards from minimal assumptions rather than downwards from the realms of speculation and desire.

Like Montaigne, Shakespeare was a voracious and opportunistic reader, neither scholarly nor systematic, and certainly not reverential. His habits of appropriation will always remain to some degree mysterious: eclectic, to be sure, and pedestrian at times, but most of all transformative. He shapes and moulds what he takes; he allows his imagination and his immediate dramatic needs to subject borrowed textuality to conceptual metamorphosis. He thereby attains a remarkable level of independence as a writer – again like Montaigne, though as a consequence, no doubt, of extremely dissimilar compositional practices. But on the whole he does not exhibit an interest in establishing consistent relations of response to his sources, and in this respect he stands in marked contrast to the author of the *Essays*, who reveals more distinct tendencies towards admiration and disdain.[87] Still, despite such differences, Montaigne and Shakespeare share one colossal achievement: that of giving us verbal creations of extraordinary power, breadth, insight and charisma. As Florio might have said, these are 'worldes of wordes', and they serve as sites for thought and feeling, for observation and experiment, and for free and open interchange with the alternate worlds from which new readers continue to emerge, invariably richer for having made the journey.[88]

Notes

1. The first of these is that of John Florio, *The Essayes or Morall, Politike and Millitarie Discourses* (London, 1603), the second that of Charles Cotton, *Essays of Michael Seigneur de Montaigne* (London, 1685–86). I quote here exclusively from Florio's translation, referring to it as the *Essayes*; I use the title *Essays* only when I refer to Montaigne's book more generally. Because Florio prepared his translation primarily from the 1595 Paris edition of Montaigne's *Essais*, my citations of the French text derive from Balsamo, Magnien, Magnien-Simonin and Legros, eds, *Les Essais*. Quotations from Shakespeare are drawn from *The Norton Shakespeare*, ed. Greenblatt et al., 3rd edn. A shorter version of this essay was published as 'Montaigne and Shakespeare' in Desan, ed., *The Oxford Handbook of Montaigne*, pp. 328–46.
2. Hoffmann, *Montaigne's Career*, argues convincingly for Montaigne's sustained authorial embeddedness within social contexts and relationships, but I would add that the essayist's remarkable independence coexisted with – and was significantly enabled by – his extensive social imbrication.
3. Strier, 'Shakespeare and the Skeptics', p. 171.
4. Grady writes that the impulse behind efforts to link Montaigne and Shakespeare is 'a widespread cultural belief that what they shared went far toward specifying and defining that transformation from theocentric to anthropocentric worldviews that had defined the Renaissance for secular Western scholars under the influence of Burckhardt' ('Afterword', pp. 174, 171). Compare Engle's comment that the modernity of Montaigne and Shakespeare might be characterised as 'disenchantment' with foundational discourses and 'meaning-bearing traditions' of their time ('*Measure for Measure* and Modernity', p. 85).
5. Capell, *Notes and Various Readings to Shakespeare*, vol. 2, pt. 4, p. 63. See *Tem* II, I, 143–68; cp. 'Des cannibales' (*Essais*, I.30, pp. 212–13).
6. Malone, ed., *Plays and Poems of William Shakspeare*, vol. 1, pt. 2 (B), p. 38.
7. The relevant section in 'Of the Caniballes' (*Essayes*, I, 30) appears on p. 102. Frampton has intriguingly proposed that Florio was involved in preparing the First Folio of 1623 and may have augmented its text of *The Tempest* by introducing a passage from Montaigne's 'Des caniballes' into Gonzalo's speech: 'The standard view has been that this [speech] represents Shakespeare's borrowing from Montaigne; the alternative is that it might represent Florio borrowing from himself' ('Who Edited Shakespeare?'). Tantalising as this possibility may be, it depends on multiple levels of speculation.
8. Yachnin, 'Eating Montaigne', p. 170.
9. Burrow, 'Montaignian Moments', pp. 240, 242.
10. Ibid. pp. 245, 248.

11. Hillman, 'Entre Shakespeare et Montaigne', pp. 151–3. Compare *Ham* V, ii, 99–161.

12. Robertson, *Montaigne and Shakespeare*; I quote from the revised edition of this book published in 1909 (31); see also pp. 38–118. Robertson's revision offers additional support for his thesis and responds to critical reviews published in the intervening years.

13. Hooker, 'The Relation of Shakespeare to Montaigne', p. 346, p. 347, pp. 350–66, p. 342.

14. George Coffin Taylor, *Shakspere's Debt*, pp. 4–5; see also pp. 49–66.

15. Relying on the *Oxford English Dictionary*, Page asserts that of Taylor's 750 words 620 were already current in English prior to 1603.

16. Eliot, 'Shakespeare and Montaigne', p. 895. *King Lear*, ed. Muir, p. 235, p. 239.

17. *King Lear*, ed. Muir, pp. 235–9. Foakes, in his more recent edition of *Lear*, agrees with Muir about Shakespeare's rare-word indebtedness; he speaks of the 'impact of Montaigne' (p. 59) and of the ways in which the *Essays* 'affected Shakespeare's thinking' in *Lear* (pp. 104–5). For a list of verbal parallels between Montaigne and *Measure for Measure*, see Eccles's edition of that play, p. 543.

18. Barkan describes Shakespeare as 'a kind of language sponge' ('What Did Shakespeare Read?' p. 45. See also Yachnin, 'Eating Montaigne', p. 167; Miola, *Shakespeare's Reading*, pp. 1–17, 152–69; Muir, *The Sources of Shakespeare's Plays*; and Mack, *Reading and Rhetoric in Montaigne and Shakespeare*. Burrow, in 'Montaignian Moments', stresses that the 'deliberative authors' on whom Shakespeare relies include not only Montaigne but Plutarch, Seneca, Cicero and others (p. 250).

19. Villey, 'Montaigne et les poètes dramatiques anglais du temps de Shakespeare', p. 381: 'Nous voudrions moins de zèle pour la gloire de Montaigne et un peu plus de preuves.' Stedefeld had argued that Shakespeare wrote *Hamlet* in order to liberate himself from Montaignian scepticism; see Stedefeld, *Hamlet*. Feis also focused on *Hamlet* but saw in the Prince a refracted image of Montaigne: the inconsistent attributes of a Renaissance humanist who simultaneously adhered to Roman Catholic dogma. See his *Shakspere and Montaigne*.

20. 'Rapprochements' and 'similitudes' are Villey's preferred terms for resemblances of any kind between Montaigne and Shakespeare; he regards source-hunting as 'une sorte de sport' (p. 382) and says of the many proposed parallels that 'pour la plupart, ils ne nous révèlent que des coïncidences de pensée entre les deux écrivains, nullement des emprunts ou même des réminiscences' (p. 383).

21. Villey, 'Montaigne et les poètes dramatiques anglais du temps de Shakespeare', p. 383: 'Cent zéros additionnés ensemble ne font toujours que zéro.' For his judgement of Capell's discovery: 'Le souvenir de Montaigne n'est pas douteux, et c'est la une constatation décisive' (p. 382).

22. Villey, 'Montaigne et les poètes dramatiques anglais du temps de Shakespeare', p. 383, p. 387.

23. Harmon, 'How Great Was Shakespeare's Debt to Montaigne?' p. 1008.

24. Ibid. p. 1008 and *passim*. Like Harmon, Friedrich was another sceptic, observing in 1949 that 'Contrary to prevailing opinion among the English, German, and French scholars of English, I am not convinced that this influence [of Montaigne on Shakespeare] amounted to much' (*Montaigne*, p. 405). See Collins, *Studies in Shakspere*, pp. 277–96.

25. Hodgen, 'Montaigne and Shakespeare Again', p. 27, p. 40. The phrases from Gonzalo's speech may be found in *Tem* II, i, 148–9. As Hodgen points out, the tactic of negative characterisation is used by Montaigne not only in 'Des cannibales', but twice in the 'An Apologie of *Raimond de Sebond*' (*Essayes*, p. 284, p. 288).

26. Prosser, 'Shakespeare, Montaigne, and the Rarer Action', pp. 261–4; the quoted lines derive from the *Essayes*, p. 243. The term 'marble-hearted', used by Shakespeare in *Lear*, also appears in 'Of Crueltie' (*Essayes*, p. 249).

27. *Tem* V, i, 25–8; Prosser, 'Shakespeare, Montaigne, and the Rarer Action', p. 262.

28. Harmon, 'How Great Was Shakespeare's Debt to Montaigne?', p. 1008. As Orgel writes about the borrowing from 'Of the Caniballes', 'Shakespeare has taken everything from Montaigne except the point' ('Shakespeare and the Cannibals', p. 54).

29. Ellrodt, 'Self-Consciousness in Montaigne and Shakespeare', pp. 41–2, 43; cf. pp. 48, 50. Ellrodt adds that 'the influence of Montaigne upon Shakespeare, if it ever existed, was at its height' in *Hamlet, Troilus and Cressida, All's Well, Measure for Measure* and *King Lear* (p. 39). He later qualifies his support even for *Lear* by arguing that 'the full tragic response calls for a heightened consciousness of identity – evident in Lear, Othello, or Macbeth – not for the kind of self-consciousness that may dissolve identity' (p. 49).

30. In *Montaigne and Shakespeare*, Ellrodt revisits these concerns, arguing that 'Shakespeare's acquaintance with the *Essays* increased his attention to the inner life and the necessity of self-knowledge in the period from *Hamlet* to *King Lear*' (p. 94); 'Montaigne and Shakespeare were indeed the first writers to open the way to clear manifestations of a new kind of self-consciousness in the early modern age' (pp. 173–4). Shannon, in *The Accommodated Animal*, maintains a similar sense of historical synchronicity in the writings of Montaigne and Shakespeare. Shannon argues for the existence of a pre-Cartesian discursive tradition 'that accommodates the presence of animals and conceives them as actors and stakeholders endowed by their creator with certain subjective interests' (p. 18).

31. Salingar, '*King Lear*, Montaigne and Harsnett'; this essay was reprinted in Salingar's monograph, *Dramatic Form in Shakespeare and the*

Jacobeans, pp. 107–39. My quotations are drawn from the latter source. Salingar's treatment of Montaigne depends primarily on the chapter 'Of the Affections of Fathers to their Children', but he also refers to 'Of the Caniballes', 'An Apologie for *Raymond Sebond*', 'Upon some Verses of *Virgil*', 'Of Vanitie', 'Of Phisiognomy' and 'Of Experience'.

32. Salingar, *Dramatic Form*, p. 108, p. 113.
33. See W. B. Drayton Henderson, 'Montaigne's *Apologie of Raymond Sebond* and *King Lear*', pp. 209–25, 40–56. Henderson claims that Montaigne's 'Of the Affections' offers 'the abstract of Lear's abdication, and the philosophy of Edmund's forged letter' (p. 47). In his edition of *Lear*, Muir likewise notes the relevance of Montaigne and offers an excerpt from the chapter in question (p. 27), but he places equal stress on Stefano Guazzo's *Civile Conversation* as translated by George Pettie (London, 1581). Guazzo's treatise includes a discussion of 'the foolishness of fathers who cling to their power and possessions'; Muir quotes relevant passages (pp. 26–7).
34. Salingar, *Dramatic Form*, p. 113, p. 133.
35. Ibid. pp. 108–9. For an examination of the reception of Montaigne in seventeenth-century England, see my book *Montaigne's English Journey*.
36. Sterling, 'Montaigne and His Writings', p. 321; Chasles, *Études sur W. Shakespeare, Marie Stuart, et l'Arétin*, p. 184: 'Une fois sur la piste des études et des préférences de Shakspeare, nous retrouvons Montaigne à tout bout de champ, dans *Hamlet*, dans *Othello*, dans *Coriolan*.' He adds that 'Le style même, le style composite de Shakspeare, si animé, si vif, si neuf, si incisif, si coloré, si hardi, offre une multitude d'analogies frappantes avec l'admirable et libre allure de Michel Montaigne' (p. 184). See also Türck, *Shakespeare und Montaigne*; Deutschbein, 'Shakespeares Hamlet und Montaigne'; Levin, *The Question of Hamlet*; and T. Olivier, 'Shakespeare and Montaigne'. Olivier represents a late instance of the enthusiasm characteristic of earlier studies.
37. For an argument that Shakespeare read Montaigne in French, see Williams, 'The *Bourn* Identity'. An entry in the *Stationers' Register* for 4 June 1600 ('*The Essais* of MICHELL lord of MONTAIGNE, translated into Englishe by JOHN FLORIO') demonstrates that Florio's translation was underway at least three years before its publication; see Edward Arber, ed., *A Transcript of the Registers of the Company of Stationers of London, 1554–1640*, 3:162. But it does not follow from this fact that manuscript copies were readily available. Gary Taylor and Rory Loughnane note that 'scribal copies of such a large book would have been expensive, and we possess no other evidence [that is, besides the theoretical supposition that Shakespeare read Florio's translation in manuscript] that it circulated in advance of publication' (*Authorship Companion*, ed. Taylor and Egan, pp. 542–3).
38. Cornwallis, *Essayes*, ed. Don Cameron Allen, p. 42. For the claim that Cornwallis read Florio's translation in manuscript, see Hooker, 'The

Relation of Shakespeare to Montaigne', pp. 347–50; Villey, 'Montaigne et les poètes dramatiques anglais du temps de Shakespeare', p. 357; Ellrodt, *Montaigne and Shakespeare*, p. 92, p. 102; Hillman, 'Entre Shakespeare et Montaigne', p. 136; Mack, 'Montaigne and Shakespeare', p. 154; Greenblatt, 'Shakespeare's Montaigne', p. xxxi. Compare Knowles, '*Hamlet* and Counter-Humanism', p. 1053, and Gillespie, *Shakespeare's Books*, p. 343. For dissenting views besides mine, see Collins, *Studies in Shakspere*, p. 286; Bennett, 'Sir William Cornwallis's Use of Montaigne', pp. 1080–1; and Shapiro, *1599*, p. 294.

39. Cornwallis, *Essayes*, p. 216.
40. *Essayes*, p. 595.
41. *Essayes*, sig. A6r. Florio mentions that 'seven or eight [translators] of great wit and worth have assayed, but found these Essayes no attempt for French apprentises or Littletonians'.
42. In *Shakespeare's Montaigne*, Greenblatt and Platt offer an appendix of eleven Shakespearean quotations which exhibit varying degrees of resemblance to ten passages from Florio's Montaigne (pp. 347–51). Three of these quotations are drawn from *Hamlet*, but two are commonplaces of the sort that Villey and Harmon rule out as candidates for evidence of borrowing. In my view the strongest verbal resemblances between *Hamlet* and the *Essayes* lie in the following collocations: 'worme' and 'emperor' (*Essayes*, p. 266; *Ham* IV, iii, 20–5); 'death', 'consummation', 'sleep' and 'dreames' (*Essayes*, p. 627; *Ham* III, i, 58–70); 'roughlie hew' and divine providence (*Essayes*, p. 559; *Ham* V, ii, 4–11). None of these, however, are as convincing as the parallels adduced by Capell and Prosser.
43. *Hamlet*, ed. Jenkins, p. 110. Cp. *Hamlet*, ed. Thompson and Taylor (2006), pp. 73–4; (2016) pp. 74–5, 146–7.
44. Hillman, 'Entre Shakespeare et Montaigne', pp.136–47; Hillman, *French Reflections in the Shakespearean Tragic*, pp. 14–22; Grady, *Shakespeare, Machiavelli, and Montaigne*, pp. 51–2, 243–65; Lee, *Shakespeare's* Hamlet *and the Controversies of Self*, esp. pp. 200–8; Lee, '"A judge that were no man"'; Nakam, 'La Mélancolie de la "Vanitas"'; Shapiro, *1599*, pp. 292–302; Patrick Gray, '"HIDE THY SELFE"', pp. 213–36; Frampton, '"To be, or not to be"'; Platt, *Shakespeare's Essays*, pp. 45–76. The arguments of Frampton and Platt depend on the increasingly cited theory that *Hamlet* Q2 (1604–5) is a Shakespearean revision of *Hamlet* Q1 (1603) – a revision that may rely in part on borrowings from Florio's newly published translation of Montaigne. I discuss the arguments of Platt and Gray later in this introduction.
45. Kirsch, *Shakespeare and the Experience of Love*, p. 124, p. 127. Kirsch's book also offers brief discussions of *Othello* and *Measure for Measure* with regard to Montaigne.
46. Adelman, *Suffocating Mothers*, p. 282, p. 78. Like Kirsch, Adelman also connects Montaigne to *Measure for Measure*.

47. Kirsch, 'Sexuality and Marriage', pp. 190, 195.
48. Kirsch, 'Virtue, Vice, and Compassion', p. 338.
49. Ibid. pp. 348, 341. Another study that sees Montaignian thought as a propaedeutic for Shakespeare is Lars Engle's 'Shakespearean Normativity in *All's Well That Ends Well*'. Engle suggests that 'in writing *All's Well* Shakespeare is exploring a relativising attitude toward sexual and marital behaviour he has learned in part from reading Montaigne' (p. 269); specifically, Shakespeare follows Montaignian practice by contextualising a particular set of social norms within a larger field of sceptical interrogation.
50. Paster, 'Montaigne, Dido, and *The Tempest*', pp. 91, 94.
51. Hendrick, 'Montaigne, Florio, and Shakespeare', pp. 125, 132.
52. Yachnin, 'Eating Montaigne', pp. 168,170–1.
53. Go, 'Montaigne's "Cannibals" and *The Tempest* Revisited', p. 473. Platt, in *Shakespeare's Essays*, builds on Go's insights in arguing that both 'Of the Caniballes' and *The Tempest* 'seem to establish firm boundaries between barbarism and civilisation, nature and art, only to collapse them. Both expose the shaky quality of European triumphalism and highlight the potential for beauty and integrity in their "canibals"' (pp. 129, 136, 144). Go's sense of the wider influence of Montaigne's 'Caniballes' on Shakespeare's play was to some extent anticipated by Gilbert, 'Montaigne and *The Tempest*'.
54. Boutcher, *The School of Montaigne in Early Modern Europe*, vol. 2, pp. 266, 270. I wish to thank Warren Boutcher for sharing parts of his book with me prior to its publication.
55. Ibid. pp. 245–6. 'Of the Institution and Education of Children' and 'Of Pedantisme' are two other Montaignian chapters to which Boutcher gives extensive, rewarding attention.
56. Trevor, 'Love, Anger, and Cruelty', pp. 53, 65–6. Trevor also suggests that Shakespeare differs from Montaigne in that he argues that 'the most savage acts of cruelty emerge from within family units that have been fractured' by abusive and choleric fathers (p. 61).
57. Bate, 'Shakespeare's Foolosophy', p. 25; Collington, 'Self-Discovery', pp. 266, 248, 250.
58. Engle, 'Sovereign Cruelty in Montaigne and *King Lear*', pp. 119, 136.
59. Dollimore, *Radical Tragedy*, 2nd edn, pp. 15, 17–18, 196, 195–202. Ellrodt makes a similar observation in 'Self-Consistency in Montaigne and Shakespeare', although in many respects he disagrees with Dollimore; the essayist and the playwright, he suggests, are 'only subversive inasmuch as they laid bare the artificial foundations of the social order' (p. 137).
60. Grady, *Shakespeare, Machiavelli, and Montaigne*, pp. 5, 52, 118, 52; Grady, 'Afterword', p. 174. Ellrodt, in 'Constance des valeurs humanistes', takes issue with Grady and others who reject all forms of essentialism in Montaigne and Shakespeare (p. 112), but nonetheless finds

various forms of commonality between these writers, including a shared abhorrence of cruelty (pp. 107–8). See also Ellrodt, 'Self-Consistency', which elaborates additional elements of authorial congruence, especially a sense that both Montaigne and most Shakespearean characters exhibit profound levels of self-consistency.

61. Holbrook, 'Introduction', p. 5; Holbrook, *Shakespeare's Individualism*, pp. 187–8, p. 193, p. 195. The quotation from Montaigne derives from 'Upon some Verses of *Virgil*', rendered by Florio as 'I greedily long to make my selfe knowne' (*Essayes*, p. 508). Ellrodt, in 'Self-Consistency', finds on the contrary that Shakespeare is 'obsessed mainly with time', while Montaigne is 'quietly obsessed with death' (p. 149).

62. Miles, *Shakespeare and the Constant Romans*, pp. 90, 85, 84. Neill similarly links this play to Montaigne and Plutarch, though his emphasis lies on discontinuous identity; see the introduction to his edition of *Anthony and Cleopatra*, pp. 81–2.

63. Carson, 'Hearing Voices', pp. 163, 152. Gordon also linked *Coriolanus* with Montaigne, noting that the chapter 'Of Glorie' reveals an awareness – much like that of Shakespeare – of the fickleness of fame and glory ('Name and Fame').

64. Cave, 'When Shakespeare Met Montaigne', p. 118. See also Nuttall, *Shakespeare the Thinker*. Burrow, in 'Montaignian Moments', *passim*, offers arguments bearing resemblances to Cave's and certainly presupposes that Shakespeare uses plays to think through ethical, judicial and political questions – especially in the latter half of his career.

65. Scholar, 'French Connections', pp. 23, 16, 19, 16.

66. Mack, 'Montaigne and Shakespeare', pp. 176–7. See also Mack's *Reading and Rhetoric*, which offers excellent comparative treatments of how these writers made use of what they read.

67. William M. Hamlin, 'The Shakespeare–Montaigne–Sextus Nexus', p. 29. See also Hamlin, *Montaigne's English Journey*, p. 110.

68. As early as 1983 Jourdan outlined a form of this comparative approach, explaining that the purpose of her study was to determine 'whether a close, binary reading of Shakespeare and Montaigne without concern for influence and without necessity therefore to respect or to speculate about chronologies can be valuably instructive'. Her interest was 'to follow Shakespeare or Montaigne in a play or an essay and to seek to enunciate their intellectual and moral postures'; see *The Sparrow and the Flea*, p. v.

69. Lee, *Shakespeare's Hamlet and the Controversies of Self*, pp. 202–3; Lee, '"A judge that were no man"', p. 38; Lee, 'Unreasonable Men?', pp. 274, 268.

70. Lee, '"A judge that were no man"', p. 48.

71. Sherman, 'Aesthetic Strategies of Skepticism', pp. 112, 109; Sherman's arguments are presented more fully in *Skepticism and Memory in Shakespeare and Donne*. Cp. also Sherman, *Skepticism in Early Modern*

English Literature. For Cavell's understanding of scepticism vis-à-vis Shakespeare, see, esp., *Disowning Knowledge* and *The Claim of Reason*, pp. 478–96.

72. Mathieu-Castellani, 'Plutarque chez Montaigne et chez Shakespeare'.
73. Cox, *Seeming Knowledge*, pp. 233, 238.
74. Mack, 'Madness, Proverbial Wisdom, and Philosophy in *King Lear*', pp. 285, 300, 284.
75. William M. Hamlin, 'Conscience and the God-Surrogate', pp. 237–60. I discuss the same issue more broadly in *Montaigne's English Journey*, pp. 110–28.
76. Maguin, '*The Tempest* and Cultural Exchange', p. 153.
77. Parker, 'Shakespeare's Argument with Montaigne', pp. 5, 17.
78. Engle, 'Shame and Reflection', pp. 252, 259, 260, 261.
79. Patrick Gray, '"HIDE THY SELFE"', pp. 219–20.
80. Ibid. pp. 227–32, p. 220, p. 219.
81. Greenblatt, 'Shakespeare's Montaigne', p. xxv, p. xxvi. Compare the *Essayes*, p. 224, for the passage in 'Of the Affections' that Shakespeare seems to have adapted into Edmund's forged letter.
82. Greenblatt, 'Shakespeare's Montaigne', p. xxviii, p. xxix. Bate, reviewing *Shakespeare's Montaigne*, writes that 'it was this book [the *Essayes*], perhaps above all others, that shaped the mind of Shakespeare in the second half of his career' ('Montaigne and Shakespeare').
83. Platt, *Shakespeare's Essays*; for 'shaping', see, e.g., p. 79, p. 164.
84. Ibid. esp. pp. 60–8 (for *Hamlet*); pp. 109–25 (for *Lear*), esp. p. 116.
85. Ibid. p. 166.
86. Greenblatt, 'Shakespeare's Montaigne', p. xxxii.
87. Montaigne also notes that he is 'wonderfull curious, to discover and know, the minde, the soule, the genuine disposition, and naturall judgement of my Authors' (*Essayes*, p. 239).
88. I allude to the title of Florio's Italian–English dictionary, *A Worlde of Wordes*, first published in London in 1598.

Introduction: Montaigne and Shakespeare as Thought-Experiment

Lars Engle

The chapters that follow associate one hyper-canonical writer with another, exploring an intellectual nexus that might matter in several ways. Though neither Montaigne nor Shakespeare suffers from lack of twenty-first-century recognition, associating them could, arguably, make Shakespeare more appropriable for French speakers and make Montaigne more salient for English speakers. For Shakespeareans, it matters whether reading Montaigne changed Shakespeare, and the more specific one can be about such changes, the better. But a general association of Montaigne with Shakespeare may also permit one to discuss Shakespeare in ways that are more difficult without that association. Again, the more specific we can be about those ways, the better. For Montaignistes, discussion of the rapid pervasive impact their author had in early seventeenth-century English culture may add a dimension, both historical and imaginative, to the afterlife of the essays. Warren Boutcher and Will Hamlin have done a great deal in recent years to permit us to be precise about that impact.[1] Hamlin, in his introduction to this book on Montaigne's and Shakespeare's 'Critical History', notes the empirical reservations one might have about claims that Montaigne influenced Shakespeare, describes the possible paths of connection between them, and gives a trenchant account of the history of scholarship associating them. In what follows, before I introduce the essays by various hands and from various points of view that await attention in this collection, I sketch thought-experiments associating Montaigne and Shakespeare: my chapter in the collection below offers a more extended and evidence-sifting experiment of the same general kind.

Most of the chapters that follow, and all the work I have done on this association, begin in the belief Shakespeare and Montaigne are each separately good to think with.[2] What special kinds of good can we discover by thinking with and about the two of them together? In brief, thinking about Shakespeare as *like* Montaigne and as *touched by* Montaigne can bring Shakespeare closer to us. Thinking about Shakespeare *reacting to* Montaigne can help us see Shakespeare *thinking, thinking about thinking,* and possibly even *thinking about the ways many of us think now.*

Two insightful and representative recent discussions of the Montaigne–Shakespeare association illustrate these two processes. The first aims at a large audience of general English-speaking readers, those of *The New Yorker*, presupposed to know Shakespeare better than Montaigne; the second addresses (in English) a smaller community of presumably bilingual scholars of the French Renaissance, presupposed to be well acquainted with Montaigne.

In a *New Yorker* essay entitled 'Montaigne on Trial', Adam Gopnik takes Philippe Desan's massive recent biography of Montaigne to task. Desan situates Montaigne as a person and writer firmly in his political life and in class-inflected personal commitments to upward social mobility and to prudent survival. At times, this approach leads Desan to indict as ahistorical and sentimental the idea that Montaigne, at least the Montaigne who publishes the first two volumes of the *Essays* in 1580, pioneers modern liberalism and the autonomy of the reflective subject. Gopnik finds Desan's demystifying tendency reductive: in Gopnik's view, Desan historicises away Montaigne's evergreen exceptionality. That exceptionality consists, for Gopnik as for others, in Montaigne's willingness to explore his own mind and world as they are, without being inhibited by preconceptions about how they ought to be. Gopnik thinks this willingness derives from Montaigne's recognition, derived no doubt from his experience in law and politics, 'that what is presented as moral logic is usually mere self-sustained ritual'.[3] Further on in the essay, Gopnik turns to the positives he thinks Montaigne finds in this idea, which on the face of it seems a discouraging one. Gopnik celebrates Montaigne's comfortable presentation of ambivalence:

> Montaigne accepts, as no other writer had, that our inner lives are double, that all emotions are mixed, and that all conclusions are inconclusive. . . . By giving life to this truth, Montaigne animates for the first time an inner human whose contradictions are identical with his conscience . . .

For Gopnik, Montaigne's unapologetic openness to the untidy behaviour of his own mind yields a new kind of writing:

> What makes him astonishing is a sort of 'show all work' ethic that forced thought as it really is, mixed in motive and meanings, onto the page. Whatever he's telling he's telling it, as Howard Cosell used to say, like it is.

From this idea of Montaigne's commitment to 'thought as it really is', Gopnik jumps to Shakespeare, and to the idea that, around 1600, we can find Shakespeare's evolving exceptionality illuminated by Montaigne's: 'Desan, writing only about the French Montaigne, avoids the question that, for an English speaker, is essential: the great question of Montaigne's relationship to Shakespeare.' And here Gopnik turns from critique to qualified appreciation of modern scholarship: 'In an introduction to a new edition of the [1603] Florio [translation of Montaigne], Stephen Greenblatt tantalizes us with the suggestion that the relation exists, and shows how richly it can be teased out – and then responsibly retreats from too much assertion with too little positive evidence, willing to mark it down to the common spirit of the time.' Asserting the freedom of writerly kinship with Montaigne, Gopnik makes what looks like a positive assertion about Montaigne and Shakespeare – one that is, presumably, in some relation to his critique of Desan's demythologised portrait of Montaigne:

> Well, essayists can go where scholars dare not tread – a key lesson to take from Montaigne – and this essayist finds it impossible to imagine that Shakespeare had not absorbed Montaigne fully, and decisively, right around 1600. It is evident not in the ideas alone but in a delighted placement of opposites in close relation, even more apparent in Shakespeare's prose than in his verse.

We note, however, that Gopnik here offers testimony about his own convictions and perceptions, what it is impossible (for Gopnik) to imagine not being the case. Gopnik's elegant prior presentation of Montaigne's demotion of public decision procedures to empty ritual by comparison to the free play of the self-aware mind, uninhibited by laws of non-self-contradiction, naturalises this subjective way of stating a literary-historical claim. Gopnik then juxtaposes Hamlet's 'What a piece of work is a man' speech with a strikingly similar passage from Florio's version of the 'Apology for Raymond Sebond', emphasising 'the sudden turns and reversals, without the mucilage of extended argument – the turn-on-a-dime movements, the interjections, the tone of a man talking to himself and being startled by what his self says back'. He also discusses the description of Jaques weeping over the stricken deer in *As You Like It* alongside Montaigne's 'On Cruelty', offering a bold summary of Montaigne's moral position in that essay (one that resembles Judith Shklar's comment in *Ordinary Vices* that Montaigne is the hero of her book, and the founder of modern liberalism, because he 'put cruelty first' among the vices).[4] Gopnik comments:

> Montaigne's point is that when it comes to cruelty we should subordinate all other 'reasoning' – stoic, of degree and dependency – to the essential fact of the stag's suffering. We can reason our way past another creature's pain, but, as we do so, such 'reason' becomes the indicted evil. . . . We are meant to find Jaques' double occupation of weeping and commenting, feeling and keeping track of his feelings, mildly comic – Shakespeare being always convinced, in his English way, that the French are hypersensitive and overintellectual. But Jaques is not a ridiculous figure. He is conscience speaking through contradiction.

At this point Gopnik returns from Shakespeare's conjectural Montaigne (who is Gopnik's Montaigne recognised by a kindred spirit) to clarify his areas of disagreement with Desan:

> After his mayoralty, combining, as it did, the trivial and the terrifying, Montaigne moved away from political action, and Desan, in the end, is hard on his politics. 'Montaigne's humanism, as it was conceptualized starting in 1585, implies a renunciation of politics,' he declares, and elsewhere he sees in Montaigne a sort of false dawn of liberalism. Montaigne's retreat was only a rich man's way of getting off the highway before history ran him over. 'Montaigne is supposed to be the best proof of . . . the victory of private judgment over systems or schools of thought,' Desan writes. 'Modern liberal thought discerns in Montaigne the starting point of its history . . . but let us make no mistake: most of the strictly philosophical readings of Montaigne are the expression of a form of (unconscious) ideological appropriation that aims to place the universal subject on a pedestal, to the detriment of its purely historical and political dimension.'

For Gopnik, this generalisation of Montaigne's step away from political life – and especially Desan's way of identifying Montaigne's idiosyncratic self-exploration with later idealisations of the autonomous subject – wrongs both Montaigne himself and what his example offers to us:

> This view is deaf to the overtones of Montaigne's self-removal. To be against violence, frightened of fanaticism, acutely conscious of the customary nature of our most devout attachments – without this foundation in realism, political action always pivots toward puritanical self-righteousness. . . . His essays insist that an honest relation to experience

is the first principle of action. . . . Ironic self-mockery, muted egotism, a knowledge of one's own absurdity that doesn't diminish the importance of one's witness, a determinedly anti-heroic stance that remains clearly ethical – all these effects and sounds of the essayist are first heard here. . . . The liberalism that came after humanism may be what keeps his memory alive and draws us to him. The humanism that has to exist before liberalism can even begin is what Montaigne is there to show us still.[5]

In Desan's defence – a defence to which academics interested in Montaigne will be eager to spring, given the enthusiasm and perseverance Desan has brought to the field, and the generous encouragement he has offered to many scholars – it should be said that he anticipates a number of Gopnik's critiques, and that he is quite willing to accept that Montaigne, especially post-1585, has the main characteristics Gopnik ascribes to him. Discussing the longer essays of Book III (first published in 1588), and especially in the revisions to the 1588 edition either incorporated in the posthumous 1595 edition or preserved in the Bordeaux exemplar, Desan comments that

> Montaigne unapologetically dared to put himself at the center of all his reflections, and he took responsibility for the preponderance of his being in a particular form – the essay – that favored exhibitionism and that he transformed into a literary genre . . . This 'last' Montaigne is the one we treasure most today, because he is self-sufficient and accepts his subjectivity as an end. (550)

So, though Gopnik might find in 'exhibitionism' a deficiency of reverence, Desan treasures what Gopnik treasures. Desan believes, however, that Montaigne adopted the humanist persona Gopnik so admires rather late in his life as a writer, and that Montaigne's political activities and aspirations motivated his early ventures into authorship. Desan and Gopnik stand on either side of a divide illustrated by the two introductions to this volume, a divide between what it is possible empirically to know or plausibly hypothesise about the author's aims and practices in the author's time – and about the actual impact one author may have had on another near-contemporary – on one hand, and on the other what present uses a mythic Montaigne may serve in relation to a mythic Shakespeare.

I dwell on Gopnik's essay because it articulates so well the appropriable Montaigne for contemporary readers: the Montaigne many of us would like Shakespeare to have recognised and cared about.

As Gopnik concedes (following Stephen Greenblatt and anticipating the very sane account of the Montaigne–Shakespeare relation by William Hamlin that precedes this introduction), we cannot prove beyond the shadow of a doubt that Shakespeare saw Montaigne's exceptionality and reacted to it. If he did, as I and others have argued, and as Gopnik also suggests in talking about Jaques in *As You Like It*, Shakespeare probably reacted somewhat aversively or parodically to aspects of Montaigne's exceptionality we moderns find attractive.[6] At the same time, Gopnik implies, Shakespeare cannot be imagined not to notice Montaigne's liberating illustration of free play of mind casting a moral searchlight outward on the horrors of the social order. But we cannot be sure he reacted to Montaigne's exceptionality *as exceptionality* at all. Shakespeare rarely if ever pays explicit homage to the literary or intellectual exceptionality of others. We are not entirely sure that he recognised even his own.[7] Detecting in Shakespeare awareness of Montaigne's special excellence helps us believe that Shakespeare saw in himself some of what we see in him.

So associating Shakespeare with Montaigne in the way Gopnik does helps us recognise Montaigne's importance and helps us believe that Shakespeare recognised his own. Our uncertainty about the degree to which Shakespeare concerns himself with literary exceptionality – an obsessive and overt concern in, for example, Chaucer, Spenser, Sidney, Marlowe and Jonson, to cite only English authors whom Shakespeare read – derives partly from Shakespeare's predominant genre. Drama, particularly drama that focuses on the lives of the great and the aristocratic, does not encourage extended appreciations or depreciations of other writers. Dramatists who want to comment on literary relations of this kind write epistles or prefaces or prologues (as Behn and Shaw and Jonson do) or write speculative essays or critical dialogues on the side (as Wilde and Dryden do) or include characters who are preoccupied with intellectual issues and discuss writers and thinkers by name (as Stoppard does). Shakespeare on the whole does not locate himself in the history of theatre or the history of thought in this way, though Hamlet's appreciation of a nameless play that sounds a lot like Marlowe's *Dido, Queen of Carthage* provides an exception, as does Shakespeare's deflating rewrite of Homer and Chaucer in *Troilus and Cressida*. Moreover, characters do pause to reflect frequently in later Shakespeare, and their reflections open windows on interior mental life of a complexity that rivals Montaigne's self-presentation in the *Essays*.

In an astute essay published a year before Gopnik's, aimed at an informed academic audience rather than dismayed Trump-era Americans looking for a survival strategy, Colin Burrow argues that Shakespeare and Montaigne can be linked in thought and furthermore points out that the Montaigne–Shakespeare juxtaposition should make us think harder about what we mean by literary influence. Thus Burrow proposes the second benefit we mentioned at the outset, the possibility that thinking about Montaigne and Shakespeare together can show us Shakespeare reacting to Montaigne and *thinking about thinking*. Burrow begins pointing out that literary historians, perhaps particularly those writing about Shakespeare, have worked with a limited and limiting concept of influence:

> [L]iterary criticism has historically not been well equipped with a vocabulary or a method for writing about relationships between two authors where thinking, rather than direct verbal borrowing, might be involved. The category 'source' as it is generally deployed in writing about Shakespeare is horribly tricked out with the defence mechanisms of empirical scholarship. The only evidence that will pass the test imposed on 'sources' by a knuckle-headed (and often also knuckle-fisted) empiricist is an exact verbal parallel. The idea that 'exact verbal parallels' might be intrinsically alien to some of the ways in which writers respond to what they read is not one that carries much weight with traditionalists.

Burrow goes on to point out how this impoverished version of influence has led to pervasive tentativeness among most critics who in their secret hearts believe in Shakespeare's sustained engagement with Montaigne:

> As a result critics with intelligent things to say about the relationship between Shakespeare and Montaigne tend now to 'finesse the question of direct influence', where 'finesse' is a delicate way of indicating that they will avoid discussing it while implying that Shakespeare shared so many premises with Montaigne that it would be strange to suppose them to be the result of coincidence.[8]

Burrow gets it exactly right in diagnosing the conflict-shirking attempt to have it both ways of the finessing critic he quotes (Lars Engle), and we can all be grateful to him for fearlessly taking on the issue of intellectual sourcing. Basically, he thinks literary studies surprisingly unable to describe precisely the kind of influence that comes from reading another author and being impressed by how that author thinks or writes. Burrow notes that in the history of Shake-speare studies 'sources' have been defined almost exclusively as pro-viders of plot – whence the complete exclusion of Montaigne from Geoffrey Bullough's *Narrative and Dramatic Sources* even when Bullough treats *The Tempest*. Burrow argues that whether or not there was what Robert Ellrodt has dubbed a 'Montaignian Moment' around 1600 when English intellectuals were taking up Montaigne, Shakespeare draws on Montaigne in scenes that show people think-ing rather than acting, scenes of suspended conversation or reflec-tion.[9] Such scenes, Burrow believes, become common in drama at the time of Montaigne's reception in England: 'one of the things Shakespeare and his contemporaries did to drama at the end of the sixteenth and at the start of the seventeenth century was to slow it down, and sickly it o'er with a pale cast of thought' (249). Mon-taigne, Burrow suggests, contributes to this, though of course he can hardly be thought to cause it single-handed. And Burrow also notes that norms of commentary in our profession have made it weirdly difficult to discuss Shakespeare as a normal intelligent responsive reader: 'Even the very simple claim that William Shakespeare was an historical agent who read books and had different thoughts about those books at different times is, in our strange world, contentious; the notion that his drama can give evidence of those personal experi-ences is doubly or trebly so' (245–6). Yet, Burrow continues, readers not only keep suggesting that Shakespeare did this kind of thinking, but their accounts of how Shakespearean thinks with Montaigne also converge: "critics have frequently suggested that there is something prickly and adversarial, as well as something sportively liberating, about the places in which Montaigne turn[s] up in Shakespeare: fake friars, ineffectual courtiers, spikey satirists, mad kings, bastards, bas-tard-makers, dispossessed princes with problems telling hawks from handsaws, prisoners, and people with nowhere to go: these are the kinds of person and occasions in which able readers of Shakespeare and of Montaigne are most likely to find parallels between the two writers' (246). Burrow offers a new, persuasive example of this kind of prickly adversarial connection, drawing out ways that the naming of Pompey Bum in *Measure for Measure* may plausibly derive from Shakespeare's reading of Montaigne 1.46, 'Of Names', in Florio, and from Shakespeare's self-referential sensitivity about social mobility across the great common–gentle divide, the sensitivity he mocks in *The Winter's Tale* by having the Clown remark 'I was a gentleman born before my father' (V, ii, 28). Burrow closes his essay with a strategically limited claim: from a moment around 1600 Shakespeare broadened the range of his drama and differentiated it from that of the immediately preceding generation:

> Montaigne was by no means the sole driver of this process; but Montaigne and the wide range of deliberative authors on whom he drew, from Plutarch to Seneca and Cicero, comprised a core of texts from which Shakespeare also drew, with which he argued, and with which he played (catlike), [in] order to fashion drama that both provoked and represented thinking in his own Montaignian moments. (250)

I call this claim 'strategically limited' not because Burrow forbears to assert that reading Montaigne at the turn of the century transformed Shakespeare all by itself: that is sanity rather than strategy. But Burrow has cannily apposed to 'the wide range of deliberative authors on whom [Montaigne] drew' (a spectrum that is phrased as though it is inclusive) the specification 'from Plutarch to Seneca and Cicero'. An attentive reader of Montaigne who does not have a link to Shakespeare in mind would surely widen that spectrum of deliberative authors to something more like 'from the Pre-Socratics to Machiavelli and Bodin'. The range of deliberative authors on whom Montaigne draws is huge, extends much further back in time than Cicero and much further forward than Plutarch, and includes extensive instructive discussion of the major lines of ancient philosophy, heroic highlighting of Socrates, much reference to Plato, copious quotation of Lucretius, and special unusual focus on Epicureanism and Pyrrhonism as viable alternatives to Stoicism, Platonism and Aristotelianism. Burrow's choice could be defended in terms of the overall distribution of references in the *Essays*, where in indexes to both Villey-Saulnier and the 2007 Pléiade Cicero is a champion in column inches, with Plutarch, Seneca, Plato and Horace neck and neck just behind him. (Many of Montaigne's references to Cicero are, in fact, references to Cicero's paraphrases of Greek philosophers.) But in naming Plutarch, Seneca and Cicero, Burrow has also chosen probably the only three of Montaigne's favourite sources that Shakespeareans would accept without quibble or query as, in Burrow's elegant phrase, 'texts . . . with which [Shakespeare] played (cat-like)'. Burrow might himself be finessing an issue about Shakespeare's responsiveness to Montaigne's philosophical reading, sidestepping the thorny issue of how, if he reads Montaigne with deep interest, Shakespeare can seem so little interested in philosophers Montaigne cares so much about. Shakespeare clearly does care about Plutarch, Cicero and Seneca, even if his economy of naming makes direct evidence of this care rather sparse. Plutarch, never named by Shakespeare, nonetheless becomes around 1599 a major empirically confirmed narrative source. Seneca, named once as a tragic dramatist by Polonius, also influences Shakespeare's conception of tragedy, as Gordon Braden has demonstrated.[10] And Cicero as an historical person – someone Montaigne repeatedly chides for being overconcerned with his own reputation – gets rejected as too egotistical to be recruited as a co-conspirator in *Julius Caesar* and referred to as a murder victim in *2 Henry VI*. Cicero the author also appears in reference to Lavinia's past instruction of young Lucius in *Titus*.

So, to finalise this thought-experiment, let us take the bull by the horns. Would it help to think that, for Shakespeare from around 1599 on, reading (some of) Plutarch and (some of) Montaigne replaces reading Holinshed and Plautus and reading or watching Marlowe in providing Shakespeare authors to think with? Holinshed and Marlowe return in *Macbeth*, a chronicle play that exposes the moral dangers of centring life on the sweet fruition of an earthly crown. Nonetheless, the discursive, character-oriented, moralising, interiority-exploring comparisons of Plutarch, and Montaigne's reflective preoccupation with his own character in a world consisting partly of books, may well *be* the world of books, and the window on thought in the non-Christian ancient world, for Shakespeare in the latter part of his career. These two authors themselves are condensers of and recorders of a world of reading Shakespeare otherwise did not have much time for. Delight in Ovid, respect for Virgil, and attention to bookish theatre poets, especially Jonson, doubtless supplemented whatever reading he did in intellectual prose.

This hypothesis accords Montaigne some of the dignity in Shakespeare's hypothetical life as a reader that Montaigne-lovers believe he deserves to have, without suggesting that Montaigne securely links Shakespeare to the many intellectual traditions Montaigne takes up. Montaigne models thoughtful selfish reading, and an anti-competitive stance towards the exigencies of political and economic and erotic life. As Montaigne says in 'Of Presumption', he is also modelling appropriate unsystematic non-scholarly reading as a mode of self-cultivation:

> I have no more made my booke, than my booke hath made me . . .
> Nature hath endowed us with a large faculty to entertaine our selves apart, and often calleth us unto it: To teach us, that *partly wee owe our selves unto society, but in the better part unto our selves.* . . .
> I listen to my humours, and harken to my conceits . . .What if I lend

mine ears, somewhat more attentively unto bookes, sith I but watch if I can filch somthing from them, wherewith to enammell and uphold mine? I never studie to make a booke; Yet have I somewhat studied, because I had already made it (if to nibble or pinch, by the head or feet, now one Author, and then another be in any sort to study) but nothing at all to forme my opinions: Yea being long since formed, assist, to second and to serve them. (II: 18, 602)

On this view, Montaigne may have nudged Shakespeare after 1600 not merely to be more thoughtful, but also more self-indulgent, more moody, more appropriative, more content to delve into simply the thing he was. If Montaigne helped make that happen, he helped with something all Shakespeareans deem important.

I have argued that Shakespeare and Montaigne together provide a banquet for thought. The chapters that follow bear this claim out. We editors have organised them into two groups according to whether they confine themselves to comparison, as the chapters in the first half do, or whether they also make influence claims, as the chapters in the second half do. We have ordered within both groups roughly in terms of the chronology of Shakespeare's works under scrutiny. Thus we begin the first section with a chapter by N. Amos Rothschild that features *Love's Labour's Lost* and a chapter by Anita Gilman Sherman that, among other plays, discusses *The Two Gentlemen of Verona*, and we end the first section with a chapter by Alison Calhoun that focuses on *King Lear* and a chapter by William M. Hamlin that discusses many plays, but pays particularly close attention to late ones. We then begin again with a chapter by Richard Dillane exploring Montaigne's influence on the philosophy embodied in Hamlet's 'To be or not to be'; following chapters discuss *Othello*, *All's Well That Ends Well* and *Antony and Cleopatra* and conclude with *The Winter's Tale*, several discussions of Montaigne's influence on *The Tempest*, and a wide-ranging critique of presentist appropriations of Montaignian and Shakespearean thought.

In 'Of Birds and Bees: Montaigne, Shakespeare and the Rhetoric of Imitation', N. Amos Rothschild focuses not on whether and where Shakespeare borrows from, alludes to or imitates Montaigne, but on how each author represents imitation. Building on the foundational work of Terence Cave and Thomas M. Greene, Rothschild situates Montaigne and Shakespeare within a broad early modern discourse on *imitatio*. He declines, however, to assess the reliability of classical and early modern taxonomies of imitative writing as descriptions of past intertextual practices, instead analysing them as constitutive rhetorical acts. '[A]long with taxonomies of imitative writing,' he observes, 'tropes function not to describe, but to fashion the distinction between [various] "versions of imitation", as well as their relative and ever-shifting cultural valuation.' For Rothschild, the tropes in question – apian, digestive, lineal, avian and cosmetic metaphors, to list a few – serve as 'rhetorical staples through which imitative texts construct their purported similarities to and differences from classical precursors in an effort to maximize their prestige and promote their visions of learning'.

Turning to the *Essayes'* engagements with this discourse, Rothschild first considers how John Florio intensifies and complicates Montaigne's interest in *imitatio* as he attempts to enhance the status of his own work as tutor and translator. Rothschild focuses particularly on the sustained exploration of imitation in the sequential chapters 'Of Pedantisme' and 'Of the Institution and Education of Children'. Through a careful evaluation of Montaigne/Florio's reworking of the taxonomies and tropes of imitative writing, Rothschild reveals how these chapters adapt the rhetoric of *imitatio* both 'to critique institutionalized pragmatic humanism as a grasping failure of imitation, and to champion instead an elitist vision of sceptically inflected civic humanism as the true philosophical incorporator of classical values'. The *Essayes*, in other words, use the 'rhetoric of imitation' to fashion a vision of aristocratic learning at once philosophically adventurous and socially conservative.

Though Shakespeare is never so direct about imitation, Rothschild notes a sustained and intense interest in the subject throughout *Love's Labour's Lost*. The pedant Holofernes is, for Rothschild, the play's embodiment of bad imitation, and it uses him 'to negotiate a middle way between the slavish imitation [he] decries and the rhetorical excesses he endorses and practices'. Moreover, the play's lords repeatedly flirt with reproducing the pedant's faults, and they must therefore humiliate Holofernes in a symbolic purging of the negative imitative traits he embodies. Rothschild's *Love's Labour's Lost* thus reveals an engagement with the discourses of imitation more subversive than that evident in the *Essayes*: the play offers not only a witty take-down of 'those who wield the hackneyed language of imitation to claim learned privilege', but provides access to forms of 'educational and cultural capital that Montaigne would deny the non-aristocratic'. And yet, as Rothschild notes in a brief coda, whatever tensions Shakespeare's engagements with the discourse of *imitatio* might reveal, in death he was quickly 'reclaimed . . . as a practitioner of, and subject for, imitation'.

Anita Gilman Sherman, in her chapter, 'The Nature of Presence: Facing Violence in Montaigne and Shakespeare', juxtaposes a few especially fraught instances of the moral predicament of a speaker who, though in the right, faces violence from an opponent commanding superior force. Can the self one presents when confronted by danger, particularly if that self does not vary from its normal state, somehow protect one against overwhelming force? At the end of his essay 'Of Physiognomy', Montaigne recalls two encounters with different groups of brigands. In the first, he narrowly escapes having his home sacked by a neighbour during the religious wars; in the second, while travelling as an envoy, he endures capture and brief imprisonment, knowing that he will likely be held for ransom or put to the sword. Looking back, he attributes his survival relatively unscathed in both person and possessions to his unusual demeanour: 'my undaunted looks, my undismayed countenance, and my liberty of speech' (III: 12, 336). Sherman comments that episodes of lawlessness 'serve Montaigne and Shakespeare philosophically' by contributing 'to a philosophical analysis of selfhood'.

Sherman asks here, as Montaigne asks himself, what was it about his character that allowed him to escape scot-free? And whence did this rare quality arise? Given that the leaders of both sets of brigands were, like Montaigne himself, well born, she notes with David Quint that one saving aspect may be class solidarity: one nobleman recognises the distinctive courage of another.[11] Sherman points to the analogous turn of events in Shakespeare's *The Two Gentleman of Verona* when Valentine, an aristocrat, is accosted by a 'wild faction' who, on account of his courage, appoint him their captain, then turn out to be banished "gentlemen" themselves (IV, i, 36, 42).

In 'Of Physiognomy', Montaigne for his part uses his recollection of what Othello calls 'hair-breadth 'scapes' as an occasion to consider once again, as he also does elsewhere, the tension in ethical practice between nature and art, that is, between temperament and deliberately cultivated habit. He also wonders if he owes his escape to how he looks. His physically ugly hero Socrates' 'childlike assurance' did not win over the Athenian jury that instead condemned him to death. Why was Socrates' 'unstudied and artless boldness' less successful than his own?

Sherman sees a similar curiosity about what works or fails in extreme situations on Shakespeare's part. She draws interesting contrasts among Barnardine's effective refusal of execution in *Measure for Measure*, Paroles's declared self-sufficiency after tacitly admitting his cowardice and treachery when confronted by his fellow soldiers in *All's Well That Ends Well*, and Falstaff's creative delight as he denies Prince Hal, Poins or anyone else any such satisfaction. Sherman argues that in these characters 'Shakespeare shows a vital "essence" that refuses to be extinguished'. Montaigne, by contrast, 'seems less sure of how that essence operates'. Sherman concludes with the suggestive claim that, despite differences, 'both writers ponder similar ethical questions' involving 'the physical body as a problem of knowledge and a slippery signifier of internal states'.

William McKenzie's chapter, 'Narcissism, Epochal Change and "Public Necessity" in *Richard II* and "Of Custom, and Not Easily Changing an Accepted Law"', sets Shakespeare's most politically daring English history play alongside Montaigne's most pointed rejection of the Protestant Reformation. McKenzie's impressively intertextual analysis begins with an unexpected linking: he ties both 'Of Custom' and *Richard II* to the myth of Narcissus and Echo, particularly as narrated by Ovid and interpreted by European commentators from the fifth to the sixteenth centuries. This myth and its traditions of imagery, according to McKenzie, are appropriated by Montaigne and Shakespeare in their contemplations of significant historical change; verbal and thematic patterns associated with the Ovidian Narcissus aid the two writers as they 'articulate the suspicion that one epoch is giving way to another'. In essence, the myth enables Montaigne and Shakespeare to better understand the anxieties attendant on recognising that a familiar, self-validating past may no longer offer meaningful guidance in the present.

Self-love and presumption are routinely attributed to Narcissus by medieval interpreters of the myth, and McKenzie notes that early modern commentaries on Ovid use similar language to describe Protestants: Narcissus is pressed into service as an emblem of the *philautia* ('self-love') of these *neosophoi impudentissimi* ('most impudent of neo-sophists'). As a consequence, Montaigne's use of these terms to describe agents of undesirable reform in 'Of Custom' not only highlights these agents' narcissism but implies that public peace is less dependent on adopting the best possible political structures than on successfully managing pride and presumption in private individuals. For Montaigne, the animating vice of would-be reformers is excessive self-conceit. As David Armitage, Conal Condren and Andrew Fitzmaurice have stressed in their introduction to *Shakespeare and Early Modern Political Thought*, while 'modern political analysis' tends to emphasise 'institutional and constitutional arrangements', in early modern Europe it was 'the character and spirit of those making up the polity' that was most crucial to its political health.

McKenzie then turns to *Richard II*, citing A. D. Nuttall's observation that the play's eponymous king is Shakespeare's 'most elaborately narcissistic' character. Shakespeare relies for Richard's depiction, of course, on the earlier *Mirror for Magistrates*, where the king is described as 'proud' and inclined to 'self love'. But despite familiar aspersions such as these, the deposition of a reigning monarch by an ancestor of the current monarch was volatile raw material for an Elizabethan playwright, and Shakespeare accordingly introduces finely balanced ambiguities. Bolingbroke's private thoughts, for instance, remain mysterious throughout, so that he can be interpreted as stumbling into rather than seeking the English throne, and Richard himself blurs the line between being usurped and abdicating. Alert to these strategies, McKenzie pays particular attention to the repeated contrast Shakespeare draws between 'shadow' and 'substance', an opposition McKenzie connects to contemporary Neoplatonism. For Henry, matter is 'substance' and ideas are 'shadows', while, for Richard, thoughts are more pressing and more substantial than the external realities they represent. In McKenzie's view, this reversal of subjective and objective prefigures modern selfhood, much as Richard's leasing-out of royal land prefigures the highly leveraged derivatives that enable the most damaging forms of present-day financial speculation. Like Montaigne, then, Shakespeare uses figurative language derived from Ovid's depiction of Narcissus as a means to articulate his sense that one epoch, the medieval, is giving way to another, the modern.

In 'Shakespeare, Montaigne and Ricœur: Identity as Narrative', a sustained and sharply focused discussion of selfhood, Zorica Bečanović-Nikolić argues that while the work of Paul Ricœur has seldom been brought to bear on the writings of Montaigne or Shakespeare, Ricœur's phenomenology of self and time helps significantly to illuminate these authors' representations of real and fictional selves. Bečanović-Nikolić begins by introducing Ricœur's distinction between *idem*-identity and *ipse*-identity. The former concept, denoting sameness over time, might be exemplified by the genetic code of a biological individual, while the latter implies no assumption about an unchanging core of selfhood and is best understood, according to Ricœur, as the creation of a narrator – the self – who assembles fragments of self-consciousness and self-behaviour that may then be seen as constituting a 'meaningful unity' even though they may simultaneously exhibit extensive internal contradiction.

Citing Hamlet's soliloquies and Montaigne's self-representations as salient examples of *ipse*-identity, Bečanović-Nikolić goes on to note that, unlike New Historicist and Cultural Materialist accounts of selfhood, Ricœur's phenomenology is fundamentally ahistorical, and in this regard it offers strikingly different possibilities for critical analysis than do the views, say, of Terry Eagleton, Catherine Belsey or Francis Barker. But Bečanović-Nikolić finds commonality between the presuppositions of Ricœur and the readings Montaigne by Charles Taylor and Erich Auerbach. Taylor aptly points to the 'terrifying inner instability' that Montaigne captures in his *Essays*, while Auerbach characterises Montaigne's apparently haphazard attempts at self-description as the 'spontaneous apprehension of the unity of his person'. Thus the famous *forme maistresse* to which Montaigne repeatedly alludes corresponds closely to what Ricœur would call his *ipse*-identity, unifying the otherwise bewildering fluctuations of his *idem*-self.

For Ricœur, the problem of the self's perpetual mutability can only be solved through narration and emplotment. Just as Montaigne, as a narrator, creates his own *ipse*-identity, so various Shakespearean characters do the same: Bečanović Nikolić mentions Prospero, Othello, Macbeth, Richard II and even King Lear as conspicuous examples of self-making through narrative, paying particular attention to John Lee's account of Hamlet's interiority. She then considers the otherness of other selves in light of the otherness of the subjective self, and in so doing raises the crucial question of the self's moral responsibility given its alterity within time. 'Moral identity, like narrative identity', she writes, 'emerges through a dialectic between permanence and change.' Shakespeare's Claudius, for instance, takes responsibility for his egregious fratricide even though he recognises that acknowledgement of his full *ipse*-identity is shared only by a God who exists outside time and flux. In closing, Bečanović-Nikolić focuses on Ricœur's concept of *attestation* as the most satisfactory overall explanation of self-constitution through the simultaneous narrative creation of identity *and* the recognition of ethical responsibility premised on dialogical acknowledgment of the other. Even here, however, Bečanović-Nikolić stresses that many related questions remain to be explored, and she valuably draws our attention to several such concerns.

In 'Genre and Gender in Montaigne and Shakespeare', which explores an important contrast between the essayist and the playwright, David Schalkwyk argues that Montaigne's 'I' and 'we' in the *Essays* are almost always male, and that when he discusses gender difference directly, Montaigne's 'they' and 'them' set women at a pronominal distance, as beings more or less unable to inhabit the subject position, the position of the person who thinks and writes, in the essay format. In theatrical writing, even for male actors impersonating female characters, Shakespeare gives his women an 'I' of their own. As Schalkwyk puts it at the outset:

> Montaigne fits more shifting within the I–myself range than any writer before him, but he nonetheless remains between these poles. And like the poles of a magnet, these pronouns attract and encompass a general we, implicitly included in the structural imaginary of the reader – an us, a possessive our, that repels or at least keeps at a distance, a they, a them, a their, defined at the basic level of grammar as different from the conjoined I of writing and the we of reading. This we is virtually always male.
>
> Theatre is an exemplary embodiment of the shifting or indexical character of pronouns that hardly ever occurs in Montaigne.

Schalkwyk supports this contrastive claim in nuanced and philosophically informed juxtapositions, setting 'Of Affectionate Relationships' alongside the wonderful exchange on male and female love between Orsino and Viola/Cesario in *Twelfth Night*, and 'On Some Verses of Virgil' alongside several passages from *Othello*, with brief cogent references to many other essays and several other plays. In each case, Shakespeare's women, whether comic heroines like Viola and Rosalind and Portia or tragic victims of gender like Desdemona and Emilia, manifest their capacity to discuss love and gender relations more perspicuously than the males they love and are married or murdered by.

Though Schalkwyk focuses on pronouns throughout, and thus describes the maleness of the grammatically implied writer/reader, the presence in the *Essays* of a great deal of untranslated Latin and occasional untranslated Greek offers cultural evidence that Schalkwyk is right in his claim that the 'we' of author and reader in Montaigne is male and elite, even if, in the 1588 and 1595 versions of *Essays*, Montaigne delights in the fact that his book has found women readers. All this might go to show that Shakespeare has more flexibility than Montaigne around gender difference. But with characteristic suppleness, Schalkwyk points out at the end of his chapter that when Montaigne actually thinks through the artificiality and injustice of male expectations about female chastity in 'On Some Verses of Virgil', Montaigne seems to 'allow for the free exercise of polyamory in sexual matters – applicable to women as much as men'. Shakespeare, he notes, offers 'few representations of this possibility' – and he closes with the point that if we admire this polyamory 'we need to focus on Cleopatra to find a path back to Montaigne'.

In her wide-ranging and ambitious chapter, 'Shakespeare, Montaigne and Moral Luck', Maria Devlin McNair argues that Montaigne and Shakespeare differ markedly in their attitudes towards what the philosopher Bernard Williams defines as 'moral luck'. McNair describes moral luck, quoting commentators on Williams, as 'the allegedly problematic or paradoxical fact that factors decisive for the moral standing of an agent are factors subject to luck'. She goes on to assert that 'Montaigne and Shakespeare disagree not only as regards the reality of moral luck but also as regards the possible dangers it might pose'. In brief, Montaigne feels moral luck is of little consequence to a well-constituted self, while Shakespeare feels that human agents sink or swim in a sea of moral instability, sometimes buoyed up by moral luck, sometimes overwhelmed by it.

In the opening part of her chapter, McNair sets this idea in a broad philosophical context, identifying Kant's assertion of the impregnability of 'good will' as the chief target of moral luck arguments. For McNair, Montaigne anticipates Kant by asserting the autonomy of his own willed enterprise of reflective self-understanding, while Shakespeare tends to illustrate various kinds of dependency of the wills of characters on their immediate circumstances, even at times contamination of the will by malice or misapprehension. Thus McNair sees in Montaigne an essentially Neostoic orientation towards the freedom from fortune of the properly disinterested human will, and in Shakespeare a basically Christian recognition of the dependency of inherently flawed and self-misdirecting human wills on divine grace (sometimes manifesting itself in comedies or romances as second chances to redeem past errors). She does not, of course, claim that Shakespeare was Christian and Montaigne pagan, but she does argue cogently that one major orientation in Montaigne (and an area of self-congratulation for him) consists of his capacity to reduce his dependence on fortune and the opinion of others to a minimum, using virtuous pagans as models. McNair does not treat Shakespeare as a person, though his career obviously depended on the opinions of a potentially fickle audience, but she does canvas his representations of a stoic Brutus, a desperate Othello, and a variety of characters in comedies and romances (Claudio, Oliver, Angelo, Posthumus, Leontes) whose moral luck turns for the better.

McNair offers a learned, informative account of Christian attitudes towards the unreliability of the will, from Saint Paul and Saint Augustine through Saint Thomas and Calvin. She sets Shakespeare in the context of Reformed Christianity, though there seems a touch of the Catholic in the penitential actions, and a touch of the Arminian in the self-rescues, Shakespeare allows some characters in comedy. Her strong argument should provoke further discussion of this contrast, in that Montaigne shows considerable awareness of what Williams calls 'constitutive moral luck' in appreciating the singularities of his own inborn temperament, his unusual education, his experience of perfect friendship, and his noble freedom from social dependency. McNair has opened up an important topic with a set of bold and well-argued claims, and she has drawn an instructive and persuasive contrast between Montaigne and Shakespeare in doing so.

Cassie Miura's wise and graceful chapter, 'Cavell's Tragic Scepticism and the Comedy of the Cuckold: *Othello* and Montaigne Revisited', takes off from Stanley Cavell's chapter 'Othello and the Stake of the Other' to argue, by contrast, that for Shakespeare as well as Montaigne scepticism is a source of comedy. Scepticism is the solution, not the problem to be solved. What Cavell calls 'the sceptical problematic' is in fact its opposite: dogmatism.

As Miura points out, Cavell's tantalising nod to Montaigne in his discussion of *Othello* is unusual for him. Cavell more typically ignores Montaigne altogether and instead maintains that Shakespeare anticipates Descartes. Here, however, Cavell draws attention to striking parallels between Shakespeare's play and Montaigne's essay 'On Some Verses of Virgil', noting as if in passing that Montaigne and Shakespeare seem to offer different approaches to 'the sceptical problematic'. Shakespeare represents the uncertainty caused by sexual jealousy as a form of inner torment, whereas Montaigne shrugs it off. Miura quotes Cavell's summary of Montaigne's position: 'We are tragic in what we take to be tragic'; infidelity in particular is 'as fit for rue and laughter as for pity and terror'.[12]

What confuses the matter in this case, Miura argues, is that Cavell ascribes to 'scepticism what he should more properly ascribe to "dogmatism"'. 'Annihilation', 'self-consuming disappointment' and 'world-consuming revenge' are the result of a state of mind Cavell himself describes in Othello as 'terrible certainty', not the *epochē* (suspension of judgement) and *ataraxia* (freedom from passion) characteristic of the sceptic.

Miura notes that Othello, like Claudio in *Much Ado*, or an early modern witch-hunter, succumbs to bad evidence filtered by destructive dogmatism. By apt contrast, Miura compares Montaigne's account in 'Of Presumption' of the man who resigned himself to the possibility that his wife might be unfaithful by marrying a prostitute powerfully to Shakespeare's Sonnet 138, in which she sees resigned comic awareness of mutual imperfection and uncertainty. She also notes Montaigne's admiration in 'Of Cannibals' for the women of the Tupinambá tribe, who not only eschew jealousy but even go so far as to seek out additional wives for their husbands. Miura argues convincingly that Cavell's discussion of *Othello* shows us the bad consequences of too little scepticism, while Shakespearean comedy offers compelling illustrations of scepticism's therapeutic potential. In *Much Ado*, for example, the opposite of Claudio, as well as Othello, is Benedick, who resigns himself happily in the end to the perils of marriage.

In her chapter, 'Feeling Indifference: Flaying Narratives in Montaigne and Shakespeare', Alison Calhoun observes that although punitive flaying was vanishingly rare in sixteenth-century England or France, if indeed it ever happened at all, the practice of flaying a condemned prisoner alive served nonetheless, as it does for Michel Foucault in *Discipline and Punish*, as a significant literary and artistic trope. Notable examples include the statue of *Saint Bartholomew Flayed* in the Duomo in Milan, erected in 1562, as well as Michelangelo's apparent self-portrait in the skin of Saint Bartholomew in his fresco for the Sistine Chapel, *The Last Judgment* (1536–41). Responding to classical biographies of the ancient Sceptic Pyrrho, as well as the figurative language of Saint Paul, Calhoun argues that Shakespeare and Montaigne use the vulnerability of human skin as an argument against fanaticism, including not only the excesses of the contemporary French Wars of Religion but also the radical implementation of Pyrrhonian scepticism.

Throughout both Montaigne's *Essays* and Shakespeare's *King Lear*, Calhoun discerns recurrent doubts about whether Pyrrhonian scepticism is a 'livable proposition'. Pyrrho's own mixed record of success at embodying his sceptical principles calls into question the plausibility of preserving in every case the sage's prized 'indifference' to what Hamlet calls 'the slings and arrows of outrageous fortune'. As Montaigne recounts, Pyrrho went to extraordinary lengths 'to make his life correspond to his doctrine'. 'If he was going somewhere, he would not change his course for any obstacle that he came on, and was saved from precipices, from being hit by carts, and from other accidents, by his friends. For to fear or avoid anything would have been to clash with his own propositions, which deprived even the senses of any choice or certainty.' Even Pyrrho, however, Montaigne observes, could not preserve such counterintuitive 'constancy' in every case. After he was seen defending himself against a dog, Pyrrho admitted, 'It is very difficult entirely to strip off the man' (II: 29, 533). Nor would it be advisable to do so, Montaigne suggests, even if we could. As he concludes in 'Of Drunkenness', 'all actions outside the ordinary limits are subject to sinister interpretation'. Pyrrho's unnatural behaviour, like Cato's in 'Of Cruelty', can be understood by this light as a form of what Christopher Brooke calls 'philosophic pride'.

Calhoun sees a misguided attempt at *epochē* in Cordelia's initial reluctance to speak, specifically in Cordelia's infuriating reply to her father, 'nothing'. Calhoun presents Cordelia's reluctance to play along as an allusion to Pyrrho's reported principle that 'we should be without opinions', leading to 'speechlessness'. Rather than insisting on such 'indifference', Calhoun suggests, Cordelia should save her own skin. Speaking *à contre cœur* or, as Cordelia puts it, heaving our hearts into our mouths can be act of tolerance, as well as self-preservation.

Completing the chapters that make no claims of influence, in 'Montaigne and Shakespeare on Belief' William M. Hamlin pursues his longstanding interest in exploring consequential differences between the thought of the French essayist and the English playwright. Attending to questions of knowing, doubting and believing, Hamlin juxtaposes varied means by which Montaigne and Shakespeare represent real or fictional humans displaying belief in propositions whose truth is conspicuously non-evident. He argues that Shakespeare finds this fundamental cognitive phenomenon significantly more attractive than does Montaigne, for whom depictions of belief often prompt ambivalent or deeply qualified assessments.

Hamlin treats several of Montaigne's principal sources in his discussion, among them Sextus Empiricus's *Outlines of Pyrrhonism* and Cicero's *Academics* and *The Nature of the Gods*. He also compares aspects of Montaigne's epistemological thought to that of Sir Francis Bacon, particularly in *The New Organon*. Despite Montaigne's vehement condemnation of reason in the 'Apology for Raymond Sebond', a tacit but equally powerful dependence on rational deliberation is evident throughout the *Essays*, and Hamlin observes that it is precisely through the exercise of such reasoning that Montaigne reaches his notably cautious evaluations of belief. This is not to deny or disregard the fact that Montaigne declares his status as a Christian believer on multiple occasions. But the ways in which Montaigne shields Christian belief from sustained critical inspection – and particularly the means whereby he modifies Pyrrhonian thought as he engages in this manoeuvre – intimate the extent to which he recognises the potential efficacy of rational investigation in ascertaining the truth-status of non-evident claims and phenomena.

Turning to characters in Shakespearean drama, Hamlin presents four brief case studies: of Hermione, Ophelia, Helen (in *All's Well*) and

Michael Williams (in *Henry V*). He contends that these figures, along with dozens of others in Shakespeare, reveal the playwright's attraction to forms of belief-adherence that can imperil the life, reputation, happiness or social stability of individuals who exhibit them. In so far as this alleged attraction is conveyed through fictional representation, its reality is undoubtedly more speculative than that of the wariness towards belief repeatedly evident in Montaigne, but Hamlin's emphasis on examples drawn from multiple dramatic genres across Shakespeare's career works to mitigate this concern, as does his attention to the potentially positive outcomes imagined by Shakespeare. Implausible, stubborn, risk-inducing belief can certainly lead to tragedy, and Shakespeare never supposes otherwise. But, like Paulina, who asks that Leontes and his companions awaken their faith, Shakespeare also suggests that belief may at times be the best means by which we can heal one another and move thereby towards more charitable, communally responsible futures.

Shifting now to chapters that allege Montaigne's impact on Shakespeare (and on Shakespeare studies), we begin with Richard Dillane's 'Making Sense of "To be or not to be"'. Dillane approaches *Hamlet* through the famously enigmatic soliloquy, finding a key to the logic of this speech in Montaigne's *Essays* and, on the basis of this discovery, a sympathy between the play as a whole and Montaigne's distinctive outlook. He notes that 'To be' is strikingly lacking in story or obvious passion and in fact takes the form of an academic argument – a form in which one expects at the least to find coherent reasoning. The speech is best understood, he writes, not as a cryptically abstract reflection on Hamlet's personal desire for revenge or suicide, but as actual philosophy.

Focusing on the soliloquy's climactic line, Dillane argues that the deduced claim 'Thus conscience does make cowards of us all' is uniquely explicable by means of the philosophy Montaigne particularly admired and helped lift from obscurity, at least for a time. Pyrrhonism is scepticism of a therapeutic kind, where human ills are blamed on our presumption as a species to know (or be able to know) what cannot in fact be known. And to such scepticism Montaigne adds the radical suggestion, deliberately counter to the spirit of Renaissance humanism, that the intellect itself is at fault. Dillane suggests that Hamlet's description of death as an 'undiscovered country' is not mere rhetorical colour but a careful assertion of death's unknownness, from which it follows that the dreaded 'something after death' is purely presumptive. Implicitly adopting Montaigne's view, Hamlet concludes that the intellect is indeed to blame.

Dillane then considers 'To be' in the context of Hamlet's other speeches and discerns a progression that reflects Pyrrhonism's dialectical technique, where factual claims are countered by their opposites in order to bring about the suspension of judgement that leads to tranquillity. In similar fashion, Hamlet describes man as godlike in rationality, but then blames rationality for cowardice and later repudiates too-precise thought altogether – at which point he becomes markedly less troubled, his vengeance ultimately succeeding in circumstances not of his making. For Dillane, this resolution to Hamlet's story reflects Montaigne's call to distrust reason and place faith in providence. On this basis, then, along with the play's complex debt to Pyrrhonism, he proposes that *Hamlet* stages the counter-humanistic thought of Montaigne.

Peter G. Platt's chapter, '"This web of our life is of a mingled yarn": Mixed Worlds and Kinds in Montaigne's 'That We Taste Nothing Purely' and Shakespeare's *All's Well That Ends Well*', argues that Shakespeare's problem plays mingle comedy and tragedy, highlight instability, and call attention to 'the moral and intellectual blendedness of the world'. Focusing especially on *All's Well That Ends Well*, Platt suggests that these plays exhibit generic and intellectual links with Montaigne's 'We Taste Nothing Purely', an essay that deals with the phenomenon of impurity, examining the nature of good mixed with evil and intimating that such mixing is connected to sexuality. Platt shows that Montaigne posits an inextricable link between pleasure and difficulty, implying that moods and emotions are blended; Montaigne recognises the impurity of desire and 'the limitations of human control'. Platt then claims that Shakespeare's problem plays engage with Montaigne's central thesis as expressed by John Florio: 'Of the pleasures and goods we have, there is none exempted from some mixture of evil and incommodity.'

Turning to a discussion of *All's Well*, Platt argues that Montaigne hovers above and haunts this play – as he does in the problem plays more generally. Demonstrating that *All's Well* 'mocks the purity of comic form' and 'evinces its impurity . . . in its paradoxes, which constantly challenge categories', Platt shows that, in Shakespeare's mingled yarns, nothing is tasted purely. He also stresses that the King of France regards nature and custom as 'blendable', emphasising social class as a key locus of impurity. The King indeed exposes the contingency of a system that, as Platt rightly notes, sustains his authority. Scepticism towards political power, and towards human knowledge more generally, runs deep in this play. Furthermore, there is 'doubt that generic restrictions – particularly those of comedy – can contain an adequate vision of human experience'.

Ultimately, as Platt concludes, 'All can never end well, really.' And in his final note Platt reinforces the idea that 'doubt, contingency, uncertainty, and mutability, and a focus on multiple selves, brave new worlds, and hybrid art forms characterise the Montaignian Shakespeare', adding that his chapter is part of a revisionist study (now published) which elaborates the thesis that Shakespeare's reading of Florio's Montaigne is fundamental to the composition of his later, post-1603 works.[13]

Like Zorica Bečanović-Nikolić, Daniel Vitkus focuses sharply on early modern selfhood in his essay entitled 'Radical Neo-Paganism: The Transmission of Discontinuous Identity from Plutarch to Montaigne to Shakespeare's *Antony and Cleopatra*'. But where Bečanović-Nikolić turns to the phenomenology of Paul Ricœur, Vitkus turns to materialist readings of English Renaissance drama such as those of Jonathan Dollimore and Hugh Grady. His argument is that Shakespeare, prompted by the writings of Ovid, Lucretius, Plutarch and, above all, Montaigne, creates in *Antony and Cleopatra* a set of theatrical characters who 'resist essentialized selfhood' and exhibit instead 'a fluidity of identity and consciousness'. For Vitkus, 'discontinuous identity' of this sort – a phenomenon by no means limited to *Antony and Cleopatra* in the Shakespearean canon – can be understood as representative of a radically new conception of subjectivity that emerged in sixteenth- and seventeenth-century European thought, strongly marking Europe's movement towards intellectual modernity.

Vitkus begins by quoting Michael Neill's observation that

> in *Hamlet* and *Troilus and Cressida* Shakespeare has already shown a fascination with the discontinuous and histrionic nature of identity explored in Montaigne's *Essays*. . . . *Antony and Cleopatra* . . . goes a step further by taking Montaigne's psychological paradoxes for granted, and in the process throwing the perplexity experienced by Hamlet and Troilus back upon the audience.

Neill's remark leads Vitkus to trace the complex transit of ideas about selfhood in Lucretius, Ovid and Plutarch up to the *Essays* of Montaigne, where, in a celebrated passage near the end of the 'Apology for Raymond Sebond', Montaigne quotes at length from Jacques Amyot's 1572 French translation of Plutarch's 'The EI at Delphi'. Plutarch, of course, is generally sceptical of materialist metaphysics, but in this essay he treats Epicurean thought quite sympathetically, and Montaigne enhances the appeal. The result is that Shakespeare would have had access here to a sustained account of subjectivity as material, ephemeral and endlessly mutable.

But it is not crucial to Vitkus's argument that Shakespeare drew upon this passage in the 'Apology', and indeed Vitkus relies on a flexible conception of influence in which distinctive trends of thought can be appropriated by various writers in various ways, particularly through creative or transformative incorporation within new discursive settings. In *Antony and Cleopatra*, then, Vitkus finds illustrations of the idea advanced by Plutarch and Montaigne that subjectivity may not be grounded in a fixed, unchanging essence. And he goes on to argue that this sense of selfhood as inherently unstable is in fact much more pronounced in Shakespeare than in Montaigne. Like the Platonist Ammonius in 'The EI at Delphi', Montaigne balances his insistence on human inconstancy with a countervailing faith in the final stability of God. But Shakespeare embraces 'Renaissance neo-paganism', which Vitkus elsewhere describes as a 'Pythagorean-Epicurean-Lucretian synthesis' characteristic, for instance, of Ovid's *Metamorphoses*. In the end, *Antony and Cleopatra* offers its audience an innovative form of tragedy that not only implies the instability of identity but also hints at 'a kind of materialist metempsychosis [enabled by] the endless cyclical metamorphosis of inspirited matter'. And to this extent the play may be seen as 'a subtle, cagey piece of "resistance literature"': a work that questions traditional Christian assumptions while simultaneously pointing towards modern, materialist presuppositions regarding consciousness and identity.

Pursuing the interest in early modern dramatic genres that has characterised much of his abundant, perceptive scholarship, Richard Hillman argues in 'Montaigne, Shakespeare and the Metamorphosis of Comedy and Tragedy' that the playwright's discovery of the *Essays* had a 'transformative impact' on the relationship between comic and tragic elements in his subsequent plays, not least within the genre dynamics of the late romances. Hillman dates this discovery to around 1600 and thus accepts the longstanding hypothesis that Florio's translation of Montaigne was circulating in manuscript at that time. But while many scholars who depend on this hypothesis concentrate on ideas or habits of reflection in Shakespeare that may be traced to Montaigne, Hillman suggests a more relaxed model of influence in which the dramatist relies selectively and unsystematically on the essayist for material which appeals to his 'sense of theatrical possibility'.

Hillman begins with *Hamlet*, drawing attention to the 'co-mingling' of comic and tragic tendencies in the play and show-ing that Montaignian essays such as the 'Apology for Raymond Sebond', 'We Taste Nothing Purely' and 'Of Experience' reinforce a sense that no absolute separation of joy and sorrow can ever be pos-sible. He then turns briefly to the problem plays, marshalling Mon-taigne's famous claim that 'the best good I have, hath some vicious tainte' in support of the view that *Troilus and Cressida*, *All's Well That Ends Well* and *Measure for Measure* depict worlds where vice and virtue not only coexist but are bound together 'so as to suggest that human experience necessarily partakes of both'. Hillman's prin-cipal interest, however, lies with the overtly tragicomic dimensions of Shakespeare's final plays, and he devotes the second half of his chapter to *The Winter's Tale* and *The Tempest*.

Regarding the latter work, Hillman notes that one major effect of Gonzalo's utopian commonwealth speech is to 'recycle Montaigne's rhetorical method in theatrical terms'. Shakespeare, in other words, mobilises the essayist's interrogation of supposed European civility to hint at an interdependence of 'natural humanity' and 'unnatural inhumanity' that we find repeatedly staged in *The Tempest*, perhaps most conspicuously when Prospero, speaking of Caliban, informs his would-be murderers that 'this thing of darkness I / Acknowl-edge mine'. As for *The Winter's Tale*, Hillman offers a sustained and intriguing argument that Montaigne's 'intertextual presence' in the play is deeply influential with respect to its generic shaping. Con-centrating on 'We Taste Nothing Purely', 'Of Three Good Women' and 'Upon Some Verses of Virgil' – essays profoundly concerned with companionate marriage – Hillman assembles an impressive cluster of Montaignian 'resonances' discernible within the reunions and metamorphoses of the play's fifth act. Paulina takes on striking prominence in this discussion, and not merely because she shares her name with Seneca's remarkable wife: one of Montaigne's 'good women' and a matron famously associated with bittersweet redemp-tion from death. Hillman simultaneously links Paulina to the faith so powerfully invoked by the essayist at the close of the 'Apology', 'If Montaigne', he writes, 'unwittingly presented Shakespeare with a figure named Paulina to mediate between tragic loss and miraculous recovery, the dramatist effectively pursued the intertextual dialogue by recuperating Montaigne's fideism for the paganism the essayist rejected.' Hillman's argument thus finally extends beyond Shake-spearean generic considerations to encompass one of the defining instances of Montaignian thought.

Richard Scholar's graceful and deeply informed chapter, 'Montaigne's *Essais*, Shakespeare's Trials and other Experiments of Moment', develops and recontextualises the suggestion from Colin Burrow quoted earlier in this introduction that we need a more capacious and more just conception of literary influence in order to account for relations between Montaigne and Shakespeare. Citing Terence Cave, Scholar notes that Shakespeare's trials have the character of *essais*; adapting a phrase from A. D. Nuttall, Scholar suggests that the Montaigne–Shakespeare relation, like many other important literary relationships, needs to be thought of as 'action at a distance'.

Scholar joins Burrow in drawing attention to how moments of reflective digression in Shakespeare remind one of Montaigne. Scholar differs from Burrow, however, in demonstrating that some such seemingly 'Montaignean moments' predate the likelihood that Shakespeare had read Montaigne in English. Leading up to a masterful discussion of Gonzalo's evocation of the commonwealth he would found and rule in *The Tempest*, Scholar adduces two such moments from earlier in Shakespeare's career as 'trials' that resemble *essais*: the scene in *Julius Caesar* in which Brutus and then Antony speak over the newly slain body of Julius Caesar, and the actual trial scene in which Shylock justifies his resolve to exact a pound of flesh from Antonio by reference to a catalogue of irrational human compulsions, including urinating involuntarily on hearing a bagpipe. Scholar finds in Montaigne strikingly similar observations about human compulsions excited by smell and hearing and the presence of particular animals to those advanced in *The Merchant of Venice*, and he persuasively links Montaigne's fascination with Plutarchan republicanism to the revelation in *Julius Caesar* that Brutus shows naivety in relying on popular commitment to republican values (as well as tactical folly in departing and allowing Antony to speak). In both cases, Scholar explores an overlap not only in the intellectual materials shared by Montaigne and Shakespeare, but the mode in which they are used: as he says, he is 'comparing and contrasting . . . not only the matter that connects our authors but also the shared manner – transformative, appropriative, experimental – that accounts for their divergences'.

These preparations allow Scholar to develop Warren Boutcher's description of Gonzalo as a scholarly courtier at work, providing a significantly altered sense of how Montaigne's influence works in this widely discussed moment by situating Gonzalo's extended appropriation of 'Des cannibales' as a 'declamation' intended as a distracting and pleasurable entertainment during a moment of trial for Alonso's court. Citing hints in this direction from William Hamlin and from

Boutcher himself, Scholar recasts Burrow and Boutcher by asserting that 'what Montaigne provides Shakespeare here is not philosophical but rhetorical in character'. Thus Gonzalo appropriates not only matter but also manner from Montaigne. Scholar believes that Montaigne's digression about the superiority of Tupinambá social relations attempts to unsettle his European readers, shaking them out of moral complacency, an essentially rhetorical rather than philosophic purpose. Given this Erasmian account of what Montaigne is up to, Scholar makes Gonzalo's failure to console, and the critique it receives from Antonio and Sebastian, all part of Shakespeare's appropriation of what Scholar calls Montaigne's own 'experiment with the praise of utopian folly'.

Lars Engle, in 'Montaigne's Shakespeare: *The Tempest* as Test-case', seizes on a co-editor's privilege to write at length, and he offers three arguments. The first is general: modern Shakespeareans have used Montaigne's apparent proto-modernity as a way to make credible claims that Shakespeare, like Montaigne, anticipates the appropriations we make of him. Engle mobilises Hume's brilliant paragraph on how moralists leap without explanation from *is*-statements to *ought*-statements to categorise Shakespeare and Montaigne (in contrast to, say, Spenser and Calvin) as *is*-oriented writers drawn to the ways actual human experiences and desires cannot easily be contained or predicted by moral systems. Engle stresses how Montaigne appeals to contemporary readers through his anti-ethnocentrism and his generally liberatory attitude towards personal shame, especially sexual and status shame. He goes on to suggest, again quite sweepingly, that Shakespeare appears to share neither Montaigne's optimism about casting off shame nor his anti-ethnocentrism.

The second argument is more particular, and Engle suggests that it may, unlike the first, be new. Following hints in recent work by Warren Boutcher and William Hamlin, Engle thinks that Shakespeare may have chosen which Montaigne essays to read on the basis of the paratexts that introduce Florio's formidable 1603 folio. Engle observes that the essays Florio and Samuel Daniel mention or allude to show up very often in speculations about Montaigne's impact on Shakespeare, and that in fact the paratexts round up all the essays that count as usual suspects for direct influence.

The third line of argument tests the idea that Shakespeare thinks hard about Montaigne in *The Tempest* by reading Prospero and Gonzalo as partial portraits of the Montaigne Shakespeare gleaned from a partial reading of Florio. Drawing on Colin Burrow, Engle argues that *The Tempest* as a play shows a preoccupation with characters in essay-like processes of thought, and that Prospero and Gonzalo are the two who do this most and who also structurally resemble Montaigne as he portrays himself, especially in the essays Florio's paratexts highlight. Engle argues that 'Prospero and Gonzalo together (like Lafew and Parolles together in *All's Well That Ends Well*) show Shakespeare understanding, evaluating and registering ambivalence towards key aspects of Montaigne'. This involves Engle in a fairly new account of what it is in Gonzalo that exempts him from Prospero's vengeful pursuit of justice against those who expelled him from Milan and tried to arrange his bloodless death at sea. Gonzalo's preservation of moral independence and personal generosity within loyal service resembles Montaigne's accounts of his preservation of honest autonomy as an envoy between princes. Engle concludes his test-case by asserting that it is 'reasonable to claim that *The Tempest* contains Shakespeare's attempt to sum up the powerful, yet hard-to-follow and hard-to-credit, example of Florio's Montaigne'.

The final chapter, also a long one, Patrick Gray's 'Falstaff's Party: Shakespeare, Montaigne and Their Liberal Censors', raises bold questions about suppositions shared by many, indeed almost all, of the other authors in the volume. Is Shakespeare 'our contemporary'? Is Montaigne? Gray returns to the questions that divide Desan and Gopnik. In what sense, if any, can either Montaigne or Shakespeare be said to anticipate present-day liberalism? Hamlin and Engle investigate differences between these two authors and conclude that, on the whole, Montaigne tends to be closer to a modern sensibility. Gender is an important exception, as Schalkwyk points out: in keeping with his experience as an actor and a playwright, Shakespeare, the English commoner, is much quicker than Montaigne, the French essayist and aristocrat, to empathise with female characters, grant them the agency of the subject position, and represent their inner life as of a complexity equal to or often surpassing that of the men with whom they share the stage.

In other respects, however, Montaigne's point of view seems closer to our own. As Hamlin explains, Shakespeare is more sympathetic to the claims of 'belief' or, to use a more charged term, 'faith'. When it comes to what the Pauline author of Hebrews describes as 'the substance of things hoped for, the evidence of things not seen', Montaigne's first impulse seems to be close scrutiny, whereas Shakespeare tends to recognise the value of 'self-subordination and intellectual humility'.[14] Engle draws attention to the contrast between Montaigne's resistance to feelings of personal shame and Shakespeare's concerns about social class, as well as fidelity within romantic relationships. Engle sees 'a Shakespeare impressed with and provoked by Montaigne, but deeply suspicious of the very possibility of a sustained Montaignian stance towards the world – a stance of free reflection largely uninterrupted by the continual pressure of negotiation and thereby largely freed from shame imposed by others from without'.[15]

Gray, by contrast, steps back from both authors to consider a third, less visible interlocutor: the perceiver, as well as the perceived. What biases do we as readers, as audience, bring to bear, when we attempt to make sense of Shakespeare and Montaigne? Tracing changes in the reception of both authors, Gray notes the late arrival of their representation as standard-bearers for beliefs associated with modernity but in practice still hotly contested: secularism, individualism and antinomianism. In the interests of securing these authors as allies, Gray argues, we have mistaken their doubts for their beliefs, reading them against the grain of their thought's development over time. We as critics want Shakespeare and Montaigne to be fellow travellers; to believe what we believe. But evidence sometimes suggests otherwise. In keeping with multiple passages in the *Essays* in which Montaigne sets out his opposition to the Protestant Reformation, recent work by George Hoffmann, for example, as well as by Philippe Desan has shown that Montaigne was in practice much more committed to the truth of Catholic dogma and its political defence than many Montaignistes both past and present have made him out to be.

A compelling array of new scholarship, meanwhile, associated with the 'religious turn' in Shakespeare studies, including work by Helen Cooper, John Cox, Sarah Beckwith, Hannibal Hamlin and Brian Cummings, among others, has demonstrated Shakespeare's substantive, sympathetic engagement with Christianity and greatly complicated – Gray would say, rendered untenable – a former critical consensus that Shakespeare is indifferent to religion.[16] By reconnecting Shakespeare to the vernacular literature of the late Middle Ages, including biblical drama, morality plays and medieval romance, as well as the Bible itself, the same body of work also calls into question the claim associated with Burckhardt that Shakespeare represents a sharp departure from English culture before the Reformation: a new articulation of individualism, a new form of more autonomous selfhood, or, in Harold Bloom's grandiose phrase, 'the invention of the human'. For Gray, as well as these other critics, Shakespeare is at least as closely tied to the Middle Ages as he is to modernity.

Thus Gray brings into sharp provocative focus a question treated in many of the chapters above, and put elegantly in Colin Burrow's preface to this volume: how reading Montaigne 'opens up a fantasy of reading as a means of experiencing the soul of another', but then forces us to ask how that fantasy accords with the 'messy realities' of reading – both our failures of attention and our propensities to self-interested appropriation.

These questions are treated both acutely and generously in two graciously provided and gracefully written afterwords that comment on the chapters, the first from a leading Montaigniste, George Hoffmann, and the second from a leading Shakespearean, Katharine Eisaman Maus. I know I speak for all three editors in expressing gratitude to all of our contributors for their perspicacity and their patience.

Notes

1. Boutcher, *The School of Montaigne in Early Modern Europe*; William M. Hamlin, *Montaigne's English Journey*.
2. See, for instance, Lupton, *Thinking with Shakespeare*; Machielson, 'Thinking with Montaigne'; and Bakewell, *How to Live*.
3. Gopnik, 'Montaigne on Trial'. I quote from the unpaginated online edition. For another excellent essay arguing that Montaigne models sanity for readers of *The New Yorker*, see Kramer, 'Me, Myself, and I', greeting the publication of the Pléiade edition of the *Essais*.
4. Shklar, *Ordinary Vices*, p. 2.
5. Gopnik quotes from Desan, *Montaigne*, p. 477 and p. 629. Cited parenthetically henceforth
6. For arguments to this effect, see Parker, 'Shakespeare's Argument', and Engle, 'Shame and Reflection'.
7. See Guillory, *Cultural Capital* on 'the cheerful resignation with which Shakespeare entrusted his book to the flood' (p. 75).
8. Burrow, *Montaignian Moments*, p. 240. Henceforth cited parenthetically in the text.
9. One might compare the Freudian moment in London just after the First World War, though neither Ellrodt nor Burrow makes that comparison.
10. See Braden, *Renaissance Tragedy and the Senecan Tradition*.
11. Quint, *Montaigne*, p. 135.
12. Cavell, *Disowning Knowledge*, pp. 138–9.
13. See Platt, *Shakespeare's Essays*.
14. Heb. 11:1; Hamlin, *Montaigne's English Journey*, p. 128.
15. Engle, 'Shame and Reflection', p. 252.
16. See, esp., Patrick Gray, 'Shakespeare versus Aristotle' and *Shakespeare and the Fall of the Roman Republic*.

Chapter 1

Of Birds and Bees: Montaigne, Shakespeare and the Rhetoric of Imitation

N. Amos Rothschild

The question of Shakespeare's debt to Montaigne has been declared by turns dead, re-energised and undecidable.[1] Rather than proposing or contesting another Montaignian source/analogue/subtext for a Shakespearean text, this chapter begins with the conviction that the very language scholars use to discuss such textual relationships – debt, source, influence, and allusion, to name a few terms – too often imposes a modern definition (and valuation) of allusiveness on works that participate in an early modern cultural conversation about textual interconnectedness.[2] This modern terminology is particularly prejudicial to the evaluation of *imitatio*, the 'central and pervasive' Renaissance precept and practice that, according to Thomas M. Greene, 'determined for two or three centuries the character of most poetic intertextuality'.[3] After all, the modern, smoking-gun standard of allusion that editors have long applied to evaluate claims about intertextuality in early modern works validates only the rote borrowing so frequently disparaged in writing on *imitatio*, while it elides the incorporative imitation such writing habitually extolled.

Sidestepping this morass, I focus not on whether and where Montaigne or Shakespeare imitates, but on how each represents imitation. Beginning with a brief glance at classical and early modern writing on *imitatio*, I analyse historical efforts to redefine and subdivide the concept not as reliable descriptions of the past's shifting intertextual practices, but as rhetorical positioning. In particular, the tropes of imitation – apian, digestive, avian and cosmetic metaphors, to list some of the most common – emerge as important rhetorical

staples through which imitative texts construct their purported similarities to and differences from classical precursors in effort both to
maximise their own prestige, and to promote their own visions of
learning. Selections from the works of Montaigne and Shakespeare
suggest they are no exceptions. In John Florio's 1603 translation
of the *Essayes*, Florio strives to bolster the status of his own twin
roles as translator and tutor, thereby heightening and complicating
Montaigne's preoccupation with *imitatio*.[4] The text's most sustained
and direct discussions of the subject – in the sequential essays 'Of
Pedantisme' (number 24) and 'Of the Institution and Education of
Children' (number 25) – work to critique institutionalised pragmatic
humanism as a grasping failure of imitation, and to champion instead
an elitist vision of sceptically inflected civic humanism as the true
philosophical incorporator of classical values. Shakespeare's corpus
offers no treatment of imitative issues so explicit; however, *Love's
Labour's Lost* embodies in the pedant Holofernes an imitative practice that would avoid slavish repetition and claim prestige through
linguistic copiousness. By humiliating Holofernes, the play rejects his
version of imitation and works to negotiate a more deserving ideal of
civic-minded learnedness – one that might somehow expel the pedantry that persistently inheres in the act of demanding preferment by
constructing the meaning and merit of *imitatio*.

Scholarship on early modern intertextuality – particularly as pertains to Shakespeare – is far too voluminous to survey in detail here.
Beyond the countless efforts to uncover specific instances of intertextual connection, scholars like Greene and Terence Cave opened
inquiry into the endlessly complex and far-reaching significance of
imitation as a pedagogical, grammatical, rhetorical, aesthetic, artistic,
musical, historiographic, political and philosophical phenomenon.[5]
More recent analysis approaches *imitatio* via revised theories of
Renaissance readership and renewed emphasis on material-historical
practices like commonplacing, thereby working to better 'respect and
account for' what John O'Brien describes as the 'disparate, heteroclite
nature' of early modern texts.[6] In the Digital Humanities, still more
recent work dares aspire to reinvigorate – even to reconcile – the old
conflict between positivist source study and 'radical intertextuality'
by harnessing computer technology capable of compiling and map-
ping a heretofore unimaginable volume of textual interconnections.[7]

However, as much as many of these scholarly approaches have
revealed about *imitatio* as theoretical precept and historical practice,
our hard-won understanding has come with some problematic side-
effects. On the one hand, work on the subject has tended either to

accept the period's own classifications of imitative writing as reasonably accurate,[8] or to adopt its figurative language in formulating alternative taxonomies and distinctions.[9] On the other hand, those that do recognise the shortcomings of Renaissance imitative categories as practical descriptions too often pass over their rhetorical significance, dismissing them as unhelpful or insufficiently/excessively nuanced.[10] In short, scholarship largely treats the language of imitation as descriptive and rarely analyses it as constitutive. To explore the ramifications of this oversight, it is useful to survey briefly some of the most prominent terms and tropes of classical and Renaissance *imitatio*.

At the outset of *The Light in Troy*, Thomas M. Greene admits that 'the concept and praxis' of *imitatio* in Renaissance Italy, France and England were 'repeatedly shifting, repeatedly redefined by the writers and artists who believed themselves to be "imitating"'. Greene offers this acknowledgement to head off potential concern about the cohesiveness and scope of his staggeringly ambitious work, proceeding to insist that 'despite all redefinitions and variations, enough remained constant to constitute a real subject'.[11] While this insight about the period's ever-shifting accounts of *imitatio* serves nicely to consolidate Greene's topic, its larger significance remains underexplored. Indeed, the unruly 'redefinitions and variations' that Greene works to corral constitute some of the many ways in which the language of imitation was adapted to fashion the worth of imitative texts.

Efforts to redefine what sorts of writing constitute praiseworthy and what problematic imitation are already evident in the work of the classical authors that early modern humanists sought to recover. Cicero claims he learned to use 'the best words' by working 'to translate the orations of the best Greek orators' into Latin; by contrast, he warns that he found imitating Latin models potentially 'prejudicial' as he 'habituated [him]self to use such [words] as were less eligible'.[12] Quintilian later demurs, defending the value of allowing students 'to paraphrase speeches of [Roman] orators' on the grounds that 'nature did not make eloquence such a poor and starveling thing, that there should be only one adequate expression for any one theme'.[13] In so doing, he redefines imitation not as judicious translation (Greek to Latin), but as expansive paraphrase (Latin to Latin) stressing diversity of expression. Clearly, each text fashions a distinct vision of laudable imitation in opposition to an alternative it deems failed or unworthy, and one text's worthy imitation may well be recast as another's vision of failure.

When these texts' early modern inheritors subdivide *imitatio*, they strive to accomplish analogous acts of textual self-portraiture.

Though the precise terminology changes from one work to another, Roger Ascham's *The Scholemaster* is characteristic.[14] In distinguishing between '*Translatio linguarum*', '*Paraphrasis*', '*Metaphrasis*', '*Epitome*', '*Imitatio*' and '*Declamatio*', Ascham holds that '[a]ll theis be used, and commended, but in order, and for respectes: as person, habilitie, place, and tyme shall require', elaborating that '[t]he five last, be fitter, for the Master, than the scholar: for men, than for children'.[15] Thus *The Scholemaster* purports to describe a hierarchy of imitative writing, and subsequent descriptions present each variety as both more advanced and more free in its relationship to its textual predecessor. Greene dismisses such categories because '[o]nce removed from the classroom' they 'are likely to seem arbitrary; parts of many imitations might well be regarded as translations, while most Renaissance "translations" are already interpretations'.[16] However, though such terminology may lack descriptive value, it certainly did rhetorical work. Indeed, if all text is 'a multi-dimensional space in which a variety of writings, none of them original, blend and clash . . . a tissue of quotations drawn from the innumerable centres of culture', as Roland Barthes claims, and if 'the writer can only imitate a gesture that is always anterior, never original', then early modern efforts to privilege *imitatio* over *paraphrasis*, *paraphrasis* over *translatio*, or *aemulatio* over *imitatio*, are slippery and inconsistent for good reason.[17] Such taxonomies and distinctions do not so much describe hierarchies of imitative writing as construct them.

Still more writers – both classical and early modern – refigure the significance of imitation tropologically. Hereafter, I re-examine a group of recurrent tropes that scholars like G. W. Pigman III have linked to *imitatio*: mellification, digestion, lineal reproduction, cosmetic ornamentation, and animal transformation or comparison. Pigman holds that 'one can identify' existent 'species' of *imitatio* 'by studying the imagery, analogies, and metaphors of writings on imitation'.[18] I would submit that, along with taxonomies of imitative writing, such tropes function not to describe but to fashion the distinctions between Pigman's 'versions of imitation', as well as their relative and ever-shifting cultural valuation.[19]

A reasonably compact introduction to some of the central tropes of imitative discourse can be found in Seneca's *Epistulae Morales* 84, a work Pigman deems 'a central text for all later discussions of imitation'.[20] Thomas Lodge's 1614 English translation renders in early modern idiom Seneca's often repeated cluster of metaphors for imitation, beginning with a famous passage likening would-be imitators to bees:

whatsoever is gathered together by reading, the pen may reduce into a bodie. We ought, as they say, to imitate Bees, which wander up and downe, and picke fit flowers to make honie: then whatsoever they have brought they dispose and place through their combes, and as our Virgil saith;
    Moist honey to make thicke they much doe strive,
    Spreading the same with sweet dew through their Hive.

Concerning them it is not apparent enough, whether they draw a moist substance from the flowers, which is presently honie; or whether that they change those things which they have gathered with a certaine mixture and propriety of their breath, into this taste. . . . But that I be not lead away to any other thing, then to that which is in hand, we also ought to imitate Bees, and to separate what things soever we have heaped together from divers reading, for distinct things are the better kept. Then using the abilitie and care of our wit, to mingle divers liquors into one taste . . . (348)[21]

Seneca/Lodge's letter acknowledges that the comparison between reader/writers and bees is, 'as they say', already commonplace.[22] According to Greene, for Seneca, 'they' are Lucretius and (to a lesser extent) Horace.[23] Lucretius apostrophises Epicurus by writing, 'From your pages, as bees in flowery glades sip every blossom, so do I crop all your golden sayings.'[24] Lucretius's apian metaphor thus defines imitation as a non-transformative gathering, a 'crop[ping]' of 'sayings'. Seneca/Lodge's metaphor is, however, decidedly more complex. While the text advises that when readers turn to writing, they should 'imitate Bees, which . . . picke fit flowers to make honie', it then admits that exactly what process bees complete to perform the miracle of mellification 'is not apparent enough'. The meaning of the tenor – imitation – depends on the nuances of an uncertain vehicle. If bees 'draw a moist substance from the flowers, which is presently honie', then the text defines successful imitation as the careful culling and artful ordering of extracted passages. If 'they change those things which they have gathered with a certaine mixture and propriety of their breath, into this taste', the letter defines imitation as the transformation and melding together of material gleaned from sundry readings (*contaminatio*). Rather than decide the issue, the letter suggests that both processes are essential; readers must 'separate what things soever [they] have heaped together from divers reading' and then use 'the abilitie and care of [their] wit, to mingle divers' snippets of text into a new whole. In short, *Epistulae Morales* 84 offers a case-in-point; Seneca/Lodge 'pick[s] a fit flower' from prior writing on imitation – the bee metaphor – and 'change[s]' it to outdo those forerunners.[25] In the process, the letter recasts as incomplete those imitative works that rely on Lucretian 'crop[ping]', rendering that practice a mere first step towards a transformative alternative it represents as more laudable.

Seneca/Lodge's second metaphor for imitation – digestion – reinforces this rhetorical negotiation.[26] The letter recommends that imitative writing must somehow 'appear to be some other thing, th[a]n that whence it was taken', noting that 'nature doth in our bodie' accomplish just such a feat

> without any helpe of us. Nourishment which we have taken, so long as it abideth in quality, and swimmeth solid in the stomacke is a burthen; but when it is changed from that which it was, then at length it passeth into strength and into bloud. The same let us doe in these things wherewith wits are nourished: that whatsoever wee have gotten, we suffer not to be whole, nor to be other mens. Let us concoct them, otherwise they will go into the memory, not into the wit. Let us faithfully agree unto them, and make them ours, that one certaine may be made of many things . . . (348–9)

Like the apian metaphor, this digestive trope serves to fashion the imitative text's similarities to and differences from classical inter-texts. In particular, the letter uses alimentary language to render con-crete the claim of transformation. Seneca/Lodge first envisions the 'burthen' of food that 'swimmeth solid in the stomacke' to figure unsuccessful imitation as a matter of failed incorporation. Against this image of failure, the letter then crafts a vision of successful imi-tation as absorption; just as when food 'is changed from that which it was, then at length it passeth into strength and into bloud', so when classical texts are adequately 'concoct[ed]', they might impart an analogous textual 'strength' to the Renaissance works that would cast themselves as their 'bloud' inheritors. Digestion thus furnishes a vehicle to negotiate the complex relationships – between self and other, subject and object, present and past – created by the processes of reading, thinking and writing. The trope naturalises these pro-cesses to construct the delicate balance of connection and distance that the letter (and the period) so desperately desires. Such alimen-tary imagery serves as a rhetorical staple through which Renaissance writers can claim prestige by linking their works to the classical texts 'wherewith wits are nourished', yet insist that the resultant work is theirs alone, and not 'other men[']s'.

Many other recurrent metaphors do the work of fashioning imita-tion, though I can only glance at a few more here. *Epistulae Morales*

84 also contains an often imitated trope of lineal descent. 'Although in thee the likenesse of some one shall appeare, whom admiration hath more deeply fastned in thee, I would that thou shouldest be like to him, not as an Image, but as a sonne,' Seneca/Lodge advises, concluding, 'An Image is a thing that is dead' (349).[27] Like the digestive trope, the comparison between 'sonne' and 'Image' constructs a distinction between successful and failed imitation; however, the familial metaphor presents the difference as a matter of 'likenesse', privileging resemblance over replica. Similarly, images of cosmetic ornamentation often represent imitative texts as concealing inadequacies by superficially beautifying themselves with insufficiently incorporated appropriated materials.[28] Tropes of animal comparison and transformation are also legion; likening authors to apes, crows, parrots or magpies fashions them as servile mimics, while likening them to swans or nightingales represents their inventiveness.[29] Broadly speaking, these tropes (along with the others described above) function to construct and condemn some writing as failed or bad imitation by aligning it with disunity, surfaces and unthinking repetition, while enshrining other writing as successful imitation by aligning it with incorporation, interiority and transformation.

The instances in which John Florio's 1603 translation of Montaigne's *Essais* engages the early modern cultural conversation about imitation are far too numerous to catalogue here, let alone to analyse in detail. The subject arises before one even reaches the essays themselves; in his letter 'To the curteous Reader', Florio queries why translation is deemed less prestigious than other forms of writing:

> If nothing can be now sayd, but hath beene saide before (as hee sayde well) if there be no new thing under the Sunne. What is that that hath beene? That that shall be: (as he sayde that was wisest) What doe the best then, but gleane after others harvest? borrow their colors, inherite their possessions? What doe they but translate? perhaps, usurpe? at least, collect? if with acknowledgement, it is well; if by stealth, it is too bad: in this, our conscience is our accuser; posteritie our judge: in that our studie is our advocate, and you Readers our jurie. (A5r–A5v)[30]

In his effort to elevate the translator, Florio instead manages to interrogate the very claims that uphold Ascham's hierarchy of imitative writing. Anticipating many aspects of Barthes's insight about the fallaciousness of original authorship, the translator suggests that distinctions between 'the best' of imitative writing – indeed of all writing – and translation are rhetorical rather than absolute. In collapsing carefully crafted divisions between 'glean[ing]' 'borrow[ing]', 'inherit[ing]', 'usurp[ing]' and 'collect[ing]', Florio resists a rhetoric of imitation that relies on such concepts to construct the meaning and merit of *imitatio* in opposition to (and at the expense of) *translatio*. In short, he defies a rhetoric that continues to bedevil the translating arts to this day.[31]

While Florio's remarks on translation offer a fitting frame to a text so preoccupied with questions of imitation, 'Of Pedantisme' and 'Of the Institution and Education of Children' treat the issue in depth. Both essays present issues of *imitatio* as entirely enmeshed with issues of education.[32] For example, 'Of Pedantisme' uses the topic and the language of imitation to define a pedantic other against which to construct an ideal erudition. 'Even as birds flutter and skip from field to field to pecke up corne or any graine, and without tasting the same, carry it in their bills, therewith to feede their little ones,' Montaigne/Florio writes, 'so doe our pedants gleane and picke learning from bookes, and never lodge it further than their lips, onely to degorge and cast it to the wind' (62). Tropological foils to the culling and conglomerating bee, the essay's birds fuse metaphors of animal comparison and (failed) digestion to represent an educational system that perpetuates problematic imitative practices; French educators have not themselves incorporated the classical learning that they purport to teach, the image suggests, and they therefore impart to their students only a shallow facsimile of erudition. These pupils learn to imitate not the 'judgement and vertue' of the ancients (62), but the grasping nature of their 'letter-puft pedants', who 'would faine raise themselves aloft, and with their litterall doctrine which floteth up and downe the superficies of their braine, arme themselves beyond other men' by 'utter[ing] lofty words, and speak[ing] golden sentences' (63). Such passages rely again on images of failed incorporation ('the superficies of the braine') and ornamentation ('golden sentences'), in this case to denigrate socially ambitious, educated commoners as walking bad imitations of both the classical models they work to emulate and the learned aristocrats they strive to join or supplant.

In fact, both essays elaborate on this condemnation of social-climbing via education, leveraging the rhetoric of imitation to elitist effect. 'Of Pedantisme' gripes that education in France has 'no other aime but profit' and scorns 'the meaner kind of people, and such as are borne to base fortune . . . who by learning & letters seeke some meane to live, and enrich themselves' (65). Likewise, 'Of the Institution and Education of Children' insists that 'learning hath not her owne true forme . . . if she fall into the hands of base and vile persons' (69) – a piece of snobbery Florio redoubles by inserting a lengthy passage translated out of Tasso.[33] Those who seek learnedness for mercenary ends disqualify themselves, the essay reasons; after all, 'a gentle-man borne of noble parentage, and heire of a house . . . aymeth at true learning . . . not so much for gaine or commoditie to himselfe . . . nor for externall shew and ornament, but to adorne and enrich his inward minde' (70). Of course, this conclusion relies on the rhetoric of internalisation to construct as 'true learning' the very sort of leisured, private education that Montaigne received and Florio provided, while a cosmetics trope serves to represent learning for economic 'profit' and/or social 'gaine or commoditie' as a false and grasping imitation thereof. The two essays thus adapt the rhetoric of *imitatio* both to critique the rise of the university-based humanist study that Anthony Grafton and Lisa Jardine have termed 'pragmatic humanism',[34] and to champion instead the *Essayes*' ideal of a private tutor-based, aristocratic education put in practice to civic benefit.

'Of the Institution and Education of Children' elaborates on this imperilled ideal with a peculiar twist on the imitative trope of lineal succession. The essay praises its dedicatee, Countess Diane de Foix, for being 'descended of so noble and learned a race' and for having 'tasted the sweetnesse [of education]' herself, then expresses confidence that she will not neglect the schooling of her son (69).[35] After all, Montaigne/Florio continues, the world

> yet possesse[s] the learned compositions of the ancient and noble Earles of *Foix*, from out whose heroicke loynes [both the Countess and her husband] take [their] of-spring. And *Francis* Lord of *Candale* [her] worthie unckle, doth dayly bring forth such fruites thereof, as the knowledge of the matchlesse qualitie of [her] house shall hereafter extend it selfe to many ages. (69)

Here the essay labours to more firmly link erudite literary production and lineal reproduction by implicitly comparing the 'learned compositions' produced by the 'ancient and noble Earles of *Foix*' with the literal descendants produced 'from out [their] heroicke loynes'. Moreover, the text reinforces this connection by adopting the language of fecundity to figure Francis of Candale's prolific writing as 'bring[ing] forth [the] fruites' of his learning. Montaigne/Florio thus virtually literalises the imitative trope of the book as son; the learned Foix write books and beget learned children, who write books and beget learned children, and so on through 'many ages', literary and literal progeny alike securing the enduring prestige of the house. The crux of this vision – and of the contention that the Countess is 'descended of so noble and learned a race' – is the elision of the labour of (often base-born) tutors like Florio to naturalise the fantasy that the elite inherit learnedness, like noble status, by blood.

The essay later expounds on its ideal of aristocratic erudition, adapting a digestive trope to praise civically applied learnedness. 'I would not onely have [a tutor] to demaund an accompt of the words contained in [a student's] lesson,' Montaigne/Florio advises,

> but of the sense and substance thereof, and judge of the profit [the pupil] hath made of it, not by the testimonie of his memorie, but by the witnesse of his life. . . . whereby he shal perceive, whether he have yet apprehended the same, and therein enfeoffed him-selfe. . . . It is a signe of cruditie and indigestion for a man to yeeld up his meate, even as he swallowed the same: the stomacke hath not wrought his full operation, unlesse it have changed forme, and altered fashion of that which was given him to boyle and decoct. (70)

As in *Epistulae Morales* 84, here alimentary language serves to negotiate the vexed relationship between reader and text. However, Montaigne's essay pushes the standard trope towards the grotesque, using the image of 'a man . . . yeeld[ing] up his meat' to present education by rote repetition as a species of failed imitation. Moreover, whereas Seneca's digestive metaphor presents successful imitation as the absorption and elision of textual precursors within a composition, Montaigne's trope constructs a different laudable alternative to 'follow[ing one's] booke' verbatim. The essay redefines absorption as enactment; to truly digest the classical models one reads, one must not only commit them to 'memorie', but also demonstrate the internalisation of their values 'by the witnesse of [one's] life'. Montaigne/Florio thus adapts the digestion trope to champion an idiosyncratic vision of civic humanism.[36]

Of course, if 'Of the Institution and Education of Children' is insistent that students incorporate and enact their learning, the essay is also anxious that they 'change [its] forme' and 'alter [its] fashion' to claim it as their own. To address this concern, the essay reworks another traditional trope of imitation: mellification. 'I would have [a tutor] make his scholler narrowly to sift all things with discretion, and harbour nothing in his head by meere authoritie, or upon trust,' Montaigne/Florio continues,

> *Aristotles* principles shall be no more axiomes unto him, then the Stoikes or Epicurians. Let this diversitie of judgements be proposed unto him, if he can, he shall be able to distinguish the truth from falsehood, if not,

he will remaine doubtfull. . . . It is requisite he indevor as much to feede him selfe with their conceits, as labour to learne their precepts; which, so hee know how to apply, let him hardly forget, where, or whence he had them. Truth and reason are common to all, and are no more proper unto him that spake them heretofore, than unto him that shall speake them hereafter. And it is no more according to *Platoes* opinion, than to mine, since both he and I understand and see alike. The bees do heere and there sucke this, and cull that flower, but afterward they produce the hony, which is peculiarly their owne, then is it no more Thyme or Majoram. So of peeces borrowed of others, he may lawfully alter, transforme, and confound them, to shape out of them a perfect peece of worke, altogether his owne. (70–1)

Here again, learning 'to apply' the 'precepts' contained in one's reading is essential. Indeed, the essay asserts that application authorises learners to claim material as their own on the grounds that '[t]ruth and reason are common to all'. The apian trope reaffirms the claim that an imitator might produce 'a perfect peece of work, altogether his owne'; the language of mellification mystifies and naturalises the processes by which the reader/writer incorporates 'peeces borrowed of others' into his own work as 'alter[ation]', 'transform[ation]' and 'confound[ing]'. Perhaps more important, though, the essay also repurposes the metaphor of mellification to fashion a vision of sceptical education. Montaigne/Florio follows convention in using the way bees 'here and there sucke this and cull that flower' to figure the characteristic humanist practice of commonplacing; however, the text also emphasises that this desultory mode of gathering exposes students to a 'diversitie of judgements', with crucial pedagogical benefits. As William M. Hamlin explains, a Montaignian 'tutor's job is not to pronounce dogmatically, but to expose the pupil to a wide range of opinion'.[37] To guard against Montaignian civic humanism calcifying into a new dogmatism, the essay thus adapts the apian trope to recast the imitative practice of *contaminatio* as cultivating dogmatism's antidote: a myriad-minded sceptical awareness (*epochē*).[38]

Shakespeare left no 'Of Pedantisme' in which he spells out his ideas about imitation.[39] He did, however, create a pedant who engages the subject explicitly.[40] In the early comedy *Love's Labour's Lost*, Lord Berowne's sonnet miscarries and finds its way to the ears of Holofernes, who delivers the following verdict:

Here are only numbers ratified, but for the
elegancy, facility and golden cadence of poesy, caret.
Ovidius Naso was the man; and why indeed 'Naso', but

For smelling out the odoriferous flowers of fancy, the
Jerks of invention? Imitari is nothing. So doth the
hound his master, the ape his keeper, the tired horse his
rider. (IV, ii, 121–7)[41]

With the assertion that 'Imitari is nothing', Holofernes dismisses
imitatio out of hand, though his definition of imitative literary production comprehends apish reproduction alone. The schoolmaster
invokes a slew of animal images to critique Berowne's sonnet's slavish adherence to Petrarchan tradition; the unthinking obedience of
'hound' and 'horse' towards 'master' and 'rider' suggests the servility
of Berowne's creation to its literary predecessor, while 'the ape' is a
well-established figure for non-transformative imitatio. Holofernes
champions instead a vision of 'poesy' embroidered with (prefer-
ably Ovidian) rhetorical 'flowers' and energised by 'facility' – a term
Terrence Cave aligns with *copia*.[42]

Of course, the pedant's perspective hardly carries the weight
of the play. Indeed, *Love's Labour's Lost* undermines repeatedly
Holofernes' strident dismissal and reductivist definition of *imitatio*. Long before the pedant first takes the stage in Act IV, the
play works to negotiate a middle way between the slavish imitation Holofernes decries and the rhetorical excesses he endorses and
practices. On the one hand, when the King and his lords withdraw
into their 'little academe' (I, i, 13), Berowne voices the play's misgivings about those who turn from life, love and nature to 'plod'
after prestige and 'base authority' by plundering 'others' books'
(I, i, 86–7).[43] On the other hand, even as Berowne deflates his fellow
bookmen's pretensions to a pure and withdrawn erudition, *Love's
Labour's Lost* points up Berowne's own infatuation with linguistic
superfluity.[44] While copiousness of expression may, as Holofernes
promises, allow *imitatio* to escape apishness, the play would seem
to join Erasmus's *De Copia* in warning that those who aspire to
such eloquence can easily 'fall instead into mere glibness, . . .
pil[ing] up a meaningless heap of words and expressions without
discrimination, and thus . . . belaboring the ears of their unfortu-
nate audience'.[45] This sort of linguistic overcompensation is, of
course, precisely Holofernes' error, and the imitative concern that
preoccupies the play. The pedant embodies the play's vision of bad
imitation, and the lords risk following his example.

When Holofernes does take the stage, he enters performing his
learning at every opportunity, and it is immediately plain that his
show of erudition is intended to purchase him a 'base authority' over

the 'undressed, unpolished, uneducated, unpruned, untrained, or rather unlettered' constable Dull (IV, ii, 15–16). His companion, the parasitical curate Nathaniel, constructs the distinction by invoking familiar metaphors:

> Sir, he hath never fed of the dainties that are bred in a book.
> He hath not eat paper, as it were; he hath not drunk ink. His intellect is not replenished. He is only an animal, only sensible in the duller parts. (IV, ii, 21–4)

Nathaniel tries to use tropes of digestion and animal comparison to do the usual work of distinction; as men who have truly absorbed their learning, the curate suggests, he and Holofernes are the bearers of an ancient virtue, and warrant preferment above the uneducated constable. However, the absurd excess of Nathaniel's tropological language undercuts his claims to an erudition worthy of veneration. Mote the page punctuates the point when he notes that the pedant and the curate 'have been at a great feast of languages and stolen the scraps' (V, i, 32–3). This pithy jibe undercuts the pedant's favourite rhetorical device – synonymy – even as it deflates Holofernes' and Nathaniel's well-gnawed tropes of incorporation; though Holofernes lauds his ability to produce innumerable synonyms as evidence of his escape from slavish imitation, he reduces the rhetorical plenitude of *copia* – a 'great feast of languages' – to witless repetition.[46] *Love's Labour's Lost* thus works to expel the pedantry that unavoidably inheres in the act of claiming status by fashioning the meaning and worth of *imitatio*.

It is essential, then, that Berowne and the other nobles ultimately confront and humiliate Holofernes in order to symbolically purge themselves of the negative imitative qualities that the schoolmaster personifies. More fitting still, they do so while Holofernes and his companions perform a Pageant of Nine Worthies, a theatrical display intended to define those qualities that are deemed culturally worthy of renown and preferment.[47] In fact, as scholars have often noted, early modern pronunciation rendered the word 'worthies' a homonym of 'wordies'.[48] The resultant pun thus crystallises the challenge that the play stages for the lords, particularly Berowne: to become truly 'worthy' of the ladies' amorous preferment (and their own gentle status), they must abjure the pedant within. Otherwise, they will remain merely 'wordies'. 'This is not generous, not gentle, not humble,' the defeated Holofernes complains (V, ii, 614). The play, however, suggests that mortifying the pedant – and more importantly expunging the grotesqueries of imitation that he embodies – is the only way that the lords can claim a learned wit worthy to be deemed 'gentle'.

Of course, the humiliation of Holofernes and the lords' education in this carefully negotiated 'gentle[ness]' are but part of *Love's Labour's Lost*'s meditation on the relationship between learning, imitation and status. As Darryll Grantley has observed, the early modern theatre was well equipped to provide an education in class mobility, as it was 'informed by the values of a relatively circumscribed social group, while at the same time operating in circumstances of consumption which challenged those values'.[49] Shakespeare's play exploits this fact with astounding self-awareness, presenting not only the 'values' of the social elite, but also a reflexive examination of the language in which those values are inscribed. Nowhere is that examination wittier (and more trenchant) than when the braggart Armado gives Costard the clown a coin as 'remuneration' for delivering a letter to Jacquenetta (III, i, 115). Costard imitates the word, taking equal pleasure in the money in his hand and the sound in his mouth:

> Now I will look to his remuneration. 'Remuneration'! O, that's the Latin word for three-farthings. Three-farthings – remuneration. 'What's the price of this inkle?' 'One penny?' 'No, I'll give you a remuneration.' Why, it carries it! Remuneration! Why, it is a fairer name than French crown. I will never buy and sell out of this word. (III, i, 119–23)

Love's Labour's Lost offers here something nearly antithetical to the *Essayes*' elitist distaste for 'the meaner kind of people . . . who by learning & letters seeke some meane to live, and enrich themselves' (65). Montaigne leverages the tropes and stereotypes by which the cultural value of learnedness is constructed to critique what he sees as the inflation and devaluation of educational capital resultant from the rise of pragmatic humanism. By contrast, *Love's Labour's Lost* not only points up (and works to expel) the pedantry that unavoidably inheres in the act of asserting distinction by means of learning, but also revels in the exchange of literal for learned currency that Costard's muddled savouring of 'the Latin word' winkingly acknowledges. Those watching have received something beyond entertainment for their penny's admission, and Shakespeare's play is determined to make certain they learn it; their coin has been metamorphosed by the alchemy of theatre into the very educational and cultural capital that Montaigne would deny the non-aristocratic— Remuneration indeed!

Much as Montaigne likened the pedantic 'university men' and 'bookish scholars' of France to so many 'birds' (62–3), so the chief of England's university wits, Robert Greene, famously compared the young playwright and actor William Shakespeare to an 'upstart crow, beautified with our feathers'.[50] Montaigne's avian trope demeans as failed imitators of classical virtue those 'who by learning & letters seeke some meane to live, and enrich themselves', thus enlisting the rhetoric of imitation to craft a socially conservative, if philosophically adventurous, vision of aristocratic learning (65). In turn, Greene – a low-born beneficiary of the very institutionalised humanism that Montaigne decries – calls on the language of *imitatio* to construct a new learned elite; he repurposes Horace's fable of the crow to recast himself and his base-born but university-educated 'fellowe Schollers' as true imitators/inheritors who must reclaim their inheritance from the inadequately learned imposter, Shakespeare.[51] The contrast between these visions of bad imitation and that advanced by *Love's Labour's Lost* is instructive. Montaigne's bad imitators are socially aspirant, institutionally educated commoners, while Greene's are actors, and especially the actor-cum-playwright Shakespeare, whom Greene berates for counterfeiting the learned wit that properly belongs to university men like Greene himself. By contrast, Shakespeare's targets are those who wield the hackneyed language of imitation to claim learned privilege in the first place. It is no small irony, then, that Ben Jonson reclaimed Shakespeare as a practitioner of, and subject for, imitation with another avian trope, swapping the stolen feathers of a Horatian crow for the more flattering plumage of a 'Sweet swan of Avon!'.[52] And that, of course, was only the beginning.

Notes

1. Grady traces the historical eulogising, reviving and redefining of scholarship on Montaigne–Shakespeare connections in his 'Afterword: Montaigne and Shakespeare in Changing Cultural Paradigms', esp. pp. 170–6. Mack has argued that the issue is 'ultimately undecidable' (*Reading and Rhetoric in Montaigne and Shakespeare*, p. 1). In the present volume, Hamlin offers an in-depth account in 'Shakespeare and Montaigne: A Critical History'.
2. On the devaluation of imitative writing through the critical language of 'allusion' and similar terminology, see Machacek, 'Allusion'.
3. Greene, *Light in Troy*, pp. 1–2. On the tension between modern terminology of 'sources' and *imitatio*, see Cave, *Cornucopian Text*, pp. 76–7. Where unavoidable in this chapter, I prefer the terms 'intertextuality'

and 'intertext' in an effort to, as Neil Kenny puts it, 'keep open – or simply pose – the question of what exactly [the relationship between texts] is in any particular instance, rather than prejudging it' ('Making Sense of Intertextuality', p. 58).

4. On Florio as mediating presence or 'Renaissance Go-Between', see Hendrick, 'Montaigne, Florio, and Shakespeare' and Pfister, 'Inglese Italianato – Italiano Anglizzato: John Florio'. For an account of Florio's Montaigne as 'not merely an English translation of a remarkable French book, but a reading of the *Essays*, indeed a reading in the service of a major act of rewriting', see William M. Hamlin, *Montaigne's English Journey*, p. 32.

5. My list of the fields *imitatio* impacted nods to Greene's opening (*Light in Troy*, p. 1). Appropriately enough, virtually all subsequent scholarship on early modern imitation negotiates its relation to Greene's monumental *The Light in Troy* and Cave's *The Cornucopian Text*. See Knight for the argument that some of Greene's and Cave's conclusions are undercut by a reliance on post-Romantic ideals of authorship and originality (pp. 90–4).

6. O'Brien, 'Introduction: The Time of Theory', p. 12. O'Brien offers an excellent account of major work on early modern intertextuality, including relevant controversies concerning Renaissance reading (pp. 11–14). For an updated account of work on intertextuality in the period and beyond, see Maxwell and Rumbold's recent collection *Shakespeare and Quotation* (pp. 11–22).

7. On the Digital Humanities' potential to reconcile source study and the 'radical intertextuality' of 'poststructuralist pioneers', see Trillini, *Casual Shakespeare*, pp. 9–12.

8. E.g., Pigman insists that 'theories of imitation help structure one's expectations as to the types of relations between text and model which one is likely to find' ('Versions of Imitation in the Renaissance', p. 2), while Kenny suggests that the 'practices of imitation . . . taught in France in humanist colleges' match the 'modes' of imitation observable in Rabelais's work ('Making Sense of Intertextuality', p. 57).

9. For instance, François Cornilliat and Gisèle Mathieu-Castellani adopt the figurative language of the period to identify three characteristic relationships between Renaissance texts and their intertexts: 'la filiation' (lineal descent), 'l'engendrement' (procreation) and 'la rivalité mimétique' (mimetic rivalry) (p. 6). Likewise, Charles and Michelle Martindale recite metaphors of mellification and reproduction as unproblematic descriptions of the early modern process of 'creative assimilation' (*Uses of Antiquity*, p. 12).

10. See Greene's dismissal of 'seem[ingly] arbitrary' pedagogical categories (*Light in Troy*, p. 51), analysed below. Pigman notes that '[t]he boundaries between the types of imitation are fluid in some theorists, and in practice it is often difficult to distinguish precisely imitation from

emulation or following' ('Versions of Imitation in the Renaissance', p. 3); however, he still does not waiver in his focus on the terminology's descriptive, rather than rhetorical, utility.

11. Greene, *Light in Troy*, p. 1.
12. Cicero, *On Oratory and Orators*, 1.34. Here I use J. S. Watson's English translation, pp. 43–4.
13. Quintilian, *Institutio Oratoria*, 10.5.5. Here I rely on H. E. Butler's English translation, p. 115.
14. For more examples of such pedagogical distinctions between types of imitative writing, see Hutton, *The Greek Anthology in France*, pp. 29–30.
15. Ascham, *The Schoolmaster*, p. 92.
16. Greene, *Light in Troy*, p. 51.
17. Here I rely on Stephen Heath's English translation of Barthes' 'Death of the Author' in *Image Music Text*, p. 146.
18. Pigman, 'Versions of Imitation in the Renaissance', p. 3.
19. Pigman's 'Versions of Imitation in the Renaissance' remains one of the most extensive accounts focused on the tropes of imitation.
20. Pigman, 'Versions of Imitation in the Renaissance', p. 4.
21. All quotations from Seneca follow Lodge's 1614 translation; they will be cited parenthetically.
22. For more instances of the bee trope, both classical and early modern, see Pigman, 'Versions of Imitation in the Renaissance', pp. 4–7, and Greene, *Light in Troy*, pp. 98–9.
23. Greene, *Light in Troy*, p. 73.
24. Lucretius, *On the Nature of the Universe*, 3.12–13. Here I use R. E. Latham's English translation, p. 67.
25. For more on this reflexive aspect of *imitatio*, see Jeanneret, *A Feast of Words*, pp. 259–60, and Greene, *Light in Troy*, pp. 16–17.
26. For a broader account of early modern 'metaphors of bibliophagy', see Jeanneret, *A Feast of Words*, pp. 131–9.
27. For more examples of the book-as-son, see Curtius, *European Literature and the Latin Middle Ages*, pp. 132–4.
28. On the ornamentation trope, see Guest, *The Understanding of Ornament in the Italian Renaissance*, pp. 251–3.
29. On 'the ape as metaphor', see Curtius, *European Literature and the Latin Middle Ages*, pp. 538–40. On the crow as emblem of 'superficial imitation', see White, *Plagiarism and Imitation during the English Renaissance*, who traces the trope to 'Horace's use of the Aesopic fable' (p. 18). On the rote repetition of parrots and magpies as opposed to the inventiveness of nightingales and swans, see Keilen, *Vulgar Eloquence*, who finds the origin of the distinction in Pliny the Elder's *Historia Naturalis* (p. 59).
30. All quotations from Montaigne follow Florio's 1603 translation; they will be cited parenthetically.

31. As Susan Bassnett explains, 'the assumption that translation is a straightforward process has also meant that the role played by the translator has been seen as relatively unimportant' (*Translation*, p. 2). On the 'fallacy of such thinking', see ibid., esp. pp. 3–15.
32. Greene notes that 'Imitatio was a literary technique that was also a pedagogical method and a critical battleground' (*Light in Troy*, p. 2).
33. The roughly nine-line insertion – which Peter Mack identifies as Florio's 'longest addition' to the *Essayes* ('Montaigne and Florio', p. 83) – personifies 'Philosophie' as a 'rich and noble Queene' who welcomes the advances of 'Princes and noble men', but 'if shee be wooed . . . by clownes, mechanicall fellowes, and such base kinde of people, she holds hir selfe disparaged and disgraced' (p. 69). Whereas Yates reads this reaffirmation of Montaigne's elitism as the work of a 'sycophant' who desires to 'sh[i]ne in a reflected glory from the aristocracy of his pupils' (*John Florio*, p. 236), Boutcher suggests that Florio pitched his translation of the passage to 'consolidate his position as a tutor in the Harrington-Russell household' (*School of Montaigne*, p. 224). Like Boutcher, I see more self-interest than sycophancy, though I would add that, as a tutor to the aristocratic elite, Florio played a necessary (though necessarily invisible) role in facilitating the social reproduction of the learned elite; after all, it was the tutor's job to ensure that the aristocratic son manifest his 'natural' learnedness (see below).
34. On civic versus pragmatic humanism, see Grafton and Jardine, *From Humanism to the Humanities*, esp. p. 199, and Armstrong, *A Ciceronian Sunburn*, pp. 2–4.
35. As Boutcher explains, an aristocratic woman often had 'agency in the appointment and briefing of the tutor for her son' (*School of Montaigne*, p. 223).
36. Here Montaigne also represents the self, and not the imitative text, as the primary product of imitation. On the *Essays*' effort to write a self by negotiating a relationship with alien discourse, see Cave, *Cornucopian Text* (esp. pp. 278–80).
37. Hamlin, What Did Montaigne's Skepticism Mean to Shakespeare and His Contemporaries?', p. 201.
38. Hamlin explains that the 'doubt' of Montaignian scepticism emphasised 'judgmental suspension [*epoché*] in the face of diverse opinion . . . It was an antidote rather than a substitute for dogmatism' (ibid. p. 199).
39. For a broader survey of Shakespeare's use of the term 'imitation', see Berggren, '"*Imitari* Is Nothing"'.
40. Shakespeare's pedant has long – and probably erroneously – been linked to Florio. For an overview of, and contribution to, the 'evidence', see Yates, *John Florio*, esp. pp. 334–5.
41. Quotations from *Love's Labour's Lost* follow William C. Carroll's edition; they will be cited parenthetically.
42. Cave, *Cornucopian Text*, p. 6.

43. In the very next scene, the braggart Armado reinforces this point when he asks Moth to cite examples of 'great men [who] have been in love' to provide him with 'More authority' that he might 'example' his own ludicrous linguistic and behavioural excesses 'by some mighty precedent' (I, ii, 54; 56; 94–5).

44. See Erickson on the obstacle presented by the lords' linguistic excess, and specifically their preoccupation with 'poetic convention' and 'standardised lyric assumptions' (esp. p. 74). I would add that *Love's Labour's Lost* figures such conventions and assumptions as a species of pedantry that the lords must expel to claim a 'worthy' learned gentility.

45. Erasmus, *De duplici copia*, p. 295. Here I rely on Betty I. Knott's English translation.

46. On the etymological confusion that led to *copia*'s dual meaning of both 'figurative abundance' and 'copy'/'endless repetition', see Cave, *Cornucopian Text*, esp. pp. 1–9.

47. On the tradition of the Nine Worthies as it relates to *Love's Labour's Lost* in particular, see Carroll's 'Appendix A' to *The Great Feast of Language in* Love's Labour's Lost (pp. 229–35).

48. Carroll notes the pun (ibid. n. 137).

49. Grantley, *Wit's Pilgrimage*, p. 208.

50. Greene, *The Life and Complete Works*, XII.144.

51. Ibid.

52. Jonson, 'To the memory of My Beloved, The AUTHOR Mr William Shakespeare And what he hath left us', l. 71, in *The Poems, The Prose Works*, vol. 8, p. 392.

Chapter 2

The Nature of Presence: Facing Violence in Montaigne and Shakespeare

Anita Gilman Sherman

Shakespeare would surely agree when Montaigne writes, 'The corruption and brigandage that enjoy dignity and established status seem to me the least endurable. We are robbed less wickedly in a forest than in a place of safety' (III: 12, 1023/801).[1] After all, Shakespeare dramatises the theft of crowns both in forests and in dignified seats of putative safety.[2] Staging brigandage in castles and courts enhances the socio-political critique implicit in the old motif from romance: the assault by brigands on the innocent wayfarer. Yet, in addition to illustrating lawlessness in both high and low places, these episodes serve Montaigne and Shakespeare philosophically. They contribute to a philosophical analysis of selfhood informed partly, in Montaigne's case, by the traditional dichotomy between nature and art. Yet, in both writers, violent assaults expose the 'natural' man to a situation of mortal danger when he must negotiate his survival with the skills at his disposal: his body and his voice. The question arises: to what extent are these survival skills natural or artificial, that is, learned performances? Although genre separates the two writers in crucial ways – Montaigne's alarming personal experiences contrasting with Shakespeare's often comic stagings – their accounts of how best to parry violence reveal a shared philosophical preoccupation with the self's presence. Perhaps thanks to his experience as an actor, Shakespeare's view of presence is more stripped down and 'instinctual' than Montaigne's.[3] His feeling that presence both relies on and derives from a kind of animal vitality or biological drive makes Shakespeare in the end less sceptical than Montaigne for whom the natural man remains a puzzle.

Two anecdotes in Montaigne's penultimate essay, 'Of Physiognomy', offer autobiographical glimpses into the natural man under threat. They occur during the French civil wars, described as 'this notable spectacle of our public death, its symptoms and its form' (1023/800). The ironic detachment of the theatrical metaphor cannot disguise Montaigne's sorrow for his country together with the intimacy of his encounters with a posse of assailants in which he narrowly averts bodily harm, possibly death.[4] Both incidents force Montaigne into a defensive posture requiring presence of mind and self. In the first, 'a neighbour, and to some extent a relative of mine' arrives at Montaigne's chateau, seeking safety from an enemy in hot pursuit. As Montaigne attempts 'naively to comfort, reassure, and refresh him', small groups of 'soldiers' catch up with their leader 'until there were twenty-five or thirty, pretending to have the enemy at their heels' (1038/812).[5] Montaigne soon realises this is a home invasion. 'Feeling that there was nothing to be gained by having begun to be pleasant if I did not go through with it,' he writes, 'and being unable to get rid of them without ruining everything, I abandoned myself to the most natural and simple course, as I always do, and gave orders for them to come in' (1038/812). A couple of paragraphs ensue in which Montaigne tries to explain to himself, as much as to us, why he reacted in this way; he mentions his trusting disposition, his prudence and his attitudes to Fortune. The narration resumes when the menacing neighbour changes his mind, remounts his horse, and retreats from the premises with his cavalcade of armed men. Suddenly, Montaigne interrupts his account with a proleptic sentence that catapults us into a bizarre future, at once shameless and convivial: 'He has often said since, for he was not afraid to tell this story, that my face and frankness had disarmed him of his treachery' (1039/813).[6] The adverb 'often' indicates that the once hostile neighbour likes to regale others with this story. The subordinate clause forestalls those readers who might expect this man to want to conceal his act of aggression. Is his bravado a continuing act of intimidation? Is Montaigne being obliged to laugh with him about it after the fact? The syntax urges us instead to dwell on Montaigne's disarming face and frankness. Somehow Montaigne's demeanour defuses the intended violence.[7] He has one of those 'lucky' faces – 'a favourable bearing, both in itself and in others' interpretation . . . one very unlike Socrates' (1036–7/811).[8]

The comparison to Socrates connects this remembered close call with the rest of the essay, since 'Of Physiognomy' focuses largely on Socrates and how he carried himself during his last days, defying the

Athenian state with his bold words and non-compliance. As is well known, Socrates occupies a huge place in Montaigne's imagination, not least for exemplifying 'the simplicity of nature' (1029/805).[9] Yet nothing is obvious about this naturalness. Of Socrates' speech to 'the judges who are deliberating over his life' (1029/805), Montaigne exclaims, 'Is that not a sober, sane plea, but at the same time natural and lowly, inconceivably lofty, truthful, frank, and just beyond all example – and employed in what a critical need!' (1031/806–7). Montaigne struggles to analyse its components. In the 1588 edition, he says, 'It is a speech which in its naturalness ranks far behind and below common opinions. It represents the pure and primary impression of Nature.'[10] But later he modifies this assessment such that the 1595 edition reads, 'In an unstudied and artless boldness and a child-like assurance it represents the pure and primary impression and ignorance of Nature' (1032/807). The addition of 'and ignorance' of Nature to his praise of Socrates for conforming to nature captures Montaigne's struggle. To what extent has Socrates trained himself to perform this naturalness? He worries about the disjunction between Socrates' beautiful soul and his ugly body. He implies that Socrates may have an unlucky face that undermines the excellence of his words. Returning to his own proclivity for following nature, he says, 'I have not, like Socrates, corrected my natural disposition by force of reason, and have not troubled my inclination at all by art. I let myself go' (1037/811). Socrates apparently laboured to correct the initial ugliness of his soul – although Montaigne, in revising the essay, no sooner quotes Socrates on this score than he discounts his words, saying, 'I hold that he was jesting according to his wont. So excellent a soul was never self-made' (1035/810). Montaigne insists that 'art cannot reach' the perfection of Socrates' 'nonchalant and mild way' of confronting death (1031–3/807–8).[11] Nevertheless, the suspicion of *sprezzatura* hangs over his redoubtable presence, tainting its naturalness.

Montaigne pursues this line of thought, contrasting Socrates' possibly schooled attitude to his death-dealing judges and the fatalistic resignation of the illiterate Gascon peasants to the plague. His own family deals with the epidemic by fleeing the area for six months (September 1586 to March 1587) and imposing on the reluctant hospitality of others.[12] The peasants, however, silently submit to death, digging their own graves. He admires their resolute presence, comparing them both to Stoic philosophers and to animals. He lauds the 'rustic, unpolished mob' as 'models of constancy, innocence and tranquility', barely pausing before adding, 'our sapience learns from the very animals the most useful teachings' (1026/803). This ambivalent way of viewing the plight of those in mortal peril carries through (as we shall see) to a few Shakespeare scenes: on the one hand, philosophical respect for holding up under misfortune, on the other hand, pity for having been reduced to such bestial straits.

The question of how best to cope with – and fend off – the threat of death continues in the second ambush when 'fifteen or twenty masked gentlemen followed by a wave of mounted archers' take him 'into the thick of a neighbouring forest' where he is 'unhorsed, my valises seized, my coffers searched, my money box taken' (1039/813). For two or three hours, they dispute over his life and ransom. 'I kept standing on my rights under the truce,' Montaigne recalls, 'which were to give up to them only the gain they had made in despoiling me . . . without promise of any other ransom' (1039/813).[13] They pack him off with a large group of musketeers to an undisclosed location when 'behold, a sudden and very unexpected change came over them'. They return Montaigne's property and set him free with gentle words. Looking back, Montaigne ponders this about-face, asking himself why these marauders changed their minds. 'The true cause', he says, 'I truly do not even now well know' (1040/813–14). But, as in the earlier incident, the leader explains himself, repeating 'that I owed my deliverance to my face and the freedom and firmness of my speech' (1040/814).[14] This unexpected outcome prompts Montaigne to consider how he carries himself and the effects of his presence:

> If my face did not answer for me, if people did not read in my eyes and my voice the innocence of my intentions, I would not have lasted so long without quarrel and without harm, considering my indiscreet freedom in saying, right or wrong, whatever comes into my head, and in judging things rashly. (1040/814)

Somehow his face, eyes and voice rescue him from the consequences of uninhibited speech. Yet, it is the very freedom and firmness of his speech that elicits the brigands' respect. Montaigne stoutly defends his rights under the truce, resisting all talk of ransom, and 'openly' confesses 'what party I belonged to and what road I was taking' (1040/814). This behaviour impresses the leader, who deems Montaigne 'undeserving of such a misadventure'. Despite Montaigne's sense that his physiognomy saves him from the rash indiscretions he utters, in this case his face together with tough talk about the law brings about the change of heart that frees him.[15] Socrates was not so lucky, doomed by his ugliness and the serenity of his challenge to the authorities.

In both incidents, Montaigne implies, the leaders shifted course midway because they saw something frank and forthright in him. Were the gangsters suddenly possessed of that 'clear and well purged sight' Montaigne praises at the essay's start (1013/793)?[16] They become, it seems, excellent readers of Montaigne, able to grasp the 'secret light' of his natural charms (1013/793). Overcome by Montaigne's presence, they drop their violent plans, as if their momentary insight into his 'nature' had the power to arrest their destructive impulses. Montaigne concedes, however, that some performative artifice entered into his reactions, especially in the second instance when he insisted on his rights even while drawing on what Florio calls his 'graces' (312). As Lawrence Kritzman puts it, 'Montaigne's makeover of the Socratic model suggests that in order to survive nature sometimes needs to be supplemented by art.'[17] Thus, the art/nature dichotomy with which the essay opens collapses by the end, as it becomes difficult to disentwine the natural man from the performer.

Comparable incidents in Shakespeare's plays explore the resourcefulness of the self under threat. In Act IV of *The Two Gentlemen of Verona* Valentine is attacked in the woods by a 'wild faction' (IV, i, 36) who are so impressed with his demeanour and presence – his made-up-on-the-spot account of having killed a man, his knowledge of 'the tongues' (IV, i, 32), and his 'goodly shape' (IV, i, 54) – that they give him a choice: join our posse or die! The upshot? Valentine becomes the captain of the outlaws, some of whom it turns out are banished 'gentlemen' (IV, i, 42). He is thus able to rescue the beautiful Silvia when his fellow bandits capture her and to intervene when they hold up Proteus and the disguised Julia. The face-to-face encounter is key to the happy resolution of the ambush, according to David Quint, who argues concerning Montaigne that his experiences reveal more about the customs of aristocratic clemency than about the essayist's individual aura. 'It is important that in both cases Montaigne is dealing with members of his own class,' Quint reminds us, 'their mutual recognition – beautifully told in the removal of the gentleman's mask – is Montaigne's substitution for that class recognition of the sacred image of valour . . . that takes place at swordpoint in the opening essay of the book'.[18] In many productions of *The Two Gentlemen* the outlaws arrive on stage masked, at least at first. Perhaps Quint is right, and one reason it works out in both the play and Montaigne's life has less to do with natural presence and more with the acknowledgement of shared values related to the masculine courage of the aristocracy.

The case of Paroles in *All's Well That Ends Well* suggests that fear rather than presence discloses the natural man. Paroles fails the test of gentlemanly valour when he is ambushed. As the boon companion of Bertram, Count of Roussillon, Paroles follows him to 'the Tuscan wars' where he plays the part of the *miles gloriosus* (II, iii, 257). We remember him for two reasons: his irresistible name and his forthright reaction to the discovery of his cowardice in the course of a cruel, but deserved prank. The scene has a whiff of Gad's Hill and its aftermath in *Henry IV, Part 1* because Paroles, like Falstaff, is humiliated by his erstwhile friends, but the differences are several as we shall see. Paroles' companions, disguised as the enemy, abduct him, threatening him with death and torture if he does not reveal military secrets. As far as Paroles is concerned, it is the end, and he does what he must to preserve himself. Surrounded by a violent posse, the terrorised Paroles talks a blue streak – no silent Stoicism in evidence. In a zany scene featuring an invented language requiring an interpreter, the blindfolded Paroles spills the beans, revealing himself as not only a coward but, worse, a traitor. When he is unmuffled and sees himself surrounded by all those whom he has denounced, he does not attempt to save face through verbal wit as Falstaff does. Instead, Paroles takes in his dismissal from the army and expulsion from the group. Alone on stage, after the others have left, he admits:

> If my heart were great
> 'Twould burst at this. Captain I'll be no more,
> But I will eat and drink and sleep as soft
> As captain shall. Simply the thing I am
> Shall make me live.
>
> (IV, iii, 307–11)

Disgraced and ostracised, Paroles declares he has the wherewithal to carry on – although the tone of this declaration is open to interpretation.[19] But the gist is clear: he will figure out how to get by. Although he lacks the presence to induce a change of heart in his captors, the chastened Paroles clings to a sense of self associated with nature that persists even when cultural notions of honour and other layers of art and artifice have been peeled away: the self conceived as an onion.[20] This is how Géralde Nakam understands Montaigne, saying that 'Montaigne disrobes man the better to know him'.[21] She argues that nudity, real and symbolic, represents truth and constitutes identity in the *Essays*.[22] Perhaps body odour substitutes for nudity in Shakespeare's theatre. Paroles ends up cadging coins from Lafeu, who pities his foul stench and disreputable appearance, saying, 'Though you are a fool and a knave, you shall eat' (V, ii, 44–5). Paroles is taken back in by his set, but only on sufferance, as if he were a mangy dog offered kitchen scraps. Will he bounce back? It is possible, as the play invites us to marvel at his self-acceptance, despite falling so low.[23]

By contrast, the prisoner Barnardine from *Measure for Measure* is the thing itself, unaccommodated man, stubbornly resisting the state's death sentence by sheer force of will for a cool nine years (IV, ii, 121). Barnardine's case undoes Montaigne's claims regarding the benefits of possessing 'a favourable bearing' (811): Barnardine's demeanour has indeed deterred the authorities from executing him, but not because he looks fair or speaks well. A convicted murderer and a drunk, he is described as a sound sleeper with 'a gravel heart' (IV, iii, 56), always hungover, whose first stage appearance is heralded as if he were emerging from a barnyard stall: 'He is coming sir, he is coming. I hear his straw rustle' (30). We learn that 'he hath evermore had the liberty of the prison. Give him leave to escape hence, he would not' – surely a sign, among other things, of animal abjection (IV, ii, 137–8). In Barnardine, the layers of art and artifice have long been stripped away. Unlike Paroles, however, he has friends who have interceded for him over the years (125). When the Duke disguised as Friar Lodowick asks about him, the Provost paints Barnardine as the opposite of Paroles, fearless and unspooked by threats and torture: 'We have very oft awaked him as if to carry to execution, and showed him a seeming warrant for it; it hath not moved him at all' (139–41). This response prompts the Duke to praise the Provost's appearance: 'There is written in your brow, Provost, honesty and constancy. If I read it not truly, my ancient skill beguiles me' (142–4).[24] The Duke presumably refers here to the ancient art of physiognomy popularised in treatises that Adriana Bontea suggests Montaigne may have read.[25] This byplay aside, when the authorities arrive to take him to 'the block', like Paroles, Barnardine clings to life. 'I will not consent to die this day, that's certain,' Barnardine declares, putting off the hangman, his assistant and the disguised Duke (IV, iii, 49). He repeats, 'I swear I will not die today, for any man's persuasion' (52). His idea that state violence requires consent is not only deep but evidently convincing, as the Duke concedes in the end that he is 'unmeet for death' (59). Barnardine may be the lowest of the low, but he has figured out how to keep the violence of the state apparatus at bay: a survival skill that we respect, even though he is represented as a brute.

Barnardine's power over his death-dealing judges depends on his stubborn nature and instinctual will to live rather than his physiognomy. His face is fungible, and not only because he is an actor. (After all, dramatic characters by definition have interchangeable faces since any performer across space and time can step into the part.) His face is fungible given that he is selected for the so-called head-trick: a device to elude Angelo's death warrant for Claudio whereby Barnardine's severed head will be substituted for Claudio's, as is Ragusine's later. 'Death's a great disguiser' (IV, ii, 173), the Duke asserts, as if a man's facial traits cease to be distinctive once he dies. The easy substitution of decapitated heads in the Duke's scheme confounds Montaigne's sense that physiognomy matters. Yet, the alleged anonymity of the death mask aside, Barnardine's reprobate presence cows those around him, suggesting a fierce individuality.

Shakespeare's variations on the theme of presence and natural instinct culminate perhaps with Falstaff's verbal self-defence after the assaults at Gad's Hill in *Henry IV, Part One*. The incident begins when Falstaff and his crew organise a night-time attack on 'pilgrims going to Canterbury with rich offerings, and traders riding to London with fat purses' (I, ii, 111–12). They succeed in robbing the travellers, but when they gather to divide the loot, they in turn are ambushed. The joke is that Prince Harry and Poins are the disguised brigands. Poins persuades Harry to join him in the prank, saying,

> The virtue of this jest will be the incomprehensible lies that this same fat rogue will tell us when we meet at supper: how thirty at least he fought with, what wards, what blows, what extremities he endured; and in the reproof of this lives the jest. (164–8)

As predicted, Falstaff lies monstrously about his valour, acting out the spirited swordplay with which he allegedly repelled the thieves. Harry finally cuts him off. 'Mark now how a plain tale shall put you down,' he says, adding, 'What trick, what device, what starting-hole canst thou now find out to hide thee from this open and apparent shame' (II, v, 235–6, 242–4)? Seemingly at bay, Falstaff fights his way out with rhetorical art, redescribing his cowardliness as animal instinct. 'By the Lord, I knew ye as well as he that made ye,' he begins (II, v, 246), adding:

> Was it for me to kill the heir-apparent? Should I turn upon the true prince? Why, thou knowest I am as valiant as Hercules, but beware instinct. The lion will not touch the true prince – instinct is a great matter. I was now a

coward on instinct. I shall think the better of myself and thee during my life – I for a valiant lion, and thou for a true prince. (II, v, 247–50)

Dazzled, he avers, by Harry's princely presence, he knows instinctively to refrain from harming him. Like those who assaulted Montaigne, Falstaff claims to have recognised a truth in Harry's person and presence that stops his arm and defuses his violent intentions. The wheel thus comes full circle as Falstaff successively occupies all the available roles in the romance scenario of brigandage – aggressor, captor, victim, trickster, thief *gloriosus* and aristocratic dispenser of clemency – together with Montaigne's bestial philosophers possessed of clear and purged vision.

In sum, Shakespeare's characters illuminate important aspects of Montaigne's essay such as the way class privilege inflects our sense of the 'human condition' (Florio's rendering of 'l'humaine condition' in 'Of Repenting').[26] Valentine's jousting with gentlemanly brigands in the forest conforms more closely to Montaigne's experience than do the struggles of Paroles and Barnardine. Paroles may be contemptible and Barnardine a brute, but they have a life force and a scrappy defiance that carries them through their ordeals. In them Shakespeare shows a vital 'essence' that refuses to be extinguished. By contrast, Montaigne – Nakam's claim notwithstanding – seems less sure of how that essence operates. He may say in 'Of Practice', 'It is not my deeds that I write down; it is myself, it is my essence' (359/274), and conclude, looking back on two wartime ambushes he barely escaped, that this 'essence' shone through in his 'deeds'. Yet his essence in practice also benefited from no small degree of cultivation: a habit of hospitality, knowledge of his rights under the law, and so on. Even as Montaigne sets out the 'natural' man as an aspirational ideal in 'Of Physiognomy', he acknowledges that aspects of cultural performance persist in extremis, even for Socrates. They certainly do for Falstaff, whose massive physical presence can never be disentwined from his rhetorical ingenuity. Despite these differences, both writers ponder similar ethical questions: how best to behave in times of violence and at what price survival? Each also grapples with the challenges of a sceptical epistemology: the physical body as a problem of knowledge and a slippery signifier of internal states.[27]

Notes

1. I use Donald Frame's translation, first including the page number from the Thibaudet-Rat edition of Montaigne's *Œuvres complètes*. I cite

John Florio's 1603 translation in the footnotes as needed, e.g. 'The corruption and the brigandage which is now in office and dignity seems to me the least tolerable. We are less injuriously robbed in the midst of a wood than a place of security' (p. 322).

2. Gadshill boasts before committing highway robbery, 'We steal as in a castle, cocksure; we have the recipe of fernseed, we walk invisible' (*1H4* II i, 79–81). Hamlet describes Claudius, the king and his uncle, as 'a cutpurse of the empire' (III, iv, 89).

3. Meredith Anne Skura explores the complicated relationship actors have to their audiences, observing that 'the actor's "response to life" affects not only his moments on stage, but also the way he positions himself in relation to the Other, to authority, to time, to desire, and to death' (p. 3). Along with the actor's talent for inhabiting multiple roles and the fluid identity this suggests, she analyses 'discomforting moments of exposure and audience-consciousness' centred on the body when he feels unmasked and naked (p. 3, p. 12).

4. See Rigolot, 'Les "visages" de Montaigne', for the shift of voice in the essay to storytelling and narrative (pp. 368–9).

5. Florio writes 'my neighbour and somewhat allied unto me' (p. 335) to translate 'mon voisin et aucunement mon alié' (p. 1038).

6. Florio writes: 'He hath since reported very often (for he was no whit scrupulous or afraid to tell this story) that my undaunted looks, my undismayed countenance, and my liberty of speech made him reject all manner of treasonable intents or treasonable designs' (p. 336) to render 'Souvent depuis, il a dict, car il ne craignoit pas de faire ce compte, que mon visage et ma franchise luy avoient arraché la trahison des points' (p. 1039).

7. Elizabeth Guild, in *Unsettling Montaigne*, brings Lévinas to bear on this moment: 'in Lévinas, the face is the fragility which instantiated and is exposed by the other's call upon the self, the archaic version of which is the hinterland of the commandment not to kill, and which must be recognised'. She explains, 'Not that Montaigne's face or look is Lévinas's symbolic "face"; the issue is, rather, the power of fragility in both kinds of face, which are different ways of asking the reader to think about intersubjective relations *in extremis*' (p. 116). Philippe Desan discusses the 'naïveté feigned for the occasion', arguing that it amounts to 'dissimulation' and constitutes 'a technique' that Montaigne associates with 'success in politics' and 'his qualities as a negotiator and diplomat' (*Montaigne*, pp. 489–90).

8. Montaigne discusses 'visages heureux' (1036) and 'un port favorable et en forme et en interpretation' (1037). Florio translates this as 'lucky and well-boding faces', rendering 'port' as 'appearance' (p. 334).

9. See, e.g., Kellermann, 'The *Essais* and Socrates'. See also Joshua Scodel who details the ways that 'by omission and adaptation' Montaigne's Socrates in 'Of Physiognomy' departs from Plato's Socrates ('The Affirmation of Paradox', p. 223).

10. I am disentangling the B-text from the later, C additions. In French it reads, 'c'est un discours en rang et an naifveté bien plus arriere et plus bas que les opinions communes: il représente la pure et premiere impression de nature' (1032).

11. Kritzman observes that 'in juxtaposing Socrates' story with his own, Montaigne discovers a new emphasis on action as either creative or adaptive – and perhaps even contingent . . . Montaigne describes himself as strikingly un-Socratic in his ability to adapt to the vicissitudes of human existence' (*The Fabulous Imagination*, p. 149).
    Note that Florio renders 'nonchallante et molle' as 'careless and effeminate' (p. 329).

12. In the summer of 1586 the League besieged Castillon, 'about five miles southwest of Montaigne' and 'the plague broke out among the besiegers' (Frame, *Montaigne*, pp. 246–7).

13. Florio writes, 'I ever stood upon the title and privilege of the truce and proclamation made in the king's name' (p. 337) to render 'Je me maintins tousjours sur le tiltre de ma trefve' (p. 1039).

14. Florio translates 'mon visage, liberté et fermeté de mes parolles' (p. 1040) as 'my undaunted looks, my undismayed countenance, and my liberty of speech' (p. 336).

15. Desan surmises that 'the fact he [Montaigne] was on a mission and was negotiating on behalf of Henry of Navarre may have produced the happy outcome of this affair . . . What could be interpreted as the success of a political negotiation is for him the result of a personality trait, a kind of political disposition opposed to rhetorical effects or other kinds of byzantine quibbles' (p. 491)

16. Hope Glidden says yes, treating the highwaymen as embedded readers with an 'idealised vantage point' on Montaigne since the artifice of textual mediation is absent ('The Face in the Text', p. 96); but Kritzman says no, arguing that, 'Montaigne attributes to the other a kind of myopia that makes him the victim of the referential fallacy. Believing that the gaze of Montaigne could not possibly be denatured, the naïve enemy falls victim to the illusion that equates his look with Being itself (*The Fabulous Imagination*, p. 146). Florio renders the phrase as 'a clear, far-seeing, and true-discerning sight' (p. 312).

17. Kritzman, *The Fabulous Imagination*, p. 150.

18. Quint, *Montaigne and the Quality of Mercy*, p. 135.

19. Compare Queen Elizabeth's angry words to Parliament on 5 November 1566: 'I will never be by violence constrained to do anything. I thank God I am endued with such qualities that were I turned out of the realm in my petticoat, I were able to live in any place in Christendom.'

20. Arthur Kirsch describes Paroles as 'a representation of the thing itself, a personification of the lowest common denominator of human nature, virtually an emblem of the corporeal demands of which Montaigne speaks' ('The Bitter and the Sweet of Tragicomedy', p. 77).

21. Nakam, *Les Essais de Montaigne*, p. 172: 'Montaigne déshabille l'homme pour mieux le faire connaître'.
22. Ibid.
23. Kirsch notes that the scene of Paroles' exposure is powerful 'because what is revealed is so familiar to him. When he is first captured, one of the lords remarks, "Is it possible that he should know what he is, and be that he is?" a line that Montaigne could have written, and the answer Parolles proceeds to enact is a profound *yes*' ('The Bitter and the Sweet of Tragicomedy', p. 76) He agrees with Marcus Nordlund who argues 'that the real function of the protracted unmasking scene cannot be to reveal the nature or properties of Parolles's self, or to expose his moral status . . . What is revealed to the audience is rather his reflexive *attitude* towards his own nature, and here we are confronted with a self-detachment of extraordinary proportions' ('Pride and Self-Love', p. 91). Nordlund highlights the 'acceptance of human frailty, weakness, even vice' that both Shakespeare and Montaigne share (ibid. p. 93).
24. This throwaway line has ironies we may savour as *Measure for Measure* develops. Compare King Duncan's remark after Cawdor's betrayal: 'There's no art / To find the mind's construction in the face. / He was a gentleman on whom I built / An absolute trust" (*Mac.* I, iv, 11–14).
25. Compare the treatises on physiognomy available in early modern England (J. A. Knapp, *Shakespeare and the Power of the Face*, pp. 11–12).
26. Glidden, e.g., observes that 'the *Essays* quite possibly began as a defensive structure erected to protect the self from dissolution, as Thomas M. Greene suggests, and that early need lends special drama to the ambush scenarios and to the threat they pose' ('The Face in the Text', p. 72). This approach – with its intuition that writing is the life force propelling Montaigne – has a way of eliding issues of privilege and the far more 'basic' life force propelling Shakespeare's losers.
27. These questions are also central to affect theory. See, e.g., Leys, 'The Turn to Affect'.

Chapter 3

Narcissism, Epochal Change and 'Public Necessity' in *Richard II* and 'Of Custom, and Not Easily Changing an Accepted Law'

William McKenzie

This chapter explores narcissism as a thematic point of contact between selected texts by Montaigne and Shakespeare. The concept of narcissism can be extended and ramified indefinitely ('the self' and 'love' are tricky enough on their own, let alone 'self-love'), so I seek to isolate and examine one particular aspect. I hope to demonstrate that Montaigne and Shakespeare both draw on phrases, images or themes from Ovid's story of Narcissus and Echo, as well as its long tradition of commentary, to examine causes or perceptions of historical change. In other words, 'narcissistic' imagery helps Montaigne and Shakespeare articulate the suspicion that one epoch is giving way to another; even that past traditions may no longer offer any meaningful guidance; and to examine the psychological stakes of this change. In the first part of this two-part essay, I examine a passage from Montaigne's 'Of Custom, and Not Easily Changing an Accepted Law' (I: 23) (Donald Frame's translation of the title), in which he attributes 'self-love' and 'presumption', terms medieval commentators explicitly associate with Narcissus, to agents of historical reforms that he abhors. By drawing contrasts between these reforms and individual agents' 'propre conscience' and 'naturelle cognoissance', Montaigne taps into a figurative logic of personal microcosm and political macrocosm which is also central to commonplaces of the 'body politic'. The implication is that individuals' conscience ideally guides right action, albeit in a somewhat uneasy, obscure dialectic with what Montaigne calls at the very end of the chapter 'public necessity'.

I argue in the second part of this essay that Shakespeare's *Richard II*, whose titular character A. D. Nuttall aptly describes as 'the most elaborately Narcissistic' of Shakespeare's protagonists, uses narcissistic imagery, especially a dichotomy of 'shadow' and 'substance' also found in Neoplatonic discourse of the period, to evaluate the influence of a pervasive idea of the body politic on self-perception: the political theology Ernst Kantorowicz calls 'the King's Two Bodies', whereby the king's physical body symbolises his regal role and kingdom.[1] I examine in turn John of Gaunt's complaints that Richard II, preoccupied with flatterers, narcissistically self-devouring, is plunging England into a new, dangerous historical moment (II, i, 1–68); the flatterer Bushy's sophistic, euphuistic analogy between sadness and 'perspective' painting (II, ii, 14–28); the deposed Richard smashing a mirror (IV, i, 288); and his soliloquy in prison (V, v, 1–66).[2] In conclusion, I suggest that the links Montaigne and Shakespeare both make between narcissism and radical historical change feed into ongoing discussions about 'early modernity' as an epoch.

As is well known, Montaigne begins 'Of Custom' by criticising custom, as if he were going to advocate throughout the chapter a radical form of individual liberalism.[3] As early as the second sentence he calls custom 'une violente et traistresse maistresse d'ecole' ('a violent and treacherous schoolteacher'): the rhyme of 'traitresse' and 'maitresse' here reproduces the subtle, ultimately 'violent', replication of habitual actions, which in turn may become accepted norms (109). Montaigne stresses repeatedly how such actions or norms may creep up on us, so that they come to seem even more 'natural' than nature itself ('forcer . . . les reigles de nature') ('to force . . . the rules of nature'), and only later disclose ('nous descouvre tantost') 'an angry tyrannous countenance' ('un furieux et tyrannique visage') (109). The implication that custom is nothing but a semi-unconscious by-product of social agreements comes through all the stronger in a well-known passage, greatly extended in the 1588 edition, that lists at conspicuous length (almost three pages) the different customs ('opinions et moeurs' [112]) held by various communities (what Montaigne calls 'regions' [111] or 'peuples' [112]) in seemingly random order, and with anaphoric force:

[A] Il est des peuples où [. . .e.g.] [B] les femmes vont à la guerre . . . où les enfans ne sont pas heritiers . . . Où les marys ont le droit de les vendre [leurs femmes] si elles sont steriles. . . (112–14)

There are peoples where . . . women accompany their husbands to the war . . . where husbands can sell their wives if they are barren. (127)

The sheer length and variety of the list implies a contradiction. Custom may determine, even tyrannically dictate, personal behaviour; but as customs are emphatically not the same everywhere, custom must somehow itself be dictated, howsoever voluntarily or involuntarily, by groups of persons.

Montaigne goes on to articulate his own position on custom in this broadly dialectical framework, acknowledging throughout, with varying degrees of candour, that his own position is itself dictated, socially, by the 'region' and 'peuple' in which he himself lives, as well as historically, even existentially, by the events that befall it. Then, near the chapter's midpoint, in a move that can surprise more modern readers, Montaigne firmly disavows any implication, nonetheless, that people should always or automatically act independently from custom, using terms familiar from the reception of Ovid's account of Narcissus and Echo: 'self-love' and 'presumption.' The passage is important, so I quote it at length, including corrections and amendments from various stages of Montaigne's text.

> [B] Mais le meilleur ~~titre~~ [C] pretexte [B] de nouvelleté est très-dangereux [C] *adeo nihil motum ex antique probabile est* Livy 34.54] [B] Si me semble-il, à le dire franchement, qu'il y a **grand amour de soy et presomption**, d'estimer ses opinions jusque-là que, pour les establir, il faille renverser une paix publique, et introduire tant de maux inevitables et une si horrible corruption de meurs que les guerres civiles apportent, et les mutations d'estat, en chose de tel pois; et les introduire en son pays propre. (120, my emphasis)

> But even the best of alleged ~~reasons~~ [C] pretexts [B] for novelty are exceedingly dangerous: [C] 'adeo nihil motum ex antiquo probabile est' [so true is it that no change from ancient ways can be approved]. [B] To speak frankly, it seems to me that there is a great deal of self-love and arrogance in judging so highly of your opinions that you are obliged to disturb the public peace in order to establish them, thereby introducing those many unavoidable evils and that horrifying moral corruption which, in matters of great importance, civil wars and political upheavals bring in their wake – introducing them moreover into your own country. (135)

'Amour de soy' ('self-love') is familiar in Christian theology from the opposition Saint Augustine poses between *amor soi* ('love of self') and *amor dei* ('love of God'), and is also present (conjugated as *amorem sui*) in the earliest known commentary on Ovid's version of the legend of Narcissus: the fifth-century *Narrationes* reprinted (often embedded into the main text) in various fourteenth- to sixteenth-century Latin editions and vernacular translations of the *Metamorphoses*.[4]

'Presomption', the title of one of Montaigne's essays (2.17), is also familiar from Christian theology; Thomas Aquinas defines *praesumptione* as when 'a man attempts things beyond his power, and especially novelties which call for greater admiration'. The charge of 'presumption' is also used to condemn Narcissus in the medieval French *Ovide Moralisé* (c. 1317–28): 'par lor fole presumption' ('by mad presumption'), Narcissus loses 'le cors et l'ame' ('body and soul') (lines 1872–3).[5]

In 'Of Custom', Montaigne associates 'amour de soy' and 'presomption' with 'guerres civiles' ('civil wars'), much as he does 'nouvelleté' ('novelty') with Protestantism. The implication that pride in one's own 'opinions' (a frequent French Catholic synonym for 'heresy') leads to the 'reversal of public peace', 'inevitable evils' and potential 'mutations of the state' aligns Montaigne with his near-contemporary Andrea Alciato, as well as Alciato's French commentator Claude Mignault. Unlike the authors of the *Ovide moralisé*, Alciato and Mignault read Narcissus not as timeless allegory, but instead in more acutely historicised terms. In his emblem of *philautia* (self-love), first printed in 1546, Alciato likens Narcissus to scholars enamored by 'nova dogmata' ('new doctrines').[6] Mignault's 1571 commentary on Alciato's emblem of *philautia* as Narcissus, printed in 1614, likens Narcissus more specifically to 'neosophoi impudentissimi' ('the most impudent of neo-sophists'), that is, in context, Protestants, or at least, those whom Mignault thinks seek to 'obliterate old ways and rationalities' ('obliterata maiorum via & ratione') and thereby 'harm the Christian republic' ('Christianiae Reipubl. communione, suo magno malo').[7] Montaigne's C-text addition echoes Mignault's rage at narcissistic *neosophoi*, even as he moves from public matters ('paix publique' ['public peace'], 'corruption des moeurs' ['moral corruption']) inwards to more private ones: 'conscience' and 'cognoissance'.

[C] Est ce pas mal mesnagé, d'advancer tant de vices certains et cognus, pour combattre des erreurs contestées et debatables? Est-il quelque pire espece de vices, que ceux qui choquent la propre conscience et naturelle cognoissance? (120)

Is it not bad husbandry to encourage so many definite and acknowledged vices in order to combat alleged and disputable error? Is there any kind of vice more wicked than those which trouble the naturally recognized sense of community? (136 – Screech's translation here tilts toward paraphrase)

In a variation on the chapter's overarching theme – persons' relationships with their social groups – Montaigne taps into a conventional

Renaissance *topos* here of the 'body politic'. Individual psychology ('conscience', 'cognoissance') is a microcosm: person and group are both alike subject to the regulatory procedures Montaigne calls 'mesnage' ('husbandry', 'management'). It follows that public peace depends on the management, howsoever achieved, of private individuals' 'amour de soy' and 'presumption'. Montaigne's rhetorical questions' reflective and parallel syntax, however, featuring intertwining antitheses, hints that this 'management' is more difficult than it seems. In the second question, especially, Montaigne arranges four problematic words – 'propre', 'conscience', 'naturelle' and 'cognoissance' – into a problematic pair of pairs. By assigning the adjective 'propre' to the noun 'conscience', Montaigne implies that each person has a personal ethical fingerprint, thereby refuting the idea, expressed, for instance, by the Folio Hamlet, that 'conscience' is a more collective form of ethical guidance, which may make 'cowards *of us all*' (F only, III, i, 82).[8] Even as he individuates conscience, however, Montaigne also universalises it as 'naturelle': a complex adjective connoting the body, humoral physiology, organic innateness. 'Cognoissance', in apposition to 'conscience', suggests a more rational faculty for deciding right action.

Navigating the limits of 'amour de soy' and 'presumption' is therefore somehow related to managing, aligning or harmonising 'conscience' and 'cognoissance'. But setting these statements as questions complicates matters. Just how rhetorical is Montaigne here? Are there indeed worse vices? Perhaps so. Writing over a period shaped and reshaped by five vicious civil wars (1571–92), Montaigne implies that such violent historical vicissitudes not only test 'conscience' and 'knowledge' in themselves, but also the ways in which such faculties should be individualised, universalised, separated or intertwined, given that their observer's ageing, mortal mind and body are no less mutable.

As a more dynamic variation of the 'body politic', as well as the dialectics of self and group set out near the start of the chapter, Montaigne comes to imply that political necessity and self-love are forms of management ('mesnage') which relate to each other as macrocosm to microcosm. This parallel is the implication, at least, as the chapter closes: an oddly downbeat ending, and yet one that Montaigne never saw fit to revise.

[A] Les Lacedemoniens mesmes, tant religieux observateurs des ordonnances de leur païs, estans pressez de leur loy qui defendoit d'eslire par deux fois Admiral un mesme personnage, et de l'autre part leurs affaires requerans de toute necessité que Lysander print de rechef cette charge, ils firent bien un Aracus Admiral, mais Lysander surintendant de la marine. Et de mesme subtilité, un de leurs ambassadeurs, estant envoyé vers les Atheniens, pour obtenir le changement de quelque ordonnance, et Pericles luy alleguant qu'il estoit defendu d'oster le tableau où une loy estoit une fois posée, luy conseilla de le tourner seulement, d'autant que cela n'estoit pas defendu. C'est ce dequoy Plutarque loue Philopaemen, qu'estant né pour commander, il sçavoit non seulement commander selon les loix, mais aux loix mesme, quand la nécessité publique le requeroit. (122–3)

The Spartans religiously observed the ordinances of their country, but, when they were caught between a law forbidding them to elect the same admiral twice and a pressing emergency requiring Lysander to reassume that office, even they elected someone called Aracus as Admiral and Lysander as 'Superintendent of the Navy'! And similar acuteness was shown by a Spartan ambassador who was dispatched to the Athenians to negotiate a change in one of their laws, only to find Pericles testifying that it was forbidden to remove a tablet once a law had been inscribed on it: he counselled him –since that was not forbidden – simply to turn the tablet round. Plutarch praises Philopoemen for being born to command, knowing how to issue commands by the laws and, when public necessity required it, to the laws. (139)

For the Lacedaemonians, who retain Lysander as *de facto* admiral despite laws forbidding such retention by simply changing his job title, or for Pericles, who simply turns a law-bearing tablet around when the law stops him from removing it, the chief criterion for right action, as its climactic position in the chapter's final sentence suggests, is always 'la necessité publique' ('public necessity'). Such straightforwardness seems belied, however, by the lengthy and complex discussions of historical changeability and cultural variation that precede it. These discussions, as well as the ending's own open-endedness, add up to the suggestion that this all-important 'necessity' is in constant mutation: both the 'amour de soy' and 'presumption' which exceed and endanger the common good and 'conscience' and 'cognaissance' which protect and uphold it must undergo continual re-evaluation.

Shakespeare's treatment of 'public necessity' in *Richard II* focuses more acutely on the form of the relation between the 'body politic' and the individual that Kantorowicz describes as 'the King's Two Bodies', a hierarchical 'political theology' whereby God is to King as King is to subject, and thereby the body of the Godlike King ('God's vicar') mystically symbolises the kingdom that he rules.[9] Like Montaigne's essay on custom, Shakespeare's play examines the possibility of radical changes to such long-established hierarchical and symbolic structures with frequent recourse to themes, images and terms recalling the Narcissus myth, as well as its associated commentary tradition. In his essay, Montaigne uses 'amour de soy' or 'presomption' to describe what he sees as the socio-psychological consequences of Protestantism, in keeping with moralising medieval interpretations of Ovid's *Metamorphoses*, still pervasive at the time, as well as a later emblem tradition. In *Richard II*, a study of a monarch accused in *the Mirror for Magistrates* of 'selfe loue' and being 'proude', Shakespeare evokes Narcissus via images of reflective surfaces; self-devouring, solipsistic self-regard; Neoplatonic terminology; and reference to flatterers. In 'the first English translation from the *Metamorphoses* in the sixteenth century', Thomas Howell compares such flatterers to Echo.[10]

These strategies are soon set to work in perhaps the play's most famous speech, frequently misused for nationalist ends, where the dying John of Gaunt complains that his nephew is subjecting England to a dangerous new epoch of instability. As York complains of a new foppishness – 'fashions in proud Italy' marked by narcissistic 'vanity' (II, ii, 21, 24) – Gaunt warns that such 'vanity' 'soon preys upon itself' (II, i, 38–9), echoing Ovid's Narcissus's 'inopem me copia fecit' ('my very plenty makes me poor', *Met.* 3.466). Much as Montaigne mobilises the trope of the body politic to claim that 'amour de soy' harms private 'conscience'/'cognoissance' and, by extension, public 'moeurs' ('mores', 'moral habits'), Shakespeare's Gaunt mobilises the conceit of 'the King's Two Bodies' to claim that Richard's narcissism will corrupt the entire kingdom ('That England that was wont to conquer others / Hath made a shameful conquest of itself' [II, i, 65–6]). Gaunt's charge of widespread narcissistic corruption has a monetary element that Montaigne's lacks. This 'dear, dear land', 'this England' (II, i, 57) has been replaced by vain (in the Latinate sense of empty) symbols: immaterial legal-financial instruments such as 'blank charters' (I, iv, 48, another echo of *The Mirror of Magistrates*), 'inky blots' and 'rotten parchment bonds' (II, i, 64).[11] The celebrated melodic phrasing of the first part of Gaunt's single, enormous, sentence, invoking England's seemingly timeless greatness through comforting anaphoric repetition (for example 'this happy breed of men, this little world' [II, i, 45]), serves by its end chiefly to emphasise its closing, jarringly broken clauses, which by analogy underscore Richard's actions' epoch-making radicalism. England 'is now leased out! I die pronouncing it! Like to a tenement or pelting farm!' blurts Gaunt in surprise as well as disgust (II, i, 59–60, punctuation modified). It would seem that Richard is not only narcissistic in his vain, self-devouring solipsism, but also in the very newness of his madness, as when Ovid's narrator pointedly describes Narcissus's 'noviatas furoris' (*Met.* 3.350). England, only '*demi*-Paradise', is 'this other Eden' (II, i, 42, emphasis added) not simply because it is idyllic, but for Gaunt because, like the Eden of the Book of Genesis, it has fallen irrevocably.

That is say, like Montaigne in 'Of Custom', Shakespeare in *Richard II* actively politicises themes or images from Ovid's Narcissus myth, couching them in terms of sudden, even epochal change. Montaigne uses the verb *choquer*; Gaunt 'dies' when his 'dear dear land' is narcissistically self-devoured. Montaigne's and Shakespeare's political revisionism here is very different from the more erotic 'narcissism' of Ovid's Narcissus, accused only of 'dura superbia' ('hard pride') because he refuses to touch the boys and girls who desire him (*Met.* 3.356–8). Instead, their take is more in keeping with Thomas Howell's in his roughly contemporary *Fable treting of Narcissus* (1560). In Howell's commentary on Ovid's Narcissus, which is much longer than his translation, he likens Echo to 'flattering folke' and Narcissus, by implication, to those like Shakespeare's Richard II who pay such flatterers too much attention.[12] 'The King is not himself but basely led / By flatterers', the King's enemy Northumberland points out, albeit not of course without an agenda of his own (II, i, 241–2).

After Gaunt's death, Shakespeare continues to develop the suggestion in his dying speech that a self-devouringly narcissistic king corrupts the kingdom that he embodies, and that his flatterers replace truth with vanity, just as they do solid land with empty paper contract. One such flatterer, Sir John Bushy, later executed for having 'misled' the King, consoles the queen after the King's voyage to Ireland to fight the Irish (III, i, 9). The Queen is, Bushy suggests, making a mountain of a molehill.

> The substance of a grief hath twenty shadows,
> Which shows like grief itself, but is not so;
> For Sorrow's eyes, glazed with blinding tears,
> Divides one thing entire to many objects,
> Like perspectives, which, rightly gazed upon,
> Show nothing but confusion; eyed awry,
> Distinguish form. So your sweet majesty,
> Looking awry upon your lord's departure,
> Find shapes of grief more than himself to wail,
> Which, looked on as it is, is naught but shadows
> Of what it is not.   (II, ii, 14–23)

Shakespeare draws his phrasing here once again from the familiar criticisms of Richard II in *The Mirror for Magistrates*: the Queen 'looks awry' (19, 21), for example, as in the *Mirror* 'Bolenbroke' seizes Richard's allies when they 'durst looke but once awry'.[13] These echoes of carelessness and flattery intermingle, however, with a new vocabulary of 'substance' (II, ii, 14) and 'shadow' (II, ii, 14, 22), familiar not only from Neoplatonic contexts (compare the first lines of Sonnet 53, 'What is thy substance, whereof are you made, / That millions of strange shadows on you tend?'), but also from Howell's (close) translation of Ovid's narrator, who rebukes Narcissus for stupidly loving his own reflection: 'The shadowe of thy selfe, it is that thou doest see / and hath no substaunce of it selfe'. The fact that sixteenth-century Neoplatonism and reception history of Ovid's Narcissus share key terms suggests that they are two ways of approaching similar questions; questions about ontology, ethics and love. These overlapping discourses' different, or potentially different, ways of using the two terms, however, leads to rich confusion. Both 'shadow' and 'substance' can be both positive and negative. 'Shadow' can denote ideal (immaterial) Platonic Form or Narcissus's 'false' (again because immaterial) reflection. 'Substance' can denote Platonic ideality or contrariwise the 'substantial' material realm of mortality and mutability that in Plato's original account distracts from that immaterial realm of essences. This context of doubled ambivalence informs Bushy's sophistic misuse of analogy. The Queen is gently chided for looking 'awry' at the King's departure, but such an angle is precisely what she should use to view a 'perspective' painting. The more general question is how people like the Queen are to 'read' her husband the King's body: physically absent put politically omnipresent; material and symbolic; shadowy and substantial.

Related questions of ontology and political power reappear in the play's *de facto* climax, the long-censored 'deposition' scene (4.1.1–318). Shocked at losing the kingdom, Richard calls for a 'glass'; and, after examining his reflection at length, smashes it.

KING RICHARD:	How soon my sorrow hath destroyed my face.
BOLINGBROKE:	The shadow of your sorrow hath destroyed
	The shadow of your face.
KING RICHARD:	Say that again!
	The shadow of my sorrow? Ha, let's see.
	'Tis very true, my grief lies all within;
	And these external manners of laments
	Are merely shadows to the unseen grief
	That swells with silence in the tortured soul.
	There lies the substance. (IV, i, 285–91)

In this interchange, Shakespeare continues to develop his earlier exploration of the intersection between Neoplatonic ontology and political theology, turning again to the same key terms, 'shadow' and 'substance'. The instability of the dichotomy becomes apparent through the contention between the two protagonists. Bolingbroke's pointed correction ('the *shadow* of your sorrow has destroyed the *shadow* of your face', emphasis added) posits an clear, straightforward split between the King's real-world physical body and its mere, reflected 'shadow', as befits the brisk, effective no-nonsense *Realpolitik* that Bolingbroke increasingly, if ambivalently, demonstrates as the play goes on (as with, say, his swift execution of Bushy and Green in III, i). With an echo of Echo, however ('Say that again! The shadow of my sorrow?'), Richard deconstructs Bolingbroke's clear dualism, realigning the kingly body with 'shadow' by introducing a third term (the 'tortured soul'), which, with near-Epicurean nuance, now becomes 'substance'. As interpreted by this exchange, Richard's smashed mirror reveals the failure of the dichotomy between shadow and substance to describe with equal validity the two adversaries' radically opposed political outlooks and sets of values. Existing structures of political theology such as the near-Platonic concept of 'the King's Two Bodies' cannot incorporate both Bolingbroke's materialism and Richard's idealism. There is, then, a historical as well as symbolic dimension to the mirror's destruction. Richard elsewhere bewails the fate of countless kings 'all murdered' (III, ii, 160), but these murders do not in the end seem to affect the underlying structure of 'fair sequence and succession' to which York makes desperate appeal (II, i, 199). Here, by contrast, in smashing his reflected, symbolic face, Richard also smashes the political theology that granted him such supernatural power in the first place, to the extent that no king in Shakespeare's seven historical plays depicting subsequent events is ever truly secure. Richard plunges us into an epoch where new, uncertain realities resist old ways of thinking.

Just as the deposition scene appears nowhere in Shakespeare's sources, so, too, Richard's shattered glass seems Shakespeare's own, wholly new invention. The most vivid explication of the themes betokened by Richard's mirror, the reversal of Bolingbroke's opposition of 'shadow' and 'substance' by turning obscurely inwards to a 'tortured soul', is perhaps Richard's prison soliloquy (V, v, 1–66). Now fully deposed, with Bolingbroke crowned Henry IV, Richard turns key notions of political theology and the 'King's Two Bodies' inside out, as if inverted in a mirror. His body used to symbolise the entire kingdom around him; now he sees a whole kingdom in himself. 'These same thoughts people this little world . . . Thus play I in one person many people / And none contented' (V, v, 9, 31–2). Richard's spatial metaphor here of a discontented inward kingdom is accompanied by an acute sense of disjunction in time. Richard traces discontinuous thoughts as he thinks them, as apparent from repeated, accelerating temporal markers ('then again', 'sometimes I am a king', 'then crushing penury' 'then I am kinged again', 'by and by . . . unkinged . . . straight am nothing' [V, v, 32–7]). These jittery switches and reversals culminate in sudden, inexplicable music played out of rhythm ('Ha, ha, keep time! How sour sweet music is / When time is broke and no proportion kept!' [V, v, 43–4]). Richard then compares this arrhythmia immediately and explicitly with the 'concord' (a term chosen ironically) of his own 'state and time' (V, v, 47). Thus, the historical rupture between one kingdom and another, more precisely the abrupt transition from one kind of kingdom to another, now devoid of York's principle of 'fair sequence and succession', finds, in a ghastly reversal or mirror-image of the logic of 'the King's Two Bodies', a more intimately personal psychological form. Richard's newly jerky, syncopated phenomenology laments lost, traditional forms of regal selfhood, anticipating in its place the fragmentary self associated with modernity.

As the long censorship of the deposition scene in the printed play-texts attests, Shakespeare's representation of a deposed and heirless monarch was not without readily apparent parallels to contemporary politics. William Lambarde's 1601 claim that Elizabeth I directly compared herself to Richard II ('I am Richard II, know ye not that?') remains disputable; more subtle resonances, however, as when Gaunt's island speech seemingly re-evokes patriotism from the 1588 defeat of the Spanish Armada, have been reasonably adduced by, for example, the play's Oxford editors.[14] Shakespeare's interpolation of the deposition scene, featuring a climactic smashing of a mirror at its centre, seems, at least at first, to call attention to the play and the history it depicts as analogous mirrors in which individuals may see, know and reform themselves. This figurative sense, common in Tudor times, is also evident in the title of one of the play's main sources, *The Mirror for Magistrates*.[15] By this light, however, Richard's smashing of the mirror hints at the loss of the possibility of any such guidance or reassurance. Any mirror-like or narcissistic identification playgoers now find with Richard comes to include, by extension, our, like his, attempts to grapple with an unknown and increasingly unknowable future.

As *Richard II* and 'Of Custom' illustrate, Shakespeare and Montaigne both draw on elements of the Narcissus myth and its commentary tradition to articulate responses to perceived sudden historical paradigm shifts. Montaigne cites 'amour de soy' and 'presumption', issuing forth in, by implication, Protestantism, to describe the mindset that he sees as driving contemporary civil war. In a [C] text expansion of this line of thought in his essay 'Of Custom', Montaigne draws on familiar analogies between individual person and social group such as the trope of the 'body politic' to attribute social discord to individual deficits of 'conscience' and 'cognoissance'. The more general sense throughout the essay, however, that people and customs determine each other dialectically, most readily in a long list of various social groups' incongruent customs, suggests that there is no fixed, objective, universal standard for knowing when individual 'presumption' and 'amour de soy' becomes excessive and thus poses a risk to the prevailing social fabric. Montaigne finds himself resorting to the somewhat vague concept 'la nécessité publique' ('public necessity') when trying to define or account for whether an action is good or not, a locution that raises more problems than it solves. Can 'la nécessité publique' itself be held to solid ethical account, given its variability across space and mutability in time? Are definitions of 'amour de soy' and 'presumption' correspondingly dynamic? Could certain forms of public necessity even necessitate certain forms of self-love?

In *Richard II*, Shakespeare uses the vertiginous reversals, reflections, doubles and contradictions characteristic of literary representations and critical interpretations of the myth of Narcissus and Echo to deconstruct the false dichotomy of 'shadow' and 'substance' that underpins Platonic distinctions between matter and idea, as well as, by extension, the concept of 'the King's Two Bodies'. Within the play, Shakespeare's characters deploy rival appropriations of figurative conceits associated with the legend of Narcissus as instruments in service of their struggle for power. Gaunt uses such imagery to warn of the new, even unprecedented dangers risked by Richard's fiscal liquidation of the kingdom. Bushy does so to curry favour with the Queen. Richard reflects his powerless idealism, and Bolingbroke his dominant realism, as they quibble over the correspondence of 'shadow' or 'substance' to Richard's face, or reflection, or soul. After power moves from Richard to Bolingbroke ('by reversion his!' as Richard unwittingly predicts [I, iv, 35]), Richard's reversal of the conceit of 'the King's Two Bodies' in his soliloquy in prison, in which he notes that after ruling material bodies, he now rules only his own immaterial 'thoughts', comes to express something like a phenomenology of modernity, a constant, bewildering, consciousness of change.

Theodor Adorno claimed that 'modernity is a qualitative, not a chronological category'.[16] The perception of epochal shift, indispensable to any contemporary understanding of 'modernity', may, in other words, occur at any point in historical time. As Silvia Federico points out, well before Shakespeare, thirteenth- and fourteenth-century contemporary poets associated Richard II with an analogous 'queer historicism' that 'violat[es] a straight(forward) development of chronology and causality'.[17] The later writers of the *Mirror for Magistrates* accused Richard of pride and 'selfe-love'. The confluence of narcissism and modernity connected with Richard may have found especial resonance in 1595, as an ageing, heirless queen sat on the throne, a year that saw the publication of Marie de Gournay's first edition of Montaigne's *Essays*, of Thomas Edward's *Narcissus* and the first productions of *Richard II*. High-profile productions starring Ben Whishaw for the BBC *Hollow Crown* films (2012) and David Tennant for the RSC (2013) chime with a contemporary modernity marked by social media's sudden and bewildering opportunities for virtual self-fashioning; the UK turning inwards to the insularity of Brexit; and the 2016 election of Donald Trump, diagnosed (Goldwater-era reservations notwithstanding) by psychologists as suffering from narcissistic personality disorder, as President of the United States of America.[18] Richard's 'blank charters' (I, iv, 48) 'inky blots' and 'rotten parchment bonds' (II, i, 64) resemble the derivatives that distort own crash-prone economies. As an investment vehicle, 'the derivative', so called because the value 'derives' from external occurrences, is for Fredric Jameson a 'historically new phenomenon in its own right'.[19] *Richard II*, by this light, offers a startlingly prescient meditation on the sensations of historical newness that occur when, like Narcissus and his reflection, signs of value perceptibly drift (in French the verb *dériver* means 'drift' as well as 'derive') from the values they once signified.[20]

Close attention to how the ramified themes of 'narcissism' and of 'modernity' interlock in texts by Montaigne and Shakespeare may not only help us reconsider their status as 'early modern' writers, but also, in light of these themes' contemporary, existential urgency, help to intimate a more meaningful scope for literary studies, an horizon adumbrated when Peter Holbrook mused upon the methodological stakes of studying Shakespeare and Montaigne in relation to each other a little over ten years ago.[21] In their richly variegated (even contradictory), theologically engaged exploration of such themes, Montaigne and Shakespeare could instruct and even help reform a contemporary conceptualisation of narcissism which, in its reliance on forced-choice questionnaires like the Narcissistic Personality Inventory, the rigidly impersonal definitions that such questionnaires presuppose, and the quantitative measurement of the data that they generate, exemplifies a mode of instrumental rationality Max Weber associates, not without some misgivings, with the modern 'disenchantment of the world'.[22] In a modernity where the 'radical' has been fearfully but conveniently denigrated, quietened and reduced, Montaigne and Shakespeare are still 'radical' writers, in so far as they open the concept of narcissism back up to broader, historically informed phenomenological horizons.

Notes

1. Nuttall, 'Ovid's Narcissus and Shakespeare's Richard II', p. 137.
2. My act, scene and line numbers refer to the 2012 Oxford edition of *Richard II*, ed. Dawson and Yachnin.
3. For ease and economy of reference, my citations from Montaigne refer back to *Les Essais*, ed. Villey and rev. Saulnier plus page number. I then give the English translation from *The Complete Essays*, trans. Screech.
4. Augustine, *The City of God* 14.28. The commentary from the *Narrationes* was, for example, reprinted in the widely used 1518 Regius edition of the *Metamorphoses* (fol. LVIv), and the 1563 Sprengius edition. See Moss, *Ovid in Renaissance France*, as well as Knoespel, *Narcissus and the Invention of Personal History*, pp. 25–9.
5. Aquinas, *Summa Theologiae* 2.2.21. See also Vinge, *The Narcissus Theme*, p. 94.
6. Alciato, *Emblemes d'Alciat*, p. 98.
7. 'Christianiae Reipubl. communione, suo magno malo'; 'obliterata maiorum via & ratione'. Alciato, *Andreae Alciati emblemata*, p. 261.
8. I refer to the 2006 Arden 3 edition of *Hamlet*, ed. Thompson and Taylor.
9. Kantorowicz, *The King's Two Bodies*.
10. Nuttall, 'Ovid's Narcissus and Shakespeare's Richard II', p. 140. Cf. Baldwin et al., *Mirror for Magistrates*, p. 103: 'The kyng ensued my rede in euery case, / whence selfe loue bred: for glory maketh proude'.
11. In *The Mirror for Magistrates*, pp. 113–14 [l. 43], Richard boasts of issuing '*Blanke charters*, othes, and shiftes *not knowne of olde*' (my emphasis).
12. '[By] thys fable some there be suppose / Ouyd mente to showe the fauinge sorte / Of flattringe folke whose vsage is to glose / With prayers swete, the men of gretiest, porte / And moste of welthe to whome the still resorte / In hope to gete, refusing nought to lye / The ende of speche as Ecco they applye' (Howell, *The fable of Ouid treting of Narcissus*, n.p.).

13. Baldwin et al., *Mirror for Magistrates*, p. 115 [l. 69].
14. Scott-Warren, 'Was Elizabeth I Richard II?'; Cp. *Richard II*, ed. Dawson and Yachnin, p. 170.
15. Lorna Hutson has compellingly considered Elizabethan theatre in general, and *Richard II* in particular, as a form of stimulating audiences' participation 'in the processes of equitable judgement', analogous to the king's own (Hutson, 'Imagining Justice', p. 139).
16. Adorno, *Minima Moralia*, p. 218.
17. Federico, 'Queer Times', p. 26.
18. See Golec de Zavala et al., 'Relationship between the Brexit Vote and Individual Predictors of Prejudice', for 'collective narcissism' and Brexit; Post, *Dreams of Glory*, for Goldwater and political narcissism; and Cruz and Buser, eds, *Clear and Present Danger*, for narcissism and Trump.
19. Jameson, *The Ancients and the Postmoderns*, p. 118.
20. Greene, *Light from Troy*, p. 15.
21. Montaigne and Shakespeare, Holbrook convincingly argues, 'share a preoccupation with the role of ideas *in life*' (Holbrook, 'Introduction', p. 8).
22. For the reliance on the Narcissistic Personality Inventory, see Campbell and Miller, eds, *Handbook of Narcissism*, p. 146. For Weber's famous phrase 'disenchantment of the World', from *Science as a Vocation*, see Weber, *From Max Weber*, p. 139.

Chapter 4

Shakespeare, Montaigne and Ricœur: Identity as Narrative

Zorica Bečanović-Nikolić

Many literary and philosophical investigations of selfhood have observed, with no small degree of fascination, that the self is not only itself but also somehow 'other'. As Rimbaud once said, 'je est un autre'.[1] For Hannah Arendt, as well, 'we are always two-in-one'.[2] Selfhood is a continual inner dialogue between consciousness, in the sense of self-awareness, and otherness.[3] We are not capable of the kind of autonomy Kant, like Seneca, idealises, but instead always find ourselves heteronomous even to ourselves. In keeping with this philosophical tradition, one associated with Aristotle as opposed to the Stoics, or Hegel as opposed to Kant, for Paul Ricœur, 'the selfhood of oneself implies otherness to such an intimate degree that one cannot be thought of without the other, that instead one passes into the other'.[4] And it is to Ricœur that Robert Ellrodt refers, albeit only briefly, in his comparative study *Montaigne et Shakespeare. L'Émergence de la conscience moderne* (Montaigne and Shakespeare: The Emergence of Modern Consciousness). Citing Ricœur, Ellrodt draws attention to the role of narrative identity in our apprehension of the vacillating nature of selfhood.[5] Although it is readily apropos, Ricœur's philosophy of time, narrative and selfhood has not often to date been brought to bear in studies of Montaigne or Shakespeare.[6] Ricœur himself, although known for his far-reaching erudition, seldom refers to either author. Nonetheless, Ellrodt's passing insight is worth pursuing. Ricœur's hermeneutic phenomenology of self and time helps to shed light on these early modern authors' representations of selfhood.

Ricœur's understanding of narrative is expansive, comprising many different modalities. The central divide that he takes up in the first volume of *Time and Narrative*, for example, is the difference between history and fiction, including not only narrative genres *sensu stricto* such as epic and the novel but also tragedy, comedy and other forms of drama. The defining characteristic of narrative for Ricœur is an underlying temporal structure, which allows him to give the term an unusually capacious scope. 'Time becomes human time,' he explains, 'to the extent that it is organised after the manner of a narrative; narrative, in turn, is meaningful to the extent that it portrays the features of temporal experience.'[7]

In order to help distinguish his more flexible, personal approach to narrative from contemporary structuralist theory such as that of Roland Barthes, as well as more limited considerations of the temporal aspects of narrative familiar from antiquity, Ricœur coins a new term, *emplotment*, which he uses to describe the lived experience of time in so far as it is mediated by an individual's distinctive and particular configuration of narrative. As William C. Dowling explains,

> much of what semiotics discovered in decentring the subject was and is, in Ricœur's opinion, true and important. For him, its limitations lie in a certain sterility or empty formalism arising from the further claim that consciousness itself is a mere epiphenomenon of underlying systems.

More precisely, 'the search for an underlying "grammar" of narrative modes', in so far as it proceeds on 'structuralist or semiotic assumptions', 'leaves out the teleological principle that gives meaning to the whole'. This *telos*, or 'final cause', of narrative, 'the internal logic that connects one event to another', we ourselves provide through what Ricœur describes as *emplotment*.[8]

In the third volume of *Time and Narrative*, elaborating on Aristotle's concepts of *mythos* and *mimesis* in his *Poetics*, as well as Saint Augustine's reflections on our experience of time in Book 11 of his *Confessions*, Ricœur responds to what he calls *aporias* in our thinking about time, akin to Kant's antinomies, and proposes narrative as a mediation between 'cosmological' and 'phenomenological' time; that is to say, between time in and of itself, in so far as we can grasp it without reference to ourselves, a bare, anonymous succession of 'before' and 'after', and time as it appears in relation to our human subjectivity: 'past-present-future'. In his *Confessions*, which Ricœur takes as a starting point, St Augustine emphasises the simultaneous availability of past, present and future to human experience. 'Neither future nor past exists,' St Augustine explains, 'and it is inexact language to speak of three times – past, present and future.' Instead, it would be more 'exact' to say that 'there are three times': 'a present of things past, a present of things present and a present of things to come'. These aspects of time exist 'in the soul' and nowhere else. 'The present considering the past is the memory, the present considering the present is immediate awareness, and the present considering the future is expectation.'[9] Thus for Saint Augustine, as M. B. Pranger explains, the soul is both *attentio* or *intentio animi*, 'that part of the mind's activity that, being concerned with the present, seems the most timeless', and *distentio animi*, 'the spreading out of the soul in the region of dissimilitude as the present expectation of the future, the present memory of things past, and the present intuition of things present'.[10] Likewise for Ricœur, *emplotment* is achieved through a threefold mimesis: prefiguration, configuration and refiguration.

As Richard Sorabji observes, Saint Augustine's sense of time as 'available altogether' has the 'paradoxical effect' of making it look 'frozen', 'like eternity', posing a problem for Ricœur's sense of the importance of narrative.[11] Ricœur turns, therefore, to Aristotle's emphasis on what he (Ricœur) calls 'the before-and-after' as a counterpoint to the absence of such succession in the thought of Saint Augustine.[12] For Ricœur, each of these thinkers, Aristotle and Saint Augustine, is inadequate on his own to the task of explaining the human experience of time.

> The conclusion to be drawn from our confrontation between Augustine and Aristotle is clear: the problem of time cannot be attacked from a single side only, whether of the soul or of movement. The distention of the soul alone cannot produce the extension of time; the dynamism of movement alone cannot generate the dialectic of the threefold present.

Narrative, Ricœur argues, is the solution to this *antinomy* or *aporia*: 'narrative poetics' is able to mediate between 'internal time-consciousness and objective succession'. According to Ricœur, *emplotment*, or 'the operation of plotting', 'may very broadly be defined as a synthesis of heterogenous elements', in keeping with the classical trope of *concordia discors* ('discordant concord or concordant discord').

> The plot is a synthesis: it unifies components as widely divergent as circumstances encountered whilst unsought, agents of actions and those who passively undergo them, accidental confrontations or expected ones, interactions which place the actors in relations ranging from conflict to cooperation, means that are well-attuned to ends or less so, and, finally, results that were not willed; gathering up all those factors into a single story turns the plot into a unity which one could call both concordant and discordant.[13]

Shakespeare's soliloquies, by this light, like Montaigne's *essais*, illuminate perplexing philosophical questions regarding the identity of self and its alterations in time. Their representation of narrative identity allows us to recognise and articulate our own.

Ricœur's subsequent study of the intersubjective nature of selfhood, *Oneself as Another*, further clarifies the complex picture of narrative identity that we encounter in the thinking of Montaigne and Shakespeare. In *Oneself as Another*, Ricœur pursues three aims, each of which he states clearly at the outset. The first is 'to indicate the primacy of reflective mediation over the immediate positing of the subject, as it is expressed in the first person singular: "I think", "I am"'.[14] The second is to distinguish two different types of identity, one of which he associates with the Latin word *idem*, the other with the Latin word *ipse*. *Idem*-identity is sameness as permanence in time, uninterrupted continuity: Ricœur uses the example of the genetic code of a biological individual.[15] *Ipse*-identity, by contrast, is selfhood, which Ricœur insists is not the same as sameness. 'The sense of *ipse* implies no assertion concerning some unchanging core of the personality,' he explains.[16] Selfhood in this sense is rather what emerges when a narrator, the self, draws together a series of changes over time into a meaningful unity. Like the plot that gives a story its coherence, *ipse*-identity is a narrative answer to the question 'Who am I?'. The third aim of *Oneself as Another* is to pair otherness and selfhood. After clarifying the difference between selfhood and sameness, *ipse*-identity and *idem*-identity, in the narrative identity of the individual self over time, Ricœur turns to the dialectic between the self and other individuals; individuals who, like the self, are subject to internal variation, as well as to encounters with other selves. Like Hegel, Ricœur sees the relation between self and other in this more profound, external sense as constitutive of the self in its ontic entirety. As also, in a different sense, for his contemporary Lévinas, for Ricœur, the other is the inescapable crux of the self's ineluctably ethical existence.

Shakespeare's Hamlet is an especially apt symbol of the contradictory wavering Ricœur sees as intrinsic to the human experience of selfhood. After hearing of his father's death by 'murder most foul', Hamlet swears that he will 'wipe away all trivial fond records' from the table of his memory, 'all saws of books, all forms, all pressures past / that youth and observation copied there' (I, v, 98–101), then accuses himself of being 'a dull, muddy-mettled rascal', 'John-a-dreams' (II, ii, 562–3), then decides, during the same monologue, that he will have the actors 'play something like the murder of [his] father' (II, ii, 591), so that Claudius's soul should be struck by the 'cunning of the scene', then changes his mind once more when he starts to doubt the authenticity of the Ghost, wondering if it might be, not his father, but instead 'a devil', preying on his 'weakness' and 'melancholy' (II, ii, 594–7). No stable position at all, only a series of passages, Montaigne might say. 'I cannot keep my subject still,' Montaigne observes, speaking of himself. His *essais* are not a stable self-portrait, but instead, as he explains, 'a record of various and changeable occurrences, and of irresolute and, when it so befalls, contradictory ideas' (III: 2, 611).

The soliloquy 'To be or not to be' (III, i, 56–89) is a paradigmatic example of the dizzying oscillation of Hamlet's thought. Every position is almost immediately rejoined and subverted by its contrary. To be can mean 'to suffer / the slings and arrows of outrageous fortune' passively, without taking action, but it can also mean 'to take arms against a sea of troubles' and 'by opposing end them'. Yet another contradictory meaning, like a nesting doll, lies inherent in this latter expression: the metonymy 'arms against a sea' does not suggest that the 'arms' in question are likely to prove victorious. Hamlet's notion of death is likewise equivocal. Is death merely a calm sleep, free from dreams, as Socrates hopes for in Plato's *Apology* (40c5–41c7)? Montaigne recounts Socrates' musing on this possibility in his *Essays*: 'If it is an annihilation of our being, it is still an improvement to enter upon a long and peaceful night. We feel nothing sweeter in life than a deep and tranquil rest and sleep, without dreams' (III, 12, 806). Then again, Hamlet speculates, death might be plagued by nightmares: 'what dreams may come, / When we have shuffled off this mortal coil, / Must give us pause'. The soliloquy is a series of inconsistent positions, a Derridian *mise en abyme*. Like Montaigne's digressive, seemingly shapeless representations of subjectivity, Hamlet's monologues are unsettled, multivalent and contradictory. 'My history needs to be adapted to the moment,' Montaigne writes. 'From day to day, from minute to minute,' he observes, 'I may presently change, not only by chance, but also by intention' (III: 12, 611). Hamlet's self, like Montaigne's, is susceptible to a myriad of transformations over time.

Unlike New Historicist and cultural materialist interpretations of the early modern sense of self, Ricœur's phenomenology is ahistorical. The picture of selfhood that emerges from his philosophy stands in sharp contrast, as well, to descriptions of Hamlet such as Terry Eagleton's, which posits 'pure deferral' as Hamlet's core: 'nothingness', a 'hollow void'.[17] At the centre of Hamlet, Francis Barker maintains, 'there is, in short, nothing'; the character's 'interiority' is merely 'gestural'.[18] As a basis for the formation of the self, the underlying act of storytelling Ricœur describes as narrative identity is instead much closer to John Lee's sense of Hamlet's self as composed through a 'Montaignesque' process of self-narration, an idea Lee picks up from Alastair MacIntyre. 'The unity of a life', MacIntyre maintains, 'is the unity of a narrative quest.'[19] 'The Prince's self', by this light, according to Lee, can be understood as 'a form of story'.[20] Catherine Belsey, for example, insists that Hamlet, 'the most discontinuous of Shakespeare's heroes', is 'not a unified subject'.[21] Lee, by contrast, cites Hazlitt: 'The character of Hamlet is made up of undulating lines; it has the yielding flexibility of "a wave o' th' sea"'. In his essay on *Hamlet*, Hazlitt's 'processional concept of character' as 'a continually changing product of self-exploration' seems to Lee 'at times to remember Montaigne'.[22] As Montaigne writes in 'Of Repenting', 'Though the lines of my picture change and vary, yet lose they not themselves.'[23] Ricœur captures this sense of the simultaneous constancy and variability of selfhood in his principle of concordant discordance.

In his essay 'Of the Inconstancy of Our Actions', Montaigne marvels at the power of time and circumstance to render character inconsistent.

> That man whom you saw so adventurous yesterday, do not think it strange to find him just as cowardly today: either anger, or necessity, or company, or wine, or the sound of a trumpet, had put his heart in his belly. His was a courage formed not by reason, but by one of these circumstances; it is no wonder if he has now been made different by other, contrary circumstances.

'Anyone who observes himself carefully', Montaigne maintains, 'can hardly find himself twice in the same state.' 'I have nothing to say about myself absolutely, simply, and solidly, without confusion and without mixture, or in one word. *Distinguo* is the most universal member of my logic' (II: 1, 242). What Ricœur calls *idem*-identity, Montaigne sees as capable of variation equally extreme as that between one individual and another altogether. 'There is as much difference between us and ourselves as between us and others.' 'We are all patchwork', he concludes, 'and so shapeless and diverse in composition that each bit, each moment, plays its own game' (II, 1, 244). In his essay 'Of Experience', Montaigne finds an analogue of the less tangible inconstancy of his character in his own changing physical appearance. 'I have pictures of myself at twenty-five and thirty-five; I compare them with one of the present: how irrevocably it is no longer myself!' (III: 13, 846)

'I do not portray being: I portray passing.' In his magisterial literary history, *Mimesis*, Erich Auerbach takes up this brief statement, the opening of Montaigne's essay, 'Of Repentance', as an occasion for a more general reflection on Montaigne's purpose, method and conclusions (III: 2, 611). What, for Montaigne, is *l'humaine condition*? As the passage Auerbach singles out emphasises, for Montaigne, 'man is a fluctuating creature subject to the changes which take place in his surroundings, his destiny, and his inner impulses'. Nonetheless, Auerbach advises, we should beware of becoming 'too entangled' in Montaigne's charming 'self-irony and modesty'. What emerges from Montaigne's 'apparently fanciful method', 'an exact and factual description of a constantly changing subject', is not 'a mass of unrelated snapshots', but instead 'a spontaneous apprehension of the unity of his person'.

'At every moment of the continual process of change', Auerbach observes, 'Montaigne possesses the coherence of his personality, and he knows it: *Il n'est personne, s'il escoute, qui ne descouvre en soy une forme sienne, une forme maistresse* ["There is no one who, if he listens to himself, does not discover in himself a pattern all his own, a ruling pattern"]' (III: 2, 615). The *forme maistresse* Montaigne emphasises here corresponds closely to what Ricœur would call Montaigne's *ipse*-identity, unifying the otherwise bewildering day-to-day, moment-to-moment fluctuations of his *idem*-identity. 'In the end', Auerbach concludes, 'there is unity and truth; in the end it is his essential being which emerges from his portrayal of the changing.'[24] Charles Taylor, too, sees Montaigne as having found 'some inner peace' in the delineation of his *forme maistresse*: 'a certain equilibrium even within the ever-changing by identifying and coming to terms with the patterns which represent his own particular way of living in flux'.[25]

As Taylor explains in his history of selfhood, *Sources of the Self*, within the context of 'ancient thought', 'the modern problem of identity is unintelligible'. For a philosopher such as Seneca, for instance, 'beneath the changing and shifting desires in the unwise soul, and over against the fluctuating fortunes of the external world, our true nature, reason, provides a foundation, unwavering and constant'. Within the genealogy of selfhood Taylor recounts, Montaigne, by contrast, is a representative 'turning point'. When he looks inwards, Montaigne, like Shakespeare's Hamlet, does not find any 'permanent, stable, unchanging core', but instead 'terrifying inner instability'.[26] As Shakespeare's Benedick says at the end of *Much Ado about Nothing*, charged with having changed his mind about the prospect of marriage, 'man is a giddy thing, and this is my conclusion' (V, iv, 106–7). Or, as Montaigne says of himself, 'I cannot keep my subject still. It goes along befuddled and staggering, with a natural drunkenness' (III: 2, 610). Elsewhere he echoes Saint Paul, as well as classical authors such as Ovid and Seneca.[27] 'We are, I know not how, double within ourselves, with the result that we do not believe what we believe, and we cannot rid ourselves of what we condemn' (II: 16, 469).

How can we make sense of the simultaneous unity and mutability that we find within ourselves? In the conclusion to the third volume of *Time and Narrative*, Ricœur sums up his position on selfhood, citing Hannah Arendt as precedent:

> To answer the question 'Who?, as Hannah Arendt has so forcefully put it, is to tell the story of a life. The story told tells about the action of the who'. And identity of this 'who' therefore itself must be a narrative identity.

'Without the recourse to narration', Ricœur explains,

> the problem of personal identity would in fact be condemned to an antinomy without solution. Either we must posit a subject identical with itself through the diversity of its different states, or, following Hume and Nietzsche, we must hold that the identical subject is nothing more than a substantialist illusion, whose elimination merely brings to light a pure manifold of cognitions, emotions and volitions.[28]

The narrator of Montaigne's *Essays*, like Shakespeare's Hamlet, is formally identifiable as *idem*, same and permanent in time. But he is also keenly aware of his own continual, consequential alterations over time. 'We float between different states of mind: we wish nothing freely, nothing absolutely, nothing constantly' (II: 1, 240). Through interlocking processes of prefiguration, configuration and refiguration, that is, through narrative, what Ricœur calls *emplotment*, Montaigne as narrator articulates his own *ipse*-identity: in his answer to the question 'Who am I?', he compares his own states of mind past, present and future, much as Hamlet registers and 'assays' different versions of himself, weighing one against the other. A flux of apparently incompatible moments thus takes on the coherence of a narrative identity: the 'natural form' (*forme naïve*; compare *forme maistresse*), complete with 'defects', that Montaigne vows to provide in his preface 'to the reader'.

Ricœur's own choice of a literary example 'to illustrate the notion of the fictive experience of time' is Proust's *Remembrance of Things*

Past.[29] Montaigne's *Essays*, however, prefigure Proust's novels, and may perhaps have even served as an inspiration, as Saint Augustine's *Confessions* did for Montaigne. Shakespeare, too, shows characters using narrative to make sense of how they themselves have changed over time: Prospero in the *The Tempest*, for example, recounting the story of his banishment from Milan to the perplexed Miranda (I, ii, 66–186), as well as Othello, recounting to the Senators of Venice a briefer version of the vivid story of his life with which he had formerly wooed Desdemona (I, iii, 128–70). Lear, by contrast, proves bewildered, precisely because he is unwilling or perhaps unable, at least at first, to allow the events of his life to cohere into a narrative. 'Who is it that can tell me who I am?' (I, iv, 227). Macbeth for his part seems to find some degree of perverse consolation in comparing life to 'a tale / Told by an idiot, full of sound and fury / Signifying nothing' (V, v, 26–8). The story that he tells, although ostensibly meaningless, serves nonetheless as a tale, a narrative. Thus, as David Bromwich points out, he comes across in the end as 'oddly *satisfied*'.[30] The analogies he posits, life as a 'way to dusty death', life as an 'hour upon the stage', although horrifying, allow him to configure or *emplot* his wife's suicide, as well as his own doomed trajectory (V, v, 23–5).

Shakespeare's royal Richards engage in similar self-reflexive scrutiny of their dramatic alterations and apparent contradictions over time. Richard III's final speech, presented in a clear-cut dialectic of questions and answers, is in effect polyphonic; Robert Ellrodt sees it, by this light, as an example of fluid modern consciousness, akin to Montaigne's.[31] For Hugh Grady, Richard II's self-deposition is a paradigmatic instance of unfixed subjectivity. Within his own apparent singularity of self-awareness, Richard II slides between multiple contradictory identities, noting their incongruity.[32] When led to abdicate and pass the crown to Bolingbroke, he muses on his own incipient incoherence, simultaneously king and yet not king. 'Well then, amen, / God save the king! although I be not he; / And yet, amen, if heaven do think him me' (IV, i, 173–5). The 'Ay, no; no, ay' speech gives immediate insight into self-reflexive and performative 'undoing' of oneself. 'Unking'd' Richard's view is blurred by tears; he cannot see, and yet he does in a different sense look inward.

> Nay, if I turn mine eyes upon myself,
> I find myself a traitor with the rest.
> For I have given here my soul's consent
> T' undeck the pompous body of a king . . . (IV, i, 247–50)

Perceiving himself as another, he no longer recognises himself. 'I . . . know not now what name to call myself!' (IV, i, 259). Names, titles, formal identities escape him. Like Hamlet, he wishes he could melt outright: 'O! that I were a mockery king of snow, / Standing before the sun of Bolingbroke, / To melt myself away in water drops' (IV, i, 260–63). He asks for a mirror to 'read himself': 'Give me the glass, and therein will I read.' 'I'll read enough,' he imagines, 'When I do see the very book indeed / Where all my sins are writ, and that's myself' (IV, i, 273–6).

Unable to accept the radical disparity by this point between his humiliating predicament and his inner grandiosity, Richard abruptly dashes the looking glass that he has asked for to the ground. 'There it is,' he notes, as if speaking of himself, 'crack'd in an hundred shivers' (IV, i, 289). 'Shivers' blurs the line between animate and inanimate object: Richard here both rejects and recognises the discarded mirror as an analogue of himself. Even in destroying the mirror, he uses it as an instrument of *emplotment*. When he is rebuffed by his daughters, Lear marvels at the dissonance between his inward sense of himself and his outward circumstances, much as Richard II does when Northumberland asks him to read aloud the charges against him. 'I have no name, no title,' Richard protests (IV, i, 255). 'Mine eyes are full of tears; I cannot see' (IV, i, 244). So, too, Lear questions his own 'eyes', as well as the connection between himself and his given name, 'Lear'.

> Does any here know me? This is not Lear:
> Does Lear walk thus? speak thus? Where are his eyes?
> Either his notion weakens, his discernings
> Are lethargied – Ha! waking? 'tis not so.
> Who is it that can tell me who I am? (I, iv, 223–7)

Even more so than Richard II, to the point of outright madness, Lear struggles to revise his longstanding narrative of himself. Richard II turns his deposition into a show of his own devising, designed to help him reconcile his past to his present and future. So, too, Lear stages a mock-trial, in an effort to forge a more coherent internal narrative. In an example of what we might now call 'distributed cognition', Lear draws upon a joint-stool to represent his daughter Goneril, much as Richard II does upon his own reflection in a mirror.

What Shakespeare reveals in these scenes with even more than usual force is a dispersed self, the kind of self that Montaigne also discerns within himself, engaged in what Ricœur describes as *emplotment*. Like

Montaigne's *essais*, which he revised repeatedly up until his death, the narratives that Lear and Richard II articulate are self-constituting, self-constructing and self-reconstructing works-in-progress, designed to mediate between the lived experience of time as Saint Augustine describes it, the private availability all at once of past, present and future within the individual mind, and the impersonal, inexorable fact of time as Aristotle describes it, the relentless, public succession Ricœur calls 'before-and-after'. Hamlet's soliloquies are an analogous exercise in self-constitution or *emplotment*. To explain this function of Hamlet's speeches, John Lee turns, not to Ricœur, but to a parallel school of thought within psychoanalysis, George E. Kelly's personal construct psychology. For Lee, Hamlet's soliloquies are not simply depictions of 'moral choice and moral dilemma', since such a reading would imply 'a static conception of who the Prince is', but instead can be better understood as demonstrations of his 'fluidity and processional nature'. 'The soliloquies do not portray a choice or dilemma, though there may be choices and dilemmas within them, but rather a part of the speaker's representation of life, in the process of construction.'[33]

'Personal construct psychology', Lee explains, 'sees man as an active, self-producing subject exploring the external and internal worlds through a series of representations or construals designed to anticipate and to render intelligible his path through the flow of time.'[34] For Shakespeare, 'personality' is not 'a quasi-concrete, unchanging and yet unrecoverable antecedent substance' but instead a 'personal adventure', 'an active process which is self-built'.[35] What George E. Kelly calls constructs, in the sense of 'representations' or 'construals', Ricœur describes in more literary language as narratives. As Lee observes, Kelly's emphasis on internal frameworks of interpretation 'lends itself to an account of the literally literary aspects of personality'. For Kelly, as for Ricœur, 'the process of producing an intelligible representation of reality' is 'closely analogous to the production of literature'.[36]

The forms of otherness that Ricœur explores in *Oneself as Another* in relation to the self comprise not only the inner temporal alterations of *ipse* within the permanence of *idem*, but also the otherness of other selves, 'other than self', which are equally constitutive of the self. For Montaigne, for example, the other individual most integral to his sense of himself was the singular friend of his youth, Étienne de La Boétie. Describing their friendship, Montaigne writes:

> In the amity I speak of, they intermix and confound themselves one in
> the other, with so universal a commixture that they wear out and can no

more find the seam that hath conjoined them together. If a man urge me to tell wherefore I loved him, I feel it cannot be expressed but by answering: Because it was he, because it was myself.[37]

For Hamlet, the equivalent is Horatio: 'Give me that man / That is not passion's slave,' he tells Horatio, 'and I will wear him / In my heart's core, ay, in my heart of heart, / As I do thee' (III, ii, 71–4).

Narrative identity provides the individual self with the internal unity and coherence over time necessary for the self to incur moral responsibility and find itself subject to the claims of ethics. The individual subject that emerges through the process of *emplotment* is the object of its own solicitude and esteem. For its sense of itself, however, it depends on its constitutive narrative being recognised by others. Self-esteem in this sense is not self-sufficient but instead depends on reciprocal relationships of care and mutual respect. As Ricœur insists, 'I cannot myself have self-esteem unless I esteem others as myself.'[38] For Ricœur, the ideal 'exchange' between 'esteem for oneself and solicitude for others' is friendship, in keeping with Aristotle's emphasis on what Ricœur calls 'similitude' in his account of friendship in his *Nicomachean Ethics*. 'It is to the stability of the best part of oneself that we owe the beautiful expression that holds the friend to be "another self" [*allos autos*] (9.4.1166a32).'[39] As Patrick Gray argues in his recent analysis of the limitations of Aristotle's concept of *anagnorisis* for making sense of characters such as Lear and Richard II, 'repentance as Shakespeare sees it' tends to be prompted by the kind of dialogical relationship with others that achieves its ideal form in such friendship: 'the reciprocal process of intersubjective self-definition Hegel calls *Anerkennung*'. 'Put in plainer language,' Gray explains, 'we come to know ourselves, to the extent that we ever do, by noticing and accepting how we are perceived by other people.'[40] Friends help us see our obligations more clearly, as well as our past ethical missteps.

On what grounds, however, are we responsible, if at all, for mistakes that we have made in the past? What is the relationship between responsibility and temporality? Ricœur differentiates three aspects, in keeping with Saint Augustine's sense of the connection between *intentio* and *distentio animi*. The retrospective aspect of responsibility concerns one's own past deeds, to which, for better or for worse, one is bound, in so far as they have contributed to the formation of one's self. The prospective aspect is responsibility for the future consequences of one's actions. These two perspectives meet and overlap in the present. To quote Saint Augustine, 'who would deny that the present time lacks extension because it passes in a point (*quia in puncto praeterit*)?'[41]

Moral identity, like narrative identity, emerges through a dialectic between permanence and change. Yet there is some possible slippage here; some potential for a gap between the two accounts, moral and narrative. Moral *emplotment* requires what Stanley Cavell calls acknowledgement. 'Holding oneself responsible', Ricœur explains, is nothing other than 'accepting to be held to be the same today as the one who acted yesterday and who will act tomorrow'.[42] But what if we refuse to accept this connection between past and present? What if we reject the self-knowledge that St Augustine in more familiar, Christian terms might call simply repentance? The retrospective aspect of responsibility troubles Shakespeare's Claudius, for example, when he tries to pray. 'My stronger guilt', he laments, 'defeats my strong intent' (*Ham* III, iii, 40).

> My fault is past – but O, what form of prayer
> Can serve my turn? 'Forgive me my foul murder?'
> That cannot be, since I am still possess'd
> Of those effects for which I did the murder –
> My crown, my own ambition, and my queen.
> May one be pardon'd and retain th'offence? (III, iii, 51–6)

Like a bird caught in birdlime, Claudius finds his 'limed soul' troubled in the present by the prospective aspect of his moral responsibility, as well as retrospective awareness of his 'offence' (III, iii, 36, 68). 'In the corrupted currents of this world', Claudius observes, it might be possible for him to escape justice. 'But 'tis not so above: / There is no shuffling, there the action lies / In his true nature' (III, iii, 60–2).

Like Richard II, who never does in the end read out the charges against him, Claudius imagines that in this life, at least, given his wealth and station, he may be able to avoid public recognition of his moral identity. God, however, is not so easy to evade. In the afterlife, Claudius imagines, we are 'compell'd / Even to the teeth and forehead of our faults / To give in evidence' (III, iii, 62–4). Even in this life, the prospect of that final encounter impinges upon Claudius's ability to enjoy the 'effects' of his crime, his 'crown', his 'ambition' and his 'queen', as we see from his anguished double-mindedness here. 'O wretched state!' he cries. As Ewan Fernie explains, 'If we are to reconstruct even an approximation of the experience of the persons of the early modern period, we must imagine them as more or less aware at any particular moment of existing simultaneously in society and before God.'[43] Claudius cannot wall himself off from fears about his likely fate: that future turns out to be instead, as St Augustine observes, already present as 'expectation'. For Claudius, as for Hamlet, the 'dreams' that may come 'when we have shuffled off this mortal coil' are in a subjective sense already present, like foreshadowing within a narrative. 'The dread of something after death' is what Saint Augustine calls 'the present of things to come', 'the present considering the future'.[44]

At the conclusion of *Oneself as Another*, Ricœur asks, 'what sort of being is the self?'[45] Neither the Cartesian *cogito* nor the Nietzschean 'anti-cogito' strike him as convincing. So he proposes to 'move beyond' what he calls 'the quarrel over the cogito, in which the "I" is by turns in a position of strength and of weakness', 'the great oscillation that causes the "I" of the "I think" to appear, by turns, to be elevated inordinately to the heights of a first truth and then cast down to the depths of a vast illusion'.[46] In place of Descartes' *cogito*, Ricœur's term for the process that constitutes the self is attestation. There is no Cartesian certainty in attestation, no hint of quasi-mathematical ratiocination. For Ricœur, the ontological core of selfhood, attestation, is not illusory. Like our personal identification of ourselves through *emplotment*, attestation presupposes individual agency. Even so, attestation cannot provide a stable foundation for subsequent, solipsistic logical speculation, as Descartes claims that the *cogito* does in his *Meditations*. Instead, selfhood can be better understood as indirect, fragmentary, and in constant flux, emerging out of ongoing narrative self-configuration, as well as, especially, the dialogical recognition of ethical responsibility.

In contrast to reason, as well as the senses, attestation relies on belief, that is, faith, in the sense here of interpersonal trust, as opposed to impersonal acceptance of a set of deracinated propositions or truth-claims in the manner of a catechism. The attestation of the individual self is secured neither through syllogisms nor by the accumulation of empirical evidence but instead, as Ricœur explains, in

> a trust in the power to say, in the power to do, in the power to recognize oneself as a character in a narrative, in the power, finally, to respond to accusation in the form of the accusative: 'It's me here' (*me voici!*), to borrow an expression dear to Levinas.[47]

Attestation by this definition is the acceptance of interpersonal as opposed to ideological interpellation, in keeping with the revised sense of interpellation Patrick Gray proposes in his reading of *Antony and Cleopatra.*[48] Perhaps the most straightforward example of such attestation is Montaigne's *Essays*, as he himself announces in his foreword 'to the Reader'.

> I desire herein to be delineated in my own genuine, simple, and ordinary fashion, without contention, art, or study; for it is myself I portray. My imperfections shall thus be read to the life, and my natural form discerned, so far-forth as public reverence hath permitted me. For if my fortune had been to have lived among those nations which yet are said to live under the sweet liberty of Nature's first and uncorrupted laws, I assure thee I would most willingly have portrayed myself fully and naked.[49]

As he lies dying, Hamlet asks Horatio to carry out this task of self-revelation for him. 'Report me and my cause aright,' he pleads (V, ii, 343). 'In this harsh world draw thy breath in pain / to tell my story' (V, ii, 353–4). What 'story', however, is Horatio to tell? Earlier in the play, having seen Laertes leap into Ophelia's grave, Hamlet leaps in after him, outraged at being displaced from his own narrative identity. 'What is he whose grief / Bears such an emphasis . . .?' he asks. 'This is I, / Hamlet the Dane!' (V, i, 243–4, 246–7). Later he apologises to Laertes and disavows this version of himself as 'madness'.

> Was't Hamlet wrong'd Laertes? Never Hamlet.
> If Hamlet from himself be ta'en away,
> And when he's not himself does wrong Laertes,
> Then Hamlet does it not, Hamlet denies it. (V, ii, 22–32)

Confronted by the memory of his past offence, Hamlet here, like Richard II, as well as Lear, momentarily balks at his own name. Having done so, however, he then settles rapidly on a different distinction, not between Hamlet and Hamlet, but instead between intention and effect, 'disclaiming' any 'purpos'd evil' (V, ii, 237). 'I have shot my arrow o'er the house / And hurt my brother' (V, ii, 238–9). Horatio takes his cue from this apology in his closing explanation of the play, when he describes the bloodshed at Elsinore to Fortinbras as 'accidental judgments, casual slaughters', and 'purposes mistook / fall'n on th'inventors' heads' (V, ii, 387–90), as well as, again, 'mischance' and 'errors' (V, ii, 399–400).

Is Horatio's 'report' accurate? Can it be understood as a Lévinasian *me voici* on the part of Hamlet, executed on his behalf by his most trusted friend after he himself, despite himself, has slipped at last into 'silence'? Or is Hamlet at the end, as T. S. Eliot says of Othello, *'cheering himself up'*? Whether or not Hamlet is guilty here of what Eliot calls *bovarysme,* 'the human will to see things as they are not', is an intriguing question.[50] We might also ask just how closely Montaigne's narrative identity, familiar from his *Essays,* does or does not correspond to his more elusive moral identity. Is there any gap between Montaigne the author and the character, 'Montaigne', who emerges from the *Essays?* His most recent biographer, Philippe Desan, argues that Montaigne was not nearly as detached from contemporary politics as he claims to be. As Desan admits, however, in the case of Montaigne, 'it is hard to distinguish between the public man and the private man'.[51] In the case of Shakespeare's characters, by contrast, the playwright goes out of his way to reveal and even emphasise comic or tragic incongruities between person and persona. That said, making sense of Shakespeare's characters' soliloquies, like Montaigne's *essais,* often can require a double vision, keenly attuned to both intended and inadvertent irony.

Does attestation require, as Ricœur sometimes seems to suggest, effective soul-searching, prompted by dialogue with others? Or can it proceed even without any such depths of self-knowledge? Future work on Shakespeare and Montaigne might explore in more detail how these authors illuminate the relation of Ricœur's description of selfhood as a process of *emplotment* and attestation to Cavell's influential account of self-awareness in Shakespeare's plays as a tension between avoidance and acknowledgment. For Ricœur, as for Lévinas, the encounter between the self and the other seems to lead as if by necessity to a recognition of ethical responsibility. Cavell, by contrast, emphasises our human capacity to disavow our moral obligations, if we so choose, albeit at tragic cost. As Erving Goffman explains, what an individual 'protects and defends and invests his feelings in' is not 'facts', but instead 'an idea about himself'. These 'ideas', what Ricœur would call narratives, 'are vulnerable, not to facts and things, but to communications'. Facts 'cannot be avoided'. 'Communications', however, 'can be bypassed, withdrawn from, disbelieved, conveniently misunderstood'.[52] Complementing Cavell's more inward-looking focus on self-deception, future work on Shakespeare and Montaigne might also consider Goffman's sense of the significance of 'face-work' or 'maintenance of face' in social interaction, as a counterpoint to Lévinas's claims about the power of 'the face-to-face', as well as Ricœur's optimism about 'the course of recognition'.[53]

Notes

1. Rimbaud, *Œuvres*, p. 345.
2. Arendt, *Essays in Understanding*, p. 358.
3. Arendt, *The Life of the Mind*, pp. 179–93.
4. Ricœur, *Oneself as Another*, p. 3.
5. Ellrodt, *Montaigne et Shakespeare*, p. 33.
6. For other recent work on Shakespeare and Ricœur, see Deitch, 'Love's Hologram'; Lawrence, *Forgiving the Gift*; Gray, *Shakespeare and the Fall of the Roman Republic*, and Smith and Lupton, eds, *Face-to-Face in Shakespearean Drama*.
7. Ricœur, *Time and Narrative: Volume 1*, p. 3.
8. On Ricœur's *Time and Narrative* as a response to contemporary French structuralism, as well as Russian formalism, see ch. 3, 'Narrativity', in Dowling, *Ricœur on Time and Narrative*. See also Bečanović-Nikolić, *Hermeneutika i poetika*, pp. 82–106.
9. Augustine, *Confessions* 11.20.26.
10. Pranger, 'Time and Narrative in Augustine's *Confessions*', p. 379. Cf. Pranger, *Eternity's Ennui*.
11. Sorabji, *Time, Creation, and the Continuum*, p. 30. See also Bečanović-Nikolić, *Hermeneutika i poetika*, pp. 26–8.
12. Ricœur, *Time and Narrative. Volume 3*, p. 19. See also Bečanović-Nikolić, *Hermeneutika i poetika*, pp. 29–32.
13. Ricœur, 'Life: A Story in Search of a Narrator', pp. 21–2. Cf. Ricœur, *Time and Narrative. Volume 2*, pp. 7–99, and Ricœur, *Time and Narrative. Volume 3*, pp. 157–79.
14. Ricœur, *Oneself as Another*, p. 1.
15. Ibid. pp. 116–17.
16. Ibid. p. 2.
17. Eagleton, *William Shakespeare*, pp. 71–2.
18. Barker, *Tremulous Private Body*, pp. 36–7.
19. MacIntyre, *After Virtue*, p. 219; cited in Lee, *Shakespeare's* Hamlet *and the Controversies of Self*, p. 204.
20. Lee, *Shakespeare's* Hamlet *and the Controversies of Self*, p. 200.
21. Belsey, *Subject of Tragedy*, pp. 41–2.
22. Lee, *Shakespeare's* Hamlet *and the Controversies of Self*, p. 144.
23. Montaigne, *Shakespeare's Montaigne*, p. 196.
24. Auerbach, *Mimesis*, pp. 292–4.
25. Taylor, *Sources of the Self*, p. 179.
26. Ibid. p. 178.
27. Rom 7:15–20; cp., e.g., Ovid, *Metamorphoses* 7: 20, Seneca, *Medea* 937–44, and Seneca, *Phaedra* 177–84.
28. Ricœur, *Time and Narrative. Volume 3*, p. 246.
29. Ricœur, *Time and Narrative. Volume 2*, p. 133.
30. Bromwich, 'What Shakespeare's Hero's Learn', p. 132.

31. Ellrodt, 'Self-Consciousness in Montaigne and Shakespeare', p. 46; Ellrodt, *Montaigne et Shakespeare*, p. 118.
32. Grady, *Shakespeare, Machiavelli, and Montaigne*, pp. 94–103.
33. Lee, *Shakespeare's* Hamlet *and the Controversies of Self*, p. 182.
34. Ibid. p. 176.
35. Ibid. p. 184.
36. Ibid. p. 175.
37. Montaigne, *Shakespeare's Montaigne*, p. 46.
38. Ricœur, *Oneself as Another*, p. 193.
39. Ibid. p. 185. Cf. Patrick Gray, *Shakespeare and the Fall of the Roman Republic*, pp. 227–42.
40. Patrick Gray, 'Shakespeare versus Aristotle', p. 89.
41. Augustine, *Confessions* 11.28.37.
42. Ricœur, *Oneself as Another*, pp. 294–5.
43. Fernie, *Shame in Shakespeare*, p. 69.
44. Augustine, *Confessions* 11.20.26.
45. Ricœur, *Oneself as Another*, p. 297.
46. Ricœur, *Oneself as Another*, p. 16, pp. 4–5. Cf. Patrick Gray, *Shakespeare and the Fall of the Roman Republic*, pp. 275–6.
47. Ricœur, *Oneself as Another*, p. 22.
48. Patrick Gray, *Shakespeare and the Fall of the Roman Republic*, pp. 220–76.
49. Montaigne, *Shakespeare's Montaigne*, p. 9.
50. Eliot, 'Shakespeare and the Stoicism of Seneca', pp. 110–11. Cf. Bromwich, 'What Shakespeare's Heroes Learn'.
51. Desan, *Montaigne*, p. xxxii.
52. Goffman, 'Face-Work', p. 43. Cf. Smith and Lupton, eds, *Face-to-Face in Shakespearean Drama*, and Knapp, ed., *Shakespeare and the Power of the Face*.
53. Ricœur, *The Course of Recognition*.

Chapter 5

Genre and Gender in Montaigne and Shakespeare

David Schalkwyk

The quest I wish to pursue in this chapter begins at the lowly level of the pronoun. It progresses from there to questions of dialogue and conversation and to the relation between genre and gender in Shakespeare and Montaigne. It asks in what ways the genre of the essay enables (or constrains) the ways in which Montaigne is able to reflect on women as a different gender, and in what ways drama allows Shakespeare different freedoms in this regard.

This leads to a further question: one that inverts the traditional issue of whether Shakespeare shares Montaigne's scepticism. What are the limits of Montaigne's scepticism? What are the things about which he does not ask questions, where doubt has no hold or simply does not arise? I am interested in what we might call the 'customary' assumptions to which Montaigne remains blind.

The Structural Imagination of *Twelfth Night* and the *Essays*

The first example is not precisely customary in the sense of being a habitual mode of thought or feeling that unconsciously drives a practice or belief. It bears the authority of ancient endorsement and of indelible personal experience: it is 'loving friendship', or *amitié*, the affective relationship that Montaigne values above all others, embodied and exemplified in his affinity with Étienne de La Boëtie. Striking about Montaigne's disquisition on friendship is that it introduces a second issue about which he admits few doubts, that of gender – the double absences of doubt, about the incomparable value of friendship and the flawed nature of women, are thus intertwined.

Other than for a single, speculative sentence in the essay, Montaigne is in absolutely no doubt that women are constitutionally incapable of the kind of affectionate bond that he values above all others.

Montaigne disallows doubt of three things. First, his friendship with De La Boëtie is unparalleled in his own time: 'so entire and so perfect that certainly you will hardly read of the like, and among men of today you see no trace of it in practice' (I: 28, 165).[1] Second, friendship, marked by free choice, complete equality, and the sharing of a single soul in one body without any consideration beyond itself, is the pinnacle of human affiliation:

> [I]n the friendship I speak of, our souls mingle and blend with each other so completely that they efface the seam that joined them, and cannot find it again . . . We sought each other before we met . . . we found ourselves so taken with each other, so well acquainted, so bound together, that from that time on nothing was so close to us as each other. (169)[2]

Finally, women are 'in truth' constitutionally excluded from the possibility of friendship, on the basis of a difference predicated upon another related but not identical contrast – between *philia* or *amitié* and *eros* or sexual love. Throughout Montaigne's essays, *eros* is a heterosexual passion, focused primarily on pleasure and beauty located almost exclusively in the body. And it is completely in line with his conception of women, who are inherently more passionate, more consumed by sexual desire, and therefore incapable of the constancy and the intellectual qualities required for *amitié* proper:

> To compare this brotherly affection with affection for women, even though it is the result of our own choice – it cannot be done; nor can we put the love of women in the same category. Its ardor, I confess . . . is more active, more scorching, and more intense. But it is an impetuous and fickle flame, undulating and variable, a fever flame, subject to fits and lulls, that holds by only one corner. In friendship it is a general and universal warmth, all gentleness and smoothness, with nothing bitter and stinging about it. What is more, in love there is nothing but a frantic desire for what flees before us. (I: 28, 166–7)

Striking about this passage is not so much the very conventional notion of *eros* as intense and inconsistent or the anticipation of the Lacanian desire, an essentially metonymic movement without the possibility of rest or satisfaction, but rather Montaigne's use of pronouns. The differentiation of men from women along active and passive lines is immediately transformed into a grammatical and rhetorical division between two distinct groups implicated in the reading or sharing of the text of the *Essays*: those collected under 'our' and 'us' in the passage above and others collected under the third-person 'them'. The very form of the *Essays* is centred on a writing I who constitutes the controlling centre of the text, both as the object of its assaying (the reflexive 'myself' that occurs some 500 times in the text) and as its driving subject, the I that Raymond Barthes and Jacques Lacan call the subject of the statement or utterance (*le sujet de l'énonciation*).

The formation of subjectivity in language, Émile Benveniste argues, occurs through the mobilisation of pronouns, especially in contrastive ways.[3] Following Ferdinand de Saussure, Benveniste argues that I gets its sense from the fact that it is used in opposition to other pronouns: the second-person you, and third-person singular he, she or it, or the third-person plural they. But it can also appropriate anything that falls within these pronominal categories under the first-person plural we. Furthermore, pronouns are 'shifters'; they have no fixed referents but change their designation on each instance of use. But despite the fact that they contain occasional dialogical exchanges, Montaigne's essays are rooted in the writing I who is not merely a grammatical subject, but also the object of their enquiry. Furthermore, unlike everyday discourse or exchanges in the theatre, or even in the movement between narrator and character in the novel, they do not shift beyond these two poles constituted by I and myself. Montaigne fits more shifting within the I–myself range than any writer before him, but he nonetheless remains between these poles. And like the poles of a magnet, these pronouns attract and encompass a general we, implicitly included in the structural imaginary of the reader – an us, a possessive our, that repels or at least keeps at a distance, a they, a them, a their, defined at the basic level of grammar as different from the conjoined I of writing and the we of reading. This we is virtually always male.[4]

Theatre is an exemplary embodiment of the shifting or indexical character of pronouns that hardly ever occurs in Montaigne: the I used by Orsino, for example, in Shakespeare's *Twelfth Night*, changes its referent the moment it is pronounced by Viola/Cesario in response to him. In the following speech from *Twelfth Night*, Orsino speaks, as it were, with Montaigne's voice (itself echoing many others from Aristotle through Galen) on the constitutional inconstancy of women:

> There is no woman's sides
> Can bide the beating of so strong a passion
> As love doth give my heart; no woman's heart
> So big, to hold so much; they lack retention.

> Alas, their love may be called appetite,
> No motion of the liver but the palate,
> That suffer surfeit, cloyment, and revolt;
> But mine is all as hungry as the sea,
> And can digest as much. Make no compare
> Between that love a woman can bear me
> And that I owe Olivia.   (II, iv, 104–13)

Orsino is talking about sexual love, asserting the constitutional incapacity of women to love beyond the fluctuating demands of mere 'appetite'. Montaigne would demur only in so far as he believes that all sexual desire, of whatever gender, is unstable and unreliable. But he does subscribe to Orsino's denigration of women as incapable of engaging constantly in any kind of relationship, including friendship:

> to tell the truth, the ordinary capacity of women is inadequate for that communion and fellowship which is the nurse of this sacred bond; nor does their soul seem firm enough to endure the strain of so tight and durable knot . . . and by the common agreement of the ancient schools is excluded from it. (I: 28, 167–8)

My main concern is the use of the exclusionary third-person *their* and *she* in Montaigne. Even the common noun 'women/woman' takes on the differential pole that Benveniste attributes to pronouns: women are implicitly displaced as subjects reading the essay into a space where they are objectified as others, unable to share in the *it* of friendship in which all men are at least potential participants.

My argument is that the genre of the essay as a process of assaying himself induces the author into what Mikhail Bakhtin calls a monological, centripetal discourse, especially in areas where his scepticism reaches its limits, and that in spite of the apparently dispersed and various voices of classical authors that so liberally inhabit the essays.[5] There is very little of what Bakhtin calls dialogism or heteroglossia (exemplified for Bakhtin in free indirect discourse), where the narrating voice resonates and is crisscrossed with different, contradictory accents and intonations, in Montaigne's style. Where he employs other voices they are set off as quotations from classical sources; they do not contaminate nor are they infected by the narrating voice in Bakhtinian dialogism. The discursive *I* of the essay accumulates a likeminded (and gendered) *we* that defines itself in opposition to the *they* of womankind.

Compare this to the expression of the same misogyny in Shakespeare. The scene quoted briefly above, immediately after Orsino mobilises the opposition between the masculine I against an incorrigible female they to Viola/Cesario, she hovers undecideably between she and he as she tries to forge a position for her own I:

VIOLA: Ay, but *I* know—
ORSINO: What dost *thou* know?
VIOLA: Too well what love women to men may owe.
In faith, *they* are as true of heart as *we*.
My father had a daughter loved a man
As it might be, perhaps, were *I* a woman,
I should your Lordship.
ORSINO: And what's *her* history?
VIOLA: A blank, my lord. *She* never told her love,
But let concealment, like a worm i' th' bud,
Feed on *her* damask cheek. *She* pined in thought,
And with a green and yellow melancholy
She sat like Patience on a monument,
Smiling at grief. Was not this love indeed?
We men may say more, swear more, but indeed
Our shows are more than will; for still *we* prove
Much in *our* vows but little in *our* love.

(II, v, 114–13; emphases mine)

Notice how Viola's irrepressible impulse to defend women against Orsino's calumny on the basis of her personal experience ('Ay, but I know . . .'), rebuffed by Orsino, forces her to transform herself into the third person in the form of a fictional sister who 'never told her love' and whose 'history' turns out to be 'a blank'. Like the female reader of Montaigne's *Essays*, she has to align herself against the they of her gender and with the we of Orsino's (and Montaigne's) distancing of women as a whole. Viola's is a moving and desperate exercise in self-alienation, only in part resolved at the end of the play.

The difference between Shakespeare and Montaigne, however, lies in the fact that Viola's imprisonment in the structures of gender difference is palpable, completely obvious, to the audience watching and listening to the play, who are able to adopt a distant, critical position regarding Orsino's pronominal hegemony. Even when she is silent, her independent embodiment on the stage speaks volumes, resisting complete incorporation into the masculine we against the feminine they.

I call this difference between the Montaignesque essay and Shake-spearean play the 'structural imagination' that each genre makes available to author and dramatist respectively. I have argued else-where that the structural imagination of his theatre enables Shake-speare to embody in the same figure what Montaigne keeps radically apart: constant, generous friend and desiring lover.[6] Viola/Cesario is both; and neither obliterates the other.

This brings us to Shakespeare's capacity to illuminate Montaigne (rather than, as is usual, vice versa). For, in the passage from 'Of Affectionate Relationships' quoted above, there is an almost hidden speculation or fantasy on the desirability of woman as friend:

> And indeed, but for that, if such a relationship, free and voluntary, could be built up, in which not only would the souls have this complete enjoy-ment, but the bodies would also share in the alliance, so that the entire man were engaged, it is certain that the resulting friendship would be fuller and more complete. (I: 28, 167)

This possibility is entertained only fleetingly, before it is dismissed with an appeal to Classical authority. It is possible, even likely, that at the end of his life Montaigne found in de Gournay precisely the friendship of a woman about which he can only (dismissively) fanta-sise in this passage.

Shakespeare's genre, then, distributes personal pronouns in a radically different way from Montaigne's, revealing the ideological violence involved in the formation of a masculine we in opposition to a female they, and allowing a female I room to speak back, even if in this scene such subjectivity is not permitted full expression.

'On Some Lines of Virgil'

The late essay 'On Some Lines of Virgil' (III: 5) is often celebrated as an especially enlightened disquisition on women: sympathetic, imaginatively tolerant and self-ironical. But the pronominal other-ing of women obstinately remains: indeed, it may even be exacer-bated, as Montaigne's reflections on his own sexuality are constantly contrasted with women as a category, defined by a driving, intrinsic sexuality that is essentially uncontainable: 'we have discovered . . . that women are incomparably more capable and ardent than we in the acts of love' (787–8) and 'If this natural violence of their desire were not somewhat held in check by the fear and honour with which they have been provided, we would be shamed' (791). The division between men and women is especially stark in the second of these quotations. Women are set apart from men in the voraciousness of their sexual appetites and readiness to have intercourse: 'There is naturally strife and wrangling between them and us: the closest communication we have with them is still tumultuous and tempestuous' (788). But they are also the vehicles of male shame and ridicule, which would be more widespread if their natural lusts were not curtailed by their universal subjection to social values of propriety, which, Montaigne reminds his readers, is no more than a male imposition: 'women are not wrong at all when they reject the rules of life that have been introduced into the world, inasmuch as it is the men who have made these without them' (787–8).

It is evident from this observation, and many have noted, that Montaigne tempers his traditional, fixed notions of female sexual intemperance with a trenchant critique of male expectations of women's sexuality and behaviour. Indeed, that supposed intemperance may be the condition of his declaration that it is unfair for men to expect them (*sic*) to behave in a way that runs contrary to their natural desires. At other moments, however, it appears that man and women share a passion for sex; only in women is it decried as an 'abomination':

> We have gone and given women continence as their particular share, and upon utmost and extreme penalties. There is no passion more pressing than this, which we want them alone to resist, not simply as a vice of its own size, but as an abomination and execration, more to be resisted than irreligion and parricide, and meanwhile we give in to it without blame or reproach . . . In short, we allure and flesh them by every means; we incessantly heat and excite their imagination. And then we bellyache. (789, 794)

This is indeed an enlightened critique of the 'double standard'. And it prefigures Montaigne's explicit declaration at the end of the essay that men and women 'are cast in the same mould; except for education and custom, the difference is not great' (831).

What difference is Montaigne considering here? In an essay that is chiefly given over to considerations of sex and sexuality, it would make sense to restrict it to a common tendency to be driven, as Plato puts it, by their respective 'animals' of genital desire (793). But if the *Essays* target anything, it is the tyranny of custom and education as a whole and our blindness to that hegemony: 'Habituation puts to sleep the eye of our judgment' (I: 23, 96).

The most celebrated of his deconstructions of custom involve his anti-ethnocentric consideration, in 'Of Cannibals', of the degree to which our blindness to the excesses and cruelty of our own practices cause us to denigrate and demonise those of different cultures: 'each man calls barbarism whatever is not his own practice; for indeed it seems we have no other test of truth and reason than the example and patterns of the opinions and customs of the country we live in' (185). 'Of Cannibals' is also structured around a rigid grammatical opposition of we and they, strengthened by the non-pronominal phrase 'those peoples' to refer to the supposed barbaric anthropophagi of the Americas. But the force of the essay uses this opposition to invert it: to show that, by the standards of Nature, people of Europe are arguably more barbaric than 'those people' of the Americas: 'So we may well call these people barbarians, in respect to the rules of reason, but not in respect to ourselves, who surpass them in every kind of barbarity' (189).

Given this openness to the otherness of 'these peoples' of the Americas, it is puzzling that, when Montaigne criticises the double standard of sexual morality imposed by men, it never strikes him that women could possibly have some role in setting standards of behaviour or norms of custom rather than merely conforming to them, thereby achieving some degree of gender neutrality or common humanity. From the very beginning of the *Essays*, women are assumed to have natures quite different from men that make them unsuitable for public life:

> It may be said that to subdue your heart to commiseration is an act of easy going indulgence and softness, which is why the weaker natures, such as those of women, children and the common herd, are the most subject to it. (I: 1, 4)

He also confines them to a particular kind of education on account of their common 'nature': 'if they want, out of curiosity, to have a share in book learning, poetry is an amusement suited to their needs; it is a wanton and subtle art, in fancy dress, wordy, all pleasure, all show, like themselves' (III: 3, 757). 'Wanton', 'fancy dress', 'wordy', 'pleasure', 'show'. Is Montaigne actually thinking when he writes this? Or is he merely being provocative with his 'rhetoric of misogyny'?[7] He does go on to recommend moral philosophy as suitable reading for women, who may benefit from it by improving themselves. Mary McKinley points out that these are the studies Montaigne himself loved; but when he speaks admiringly of Lucretius, for instance, quoting Seneca, he praises such poetry for its virile strength ('*Contextus totus virilis est*'): 'it is solid and has sinews' (III: 12, 807).[8]

The grounds on which he excludes women from engaging in anything other than poetry, history and moral philosophy are complicated. The excluded areas are not only useless, they also render women more easily manipulated by men (like other 'weaker natures', 'children' and 'common-people'):

> When I see them intent on rhetoric, astrology, logic and similar drugs, so vain and useless for their needs, I begin to fear that the men who advise them to do this, do so as a means of gaining authority over them under this pretext. For what other excuse could I find for them? (II: 3, 757)

Why should rhetoric and logic be 'vain and useless' 'drugs'? Are they such only for women, or for men too? The referent of Montaigne's 'them' is uncertain here. Does it include men or women, or both?

Shakespeare offers a very different perspective, not on women as highly sexualised objects meant, in essence, for 'pleasure', but as relatively free agents able to escape the very snares of patriarchy that Montaigne decries. This is again a matter of genre and its relation to gender. Shakespearean romantic comedy gives women the social and personal space not merely to follow (or forge) the choice of their desires, but also to intervene in ways that Montaigne hardly considers possible. Shakespeare's female characters are articulate, savvy, cunning, with a capacity to adopt and adapt the roles usually reserved for men in ways that outstrip males. Think of Viola's command of rhetoric and her embodiment of the kind of constant friendship Montaigne delimits as the preserve of men while harbouring her erotic desires; of Rosalind's similar command of language and capacity to mock the clichés of *eros* while playing Cupid's part; and especially of Portia as the learned legal doctor who uses every rhetorical, logical and legal device not only to press her arguments against Shylock but also to outwit her husband. That the 'green spaces' of the romantic comedies are temporary interludes that allow for flexible desire and the adoption of alternative roles means that Shakespeare remains bound by a culture that would keep women where Montaigne places them, but his theatre and the peculiar generic form of his comedies gives him the structural imagination to embody alternatives. This is, of course, overdetermined on Shakespeare's stage, for not only does cross-dressing allow 'women' to play powerful, male roles, but the male actor beneath the costume is also able to enact a powerful bond of comradeship with other (male) actors.[9]

As always with the French essayist, though, there are complications. Adopting a strategy of reading Montaigne and Shakespeare across each other allows us to interrogate (as many have done) the ethics of Portia's employment of the 'trivial drugs' of rhetoric and forensic legal argument. The fine rhetoric of her plea on behalf of mercy may be considered spurious, since she shows no such pity to Shylock. Her use of legal argument is questionable, since she moves from declaring that there is no legal impediment to Shylock's exacting his contractual penalty to the retributive law against aliens. Finally, the conversion of Shylock as a punishment redoubles the ethnocentrism that Montaigne attacks in other contexts (although he has very little to say about Jews). The point is that use of such devices and forms of learning leads all humans astray, securing them in their ignorance and arrogance:

> Men's opinions are accepted in the train of ancient beliefs, by authority and on credit, as if they were religion and law. They accept as by rote what is commonly held about it. They accept this truth, with all its structure and apparatus of argument and proofs, as a firm and solid body, no longer shakeable, no longer to be judged. On the contrary everyone competes in plastering up and confirming this accepted belief, with all the power of their reason, which is a supple tool, pliable, and adaptable to any form. Thus the world is filled and soaked in twaddle and lies. (II: 12, 489)

Does Montaigne have this general castigation of the 'powers of reason' in mind when he limits women to history, poetry and moral philosophy? There is no way of knowing.

Many discussions of Montaigne's scepticism appear to assume that he is in full control of his arguments and digressions. Isabelle Krier, for example, sees the contradiction of the essays as a deliberate strategy to perplex the reader and thereby exercise his peculiar brand of scepticism.[10] But perhaps such complications and contradictions escape Montaigne's conscious intention. I have mentioned Montaigne (or rather the I of the *Essays*) in his capacity as *le sujet de l'énonciation*. What of that subject position as *le sujet de de l'énoncé*, 'the subject not insofar as it produces discourse but insofar as it is produced [*fait*], cornered even [*fait comme un rat*], by discourse'?[11] To adopt a psychoanalytical perspective on Montaigne's writing would mean reading against the grain of the *Essays'* against-the-grain writing. This is not the easiest task, but it would allow for a multiplication of voices, especially within the writing subject, that offers not an identical form of dialogism to Shakespeare's drama, but a different kind of unconscious, undeliberate counterpoint. We might then acknowledge the overt expressions of misogyny as a kind of locker-room talk, signs of the writing self's complicity in the grammar of a communal, but also exclusionary we. Such a reading would be entirely in keeping with Montaigne's conscious sense of himself and others as radically unstable, incomplete and contradictory, and the *Essays* as akin to Ludwig Wittgenstein's journeyings in the *Philosophical Investigations*:[12] 'I do not find myself in the place where I look; and I find myself more by chance encounter than by searching my judgment' (I: 10, 31).

Philippe Desan offers a psychoanalytical reading in 'The Book, the Friend, and the Woman: Montaigne's Circular Exchanges', which argues that Montaigne can be found only in exchange or contradiction with the 'Other', particularly the Others of the book, the friend, and the woman. In his reading the friend always belongs to the past, as a nostalgic ideal forever lost, whereas 'placed in the future, the woman is, in fact, the object of desire par excellence'. [13] Moreover, the pleasure of desire, in a standard Lacanian reading, involves endless deferral and absence. This reading certainly accounts for the 'blankness' of women in the essays, like the pining sister in Viola's story of female love: both as silence and as a slate onto which male fantasy may be projected. But the most notable absence in the *Essays* is Montaigne's wife. That absence, however, is literal. It is not the absence construed by Lacanian desire or fantasy.

Does she represent marriage – that completely desexualised union, constrained by concerns completely other to the character and desires of the parties and which, however much it may approach the consanguinity of friendship – 'A good marriage, if such there be, rejects the company and conditions of love. It tries to reproduce those of friendship' (III: 5, 1041) – contradicts the criteria, insisted upon in the earlier essay, of absolute freedom and equality between friends? Montaigne betrays a curious prudishness in his disgust at the thought that marriage should know anything of *eros*:

> it is a kind of incest to employ . . . the efforts and extravagances of amorous licence . . . A man, says Aristotle, should touch his wife prudently and soberly, lest if he caresses her too lasciviously the pleasure should transport her outside the bounds of reason. (III: 5, 783)

The reader remains caught in the grammatical snare of the *Essays*, from which there is no escape, in which the we of men is ranged against the they of women; but more disturbing is the notion of women as intrinsically lascivious, irrational beings, who need to be saved by the disciplined consideration of men – at least in marriage.

If Cupid plays no part in either marriage or friendship, then how does Montaigne characterise him? It is telling that when he comes to write directly of Cupid, he puts aside books and customary authority: 'Now then, leaving books aside and speaking more materially and simply, I find after all love is nothing else but the thirst for sexual enjoyment within the desired object, and Venus nothing else but the pleasure of discharging our vessels' (III: 5, 811).[14] Nowhere is the exclusion of women more complete than in this male 'unloading of our balls'. Despite his putting aside books, this is a direct echo of Lucretius, for whom erotic passion is likewise a frenzied impulse to unload semen in as many receptacles as possible. But even though Lucretius addresses *On the Nature of Things* to a man, Memmius, his account of desire does not range men against women, as Montaigne does. Instead, he writes of 'lovers' and 'couples', including both sexes in his descriptions of erotic passion, and insisting on mutual pleasure: 'couples enchained by mutual pleasure are often tortured in common chains . . . So I insist that sexual pleasure is shared.'[15] Nor does Lucretius attribute to women any greater lasciviousness or irrationality in desire than men. Both are equally prone to mad frenzy; each requires mutual sexual pleasure. His we is inclusive; his they not exclusionary.

This brings us to my final example from Shakespeare, *Othello*, one play in which received ideas about female sexual voracity are expressed openly and frequently. But such views are confined to the play's villain – until he infects Othello with his 'thoughts'. My first example is entirely in keeping with the dialogism of theatre, in that it employs the plural pronoun you in a direct address to women, who have the opportunity to respond:

> IAGO: Come on, come on! You are pictures out of door,
> bells in your parlors, wildcats in your kitchens,
> saints in your injuries, devils being offended, players
> in your huswifery, and huswives in your beds.
> DESDEMONA: Oh, fie upon thee, slanderer.
>
> (II, i, 122–6)

The second is between two men, Iago and Othello:

> IAGO: Look to 't.
> I know our country disposition well.
> In Venice they do let God see the pranks
> They dare not show their husbands. Their best conscience
> Is not to leave 't undone, but keep 't unknown.
>
> (III, iii, 231–5)

We have now shifted from you to they and our, into a situation where cormorant female sexuality is again displaced onto a distanced other unable to speak as an I or we in defence. But Othello is also distanced through Iago's our: as a 'an extravagant and wheeling stranger / Of here and everywhere' (I, i, 150–1) he is not included within the compass of the pronoun, but rather debarred on the grounds of race, origin and ignorance.

My third example returns to the opposition between a male we and a female they, now rooted in the incorrigible singular I of male passion:

> OTHELLO: She's gone, I am abused, and my relief
> Must be to loathe her. O curse of marriage,
> That we can call these delicate creatures ours
> And not their appetites! I had rather be a toad
> And live upon the vapor of a dungeon
> Than keep a corner in the thing I love
> For others' uses.   (III, iii, 308–14)

Beginning with the opposition of individuals – '*she*'s gone, *I* am abused' – Othello moves into a generalised statement about marriage, women and the universal incapacity of men to own and control female desire. But the solidarity that binds men is broken through the 'others' whose 'use' of the woman produces so much anguished alienation.

There are more voices in the play that further complicate its gender binaries. They constitute my final example and are worth quoting at some length.

> DESDEMONA: . . . O these men, these men!
> Dost thou in conscience think – tell me, Emilia –
> That there be women do abuse their husbands
> In such gross kind?
> EMILIA: There be some such, no question.
> DESDEMONA: Wouldst thou do such a deed for all the world?
> EMILIA: Why, would not you?
> DESDEMONA: No, by this heavenly light!
> EMILIA: Nor I neither, by this heavenly light.
> I might do 't as well i' th' dark.
>
> . . .
>
> DESDEMONA: I do not think there is any such woman.
> EMILIA: Yes, a dozen; and as many to th' vantage as
> would store the world they played for.
> But I do think it is their husbands' faults

> If wives do fall. Say that they slack their duties,
> And pour our treasures into foreign laps;
> Or else break out in peevish jealousies,
> Throwing restraint upon us. Or say they strike us,
> Or scant our former having in despite.
> Why, we have galls, and though we have some grace,
> Yet have we some revenge. Let husbands know
> Their wives have sense like them. They see, and smell,
> And have their palates both for sweet and sour,
> As husbands have.   (IV, iii, 65–107)

The movement between pronominal and nominal inclusions and exclusions takes complex, shifting trajectories before settling into an absolute dichotomy between a female we and a male they that nonetheless speaks for a common, fallen humanity. 'O these men, these men', Desdemona exclaims, in a despairing, exclusionary move, before immediately distancing herself from the women 'who abuse their husbands'. But she also excludes herself from Emilia, who displays an at least ambivalent, comic attitude to being included in the class of women who 'would do it i'th' dark'. By the time Emilia affirms that the class of women who would betray their husbands is much greater than Desdemona naively believes, we are close to Montaigne's affirmation that 'If the ferocity of their desires were not somewhat reined in by that fear for their honour with which all women are endowed, we would all be laughing-stocks' (968). And we move even closer to him in her Shylock-like affirmation not merely of a shared humanity, but of a mutual desire for revenge by mimicking the language of instruction, for indulging too in 'sport', 'affection' and 'frailty':

> What is it that they do
> When they change us for others? Is it sport?
> I think it is. And doth affection breed it?
> I think it doth. Is 't frailty that thus errs?
> It is so too. And have not we affections,
> Desires for sport, and frailty, as men have?
> Then let them use us well. Else let them know,
> The ills we do, their ills instruct us so.
>
> (IV, iii, 108–115)

But notice, *contra* Montaigne, the instability of pronominal use in this speech, as Emilia shifts between an alignment with the common experience of all women and a distancing of herself from the they of the 'their wives', and between the othering they of 'husbands' and the implicit we of all human beings. But Shakespeare is yet more nuanced. After the temporary solidarity as women of Emilia and Desdemona, the latter leaves the company of women as incorporated by her servant, both dismissing her and declaring her difference (with the help of God): 'Good night, good night. God me such uses send, / Not to pick bad from bad, but by bad mend' (IV, iii, 116–17).

I am arguing that the affinities and dislocations of Shakespeare and Montaigne should not be confined to textual echoes and corresponding ideas or attitudes but rather through the filter of generic difference, where especially issues of gender are deeply informed by the constraints and possibilities of genre. The destructive intensity of Othello's passion – both in his love for Desdemona ('Perdition catch my soul / But I do love thee! And when I love thee not, Chaos is come again' (III, iii, 100–3)) and in his rage and despair that the 'appetite' is not his to possess or control – appears to underwrite both Montaigne's view that erotic intensity is completely out of place in marriage and his contempt for the ravages of jealousy, 'the most vain and turbulent distemper which ever afflicts our human souls' (III: 12, 975). But the flexible, interactive dialogism of the theatre, where the inclusions and exclusions of pronoun use allow, ironically, for greater shifts between and within gender identities than the *Essays'* tendency towards a monological folding together of I and we to the exclusion of a female they.

But if genre traps Montaigne, so does it Shakespeare. Montaigne's argument against sexual passion in marriage opens up his celebration of a common sexuality that may find its satisfaction in the sharing of pleasure and wit, in the joyful seizing of opportunity ('If someone asked me the first thing in love, I would answer that it is knowing how to seize the right time; the second likewise, and the third too . . .' (III: 5, 799)). There is a degree of admiration in Montaigne's account of the boundless nature of female sexuality, and his view that the desire to curtail the will of women is not only futile but insane: 'Is it their will that we want our women to curb? . . . It is not in them, nor perhaps Chasity herself, since she is a women, to keep themselves from lust and desire' (799). The 'natural' outcome, then, is, while celebrating marriage as an asexual condition of mutual respect and friendship, to allow for the free exercise of polyamory in sexual matters – applicable to women as much as men. For, finally, 'males and females are finally cast in the same mould: except for education and custom, the difference is not that great' (831). And we know that for Montaigne custom and education rest on no given foundation in nature.

If Montaigne can entertain for both men and women a free exercise of sexual desire and enjoyment outside marriage, Shakespeare offers few representations of this possibility in his romantic comedies. We need to focus on Cleopatra to find a path back to Montaigne. But that is a topic for another essay.

Notes

1. All quotations, unless stated otherwise, are from Montaigne, *The Complete Works*, trans. Frame.
2. But note recent scepticism about the historical veracity of that relationship which suggests that is a posthumous 'literary construction': Magnien, 'La Boétie and Montaigne' and Desan, 'The Book, the Friend, and the Woman'. It is also striking that while Montaigne strives to eliminate desire from such friendship, he soon succumbs to the inevitability of a felt longing and absence. Despite insisting that friends are 'one soul in two bodies' and 'hold everything in common', he nonetheless insists that in 'this perfect friendship . . . each one gives himself so wholly to his friend that he has nothing left . . . he is sorry that he is not double, triple, or quadruple, and that he has so several souls and several wills, to distribute them all on this one object' (172).
3. Benveniste, *Problems in General Linguistics*.
4. There are, of course, essays addressed to women, to Marguerite de Valois, Madame de Foix and Madame d'Estissac, where some uses of the first-person plural pronoun may include women, but these are exceptional. It is clear that Montaigne wanted women to read his *Essays*, from remarks in III: 5, but it seems that they remain as outsiders, observing a discourse directed by one man to other men. (I am indebted to William M. Hamlin for this observation.)
5. Bakhtin, *Dialogic Imagination*.
6. See Schalkwyk, 'The Discourses of Friendship and the Structural Imagination of Shakespeare's Theater'. This essay argues that Montaigne may have found the embodiment of this fantasy in his friendship at the end of his life with Marie de Gournay, who edited the posthumous edition of the *Essays*.
7. See Floyd Gray, 'The Women in Montaigne's Life'.
8. McKinley, 'Montaigne on Women', p. 584.
9. I am grateful to Elena Pellone for drawing my attention to this point.
10. Krier, *Montaigne et la genre instable*, p. 19, quoted in McKinley, 'Montaigne on Women', p. 587.
11. Lacan and Miller, *My Teaching*, p. 36.
12. Wittgenstein, *Philosophical Investigations*: the remarks are 'number of sketches of landscapes . . . made in the course of . . . long and involved

journeying . . . an album . . . of a wide field of thought criss-cross in every direction'.

13. Desan, 'The Book, the Friend, and the Woman', p. 225, pp. 229–30.
14. Screech has: 'unloading our balls' (1074).
15. Lucretius, *On the Nature of Things* 4.1201–9.

Chapter 6

Shakespeare, Montaigne and Moral Luck

Maria Devlin McNair

The term 'moral luck' refers to the 'apparent and allegedly problematic or paradoxical fact that factors decisive for the moral standing of an agent are factors subject to luck'.[1] While we feel intuitively that agents cannot be morally judged for what they cannot help, the factors that influence our judgements commonly lie outside the agent's control. Montaigne and Shakespeare disagree not only as regards the reality of moral luck but also as regards the possible dangers it might pose.

Montaigne rejects moral luck in so far as he adopts a Stoic ethos, which locates the ground of moral judgement in the agent's autonomous will.[2] The agent's will, or more broadly his character, is also the ground of value. The highest value lies in excellence of the self. This excellence would be at risk if accidents could occasion remorse; the possibility of moral luck is rejected, however, in that agents are held responsible only for what they can control. The Christian ethos dramatised by Shakespeare also holds that agents are judged by their wills but insists that the will is *not* autonomous. The state of an agent's will depends partially on external factors. Moral luck is real, then, in so far as one's moral status is partly determined by something outside oneself. Christianity takes the highest value to lie outside the agent, not in one's own excellence but instead in one's relations with others. When those interpersonal relations are compromised by sinful forms of willing, full reconciliation often requires moral luck. While for Montaigne, the greatest threat would be to suffer bad moral luck, the greatest threat for Shakespeare would be to miss out on good moral luck.

Neostoicism, a late sixteenth-century movement promulgated by Justus Lipsius, Guillaume Du Vair and Montaigne, attempted to revive classical Stoicism, especially Senecan Stoicism, within a Christian context.[3] As the problem of moral luck reveals, however, Christianity and Stoicism are incompatible. Both systems can be considered intentionalist. That is to say, both moral paradigms hold that the most important factor in moral judgements is the intention or will of the agent. But Stoicism and Christianity disagree markedly about the possibility of self-sufficiency, including especially the degree of control a moral agent possesses over his own will.

Stoicism identifies virtue with 'knowledge of what is good'.[4] The 'perfection of one's rational nature is the condition of being virtuous and it is exercising this, and this alone, which is good'.[5] Virtue is the grounds for value. A good life is one lived in accordance with one's reasoned judgements, regardless of what one is able to accomplish thereby. It is in the 'inner world alone' that man 'can hope to achieve total happiness'.[6] This happiness is, in theory, available to everyone, since it requires only reason, and reason is taken to be a 'universal human attribute'.[7] In contemporary philosophy, these views find parallels in the philosophy of Immanuel Kant.

> The good will is good not through what it effects or accomplishes, not through its efficacy for attaining any intended end, but only through its willing, i.e., good in itself, and considered for itself, without comparison, it is to be estimated far higher than anything that could be brought about by it in favour of any inclination, or indeed, if you prefer, of the sum of all inclinations. Even if through the peculiar disfavour of fate, or through the meagre endowment of a stepmotherly nature, this will were entirely lacking in the resources to carry out its aim, if with its greatest effort nothing of it were accomplished, and only the good will were left over (to be sure, not a mere wish, but as the summoning up of all the means insofar as they are in our control): then it would shine like a jewel for itself, as something that has its full worth in itself. Utility or fruitlessness can neither add to nor subtract anything from this worth.[8]

Kant holds, in sum, that the only unconditional good is a good will: one that acts in accordance with, and for the sake of, the moral law as determined by reason. 'There is nothing it is possible to think of anywhere in the world,' he maintains, 'or indeed anything at all outside it, that can be held to be good without limitation, excepting only a good will.'[9] The will's autonomy makes it capable of acting on the moral law, and this autonomy belongs to every human being.[10] On Kant's view, 'the moral law will create in us a special moral motive – respect for the law – which is as universal in humankind as is awareness of the law itself'.[11]

Two features of the Stoic system make it particularly invulnerable to luck. First, the means to make oneself both good and happy belong to every person by virtue of his rational human nature. Second, those means are wholly internal. Stoicism draws a sharp distinction between the external world, which is controlled by fortune or fate, and the internal world, which is controlled wholly by the agent himself. Nothing can take away my happiness, for it depends only on my virtue and virtue depends on my inner reason. Virtue is thus a form of 'self-sufficiency which, by freeing the individual from all dependence on things external to himself, makes him invulnerable to fortune', making it the 'ultimate resource by which the ego could minimise its vulnerability to adversity'.[12] The good willer, even under the most devastating attacks of fortune, retains the ultimate value, his own excellence of self.[13]

Christianity shares the Stoic and Kantian view that moral judgements are dependent upon the agent's will: 'whosoever looketh on a woman to lust after her, hath committed adultery with her already in his heart' (Matt. 5:28).[14] But Christianity denies that the will is fully autonomous. The Stoics, identifying virtue with knowledge, held that 'a person who knows what is good will necessarily act rightly'.[15] On the Christian view, by contrast, it is part of fallen human nature to know what is good without being able to will it: 'For I do not the good thing, which I would, but the evil, which I would not, that do I' (Rom. 7:19).[16]

Augustine in particular emphasises the loss of human moral freedom as a result of the Fall of Man. From his perspective, no merely human effort can enable a person to carry out the moral law.[17] Augustine's views exerted a major influence on the Reformation. The Church of England's Thirty-Nine Articles declared that any good will within us is the result of Christ's prevenient grace:

> man after the fall of Adam . . . can not turne and prepare hym selfe by his owne natural strength and good workes, to faith and calling vppon GOD: Wherfore we haue no power to do good workes pleasaunt and acceptable to GOD, without the grace of God by Christe preuentyng vs, that we may haue a good wyll, & workyng with vs, when we haue that good wyll.[18]

Other theologians, notably Thomas Aquinas, allow a greater degree of freedom in the will and the possibility of cooperating with God's grace.[19] But no Christian theology would concede that humans are capable of willing rightly alone and unaided. All human goodness depends to some extent on divine assistance.

Calvin's theory of predestination, adapted in the Thirty-Nine Articles as 'predestination to lyfe', was an absolute refutation of Stoic notions of self-sufficiency. No human had power to secure eternal happiness for himself, any more than he had power to secure goodness. He had not even the power to know why anyone else secured it. Why God saved some and damned others was, from his perspective, unknowable: from the human point of view, rather like a matter of luck. Christianity in general in the sixteenth century had a vexed and changing relationship to the concept of luck. Brian Cummings shows that, while theological texts earlier in the century used the term 'luck' with frequency, later texts firmly condemn any suggestion that chance plays any role whatsoever in human affairs.[20] What appears to be luck is in fact the work of God.[21] But, in either case, the salient point remains. On our own, we can attain neither goodness nor salvation. Cummings quotes one prayer book that enjoins, 'praye God continually, that he wyll graunt . . . a luckie, and good end of this lyfe'.[22] The prevailing assumption, as Cummings explains, is that 'life is a matter of God's luck, of sublimely, or even providentially, "good luck"'.[23] Christian dependence on 'luck' of this sort – where luck is understood as a form of grace – creates an entirely different role for moral luck in Shakespeare's plays than what we encounter in the essays of Montaigne, which hew more closely, by contrast, to the countervailing influence of Stoicism.

Montaigne

Montaigne's *Essays* were a significant source of European Neostoicism. The writer he quotes most often is Seneca, the Stoic philosopher who eclipsed Cicero as the key figure for Neostoicism. He expresses his admiration for Seneca in 'On Bookes', 'A Defence of Seneca and Plutarch' and in 'Of Three Good Women', in which he also expresses his admiration for Stoic suicide. In 'That we should not judge of our Happinesse untill after our death', he emphasises the power of fortune, as well as the importance of indifference to external things and a tranquil inward spirit, referring several times to Seneca. He also quotes Seneca extensively in 'That to Philosophise is to learn how to die', in which he works to secure an attitude of Stoic tranquillity towards death. Across his *Essays* as a whole, Montaigne's admiration for Stoicism is far from consistent or uniform: Pierre Villey, for example, proposes a trajectory of affirmation, scepticism and qualified admiration for Stoicism over the long course of Montaigne's writing life.[24] By and large, however, in discussions of morality, Montaigne consistently adopts several key Stoic principles: morality depends upon the inward will; luck cannot affect morality because luck cannot affect what is internal; this internal morality guarantees human agents a source of value that is invulnerable to luck.

In one essay, Montaigne claims that we cannot be bound to promises that are 'beyond our strength and meanes' to perform. We cannot be morally obligated to do what is not within our power, and 'nothing is truly in our power', he writes, 'except our will . . . on it only are all the rules of man's dutie grounded and established'.[25] The reason that the will is the only ground of moral obligation and moral judgement is that it is the only thing we fully control. This is an intentionalist view of morality; we are praiseworthy or blameworthy, good or bad, according to what we will or intend. The title of the essay is 'That our Intention judgeth our Actions', and we find the intentionalist view of morality in a number of Montaigne's essays.[26] In 'Of Cato the Younger', for example, he maintains that 'Vertue alloweth of nothing but what is done by her, and for her alone' (114).

> There are no more vertuous actions knowne; those that beare a shew of vertue have no essence of it: for profit, glorie, custome, feare, and other like strange causes direct us to produce them. Justice, valour, integritie, which we then exercise, may by others consideration, and by the countenance they publikly beare, be termed so: but with the true workman it is no vertue at all. (114)

Discussing chastity in 'Upon Some Verses of *Virgil*', he finds that the intention behind the action is key in judging it: 'the knot of the judgement of this duty consisteth principally in the will' (487). In 'Of Crueltie', he rejects the idea that good behaviour alone qualifies as virtue if it comes about accidentally through defects rather than through a desire to be virtuous:

> I see that many vertues, as chastitie, sobrietie, and temperance, may come unto us by meanes of corporall defects and imbecilities. Constancie in dangers (if it may be termed constancie) contempt of death, patiencie in misfortunes, may happen and are often seen in men, for want of good judgement in such accidents, and that they are not apprehended for such as they are indeed. *Lacke of apprehension and stupiditie . . . counterfeit vertuous effects.* As I have often seen come to passe, that some men are commended for things they rather deserve to be blamed. (235)

Throughout Montaigne's *Essays*, we also find an insistence that humans have no control over events. As he proclaims, for example, in the early essay 'Divers Events From one selfsame counsell', 'contrary to all projects, devices, counsels and precautions, fortune doth ever keepe a full sway and possession of all' (57). The power he attributes to 'fortune' becomes a recurring theme.[27] Montaigne offers an extended discussion of fortune, for example, and its relationship to moral praise and blame in 'Of Repenting'. In this essay, he claims that repentance – understood as 'remorse accompanied by strong guilt feelings' – properly applies only to what the agent can control: '*repentance doth not properly concern what is not in our power*' (455). What does lie within are our power are the intentional actions of deliberating and choosing.[28] To the extent that we can control these internal processes, our reasoning and willing are what merit blame and occasion repentance. If an agent deliberates well and chooses well, he deserves no blame, even if fortune thwarts his intended goal:

> many good fortunes have slipt me for want of good discretion, yet did my projects make good choice, according to the occurrences presented unto them . . . I finde that in my former deliberations, I proceeded, after my rules, discreetely for the subjects state propounded to mee . . . I respect not what now it is, but what it was, when I consulted of it . . . I have in my time runne into some grosse, absurde, and important errors; not for want of good advise, but of good happe. There are secret and indivinable parts in the objects men doe handle . . . If my wit could neyther finde nor presage them, I am not offended with it; the function thereof is contained within it's owne limits. If the successe beate me, and favour the side I refused, there is no remedy; I fall not out with my selfe: I accuse my fortune, not my endeavour: that's not called repentance. (456)

That said, Montaigne does offer different views on the extent to which our desires and choices can deviate from the *forme maitresse*, 'a swaying forme' that every person is born with (454).[29] Montaigne makes his claim about repentance and control in the context of discussing this form:

> For my part, I may in generall wish to be other then I am; I may condemne and mislike my universall forme, I may beseech God to grant me an undefiled reformation, and excuse my naturall weakenesse: but meeseemeth I ought not to tearme this repentance, no more then the displeasure of being neither Angell nor *Cato*. My actions are squared to what I am and confirmed to my condition. I cannot doe better. (455)

Montaigne does not believe that he himself is capable of attaining perfect rationality and perfect virtue. He does maintain the intentionalist standpoint, however, that a moral agent cannot be blamed for what he is not capable of doing.

In sum, Montaigne holds himself responsible only for what he can control. He cannot control the outcomes of his actions – what he calls 'fortune' – but he can control his 'endevour', that is, his efforts to deliberate well according to the available information. Once he has done these deliberations and made 'good choice', he may rest satisfied with himself no matter what the outcome proves to be. As the Stoics identified the human person with reason, Montaigne identifies the potentially blameworthy agent with his 'wit'. If his reasoning is blameless, so is the agent. In refusing to let fortune 'accuse' him, or make him subject to blame, Montaigne rejects the possibility of moral luck.[30]

Montaigne aligns himself here with the mainstream of classical thought. In her study of remorse in ancient Greek and Roman writings, Laurel Fulkerson finds that 'ancient theorists seem to suggest that acting with correct intentions and whatever knowledge could reasonably have been available will mean that the virtuous man need never feel any regrets'.[31] Montaigne, by this light, anticipates the twentieth-century Kantian philosopher John Rawls, who advocated as his 'guiding principle' that 'a rational individual is always to act so that he need never blame himself no matter how things finally transpire'.[32] One can escape blame for how things transpire if, as Montaigne affirms, blame accrues only to intentional actions like deliberating and choosing.

Montaigne places a premium on never needing to blame himself. The place of repentance in Montaigne's life, as Max Guana argues, 'was as small as he could make it'.[33] Montaigne's Rawlsian calculus 'is specifically designed to eliminate from his life the guilt-feelings attendant on avoidable bad outcomes'. His sense of the limits that his temperament imposes work to distance him still further from 'unnecessary and crippling remorse'.[34] Guana finds that Montaigne adopts a determinist view not only as regards external events, which are more obviously subject to fortune, but also as regards our own character (the *forme maitresse*), from which we draw our abilities and motivations. Montaigne's intentionalism does not simply or incidentally happen to entail a reduction of scope for blame; as Gauna explains, Montaigne deliberately seeks to rationalize reduction of blame precisely because the experience of repentance is so psychologically painful. As Montaigne writes in 'Of Repenting', '*Vice leaveth, as an ulcer in the flesh, a repentance in the soule, which still scratcheth and bloodieth it selfe. For reason effaceth other griefes and sorrowes,* but engendereth those of repentance: the more yrkesome because inward' (452).

If moral luck were admitted, it would upset Montaigne's conceptual framework and pose a considerable threat to his psychological well-being. Accidents could prompt the inner torment of remorse, especially in a world believed to be under fortune's sway. Montaigne protects himself from this threat by rejecting the possibility of moral luck. Instead, he insists on the satisfaction of a good conscience, which he sees as highly reliable, independent of circumstance:

> There is truely I wot not what kinde or congratulation of well doing which rejoyceth in ourselves, and a generous jollitie that accompanieth a good conscience . . . [a] selfe-[joying] delight and satisfaction. It is no small pleasure for one to feele himselfe preserved from the contagion of an age so infected as ours, and to say to himselfe; could a man enter and see even into my soule, yet shold he not finde me guilty either of the affliction or ruine of any body, nor culpable of envie or revenge, nor of publike offence . . . These testimonies of an unspotted conscience are very pleasing, which naturall joy is a great benefit unto us: and the onely payment never faileth us. To ground the recompence of vertuous actions upon the approbation of others is to undertake a most uncertaine or troubled foundation[.] (452)

In his Roman plays, Shakespeare depicts characters who share this view. They, too, seek to 'rejoice in themselves' and to avoid basing their self-regard on the uncertain foundation of other people or on the external world in general. In his study of constancy in Shakespeare's Roman plays, Geoffrey Miles describes Senecan constancy as the 'virtue of a heroic individual who . . . is primarily concerned with his own self-sufficiency and self-perfection'.[35] Heroic Roman individuals ensure their self-sufficiency by locating perfection in their own states of mind. I focus here on Brutus in *Julius Caesar*. Brutus's greatest concern is to maintain the nobility of his own motivations.

Shakespeare's Romans

In 'Divers events from one selfsame counsell', Montaigne emphasizes the uncertainty of 'military enterprises': 'no man is so blinde but seeth what share fortune hath in them: even in our counsels and deliberations, some chance or good lucke must needs be joyned to them' (57). Given these 'divers accidents', Montaigne's advice is 'to follow the partie, wherein is most honestie and justice' (57). He cites the example of two rulers who pardoned traitors. One made a loyal friend from the pardoned traitor; the other was later assassinated. Montaigne writes,

> If [one] had but ill successe, his good intent is not to be blamed; and no man knoweth, had [he] taken the contrary way, whether he should have escaped the end, to which destinie called him; and then had he lost the glorie and commendations of so seld-seene humanitie. (57)

When (as the term 'destinie' suggests) you cannot control events, the best policy is to prioritise 'good intent'. That way, no matter how things turn out, you can be sure of earning 'glorie' for your virtue. In *Julius Caesar*, Brutus adopts this policy. Faced with the uncertainty of military enterprises, 'accidental evils',[36] and the 'providence of some high powers / That govern us below', Brutus makes his guiding principle the preservation of 'good intent' (IV, iii, 145; V, i, 109–10).[37]

Like the Stoics he seeks to emulate, Brutus is an intentionalist. In meditating on the assassination, he begins by citing the 'general' cause that motivates him: preserving Rome's liberty (II, i, 12). After the assassination, he likewise insists that the act should be judged by the motives behind it. When Antony hopes they can offer 'reasons / Why and wherein Caesar was dangerous', Brutus replies, 'Or else were this a savage spectacle' (III, iv, 223–4, 225). Brutus believes that their 'reasons are so full of good regard' that they can turn the otherwise savage attack into an honourable act of patriotism (III, iv, 226). Because their 'purpose' was 'necessary and not envious', they should be called 'purgers, not murderers' (II, i, 178–80). Brutus's later actions, as well, are guided by his desire to maintain purity of purpose. He makes a tactical mistake in allowing Antony to live; he arguably makes another when he refuses to secure necessary resources for war by seizing them. Had he done otherwise, however, he would have cast doubt on his motive for killing Caesar and, by extension, on his entire character.

The most desirable character trait for a Roman was constancy, which comprehended both steadfastness and consistency. As Laurel Fulkerson explains, 'in both philosophy and lay texts from antiquity', 'virtuous action' is 'closely connected' with 'consistency': 'one must have a stable disposition in order to act well'.[38] If Brutus were to claim a noble, disinterested motive for killing Caesar, but betray pragmatic, self-serving motives by killing off Antony and seizing goods, this inconsistency would indicate that he lacked the stable disposition necessary for virtue. The virtue of his motive in killing Caesar would then be cast in doubt. If he wishes to prove the nobility of his past motives, he must admit only similar motives in the future. He must also refrain from expressing any kind of regret or remorse about his past actions.

When Brutus joins the conspiracy, he makes himself a prime candidate for the type of moral luck Thomas Nagel terms 'resultant luck'. 'If the American Revolution', for example, he proposes, 'had been a bloody failure resulting in greater repression, then Jefferson, Franklin and Washington would still have made a noble attempt, and might not even have regretted it on their way to the scaffold, but they would also have had to blame themselves for what they had helped bring on their compatriots.'[39] Brutus's attempt has been a failure. He helped assassinate Caesar in the hopes of securing political liberty for the Roman Republic. Now, Rome threatens to fall under the domination of Octavius Caesar and Mark Antony – whose life Brutus preserved. Brutus refuses to allow the outcome to inspire any self-reproach, however, because such remorse might cast doubt upon his original motives. In his *Lives* – a key source for *Julius Caesar* – Plutarch tells the story of Timoleon. Timoleon had his tyrannical brother killed but then became deeply distraught and went into self-imposed exile. Plutarch finds this reversal of feeling highly disturbing, holding that '[to] regret noble actions once they are complete suggests that one was doing them for the wrong reasons'.[40]

Brutus wants above all to be able to believe that he acted for the right reasons. When he castigates Cassius for taking bribes and seizing goods, what is at stake is the motive for the assassination: 'Did not great Julius bleed for justice' sake? / What villain touch'd his body, that did stab, / And not for justice? What . . . shall we now / Contaminate our fingers with base bribes . . . ?' (IV, iii, 19–24). He does not wish to contaminate his purported motive of justice by revealing motives of gain. Likewise, he does not wish to suggest that he acted for the wrong reasons by expressing any sort of regret about his actions. His noble purposes provide him with the satisfaction of self-regard. Brutus values this sense of his own righteousness so highly, moreover, that he is willing to die to preserve it.

When the battle has gone decisively against them, Brutus prepares to commit suicide. 'Suicide is the ultimate act of Stoic constancy,' Miles writes. 'It asserts an immutable virtue which would rather die than change or compromise, a rocklike invulnerability and a godlike superiority to fortune.'[41] With this degree of constancy, Brutus can prove to himself and to others that he possessed the virtue required to undertake the assassination for noble purposes. His last words insist once more that he acted with good intentions: 'Caesar, now be still: / I kill'd not thee with half so good a will' (V, v, 50–1). Antony's posthumous praise is based on this claim that Brutus acted on the basis of a good will.

> This was the noblest Roman of them all:
> All the conspirators save only he
> Did that they did in envy of great Caesar;
> He only, in a general honest thought
> And common good to all, made one of them.
>
>   (V, v, 68–72).

By his own account and others', Brutus has proved his 'superiority to fortune'. He has evaded the threat of moral luck. 'I shall have glory by this losing day,' he claims, 'More than Octavius and Mark Antony / By this vile conquest shall attain unto', because, like Montaigne, he has relocated the grounds of glory from external success to the internal world of character and 'good intent' (V, v, 36–8). His intentionalism secures his moral autonomy and with it his psychic autonomy. He can think of himself as self-sufficient. Even so, escaping one threat can introduce another. When the intentionalist's plans go awry, he might protect himself from self-reproach by taking satisfaction in his good deliberations. The cost, however, as Bernard Williams notes, is that 'he finds nothing to be *learned* from the case'.[42] As Patrick Gray explains, to be 'constant' in the Stoic sense 'is also to be dangerously oblivious'.[43]

In ancient Greek and Roman culture, there was a time when one ought to cease learning. Learning, in the sense of rethinking or changing one's mind (*metanoia*), was appropriate in youth, but '[w]ith maturity . . . comes the responsibility to have got it right the first time'. It was deemed possible, and therefore obligatory, to achieve full moral and intellectual maturity. Writers like Plutarch held that 'men ought to ensure that their virtue is sufficiently developed before they enter public life'. A remorseful person was seen as 'a person who has failed to act well rather than one who has learned a lesson'. Fulkerson contrasts this culture with that of Christianity. A Christian never takes himself to be fully mature but always on a journey of spiritual growth, in which remorse becomes valuable evidence that one is progressing.[44]

Montaigne, like all persons educated by the Renaissance humanist curriculum, found himself grappling with both cultures at once,

pagan and Christian. In keeping with this tension, while he sometimes leans heavily towards Stoic intentionalism, he also at other
times questions or qualifies Stoic views.[45] In his 'An Apologie of *Raymond Sebond*', Montaigne rejects Stoic delusions of self-sufficiency
in favour of a Christian sense of our moral dependence on divine
assistance. We cannot be virtuous, he insists, without help from God.

> *'Oh, what a vile and abject thing is man* (saith he) *unlesse he raise him-
> selfe above humanity!'* Observe here a notable speech and a profitable
> desire; but likewise absurd. For to make the handfull greater than the
> hand, and the embraced greater than the arme . . . is impossible and
> monstrous: nor that man should mount over and above himselfe or
> humanity . . . He shall raise himself up, if it please God to lend him his
> helping hand. He may elevate himselfe by forsaking and renouncing his
> owne meanes, and suffering himselfe to be elevated and raised by meere
> heavenly meanes. It is for our Christian faith, not for his Stoicke vertue,
> to pretend or aspire to this divine Metamorphosis, or miraculous trans-
> mutation. (341)

Shakespeare, too, undermines Stoic claims in his Roman plays. As
Patrick Gray argues, the tragic protagonists of his Roman plays strive
to transcend the limits of their own physical bodies, as well as their
susceptibility to passions such as pity, grief, and fear, and instead
come crashing back down to earth. The 'frailty' that they hope to
escape proves instead an intransigent given of the human condition.[46]

Characters in other plays, as well, such as Othello who imagine
themselves 'all-in-all sufficient' bring down tragedy upon themselves
and others.[47] Shakespeare presents a more desirable alternative –
acknowledgement of our intrinsic vulnerability, dependency and
moral fault – in a group of plays whose ethos is Christian rather than
Stoic and whose plots turn on luck.

Shakespeare's Providential Plays

When it comes to religion, scholars have found as much diversity in
Shakespeare as Montaigne finds in himself: as Alison Shell observes,
'Shakespeare's writing has been seen as both profoundly religious,
giving everyday life a sacramental quality, and as profoundly secular, foreshadowing the kind of humanism that sees no necessity for
God.'[48] Reformed Christianity was the dominant cultural framework in Shakespeare's England, and its influence is everywhere in

Shakespeare's plays, from his language to his story-structures and themes to the ethical values his plays implicitly endorse.[49] Like Montaigne, Shakespeare grapples simultaneously with classical philosophy and Christianity. More so than Montaigne, however, as Patrick Gray and Helen Clifford suggest, Shakespeare 'tends to side with those classical schools of thought about ethics which are more compatible with Christianity against those which are less so'.[50] In particular, Shakespeare rejects Stoic notions of perfection, constancy and self-sufficiency. His plays suggest that humans are not capable of perfection. If we are to improve at all, it must be by openness to change, not resistance to it; even then, the opportunity to improve is often dependent on luck.

In Shakespeare's comedies, tragicomedies and romances, the 'happy ending' tends to comprise repentance, forgiveness and reconciliation.[51] The ultimate value lies not in individual excellence but in relationships with others. For a Christian, heaven consists of union with God and with others in God; the closest earthly analogue is union with others.[52] But this union can be destroyed by one's actions. Moral evil is not confined to imperfect intentions; it is also found in the suffering that one's actions bring to others. Our moral status is affected not merely by what we will but also what we cause. It is not enough to recognise and repent of sinful intentions; one must also try to make reparations for the harm one has done. But what can and cannot be repaired is often beyond the agent's control. For a full reconciliation to take place, conversion of the sinful will is necessary, but it is often not sufficient. And although luck may not be sufficient to reconcile estranged persons, in Shakespeare's plays, it is often necessary. Under these circumstances, the greatest threat lies in missing out on good moral luck.

Luck plays a key role in a number of Shakespeare's plots. An agent attempts to commit some harm, but luck – meaning in this case events beyond that agent's control, whether orchestrated by other moral agents or not – prevents the harm from occurring. In *Measure for Measure*, for example, Angelo attempts to seduce Isabella and to execute her brother Claudio after promising to spare him. Unbeknown to Angelo, however, the disguised Duke stays the order for Claudio's execution; he also has Marianna, Angelo's estranged fiancée, keep the tryst with Angelo instead of Isabella. Because his intended crimes did not succeed, Angelo is ultimately pardoned. In this respect, he seems to enjoy good moral luck.

A strict intentionalist would claim that the results of Angelo's actions make no moral difference; what matters was his intent.

Augustine, for instance, advances such a view in his discussion of chastity. Suppose, he says, that a midwife has 'destroyed the hymen of some girl . . . I suppose no one is so foolish as to believe that, by this destruction of the integrity of one organ, the virgin has lost anything even of her bodily sanctity.' But suppose, on the other hand, 'a virgin violates the oath she has sworn to God, and goes to meet her seducer with the *intention* of yielding to him'.

> Shall we say that as she goes she is possessed even of bodily sanctity, when already she has lost and destroyed that sanctity of soul which sanctifies the body? . . . Let us rather draw this conclusion, that while the sanctity of the soul remains even when the body is violated, the sanctity of the body is not lost; and that, in like manner, the sanctity of the body is lost when the sanctity of the soul is violated, though the body itself remains intact.[53]

This is the intentionalist view. It is intention that determines moral status. If you *would* commit a sin, as the virgin would yield to her seducer, then your soul's sanctity is violated as surely as if you *had* committed the sin. But Isabella in *Measure* argues against this view. She claims that Angelo should not be held guilty for attempting to seduce her because 'His act did not o'ertake his bad intent' (V, i, 453). Although Angelo had blameworthy intentions, he ought not be punished because he did not realise those intentions in action. The Duke grants the petition and pardons Angelo.

We find similar outcomes in *All's Well That Ends Well*, *Much Ado about Nothing*, *The Winter's Tale* and *Cymbeline*. Male protagonists seduce unwilling women, wrongfully accuse innocent women, and either risk or seek a woman's death. Happily, however, the worst possible consequences of these actions are, by chance, averted, and the would-be culprits ultimately reconciled with their community. *As You Like It* features a similar plotline involving two male protagonists.[54] Oliver gives orders for his brother, Orlando, to be murdered; to his consternation, Orlando escapes. This escape affords Oliver the opportunity to undergo a conversion later in the play and to be reconciled with Orlando; he is never punished for the attempted murder. Such plays reveal a moral role for luck in a number of ways. First, whether we are moved to repent of a crime depends partly on the actions of others. Second, whether we commit a certain crime depends partly on circumstance. Third, whether we are able to make reparations for the crime depends likewise on events beyond our control – on luck.

In *Measure for Measure*, Escalus argues that it is unjust for Angelo to condemn Claudio for fornication when he himself, 'Had time cohered with place', might have done the same (II, i, 11). Angelo counters that the law can only judge what it can see: 'What's open made to justice, / That justice seizes' (II, i, 21–2). The play suggests that what is 'open made to justice' is partly a matter of luck. Montaigne does not hold this view. As William M. Hamlin explains, Montaigne tends to believe that guilt will reveal itself: conscience 'consistently overrides any conscious effort to suppress its overt and public expression'.[55] Shakespeare is less sure. In many of his plays, 'conscience requires provocation; it needs to be nudged'.[56] Conscience is 'nudged' by what Hamlin terms 'god-surrogates': staged mimetic representations of truth.

These stagings are required because the human will needs help. It is not that Shakespeare's plays express a Calvininist doctrine of total human depravity.[57] As Aquinas argued that humans can and must cooperate with grace, characters in Shakespeare's plays can and do 'cooperate' with their lucky breaks by confessing and repenting of their intended crimes. But just as prevenient grace is required to begin the process of sanctification, god-surrogates often begin the process of confession in the plays. Paulina in *The Winter's Tale* and Helena in *All's Well* stage elaborate scenes in which a woman believed dead is revealed to be alive so that the man who caused her 'death' will be moved to contrition. The Duke similarly stages a public trial in *Measure* to prompt Angelo's confession and conversion. Without these external promptings, the characters might never have repented of their crimes.

Similarly, Angelo might never have had a crime to confess if external circumstances had not put him in a position that made his crime possible. As C. S. Lewis writes, 'One man may be so placed that his anger sheds the blood of thousands, and another so placed that however angry he gets he will only be laughed at. But the little mark on the soul may be much the same in both.'[58] If Angelo had not been made deputy, he would never have had the chance to blackmail Isabella. If Don John and Iachimo had not lied, then Claudio and Posthumous might never have turned against Hero and Imogen. Their crimes were occasioned by bad luck.

Does such luck matter from God's point of view? Some philosophers argue that a just God would punish humans for sins they would have committed as much as for sins they have committed. Judith Jarvis Thomson puts forward this view in the hypothetical case of two judges. Judge Actual is offered a bribe and takes it; Judge

Counterfactual is never offered one and so never takes one – but he would have taken one if it had been offered. '[D]o we regard Actual with a moral indignation that would be out of place in respect to Counterfactual? I hardly think so,' Thomson affirms. 'Would you have God throw Actual into a deeper circle of hell than Counter-factual?' Thomson asks. 'That would be rank injustice.'[59] God can know, as no human can, what a person would do if given the occa-sion; God could be the ultimate intentionalist. We do find intention-alist judgements in theological works like *City of God*, cited above, and the *Summa Theologica*.[60] Nevertheless, Christianity does not take intentionalism to be the whole story.

After the interview that sparks Angelo's desire for her, Isabella departs, saying, 'Heaven keep your honour safe!' Angelo replies 'Amen' and continues to himself, 'For I am that way going to temptation, / Where prayers cross' (II, ii, 157–60). As he is tempted to pursue Isabella, his prayer to satisfy his newfound desire crosses or conflicts with another prayer; the most obvious candidate is the petition of the Lord's Prayer that asks, 'Lead us not into tempta-tion.' Why ask God not to allow you to face temptation?[61] An inten-tionalist would say that it does not matter whether you do face temptation, only what you *would* do if you did. Yet Christ gives his disciples the Lord's Prayer and enjoins them, 'Watch, and pray, that ye enter not into temptation' (Matt. 26:41; cp. Luke 22:40). Such prayers suggest that there is a difference between would do and have done. We find the same suggestion in *Cymbeline*. Posthumous berates the gods for not intervening to save Imogen after he ordered her death, but then reflects, 'But, alack, / You snatch some hence for little faults; that's love, / To have them fall no more' (5.1.11–13). The gods know that a person would commit greater faults if allowed to keep on living, so they 'snatch' her away before she can commit them. Such an intervention would only be an act of love if there were some difference between 'would fall' and 'have fallen'.

John Calvin makes this very claim. In a sermon on Peter's denial of Christ, he writes,

> If Saint Peter had bene te[m]pted an hundred times . . . he would haue denied Iesus Christe an hundred tymes, and a thowsande . . . Loe in what case he had bene, if God had not had compassion vpon him: but he spared hym, and woulde not proue him any further.[62]

If Peter had been tempted more times, he would have fallen more times, but God had compassion on him and spared him the test. Calvin regards this reprieve as a meaningful gift of grace and favour: 'if hee had bene troubled with any other temptations, hee woulde none otherwise haue resisted them, and that had bene to haue cast him to the déepest place of hell, if God had not so greatly fauoured him.'

Montaigne rejects the notion that we could deserve any credit for not yielding to a temptation we do not face:

> I hate that accidentall repentance which olde age brings with it. Hee that in ancient times said he was beholden to yeares because they had ridde him of voluptuousnesse, was not of mine opinion . . . *Oh miserable kinde of remedie to bee beholden unto sicknesse for our health.* It is not for our mishap, but for the good successe of our judgement to performe this office. (456–7)

Montaigne explores this question at length in 'Of Crueltie', asking whether we should give credit to people whose good behaviour proceeds from a naturally happy disposition and not from any intentional efforts to act virtuously. Like C. S. Lewis, Montaigne finds this kind of character less meritorious than someone who struggles to resist temptation and attain virtue, much less someone who through such struggles eventually overcomes his vicious desires.[63] If all we cared about was the perfection of our judgement, we might not care whether 'mishap', or luck, kept our errors in judgement from harming others. For the Christian, however, the virtues belonging to the reason and the will are merely the means to an end.

Citing Melanchthon, William J. Bouwsma points out that Christianity is not primarily concerned with virtue in and of itself: 'the pursuit of instruction on this topic in the Scriptures is "more philosophical than Christian"'.[64] The ultimate goal of Christianity is not virtue but instead a relationship of love with other people, as well as God himself. Why does it matter, morally speaking, whether you actually fail a test, as opposed to whether you would have failed, if not for some sort of felicitous intervention? It matters because other people matter. A sinner owes a debt not only to God but also to other people, other human beings, and what it takes to pay that debt is different if you merely would have harmed them than if you actually did. If luck helps us pay that debt, Shakespeare's plays suggest, we ought to be grateful for luck.

According to the penitential theology operative in late medieval England, sin had to be considered in terms of punishment, as well as guilt. Guilt required the internal action of repentance; punishment required the external action of penance and restitution. The influential theologian Christopher St German, for example, insisted in the 1530s that restitution was owed not only to God but also to the humans harmed by the sin: 'prayers be right expedient and helthfull to the soule: yet they serue not in al cases, as to discharge debtes or restitutions'.[65] And in the plays under discussion, we do find sinners making attempts at restitution. After Claudio, Leontes and Posthumous lose faith in a faithful woman, they acknowledge their culpability.[66] They submit themselves for correction – to Leonato, to Paulina, to the purgatory of war – and they attempt some form of reparation. Imperfect though these attempts may be, they make possible the reunions and reconciliations at the plays' conclusions. These endings would have been impossible if, in a fit of Stoic nobility, the men had killed themselves instead.

That said, the conciliatory endings of these plays also would have been impossible if the women in question had actually been killed. To turn tragedy into comedy, Shakespeare suggests, repentance and reparation are utterly necessary. But they are not sufficient. Contrition cannot rebuild a relationship if one of the partners has been killed.[67] When Claudio submits himself for penance, Leonato responds, 'I cannot bid you bid my daughter live' (V, i, 264). If Othello had chosen not to commit suicide but to return to Venice and submit himself to Brabantio, he could not have made the reparation that Claudio was able to make. He could not have expressed sorrow, asked Desdemona for forgiveness, renewed his marriage vows, and embarked on a new life with her. He was not fortunate enough to be saved from the results of his own worst intentions.[68] The fact that in some plays it is possible to repair some of the damage done is, from the sinner's point of view, a matter of luck – or grace. The Duke in *Measure* has been described as a figure of Providence.[69] In plays with similar 'lucky' plots, the twists and turns that prevent intended crimes are not accidents at all but God's will.[70] If we are to recover from our falls, we require the good luck of grace. In Shakespeare's plays, a happy ending depends on good hap.

Conclusion

Philosophers continue to debate whether moral luck is 'real', and their contention may well be irresolvable.[71] Even if Shakespeare and Montaigne do not resolve the question of the existence of moral luck, however, they do clarify what is at stake in the debate. Montaigne's depiction of the satisfactions of conscience is compelling, especially when paired with his depiction of a world so rocked by fortune that such satisfaction is the only consolation we can conceivably guarantee. Self-regard is the satisfaction Brutus seeks when events go against him, and he refuses to compromise it through self-reproach. To show remorse for his decision, or even regret for the outcome, would put him in a position from which his culture affords him no exit. For Romans who held it possible to attain perfect virtue, acknowledging a failure meant acknowledging that one had not attained that virtue and perhaps never would: as Fulkerson explains, remorse was held to indicate a 'chronic, and crippling, defect of character'. For this reason, 'the most common ancient reaction to a mistake, or even a change of mind, is to ignore it or argue it away'.[72] A common way to argue away a mistake is to claim that one cannot be blamed for what one cannot control – that there is, in other words, no such thing as moral luck.

What changes in a Christian culture is that new frameworks become available to cope with failure. The 'ulcer in the flesh' occasioned by remorse can find remedy in God's forgiveness. Reformation preachers taught that feeling pained by one's sins was the first step toward repentance and reconciliation with God.[73] It was also the first step towards reconciliation with one's community. As historian Cynthia Herrup points out, Shakespeare lived in a 'religious milieu that repeatedly emphasised that everyone was a sinner'.[74] This religious mindset, Herrup argues, helps to explain the relative leniency of pre-industrial England's criminal sentencing.[75] Because human nature was seen as irreducibly flawed, 'a law without room for more than occasional mercy' was perceived as 'a mockery of justice'.[76] Mercy was especially likely to be extended to those who were willing to admit their guilt. Sentencing drew a non-accidental parallel between religious and legal confession: 'God forgave those who were contrite, and in most cases the law would not demand a life from those who had asked their peers to forgive them.'[77]

In Shakespeare's plays, characters ask forgiveness even for what was not entirely their fault. In *Much Ado about Nothing*, when Claudio learns that Don John tricked him into believing that Hero was unfaithful, he tells Hero's father, Leonato, 'Choose your revenge yourself; / Impose me to what penance your invention / Can lay upon my sin: yet sinn'd I not / But in mistaking' (V, i, 257–60). The syntax is slightly ambiguous: does Claudio believe that he only made a mistake and did not commit a sin? Or does he believe that the mistake was a sin? His term 'penance' hints towards the latter. He accepts that one's moral status may be compromised by luck. But conversely, luck can also help restore it. It is thanks to luck that he learns the truth and becomes not simply 'the man who unjustly rejected Hero' but 'the man who unjustly rejected Hero but then repented and married her with (possibly) new appreciation of his flaws and her value'.

As Bernard Williams observes, 'One's history as an agent is a web in which anything that is the product of the will is surrounded and held up and partly formed by things that are not.' 'If one attaches importance to the sense of what one is in terms of what one has done and what in the world one is responsible for,' Williams argues, 'one must accept much that makes its claim on that sense solely in virtue of its being actual' – even where what becomes actual is partly a matter of luck.[78] God's providence creates a similar web in which choice and luck, one's own will and God's will, are inseparably bound together, as are good and evil. God's providence 'permit[s] certain defects in particular effects,' write Aquinas, 'for if all evil were prevented, much good would be absent from the universe . . . Thus Augustine says (Enchiridion 2): "Almighty God would in no wise permit evil to exist in His works, unless He were so almighty and so good as to produce good even from evil."'[79] In Shakespeare's narratives, we see how complex webs of both intention and accident shape 'what one is' and how an evil choice can be remedied and redeemed, if we are blessed with good luck.

Notes

1. Walker, 'Moral Luck', p. 14. Nagel, *Mortal Questions* and Williams, 'Moral Luck', in *Moral Luck*, were seminal in beginning the contemporary philosophical conversation around moral luck. For an excellent collection of articles on moral luck, see Statman, ed., *Moral Luck*. The seminal discussion of moral luck in relation to ancient philosophy is Nussbaum, *Fragility of Goodness*.
2. For a useful overview of Stoicism and its Renaissance revivals, see Sellars, ed., *Routledge Handbook of the Stoic Tradition*. Braden, *Renaissance Tragedy and the Senecan Tradition* is a seminal study of the influence of Seneca and Senecan Stoicism on early modern English drama. See also Miles, *Shakespeare and the Constant Romans*, and Patrick Gray, *Shakespeare and the Fall of the Roman Republic*.
3. Miles notes that the 'most obvious feature of the new movement is its stress on Seneca rather than Cicero' (*Shakespeare and the Constant Romans*, p. 69). Lipsius edited and published a new edition of Seneca's writings, and his dialogue *De constantia in publicis malis*, inspired by Seneca's work *De constantia sapientis*, was highly influential throughout

Europe, with eight editions and translations into numerous languages. A distinctive feature of Seneca's Stoicism was his emphasis – itself borrowed from Epicurean philosophy – on the isolated individual's self-sufficiency, rather than a Ciceronian emphasis on public duties and expanding circles of concern for others. See Patrick Gray, *Shakespeare and the Fall of the Roman Republic*, pp. 57–8.

4. Miles, *Shakespeare and the Constant Romans*, p. 10.
5. Baltzly, 'Stoicism'.
6. Bouwsma, 'Two Faces', p. 28.
7. Bouwsma, 'Two Faces', p. 10. Of course, very few people were admitted to have attained the perfection of the Stoic *sapiens*, as few people attain a perfect Kantian good will; for classical reflections on the rarity of the Stoic sage, see Patrick Gray, *Shakespeare and the Fall of the Roman Republic*, pp. 54–7. The paucity of achieved examples of Stoic perfection is not, however, due to the fact that luck deprived potential sages of the resources necessary even to begin. This view stands in contrast to Aristotle's, which acknowledges the necessity of good luck and external goods to the practice of virtues such as magnanimity and prudential statesmanship.
8. Kant, *Groundwork*, 4: 394.
9. Ibid. 393.
10. 'Kant defines autonomy principally as 'the property of the will by which it is a law to itself (independently of any property of the objects of volition)' (*Groundwork*, 4: 440). According to Kant, the will of a moral agent is autonomous in that 'it both gives itself the moral law (it is self-legislating) and that it can constrain or motivate itself to follow the law (it is self-constraining or self-motivating)': Denis and Wilson, 'Kant and Hume on Morality'. On Kant and Neostoicism, see Schneewind, *Invention of Autonomy*.
11. Schneewind, *Moral Philosophy from Montaigne to Kant*, 1: 29.
12. Bouwsma, 'Two Faces', p. 28.
13. Williams discusses the importance, if one desires immunity from luck, of making morality not just one value but the supreme value: see Williams, *Moral Luck*, p. 21.
14. All quotations from the Bible are taken from the 1560 Geneva Bible, spelling modernised.
15. Miles, *Shakespeare and the Constant Romans*, p. 10.
16. In Paul's case, we might also say that it is possible to have a second-order will for the good without having a first-order will for it. For Christian perspectives on first- and second-order desires in the will, see Stump, *Wandering in Darkness*, esp. ch. 8, 'Other-Worldly Redemption'.
17. 'So great a sin was committed, that by it the human nature was altered for the worse, and was transmitted also to their posterity, liable to sin and subject to death. And the kingdom of death so reigned over men, that the deserved penalty of sin would have hurled all headlong even

into the second death, of which there is no end, had not the undeserved grace of God saved some therefrom' (Augustine, *City of God* 14.1). See Schneewind, *Moral Philosophy from Montaigne to Kant*, for a comparison of Augustine's views on moral autonomy to those of Aquinas.

18. *Articles Whereupon It Was Agreed by the Archbishoppes and Bishoppes of Both Prouinces and the Whole Cleargie*, STC (2nd ed.) / 10039.3 ed. (London 1571), Article X.

19. See Schneewind, *Moral Philosophy from Montaigne to Kant*, for a comparison of Augustine's views on moral autonomy to those of Aquinas.

20. See ch. 6, 'Hamlet's Luck', in Cummings, *Mortal Thoughts*.

21. Thomas Aquinas makes this point in *Summa Theologica* I.22.2. Answering Objection 1, 'It seems that everything is not subject to divine providence. For nothing foreseen can happen by chance. If then everything was foreseen by God, nothing would happen by chance. And thus hazard and luck would disappear; which is against common opinion,' he replies, 'There is a difference between universal and particular causes. A thing can escape the order of a particular cause; but not the order of a universal cause . . . So far then as an effect escapes the order of a particular cause, it is said to be casual or fortuitous in respect to that cause; but if we regard the universal cause, outside whose range no effect can happen, it is said to be foreseen.'

22. Weid, *A simple, and religious consultation*, 2I8v–2K1r, cited in Cummings, *Mortal Thoughts*, p. 221.

23. Ibid., p. 221.

24. Villey, *Les Sources et l'évolution*.

25. *Essays*, trans. Florio, 1613 edn, p. 14 (spelling and punctuation modified). All citations from Montaigne in English are from this edition.

26. Montaigne's intentionalism underlies, for instance, his opinion that only acts that are knowingly chosen – not acts resulting from 'stupiditie' – can be virtuous: 'I see that many vertues, as chastitie, sobrietie, and temperance, may come unto us by meanes of corporall defects and imbecilities. Constancie in dangers (if it may be termed constancie) contempt of death, patiencie in misfortunes, may happen and are often seen in men, for want of good judgement in such accidents, and that they are not apprehended for such as they are indeed. *Lacke of apprehension and stupiditie counterfeit vertuous effects*. As I have often seen come to passe, that some men are commended for things they rather deserve to be blamed' ('Of Crueltie', 235; also cited p. 144).

27. See, esp., 'That Fortune is oftentimes met withall in pursuit of Reason'.

28. I refer to deliberating, reasoning, choosing, willing, etc, as 'intentional actions' because they are uniquely subject to the agent's intentions in a way that actions that involve physical behaviours are not; if I wish to deliberate, I have only to intend to deliberate. There are not, generally speaking, external events that could impede my successful completion of this action.

29. Guana, *Montaigne and the Ethics of Compassion*, takes Montaigne's views on the *forme maistresse* to be one way in which Montaigne rejects moral luck.

30. In the same essay, Montaigne explicitly links his refusal to grieve for what he cannot control to Stoic philosophy: 'When sutes or businesses bee over-past, howsoever it bee, I greeve little at them. For, the imagination that they must necessarily happen so, puts mee out of paine; Behould them in the course of the Universe, and enchained in Stoycall causes, Your fantazie cannot by wish or imagination remoove one point of them, but the whole order of things must reverse both what is past and what is to come' (456).

31. Fulkerson, *No Regrets*, p. 19.

32. Rawls, *Theory of Justice*, p. 422, cited in Gauna, *Montaigne and the Ethics of Compassion*, p. 135. Guana draws this connection between Montaigne and Rawls.

33. Guana, *Montaigne and the Ethics of Compassion*, p. 127.

34. Ibid., p. 138, p. 135.

35. Miles, *Shakespeare and the Constant Romans*, p. 14.

36. When Brutus tells Cassius that he is 'sick with many griefs', Cassius reproaches him, 'Of your philosophy you make no use, / If you give place to accidental evils' (IV, iii, 144–5). The 'philosophy' referred to here is Stoicism, specifically the Senecan Stoicism that idealises detachment, tranquility, and, through these, the steadfast endurance of suffering. Miles notes that when Shakespeare uses the general term 'philosophy', it is often in a generalised Stoic sense, referring to 'an attitude of patient endurance, absence of passion, indifference to externals' (p. 12). As Gray argues, Brutus aspires to be the Stoic *sapiens*, a paragon of philosophical detachment. This aspiration is compromised by his friendship with his Cassius, his love for his wife, and his concern for the well-being of his fellow Roman citizens. See ch. 1, '"A beast without a heart": *Pietas* and Pity in *Julius Caesar*', in Patrick Gray, *Shakespeare and the Fall of the Roman Republic*.

37. All citations from Shakespeare are from *The Norton Shakespeare*, 3rd edn, ed. Greenblatt et al.

38. Fulkerson, *No Regrets*, p. 8.

39. Nagel, *Mortal Questions*, p. 30.

40. Fulkerson, *No Regrets*, 201.

41. Miles, *Shakespeare and the Constant Romans*, p. 53.

42. Williams, 'Moral Luck', 33, in Williams, *Moral Luck*; cp. Bromwich, 'What Shakespeare's Heroes Learn' and Patrick Gray, 'Shakespeare versus Aristotle'.

43. Patrick Gray, *Shakespeare and the Fall of the Roman Republic*, pp. 130–1.

44. Fulkerson, *No Regrets*, 187, 197, 6; see conclusion for discussion of Christianity's comprehensive re-evaluation of the value of remorse.

45. Montaigne's essays 'On Drunkeness' and esp. 'Of Experience' challenge the Stoic notion that it is possible or desirable to achieve total tranquility and suppression of the passions. For a discussion of the more practicable ethics that Montaigne ultimately endorses, see 'A Montaignian ethic?' in Schneewind, *Invention of Autonomy*, pp. 50ff. and ch. 10, 'Exploring "l'humaine condition"', in Charles Taylor, *Sources of the Self*. A brief account of Shakespeare's doubts about Stoicism can be found in Gray and Clifford, 'Shakespeare', and a much more extensive discussion in Patrick Gray, *Shakespeare and the Fall of the Roman Republic*.
46. Patrick Gray, *Shakespeare and the Fall of the Roman Republic*, 1.
47. On parallels between *Othello* and Shakespeare's Roman plays, see Altman, *Improbability of Othello*.
48. Shell, *Shakespeare and Religion*, p. 2. See also Cummings, 'Religion', in Kinney, ed., *Oxford Handbook of Shakespeare*.
49. On Christianity and Shakespeare's language, see, e.g., Swift, *Shakespeare's Common Prayers*, and Hannibal Hamlin, *The Bible in Shakespeare*. On Christianity and Shakespeare's story-structures and themes, see, e.g., Gless, *Measure for Measure*, Lupton, *Citizen-Saints*, Greenblatt, *Hamlet in Purgatory*, Cummings, *Mortal Thoughts*, and Cox, *Seeming Knowledge*. On Christianity and Shakespeare's own ethical perspective, see, e.g., Hunter, *Shakespeare and the Comedy of Forgiveness*, Friedman, *'The World Must Be Peopled'*, and Beckwith, *Shakespeare and the Grammar of Forgiveness*.
50. Gray and Clifford, 'Shakespeare'.
51. My argument does not turn on the genres assigned to the plays, but it is useful to recognise the plays' connection to New Comedy and romance because these genres frequently invoke providence as the cause of happy 'accidents'. For accounts of the role of luck, fortune and providence in romance and New Comedy, see Salingar, *Shakespeare and the Traditions of Comedy*, Miola, *Shakespeare and Classical Comedy*, and Hardin, *Plautus and the English Renaissance of Comedy*.
52. Augustine describes these parallel forms of blessedness in *City of God*: 'Domestic peace is the well-ordered concord between those of the family who rule and those who obey. Civil peace is a similar concord among the citizens. The peace of the celestial city is the perfectly ordered and harmonious enjoyment of God, and of one another in God' (Augustine, *City of God* 2.14.13).
53. Augustine, *City of God* 1.18.
54. In *As You Like It*, Orlando's escape from Oliver's attempted murder is not simply providential chance; the faithful Adam warns him of Oliver's intentions. But Orlando's chance meeting with his brother, which prompts their reconciliation, and Duke Frederick's conversion after meeting a religious man, suggest the possibility of providential influence.
55. William M. Hamlin, 'Conscience and the God-Surrogate in Montaigne and *Measure for Measure*', pp. 241, 238. I draw here on Hamlin's

argument that Montaigne displays, overall, a greater trust in the revelatory power of conscience than Shakespeare does.

56. Ibid., p. 244. Cp. Patrick Gray, 'Shakespeare versus Aristotle'.
57. For an account of how Shakespeare modifies and corrects the Calvinism of his day, see Hillier, 'Hamlet the rough-hewer'. For Shakespeare's opposition to Calvinist determinism, see ch. 9, 'Sanctity', in Parvini, *Shakespeare's Moral Compass*.
58. C. S. Lewis, *Mere Christianity*, p. 93.
59. Thomson, 'Morality and Bad Luck', pp. 214–15.
60. See, esp., 1-2.1.3 and 1-2.18.6.
61. According to the Catholic Catechism, 'the Greek means both "do not allow us to enter into temptation" and "do not let us yield to temptation"'. So the meaning is not confined to a petition that God help us not to succumb to temptation but petitions also that God help us to avoid occasions of temptation altogether. A similar view is expressed in the Act of Contrition which affirms, 'I firmly intend, with your help, to do penance, to sin no more, and to avoid whatever leads me to sin.' http://www.vatican.va/archive/ccc_css/archive/catechism/p4s2a3.htm
62. Calvin, *Diuerse sermons of Master John Caluin* (London, 1581), STC (2nd ed./4437, accessed via EEBO. For the influence of Calvin's writings (in English translation) on Shakespeare's work, see Hannibal Hamlin, *The Bible in Shakespeare*.
63. Cp. bk 3, ch. 4, 'Morality and Psychoanalysis', in Lewis, *Mere Christianity*.
64. Bouwsma, 'Two Faces', p. 44.
65. German, *Salem and Bizance*, 10: 345; cited in Hutson, *Invention of Suspicion*, p. 53.
66. On 'acknowledgement' in Shakespeare's works, see Cavell, *Disowning Knowledge*, as well as Patrick Gray, 'Shakespeare versus Aristotle'.
67. Aristotle carefully considers the extent of our dependence upon external goods such as, esp., friends, for a happy and flourishing life in his treatises on ethics. See Nussbaum, *Fragility of Goodness*, as well as Patrick Gray, *Shakespeare and the Fall of the Roman Republic*, pp. 235ff.
68. On Othello as a victim of bad moral luck, see Escobedo, '"Unlucky Deeds"', as well as Altman, *Improbability of Othello*.
69. See Kirsch, 'Integrity of Measure for Measure', and Gless, *Measure for Measure*.
70. On providential order in Shakespeare's late plays, see Boitani, *The Gospel according to Shakespeare*.
71. See the work of Cushman, esp. Cushman and Young, 'Psychology of Dilemmas', and Cushman and Greene, 'Finding Faults'.
72. Fulkerson, *No Regrets*, p. 9.
73. '*A godly sorrow whereby a man is grieved for his sins, because they are sins, is the beginning of repentance*' (William Perkins, 1556–1602, pp. 122–3). According to Perkins and other Reformation divines, 'godly

sorrow' plays a crucial role in repentance, as well as the process of sanctification.
74. Herrup, 'Law and Morality in Seventeenth-Century England', p. 110.
75. Herrup finds a significant 'gap between known crimes and criminal sentences': 'less than half of those liable for execution were ever ordered to the gallows': ibid., pp. 102, 106.
76. Ibid. p. 111.
77. Ibid. p. 119.
78. Williams, *Moral Luck*, pp. 29–30.
79. 1.22.2, reply to objection 2.

Chapter 7

Cavell's Tragic Scepticism and the Comedy of the Cuckold: *Othello* and Montaigne Revisited
Cassie M. Miura

This chapter challenges the intrinsic connection Stanley Cavell posits between philosophical scepticism and tragedy in Shakespeare's plays by expanding on his suggestion in 'Othello and the Stake of the Other' that Montaigne offers a different approach from Shakespeare to doubt, sexual jealousy and witchcraft.[1] Both Shakespeare's *Othello* and Montaigne's *Essays* show that comedy as well as tragedy can articulate the quandary Cavell calls 'the sceptical problematic'. Cavell hints at this possibility when he notes that in the *Essays* Montaigne suggests that topics such as jealousy 'should be food for thought and moderation, not for torture and murder': 'they are not tragic unless one makes them so' (139). For Shakespeare's protagonists, however, Cavell suggests, such rethinking proves impossible. In comparing *Othello* here to Montaigne's essay 'On Some Verses of Virgil', Cavell indirectly draws attention to the surprising omission of Montaigne, more generally speaking, in his reflections on philosophical scepticism. Although I do not wish to dispute the claim that scepticism permeates many of Shakespeare's tragedies, I do wish to dispute the impression Cavell gives that early modern scepticism is somehow necessarily tragic.[2] This distinction is important because it has become commonplace for scholars studying early modern literature and intellectual history who do not necessarily share Cavell's investments in, for example, language philosophy or Wittgenstein nonetheless to affirm and reproduce his representation of scepticism as inherently tragic.[3] If early modern thinkers did not regard despair and death as the inevitable results of scepticism, then Shakespeare's decision to make them seem foregone conclusions becomes all the more significant.

In the introduction to *Disowning Knowledge in Seven Plays of Shakespeare*, Cavell indicates that he is much more interested in Shakespeare as a precursor to Descartes than he is in Shakespeare as a successor of Montaigne. 'However strong the presence of Montaigne and Montaigne's scepticism is in various of Shakespeare's plays,' Cavell explains, 'the sceptical problematic I have in mind is given its philosophical refinement in Descartes's way of raising the questions of God's existence and of the immortality of the soul' (3). Shakespeare's *Othello* anticipates Descartes' *Meditations on First Philosophy* by almost forty years; nevertheless, and in lieu of a more developed historical argument, Cavell maintains that Cartesian scepticism is 'already in full existence in Shakespeare, from the time of the great tragedies of the first years of the seventeenth century' (3). Cavell objects to what he describes as a pervasive 'misunderstanding' of his project: 'the application of some philosophically independent problematic of scepticism to a fragmentary parade of Shakespearean texts' (1). His insistence that Shakespeare intervenes in a sceptical tradition of the future is in keeping, however, with precisely this objection that he is indifferent to intellectual history, as is his relative disregard for scepticism's past. To characterise the difference between Montaigne's and Shakespeare's responses to the early modern recovery of ancient scepticism, all that Cavell offers the reader is the statement that 'the issue posed is no longer, or not alone, as with the earlier scepticism, how to conduct oneself best in an uncertain world; the issue suggested is how to live at all in a groundless world' (2). What does Cavell mean by the 'earlier scepticism', apart from Montaigne? Does he intend to invoke the Academic tradition which considers knowledge of external things to be unattainable or the Pyrrhonian tradition which calls even this claim into doubt? Cavell deliberately obscures such distinctions; I return to them here, however, in order to suggest that his sense of a 'newer scepticism' not only reasserts the negative dogmatism of the Academic position but also, more importantly, precludes the therapeutic objectives of the Pyrrhonian.

For Cavell, the sceptic is not one who poses the question 'whether I know with certainty of the existence of the external world and of myself and others in it', but one for whom such questions induce a crisis (3). Whereas Pyrrhonian scepticism, as expounded by Montaigne, as well as Sextus Empiricus, is zetetic, an open-ended form of inquiry, Cavell's sceptic demands immediate satisfaction of a violent desire for absolute knowledge.[4] I see this desire, to which Othello

ultimately succumbs, as the very same desire that Pyrrhonism prepares the sceptic to relinquish. In place of *epochē* (suspension of
judgement) and *ataraxia* (tranquillity of mind), Cavell posits 'annihilation', 'self-consuming disappointment' and 'world-consuming
revenge' as the defining characteristics of the sceptical problematic in
Shakespearean tragedy (6). In so far as Cavell concerns himself with
the psychological and existential impact of doubt, with scepticism
regarding the problem of other minds and the external world, he
ends where Montaigne begins. In the case of Shakespeare's *Othello*,
it is not scepticism but rather its opposite, dogmatism, that underlies
Othello's characteristic, masculine refusal to acknowledge a feminine
other as other, separate from the self.

Cavell's most surprising claim about the play, meanwhile, is
that Othello's misgivings about Desdemona's virtue, as well as his
demands for evidence of her guilt, serve only to mask his true murderous intentions. Even though Cavell wants to read Othello as an
exemplar of masculine doubt, his analysis returns repeatedly to what
Othello knows for certain. Take, for example, his blithe dismissal of
Iago as the source of Othello's suspicions: 'however far he believes
Iago's tidings, he cannot just believe them; somewhere he also *knows*
them to be false' (133). According to Cavell, Desdemona's willingness to sacrifice her chastity to Othello is a revelation of female sexuality that shatters Othello's conception of himself as a perfect and
uncontaminated soul (I, ii, 31). Othello's 'professions of scepticism
over her faithfulness' are 'a cover story', he maintains, 'for a deeper
conviction': 'a terrible doubt covering a yet more terrible certainty,
an unstable certainty' (138). If scepticism is merely a facade, then
its relationship both to tragedy and to the philosophical problem of
other minds needs further clarification. According to Cavell's argument here, the motivation for Othello's scepticism is, strictly speaking, not epistemological at all. As Cavell sees him, Othello doubts
neither Desdemona's virtue nor her existence as other: 'Othello certainly knows that Desdemona exists', even though he is unable to
live with this knowledge (137).[5] By casting doubt on our ability to
fully understand Othello's doubt, Cavell concludes his reading of the
play with the articulation of a riddle based on the 'conversion of
metaphysical finitude into intellectual lack' (138). The sceptic represents the human compulsion to demand a level of certainty that
transcends the limits of human knowledge. What we find in Cavell's
essay, however, is a characteristic reversal of the beginning and ends
of Pyrrhonian scepticism, a reversal which bears directly on his conception of tragedy.

More so than many Shakespeare scholars, Cavell is attuned to moments of *Othello* when the high romanticism of the tragic hero is undercut by the cynical wit of characters such as Iago or even Desdemona. His concession that 'the play obeys the rhythm of farce, not tragedy' suggests that the connection he sees between scepticism and tragedy in *Othello* is tenuous (132). As a stock character in both ancient comedy and medieval fabliaux, the cuckold often serves as an object of derision who lacks essential knowledge of himself and power to control and satisfy his beloved, usually a much younger woman.[6] Since the comic resolution of this familiar plot collapses, however, when Desdemona's marriage bed becomes the scene of her death, Cavell suggests that *Othello* can be read instead as a meta-commentary on the genre of tragedy. 'One might say', he argues, 'that by beginning with a sexual scene denied our sight, this play opens exactly as a normal comedy closes, as if turning comedy inside out' (132–3).[7] In his brief engagement with 'On Some Verses of Virgil', Cavell proposes that the contrast between comedy and tragedy may elucidate distinctions between Montaigne's and Shakespeare's respective treatments of the relation between scepticism and sexual jealousy. 'We are tragic in what we take to be tragic'; infidelity in particular is 'as fit for rue and laughter as for pity and terror' (138–9). Whereas Cavell goes on to maintain that one must look beyond early modernity to find a comic resolution to the problem of scepticism, I will argue here that we can find it already present, as his passing reference suggests, in Montaigne's *Essays*. Unlike Descartes, whose methodical doubt still produces, or at least, claims to produce, certain knowledge in the domains of theology and science, Montaigne relinquishes this end in favour of tranquillity.

Much of what makes *Othello* tragic is not scepticism, however, but instead the symbolic value ascribed to virginity. Cavell demonstrates his capacity for the very same kind of humour that Othello cannot grasp when he remarks that, 'on such issues, farce and tragedy are separated by the thickness of a membrane' (135). Throughout the play Desdemona's chastity serves as the necessary precondition for Othello's tragic and heroic vision of himself, but this vision is by no means stable: we can easily imagine alternatives familiar from comedy. Even if audiences speculate that Desdemona and Othello may have never properly consummated their marriage, Desdemona's discussion of sex threatens Othello, since the play suggests that male desire for absolute knowledge depends in large part on female ignorance. A subtle exchange between Iago and Desdemona just before Othello returns from his campaign at the beginning of Act II establishes not only Desdemona's understanding of the coarse nature of Iago's sexual jokes at her and Emilia's expense but also her ability to match Iago jest for jest. Cavell makes passing reference to 'that dirty banter between her and Iago' in order to suggest that Othello does not recognise Desdemona as a woman of 'flesh and blood', but unfortunately overlooks its epistemological significance (136). In these playful exchanges, we gain access to a discourse that deliberately blurs the lines between truth and falsehood, knowledge and ignorance. Rather than insisting on a single official significance, puns allow multiple meanings to proliferate and coexist.

Part of what Othello cannot see in Desdemona, which Iago can, is an ability to understand sexual innuendo, which inherently entails holding competing representations of herself simultaneously in mind. When Iago claims that Emilia and Desdemona 'are pictures out of doors, / Bells in your parlours; wildcats in your kitchens, / Saints in your injuries; devils being offended, / Players in your housewifery and housewives in your beds', he exploits a level of ambiguity that Othello can neither comprehend nor tolerate (II, i, 112–15). These misogynistic jokes not only confirm Iago's cynical disregard for romantic love but also afford Desdemona greater complexity as a character. The claim that 'I am not merry, but I do beguile / The thing I am by seeming otherwise' links Desdemona's capacity to engage in deceit directly to her capacity to engage in witty repartee (II, i, 125–6). Iago's charge that 'You rise to play, and go to bed to work' may not accurately reflect Desdemona's sexual habits or the nature of her relationship with Othello; nevertheless, she derives pleasure from her exchange with Iago and urges him three times to continue (II, i, 118).

Reading the powerful image of Othello and Desdemona lying dead on their bridal bed as emblematic of the 'truth of scepticism', Cavell concludes that 'what this man lacked was not certainty. He knew everything but he could not yield to what he knew to be commanded by it' (141). If Montaigne could comment, he might assert that what Othello so crucially lacked was indeed not certainty, but a sense of humour. As Michael Fischer explains, Cavell's *Othello* 'smothers the laughter' that 'elements of farce might have triggered': 'in another context, another man might have delighted in Desdemona's capacity for pleasure. Othello uses it against her'.[8] When Desdemona goads Iago to continue his discourse on female sexuality, she seems almost to invoke Montaigne's signature method (the *essai*): 'Come on, assay' (II, i, 123). The exhortation brings to mind an anecdote from Montaigne's 'Of Presumption', an essay Cavell overlooks, in which an old man overcomes his fear of being made a cuckold by deliberately marrying a prostitute.

Like Shakespeare, Montaigne ties scepticism to male anxieties about marriage. He takes more care, however, than Shakespeare does to imagine outcomes that might circumvent the disastrous consequences of sexual jealousy. Unlike Othello, who is ultimately consumed by this passion, Montaigne's cuckold relinquishes the desire for absolute certainty and control which the essay in which he appears presents as the height of human 'presumption'. Making frequent recourse to statements such as 'there is virtually nothing that I know I know' or 'I am as doubtful of myself as of anything else', Montaigne uses scepticism to quiet the demand for knowledge, a passion that at its height can pursue satisfaction even through the use of force (II: 17, 583). In her recent work on early modern cuckoldry and belief, Claire McEachern argues that horns indicate

> stirrings of Cartesian scepticism, or the death rattle of Pyrrhonism, or whatever else might have been making an early modern subject uneasy. In other words, they allow the audience to laugh off or neutralise some anxiety, transmuting some deeper fear into a more lighthearted one ('mere' adultery, ho ho).[9]

Since Othello does not jest about his imaginary horns, laughter is not available to mitigate the anxiety produced by his doubt.[10] Juxtaposing Shakespeare's play and Montaigne's essay, we see that Montaigne undercuts the kind of tragic romanticism Othello represents by depicting a prostitute who falls short of Desdemona's virtue in every way. Shakespeare gives us a cautionary tale of murder and suicide; Montaigne, by contrast, offers a comic vision of married love that approximates sceptical tranquillity.

When Montaigne writes in 'Of Presumption' that 'the most painful situation for me is to be in suspense about urgent matters, and tossed between fear and hope', he recognises in himself the same internal conflict that leads Othello to kill Desdemona rather than persist in a state of deliberation over her guilt. Unlike Othello, however, Montaigne retreats from such violence, preferring other means to preserve his peace of mind (II: 17, 593). Addressing emotions that commonly disturb the soul, he concludes that 'the miser is worse off for his passion than the poor man, and the jealous man than the cuckold' (II: 17, 593–4). By refashioning the cuckold into an emblem of sceptical tranquillity, Montaigne's comic anecdote aims to sever the inextricable tie between male honour and female chastity. He writes:

> Is there not a certain philosophical air about the case of a gentleman known to many? He married well along in years, having spent his youth in gay company, a great storyteller, a merry lad. Remembering how the subject of cuckoldry had given him material for talking and jesting about others, to take cover he married a woman whom he picked up in the place where each man can find one for his money, and made a compact with her that they would use these greetings: 'Good morning, whore.' 'Good morning, cuckold.' And there was nothing about which he talked more often and openly to visitors at his home than this arrangement of his; by which he checked the secret gossip of mockers, and blunted the point of this reproach. (II: 17, 594)

Montaigne's representation of married love here is deeply cynical, but it allows its male protagonist to remain 'merry' and 'gay'. Like Montaigne himself, who reports that he would rather be robbed than lose sleep over money, this gentleman would rather be made a cuckold than agonise over his lover's faith. McEachern makes an important distinction when she writes that 'a cuckold who knows himself to be such isn't in fact a cuckold, but a wittol, someone "in the know"'.[11] By representing tranquillity as part of a comic resolution, Montaigne affirms the limits of human knowledge, especially with respect to male fantasies of control, and advances his larger critique of human presumption.

Montaigne may be said then to confirm Cavell's assertion that the sceptic actually prefers to know that his lover is 'an adulterous whore', since this knowledge would put an end to his doubt (161). As Iago says, 'That cuckold lives in bliss / Who, certain of his fate, loves not his wronger; / But O, what damned minutes tells he o'er / Who dotes yet doubts; suspects yet strongly loves!' (III, ii, 169–70). In this case, however, the object of the sceptic's doubt is neither the woman nor her virtue but virtue itself. Despite the lowly nature of Montaigne's cuckold, he has a 'certain philosophical air' because he divests virginity and chastity of their metaphysical value. Desdemona's sexuality undermines Othello's sense of self, whereas Montaigne's sceptic evinces no such anxiety. Like Iago, who insists of Desdemona that, 'Blest fig's end! The wine she drinks is made of grapes', Montaigne refuses to exclude women and female sexuality from that which constitutes the human (2.1.249–50). The only manuscript addition, for example, that Montaigne makes to this anecdote after 1588 is the insertion of the word 'putain [whore]', a feminine obscenity that perfectly complements the masculine 'cocu [cuckold]'. The cuckold and the whore each affirm the other's identity: through a daily ritual, exchanging greetings that would more typically be received as outrageous insults, they acknowledge a shared sense of imperfection. When Cavell speaks of the problem of other minds, the kind of exchange that Montaigne describes here is the very form of acknowledgement that Cavell's version of scepticism renders impossible. Montaigne's lovers, for obvious reasons, cannot exemplify intimacy or trust, but they go on living and loving while Othello and Desdemona do not.

Although Cavell's engagement with Montaigne is relatively limited, he does explore the possibility that comedy could express 'the sceptical problematic' by a different light in his *Pursuits of Happiness*. Citing Montaigne as a touchstone, Cavell turns here to early twentieth-century Hollywood comedies of remarriage, which he views as the natural extension of Shakespearean romantic comedy. Again, however, Montaigne anticipates much of what he finds. Cavell writes:

> I have had occasion in speaking of the career of Othello to invoke Montaigne's horrified fascination by the human being's horror of itself, as if to say: life is hard, but then let us not burden it further by choosing tragically to call it tragic where we are free to choose otherwise. I understand Montaigne's alternative to horror to be the achievement of what he calls at the end a gay and sociable wisdom. I take this gaiety as the attitude on which what I am calling diurnal comedy depends.[12]

When considering the role of judgment in a sceptical framework, Cavell's reassertion of the choice between comic and tragic modes of representation is significant. Since sceptics do not believe they have any secure knowledge of an objective reality, they rely instead on avowedly subjective perceptions to navigate the world around them and to establish relationships with others. For Montaigne, the freedom to frame human ignorance and frailty as a subject of laughter is an attractive prospect, a possibility that draws him to engage with classical Scepticism in the first place. Throughout his reading of *Othello*, Cavell suggests that Shakespeare ultimately rejects Montaigne's comic vision of scepticism because it requires an inhuman ability to moderate passionate excess. Tragedy reveals Pyrrhonian scepticism's failure to attain its signature aim.

Responding to Cavell's work, some scholars turn to Shakespeare's comedies for the kind of practical resolution to what Cavell calls 'the skeptical problematic' that tragedies by the nature of the genre withhold. John Lee suggests that 'anyone looking for a Montaign-esque play might do well to restrict their research to the comedies and, perhaps especially, to the late plays with their turns away from, or recuperations of the effects of, tragedy'.[13] David Schalkwyk, too, argues that 'in Shakespearean comedy theatrical laughter may disarm skeptical doubt; in Shakespearean romance acknowledgement may replace an inappropriate demand for knowledge'.[14] Derek Gottlieb proposes that 'if tragedy is the drama of avoidance, Shakespeare's comedies can be read as the drama of acknowledgment'.[15]

The resolutions of Shakespeare's comedies tend to depend, how-ever, on the revelation of evidence that is in effect beyond doubt rather than reimagining doubt, as Montaigne does, as a possible source of tranquillity within romantic love. William Hamlin notes that *Much Ado about Nothing*, for example, like *Othello*, features a sceptical critique of the reliability of sense perception: Claudio's misjudgement of Hero's apparent infidelity, like Othello's of what he believes is 'ocular proof' of Desdemona's, reveals the limits of the empirical criterion Hamlin describes as 'specular authority'.[16] The happy ending of Claudio and Hero's love story depends, however, on a series of events more 'miraculous' than plausible: Hero's apparent death and unexpected reappearance.

For both Schalkwyk and Gottlieb, the marriage of Beatrice and Benedick in *Much Ado about Nothing* is evidence that the couple has adequately overcome their initial doubts about each other. For Gottlieb, the revelation of the sonnets, in particular, confirming their true feelings is 'miraculous'.[17] Doubt is understood as an impediment to marriage that must be removed rather than a capacity that makes marriage possible. Not all of us have physical proof, however, as striking as sonnets composed by our beloved in secret that our love is reciprocated. For the philosophically minded, moreover, material evidence of whatsoever kind, even such heartfelt professions, can-not altogether remedy internal uncertainty about the true nature of the external world, including not least doubts about the contents of other minds.

Comedy and tragedy can be understood not only as genres or sets of literary conventions but also in looser sense as rival approaches to the experience of doubt. Resisting the impulse to posit certainty, comic scepticism accepts our epistemological limitations, forfeit-ing unfounded claims to know the minds of others. As Schalkwyk observes, *Much Ado* 'not only declares via its protagonist that "man is but a giddy thing" but also registers its acceptance of that condition'.[18] Hamlin sees in Renaissance comedies more generally 'a collective sense of human weakness and mental frailty'.[19] Comic scepticism in this sense, as a way of life, need not be confined to the comic genre. In the story of the cuckold and the prostitute Montaigne recounts, the cuckold's doubts are answered not with truth but with laughter. This comic response acknowledges the finitude and fallibility of human knowledge and signals inner freedom from the perturbation engendered by the now more settled sceptic's previous 'presumption'.

Perhaps the closest parallel to Montaigne's comic anecdote to be found in Shakespeare's works is Sonnet 138, in which two lovers likewise set aside concerns about fidelity and veracity in order to stay together. 'When my love swears that she is made of truth, / I do believe her, though I know she lies': the speaker seems to vacillate here between reason and wilful delusion. These dichotomies are undercut, however, when we learn that he lies about his age in the same way that she lies about her fidelity.[20] 'Therefore I lie with her, and she with me, / And in our faults by lies we flattered be': the playful pun here in the sonnet's closing couplet suggests that, although the relationship is shot through with deceit, the reciprocal and understood nature of that deceit allows for a form of honesty that is tragically absent in *Othello*. Comedy allows us to hold ourselves and others to a less exacting measure than tragedy. In Sonnet 138, the speaker accepts his beloved, 'warts and all', because he also recognises his own shortcomings: his self-image is not as grandiose and therefore not as fragile as Othello's.

A consideration of Shakespeare and Montaigne need not rely on patterns of direct transmission in order to shed light on the broader question of how early modern scepticism began to inflect new literary genres and cultural contexts. That said, the resemblances between Shakespeare's *Othello* and Montaigne's essay 'On Some Verses of Virgil' that Cavell points out are indeed uncanny and suggest at least the possibility that Shakespeare's play is in part an intentional response to Montaigne's essay.[21] As Cavell notes, 'On Some Verses of Virgil'

> concerns the compatibility of sex with marriage, of sex with age; it remarks upon, and upon the relations among jealousy, chastity, imagination, doubts about virginity; upon the strength of language and the honesty of language; and includes mention of a Turk and of certain instances of necrophilia. One just about runs through the topics of *Othello* if to this essay one adds Montaigne's early essay 'Of the Power of the Imagination'

which contains a Moor and speaks of a king of Egypt who, finding himself impotent with his bride, threatened to kill her, thinking it was some sort of sorcery. (139)

In 'On Some Verses of Virgil', Montaigne not only comments on the double standards that regularly attend sexual acts performed by men and women, especially within the confines of marriage, but also sets out a vision of philosophy as a means of attaining pleasure. This pleasure appears ethically suspect in *Othello* and informs what Cavell describes as Shakespeare's 'rebuke' of Montaigne (140).

While it may seem odd to regard the essay as a comic mode or genre, Montaigne regularly associates laughter with the therapeutic ends of Pyrrhonian scepticism. 'I tickle myself', he confesses in 'On Some Verses of Virgil': 'I, who have no other aim but to live and be merry, would run from one end of the world to the other to seek out some one good year of pleasant and cheerful tranquillity' (III: 5, 775, 777). Much as Montaigne imagines humorous ways to blunt the cuckold's experience of jealousy, so too he imagines here the possibility of a philosophy that does not end in violence or despair. Citing Montaigne's 'gay and sociable wisdom' as evidence of a desire to disrupt the potentially tragic repercussions of scepticism, Cavell raises serious questions about the authenticity and viability of Montaigne's comic vision (III: 13, 1044). Although he aims to restore a sense of dignity that Montaigne's lowly portrait of human nature denies, Cavell in doing so ignores the therapeutic ends of classical Scepticism treating it instead as symptomatic of the very fears it was developed to assuage.[22] Through his reading of Shakespeare, Cavell conflates scepticism with tragedy, as if scepticism were inherently a state of torment. *Othello* is certainly a tragedy, but scepticism does not account for and indeed might have averted the play's troubling conclusion.

Montaigne's confidence that scepticism can moderate strong emotions such as sexual jealousy may well assume too much of the capacities of ordinary men and women, as well as the effectiveness of such philosophising. Cavell raises this concern when he says,

> But to whom is this advice usable? And how do we understand why it cannot be taken by those in directest need of it? . . . Is Montaigne's attitude fully earned, itself without a tint of the wish for exemption from the human? (140)

The seeming absurdity of Montaigne's position is apparent in his account of the happy cuckold; in light of Shakespeare's *Othello*, it does become difficult to imagine a real-life scenario in which a man would enter gleefully into a marriage with a woman whom he knows to be unfaithful.[23] That said, Montaigne's effort to quiet the stings of sexual jealousy is not a rejection of 'the human' altogether. The only 'exemption' that Montaigne seeks is from the dominant perspective of a European male.

In his description of the New World, Montaigne praises the tribe of the Tupinambá specifically because their culture does not require monogamy. In 'Of Cannibals', the one essay almost all scholars agree Shakespeare knew first-hand, Montaigne notes that, although men and women in the tribe do not enjoy the same degrees of sexual freedom,

> it is a remarkably beautiful thing about their marriage that the same jealousy our wives have to keep us from the affection and kindness of other women, theirs have to win this for them . . . they strive and scheme to have as many companions as they can, since that is a sign of their husband's valour. (I: 31, 192)[24]

Unlike Cavell, who cannot dismiss the lived experience of sexual jealousy and its tragic consequences, Montaigne uses an account of the New World as an opportunity to reflect on the limitations of this objection, presenting it as tied to a masculine subject position. Confronted with sexual indiscretion, women, especially those in other cultures, might perhaps look the other way. Shakespeare hints at a more scandalous version of this perspective when Emilia demands of Desdemona, 'Who would not make her husband a cuckold to make him a monarch?', although her argument ultimately falls upon deaf ears (IV, iii, 74–5).

Imagining how Montaigne might respond to Cavell's examination of witchcraft in *Othello* helps to clarify how scepticism can constitute an ethical solution rather than an epistemological problem. Recalling Brabantio's accusation that in order to win Desdemona, Othello 'practised on her with foul charms, / Abused her delicate youth with drugs and minerals', Cavell suggests that Othello's final judgement of Desdemona resembles a witch trial (I, ii, 73–4). He draws attention, in particular, to 'the crazed logic Othello's rage for proof and for "satisfaction" seems to require', which he compares to 'testing for a woman's witchcraft by seeing whether she will drown, declaring that if she does, she was innocent, but if she does not, she is to be put to death for a witch' (141). By comparing Othello to an inquisitor, Cavell ties masculine desire for proof directly to the death of others, usually female, and invites us to consider a larger question. Does scepticism lead to violence, especially violence against women?

If Shakespeare, as Cavell suggests, figures Desdemona as an innocent woman accused of witchcraft, a victim forced to stand trial for charges that are difficult or impossible to substantiate, then Othello can be seen acting on the very evidence that a sceptic should refuse to take as definitive proof. In 'Of Cripples', for instance, Montaigne introduces a group of women that he met who had been imprisoned for witchcraft. 'In the end,' he writes, 'and in all conscience, I would have prescribed them rather hellebore than hemlock' (III.2.961): that is to say, he would have deemed them insane and prescribed medicine (hellebore) rather than so dangerous to society at large as to merit capital punishment (hemlock). In his capacity as judge, Montaigne had access to many versions of the kind of 'ocular proof' Othello demands of Iago. 'I saw both proofs and free confessions,' he explains; 'I talked and asked questions all I wanted' (*Oth* III, iii, 370; Montaigne III: 2, 961). Whereas Othello presses for unattainable certainty, Montaigne refrains from acting on imperfect knowledge. 'The proofs and reasons that are founded on experience and fact I do not attempt to disentangle,' he explains. 'After all, it is putting a very high price on one's conjectures to have a man roasted alive because of them' (III: 2, 962). In ethical terms, scepticism prevents Montaigne from assenting to violence at another's expense. If Othello truly had been a sceptic, he too might have suspended his judgement on the matter of Desdemona's guilt, on the matter of whether the female other can be known or not. This experience of doubt would not have required then that he bid 'Farewell the tranquil mind, farewell content!' (III, iii, 351).

Notes

1. Cavell's essay originally appeared as part of a chapter titled 'Between Acknowledgement and Avoidance' in *The Claim of Reason*. Parenthetical citations are to the version reprinted in *Disowning Knowledge* as 'Othello and the Stake of the Other'.
2. For extended treatments of the relation between Shakespeare's scepticism and tragedy, see, esp., Bradshaw, *Shakespeare's Scepticism*, and Bell, *Shakespeare's Tragic Skepticism*.
3. For more recent and more sympathetic treatment of Shakespeare's reception of classical scepticism, see Cox, *Seeming Knowledge*; Kuzner, *Shakespeare as a Way of Life*, and Benfell, 'Disowning Certainty'.
4. On the zetetic quality of Montaigne's scepticism, see William M. Hamlin, 'The Shakespeare-Montaigne-Sextus Nexus', pp. 28–9.

5. Scholars do not agree on Othello's scepticism. See DiSanto, 'Nothing if Not Critical', p. 365, who views Iago as the real sceptic in the play and Cox, 'Suspicion and Belief in the Early Comedies', p. 70, who argues that what Cavell calls scepticism might more accurately be called suspicion.

6. On *Othello* and the trope of the jealous husband in Roman comedy, see Rogers, '*Othello*: Comedy in Reverse', p. 210.

7. On *Othello* as farce, see Bell, *Shakespeare's Tragic Skepticism*, pp. 87–91, and Bradshaw, *Shakespeare's Scepticism*, p. 16.

8. Fischer, *Stanley Cavell and Literary Skepticism*, p. 91.

9. McEachern, *Believing in Shakespeare*, p. 135.

10. After hitting his head during an epileptic seizure, Othello demands of Iago, 'Dost thou mock me?' (IV, i, 59).

11. McEachern, *Believing in Shakespeare*, p. 139.

12. Cavell, *Pursuits of Happiness*, p. 238.

13. Lee, '"A judge that were no man"', p. 37.

14. Schalkwyk, 'Cavell, Wittgenstein, Shakespeare, and Skepticism', p. 629.

15. Gottlieb, *Skepticism and Belonging in Shakespeare's Comedy*, p. 20.

16. William M. Hamlin, *Tragedy and Scepticism in Shakespeare's England*, pp. 129–30.

17. Gottlieb, *Skepticism and Belonging in Shakespeare's Comedy*, p. 20.

18. Schalkwyk, 'Cavell, Wittgenstein, Shakespeare, and Skepticism', p. 609.

19. William M. Hamlin, *Tragedy and Scepticism in Shakespeare's England*, 124.

20. For a fuller treatment of the role of Pyrrhonian scepticism in Sonnet 138, see Kellogg, 'Pyrrhonist Uncertainty in Shakespeare's Sonnets', pp. 418–20, and Tartamella, *Rethinking Shakespeare's Skepticism*, pp. 173–88.

21. For others who have posited 'On Some Verses of Virgil' as a possible source text for *Othello*, see Engle, 'Sovereign Cruelty in Montaigne and *King Lear*', pp. 134–5; Kirsch, *Shakespeare and the Experience of Love*, pp. 38–9; and Adelman, *Suffocating Mothers*, p. 78.

22. On the therapeutic function of ancient scepticism, see, esp., Nussbaum, *Therapy of Desire*, ch. 8.

23. Comparing Sonnet 138 to *The Taming of the Shrew*, Tartamella, *Rethinking Shakespeare's Skepticism*, pp. 202–12, offers a compelling reading of Kate's final speech as an example of knowing deception within a similarly sceptical and comic framework.

24. An important complication of the general consensus that Shakespeare responds relatively directly to Montaigne's essay 'Of Cannibals' in *The Tempest* can be found in Boutcher, *School of Montaigne*, 2: 264–71. As Boutcher explains, Shakespeare's *The Tempest* also responds to Samuel Daniel's distinctive appropriation of the same key passage in his play *The Queen's Arcadia*. Gonzalo, by this light, can be understood as 'a stage caricature of the persona given to the English Montaigne by Daniel and Florio: that of a knight-adventurer making sallies out upon custom in daring intellectual exercises' (p. 270).

Chapter 8

Feeling Indifference: Flaying Narratives in Montaigne and Shakespeare

Alison Calhoun

Flaying the condemned alive, though a form of torture rarely if ever performed in sixteenth-century England or France, nonetheless served as a significant topos during the Renaissance within Christian and philosophical textual traditions.[1] This chapter looks at some of the striking resonances between narratives of flaying in Shakespeare's *King Lear* and Montaigne's 'Of Vertue' and 'On Experience', exploring how both authors respond to an ambiguous tale about skinning found in biographical sources for scepticism's figurehead, Pyrrho. This Pyrrhonian tale of flayed skin raises questions about the body, virtue and belief. The topos becomes more polemical, as well, when read in the context of the Pauline tradition. Both Pyrrho and Paul were almost certainly significant points of reference for both Shakespeare and Montaigne. The Pyrrhonian/Pauline figure of flaying is a vehicle through which Shakespeare as well as Montaigne, each in his own distinctive mode, proposes a critique of fanaticism, a critique which may have originated in the roots of early scepticism. Through the universal vulnerability of the skin, both authors encourage us to consider alternative paths to tranquillity through pacifism, self-preservation and tolerance.

Pyrrho's great virtue was supposed to be his mastery of the suspension of judgement (*epochē*), which he used as a gateway to a coveted state of indifference or freedom from worry (*ataraxia*). Although many ancient sources report that he did so incredibly well, we do nonetheless have biographical fragments that suggest Pyrrho sometimes faltered. In the history of scepticism, these failures provide a possibility of reading more continuity between 'early', 'pure' Pyrrhonian scepticism and 'late', 'academic' scepticism, as in Sextus

Empiricus's *Outlines of Pyrrhonism*. As Richard Bett demonstrates, a cautionary reading of the fallibility of Pyrrho would prove that our contemporary distinction between the early Pyrrhonian concept of virtue as 'unwaveringness' (constancy) and later, or 'academic', scepticism's concept of adhering to appearances is one that the sceptical readers in the Renaissance may not have made. A very visual and material example of this coexistence is the likelihood that Shakespeare and Montaigne would have read the 'Life of Pyrrho' from the Henri Estienne's 1562 Greek–Latin edition of Sextus Empiricus's *Outlines*, which had Diogenes' 'Life of Pyrrho' printed at the back.[2] Montaigne and Shakespeare display readings that bring to bear both the early and the late traditions.

The absence of belief in Pyrrho's model stems in part from his biographical material in Diogenes Laertius's *Lives*.[3] The following series of anecdotes, for instance, is part of a larger fragment from Diogenes' 'Life of Pyrrho', as adapted by Montaigne in his essay 'On Virtue'. In the 1603 English translation by John Florio, we read:

> *Pyrrho*, who framed so pleasant a science of ignorance, assaied (as all other true philosophers) to fashion his life answerable to his doctrine. And forasmuch as he maintained the weaknesse of mans judgement to be so extreame as it could take nor resolution nor inclination: and would perpetually suspend it, ballancing, beholding and receiving all things as indifferent . . . (405)[4]

Yet Pyrrho took this suspension of judgement to such an absurd extreme that he can seem at times like a raving lunatic. In the passages that follow, derived from Antigonus, Montaigne continues:

> it is reported of him that . . . if he went any where, he would not goe an inche out of his path what let or obstacle soever came in his way; being kept from falls, from cartes, or other accidents by his friends . . . He sometimes suffered himselfe to be cut and cauterized with such constancy as he was never seen so much as to shrug, twitch, move, or winke with his eyes. It is something to bring the minde to these imagination, but more to joine the effects unto it . . . verily in these enterprises so farre from common use, it is almost incredible to be done.[5](405)

So far, Montaigne grants that Pyrrho was able to do the impossible, though perhaps as a result of an unusual, natural immunity: suspend judgement, even facing death, thanks to a little help from 'his friends'. But the next part of the narrative turns to proof that there were a few instances where Pyrrho fell short of this ideal. The anecdotes Montaigne borrows here are found in Aristocles, as well as in Diogenes Laertius, and Aristocles attributes them to Antigonus; for the sake of clarity, these particular incidents will be referred to in what follows as the Antigonian passages.[6] The significance of Montaigne's and Shakespeare's use of these Antigonian passages, regardless of where they read them, is that they illuminate key ambiguities complicating later interpretation of early, Pyrrhonian scepticism. Their allusions prove that their study of scepticism probably involved a combination of Sextus Empiricus and Diogenes Laertius, as well as other texts which incorporate fragments and anecdotes about Pyrrho's life:[7]

> The reason is this, that he was sometimes found in his house bitterly scolding with his sister for which being reproved as he that wronged his indifferencie . . . Another time, being found to defend himselfe from a dog: '*It is*,' replied he, '*very hard altogether to dispoile and shake off man*;' and man must endevour and enforce himselfe to resist and confront all things, first by effects, but if the worst befall, by reason and by discourse. (405)

When he learned his sister was mistreated, Pyrrho reacted with anger. When faced with an attacking dog, he fled out of fear. Surely these were failures of *epochē*?

Bett demonstrates that the quandary the Antigonian passages raise is that we have no way of knowing if their intention was prescriptive or cautionary.[8] Is Pyrrho telling us that we should try to strip ourselves of our humanity in order to follow in his footsteps as a good Pyrrhonian sceptic and achieve freedom from worry? Or is the passage meant to demonstrate that, because perfect indifference is impossible (in this case, dangerous), it is within the guidelines of basic Pyrrhonian practice to make exceptions in order to save one's own skin?

Ultimately, the question is this: is Pyrrhonian scepticism a liveable proposition? Montaigne examines the raw, embodied practice of scepticism in his highly personal reflections on the relationship between living and pain, as does Shakespeare in his representation of the challenges that face Lear, Tom and Cordelia in his tragedy *King Lear*.

Montaigne's Scepticism and Skinning

Montaigne quotes from Diogenes Laertius's 'Life of Pyrrho' at length in 'On Vertue', an essay less focused on offering Pyrrho as a model than it is on elaborating Montaigne's resistance to both classical efforts to define virtue in terms of suicidal constancy and Christian efforts to define it in terms of fanatical belief. Pyrrho does provide him, nonetheless, with a speedy entrée to the subject. In Diogenes, differing accounts from various fragments come together to paint a portrait of Pyrrho as a celebrity in the pursuit of *ataraxia*, displaying an almost inhuman, android-like degree of indifference. He is famously described as not having so much as flinched during a surgery.[9] But Laertius also includes examples of occasions Pyrrho failed to maintain such perfect indifference: quarrelling with his sister, fleeing from an attacking dog. How did the sage account for these shortfalls? In the text, Pyrrho exclaims: 'It is very difficult entirely to despoil and shake off man' (405) ['Il est, dit-il, tres-difficile de despouiller entierement l'homme'] (II: 29, 706).

The verb used in Montaigne's presentation of the story is *despouiller*: flaying or skinning. This one word provides the keynote to the rest of the essay. Montaigne goes on to share two accounts of literal 'putting off' of the man: two instances of men who sever their penises in protest against their wives or lovers. Next he moves to suicidal women: one a battered wife from Dordogne who jumps off a bridge, the others from India and 'Oriental nations' who perform *sati*. These women honour their husbands' deaths through cleansing ceremonies followed by self-immolation or other forms of suicide. In this account, another sense of *despouiller* appears, *despouiller* as undressing: 'she strips herself all naked' (406) ['elle se despouille toute nue' (II: 29, 708)]. Finally, Montaigne moves to a series of Indian philosophers, Bedouin soldiers and quarrelling monks, all depicted as suicidal.

Gymnosophists burn themselves alive the minute they reach old age or fall ill. Bedouins believe in *fatum* (or predestination) and go to the battlefield practically naked and unarmed. Monks nearly walk through fire to settle a theological battle. Only in the last example, which Montaigne adds in his final edits to the *Essays*, do we have a case of murder instead of self-harm: the 'Assassins', whom he describes as 'a nation depending of Phoenicia', and 'esteemed among the Mahometists of a soveraigne devotion and puritie of maners' [nation dependante de la Phoenicie . . . estimés entre les Mahumetans d'une souveraine devotion et pureté de meurs].

> They hold that the readiest and shortest way to gaine Paradise is to kill some one of a contrary religion; therefore hath it often beene seene that one or two in their bare doublets have undertaken to assault mighty

enemies with the price of an assured death and without any care of their own danger. (408)

Ils tiennent que le plus certain moyen de meriter Paradis, c'est tuer quelqu'un de religion contraire. Parquoy mesprisant tous les dangiers propres, pour une si utile execution, un ou deux se sont veus souvent, au pris d'une certaine mort, se presenter à assassiner (nous avons emprunté ce mot de leur nom) leur ennemi au milieu de ses forces. (II: 29, 711)

Shakespeare seems to draw on similar moments of foolhardiness in the face of danger in his *Coriolanus*, whose eponymous character displays vivid, wilful indifference to his own physical safety. He describes his own loss of blood, for example, as medicinal rather than debilitating: 'rather physical / Than dangerous' (I, v, 16–17). As in Shakespeare's *Coriolanus*, so, too, in Montaigne's 'Of Vertue', acts of bold violence are not presented as truly virtuous but instead as acts of hubris.[10]

Montaigne emphasises the utility of these tales by relating them to the reader's own skin. Those who choose to assassinate their enemy '*au milieu de ses forces*' are examples of those who 'disregard the dangers they are imposing on themselves' ['mesprisent tous les dangiers propres' (II: 29, 711)]; in this sense, even murder is a violation or risk of violation of the perpetrator's self. Connecting this final message back through the suicides and self-mutilators to Pyrrho, Montaigne's position seems to be that *mépris* – indifference – is a major error. So, too, in Shakespeare's *Coriolanus*, the protagonist's 'noble carelessness' (II, ii, 14) proves self-destructive. To be 'a soldier / Even to Cato's wish' (I, iv, 56–7) is, like Cato, to commit a kind of suicide.

These stories become all the more suggestive when we consider the Pauline intertext, specifically Paul's letters where he discusses stripping off or putting away 'the old man'. In his Letter to the Ephesians, Paul compares the church to the body of Christ, its head: 'From whom the whole body, being compacted and fitly joined together, by what every joint supplieth, according to the operation in the measure of every part, maketh increase of the body, unto the edifying of itself in charity' (Eph. 4:6). But he then prescribes shedding one's skin: 'put off, according to former conversation, the old man, who is corrupted according to the desire of error' (Eph. 4:18). In his Letter to the Colossians, Paul again writes:

Lie not one to another: seeing that ye have put off the old man with his works, and have put on the new, which is renewed in knowledge after the image of him that created him, where is neither Grecian nor Jew, circumcision nor uncircumcision, Barbarian, Scythian, bond, free: But Christ is all, and in all things. (Col. 3:9–11)

Skin in the Pauline usage is disposable, replaceable.

Shaped by Paul's aversion to the flesh, post-classical Pyrrhonism is prescriptive: flaying the old skin in this Christian context is not merely possible but actually necessary in order to secure salvation. In the mouth of a defeated sceptic, however, as in the passage cited above from Laertius, where Pyrrho concedes that he was startled by a dog, such figures of speech serve to remind us that our skin is far from disposable. It is, as Pyrrho says, 'very difficult to entirely strip away the man' ['tres-difficile de despouiller entierement l'homme']. Nor would we, were we to remove the ones we have, as in the case of ideologies as well as garments, magically generate second skins. Paul suggests that flaying will somehow lead to a more sensitive layer of skin, whereas Pyrrho focuses on the extreme fragility of the outer layer. Of the two, Montaigne chooses the more cautious perspective, arguing that our skin is much less elastic and flexible than our reason. Our beliefs are potentially pliable and malleable. Our skin, on the other hand, will not stretch as far as fanaticism calls for.

The relationship between this Pyrrhonian moment, its Pauline intertext, and Montaigne's later reflections can be discerned at the end of Montaigne's final essay, 'On Experience'. Montaigne writes: 'They will bee exempted from them and escape man. It is meere folly: in steade of transforming themselves into angels, they transchange themselves into beasts: in lieu of advancing, they abase themselves' (664) ['Ils veulent se mettre hors d'eux et eschapper à l'homme. C'est folie: au lieu de se transformer en anges, ils se transforment en bestes; au lieu de se hausser, ils s'abattent' (III: 13, 1115)]. As David Quint notes, these lines, borrowed from Giovanni Pico della Mirandola, warn that when human beings attempt to transcend their humanity, to become angels, for example, they not only fall short of this ideal but fall even further than they were before, becoming more like beasts.[11] Our skin keeps us grounded, by this light, in a human casing that prevents hubris and encourages vulnerability. Not long after this general assessment of the limits of human nature, Montaigne turns to a more personal matter, his suffering from kidney stones, and sets the stage for his account of his own quasi-Pauline 'thorn in the flesh' (2 Cor. 12:8).

Montaigne's discussion of his own intimate acquaintance with physical frailty brings with it other intertexts, as well, related to flaying. Robert Aulotte sees a link to Marsyas, the flute player whom Apollo flayed for daring to challenge him to a competition.[12] Montaigne's description of suffering reflects Christian intertexts and iconography, however, as well as pagan, ranging from the scourging that preceded Christ's Crucifixion to the story of the martyrdom of Saint Bartholomew, whom Eusebius of Caesarea and Saint Jerome report was tortured and killed for his evangelising in India by being flayed alive and hanged upside-down. Saint Bartholomew in particular appears as a significant element in the Renaissance imaginary, with Milan Cathedral's statue of *St Bartholomew Flayed* by Marco d'Agrate (erected in 1562), which closely resembles the ground-breaking anatomical drawings from Vesalius's *De humani corporis* (1543), and which Montaigne would likely have seen during his travels to Italy. Familiarity with skinning in this period can be discerned in the eerie flayed skin, as well, that appears in Michelangelo's fresco for the Sistine Chapel, *The Last Judgment* (1536–41). Saint Bartholomew is himself intact in the centre of the image but holds a skin envelope in his left hand whose visage bears an uncanny resemblance to the artist, Michelangelo.[13] This identification with Bartholomew, possibly intentional, suggests that Michelangelo saw some analogy between painting and being flayed: art is a process of suffering and laying oneself bare. Returning to his interest in 'Of Virtue' in the motives for martyrdom, Montaigne admits here that those who find his suffering due to kidney stones courageous flatter him: 'It is some pleasure for a man to heare others say to him: Loe there a patterne of true fortitude; loe there a mirrour of matchlesse patience' (649) ['Il y a plaisir à ouyr dire de soy: Voylà bien de la force, voylà bien de la patience' (III: 13, 1091)].

> Thou art seen to sweat with labour, to grow pale and wane, to wax red, to quake and tremble, to cast and vomite blood, to endure strange contractions, to brooke convulsions, to trill downe brackish and great teares, to make thicke, muddie, blacke, bloodie and fearefull urine, or to have it stoppt by some sharpe or rugged stone which pricketh and cruelly wringeth the necke of the yarde: entertaining in the meanwhile the by-standers with an ordinarie and undanted countenance, by pawses jeasting and by entremissions dallying with thy servants: keeping a partie in a continued discourse; with words now and then excusing thy griefe, and abating thy painful sufferance. (649–50)

> On te voit suer d'ahan, pallir, rougir, trembler, vomir jusques au sang, souffrir des contractions et convulsions estranges, degouter par foys de grosses larmes des yeux, rendre les urines espesses, noires, et effroyables,

ou les avoir arrestées par quelque pierre espineuse et herissée qui te pouinct et escorche cruellement le col de la verge, entretenant cependant les assistans d'une contenance commune, bouffonnant à pauses avec tes gens, tenant ta partie en un discours tendu, excusant de parolle ta douleur et rabatant de ta souffrance. (III: 13, 1091)

Such flattery, however, he implies, is misguided. Not everyone spends their days suffering painful ailments like Montaigne. What he suggests here is not that we praise him for tolerating or downplaying his own suffering, but rather that we take away from his account what he himself has learned, which is that, if or rather when we are put into dangerous situations, our aim should always be to protect our own skin. We should focus on self-preservation, the fragility of our bodies, before we consider questions of blind courage, extreme belief or divine virtue. If we read this passage in dialogue with his essay 'On Virtue', Montaigne wants the reader to recognise the danger of dissimulating or even downplaying suffering ('excusing' or 'abating' suffering). Praise of senselessness can lead to the harmful morality of religious fanatics, exemplified in the stories he recounts of suicide. If the *Essays* are Montaigne's flayed skin, as Montaigne proposes, in a sense, when he claims the book is 'consubstantiall to his author' (p. 385), he may have hoped that his ultimate sacrifice would convert one or two noble readers into pacifists by re-sensitising them to real suffering, teaching them what David Quint calls a 'morality of yielding'.[14]

Shakespeare's Scepticism and Skinning

While Montaigne is clearly in dialogue with Pyrrho via Diogenes Laertius, the Pyrrhonian influence in Shakespeare's *King Lear* is less obvious. Until now, the passages I want to reread have been associated with Cynicism in Diogenes Laertius rather than his representation of scepticism, as well as beliefs about the afterlife in the Christian tradition.[15] I read them, however, in the context of Montaigne's critique of what could be described as a Pauline, that is to say, a pure or radical, form of Pyrrhonism, indifferent to the body. Paul and Pyrrho play an important role in Shakespeare's development of Lear, Tom and Cordelia. The affinities between Shakespeare's and Montaigne's treatment of Pyrrhonian and Pauline intertexts issue from a shared desire to ground abstract claims in the fallible realm of human psychology and concrete behaviour. This perspective on philosophy is in keeping with the tendency throughout the Renaissance to approach philosophical doctrine through life writing rather than formal logic. As James Kuzner suggests, Shakespeare as well as Montaigne are interested in philosophy as a way of life rather than in philosophy as a deracinated game.[16] For Shakespeare, however, as Cavell points out, thoroughgoing scepticism proves in practice more problematic than beneficial. Like Pyrrho, Shakespeare's tragic protagonists find it difficult, indeed impossible, as well as self-destructive to live out the demands of scepticism.

Shakespeare's *King Lear*, with its scenes of suffering, torture and cruelty, inhabits a similar affective realm as Montaigne's passages on flaying. Like Montaigne, Lear questions Pyrrhonian and Pauline therapies by focusing on the paradoxical nature of attempting to embody perfect indifference (*epochē*). In Act IV, scene vi, Lear tells Gloucester about the relationship between appearances, the body and judgement. This scene in *Lear* could be a gloss of the Antigonian fragment, inspired by Shakespeare's reading of Diogenes Laertius or, more likely, Montaigne's borrowing of that fragment in his essay 'Of Vertue'. In Lear's dialogue with the blinded Gloucester about the faulty relationship between appearances, or what we perceive based on our eyesight, and our judgement, he says:

> LEAR: What, art mad? A man may see how the world goes with no eyes.
> Look with thine ears. See how yond justice rails upon yond
> simple thief. Hark in thine ear. Change places and, handy-dandy,
> which is the justice, which is the thief? Thou hast seen a
> farmer's dog bark at a beggar?
> EARL OF GLOUCESTER: Ay, sir.
> LEAR: And the creature run from the cur? There thou mightst behold
> the great image of authority: a dog's obeyed in office.
> Thou rascal beadle, hold thy bloody hand!
> Why dost thou lash that whore? Strip thine own back.
> Thou hotly lusts to use her in that kind
> For which thou whip'st her. The usurer hangs the cozener.
> Through tatter'd clothes small vices do appear;
> Robes and furr'd gowns hide all. Plate sin with gold,
> And the strong lance of justice hurtless breaks;
> Arm it in rags, a pygmy's straw does pierce it.
> None does offend, none – I say none! I'll able 'em.
> Take that of me, my friend, who have the power
> To seal th' accuser's lips. Get thee glass eyes
> And, like a scurvy politician, seem
> To see the things thou dost not. Now, now, now, now!
> Pull off my boots. Harder, harder! So.   (IV, vi, 146–69)[17]

Parts of this dialogue rehearse the passage in Montaigne's essay 'How one ought to governe his Will' where he likewise questions the value of judgements based solely on the outer trappings of a person or thing.[18] Lear's example of a 'creature' fleeing a dog, the command, 'strip thine own back', and the order to 'pull off' his boots evoke Pyrrho's morally ambiguous failure to ignore an attacking dog in the Antigonian fragment. That this image is closely coupled with an example of scourging, an analogue of flaying, and that this punishment is being administered by a church official, a 'rascal beadle', suggests the possible influence of Montaigne's critique of religious fanaticism, or at least a sympathetic point of view. Lear can be understood here as philosophising in Pyrrhonian terms if we interpret Pyrrho's confession of weakness as cautionary: sometimes we judge and act based on our senses, and to do so is not only human, but often reasonable; even virtuous.

Gloucester's presence in this scene provides a graphic physical demonstration of this larger philosophical point. Gloucester is blind because his eyes have been violently ripped out. Despite the cruel intentions of his persecutors, however, this mutilation has not stripped away his humanity. Gloucester retains his emotions: he tells Lear that, despite his mere casings for eyes, he still sees the world 'feelingly' (IV, 6, 145). As Montaigne writes, echoing Pyrrho, trying to get out of ourselves, our sensitive skins, our trappings, is madness (III: 13, 1115).

On the heath, Lear works through a similar line of thought about skin, skinning and coverings, in order to continue to debate the Pyrrhonian problem. Is it even possible to rid ourselves of our skin? That is, 'to entirely strip away the man'? Many readings of this scene align 'poor Tom' with Diogenes the Cynic.[19] Looking again at Shakespeare's sources, however, as well as Tom himself as, in Lear's words, 'unaccommodated man' (III, iv, 105), a connection to Pyrrho becomes apparent. Tom is based in part on the example of Diogenes of Sinope; this paradigmatic Cynic is the kind of philosopher Lear wants to imitate. Like David Hershinow, although Hershinow is more interested in the influence of Cynicism than scepticism, I, too, would note the importance of life writing and biographical anecdotes to the Renaissance understanding of ancient philosophy, as well as foreground Diogenes Laertius as an especially important classical source, most likely mediated in Shakespeare's case by his reading of Montaigne. To date, however, such interpretations have overlooked an additional layer of complexity, an allusion to the life of Pyrrho which informs the vision of ancient philosophy apparent

in Shakespeare's tragedy, as well as the resonance of his work with
Montaigne's.

Out on a heath in the middle of a terrible storm, Lear meets Edgar
disguised as a madman, Tom o'Bedlam. The passage in which despoiling comes into play is when Lear, noticing that Tom is naked, wonders
to what extent he, too, should disrobe. If we take the passage in which
Lear discusses 'unaccommodated man' as an allusion to the cynicism of
Diogenes without adding a possible Pyrrhonian and Pauline intertext,
we read it as prescriptive (as we might the Antigonian passage) instead
of cautionary:

> Why, thou wert better in thy grave than to answer with thy
> uncover'd body this extremity of the skies. Is man no more than
> this? Consider him well. Thou ow'st the worm no silk, the beast
> no hide, the sheep no wool, the cat no perfume. Ha! Here's three
> on's are sophisticated! Thou art the thing itself;
> unaccommodated man is no more but such a poor, bare, forked
> animal as thou art. Off, off, you lendings! Come, unbutton here.
> [*tears at his clothes*]   (III, iv, 100–8)

If we characterise Tom as Cynic, in other words, and Lear as his aspir-
ing follower, we miss the error of fanatical belief that Shakespeare,
like Montaigne, seeks to underscore. Moreover, without the flaying
intertext, we might hear relief in Lear's voice as he questions 'Is man
no more than this?' rather than frustration and caution inspired by
the impossibility of shaking off humanity. In saying that this passage
is more Pyrrhonian and reactive to Paul than it is cynicism means
reading irony into the phrase 'Thou art the thing itself.' The 'thing',
that is to say, 'unaccommodated man', comes across as weak, since
it is a human being cloaked in vulnerable skin. Hershinow adds to
this irony the possible reference to Plato's inadequate definition of
'man' in Erasmus's *Apothegmes*.[20] If, like Hershinow, we read these
lines as suggesting a Lear who expects to become like Diogenes the
Cynic by imitating Tom and stripping himself naked, we would interpret this scene as a kind of Pauline conversion: Lear disrobes and he
gives up his old life to follow the Cynic, Tom. When we read these
lines in a Montaignian light, however, the exclamation point makes
more sense. Despite Lear's urgent desire to be 'un-manned' or an
'unaccommodated man', no amount of unbuttoning, unmasking or
undressing will allow him to escape the weakness of his human skin.

Lear's initial question has the ring of a cautionary Pyrrhonism.
Can we rid ourselves of our humanity? Of all the cast, the character

of Cordelia, however, is most frequently associated with scepticism, and it is Cordelia and her fate that offer a response to this question.[21] Cordelia is a negative example, embodying the undesirable consequences in practice of attempting to attain freedom from inner distress *(ataraxia)* through a refusal to speak *(aphasia)*. This understanding of Cordelia sits in considerable tension with readings of her as a Christ figure, in so far as it suggests that, within the sceptical tradition, there might have been a way for her to have avoided her suffering and death.

In light of our findings, it is possible to reread Cordelia, especially her initial response in Act I, scene i and Lear's reaction to her corpse in the final scene of Act V, as Shakespeare's response to those who interpret these skinning passages as legitimate, practical ways of demonstrating true belief. The error, Shakespeare indicates, is to understand scepticism or Christian faith as unwavering, inflexible adherence to belief without any compromise in the face of certain sensory or customary situations, akin to the Stoic virtue of 'constancy'. Cordelia, like Coriolanus, is in this sense Shakespeare's version of Montaigne's suicide bombers, the Assassins.[22] She demonstrates one of the extremes possible if we interpret the Antigonian passages as prescriptive instead of cautionary: what Montaigne would describe as 'circumscribing oneself' instead of 'pressing upward and forward.'[23]

Cordelia speaks in sceptical terms during her initial response to her father. When Lear asks each daughter to demonstrate her love in speech, his wicked daughters speak fluently and to the point, whereas his most beloved and loving daughter freezes and says very little. When at last she does speak, moreover, her halting diction closely resembles the sceptical practice of suspension of judgement *(epochē)*:

> LEAR: Nothing?
> CORDELIA: Nothing.
> LEAR: Nothing can come of nothing. Speak again.
> CORDELIA: Unhappy that I am, I cannot heave
> My heart into my mouth. I love your Majesty
> According to my bond; no more nor less.[24]

(I, i, 88–93)

'No more nor less': as has not been noticed to date, Cordelia's lines here seem to have been lifted from Aristocles via Eusebius of Caesarea, a source which Shakespeare may have encountered indirectly through Sextus's gloss:

> He [Timon, Pyrrho's only real follower] says that he [Pyrrho] reveals
> that things are equally indifferent and unstable and indeterminate; for
> this reason neither our sensations nor our opinions tell the truth or lie.
> For this reason, then, we should not trust them, but we should be with-
> out opinions and without inclinations and without wavering, saying
> about each single thing that it no more is than is not or both is and is not
> or neither is nor is not (*ou mallon estin ê ouk estin ê kai esti kai ouk estin
> ê oute estin oute ouk estin*). Timon says that the result for those who are
> so disposed will be first speechlessness (*aphasia*), but then freedom from
> worry (*ataraxia*); and Aenesidemus says pleasure.[25]

The question for Cordelia is whether this *epochē*, which does
indeed lead to *aphasia* in the sense of speechlessness, then leads
her to ataraxia (freedom from worry) or any kind of pleasure. I
think not. Instead, from the very opening scene of the play, Shakespeare develops the character of Cordelia as an example of what
scepticism might look like if we refused to compromise in times of
urgent need. The Pauline text makes it more readily an analogy to
the religious fanatic, and the Montaignian intertext makes it both.
Cordelia's fate in the play, in other words, can be understood in
light of Kuzner's as well as Cavell's work on Shakespeare's representation of the lived experience of scepticism. Like Kuzner, who
draws upon Hadot, who draws in turn upon Hellenistic thinkers
such as Pyrrho, I see Shakespeare as well as Montaigne as interested in philosophy as practice rather than philosophy as theory. In
contrast to Kuzner, however, I believe Shakespeare sees scepticism
as in the end more dangerous than beneficial, a pattern we can see
exemplified in Cordelia.[26]

More pointedly, when Cordelia insists that she cannot 'heave [her]
heart into [her] mouth', Shakespeare highlights her error in thinking that the primary purpose of speech or in her case, the refusal to
speak, is to safeguard her own emotions. She would be better served
using her capacity for language to save her own skin. As Montaigne
explains: 'man must endevour and enforce himselfe to resist and confront all things, first by effects, but if the worst befall, by reason and
by discourse' (405) ['se faut mettre en devoir et efforcer de combattre les choses, premierement par les effects, mais, au pis aller, par la
raison et par les discours' (II: 29, 706)].

Cordelia's death is Shakespeare's final reaction to the Antigonian
passages, a reprise of Cordelia's hesitation in the opening scene, as well
as a response to the agitated question Lear poses to Tom: 'Is man no
more than this?' The first sign Shakespeare might be looking back to
some of the initial sceptical intertext from Act I is when Lear refers to

the men around him as 'men of stone'. He begins to paint the embodied weakness of Cordelia and Lear himself in comparison to her murderers. Lear's references to eyes and tongues here recall the two main philosophical problems at stake: an epistemological question, whether sense-impressions are reliable, and an ethical question, whether discourse should be used to follow appearances when the need is life-threatening.

> Howl, howl, howl, howl! O, you are men of stone.
> Had I your tongues and eyes, I'ld use them so
> That heaven's vault should crack. She's gone for ever!
> I know when one is dead, and when one lives.
> She's dead as earth. Lend me a looking glass.
> If that her breath will mist or stain the stone,
> Why, then she lives.   (V, iii, 255–61)

Lear echoes Act I again when he describes Cordelia's voice as soft and womanly, as he declares his futile desire to hear what she is saying: 'What is't thou say'st? Her voice was ever soft, / Gentle, and low- an excellent thing in woman' (V, iii, 270–1). As a corpse, Cordelia does not speak. As a living being, however, she was equally speechless. As in the case of Coriolanus, who refuses to make the speeches that he needs to make, first, to become consul, then, second, to preserve his own life, Cordelia's silence reveals the dangers of the perfect *ou mallon,* perfect indifference, ultimately in the form of death.[27]

Lear then circles back to Tom as 'unaccommodated man'. Shocked by the visual appearance of Cordelia's body, Lear asks once again to be unbuttoned:

> And my poor fool is hang'd! No, no, no life!
> Why should a dog, a horse, a rat, have life,
> And thou no breath at all? Thou'lt come no more,
> Never, never, never, never, never!
> Pray you undo this button. Thank you, sir.
> Do you see this? Look on her! look! her lips!
> Look there, look there! *He dies.*
>
>   (V, iii, 304–9)

The Antigonian passages in Diogenes Laertius that Montaigne mentions in his *Essays* suggest a reading of these lines as a demonstration of the futility of Cordelia's speechlessness as well as Lear's unbuttoning. One cause of this tragedy was that Cordelia did not make herself heard or seen. She may not have wanted to speak from the heart, falsely converting her love into the impurity of words, but doing so would have protected her from physical harm. At the end of it all, Shakespeare's strongest message is cautionary.

It could also be said, however, that Shakespeare explores both of the possibilities of the Antigonian fragment. The frustrations of the cautionary interpretation are expressed in the dialogue between Lear and Tom; the problems with the prescriptive interpretation, in Cordelia's fate. This reading of Cordelia in light of Pyrrho, especially a Montaignian Pyrrho who explored the pitfalls of a living scepticism, suggests that Shakespeare's understanding of sceptical tradition was as complex and ambivalent as Montaigne's. Like Montaigne, Shakespeare sees a continuity between early Pyrrhonian and later, academic scepticism. Like Montaigne, Shakespeare distrusts fanaticism, including even thoroughgoing scepticism, which appears here as one possible form of the fanatic's 'constant' refusal to compromise.

Feeling Indifference, Acting against Our Hearts

In practice, flaying was rarely, if ever, used as punishment in premodern France and England. But its status as a feature of modern folklore, and its severity in the scant cases that did exist, made it a cultural staple. The case Foucault refers to from the late eighteenth century, the flaying of Damiens that opens *Discipline and Punish*, is a good example. The eyewitness Foucault quotes notes that it proved surprisingly difficult to skin Damiens alive:

> Though a strong, sturdy fellow, this executioner found it so difficult to tear away the pieces of flesh that he set about the same spot two or three times, twisting the pincers as he did so, and what he took away formed at each part a wound about the size of a six-pound crown piece.[28]

By focusing on the skin as both a liminal site for our humanity and a site of punishment where we feel pain, Montaigne and Shakespeare anticipate Foucault's interpretation of torture as 'epistemologico-juridical'. Foucault posits that, in the context of the modern penal system, the disappearance of spectacle and with it our connection to the condemned body has led us to 'take away life, but prevent the patient from feeling it; deprive the prisoner of all rights, [without inflicting] pain'.[29] In channelling suffering in his writing about the skin, Montaigne's goal, by contrast, was to keep our minds on the relationship between our actions, our ethics and our bodies; to strike at what he calls in 'Of the Institution and Education of Children' 'les nerfs' instead of 'le cœur' – the sinews rather than the heart – reinforcing a desire to circumvent the Pauline 'blindness of the hearts' of his readership by appealing to other senses and organs. Montaigne's didactic goal of affecting the body and its nerves over the heart and its passions is striking because, in the dictionaries, *tolerer* [to tolerate] is often characterised as acceptance *à contre cœur* [against one's heart]. [30] For Shakespeare's choice of the name Cordelia, this conflict between tolerance and the heart, surviving and perfect indifference, is epitomised in her name's relationship to varying iterations of the heart from the Latin *cor/cordis* [heart] to the English 'cordial' meaning of the heart or heartfelt. Tolerance in Shakespeare's *Lear*, by this light, is to go against Cordelia: *contre cœur*. We learn that by not following her model, we might arrive at a better outcome than her tragic death.

If we cannot strip off our humanity, how do we reconcile our human weakness with belief, whether philosophical scepticism or Christian faith? Cordelia's lesson appears to be that we speak against our hearts when necessary (*tolerer*), in the interest of self-preservation. We may be going *contre cœur*, but we are following the senses in order to save our skin, and perhaps even performing an act of tolerance. In this sense, when the Duke of Albany concludes the play, cautioning us to 'Speak what we feel, not what we ought to say', he reflects the equivalent of Montaigne's appealing to the nerves instead of to the heart. [31] Reading the word 'feel' as bodily (no more than skin deep) instead of emotional sheds new light on the sceptical message behind Albany's final moral statement: the 'ought' is the heart, and the 'feel' is the nerves and the sinews. In Pyrrhonian terms, we should use discourse and logic to save our skin, even if in doing so we display less than perfect indifference.

Notes

1. Tracy (ed.), *Flaying in the Pre-Modern World*, p. 7.
2. See Calhoun, *Montaigne and the Lives of the Philosophers*, pp. 85–6.
3. The interpretation of Pyrrho as a figure without belief is sometimes referred to as the 'indeterminacy theory' in Bett, *Pyrrho*, p. 57.
4. All references to the *Essays* are from Montaigne, ed. Viley and Salunier and will be cited in parentheses by book number, chapter number and page number. All English translations of Montaigne's *Essays* are from Montaigne, *Essayes*, trans. Florio and are cited by page number only.
5. For more on their original source, see Bett, *Pyrrho*, p. 84.
6. For more on the interest of the provenance of the Antigonian passage, see Bett, *Pyrrho*, p. 66.

7. Another such source we will explore below is Eusebius's *Praeparatio evangelica*.
8. In Bett, *Pyrrho*.
9. Diogenes Laertius, *Lives of Eminent Philosophers* 9.66.
10. I would like to thank Patrick Gray for this reference, for which there are others in *Cor* I, iii and ix, and V, vi.
11. See Quint's discussion in *Montaigne and the Quality of Mercy*, p. x.
12. Aulotte, *Amyot et Plutarque*, p. 104.
13. For a recent discussion of Michelangelo's self-portraits in *The Last Judgment* and a full bibliography regarding the debate about the tonsured self-portrait, see Barnes, 'Self-Portraits in Michelangelo's *Last Judgment*', pp. 969–86, esp. n. 8.
14. See Quint, *Montaigne and the Quality of Mercy*, pp. x–xi.
15. For Cynicism, see E. M. M. Taylor, 'Lear's Philosopher'; Donawerth, 'Diogenes the Cynic and Lear's Definition of Man'; Butler, 'Who Are King Lear's Philosophers?'; Doloff, 'The Alexander/Diogenes Paradigm in *King Lear*'; Shannon, 'Animal Sovereignty, Human Negative Exceptionalism, and the Natural History of *King Lear*'; and Hershinow, 'Diogenes the Cynic and Shakespeare's Bitter Fool', p. 5. For the Christian tradition, see Hoffman, 'Montaigne, Lear, and the Question of the Afterlife'.
16. In keeping with Kuzner and in contrast to Cavell, this study of these early modern authors' sceptical discourse looks backward to the nuances of different forms of ancient Scepticism rather than forward to the doubt of Descartes.
17. All references to *Lear* follow the Arden 3 edition ed. Foakes.
18. '[B] Nous ne sçavons pas distinguer la peau de la chemise. [C] C'est assés de s'enfariner le visage, sans s'enfariner la poictrine. [B] J'en vois qui se transforment et se transsubstantient en autant de nouvelles figures et de nouveaux estres qu'ils entreprennent de charges, et qui se prelatent jusques au foye et aux intestins, et entreinent leur office jusques en leur garderobe' (III: 10, 1011–12).
19. I have cited several, though would add that my analysis aligns significantly with Hershinow, because I also identify the Cynical as problematic, unbeneficial and ironic.
20. See Hershinow, 'Diogenes the Cynic and Shakespeare's Bitter Fool' for more on what Hershinow calls the 'composite Cynic stance'.
21. See Cavell, *Disowning Knowledge*, ch. 2.
22. See Quint, 'Montaigne and the Suicide Bombers'.
23. 'La grandeur de l'ame n'est pas tant tirer à mont et tirer avant comme sçavoir se ranger et circonscrire. Elle tient pour grand tout ce qui est assez, et montre sa hauteur à aimer mieux les choses moyennes que les eminentes' (III: 13, 1110).
24. Note that there are Pauline undertones to the reaction of Lear when he mentions barbarous Scythian; compare Paul's ideal that among Christians, there is no difference between Jew, Greek, barbarian or Scythian (Col. 3:9–11).

25. Aristocles in Eusebius's *Praeparatio evangelica* 14.18.1–5, cited in and translated by Bett, *Pyrrho*, p. 16. I assume here that Shakespeare was familiar with these notions through his reading of Montaigne, but there is support for the idea that Shakespeare, too, read Sextus Empiricus. On the case for Shakespeare's reading of Sextus, see Hamlin, *Tragedy and Scepticism in Shakespeare's England and* 'A Lost Translation Found? An Edition of *The Sceptick (ca. 1590)*'.

26. For Shakespeare's Hamlet as endangered by the practice of a kind of Scepticism, like the Cordelia I paint here, see Patrick Gray, 'HIDE THY SELFE'.

27. Note that this turn of phrase is Sextus's rather than necessarily Pyrrho's. See Bett, *Pyrrho*, p. 31.

28. Foucault, *Discipline and Punish*, p. 4.

29. Ibid. p. 11.

30. Defining *tolerer as* 'against the heart' is certainly the case by 1695 in France. See Bossuet, *Méditations sur l'Évangile*, p. 231.

31. This understanding of 'feel' as related to the bodily senses rather than the passions is in keeping with the use of 'feel' as a synonym for 'touch' in this period.

Chapter 9

On Belief in Montaigne and Shakespeare
William M. Hamlin

Les uns font accroire au monde qu'ils croyent ce qu'ils ne croyent pas. Les autres, en plus grand nombre, se le font accroire à eux mesmes, ne sçachants pas penetrer que c'est que croire.[1]

Debate about Shakespeare's literary and intellectual ties to Montaigne has taken a decided turn in recent decades, shifting from a predominant emphasis on influence (Montaigne as 'source') to a more fundamental consideration of affinity and dissonance between two extraordinary writers. Discussions of scepticism, meanwhile, have retained their longstanding centrality in Montaigne studies while growing increasingly prominent in Shakespearean scholarship. I propose to draw these trends into alignment by adopting an epistemological perspective and suggesting that belief is presented in Shakespeare's works as a much more attractive feature of human cognitive behaviour than it is in the *Essays* of Montaigne.[2] In grounding this argument I depend not so much on cognitive psychology or contemporary theories of mind as on historically influential contemplations of knowing, doubting and believing.[3]

Belief has been defined in many ways, and in the following pages I will refer to several important definitions, but for the purposes of this chapter I will rely on a broad, uncontroversial understanding of the term that accords with common usage: 'belief' designates the cognitive state in which a proposition or phenomenon whose truth or existence is not evident is nonetheless accepted as true or real.[4] And by 'evident' I do not limit my meaning to the self-evident (i.e., the formally true or internally demonstrable). That which is consistently manifest to sense-perception or open to empirical confirmation through scientific or documentary analysis also meets the evidential standard by which I abide; there is no need here for Cartesian rigour and I certainly won't posit a *malin génie*.[5] But while I admire David Hume's argument that belief, in essence, is 'a lively idea related to or associated with a present impression [in the mind]', I intend to bring questions of truth to bear on the matter of belief, acknowledging all the while that common understandings of truth-status are often quite distinct from those debated by theorists of knowledge.[6] In accordance with the terms I propose, then, believing what we know to be true is gratuitous: people do not believe that Bolivia is landlocked, that pterodactyls once existed, that three is the square root of nine, that the Earth orbits the Sun, and so on. Or, if they do, their beliefs are indistinguishable from their knowledge, and therefore trivial. Likewise, people do not believe what they know to be false, although they may pretend to do so, as Shakespeare demonstrates in Sonnet 138:

> When my love swears that she is made of truth,
> I do believe her, though I know she lies,
> That she might think me some untutored youth,
> Unlearnèd in the world's false subtleties.[7]

In cases, however, where people commit themselves to the truth of ideas or propositions whose truth-status is unknown, unwarranted or apparently indeterminable, their acts of belief extend beyond the reach of whatever reasons they offer in justification or support. And to this extent, non-trivial belief puts people at risk, makes them vulnerable, exposes them to potential mockery, shame, correction. Shakespeare, I suggest, admires this phenomenon – this embracing as true that which may be false – more than does Montaigne. His view may perhaps resemble that of Saint Augustine, whose commentaries on the Gospel of John include the argument that understanding flows from belief rather than the other way around.[8] At all events, Shakespeare strikes me as sympathetic to belief in a way that Montaigne is not, even though Montaigne is a professed believer in a complex metaphysical system to which Shakespeare's attitude remains far less clear.

But is such an opinion susceptible to demonstration, or is it merely impressionistic? Montaigne certainly displays concern for the potential perils of dogmatic belief and ideological interpellation with an intensity that Shakespeare tends not to exhibit, but this difference between the two writers is far from absolute and, as Lars Engle has argued in an important essay on *King Lear*, Shakespeare shares with Montaigne an evident hatred of cruelty, recognising that 'commitment to abstract principles' can sometimes facilitate the unleashing of cruelty among those who have power to hurt.[9] Commitment to abstract principles is not in every instance a form of belief, but I do not think we are much inclined to balk at the notion that Edmund believes in Nature's 'law' (as opposed to 'custom' and 'the curiosity of nations') or that Iago believes in self-determination (as opposed to 'obsequious bondage' to social superiors).[10] Nonetheless, I would suggest that specific instances of belief exhibited by Richard II, John of Gaunt, the Bishop of Carlisle, Portia (in *The Merchant of Venice*), Bassanio, Hotspur, Friar Francis (in *Much Ado about Nothing*), Fluellen, Michael Williams, Orlando, Hamlet, Ophelia, Viola, Lafeu, Helen (in *All's Well That Ends Well*), Duke Vincentio, Mariana, Emilia (in *Othello*), Edgar, Kent, Banquo, Hermione, Camillo, Paulina, Gonzalo and dozens of other Shakespearean figures are meant to be perceived as essentially admirable, even charismatic, and that, by contrast, the disruptive beliefs of Leontes, Posthumus, Gloucester, Othello, Bertram, Claudio (in *Much Ado*) and perhaps even Edmund are presented as temporary, aberrant and possibly at odds with deeper predispositions that may not yet have been subjected to adequate self-scrutiny. In ways such as these, then, I would claim that Shakespearean depictions of belief convey a stronger level of authorial sympathy than do comparable depictions in Montaigne.

But belief in Montaigne is difficult to investigate – and not merely because we are concerned with an historical individual rather than with fictional characters, and thus with a body of evidence that includes but exceeds the words Montaigne has left us. The Shakespearean entity we call 'Kent', after all, is essentially finite inasmuch as it is comprised of the words spoken by Kent, the actions attributed to Kent and the ways in which Kent is perceived and discussed by other similar entities within the same verbal object.[11] We can therefore speak with considerable confidence about beliefs that Kent holds with respect to monarchical authority, social subordination, loyalty, service and so forth, and we can make defensible inferences about Shakespeare's attitude towards these beliefs. This is not the case with Montaigne. Not only did he exist for almost sixty years in more or less the same ways that we exist, but the vast majority of what he perceived, thought, said, knew and believed during that existence has vanished from the possibility of our apprehension. Whether what remains is reliably representative of Montaigne is a question we cannot answer with certainty, since we do not know what we do not know. Even if the archives yield new writings by Montaigne or new allusions to his life and work, this will not change the fact that most of Montaigne is irretrievable. We must also acknowledge that in his essays he often contradicts himself – indeed, that he does so consciously – and that at one point he perceptively notes that 'we are, I know not how, double within ourselves, with the result that we do not believe what we believe, and cannot rid ourselves of what we condemn' (469). He emphasises, moreover, that he sometimes refrains from saying all that he thinks: 'I speak the truth, not my fill of it, but as much as I dare speak' (611). Still, despite such complications, most scholars would find it plausible to claim that Montaigne displays belief in multiple non-evident and therefore debatable propositions: that cruelty is indefensible; that ascetic renunciation is foolish; that pride, presumption, inconstancy and self-deception are ubiquitous, transhistorical human traits; that people are endowed with immaterial, immortal souls which are somehow linked to an omniscient, all-powerful deity; and that this deity intervenes in the fallen realm of humanity by extending grace that enables faith and by revealing inviolable truths in a vast collection of texts known as Holy Scripture.

What, then, is the problem? Are these beliefs not attractive? Even if some of them might prove to be instances of false consciousness, are they not essentially benign? If Montaigne were a Shakespearean character holding beliefs of this sort, would we not find him sympathetic? Would we not suspect that Shakespeare looked favourably upon his tendencies towards commitment, risk and self-exposure? One way to approach these questions is to examine how Montaigne reaches his beliefs – and how he imagines that others typically reach theirs. In this way, perhaps, we can move towards a fuller understanding of central differences between the ways in which belief is assessed in Montaigne and in Shakespeare.

Take, for example, the first moment in the 'Apology for Raymond Sebond' where Judaeo-Christian belief is mentioned in an explicitly sceptical context:

> We are much better if we let ourselves be led without inquisitiveness in the way of the world. A soul guaranteed against prejudice is marvellously advanced toward tranquility. People who judge and check their judges never submit to them as they ought. How much more docile and easily led, both by the laws of religion and by political laws, are the simple and incurious minds, than those minds that survey divine and human causes like pedagogues! There is nothing in man's invention that has so much verisimilitude and usefulness [as Pyrrhonian scepticism]. It presents man naked and empty, acknowledging his natural weakness, fit to receive from above some outside power; stripped of human knowledge, and all the more apt to lodge divine knowledge in himself,

> annihilating his judgment to make more room for faith; neither disbe-
> lieving nor setting up any doctrine against the common observances;
> humble, obedient, teachable, zealous; a sworn enemy of heresy, and
> consequently free from the vain and irreligious opinions introduced by
> false sects. He is a blank tablet prepared to take from the finger of God
> such forms as he shall be pleased to engrave on it. (375)

The link established here between Pyrrhonism and divine enlightenment is nowhere present in the principal source on which Montaigne
relies in his account of sceptical practice. For Sextus Empiricus, the
'causal principle of scepticism is the hope of becoming tranquil'.[12]
But for Montaigne, the modern-day Pyrrhonist disables critical
judgement so as to make room for faith. It is true that Sextus repeatedly stresses that sceptics live in accordance with the laws, customs
and teachings of the cultures they inhabit, but living in this way is
explicitly distinguished from holding opinions about those customs
(e.g. 9, 143). And in this respect Sextus's treatment of scepticism
differs sharply from that provided in another major source, Cicero's
The Nature of the Gods, to which Montaigne alludes several times
prior to the passage I have quoted from the 'Apology'. Gaius Cotta,
Cicero's spokesman for Academic scepticism, presents devastating
critiques of Epicurean and Stoic thought, but when Quintus Balbus (a stalwart Stoic) reminds him of his religious affiliations, Cotta
offers the following clarification:

> I take considerably to heart your authority, Balbus, and the comments
> at the close of your discourse, in which you urged me to remember that
> I am not just Cotta, but also a priest. The point you were making, I
> imagine, was that I should defend the beliefs about the immortal gods
> which we have inherited from our ancestors, together with our sacrifices,
> ceremonies, and religious observances. I shall indeed defend them, and
> I have always done so; no words from any person, whether learned or
> unlearned, will ever budge me from the views which I inherited from our
> ancestors concerning the worship of the immortal gods.[13]

In stating his willingness to defend Roman beliefs about the gods,
Cotta goes well beyond the attitude of living-in-accordance-with outlined by Sextus, and indeed he later informs Balbus that he believes
these gods exist – though not because the Stoics say they do (113).
Such belief in non-evident phenomena certainly amounts to 'opinion' (that is, dogmatic assertion) from the Pyrrhonian perspective,
and it serves as a better analogue to religious attitudes expressed by
Montaigne than does the more cautious orientation described by

Sextus, even though it is Sextus's view to which Montaigne primarily alludes in the 'Apology'.[14]

This is not the place to offer an account of epistemological differences between Pyrrhonian and Academic scepticism; several excellent studies of the topic have been published during the past half-century.[15] Suffice it to say here that while Montaigne is well aware of various key distinctions – 'the Academics [have] despaired of their quest' whereas 'Pyrrho and other Skeptics . . . are still in search of the truth' (371) – he tends nevertheless to situate both sceptical schools in opposition to the Stoics, Epicureans, Peripatetics and other purveyors of positive knowledge. 'Of three general sects of philosophy,' he writes, 'two make express profession of doubt and ignorance; and in that of the dogmatists, which is the third, it is easy to discover that most of them have put on the mask of assurance only to look better' (375). This tendency indeed extends to Montaigne's view of their attitude towards social existence, in so far as both schools find themselves obliged 'to bow to civil law' (380).[16] In short, Montaigne's partial conflation of Academic and Pyrrhonian scepticism allows him to present his subscription to Judaeo-Christian truth as social conformity in the Sextian mode, even though his characterisation of this conformity is often much closer to the model of active belief we see in Cicero's Cotta.[17]

It is worth remembering, too, that a great many of Montaigne's post-1588 additions to the *Essays* derive from the writings of Cicero (especially from the *Academics*, *The Nature of the Gods* and *The Tusculan Disputations*), whereas no conclusive evidence indicates that Montaigne continued to read Sextus after the initial publication of his book in 1580. A weakening or dilution of Montaigne's understanding of the Pyrrhonian orientation towards social conformity thus seems an inference we may plausibly draw given what we know of his reading habits and his manner of broaching Judaeo-Christian belief within the epistemological context of ancient scepticism.

A related point may be made with regard to another Montaignian passage several pages earlier in the 'Apology'. After condemning pride and curiosity as the traits that led most directly to the Fall, Montaigne volunteers the following pronouncement:

> Our powers are so far from conceiving the sublimity of God, that of the works of our creator those bear his stamp most clearly, and are most his, that we understand least. To Christians it is an occasion for belief to encounter something incredible. It is the more according to reason as it is contrary to human reason. (368–9)[18]

It is not often in the *Essays* that we encounter blatantly unfalsifiable claims such as these, but the notion that we should exercise our belief in the face of that which we least understand seems oddly appropriate as a prelude to the way in which Montaigne subsequently distorts Pyrrhonian epistemology. It is as though he conceives of the human capacity for belief as a muscle that requires occasional flexing – a muscle we would not possess if we were not likely to confront scenarios where its presence will be crucial to our successful negotiation of mystery, ignorance or uncertainty. When we rule out belief as a viable response, we are left in the position of those who restrict the will of God and the power of Nature to the limits and irregularities of their own intellectual capacities. And for Montaigne this is never a promising attitude.[19] Yet it remains the case that belief is ineradicably stigmatised in the *Essays*, since there are so many humans who believe out of desire, convention, cowardice, infirmity, sloth or exhausted acquiescence rather than out of sustained inquiry and reflection: 'This is why children, common people, women, and sick people are most subject to being led by the ears' (132).[20] It is an 'annoying malady', Montaigne says elsewhere, 'to think yourself so wise that you persuade yourself that no one can believe the contrary' (231). 'To what notions will the laxness of human credulity not submit!' (698). Those who believe because they lack the resilience of mind to resist impressions proffered by mere allegation (or entertained with mere satisfaction) will always taint the general concept of belief, if not specific beliefs themselves.[21]

Montaigne's allusion to people who reduce God and Nature to the measure of their own 'capacity and confidence' (132) invites comparison to Sir Francis Bacon's famous discussion of the 'Idols' in his *New Organon*, and particularly to his aphorisms concerning Idols of the Tribe.[22] Resorting to a characteristically iconoclastic style, Bacon argues that

> it is a false assertion that the sense of man is the measure of things. On the contrary, all perceptions as well of the sense as of the mind are according to the measure of the individual and not according to the measure of the universe. And the human understanding is like a false mirror, which, receiving rays irregularly, distorts and discolours the nature of things by mingling its own nature with it. (48)

Because the Idols of the Tribe, in Bacon's view, constitute innate problems of human understanding, they are not subject (as are the Idols of the Theatre) to complete eradication, although their damage can be mitigated through the exercise of restraint, repeated observation, cautious empirical reasoning and the formation of maxims through 'true induction' (e.g. 41, 48). But when it comes to the 'playbooks of philosophical systems' (58), Bacon is severe, particularly with respect to systems incorporating an 'admixture of theology':

> some of the moderns have with extreme levity indulged so far as to attempt to found a system of natural philosophy on the first chapter of Genesis, on the Book of Job, and other parts of the sacred writings, seeking for the dead among the living; which also makes the inhibition and repression of it the more important, because from this unwholesome mixture of things human and divine there arises not only a fantastic philosophy but also a heretical religion. Very meet it is therefore that we be sober-minded, and give to faith that only which is faith's. (62)

Repeating a formulation offered in his Preface to 'The Great Instauration', Bacon delivers a pre-emptive strike here, forcefully segregating 'things human' from 'things divine' in such a manner as to facilitate the reformation and advancement of learning.[23] And one senses that the ontological division he imagines is even more pronounced than that which we encounter in Montaigne. For Bacon, presumably, belief within the sphere of 'things human' will operate (i.e., to the extent that it will operate at all) in concert with the rules and practices of his 'instauration', whereas, for Montaigne, belief appropriate to the sphere of 'things divine' can at times serve as a model for belief within the human sphere, since both spheres predicate human ignorance and presumption.[24] Montaigne, moreover, approaches 'things divine' (at least in the 'Apology') from the premises of Pyrrhonian scepticism, and thus his readers often experience a sense of deflation as they encounter the apparent non sequitur of his movement into what Richard Popkin has termed 'Christian Pyrrhonism': a fideistic leap redescribed as sceptical tranquility.[25] Sextus Empiricus would never have countenanced such a deployment of Pyrrhonian argumentation. Here, for instance, is the sort of consideration Sextus extends to deity:

> Since the majority have asserted that god is a most active cause, let us first consider god, remarking by way of preface that, following ordinary life without opinions, we say that there are gods and we are pious toward the gods and say that they are provident: . . . [but] even granting that god is indeed conceivable, it is necessary to suspend judgement about whether gods exist or not, so far as the Dogmatists are concerned. For it is not clear that gods exist: . . . we will not be able to say how it is

apprehended that there are gods, since it is neither apparent in itself nor apprehended by way of any effects. For this reason too, then, it is inapprehensible whether there are any gods.[26]

Sextus subjects 'things divine' to the same rational scrutiny he reserves for all other non-evident phenomena, and to this extent we may say that he imagines a single, undivided ontological realm, one in which Pyrrhonian inquiry can be pursued in every direction. But this appears not to be an option for Montaigne or for Bacon, nor indeed for Gianfrancesco Pico della Mirandola, one of Sextus's first Renaissance readers: Pico regarded Christianity as 'immune to sceptical infection because it does not depend on the dogmatic philosophies that Sextus had refuted'.[27] In the end, it would seem that the ideological force field of Judaeo-Christian thought is sufficiently powerful in early modern Europe to preclude the possibility of thoroughgoing, openly avowed investigation from a strict Pyrrhonian standpoint.[28] And one consequence of this seeming fact is that large realms of experience and imagination are reserved for belief that functions as knowledge rather than for knowledge that obviates belief.

With Shakespeare, for whom caveats concerning biographical irretrievability are even more pertinent than they are with Montaigne, the question at issue might be seen as coming down to this: are the beliefs of specific characters typically accompanied by the sort of reflective humility that Montaigne recommends, but without being compromised by indolence, uncritical credulity, or inability to comprehend what is at stake? There is, of course, no single answer to such a question, but on the whole I would say yes, they are. Hermione, for instance, fully grasps the long-term implications of her husband's outrageous accusation, yet she answers him with astonishing composure and generosity:

> How will this grieve you
> When you shall come to clearer knowledge, that
> You thus have published me! Gentle my lord,
> You scarce can right me throughly then to say
> You did mistake.
>
> (*WT* II, i, 97–101)

Hermione believes that Leontes will regain his senses and find himself tormented by his grotesque misprision. But she knows that her marital relationship has been forever altered. Even at this early stage in the arc of her husband's pathology, it is evident to her that nothing he might later say or do can ever compensate for the damage he has inflicted.

Yet while he will be unable to change the past by repenting his errors of judgement, Leontes will seek to 'right' Hermione as 'throughly' as is humanly possible. This, I suggest, is what she believes.

But if Hermione seems too otherworldly to serve as a representative example of Shakespearean attitudes towards belief, take Ophelia, particularly in this crucial interchange with Hamlet:

HAMLET:　I did love you once.
OPHELIA:　Indeed, my lord, you made me believe so.
HAMLET:　You should not have believed me, for virtue cannot so inoculate our old stock but we shall relish of it. I loved you not.
OPHELIA:　I was the more deceived.

(*Ham* III, i, 113–18)

That Hamlet is lying when he says 'I loved you not' seems beyond reasonable doubt, but for our purposes what matters is that Ophelia takes him at his word, acknowledging without hesitation that she was deceived in her belief that he loved her. Nothing about this confession suggests that Shakespeare wants us to think less of Ophelia for having made herself vulnerable. On the contrary, our sense that Hamlet abuses her is largely premised on our recognition and approval of her venturous sensitivity — her capacity, that is, for extending and enduring belief. Or take Helen in *All's Well That Ends Well*, specifically at the moment when she seeks the Countess's permission to visit the ailing King in Paris:

COUNTESS: He and his physicians
Are of a mind: he, that they cannot help him;
They, that they cannot help. How shall they credit
A poor unlearnèd virgin when the schools,
Embowelled of their doctrine, have left off
The danger to itself?
HELEN: There's something in't
More than my father's skill, which was the greatest
Of his profession, that his good receipt
Shall for my legacy be sanctified
By th' luckiest stars in heaven. And would your honour
But give me leave to try success, I'd venture
The well-lost life of mine on his grace's cure
By such a day, an hour.
COUNTESS: Dost thou believe't?
HELEN: Ay, madam, knowingly.

(*AW* I, iii, 222–35)

Helen is not saying that she knows her cure will work; she's saying that she believes it will work as though she knew this for a truth. She believes it knowingly, so to speak. And soon afterwards the King is prepared to mirror her belief, having been as impressed by it as was the Countess. Upon posing a similar question ('Art thou so confident?' (II, i, 157)) and receiving similarly devout assurances, he agrees to Helen's terms and commits himself to her care: 'More should I question thee, and more I must, / Though more to know could not be more to trust'   (*AW* II, i, 204–5). The King's trust is structurally identical to belief as I have defined it, which is to say that it exceeds whatever rational or evidential grounds might be marshalled to warrant its legitimacy. And the King is aware of this – acutely conscious that he is risking his reputation, just as Helen is risking her life. But he trusts Helen knowingly.

One final example. When Michael Williams engages in debate with the disguised King Henry on the night before Agincourt, he begins by asserting that 'there are few die well that die in a battle'; he then adds that 'if these men do not die well, it will be a black matter for the King that led them to it – who to disobey were against all proportion of subjection' (*H5* IV, i, 131–5). Williams thus disputes the reassuring claim of Bates ('our obedience to the King wipes the crime of it out of us' (123–4)) while simultaneously bringing the King's responsibility into sharp focus. Henry counters this move by declaring that '[t]he King is not bound to answer the particular endings of his soldiers' (143–4). But then, perhaps recognising the doubtful validity of this remark in its current context, he adds that 'War is [God's] beadle. War is his vengeance' (155).[29] As a dogmatic assertion on a non-evident matter, such a claim changes everything, for if it is true, Williams's critique of the King is nullified; soldiers who fail to 'die well' are simply being punished for prior guilt. Henry has produced a watertight, unfalsifiable explanation for battlefield mortality, and he seals his victory with rhetorical flair: 'Every subject's duty is the King's, but every subject's soul is his own' (161–2).

There is no suggestion in this scene that Williams lacks the intelligence or presence of mind to pursue debate with his mysterious interlocutor, but he elects not to do so, instead conceding that ''Tis certain, every man that dies ill, the ill upon his own head. The King is not to answer it' (170–1). This concession carries the force of a belief claim. Williams might have responded that Henry's formulation, despite its tidiness, seems unsatisfactory in the face of various potential scenarios, for instance the case of a soldier who receives the sacrament of penance before battle (and who is therefore 'unspotted' [148]), but who nonetheless 'dies ill' because his subsequent behaviour in combat is 'uncharitable' – even though such behaviour is inescapable when 'blood is [one's] argument' and disobedience to the King 'against all proportion of subjection' (131–5). But Williams eschews rational disputation and extends belief to a non-evident claim. It's difficult not to suspect that Montaigne would be more troubled by this volte-face than Shakespeare seems to be; at the very least I imagine that he would make it clear that responses other than the one on which Williams settles can easily be conceived. Establishing multiple perspectives, after all, is one of the essayist's most fundamental modes of contemplation. But Shakespeare allows Williams's dignity to remain unruffled, and many readers have found themselves drawn to this character's forthright manner and willingness to subordinate himself to mystery. Williams's belief, though incompatible with Pyrrhonian practice – or, for that matter, with W. K. Clifford's uncompromising principle that 'it is wrong always, everywhere, and for anyone to believe anything on insufficient evidence' – proceeds not from gullibility but from reflective commitment to an assertion laying claim to his sense of intercommunal responsibility, a concern to which Shakespeare has shown us Williams is highly attuned.[30]

It must, of course, be added that believing is more dramatic than knowing, and we should never discount such a factor when considering Shakespeare or any playwright. But in the end it is not at all surprising that belief is absent from the epistemological hierarchy described by Cicero and paraphrased with approbation by Montaigne:

> Zeno pictured in a gesture his conception of this division of the faculties of the soul: the hand spread and open was appearance; the hand half shut and the fingers a little hooked, consent; the closed fist, comprehension; when with his left hand he closed his fist still tighter, knowledge. (372)[31]

In an explanatory schema such as this, belief can have no place. For Cicero, an idea's appearance of truthfulness serves as a prerequisite for our consent to that idea, where consent is not belief but provisional acceptance that the idea's apparent truth is genuine; consent in turn serves as a prerequisite for comprehension – and comprehension for knowledge. Belief, meanwhile, has been excluded from visual representation and indeed reasoned out of existence.[32]

But belief *does* exist, as we all know. And because it can lead to tragedy, as with Othello, Leontes, Lear, Gloucester, Posthumus and others, we admire Montaigne's cautionary wisdom: 'in a slippery and treacherous place let us suspend our belief' (378); 'it is better to lean toward doubt than toward assurance in things difficult to prove and dangerous to believe' (789–90). Acknowledging our durable pre-disposition towards folly, Montaigne steers us away from self-righteousness, overconfidence, fanaticism and precipitous acceptance of questionable claims. Shakespeare, meanwhile, though equally conscious of our fallibility, is finally more interested in the collective healing and enhanced solidarity we stand to gain by mutual trust, self-subordination, and the extension of belief to ideas whose truth we cannot prove. This is not to deny or forget that Montaigne is aware of and embraces a more refined form of belief: a belief tempered by scepticism and humility, similar in many ways to the learned ignorance adumbrated by Erasmus in his *Praise of Folly* and sharply implied by the extract from the 'Apology' that I have chosen as an epigraph to this chapter.[33] But belief of this sort is hard won – the result of sustained dialectical interchange between practices of doubt and affirmation. It is not the belief that Montaigne found commonly exemplified in the world he inhabited.[34]

In that world, from our perspective more than four centuries later, we can identify what might be described as a substratum of pre-critical assumptions, biases, persuasions, acceptances, trustings, intuitions and thought-habits: a set of conceptual 'givens' or 'hinge-commitments' that serve as crucial prerequisites for critical reflection but which are themselves stubbornly resistant to rational scrutiny within such reflection.[35] No doubt there are similar givens in my own thinking – and in that of every other person, regardless of time or place. To be sure, we find more evidence for this claim in the writings of Montaigne and Bacon than we do in those of Shakespeare, but I suspect that this may be explained primarily with reference to genre rather than to essential differences in cognition. Shakespeare, I would argue, is largely sympathetic to opinions and beliefs that emerge from within this pre-reflective realm, and which indeed appear to function quite regularly as presuppositions in Montaigne's own cerebral and creaturely life. Montaigne, meanwhile, strikes me as much less sympathetic to such forms of belief, and this tendency appears to derive from greater general reliance on rational inspection of the very sort he condemns in the 'Apology' yet elsewhere confesses he often relies on, for instance in 'It is folly to measure the true and false by our own capacity' (132–3). So while Montaigne is dependent on pre-critical assumptions for the activation of his routine habits of inquiry, he displays a markedly vexed attitude towards them and indeed cannot assimilate them within his mature outlook without having first assayed them: having subjected them, that is, to the operations of his critical intellect. Particularly in this way, then, Montaigne's intellectual ambition is at once more exacting, more expansive and more historically responsive than that of Shakespeare, and he frequently concerns himself with what we stand to lose through unexamined, precipitous or self-serving belief. Shakespeare's imaginative resources, however, are more powerful and pervasive than Montaigne's, and within the scope of his fictions he extends tremendous admiration towards the believing temperament that, while it always bears the potential of drawing us into catastrophe, may also create the very conditions within which charitable forms of coexistence, otherwise unattainable, may finally be achieved.

Notes

1. Montaigne, *Essais*, ed. Villey and rev. Saulnier, II: 12, p. 442. In Frame's translation: 'Some make the world believe that they believe what they do not believe. Others, in greater number, make themselves believe it, being unable to penetrate what it means to believe' (p. 322). Subsequent quotations from Montaigne are drawn from Frame's translation; I use in-text citation hereafter. All quotations from Shakespeare derive from *The Norton Shakespeare*, 3rd edn, ed. Stephen Greenblatt et al. I wish to thank Lars Engle, Patrick Gray, Jordana Lobo-Pires, Howard Marchitello, Amos Rothschild, Richard Strier and Suzanne Tartamella for their detailed and thoughtful responses to this chapter.
2. I have touched upon this idea once previously, in 'Conscience and the God-surrogate', pp. 237–60, esp. p. 258.
3. E.g., Cicero, *The Nature of the Gods*; Paul's letters to the Romans and Corinthians (e.g., Rom. 8:24–5, 1 Cor. 13:12, 2 Cor. 4:18, 2 Cor. 5:7); Sextus Empiricus, *Outlines of Scepticism*; Bacon, *New Organon*; Descartes, *Philosophical Writings*; Pascal, *Pensées* and *Discussion with Monsieur de Sacy*; Hume, *Treatise of Human Nature*; Emerson, 'Montaigne; Or, the Skeptic'; Clifford, 'The Ethics of Belief'; James, 'The Will to Believe'; Russell, *The Problems of Philosophy*; Wittgenstein, *On Certainty*; C. S. Lewis, *Mere Christianity*; and Bernard Williams, 'Deciding to Believe', pp. 136–51. Although I disagree with David Wootton's implication that Montaigne's protestations of Roman Catholic orthodoxy are merely 'concessions to the censor' (p. 559), I have learned much from *The Invention of Science*, esp. chs 7–11, 13 and 17.
4. See, e.g., 'belief' in the *OED*. I: 'Mental conviction'; I.2: 'The mental action, condition, or habit of trusting to or having confidence in a person or thing; trust, dependence, reliance, confidence, faith'; I.4.a:

'Something believed; a proposition or set of propositions held to be true'; I.5.b: 'Acceptance or conviction of the existence or occurrence of something'; I.6: 'Acceptance that a statement, supposed fact, etc., is true; a religious, philosophical, or personal conviction; an opinion, a persuasion'; I.7: 'Assent to a proposition, statement, or fact, esp. on the grounds of testimony or authority, or in the absence of proof or conclusive evidence.' That belief is a propositional attitude is a standard view among contemporary philosophers. The *Stanford Encyclopedia of Philosophy* defines belief as 'the attitude we have, roughly, whenever we take something to be the case or regard it as true' (https://plato.stanford.edu/entries/belief/). Belief is generally regarded as a much larger category than knowledge; the latter is typically understood as belief that is both justified and true.

5. Non-evidence of the truth or reality of propositions or phenomena is also usually taken to include a lack of plausible justification (i.e., above and beyond the lack of self-evidence or empirical demonstration). See the discussion of evidentialism in the *Stanford Encyclopedia*'s entry on epistemology in religion (https://plato.stanford.edu/entries/religion-epistemology/).

6. Hume, *Treatise*, p. 67; see pp. 65–85 for Hume's full argument. I will speak for the most part of *belief* rather than of *faith*, as I view the latter as a species of the former (cp. *KL* I, i, 219–21); belief is the more representative term in a broad epistemological context. Faith can also carry connotations of feeling or sensation which are seldom associated with belief; see, for example, Pascal's claim that 'It is the heart that feels God, not reason: that is what faith is. God felt by the heart, not by reason' (*Pensées*, fragment 680, p. 157). And see C. S. Lewis, *Mere Christianity*, pp. 138–50. I will also speak of *trust*, which is structurally similar to belief but more typically embedded within complex interpersonal relations – and less oriented towards concerns of truth. For conceptions of truth in Montaigne and in the philosophical presuppositions of early modern Europe, see Maclean, 'Montaigne and the Truth of the Schools', pp. 142–62.

7. *Norton Shakespeare*, p. 2297. I exclude cases of self-deception from this category because the self-deceived person erects barriers to self-knowledge: for example, the dogmatist considers himself open-minded because he prevents himself from knowing his unwillingness to entertain alternative viewpoints.

8. 'Do you want to understand? Believe. For God said through the prophet' [Isaiah 7.9]: 'Unless you believe, you will not understand . . . Therefore, seek not to understand so that you may believe, but believe so that you may understand' (*The Fathers of the Church, Volume 88: Tractates on the Gospel of John 28–54*, ed. John W. Rettig [New York: Catholic University Press of America, 2010], pp. 17–18). Compare the prayer of Saint Anselm: 'Grant me to understand you to be as I believe

you to be' (*Proslogion*, p. 117). Emerson presents a less potent concep-
tion of belief, though one still reliant upon an unfalsifiable premise:
'Belief consists in accepting the affirmations of the soul' ('Montaigne;
Or, the Skeptic', p. 299).

9. Engle, 'Sovereign Cruelty', p. 119.
10. *KL* I, ii, 1–4; *Oth* I, i, 40–63.
11. To be precise, I should say 'objects', since Kent exists in both the 1608
    Quarto and 1623 Folio texts of *Lear*. But Kent's finitude remains
    unchanged.
12. Sextus, *Outlines*, p. 5. For a partial English translation of Sextus cir-
    culating in England around 1590, see my article 'A Lost Translation
    Found?'
13. Cicero, *The Nature of the Gods*, p. 109.
14. For example, Montaigne, *Essays*, trans. Frame, pp. 374, 380. Compare
    Sextus, *Outlines*, p. 9. In his impressive recent book, *The Birth of Mod-
    ern Belief*, Ethan Shagan argues that Montaigne reduces all belief to
    the level of opinion (pp. 169–79); this claim, exaggerated though it is,
    nonetheless describes a strong and distinctive current in Montaignian
    thought.
15. See Hankinson, *Sceptics*; Larmore, 'Scepticism'; Schmitt, *Cicero Scep-
    ticus*; and Popkin, *History of Scepticism from Savonarola to Bayle*. For
    a brief discussion, see my recent treatment of the topic in *Montaigne: A
    Very Short Introduction*, pp. 84–100.
16. Compare Montaigne's memorable comment about La Boétie: 'if he had
    had the choice, he would rather have been born in Venice than in Sar-
    lat, and with reason. But he had another maxim sovereignly imprinted
    in his soul, to obey and submit most religiously to the laws under which
    he was born' (p. 144; cp. p. 86 on 'the universal law of laws').
17. See Charles Schmitt, *Cicero Scepticus*, pp. 7–8 and 73–7 on the fre-
    quency with which early modern writers blur distinctions between Pyr-
    rhonism and Academic scepticism.
18. Marie de Gournay paraphrases this passage with clear approbation
    in her preface to the 1595 posthumous edition of Montaigne, adding
    that 'God is neither here nor there if there is no miracle'; see Gournay,
    Preface, trans. and ed. Hillman and Quesnel, pp. 56–7.
19. See, for example, 'It is folly to measure the true and false by our own
    capacity' (pp. 132– 5).
20. And if it is true, as Montaigne speculates in the 'Apology', that Nature
    'enfolds within the bounds of her ordinary progress, like all other
    things, also the beliefs, judgments, and opinions of men; if they have
    their rotation, their season, their birth, their death, like cabbages', then
    'what magisterial and permanent authority are we attributing to them?'
    (p. 433).
21. Compare Montaigne's remark that 'nothing is so firmly believed as
    what is least known, nor are any people so confident as those who tell

us fables' (p. 160). Paraphrasing Pliny the Elder and Tacitus, Montaigne also writes that 'Men put greater faith in those things that they do not understand. By a twist of the human mind, obscure things are more readily believed' (p. 789). In *Venus and Adonis*, Shakespeare describes a similar phenomenon but emphasises active interpretation rather than passive acquiescence: 'Look how the world's poor people are amazèd / At apparitions, signs, and prodigies, / Whereon with fearful eyes they long have gazèd, / Infusing them with dreadful prophecies' (ll. 925–8). Hume, in his *Treatise*, usefully defines 'credulity' as 'too easy faith in testimony of others' (p. 78).

22. Bacon, *New Organon*, pp. 47–67.

23. Ibid. pp. 14–15. For Bacon's complex allusion to Christ's response to Pharisaic interrogation in the synoptic gospels, see Matt. 22:15–22, Mark 12:13–17 and Luke 20:20–6; cp. Rom. 13:1–7, Tit. 1:3.

24. Compare 'Of Custom', where Montaigne avers in a post-1588 addition that 'divine Providence' operates in ways that are by definition 'above our categories and our powers' (p. 88); he then quotes the latter half of the same passage from *The Nature of the Gods* that I have included above.

25. Popkin, *History of Scepticism*, p. 56; compare Brahami, *Le Scepticisme de Montaigne*, pp. 29–57. See also my essay 'On Continuities between Skepticism and Early Ethnography', esp. p. 374.

26. Sextus, *Outlines*, pp. 143, 144 and 146.

27. Copenhaver and Schmitt, *Renaissance Philosophy*, p. 246. Montaigne makes a misogynistic joke in 'On Some Verses of Virgil' that points to the same ontological division: he says he can't imagine that a woman could be bothered by the assiduous sexual advances of her husband, 'for I believe in miracles only in matters of faith' (p. 650).

28. Although Hobbes does not rely on Pyrrhonian premises in his dismissal of polytheistic belief systems, the immunity of Judaeo-Christian revelation from his otherwise withering account of the origins of human religion reflects the attitude I speak of here (*Leviathan*, pp. 93–104).

29. Henry himself has stated, earlier in the play, that the 'guiltless drops' of blood that fall when mighty kingdoms contend with one another 'Are every one a woe, a sore complaint / 'Gainst him whose wrongs gives edge unto the swords / That makes such waste in brief mortality' (*H5* I, ii, 25–8).

30. Clifford, 'Ethics of Belief', p. 18. Not only is Williams oriented towards issues of responsibility; he is also alert to epistemological distinctions, as when he responds to Henry's claim that the war in France is just and honourable: 'That's more than we know' (*H5* IV, i, 120). As far as I can discern, Williams never extends belief to Henry's assertion.

31. Montaigne takes this passage from the *Academics*, 2.47; see Cicero, *De Natura Deorum* and *Academica*, trans. Rackham, pp. 652–5.

32. Comprehension, within this hierarchy, might be characterised as the understanding enabled by consent to the potential validity of an idea's

apparent truth. For example, once Copernicus extends provisional acceptance to the idea that the Earth is located within a heliocentric rather than a geocentric system, he discovers that this account yields new and powerful forms of understanding; these, in turn, serve as warrants for knowledge. But belief, as I have argued throughout this chapter, is not provisional consent but commitment to the truth of an idea or proposition whose truth is non-evident.

33. Erasmus, *Praise of Folly and Other Writings*, pp. 46–51, 80–7. If we can trust Erasmus's claims in his letter to Martin Dorp, however, the great humanist is more blithely confident than is Montaigne in the potential for the revelations of Holy Scripture to serve usefully in settling conflicts within what Bacon calls the realm of 'things human': see esp. p. 239 in Adams's edition.

34. For a valuable discussion of the dialectic between scepticism and faith in the 'Apology', see Hartle, *Michel de Montaigne*, pp. 121–48.

35. McEachern speaks of such phenomena (both in early modern Europe and in the present) as simultaneously cognitive and physiological: things 'felt in the bones or the pit of one's stomach, something we feel sure of or feel ourselves feeling our way towards, even if we cannot, precisely, articulate the reasons for our motion toward conviction'. See *Believing in Shakespeare*, esp. Part I ('Believing', pp. 3–76; here, p. 55). See also Russell's discussion of this matter; Russell writes of the 'instinctive beliefs' on which we must necessarily rely as we form arguments leading to knowledge claims (*Problems*, pp. 11–12). Discussions of 'hinge-commitments' stem from Wittgenstein's efforts to refute scepticism in *On Certainty*.

Chapter 10

Making Sense of 'To be or not to be'
Richard Dillane

The special fascination of *Hamlet* the play and Hamlet the character is felt most strongly in his elusive central soliloquy. Interpretations abound, and modern appraisals of the speech as 'mercurial', 'evasive', 'confused and ambiguous' and 'lacking in logical and syntactic cohesion' hardly improve on Samuel Johnson's remark that the soliloquy 'is connected rather in the speaker's mind than on his tongue'.[1] According to Royal Shakespeare Company sage John Barton, however, 'in a set speech the actor always needs to go for the *argument* if he is to take his audience with him' (his emphasis), and 'To be' is especially tantalising in this respect in its resemblance to academic *disputatio*: an abstract binary choice developed stepwise on both sides towards a concluding 'thus' was a standard form of dialectic for students across early modern Europe.[2] It was Shakespeare's idea to convert the time-biding revenger of legend into a procrastinating university man. In giving him a speech of such markedly academic tenor, for a play that would very soon be performed at England's two universities, Shakespeare sets up coherence as a particular expectation.[3] Even at the time the speech may have been perplexing to many: witness the 'bad' quarto version cobbled from an actor's memory and daftly blaming our reluctance to die on our joyful hope of heaven.[4] But if 'To be' has a coherence it hinges on a trope of thought that was current at the time of writing and perhaps not thereafter, and a lucid reading may indeed be obtained, one that suits both Hamlet's tone and Shakespeare's cultural context, with a key from Montaigne's *Essays*.

* * *

The inadequacy of extant interpretations of 'To be' (*Ham* III, i, 55–89) is hard to summarise as they are so various.[5] What follows is a composite reading to which objections of a general order apply.

Shortly before 'To be', Hamlet reaches a pitch of resolve, not yet to kill Claudius but to make sure of his guilt: 'The play's the thing / Wherein I'll catch the conscience of the king!' (II, ii, 604–5). And just as the mania of 'Well said old mole!' in Act I gave way to piteous sighs for Ophelia in her closet, and his thrill at the players' arrival in Act II to 'what a rogue and peasant slave am I!', Hamlet's fire has again cooled. The thought of his obligation, if the play succeeds, to skewer his uncle/'father'/king has thrown him into a morbid funk. Revenge now seems both a moral trap and a suicide mission. Hamlet ponders the task as if it were suicide and finds that his conscience, suddenly unpersuaded of the value of revenge and making him dread its consequence in the hereafter, dampens the will to follow through. 'To be or not to be' and 'suffer or take arms' represent the choice to live unrevenged or die attempting Claudius's life, although whether 'be' means live or act is debated. In short, the knowledge that death promises morally punitive 'dreams' makes us prefer life and therefore inaction, which to some is a form of non-being.

Nothing of this interpretation survives attention to the text. Despite its focus on death the rhetoric is not obviously charged with emotion; it is free, for example, of exclamations like 'O God', 'ah fie', 'what a rogue' and 'what an ass'. Nor does Hamlet mention revenge, Claudius or even himself; the discussion is studiously unspecific. Also, if conscience prevents Hamlet exacting revenge because revenge might be wrong, or effectively suicide, then conscience is doing its job and it is not cowardly to heed it.[6] The play gives little sign, moreover, that Hamlet doubts the rightness of revenge in principle, and every sign that as a Christian he regards suicide as a closed option. In any case the speech does not suggest that its 'dreams' are punishments.

It is doubtful that Hamlet's 'question' amounts to whether or not he should proceed with revenge and thereby court his own death. If ending 'a sea of troubles' is, in short, 'to die', then the sea of troubles is life, not a set of difficulties, however appreciable, such as Hamlet's with Claudius. And, as Harold Skulsky points out, if death is the result but not the purpose of taking arms, then taking arms and suffering fortune are not opposites. The nub of the choice is whether to suffer one's fortune, and the only way not to suffer fortune is to subtract oneself from the world – which is what the arms are for.[7]

It is equally unlikely, however, that Hamlet is considering killing himself. Such contemplation would repeat a question already answered in the first soliloquy by God's interdict, and thus also imply a crisis of faith, of which there is no sign. Ophelia is placed in the lobby because Hamlet's ruminative presence there is normal (II, ii, 160–2), and if the First Quarto remembers the first production Burbage entered for this speech 'poring upon a book': hardly a picture of desperation.

The mistake on both sides is to constrain the speech to particulars, either of the plot or Hamlet's supposed mental state, when its most striking quality, apparent in the metronomic infinitives 'to be', 'to suffer', 'to die' and so forth, is one of philosophical abstractness. Why adopt this register if it is not what the meaning demands? It is an odd way to feign madness and not one that 'lacks form' (III, i, 163). The speech must have a plot purpose and a psychology, but to interpret it with a view to those requirements rather than by its own lights, such that what is famously distinctive counts for mere style, and when sense is not improved, seems unsound.[8]

Even less helpful is the almost universal belief that 'nobler in the mind' signifies a moral question, namely, ought one rather bear one's troubles in patience or boldly and strenuously confront them, even if the endeavour is futile? This is plausibly the dilemma of a mindful prince and crux of a weighty drama but it strains the text. It would make 'suffer or take arms' a non sequitur to the opening line because passivism and activism are both modes of being, leaving 'not to be' without a correlate. And if the meaning is 'nobler', 'in the mind' is redundant. To sustain the moral reading, critics argue variously that the questions are different,[9] that confronting troubles is tantamount to dying,[10] that troubles end us and not we them,[11] that to be is to act,[12] that 'in the mind' belongs with 'to suffer',[13] and so on. No solution of any sort is required, however, if the speech is what it seems: philosophy.

The option to commit suicide comes with being human. Only we, 'crawling between earth and heaven' with both godlike reason and animal mortality, can decide whether to go on living. Indeed decide we must: as Seneca stoically observes, 'Humanity is well situated because no man is unhappy except by his own fault. Live if you so desire; if not you may return from whence you came' (Letter 70).[14] Seneca is debating what conditions in life justify suicide; Hamlet raises the same question but with the added consideration, not Stoic but Christian, and contained in the phrases 'slings and arrows of fortune', 'whips and scorns of time' and 'shocks that flesh is heir to', that life is innately wretched. He asks whether bearing the human condition at all is rational, not in order to decide a course of action but to posit our condition as problematic (since we are innately rational), and from there develop an argument. The phrase 'nobler in the mind' recalls Hamlet's own 'how noble in reason' (II, ii, 304) and anticipates Ophelia's 'O what a noble mind is here o'erthrown' (III, i, 150), both referring to intellect. Far from being redundant, the words 'in the mind' are key. The curious lexical choice is 'nobler'. As I will show, it is used in irony.

The other obstacle is 'conscience'. Some editors defend the moral meaning because it was predominant at the time, including within *Hamlet*, and because in the Christian account conscience is what dissuades us from acts we will pay for in the afterlife.[15] Philosophy, however, suspends doctrinal moral values, and clearly 'To be' presents suicide not with disapproval but as a welcome release, the virile retort to life's insults, a feat one may accomplish with a mere bodkin and that we are 'cowards' to eschew.[16] If 'conscience' means our moral awareness that suicide is wrong, it introduces an incongruent, even antithetical idea, which has the effect of divorcing the conclusion from the argument. Moreover, 'conscience does make cowards of us all' would suggest that Hamlet – a Christian addressing Christians – laments morality's prevention of mass suicide.

Other readings of 'conscience' in this context as 'consciousness' and 'introspection' imply that what deters us from self-slaughter is personal reflection on the nature of death, again preferring psychological to philosophical interpretation.[17] But Hamlet says that all of us are made cowards by conscience, not just those who introspect, and if reflections on death have any basis it is not cowardly to heed them. The word 'cowards' imputes a fault, and 'of us all' implies that the fault is man's *qua* man, not a contingent or individual flaw.

* * *

Montaigne expresses particular enthusiasm for the ancient Greek philosophy of Pyrrhonism which had recently been recovered from obscurity. Said to have been inspired by contact between its originator, Pyrrho, and Indian sadhus, possibly Buddhist, Pyrrhonism is the practice of seeking tranquillity through doubt.[18] The Pyrrhonist systematically challenges truth-claims, with the nominal aim of establishing fact but with the effect of exposing uncertainty, which generates a state of indecision, leading pleasantly in turn to one of *ataraxia*, a Greek analogue of Buddhist *nirvana*.[19] Sextus Empiricus compares the transforming experience to that of the painter Apelles, of whom

> it is said that once upon a time, when he was painting a horse and wished to depict the horse's froth, he failed so completely that he gave up and threw his sponge at the picture – the sponge on which he used to wipe

the paints from his brush – and that in striking the picture the sponge produced the desired effect.[20]

Likewise, we gather, seeking contentment through knowledge succeeds by failing.

Pyrrhonists are sceptics, but not as the word is commonly used or understood.[21] A sceptic in the everyday sense, denying for example that goblins exist, makes a battleground of the question. To the Pyrrhonist, by contrast, the undecideability of the question renders all thoughts about it pointless and pernicious, whether opinions or feelings. Finding claim and counterclaim of equal weight he becomes entirely neutral to the matter. Nor, as is often thought of sceptics, is he glum or jaundiced: his scepticism is remedy, not plight. It cures him of both the frustration of trying to know and the delusion that he already knows.[22] Lastly, Pyrrhonism does not claim that nothing can be known. It distinguishes between the evident, or experiential, and the non-evident, or non-experiential. Matters belonging to experience, such as the sweetness of honey and seeming crookedness of sticks in water, are not contested, and in daily life Pyrrhonists accede to instinct, custom and practical teaching.[23] Their philosophical equivocation is reserved for matters to which experience cannot speak, such as whether honey's sweetness is intrinsic or subjective, whether gods exist and, which is relevant here, what being dead is like.[24]

Although prominent in late antiquity, Pyrrhonism then faded from view for a millennium. It re-entered European conversation in the late sixteenth century with the publication in 1562 of a Latin translation of Sextus Empiricus's second-century CE Greek volume *Outlines of Pyrrhonism*, and of Sextus's complete works in 1569.[25] Over the next century, however, with the emergence of new philosophies, beginning with Cartesian rationalism, and of the scientific method, Pyrrhonism fell back into relative obscurity where it remains.[26] During this short-lived revival, Pyrrhonism's principal champion was Montaigne. The success of Montaigne's book *Essays* through the 1580s and 1590s, coupled with the uptake of Sextus's *Outlines* in institutions of learning, meant that by around 1600 Pyrrhonism was known to English scholars and literati, although not always well distinguished from Academic or less defined scepticism.[27]

Pyrrhonism's value to Montaigne lay in its intellectual humility and radical empiricism, which chime with and philosophically authenticate his overarching claim that the way to live is to embrace one's human and worldly limitations: as he quotes Plutarch at the very end of the *Essays*, 'You are god insomuch / As you know yourself man'.[28] In evoking Pyrrhonism, however, Montaigne somewhat distorts it. For example, from the chapter on Pyrrho in Diogenes Laertius's *Lives of Eminent Philosophers*, included in the publications of Sextus, Montaigne recounts this vignette and draws a startling lesson:

> The philosopher Pyrrho, aboard ship once in a great storm, pointed out as an encouragement and example to those most terrified around him a pig that happened to be there not in the least perturbed by the storm. Dare we infer that the gift of reason we make such a song and dance about, and think makes us lords of creation, was actually put in us for our torment? What use is knowledge if it makes us more cowardly, if we lose the ease and tranquility we would enjoy without it, and if it makes us worse than Pyrrho's pig? (I, 40, 263)[29]

Montaigne's inference seems at first without merit. How are reason and knowledge to blame for terror? How does the pig's ignorance of its peril make it superior to humans? The key, as we might expect, is scepticism. If something is unknowable, better brainpower is of no advantage in knowing it and instead becomes a handicap if its speculations cause fear and trembling. What terrifies Pyrrho's companions is their potential fate, death, but since death itself is unknowable, being almost by definition beyond experience, the true object of their dread is the idea of death, born of reason.[30]

This logic is not strictly Pyrrhonist. Pyrrho's gesture simply means that the pig, unburdened by complex ideas, enjoys a natural *ataraxia*. In concluding that humanity might be better off unburdened by reason itself, Montaigne goes dramatically further. Pyrrhonism as Sextus presents it favours reason because dialectic reveals the equipollence of opposites, the apprehension of which leads to indecision and thence to tranquillity. Montaigne's professed antipathy to reason, on the other hand, exhaustively dilated in his 'Apology for Raymond Sebond' and iterated through the *Essays*, is a reaction to the Renaissance recovery of classical optimism which exalts man for the potency and compass of his intellect.[31] Regarding this development as vain, hubristic and the path to atheism and social disintegration (as France gored itself over a re-conception of Christianity), Montaigne argues that human reason is puny and limited, that it presumes and speculates beyond its reach and in doing so *creates* objects of spurious worry such as notions of what follows death.

> People (says an ancient Greek maxim) are troubled by what they think of things, not by the things themselves. (I, 40, 258)

Our intellect can frame a hundred alternative worlds, and then discover their laws and workings: it needs neither ground nor substance. Give it rein, it builds just as well in a vacuum as on earth, and as well with vacancy as with stuff. (III, 11, 1072)

If man alone in all creation has the free imagination and untethered intellect to conceive of what is, what is not, and whatever he likes whether fact or fiction, it is an advantage dearly bought and little to his glory, since it constitutes the main source of his besetting ills: sin, sickness, hesitancy, confusion and despair.[32] (II, 12, 481–2)

I find that we not only guard ourselves lamely from deception but actively seek to impale ourselves on it. (III, 11, 1073)

It is pathetic how we gull ourselves with pranks of our own invention . . . like children spooked by a friend's face they themselves blackened with soot. (II, 12, 559)

Presumption is our natural, original disease. (II, 12, 473)

*   *   *

If Hamlet's 'To be' soliloquy has a definite sense, then in missing it we must be subject to stubborn misconceptions, as with 'nobler in the mind'. Because Hamlet is Christian and has heard a first-hand account of purgatory from his dead father's spirit, it has been firmly assumed that 'something after death' is for him a serious prospect, one that 'To be' gravely contemplates. If so, 'The undiscovered country from whose bourn / No traveller returns' is simply a passing metaphor. In the sense of virgin territory, however, death is not undiscovered: the dead are innumerable. But 'discover' also means reveal or disclose, as in *Much Ado about Nothing* when Antonio tells Leonato 'the prince discovered to Claudio that he loved my niece your daughter' (I, ii, 11–12), and death is undiscovered in this sense for the reason Hamlet gives, that no traveller returns: they cannot communicate to those left behind.[33] The thrust of the metaphor, in other words, is not that death is final but that the living know nothing of it. If death is a 'country' (region) its 'bourn' (boundary) is its border with life, its threshold. At this bourn we see travellers stop breathing, lose their pulse and then . . . what? There is no more data. Whether there is an after, let alone a something after, we are irremediably ignorant: 'All we can ever know about death is that a living person becomes strangely still.'[34]

What we dread, then, is not something that subsists after death of which we are darkly aware but an idea or projection of what could follow death, exactly as Pyrrho implies is the case with his tempest-tossed companions by pointing out to them the blithe, unspeculative pig. And just as Montaigne dared his readers conclude from Pyrrho's example that 'knowledge [*cognoissance*] . . . makes us more cowardly', Hamlet concludes that 'conscience does make cowards of us all'. Both of them impugn the faculty that separates man from beast: reason. Hence the 'of us all'.[35] The arguments, too, are a match: Montaigne's, augmenting Pyrrhonism, is 'We dread death – death is unknown – so reason is to blame', and Hamlet's is 'We dread "something after death" – death is "undiscovered" – so "conscience" is to blame'. The only difference is that because Hamlet discusses voluntary rather than accidental death his conclusion pertains to failure of will and not simply of composure, and thus applies to any mortal enterprise losing the name of action, such as his revenge.[36]

Hamlet's logic is as follows. Being rational we choose between suffering and suicide, and while the rational default should be suicide, the possibility of 'something after death' makes us rationally prefer the agony of life. Since, however, 'something after death' is wholly speculated, the blame for our craven choice to live lies with the speculative faculty, reason.[37]

This reading brings to life Montaigne's perhaps mischievous but pointedly counter-humanist suggestion that we were given intellect not as a boon but a torment, and it has implications for performance. If the first line is not a meditative insight but the premise of an argument, and the rest is close reasoning, then something brisker than solemn reflectiveness is called for. Also, and perhaps more upsetting of tradition, the tone may not be one of deep earnest. If Hamlet's point is that what we dread in death are 'pranks of our own invention' – notions of things rather than the things themselves – then all mention of afterlife is in inverted commas. The 'dreams', the 'something' and the 'others' (the ills, that is, not of life but death), each tellingly paired with a sceptical qualifier ('perchance', 'undiscovered' and 'that we know not of'), are occasions not of foreboding but sarcasm. Also insincere, therefore, are our 'respect' and 'regard' for these projected ills, comparably to Troilus's withering cry that 'reason and respect / Make livers pale and lustihood deject' (*TC* II, ii, 49–50). In fact, as might be expected in a set-piece argument, as opposed to an extemporised passion, the beginning prepares for the end: 'take arms' conspires with 'nobler' to link ending one's troubles with valour because the aim is to show, by damning contrast, that *not* ending one's troubles is 'nobler' in the mind; that reason is pusil-lanimous. The assonance of 'conscience', 'cowards' and 'sicklied' is the sound of caustic, sardonic self-indictment, 'not for his own faults but for those of humankind'.[38]

If it seems unchristian to doubt the hereafter, it is important to remember that scepticism does not issue in denial but in the absence of opinion. It is no less presumptuous to suggest that nothing follows death as that something does. Indeed, Montaigne famously appro-priates scepticism for Christianity, arguing that a mind purged of 'human' knowledge is 'readier to accommodate the divine' (II, 12, 534); Hamlet, too, speaks ingenuously of 'a divinity that shapes our ends / Rough-hew them how we will' (V, ii, 10–11). Since neither scep-ticism nor Christianity allows Hamlet to suggest that in death there is nothing to dread, his scathing word 'cowards', describing our dread of 'something' and demonising 'conscience', is only explicable by vir-tue of the Pyrrhonist insight that, *whether or not* anything awaits us in death, its status as unknowable makes dreading it fatuous. And this insight has a second source in the *Essays* which on separate grounds is noticeably echoed in 'To be': the words of Socrates.

Socrates was Montaigne's avowed philosophical hero; more spe-cifically, Socrates the de facto sceptic, whom we find in Plato's early dialogues, as opposed to the rationalist system-builder encountered in *The Republic*. In 'On Physiognomy', Montaigne quotes a passage from Plato's *Apology* in which Socrates compares death to sleep, sleep that is best when dreamless.[39] Several critics regard Montaigne's quo-tation of Plato here as the probable source of some of Hamlet's lines:

> to die, to sleep,
> No more, and by a sleep to say we end
> The heartache and the thousand natural shocks
> That flesh is heir to; 'tis a consummation
> Devoutly to be wished, to die, to sleep.
> To sleep, perchance to dream – ay there's the rub
>
> (*Ham* III, I, 61–7)

The resemblance is noted in particular because the word 'consum-mation' is also in the quotation of Socrates as it appears in John Florio's 1603 translation of the *Essays*; an indication to some that Shakespeare had read Florio in manuscript.[40] According to the 'good' quarto (Q2), however, thought to derive from Shakespeare's own draft, Hamlet's word is 'consumation' – from 'to consume', not 'to consummate' – which better captures Montaigne's *anéantissement* (annihilation), as well as Plato's *meden einai* (being nothing), and which restates 'not to be'.[41] This does not exclude a debt to Florio but it brings out a deeper link to the Socrates quotation than those of metaphor and vocabulary.

> I know I have neither viewed death, nor visited it, nor met anyone experienced in it from whom to learn. Those who dread it presuppose to know it. I neither know what it is, nor what they do there. It could be something neutral, perhaps something desirable. . . . If it is an annihilation of one's being, it is still an improvement to enter a long and peaceful night. We find nothing sweeter in life than quiet rest and deep, dreamless sleep. What I know is bad . . . I carefully avoid. What I do not know is good or bad, I cannot dread. (III: 12, 1099–100)[42]

The logic here – that since the nature of death is beyond anyone's ken it makes no sense to dread it, and that to dread it is to presume what it is – is the implicit logic of the Pyrrho's pig anecdote which, taken to Montaigne's antirational conclusion, unlocks 'To be or not to be'. Both passages press Montaigne's theme that human woes and failings arise from intellectual overreach. Since one of them also shares with 'To be' a distinctive metaphor and the conceptual ingredient of death as utter non-existence, not asserted as fact but mooted in argument, it is hard to doubt that inspiration for the Hamlet soliloquy came from the *Essays*.[43]

*   *   *

Does Hamlet really think intellect a crippling handicap? Not entirely. The idea that thought vitiates action is recurrent in Shakespeare. 'To be' takes the form of a proof but its purpose in being so is not to press the point beyond question: if it were, we would have to take the endorsement of suicide seriously, which Hamlet's faith precludes. The purpose is ironic: the realisation of reason's harm through pure reasoning; our brainy hero denouncing brains. Similarly, Hamlet himself is not Pyrrhonist because he subscribes to such non-evident propositions as his uncle's criminality and mother's concupiscence. The Pyrrhonism in 'To be' is momentary and point-making rather than principled. It is also a 'modish posture' recognisable to a generation of students for whom Sextus and Montaigne were recent and influential sources.[44]

On a wider view, however, Hamlet's thoughts evolve in a discernibly Pyrrhonist sequence, of which 'To be' is one step. Under such synonyms as 'sense', 'judgement', 'understanding', 'apprehension' and 'conception', the motif of reason recurs throughout the play. It also unites three of Hamlet's speeches as a trio of claim, counterclaim and suspension of judgement, leading afterwards to tranquillity. In 'What a piece of work is a man' (II, ii, 303–10), our surpassing intellect, under the description of noble reason, infinite faculty and godlike apprehension, is said to make us the paragon of animals – a gushing extolment which is instantly subverted by 'and yet to me what is this quintessence of dust?' and then contradicted by a crushing proof that reason makes us cowards.[45] This violent ambivalence towards our highest faculty erupts in the final soliloquy 'How all occasions do inform against me' (IV, iv, 32–66), which begins with an exasperated Hamlet reminding himself, in view of the fact that it has dulled his revenge, that thinking is human and that God surely means us to think, and which ends in emulation of Fortinbras with the resolve to value only 'bloody' thoughts and scorn 'the invisible [that is, non-evident] event'. This renouncement, though hardly *epochē*, nonetheless begets an ataraxic calm. Disburdened of any theory as to what death 'is', and as a consequence, as we see in the cheery graveyard scene, without dread, Hamlet returns to Denmark serenely prepared for a showdown he himself does not bring about but rather awaits, trusting to higher direction. Like Apelles hurling his sponge, Hamlet advances his cause by abjuring rational control of it.[46]

This understanding of 'To be' and its place in the play may shed light on the conception of *Hamlet* as a tragedy. The hero is not (or not only) the Romantics' anguished individual but Renaissance Man, personifying the humanistic myth that man, gifted with reason, is somewhat his own and the world's master, having the capacity through rational action to determine the course of history: in this case the Danish succession. In him that myth is not affirmed but dismantled. Brought to a painful and even guilty awareness of reason's propensity to stall action, Hamlet forswears its counsel and makes himself the instrument of providence, whereupon things go swimmingly. Even with his own death upon him he is not dismayed, having by then achieved the pacific sceptical insight – discarding rational optimism – that 'Since no man knows aught of what he leaves, what is't to leave betimes?': it makes no odds when you depart a world you cannot rationally grasp, or, it follows, affect through rational action.[47] Like the *Essays*, *Hamlet* teaches that we do better to live our situated humanity than overrate 'how like a god' we are.

The crux of this plan is the hero confronting his predicament, represented in the spectacular irony of reason shaming itself. Neither vague nor incoherent, Hamlet's great soliloquy makes taut sense under a trademark logic that was current almost peculiarly at Shakespeare's height and available to him through the already influential work of Montaigne, whose variation of it Hamlet exactly replicates. Schopenhauer comes closest: Hamlet 'merely states that considering the nature of the world death would be certainly preferable if we were sure that by it we should be annihilated. But there lies the rub.'[48] Even for Schopenhauer, however, the speech's ultimate point is that dread of an unknown futurity thwarts action.[49] In reality the argument has a further step. In so far as death is an 'event horizon', something after it can only be supposition, of which dread is inane: hence the indictment of thought. Hamlet's 'To be' soliloquy, not so much a morbid descant as mordant calculus, is the chief component of a larger exercise that questions reason's good to man. To this extent, *Hamlet* is a staging of Montaigne's critique of humanism.

Appendix

As Hunter Kellenberger shows, Shakespeare's contemporaries often confused 'consumation' and 'consummation' while Shakespeare himself does not. 'Consummation' only appears in editions of his plays dated after his death, replacing 'consumation' where it occurs in verse and in both contexts introducing confusion (in prose 'consumation' became 'consumption', a better match for sense).[50] Even so, 'consummation' is bound to be heard in the theatre, especially followed by 'devoutly'.

In the Gospel of St John in Latin, *consummatum est* is Jesus' last utterance on the cross, a translation of *tetelestai* which means 'completed' in a contractual sense, as does *quietus est*, so that 'To be' simultaneously trades on the conceit that death quits a debt and suggests Hamlet-as-Christ. Since the frailty Hamlet embodies and suffers for is not sinfulness but rationality, however, his resemblance to Christ is ironic. He is, in effect, a fall guy for humanism.

In a speech condemning man's failure in action, the metaphor of sexual impotence practically suggests itself. Accordingly, the 'will' that is 'puzzled' at the prospect of an irremeable 'country' of 'death' is plain bawdy, but the metaphor is set up earlier in the speech.[51] 'Consummation' in the marital sense completes death's rise from being only neutrally attractive (be or not be) through beneficial (ending one's troubles) and easy (no more than sleep) to irresistible (ardently to be wished). The bare bodkin is the prick that, were it not puzzled, would do the consummating. Also suggestive, we can presume, is the 'bourn' at which failure occurs. As 'stream' or 'burn' ('Come o'er the bourn, Bessy, to me / Her boat hath a leak . . . she dares not come over', *KL* 3.6.25–8), 'bourn' suggests a vale and thus vagina, as a 'sist'ring vale' has a 'concave womb' (*LC* 1–2). 'Burn', however, further connotes disease.[52] In sum, irresolution in the face of death is pictured as flaccidity induced by a repellent female sexuality, which is consistent with Hamlet's attitude to Gertrude's 'enseaméd bed' and with the dialogue with Ophelia which follows 'To be' and has often been thought discontinuous to it. The soliloquy's metaphor, in which the male erection represents the drive to act, and femaleness is its undoing, finds visceral expression in 'Get thee to a nunnery'.

Not one myself, I thank the professional scholars who generously answered and encouraged me when contacted: Colin McGinn who urged me to write up my idea, Terence Cave who received the most enquiries, Andrew Hadfield who arranged my Visiting Fellowship, William Hamlin whose kind interest and feedback has led to publication, and others including Carol Atack, Alan Bailey, Richard Bett, Colin Burrow, Saul Frampton, Adrian Kuzminski, Stephen Priest, Travis Williams and Jessica Winston.

Notes

1. McGinn, *Shakespeare's Philosophy*, p. 54; Mercer, *Hamlet and the Acting of Revenge*, p. 204; G. Wilson Knight, *The Wheel of Fire*, p. 304; Clemen, *Shakespeare's Soliloquies*, p. 134; *Hamlet*, ed. Johnson, p. 207n.
2. Barton, *Playing Shakespeare*, p. 92 (originally a television series); Burrow, *Shakespeare and Classical Antiquity*, p. 42.
3. The Q1 title page tells us that *Hamlet* had been performed at Oxford and Cambridge; this need not mean the Q1 text (ed. Jenkins, p. 14n). Faustus's farewell to '*on kai me on*' (Marlowe, *Dr Faustus*, ed. Jump, I, I, 12) confirms that 'being and not being' was at the time an archetypal scholarly topic.
4. That Q1 is based on the memory of a bit-part actor is shown by Irace (*The First Quarto of Hamlet*, p. 7).
5. Line numbers are from *The Riverside Shakespeare*, 2nd edn, 1997.
6. Hamlet is neither evil like Richard III ('Conscience is but a word that cowards use', *R3* V, iii, 309) nor raging like Laertes ('Conscience and grace to the profoundest pit!', *Ham* IV, v, 133).
7. Skulsky, 'Revenge, Honor, and Conscience in *Hamlet*', p. 82. To shuffle off this mortal coil cannot simply mean 'die' (e.g. Bruster, *To Be or Not*

to Be, p. 25). The whole interest is in how enterprises lose the name of action – that is, intent. See n.11.

8. Descriptions of the speech as 'quasi-formal' and 'quasi-philosophical' (*Hamlet*, ed. Jenkins p. 149; Newell, *The Soliloquies in Hamlet*, p. 80) are typical. Similarly, Bruster thinks it 'messy' but in 'the language of the philosopher' (*To Be or Not to Be*, pp. 8, 98).

9. For example Knights, *An Approach to Hamlet*, p. 78; *Hamlet*, ed. Johnson, p. 207n.; Alexander, *Poison, Play, and Duel*, p. 73. For Knights, the choice to suffer or take arms is secondary to that of one's 'essential being'; for Johnson, the suffer/ take arms choice depends on whether *after death* we are 'to be or not to be'; for Alexander, both suffering and taking arms constitute 'to be' while 'not to be' is simply 'to die'.

10. For example Muir, *Hamlet*, p. 34; Richards, 'The Meaning of Hamlet's Soliloquy', p. 749; Haydn, *The Counter-Renaissance*, p. 629. This solution is a convenient presumption of likelihood. Note Skulsky's objection.

11. For example *Hamlet*, ed. Jenkins, pp. 487, 490; ed. Hibbard, p. 240. This ignores the intentionality of 'end them', 'end the heartache', 'shuffled off', 'quietus make' and 'fly to others'.

12. For example Traversi, *An Approach to Shakespeare*, p. 53; Murry, *Things to Come*, p. 231; Prosser, *Hamlet and Revenge*, pp. 160–1. If non-being means inaction, how is 'to die' relevant? If the assumption is that action results in death (again: must it?), then, perversely, to be is to die and not to be is to live.

13. For example *Hamlet*, ed. Dowden, p. 99n.; ed. Dover Wilson, p. 191; Bruster, *To Be or Not to Be*, p. 17: 'in the mind to suffer' is inelegant, ruins the symmetry of 'to be/not to be' with 'to suffer/to take arms' and forgets the grunts and sweats of fardel-bearing.

14. The first appearance of Letter 70 in English (in full) was Thomas Lodge's *Workes* of Seneca, published in 1614 but notified in the Stationers' Register in 1600 when it was possibly under way.

15. For example Muir, *Shakespeare's Tragic Sequence*, p. 81; *Hamlet*, ed. Jenkins, pp. 487–8; ed. Edwards, p. 147n.

16. That a little bodkin (compare 'pipkin', 'lambkin') may bring everlasting *quietus* echoes the quoted passage of Seneca, which continues: 'A gaping wound is not necessary – a lancet [*scalpello*, diminutive of *scalprum*] will open the way to that great freedom, and tranquility can be purchased at the cost of a pinprick' (see Honigmann and West, 'With a Bare Bodkin').

17. For example Bradley, *Shakespearean Tragedy*, p. 98n.; Spencer, *Shakespeare and the Nature of Man*, p. 269n.; *Hamlet*, ed. Dover Wilson, p. 267; Schücking, *The Meaning of Hamlet*, p. 119.

18. Sextus, *Outlines* I, 4, 6, trans. Mates. That Pyrrho met and was inspired by Indian gymnosophists is reported by Diogenes Laertius (*Lives of Eminent Philosophers* 9.61.63) on the basis of earlier sources.

19. Sextus, *Outlines* I, 4, trans. Mates. The *nirvana/ataraxia* parallel is recognised by Kuzminski, *Pyrrhonism*, p. 53, Christopher I. Beckwith, *Greek Buddha*, p. 42 and others. 'Indecision' covers both *aporia* (puzzlement) and *epochē* (suspended judgement).

20. Sextus, *Outlines* I, 12, trans. Mates.

21. I leave aside the original sense of *skeptikoi* (enquirers) claimed by Sextus for Pyrrhonists.

22. Scepticism-as-pessimism, as for example in Cavell, *Disowning Knowledge* (ch. 1), Bell, *Shakespeare's Tragic Skepticism* (Introduction) and Shapiro, *1599* (pp. 331–4), is unwelcome doubt which attests a craving for certainty. For Pyrrhonists the craving is the problem, and doubt relieves it.

23. Sextus, *Outlines* I, 10, 11. Indiscriminate doubt (with allowance for probability) is the scepticism of Plato's Academy in its middle and late periods, and of Cicero's *Academica*.

24. Sextus, *Outlines* III, 3, 23, 24.

25. Early modern interest in Pyrrhonism began earlier but the 1562 event was decisive: see Popkin, *The History of Scepticism*, ch. 2.

26. Both Cartesianism and the new science were responses to the sceptic challenge, reasserting in different ways the possibility of knowledge. Scepticism remained central to philosophy but decidedly not in its therapeutic Pyrrhonian form.

27. Cave, *How to Read Montaigne* (ch. 3) and Hamlin, *Tragedy and Scepticism in Shakespeare's England*. For the availability of Sextus in England, see Hamlin, *Tragedy and Scepticism in Shakespeare's England*, pp. 32–5 and 47.

28. III: 13, 1166.

29. Except where indicated, translations from the *Essays* are mine, based on the 1595 edition that Shakespeare is likely, directly or indirectly, to have encountered. Page references are to the 2007 Pléiade edition. The phrase 'if it makes us more cowardly' ('si nous en devenons plus lasches') does not appear in pre-1595 editions or modern ones based on the Bordeaux copy (in which I: 40 is I: 14).

30. 'Unknowable' takes a liberty: Pyrrhonism does not claim that the non-evident is ipso facto unknowable; it suspends judgement case by case. Since, however, its armoury of doubt-inducing refutations leaves no gaps (Sextus, *Outlines* I, 14–16), and generalised *epochē* is its aim, the distinction disappears.

31. See Haydn, *The Counter-Renaissance* (p. xv), for whom anti-rationalism defines the 'counter-Renaissance'. Montaigne, quoting Cicero, writes that 'It would have been better for Man not to been given it [*sc.* reason] at all than to have been given it with such munificence' (II: 12, 512, trans. Screech).

32. A similar list includes 'worry about what will happen to us, even after life' (II: 12, 511).

33. Hamlet has already said that the ghost may not be of the dead but a devil in 'pleasing shape' (II, ii, 598–600).
34. Rowe, *What Should I Believe?*, p. 39. Irremediably, that is, if the nature of death is that no traveller returns.
35. For 'conscience' in this sense, compare *Tim* II, ii, 175–6: 'Why dost thou weep? Canst thou the conscience lack / To think I shall lack friends?'; in other words, 'What's the matter? Have you so lost your faculties you think my friends won't help?' (the point being that Timon, not Flavius, is thus deluded).
36. It is worth noting, however, that the chapter of the *Essays* in which the 'Pyrrho's pig' passage occurs, and whose title Hamlet distinctly echoes at II, ii, 249–50, includes discussion of suicide and more or less quotes Seneca's Letter 70: 'No-one suffers long but by his own fault' (I: 40, 277).
37. The mind's propensity to reify is similarly deprecated by Theseus in *A Midsummer Night's Dream*: 'imagination bodies forth / The forms of things unknown . . . if it would but apprehend some joy / It comprehends some bringer of that joy' (V, i, 14–20).
38. Craig, 'Hamlet's Book', p. 30.
39. Plato, *Apology* 40c5 – 41c7.
40. For example Brandes, *William Shakespeare*, p. 354; *Hamlet*, ed. Dover Wilson, p. 191; Levin, *The Question of Hamlet*, p. 72; Schücking, *The Meaning of Hamlet*, p. 115. *Essayes*, trans. Florio, p. 627.
41. See Kellenberger, '"Consummation" or "Consumation" in Shakespeare'. Hamlet's 'consummation' is a later editorial change (F or the undated Q4, whichever came first) which obfuscates the sense. If the appeal of death is relief from suffering in non-existence, and the rub is that death may not be non-existence, the suggestion that death improves one's existence is sorely confusing. That said, as a homonym of 'consumation', 'consummation' clearly adds meaning: see Appendix.
42. Other Renaissance writers (e.g. Cardano, *Cardanus Comforte*, 26r following) reference Socrates' speech but omit the epistemological aspects.
43. To summarise: like Seneca's Letter 70, Hamlet discusses suicide as a rational end to suffering, a victory of will over fortune, achievable by pinprick and something we are weak to eschew; like Montaigne's Socrates he speculatively equates death to nonbeing, likens it favourably to dreamless sleep and regards it as unknown on the basis that the dead are unavailable to us; like Montaigne's 'Pyrrho's pig' passage he suggests that dread of death is presumptuous and contemptible and blames it on intellect,
44. Knowles, '*Hamlet* and Counter-Humanism', p. 1056. Nosworthy argues plausibly that the play 'was addressed, in the first place, to a university audience' (*Shakespeare's Occasional Plays*, p. 4).
45. The reversed order of these speeches in Q1 disrupts their relationship.

46. Hamlet's fideistic fatalism explains what has seemed baffling: the almost happenstance nature of his eventual revenge. Providence is at work.
47. V, ii, 223–4, Johnson's emendation but not his interpretation: not just the future but the present is unknown. That we lose nothing by dying early is a point made repeatedly in Seneca's Letter 70.
48. 'On Suicide', p. 222.
49. 'There is something in us, however, which tells us . . . that [death] is not the end of things': Schopenhauer, *The World as Will and Representation*, p. 324.
50. Besides *Hamlet*: *Cym* IV, ii, 280 and *KL* IV, vi, 129 (prose). Lear's 'consumation' was 'consummation' for one edition, the 1619 Q2.
51. See Partridge, *Shakespeare's Bawdy* (which also lists 'conscience'). When Enobarbus says that Cleopatra's presence on the battlefield 'needs must puzzle Antony' (*AC* III, vii, 10) he means 'emasculate', not 'perplex'.
52. 'Bourn' thus combines two English meanings behind a French one. See Williams, 'The *Bourn* Identity'.

Chapter 11

'The Web of our Life is of a Mingled Yarn': Mixed Worlds and Kinds in Montaigne's 'We Taste Nothing Purely' and Shakespeare's *All's Well That Ends Well*

Peter G. Platt

The so-called problem plays of Shakespeare highlight instability, focusing on the moral and intellectual blendedness of the world by calling attention to this complexity in their hybrid forms. Exploring playworlds that are 'mingled yarns' of 'good and ill together', these plays also blend comedy and tragedy.[1] They seem especially connected to Montaigne's 'We taste nothing purely' (II: 20), both intellectually and generically.[2] Indeed, I would argue that *All's Well That Ends Well* in particular can be seen as a dramatic essay – a tasting – of the opening sentences of Montaigne's essay:[3]

> The weakness of our condition causeth that things in their natural simplicity and purity cannot fall into our use. The elements we enjoy are altered, metals likewise, yea gold must be empared with some other stuff to make it fit for our service.[4]

These strangely hybrid, 'impure' plays have been linked since the late nineteenth century. In his *Shakespere* [*sic*] *and His Predecessors* (1896), F. S. Boas grouped three plays together as problem plays or unpleasant, dark comedies – *Measure for Measure, All's Well That Ends Well* and *Troilus and Cressida*. Boas claimed 'the issues raised [in these plays] preclude a completely satisfactory outcome' so that there is no 'settlement of difficulties'.[5]

It is not a stretch to imagine Montaigne's 'We taste nothing purely' shaping plays that, in their form and central ideas, both are impure and are about impurity. According to Boas, 'throughout these plays [*Measure* and *All's Well*] we move along dim, untrodden paths, and at the close our feeling is neither of simple joy nor pain; we are excited, fascinated, perplexed, for the issues raised preclude a completely satisfactory outcome.'[6] Much more recently, Lars Engle has claimed that, in the problem plays, there is 'an acknowledgment of the impure negotiation of purposes that renders any final judgment on anything questionable, and an apparent disposition to take some comfort from that acknowledgment'.[7] Indeed, the plays seem to engage with Montaigne's central thesis, laid out in the opening paragraphs of the essay: '*Of the pleasures and goods we have, there is none exempted from some mixture of evil and incommodity*' (190; 389).

In 'We taste nothing purely', 'goods' are mixed with 'evil', and 'pleasures' with 'incommodity', inconvenience and difficulty. Not surprisingly, early in the essay Montaigne moves on to a meditation on the way this blendedness of 'pleasures' and 'evill' is connected to sex:

> Our exceeding voluptuousness hath some air of groaning and wailing. Would you not say it dyeth with anguish? Yea, when we forge its image in her excellency, we deck it with epithets of sickish and dolorous qualities: languor, effeminacy, weakness, fainting, and *Morbidezza*, a great testimony of their consanguinity and consubstantiality. (190; 389)

The sexual act is filled with both 'voluptuousness' and pleasure on the one hand and 'groaning', 'wailing' and 'anguish' on the other. Its representations, too, are characterised by 'consanguinity and consubstantiality': the image of desire at its peak ('excellency') is nevertheless decked with 'sickish and dolorous qualities', as well as '*Morbidezza*' (which Florio glosses in his dictionary as 'wantonnesse, ranknesse, softnes').[8]

Sex and its representations turn out to be synecdoches for the general 'consanguinity and consubstantiality' of human experience. All moods are blended, 'excessive joy hath more severity than jollity; extreme and full content, more settledness than cheerfulness. . . . Ease consumeth us' (190; 389). Montaigne then quotes 'an old Greek verse' that claims, '"The gods sell us all the goods they give us." That is to say, they give us not one pure and perfect, and that which we buy not with the cost of some evil' (190–1; 389).[9] Nothing is pure – and nothing is without some cost.

Montaigne next discusses the inextricability of pleasure and pain, or at least pleasure and difficulty. 'Travell [travail] and pleasure', seeming opposites and

> most unlike in nature, are notwithstanding followed together by a kind I wot not what natural conjunction. *Socrates* sayeth that some god attempted to huddle up together and confound sorrow and voluptuousness, but being unable to effect it, he bethought himself to couple them together, at least by the tail. (191; 389)

Similarly, Montaigne invokes Metrodorus' claim that 'in sadness there is some alloy of pleasure', and more specifically – alluding to Attalus in Seneca – asserts that 'the remembrance of our last [lost] friends is as pleasing to us as bitterness in wine that is over old . . . and as of sweetly-sour apples' (191; 389). Joy and sorrow, then, are blended emotions: 'the extremity of laughing intermingles itself with tears' (191–2; 389). Painters, Montaigne says, confirm this intermingling, being

> of opinion that *the motions and wrinkles in the face which serve to weep serve also to laugh*. Verily, before one or other be determined to express which, behold the picture['s] success; you are in doubt toward which one inclineth. (191; 389)

As before with poetic descriptions of sex, pictorial representations – like the thing represented –reveal the doubleness of the world.

At this point, Montaigne returns to sex, asserting that no man could bear pure, unmitigated desire:

> Let us suppose all his several members were for ever possessed with a pleasure like unto that of generation, even in the highest point that may be — I find him unable to bear so pure, so constant, and so universal a sensuality. (192; 389)

Even if he could taste desire purely, Montaigne continues, he would not want to: 'Truly, he flies when he is even upon the nick and naturally hasteneth to escape it, as from a step whereon he cannot stay or contain himself, and feareth to sinketh into it' (192; 389).

This meditation on sexuality is followed by a broader yet more personal exploration of his own ethical blendedness, one that Shakespeare seems to echo in *All's Well*: 'When I religiously confess myself unto myself, I find the best good I have hath some vicious taint'

(192; 389). Montaigne suspects that even Plato, as he listened for the music of the spheres, would have 'heard some harsh tune of human mixture, but an obscure tune, and only sensible unto himself' (192; 389). He concludes this section by claiming that '*Man all in all is but a botching and parti-coloured work*' (192; 389).[10]

Montaigne's essay ends by returning to a more general meditation on the problems raised by the mixed quality of human experience. As a result of these difficulties, Montaigne recommends that 'human enterprises should be managed more grossly and superficially and have a good and great part of them left for the rights of fortune' (193; 390). Recognising the limitations of human control, we should try not to analyse things 'so nicely and so profoundly. A man loseth himself about the considerations of so many contrary lusters and diverse forms' (193; 390). Quoting Livy, Montaigne notes, '*Their minds were astonished while they revolved things so different*' (193; 390). As an example of such astonishment, Montaigne mentions the story of Cicero's Simonides's pondering King Hieron's question, 'What is the being and nature of God?' Faced with 'sundry subtle and sharp considerations unto him' and 'doubting which might be the likeliest, he altogether despaireth of the truth' (193; 390).

This is a model for all of us: 'Whosoever searcheth all the circumstances and embraceth all the consequences thereof, hindereth his election' (193; 390). In order not to be paralysed by possibility, we should not only submit to 'the rights of fortune' but also think with a more narrow scope:

> *A mean engine doth equally conduct and sufficeth for the executions of great and little weights.* It is commonly seen that the best husbands [i.e., managers] and the thriftiest are those who cannot tell how they are so, and that these cunning arithmeticians do seldom thrive by it. (193; 390)

The essay concludes, then, on a note of resignation: nothing is pure, and the ability to negotiate this impurity is compromised by our very impurity. Those who reason less intricately get closer to the answers. The rest, with Simonides, most likely 'despaireth of the truth'.

The self-conscious title of *All's Well That Ends Well* both suggests and mocks the purity of comic form and the world.[11] One of the central ways in which *All's Well* evinces its impurity is in its paradoxes, which constantly challenge categories. A crucial paradox surrounds nature and nurture or custom, which the play suggests are a mingled yarn. Nowhere is this more clear than in the King's speech to Bertram about blood in Act II, scene iii. Having been cured by Helena, the

King makes good on his bargain to give to Helena 'with thy kingly hand / What husband in thy power I will command' (II, i, 192–3). When Helena picks Bertram, the latter is horrified both because he has not chosen her himself – 'In such a business give me leave to use / The help of mine own eyes' (II, iii, 103–4) – and because he considers the class difference insurmountable: 'She had her breeding at my father's charge. / A poor physician's daughter, my wife? Disdain / Rather corrupt me ever' (110–12). The King's response shows that he – like the Countess – sees nature and custom to be blendable, mixable, interchangeable.

> 'Tis only the title thou disdain'st in her, the which
> I can build up. Strange is it that our bloods,
> Of colour, weight, and heat, poured all together,
> Would quite confound distinction, yet stands off
> In differences so mighty. If she be
> All that is virtuous, save what thou dislik'st –
> 'A poor physician's daughter' – thou dislik'st
> Of virtue for the name. But do not so.
> From lowest place when virtuous things proceed,
> The place is dignified by th'doer's deed.
> Where great additions swell's, and virtue none,
> It is a dropsied honour. Good alone
> Is good without a name; vileness is so;
> The property by what it is should go,
> Not by the title. She is young, wise, fair.
> In these to nature she's immediate heir,
> And these breed honour. That is honour's scorn
> Which challenges itself as honour's born
> And is not like the sire; honours thrive,
> When rather from our acts we them derive
> Than our foregoers. The mere word's a slave,
> Debauched on every tomb, on every grave
> A lying trophy, and as oft is dumb
> Where dust and damned oblivion is the tomb
> Of honoured bones indeed. What should be said?
> If thou canst like this creature as a maid,
> I can create the rest. Virtue and she
> Is her own dower; honour and wealth from me. (II, iii, 113–40)

This extraordinary speech continues the Montaignian theme of Act II scene ii in *All's Well*: we taste nothing purely, even – perhaps especially – social class. Yarns are not the only thing envisioned as mingled in this play: for the King, mingled blood is indistinguishable blood, and his deconstruction of nobility asserts that noble 'blood' and birthright are not intrinsically connected to noble action. Convinced that Helena is 'All that is virtuous', the King promises Bertram that, by royal fiat, he can adjust the class distinction that is merely conventional and customary: he can easily 'build up' the title that Bertram is so disturbed by.

The King goes further, though, and pokes holes in the entire system – the system that, interestingly, holds up his claim to power. Titles, names, words are 'lying trophies' unless there is honour – and honourable deeds – behind them. Further, they are sources of disease rather than health: 'Where great additions swell's, and virtue none, / It is a dropsied honour.' But far from being a Montaignian hero, Bertram is utterly unmoved by the ideas akin to those of the French essayist delivered to him by his monarch: 'I cannot love her, nor will strive to do't' (II, iii, 141). And the King is forced to reassert the system whose mutability and fragility he has just exposed: 'My honour's at the stake, which to defeat / I must produce my power' (II, iii, 145–6). Bertram's resistance to the royal proclamation has threatened the King's very traditional 'honour', and he must reassert his royal authority and 'produce' his 'power'. He forces Bertram to marry Helena, and Bertram pretends to agree: 'Pardon, my gracious lord, for I submit / My fancy to your eyes' (163–4). But Bertram will leave France in order to fight in the Italian wars before consummating his marriage – indeed, without giving Helena a kiss.

The scepticism towards political power runs throughout the play, in scenes both before and after this one, and royal authority is deeply connected to the play's focus on the world's categorical impurity. The levelling tendency of *All's Well*, put forth by the King himself in Act II scene iii, begins with the King's health issues, especially if the fistula is located in the anus – which then and now it almost certainly would have been.[12] The King is one of us – suffering pain and indignity, as well as life-threatening disease. As Montaigne reminded us on the final page of the *Essays*, '*And sit we upon the highest throne of the world, yet sit we upon our own tail*' (3: 13, 340; 664).[13] *All's Well*'s King, as the play opens, presumably cannot even 'sit . . . upon' his 'own tail'. Although the King and Helena ultimately reach a harmonious arrangement in Act II scene i, the omnipotence of the King is nevertheless challenged in this scene. The King initially rejects Helena's help because

> our most learned doctors leave us, and
> The congregated College have concluded
> That laboring art can never ransom nature
> From her inaidable estate. (II, i, 114–17)

Despite what he argues elsewhere, here the King asserts that nature trumps 'labouring art', culture and convention. But Helena responds by chiding the King for eschewing potentially divine help:

> Inspirèd merit so by breath is barred.
> It is not so with him that all things knows
> As 'tis with us that square our guess by shows;
> But most it is presumption in us when
> The help of heaven we count the act of men. (II, i, 147–51)

Helena chides the King for his presuming to know all that God can do, challenging the idea of the King as being 'God's substitute' (*R2* I, ii, 37) that was crucial to James I's political ideology. But Helena is also suggesting that she, and not the King, has the divinely 'inspirèd merit' that is being barred by the King's very human 'breath'. In highlighting the limitations and impurity at the heart of human power, Helena is at her most Montaignian, especially when she reminds the King of God's tendency to use weak agents to convey his power and message:

> He that of greatest works is finisher
> Oft does them by the weakest minister.
> So holy writ in babes hath judgement shown
> When judges have been babes; great floods have flow'n
> From simple sources, and great seas have dried.
> When miracles by th'greatest have been denied. (II, i, 134–9)

Montaigne, in fact, said as much:

> The participation which we have of the knowledge of truth, whatsoever she is, it is not by our strength we have gotten it. God hath sufficiently taught it us, in that he hath made choice of the simple, common, and ignorant to teach us his wonderful secrets. (II: 12, 147; 289)

But because in Shakespeare we taste nothing purely, Helena's implication that she is the 'weakest minister' and that she and not the King has received the divine breath merely shifts the arrogance that Montaigne is constantly chiding us for:

> Is it possible to imagine anything so ridiculous as this miserable and wretched creature, which is not so much as master of himself, exposed and subject to offences of all things, and yet dareth to call himself master and emperour of this universe? (II: 12, 142; 258)

The venerable courtier Lafeu's Montaignian response to Helena's 'miracle' cure continues the play's sceptical approach to human knowledge:

> They say that miracles are past, and we have our philosophical persons to make modern and familiar things supernatural and causeless. Hence it is that we make trifles of terrors, ensconcing ourselves into seeming knowledge when we should submit ourselves to an unknown fear. (II, iii, 1–5)[14]

Lafeu also tells us that a ballad has been written about the King's healing that confirms Helena's earlier claim (though without the hint of arrogance); its title is 'A showing of a heavenly effect in an earthly actor' (II, iii, 22–3). In this impure, uncertain world, the ways of God are largely 'unknown' and 'causeless'; when they are partially revealed, they are evinced in unpredictable ways.[15]

The brothers Dumaine, even more than Helena and Lafeu, are the true Montaignists of *All's Well*. Their meditations on the 'mingled yarn' of human affairs come directly out of a discussion of Bertram's peccadillos. Discussing the report of Helena's death, the brothers have the following exchange leading up to the 'mingled yarn' quotation, which I include for context:

> SECOND LORD DUMAINE: I am heartily sorry that he'll be glad of this.
> FIRST LORD DUMAINE: How mightily sometimes we make us comforts of our losses.
> SECOND LORD DUMAINE: And how mightily some other times we drown our gain in tears. The great dignity that his valour hath here acquired for him shall at home be encountered with a shame as ample.
> FIRST LORD DUMAINE: The web of our life is of a mingled yarn, good and ill together. Our virtues would be proud if our faults whipped them not, and our crimes would despair if they were not cherished by our virtues.
> (IV, iii, 61–72)

Comforts in loss, tears in gain, shame in dignity and valour – many mingled yarns populate this play.[16]

Yet another of the play's mingled yarns is its ending, which Shakespeare connects to the impurity of its intellectual content. The play tries to end well, and, as Bard Cosman has noted, at least the King has a well end.[17] But the efforts to rehabilitate the superficial and lying Parolles by having him at least partly forgiven by his chief critic, Lafeu, are undermined by the seemingly unredeemable Bertram. Helena tries to forgive Bertram, but she has also beaten him at his game by solving his riddle: she has his ring and presumably is carrying his child. Having learned her Montaignian lessons about the impurity of human experience – especially where love is concerned – she tells the King and Bertram that she is 'but the shadow of a wife you see, / The name and not the thing' (V, iii, 303–4). Before, of course, she was the thing itself that needed a mere title; her reduction to a shadow and name hardly seems comically promising. Striving for comic happiness, Bertram responds, 'Both, both. O, pardon!' (305). But that gesture is compromised by his address – not to Helena but to the King – that focuses on the conditional: 'If she, my liege, can make me know this clearly, / I'll love her dearly, ever ever dearly' (312–13). Renaissance literature is filled with questions of paternity, and Bertram seems to have a loophole if he wants one.

The King, too, does not give us the closure we might hope for – either in his closing speech or in the Epilogue. Befitting this play in which we taste nothing purely, the King cannot be sure that this comedy will end well, despite his reaching for the rhymed couplet that should help achieve his goal: 'All yet seems well; and if it end so meet, / The bitter past, more welcome is the sweet' (329–30). The King's 'seems' is important because it registers doubt about whether all actually is well.[18] Further, his 'if' reminds us of Bertram's 'if', reminds us not only that all may not be well but that the problems may not have ended: to reformulate the phrase yet again, all may be well if it ends well. With this conclusion that points beyond the frame of the play, Shakespeare reveals a doubt that generic restrictions – particularly those of comedy – can contain an adequate version of human experience.[19]

And there's one more twist. The title is invoked a final time in the epilogue:

> The King's a beggar now the play is done.
> All is well ended if this suit be won:
> That you express content, which we will pay
> With strife to please you, day exceeding day. (V, iii, 1–4)

The King has become a beggar – a beggar for applause. This move reminds us that kings on stage were not royalty, were relative beggars – indeed, actors were linked by statute in Shakespeare's day to 'rogues, vagabonds, and sturdy beggars'.[20] And, of course, this move can be connected to the King's astonishing views on class and nobility in Act II; no one's blood is distinguishable from anyone else's, and thus a King can easily become a beggar, as Hamlet has taught us.[21]

Bringing back the conditional 'if', these lines also underscore that theatrical success was and is about audience satisfaction; comedies and happy endings typically provide the most pleasure. Thus, there is another potentially cynical angle on the end of this play: the drama ends well if people like it and come back to the Globe, paying to see it and other plays by Shakespeare and his company. So it is ironically fitting that, admitting it both seeks witnesses who will 'express content' and strives 'to please' them, *All's Well* has been deemed unpleasant, broken and 'unsmiling', indeed 'one of Shakespeare's least performed and least loved comedies'.[22] As with so much else in this play – and the problem plays more generally – Montaigne seems to be hovering and haunting: 'Excessive joy hath more severity than jollity; extreme and full content, more settledness than cheerfulness' (II: 20, 190; 389). The incompleteness that one finds in Montaigne and Shakespeare is often less than pleasant; open-endedness can suggest ongoing searches but also brokenness.[23] To essay – to taste – is to taste impurely. All can never end well, really.

Notes

1. This chapter has also been published in *Shakespeare's Essays: Sampling Montaigne from* Hamlet *to* The Tempest (Edinburgh University Press, 2020). It is a revisionist study arguing that the *Essays* of Montaigne – made available to Shakespeare and the English-reading world via John Florio's translated *Essayes* in 1603 – were a crucial factor in the composition of later Shakespearean drama, filled as it is with doubt, contingency, uncertainty and mutability. A focus on multiple selves, brave new worlds, and hybrid art forms characterises Shakespeare's essaying of the *Essays*.

. Shakespeare, *All's Well That Ends Well*, III, iii, 69–70, in *The Norton Shakespeare*, 2nd edn, ed. Stephen Greenblatt et al. Unless otherwise noted, all further citations from the plays of Shakespeare are to this edition and are annotated within the text.

2. Linking the problem plays to Montaigne – though not specifically this essay – A. P. Rossiter has called attention to the plays' 'shiftingness': 'All the firm points of view or *points d'appui* fail one, or are felt to be fallible: in Ulysses, Isabella, Helena; even in Order, as represented by the Duke. Hence the "problem"-quality, and the ease with which any critic who takes a firm line is cancelled out by another. To pursue this shiftingness I should have to explore at length the world of the 1590s: of Donne, of Chapman, Marston, Jonson and the young Middleton. But this much I can say: it was a world in which human experience,

thought and feeling seemed only describable in terms of *paradox*: the greatest of all, man himself' ('The Problem Plays', p. 28). More recently, see Hugh Grady who in *Shakespeare and Impure Aesthetics* explores an 'impure aesthetics' that focuses on an artwork as 'disunified, as constituted by internal clashes of discourse and by the insubordination of repressed materials. . . . [T]he aesthetic is intrinsically "impure" – it is a place-holder for what is repressed elsewhere in the system; it develops as an autonomous practice but participates in the market economy, the social-status system, the political world, the religious communities, and private life' (pp. 4, 21).

3. See 'Essayer', in Cotgrave, *A Dictionarie*.
4. Montaigne, 'We taste nothing purely' (II: 20), in *Shakespeare's Montaigne*, ed. Greenblatt and Platt. Where available, quotations from Florio's Montaigne will come from this edition; citations will be included in the text and will list, first, this edition's page number and, second, the page number of the 1603 edition (190; 389–90). For a parallel idea and phrasing, see Montaigne's 'Of Experience' (III: 13): 'Our life is composed, as is the harmonie of the World, of contrarie things; so of divers tunes, some pleasant, some harsh, some sharpe, some flat, some low and some high: What would that Musition say, that should love but some one of them?' (*Essayes*, trans. Florio, pp. 648–9).
5. Boas, *Shakspere and His Predecessors*, p. 345. See also E. K. Chambers, who, in his *Shakespeare: A Survey*, writes: 'They are all [*Measure, All's Well* and *Troilus*] unpleasant plays, the utterances of a puzzled and disturbed spirit, full of questionings, sceptical of its own ideals, looking with new misgiving into the ambiguous shadows of a world over which a cloud has passed and made a goblin of the sun' (p. 210). Chambers's introductions to Shakespeare's plays, collected in this book, were originally published between 1904 and 1908, so we can safely assume the influence of Boas (the clustering of these three plays) and of George Bernard Shaw, whose *Plays Pleasant and Unpleasant* was published in 1898. Shaw mentioned the three Shakespearearean problem plays by title – and called them 'unpopular plays' – in his preface to this collection (p. ix).
6. Boas, *Shakspere and His Predecessors*, p. 345.
7. Engle, '*Measure for Measure* and Modernity', p. 89.
8. Florio, *A Worlde of Wordes*.
9. The Greek verse comes from Epicharmus, 'preserved in Xenophon's *Memorabilia*, II, i, 20' (Montaigne, *Essays*, ed. Zeitlin, 2: 581n).
10. Shakespeare's Feste, the 'parti-coloured', motley Fool in *Twelfth Night*, though a pre-1603 character, shares Montaigne's view (and Florio's metaphor): 'bid the dishonest man mend himself: if he mend, he is no longer dishonest; if he cannot, let the botcher mend him. Any thing that's mended is but patch'd; virtue that transgresses is but patch'd with sin, and sin that amends is but patch'd with virtue' (I, v, 45–9).

11. G. Wilson Knight, in his 'The Third Eye: An Essay on *All's Well That Ends Well*', notes that 'the play is more than a problem play like *Troilus and Cressida* and *Measure for Measure*' (p. 102). Nonetheless, he, too, highlights the play's ambivalence and uncertainty, on many levels: 'The more important thinking here avoids questions of right and wrong as sharply opposed absolutes – the Clown is there to point the difference – and concentrates rather on a territory where exactitudes are impossible because ethical ideals and human stuff, personal or communal, are in such conflict that some compromise, some unwritten code for living and action, must be devised' (p. 103).
12. See Cosman, 'Shakespeare's Treatment of Anal Fistula'.
13. See Mack, *Reading and Rhetoric in Shakespeare and Montaigne*: 'The later Montaigne shares Shakespeare's interest in the experiences and actions of ordinary people . . . Montaigne uses the necessity of bodily functions to equate rulers with ordinary people' (pp. 134, 135).
14. Montaigne would almost certainly agree: 'Whence it followeth, that nothing is so firmly believed, as that which a man knoweth least; nor are there people more assured in their reports, then such as tell-vs fables, as Alchumists, Prognosticators, Fortune-tellers, Palmesters, Phisitians, *id genus omne*, and such like. To which, if I durst, I would joyne a rable of men, that are ordinarie interpreters and controulers of Gods secret desseignes, presuming to finde out the causes of every accident, and to prie into the secrets of Gods divine will, the incomprehensible motives of his workes' (Montaigne, 'That a Man Ought to Meddle with Iudging of Divine Lawes' [I: 32, I: 31 in *Essayes*, trans. Florio, p. 107]).
15. Horkheimer and Adorno in their *Dialectic of Enlightenment* provide the same critique of 'enlightenment' as Lafeu does of 'seeming knowledge', invoking Francis Bacon as they do so:

> '[Knowledge's] concern is not "satisfaction, which men call truth," but "operation," the effective procedure. The "true end, scope or office of knowledge" does not consist in "any plausible, delectable, reverend or admired discourse, or any satisfactory arguments, but in effecting and working, and in discovery of particulars not revealed before, for the better endowment and help of man's life." There shall be neither mystery nor any desire to reveal mystery . . . From now on matter was finally to be controlled without the illusion of immanent powers or hidden properties. For enlightenment, anything which does not conform to the standard of calculability and utility must be viewed with suspicion . . . The supernatural, spirits and demons, are taken to be reflections of human beings who allow themselves to be frightened by natural phenomena (pp. 2, 3, 4).

16. Mary Floyd-Wilson sees another doubleness at work in *All's Well* – that of proto-science and the occult. For a fascinating reading of the problems of hidden knowledge in the play, see her *Occult Knowledge, Science, and Gender in the Shakespearean Stage*, pp. 28–46.

17. Cosman, 'Shakespeare's Treatment of Anal Fistula', p. 916.
18. Donaldson nicely notes the paradoxes and impurities of the play: 'The ending seems no ending, as the maid seems no maid, Parolles is a knave and no knave, as Bertram loved Diana and he loved her not, and as the dead wife seems suddenly and miraculously alive' ('Shakespeare's Play of Endings', p. 51).
19. See Donaldson: '*All's Well That Ends Well* speaks constantly of an end which is not finally realised within its dramatic framework, but pushed forward beyond the play into an undramatised future . . . *All's Well*['s] . . . problems of *ending* . . . [are] not merely formal problems but also the problems of life itself' ('Shakespeare's Play of Endings', pp. 52, 54). See also Kay, '"To hear the rest untold"', esp. pp. 217–18.
20. See the 29 June 1572 *An Acte for the punishment of Vacabondes and for Releif of the Poore & Impotent* (14 *Eliz.* C. 5), quoted in Chambers, *The Elizabethan Stage*: 'all Fencers Bearewardes Comon Players in Enterludes & Minstrels, not belonging to any Baron of this Realme or towardes any other honorable Personage of greater Degree; all Juglers Pedlars Tynkers and Petye Chapmen . . . shall wander abroad and have not Lycence of two Justices of the Peace at the leaste, whereof one to be of the Quorum, when and in what Shier they shall happen to wander . . . shalbee taken adjudged and deemed Roges, Vacaboundes and Sturdy Beggers . . .' (4: 270).
21. See *Ham* II, ii, 245–57 and IV, iii, 22–5.
22. Chambers, *Shakespeare: A Survey*, p. 207, and Bate, 'Introduction', p. vii.
23. This is akin to what John O'Brien, in 'Montaigne and Antiquity', has called an 'aesthetic of *non-finito*' (p. 69).

Chapter 12

Radical Neo-Paganism: The Transmission of Discontinuous Identity from Plutarch to Montaigne to Shakespeare's *Antony and Cleopatra*

Daniel Vitkus

One of the claims made by Jonathan Dollimore in *Radical Tragedy* is that Jacobean tragedy exposed its audiences to a radical philosophical concept, what Dollimore calls 'discontinuous identity'.[1] In his description and analysis of discontinuous identity in John Marston's play *Antonio's Revenge* (1601), Dollimore offers this observation, which might also be applied to Shakespeare's *Antony and Cleopatra*:

> The characters of this play attempt to disengage themselves from hostile circumstance but cannot; they internalise the confusions and contradictions of their world, becoming themselves confused and contradictory. Faced with a dislocated world, individual consciousness itself becomes dislocated.[2]

The concept of discontinuous identity is an important element in the anti-essentialist definition of selfhood that emerged in early modernity, but the idea of an inconstant, mutable self has a long, complex history in the Western tradition, going back to antiquity. One possible starting point for tracing its genealogy may be found in Plutarch's Heraclitean description of temporal being as mutation in the *Moralia*, an account of being and becoming that was adapted by Michel de Montaigne, where it appears at the conclusion of his 'Apology for Raymond Sebond'. This chapter argues that in *Antony and Cleopatra*, provoked by John Florio's translation of Montaigne, and inspired by an eclectic variety of pagan materialist philosophers, Shakespeare created theatrical characters in *Antony and Cleopatra* who resist essentialised selfhood and exhibit a fluidity of identity and consciousness. Here I am in strong agreement with the case made by Hugh Grady, who has argued that Montaigne and Shakespeare are both

> key pioneers of an epochal shift in Western culture productive of new ways of constituting and thinking about the private, the domestic, and the subjective – a shift that is now commonly seen as one of the crucial characteristics of an emerging modernity in the Renaissance.[3]

Through the adaptive strategies of Montaigne and Shakespeare, whose innovative writing was guided by an early modern version of Renaissance humanism, we see a radically new and 'modern' definition of subjectivity emerging.

In his superb introduction to the Oxford edition of *Antony and Cleopatra*, Michael Neill describes the dramatic effect of Shakespeare's appropriation of Montaigne:

> In plays like *Hamlet* and *Troilus and Cressida* Shakespeare has already shown a fascination with the discontinuous and histrionic nature of identity explored in Montaigne's *Essays*. . . . *Antony and Cleopatra* . . . goes a step further by simply taking Montaigne's psychological paradoxes for granted, and in the process throwing the perplexity experienced by Hamlet and Troilus back upon the audience.[4]

Drawing on Janet Adelman's brilliant reading of *Antony and Cleopatra* in *The Common Liar*, Neill goes on to provide a convincing account, not only of the pattern of discontinuous identity in the play, but of the 'properties of the self' that are exhibited by the tragic couple, both in terms of identity as defined by external action in the public gaze and by an 'elasticity of becoming'.[5] While the former tends to be associated with masculine virtu(e), and the latter is frequently connected to Cleopatra (and to her feminine manifestations of 'infinite variety'), both characters exhibit a slipperiness and an inconsistency that resists stable identity while offering a model for understanding human identity in general as unstable. It is both a humanist rebooting of ancient philosophy and the beginning of something new and more fundamentally anti-essentialist – the modern, secular understanding of subjectivity as material (not metaphysical), ephemeral (not immortal-in-identity) and ever-changing (not necessarily rooted in an essentialised, unique and separate 'soul' or 'spirit').

Renaissance humanists found in ancient philosophers and authors like Lucretius and Ovid a description of inanimate matter (including mind as matter) as 'eterne in mutabilitie' (as Edmund Spenser famously termed it).[6] This sense of a material world in flux, to which human consciousness and vitality are also subject, was described by Plutarch in 'The EI at Delphi'. Plutarch's text was then transmitted, via Jacques Amyot's translation, to Montaigne, who, in his 'Apology for Raymond Sebond', the longest and most philosophically oriented of his essays, placed Plutarch's radical description of mutability and instability at the conclusion of that essay.[7] Although the entire section taken from Plutarch is too long to be quoted in full, here are two key passages from Florio's English translation of Montaigne's 'Apology':

[T]here is no constant existence, neither of our being, nor of the objects. And we, and our judgment, and all mortal things else, do incessantly roll, turn, and pass away. Thus can nothing be certainly established, nor of the one, nor of the other; both the judging and the judged being in continual alteration and motion. We have no communication with being; for every human nature is ever in the middle between being born and dying; giving nothing of itself but an obscure appearance and shadow, and an uncertain and weak opinion. And if perhaps you fix your thought to take its being, it would be even as if one should go about to [grasp] the water: for how much the more he shall close and press that, which by its own nature is ever gliding, so much the more he shall lose what he would hold and fasten. Thus, seeing all things are subject to pass from one change to another, reason, which therein seeketh a real subsistence, finds herself deceived as unable to apprehend anything subsistent and permanent: forsomuch as each thing either commeth to a being and is not yet altogether, or beginneth to die before it be born.[8]

Citing the ancient Greek writer Epicharmus, Plutarch explains how, from moment to moment, the flow of life and matter in temporality does not allow for human identity to remain stable or consistent:

[H]e who yesternight was bidden to dinner this day, cometh today unbidden, since they are no more themselves, but are become others. And that one mortal substance could not twice be found in one self state: for by the suddenness and lightness of change, sometimes it wasteth and other times it reassembleth; now it comes, and now it goes. In such sort that he who beginneth to be born never comes to the perfection of being. For this being born never cometh to an end, nor ever stayeth as being at an end, but after the seed proceedeth continually in change and alteration from one to another.[9]

In *Antony and Cleopatra*, Shakespeare does not directly echo Florio's translation of Montaigne (as he does in other plays) but rather figures forth the concept of discontinuous identity through the histrionics of his main characters, Antony and Cleopatra. It is part and parcel of the dazzling artistic and intellectual virtuosity demonstrated in Shakespeare's play that the author would set out to create compelling theatrical characters who lack a stable identity. This seemingly perverse strategy is consistent, however, with the fundamental pattern of meaning in the play, which is designed to show how human existence and understanding are inconstant and discontinuous. And in *Antony and Cleopatra* Shakespeare goes further than Montaigne, producing a more deeply radical text, because, while Shakespeare shares Montaigne's profound scepticism about the human capacity for stable identity, the author of *Antony and Cleopatra* does not combine that scepticism with a countervailing faith in the divine perfection of the incomprehensible one God (Montaigne: 'that infinite beauty, power, and goodness – how can it allow any correspondence or likeness with anything as abject as we are . . . ?' [472][10]). Nor does *Antony and Cleopatra* acknowledge providentialist Christian dogma (for Montaigne, 'The hand with which [God] governs lends itself to all things with the same tenor' [479]). But these concepts function as Montaigne's core certainties in the 'Apology'.

Nothing could be further from the tone and spirit of *Antony and Cleopatra* than certain statements in 'The Apology': for example, Montaigne's condemnation of suicide as treacherous, cowardly and 'unjust' (472), or this passage, which stands in direct opposition to the pagan-Epicurean values embodied by Shakespeare's protagonists:

> If the pleasures that you promise us in the other life are of the kind I have tasted here below, that has nothing in common with infinity. Even if all my five natural senses were filled to overflowing with delight, and this soul possessed of all the contentment it can desire or hope for, we know what it is capable of: that would still be nothing.
> If there is anything of mine in it, there is nothing divine. (467)

Shakespeare passed over this kind of dualistic asceticism, but he found and appropriated other elements in Montaigne (and in Montaigne's Plutarch) where the joyful energy in material pleasure, moving through life and the senses, might be discerned.

Both Montaigne and Shakespeare, as Renaissance humanists and radical intellectual and artistic innovators, appropriated elements from the ancient and contemporary texts they had read, not in the manner of traditional scholarly or philosophical discourse, but in ground-breaking, modern ways that were eclectic and creative. What Shakespeare does with Montaigne (and with Plutarch) is typical of his appropriations and transformations from non-narrative sources: Shakespeare never incorporates a thinker's entire work, never swallows it whole, and never reproduces the overarching principles found in such sources in a comprehensive way, as if he were a doctrinaire disciple of a certain philosopher or philosophical school. Instead, when Shakespeare is inspired by something from Plutarch or Montaigne, he seizes on a portion of that text and reworks it into a new form, restating, applying and modifying the philosophical concepts to fit the shape of a dramatic dialogue or soliloquy. Rather than cutting and pasting a written passage, which is in large part what Montaigne does in his layered essays that exhibit many of the features of the commonplace book, Shakespeare adopts and transforms the philosophical source into an image, an action or a short speech that is integrated within his own dramatic plot and plan. Of course, the essay as a written form to be read and tragic drama as a script for performance are widely divergent genres: they call for very different formal and representational strategies, and this imperative goes a long way towards explaining why Montaigne and Shakespeare handle philosophy differently.[11] In the case of Shakespeare the playwright, he can demonstrate his ideas through a coordinated complex of spoken words, actions and images on stage, while Montaigne speaks more personally and intimately to his readers. In describing Shakespeare and his adaptation of philosophy, we cannot simply say that he is an Epicurean materialist withdrawing from politics, a Plutarchan anti-Epicurean, a Pyrrhonian sceptic or a Christian fideist, though we may find elements of these philosophical positions articulated or demonstrated throughout Shakespeare's work and in the mouths of various characters. On the other hand, though he is no flat-footed philosopher conforming to predetermined scholastic forms and conventions, Montaigne's first-person discourse and personalising, autobiographical tendencies make it easier to categorise his philosophical positions on various questions and to discern the overarching pattern of his orientation towards various philosophical schools.[12] Easier than Shakespeare, at least, who left no essays written in the first person. But Montaigne is nonetheless a slippery figure whose intricately layered *Essays* contain contradictions and tensions that are never fully resolved.[13] An important example of this complexity is the 'Apology' itself, which sets out to apologise for something that Montaigne is actually quite reluctant to support, then proceeds to move back and forth from, on the one hand, Montagne's radical Pyrrhonian scepticism and his vigorous attack on human presumption to, on the other, an unflinching presumption of faith in the truth of Roman Catholic teachings about an absolute, all-knowing God.[14]

Where Shakespeare's humanism in *Antony and Cleopatra* diverges from Montaigne's humanism in the *Essays* most notably is in Shakespeare's reconstruction and celebration of a pre-Christian, classical 'world'. Shakespeare drew on North's translation of Plutarch's *Lives* as his primary source for the events of the play, but in thinking about the ancient Mediterranean world and the changes wrought by the Roman civil wars and the subsequent rise of Octavius to become sole ruler and emperor, Shakespeare was moved to produce, and even celebrate, a certain eclectic, imaginary version of 'paganism'. It was certainly not an accurate representation of ancient pagan culture or history – rather, it was a creative, nostalgic reconstruction (or, to use Barbara Bono's term, a 'transvaluation') designed to speak to audiences in Jacobean London.[15] Such transformation is typical of Renaissance humanism and its art. What sets the author of *Antony and Cleopatra* apart from most Renaissance humanists, however, including Montaigne, is his refusal to engage in the kind of treatment of ancient paganism that would result in a syncretic mixture of pagan thought or ancient history erring on the side of an explicitly moralising Christian worldview or attitude. In this regard, the author of *Antony and Cleopatra*, like Horatio, is 'more an antique Roman than a Dane'. We might even say that Shakespeare, like Antony and Cleopatra, came to view Roman virtue and imperial might from an Egyptian perspective.

Wavering between Roman and Egyptian behaviours, Antony and Cleopatra exhibit both the Roman virtue of noble suicide that shows the courage to undo the self but also the festive, Bacchanalian excess that enacts a loss of self in the divine intoxication that is possession by the god and unification with the other celebrants. When Antony faces defeat and death, he accounts for his changing identity in images of dissolution that invoke the sacred, elemental nature of shifting earth, water and air. Just before his suicide attempt, he confides in Eros, comparing his self to a 'cloud' or 'vapour' that shifts its shape:

> . . . even with a thought
> The rack dislimns, and makes it indistinct
> As water is in water.

> . . . now thy captain is
> Even such a body: here I am Anthony,
> Yet cannot hold this visible shape, my knave.
> . . . Nay, weep not, gentle Eros, there is left us
> Ourselves to end ourselves. (IV, xv, 9–22)

This paradoxical doing and undoing results in a 'discandying', an oscillation back and forth that melts away the self into death and non-being. As Neill puts it, 'the undoing of the self is figured as a terminal act of self-realisation'.[16] But this alteration is the nature of life as well as death and suicide: inspirited matter grows, changes, then resolves itself into a dew at the time of death. Antony or Cleopatra are both presented or described as a potentially divine beings, poised to morph into a daemon or god; and at the same time they are merely fragile sacks of mud and water, whose serpentine skin-shedding and passing leaves only the faint trail of slime on the 'fig-leaves' or the 'caves of Nile' (V, ii, 349–51).

Shakespeare's play, in the way that it sometimes inflates Antony and Cleopatra to the status of deity, and in the way that it associates their quasi-divinity with the generative force in Nature, draws on pagan traditions that had gained new attention during the Renaissance. In her correspondence with Isis and Venus, Shakespeare's Cleopatra can sometimes be seen as a kind of earth mother personifying the endless variety and sexual energy in nature. Shakespeare's play suggests that Cleopatra, who is at one level a mere squeaking boy-actor, is also a larger-than-life figure, a *Venus genetrix* or *Aphrodite armata*.

Janet Adelman has observed that 'Throughout the play, Antony and Cleopatra are presented as extremes of martial and venereal virtue; it is inevitable that they be seen as analogous to Mars and Venus' (82). Another classical myth that seems to be part of the web of Shakespearean intertextuality is the story of how the jealous husband of Venus, Vulcan, catches Mars and his wife in his net. This fable is recounted in Lucretius's *On the Nature of Things* and given an eclectic Renaissance interpretation by George Sandys in his English translation of Ovid. There is a kind of Pythagorean–Epicurean–Lucretian synthesis in Ovid's *Metamorphoses*, where, in the fifteenth and final book, a long speech is given to Pythagoras, and in which the Lucretian discourse of natural philosophy is deployed to describe a series of fantastical transformations from one state to another. Clearly, Montaigne was not a believer in reincarnation, and in many ways he positioned himself as an anti-materialist in the sense that he strongly endorsed the unshakable 'truth' of a transcendent, metaphysical realm inhabited by God and the notion of the immortal soul. But, at the same time, he articulated many emergent, subversive ideas that were developed from texts by Lucretius and other materialist or sceptical thinkers. After all, Montaigne's self-declared inconsistency is consistent with his endorsement of discontinuous identity and with his autobiographical description of selfhood in constant motion. This is quite clear in this well-known passage from 'Of Repenting': 'I cannot settle my object. It goeth so unquietly and staggering, with a natural drunkenness. I take it in this plight, as it is in the instant I amuse myself about it. I describe not the essence but the passage' (196). Such moments of radical implication are the ludic extremes that counter-balance Montaigne's tendencies towards melancholy and his almost misanthropic, fideistic attack on human reason, an approach which drives much of the 'Apology' and leads him to sneer, 'Puff-up thyself, poor man – yea, swell and swell again' (164).

In Plutarch's *Moralia*, Montaigne found one of his favourite sources for borrowing from the classical past: he refers to or quotes from the *Moralia* 459 times in the *Essays*, by one scholar's count.[17] Plutarch's *Moralia* also constitutes an important formal model for Montaigne's *Essays*: the ancient philosopher wrote in a form of philosophical discourse that quoted from and synthesised various philosophical predecessors and used references to mythology, past history and current events. A follower of the Platonic school, Plutarch was an enthusiastic anti-Epicurean (see, for the most obvious example of this in the *Moralia*, Plutarch's extended polemic against the Epicurean philosopher Colotes), but this opposition did not prevent him from citing the Epicurean Lucretius to support a point.[18] For instance, the following lines appear in the section from Plutarch's 'On the EI at Delphi' that Montaigne places at the conclusion of his 'Apology':

> Of th'universal world, age doth the nature change,
> And all things from one state must to another range.
> No one thing like itself remains; all things do pass.
> Nature doth change, and drive to change, each thing that was.[19]

A series of authorial and cultural mediations leads from Lucretius and Plutarch's ancient descriptions of discontinuous identity, through Montaigne and the culture of Renaissance humanism, to the theatrical representation of unstable 'character' in Shakespeare's *Antony and Cleopatra*; and along the way a complex process of selective appropriation and synthesis occurs.

In order to reach a better understanding of *Antony and Cleopatra* as a play, not only of character psychology, but of ideas, we must not neglect the importance of another text from Plutarch's *Moralia*, a section titled 'Of Isis and Osiris'.[20] Ancient texts by authors such as Lucretius, Plutarch or Apuleius as well as Renaissance translations and reinterpretations of ancient myth by authors such as Edmund Spenser and Giordano Bruno provided Shakespeare and his contemporaries with a conceptual framework that defined Egypt as the site of a kind of dark ecology of excess that defies Christian metaphysical dualism, asceticism and anti-materialism. In *Antony and Cleopatra*, the natural, elemental imagery and the references to pagan deity and apotheosis come together to form a celebration of the divine, metamorphic life force that Egypt represents, and which the Roman empire under Octavius Caesar will attempt to incorporate, control and repress.

Direct allusions to a Christian frame of reference (for judging moral behaviour, for measuring the spiritual condition of those who are about to die, etc.) are markedly rare in *Antony and Cleopatra*: nature, life, death, suicide and the afterlife are all treated from a pagan point of view. The Christian notion of sin, for example, is introduced only once, when Cleopatra asks, 'is it sin / To rush into the house of death / Ere death dare come to us?' (IV, xvi, 81–3), and this question is raised only to be immediately and emphatically refuted when the Egyptian queen strongly advocates the 'brave' and 'noble' course of suicide, 'after the high Roman fashion' (IV, xvi, 88). Sex is also sacred in Cleopatra's pagan realm, for 'The holy priests / Bless her when she is riggish' (II, ii, 246–7), and death, for Cleopatra, will not involve the Christian eschatology of heaven and hell. Instead, her final performance invokes the possibility of transcendence and reunion with Antony in the Elysian Fields of the classical afterlife.[21]

All this is not to say that Shakespeare avoids 'biblical language' in *Antony and Cleopatra*. Such language, as many scholars have convincingly shown, was a deeply embedded source of inspiration for Shakespeare's style and idiom, and it is apparent throughout his writings.[22] In *The Bible in Shakespeare*, Hannibal Hamlin shows us that *Antony and Cleopatra* 'contains significant anachronistic allusions to the Bible',[23] but after cataloguing and analysing these (mostly indirect) references, nearly all of which refer to the Book of Revelation, Hamlin rightly concludes that 'These biblical allusions do not by any means make *Antony and Cleopatra* a "Christian play"'.[24] Rather, Shakespeare's usage of biblical language and allusion in the play is strongly ironic and playful. We would be wise to understand the play as a 'dark parody . . . of Christian beliefs and doctrines' rather than to wrest its meaning to fit a didactic Christian model, complete with metaphysical dualism.[25] The pattern of biblical allusion that likens Antony to Christ or Cleopatra to the Whore of Babylon certainly helps to produce a suggestive richness and intertextual complexity, but these analogies are not to be taken literally. When the play's ironic appropriations of the Bible hint, anachronistically, at the apocalypse to come, they do so in order to mourn the passing of an older pagan order. Rather than celebrating the arrival of the Christian era as a universal improvement that makes salvation possible or glorying in the dawning light of a Truth that extinguishes pagan darkness, Shakespeare's play aligns the coming of the new Christian-imperial order with the tragic defeat of the play's two protagonists, and with the victory of the calculating dictator Octavius Caesar.[26]

Anticipating his triumph over the defeated Antony, Caesar declares that 'the time of universal peace is near' (IV, vi, 4). But it is personal ambition, exploiting every opportunity to monopolise worldly, geopolitical power, that drives the calculating, Machiavellian Caesar, not piety. Caesar's victory enables the tragic passing of the pagan era and prepares the 'three-nooked world' for the *Pax Romana*, which was (according to Christian tradition) a prefiguration and preparation for the coming of Christ, the 'prince of peace', into the world. Shakespeare's play chronicles the transition from one epoch to another, marking the beginning of a new Christian age that will witness the silencing of the oracles and the imposition of a state-sponsored monotheism over the rich, polytheistic belief systems of the Mediterranean world.[27]

When the god Hercules abandons Antony in Act IV, scene iii, this desertion is not only an indication of Antony's waning power but also a sign of the times. The epic age of gods, daemons and heroes is passing, and a new era of imperial administration and instrumental reason under Octavius Caesar is about to begin. This historical event comes to symbolise a shift in values from 'infinite variety', subjective fluidity and overflowing bounty to a Roman attitude that quantifies, judges, sets strict limits, and establishes imperial order and control. At the same time, the play has established a model for discontinuous identity that is at odds with all that Caesar stands for as the new emperor who will assert order, essence and stability as a political and ideological strategy that seeks to occlude and deny the mutability of selfhood enacted by his hybridising rivals for imperial power, Antony and Cleopatra.

Antony's posthumous status as a wonder of the world, described by Cleopatra as a being whose 'face was as the heavens' and whose 'legs bestrid the ocean' (V, ii, 79, 82) suggests that he was a god among men, and a man who might become a god in the afterlife, following the model of 'the god Hercules' (IV, iii, 14). While demonstrating the frail, mortal humanity of his protagonists, Shakespeare's play simultaneously expresses the theory of euhemerism, which claims that myths are based on traditional accounts of real people or events and that the gods were once heroes who walked the earth. And yet, the passing of the pagan era implies an end to this type of transmutability and transcendence. According to Christian historiography regarding the Roman Empire, which was well known in Shakespeare's day, the Pax Romana brings, not the euhemeristic translation of human heroes to gods, but the opposite: a top-down incarnation of godhead in human form as the son of the one true God descends into the flesh. This stingy downsizing of divinity, which also denied divine status to humanity while on earth, is heralded by Caesar's sober and calculating seizure of absolute power. Ironically, the two exceptions that would prove the rule would be, first, the deification of Julius Caesar in 42 BCE, two years after his assassination; and later, Augustus Caesar's adoption of the title *Divi Filius* (son of a god), and later his deification while still living when he permitted the imperial cults to be established in the Eastern provinces of the empire and elsewhere. Christian historiographers were later to characterise the imperial cults as the last, corrupt efforts of pagan religion to resist the inevitable coming of Christianity (which would bring the demonisation of daemons, among other things). According to Christian apologists, when the 'apostate' emperor Julian attempted to revive the oracle at Delphi, the oracle produced its final answer: 'Tell the emperor that the Diadalic hall has fallen. No longer does Phoebus have his chamber, nor mantic laurel, nor prophetic spring; and the speaking water has been silenced.'[28]

Plutarch, who lived in the time between the reigns of Augustus and Julian, was interested in the fate of the Delphic oracle. Another of his dialogues, 'Of the Oracles that Have Ceased to Give Answer', which also appears in Holland's 1603 translation of Plutarch's *Moralia*, tries to account for this silencing: 'the Oracles are become mute and lie still without any validity because the Daemons which were wont to govern them be retired and gone, like as instruments of music yield no sound and harmony when musicians handle them not'.[29] In this dialogue, Plutarch seeks to explain the mystical pronouncement, 'That the Great Pan is dead',[30] and he debates various causes for the silencing of the oracles. Plutarch's interlocutors give reasons for this phenomenon by asserting that the oracles are manifestations of 'daemons', divine spirits whose powers wax and wane over time. While providing this explanation for the silencing of the oracles in Greece, the dialogue offered Shakespeare a model for the apotheosis of Antony and Cleopatra:

> Hesiodus was the first who purely and distinctly hath set down four kinds of reasonable natures, to wit, the Gods; then the Daemons, and those many in number and all good; the Heroes, and Men; for the Demi-gods are ranged in the number of those heroic worthies. But others hold that there is a transmutation as well of bodies as of souls, and like as we may observe, that of earth is engendered of water, of water air, and of air fire, whiles the nature of the substance still mounteth on high: even so the better souls are changed, first from men to Heroes or demi-gods, and afterwards from them to Daemons, and of Daemons some few after long time, being well refined and purified by virtue, came to participate the divination of the gods. Yet unto some it befalleth, that not being able to hold and contain, they suffer themselves to slide and fall into mortal bodies again, where they lead an obscure and dark life, like unto a smoky vapor.[31]

This classical, pagan system describes an afterlife and a spirit world in which beings can pass from one spiritual state to another, from mortal to hero to daemon to deity, as well as a spiritual hierarchy that is related to and correspondent with the elemental transmutations of the material world.

It is indicative of the larger pattern of uncertainty in the play, described in detail by Adelman, that we never know whether the deaths of Antony and Cleopatra are pathways to reincarnation and apotheosis, or whether they merely suffer the way of all flesh and matter, in spite of their claims to an immortal reunion. Perhaps their immortality, and the preservation of their greatness, is a product of fame and poetry: both protagonists have a firm eye on their future reputation. In any case, their lives beyond suicide and death are never described in Christian terms.

The instability of matter in nature, the shifting forms and substances that characterise all life and even the changes that transport souls into a new life beyond death: these phenomena are linked by Shakespeare to the insubstantiality of human identity. Identity in *Antony and Cleopatra* is both discontinuous and performative. The Renaissance tradition of correspondence produced a worldview that linked nature to humankind and humankind to the cosmos. These connections could be employed ideologically to reinforce notions of order and hierarchy, as in the case of Ulysses' speech on order in *Troilus and Cressida*, but Shakespeare could also use the logic of correspondence to describe a system of disorder and change. Many of Shakespeare's contemporaries believed that esoteric knowledge originating in Egypt with Hermes Trismegistus and others was the key to understanding Nature, and the pagan cults of ancient Egypt were believed to involve the stewardship of that knowledge and to comprise the origins of 'religion'. The Renaissance neo-paganism that Shakespeare drew upon was an eclectic tradition that combined mythic and philosophical approaches to the concept of identity. Both the elemental imagery and the representations of fluctuation in desire express the notion of human identity as discontinuous role-playing.

In 'Of Isis and Osiris', Plutarch's Isis is a divine personification of the natural mutability and discontinuous identity he also described in 'The EI at Delphi': 'For her whole power consisteth and is employed in matter which receiveth all forms and becometh all manner of things: to wit, light, darkness, day, night, fire, water, life, death, beginning and end'.[32] As much as Cleopatra is associated with Isis, she comes to represent the divine force that drives 'natural' human mutability as well as the transformations, dissolutions and rebirths that form a cyclical pattern in Nature writ large.

In addition to the passages from 'The Apology for Raymond Sebond' that draw on Plutarch, we should also look at the following part of Montaigne's essay 'Of the inconstancie of our Actions', as translated by Florio, a subject matter that is highly relevant to the behaviour of Antony and Cleopatra in Shakespeare's play:

> Authors do ill and take a wrong course, willfully to opinionate them-selves about framing a constant and solid contexture of us. They choose an universal ayre [i.e. characteristic], and following that image, range and interpret all a man's actions, which if they cannot wrest suf-ficiently, they remit them unto dissimulation. Augustus hath escaped their hands: for there is so apparent, so sudden and continual a variety of actions found in him, through the course of his life, that even the boldest judges and strictest censurers have been fain to give him over and leave him undecided. There is nothing I so hardly believe to be in man as constancy, and nothing so easy to be found in him as incon-stancy. He that should distinctly, and part by part, judge of him, should often jump to speak truth. View all antiquity over, and you shall find it a hard matter to choose out a dozen of men that have directed their life unto one certain, settled, and assured course, which is the surest drift of wisdom.[33]

In the concluding section of that essay, Montaigne goes on to say:

> He whom you saw yesterday so boldly venturous, wonder not if you see him a dastardly meacock tomorrow next . . . We are all framed of flaps and patches, and of so shapeless and diverse a contexture that every piece [bit or fragment], and every moment, playeth his part. And there is as much difference found between us and ourselves as there is between ourselves and others. . . . It is no part of a well grounded judgment simply to judge ourselves by our exterior actions: a man must thoroughly sound himself, and dive into his heart, and there see by what wards and springs the motions stir. But forasmuch as it is a hazardous and high enterprise, I would not have so many meddle with it as do.[34]

This description of the difficulty involved in observing and making judgements based on 'exterior actions' emphasises that such self-analysis is something that we cannot easily do for ourselves, and therefore it must be even more challenging when we attempt to judge and categorise others. From Philo's opening call to 'behold and see' (I, i, 13) to Caesar's final command to 'see / High order in this great solemnity' (V, ii, 363–4), Shakespeare's *Antony and Cleopatra* repeatedly asks its audience to observe, measure and judge its main characters, but their efforts to define themselves, the efforts of the minor characters to judge or understand them, and the efforts of the audience to gain privileged access to the interiority of these characters are all repeatedly frustrated or problematised. How, the play asks, can we latch on to a fixed identity, for ourselves or for our understanding of others? The self, identity, consciousness, subjectivity: these things are seen by Montaigne (when he draws on Plutarch) as constantly in motion, and it is that kind of modern instability, described so strikingly and decisively in the conclusion of Montaigne's 'Apology', that Shakespeare dramatises in *Antony and Cleopatra*. It is a version of the 'perpetual motion' that Michel Jeanneret sees as central to many works of Renaissance art when he argues that 'Renaissance thinkers, far more sensitive to emerging forces than to rigorous forms, placed their confidence in movement and exerted an expansive creative energy that is the source of our modernity'.[35] Thus *Antony and Cleopatra* presented its audiences with an innovative form of tragedy that includes, not only the assertion that identity is unstable, but also the suggestion that a kind of materialist metempsychosis occurs through the endless cyclical metamorphosis of inspirited matter. Given that this pagan worldview, exemplified by Shakespeare's unstable characters Antony and Cleopatra, suffers a tragic defeat with the triumph of Octavius, with the advent of the imperial Pax

Romana, and with the coming, after the incarnation of Christ, of 'the time of universal peace', we might categorise Shakespeare's play as a subtle, cagey piece of 'resistance literature', one that audaciously encourages its audience to question traditional Christian forms of dualism and essentialism. In the place of conventional Christian ideology promoting monotheism and autocracy, playgoers are offered a radical remix of ancient pagan thought that undermines Christian theology and morality. At the same time, Shakespeare's dramatisation of discontinuous identity and neo-pagan materialism in *Antony and Cleopatra* points the way towards a modern materialism that rejects essence, celebrates flux and declares all matter sacred.

Notes

1. See Dollimore, *Radical Tragedy*, pp. 29–50, for his description of how 'discontinuous identity' was figured in the drama of Shakespeare and his contemporaries.
2. Ibid. p. 31.
3. Grady, *Shakespeare, Machiavelli, and Montaigne*, p. 119. Grady's argument, which exists in its fullest form in his book *Shakespeare, Machiavelli, and Montaigne*, is challenged by John Lee in '"A judge that were no man"'. I agree with many of Lee's claims, including his stress on the difference between Montaigne's essay form and that of Shakespeare's dramatic texts, as well as his concluding assertion that 'Shakespeare is an opportunist; he uses Montaigne locally and selfishly, making use of Montaigne to serve his own ends' (p. 53), but I am not convinced by Lee's assertion that a 'ruling form' of Montaignian selfhood somehow Platonically transcends the vicissitudes of discontinuous identity in both Montaigne and in Shakespeare's *Hamlet*, nor by his claim that Montaigne's essays never 'descend into crises of identity because they are not about the loss or impossibility of identity but rather about the creation of a sense of self . . . which only God may give us direct knowledge of' (p. 45).
4. *The Tragedy of Antony and Cleopatra*, ed. Neill, p. 82.
5. Ibid. p. 112.
6. Scholars have long recognised in Spenser's work not only the allegorical adaptation of classical mythology as cosmological and natural wisdom about inanimate and ever-changing matter (see the Garden of Adonis in Book 3 of *The Faerie Queene*, for instance), but also his references to ancient wisdom, based in Egypt, that had purportedly unlocked the secrets of nature, and his mingling of elements from the Neoplatonists, Lucretius, Ovid and others. See Allen, *Doubt's Boundless Sea*; Barbour, *English Epicures and Stoics*; Hyman, 'Seizing Flowers in Spenser's Bower and Garden'; Greenlaw, 'Spenser and Lucretius'; and Esolen,

'Spenserian Chaos', on the aspects of Epicurean thought that are found in the work of Spenser and other English Renaissance writers.

7. Montaigne's quotations from Plutarch's dialogue 'The EI at Delphi' are taken almost verbatim from Jacques Amyot's 1572 French translation of Plutarch's *Moralia*. Amyot's earlier French translation of Plutarch's *Lives* was the basis for Sir Thomas North's English translation, which Shakespeare uses as his main source for the plot of *Antony and Cleopatra* and for many of its details. At the time he wrote *Antony and Cleopatra*, Shakespeare would have also had access to Philemon Holland's English translation of Plutarch's *Moralia*, which Holland titled *The Philosophie commonlie called the morals* (1603).

8. *Essayes*, trans. Florio, pp. 185–6.

9. Plutarch, *The Philosophie*, trans. Holland, p. 186.

10. *Complete Works*, trans. Frame, p. 472. Subsequent references are given in the text.

11. As Parker ('Shakespeare's Argument with Montaigne') and Lee ("A judge that were no man"') have both pointed out.

12. See Gray, '"HIDE THY SELFE"', for an astute discussion of the different ways that Montaigne and Shakespeare handled Epicurean ethical principles.

13. Various scholars have pointed to Montaigne's form of writing in the essays as an unconventional version of philosophical expression: a layered textual record of his intellectual mobility, rather than an attempt to arrive at a conclusion or establish a coherent, fixed position. See Hartle on Montaigne as a non-traditional 'accidental philosopher' and Starobinski on 'Montaigne in motion'.

14. Donald Frame declares that 'The Apology' is 'perplexing mainly because it belies its title' and goes on to observe: 'Sebond . . . has argued that man could learn all about God and religion by reading in the book of God's creation, the world. Montaigne shows his complete disagreement here. . . . The best he can bring himself to say in the page or two that can be called a defense is that Sebond means well' (*Complete Works*, trans. Frame, p. 386)

15. I am indebted to Bono's perceptive account of how Shakespeare, in *Antony and Cleopatra*, carried out a 'literary transvaluation' of various texts by Plutarch, one that appropriated a variety of classical precedents (including Plutarch's 'focus on the irreducible qualities of Antony's nature' [*Literary Transvaluation*, p. 153]) in order to produce a tragicomic 'Shakespearean synthesis'. For Bono's discussion of how Shakespeare transformed various aspects of Virgil, Plutarch and Lucretius in *Antony and Cleopatra*, see pp. 149–219.

16. *The Tragedy of Antony and Cleopatra*, ed. Neill, p. 122.

17. Konstantinovic, *Montaigne et Plutarque*, p. 28. On the connections between Montaigne and Plutarch, see ibid. and Panichi, 'Montaigne and Plutarch'.

18. For a helpful contextualisation and analysis of Plutarch's polemic against the Epicurean Colotes, see Kechagia, *Plutarch against Colotes*.

19. Lucretius, *De Rerum Natura*, v. 837, quoted in *Shakespeare's Montaigne*, trans. Florio, ed. Greenblatt and Platt, p. 187.

20. On the associations between Antony and Osiris, and Cleopatra and Isis, in Plutarch and Shakespeare, see Lloyd, 'Cleopatra as Isis', and Brenk, 'Antony-Osiris, Cleopatra-Isis'.

21. For a diametrically opposed reading of *Antony and Cleopatra*, see Gray, *Shakespeare and the Fall of the Roman Republic*.

22. See Battenhouse, *Shakespearean Tragedy*; Fisch, *The Biblical Presence in Shakespeare, Milton, and Blake*; Shaheen, *Biblical References in Shakespeare's Plays*; and Hannibal Hamlin, *The Bible in Shakespeare*.

23. Hannibal Hamlin, *The Bible in Shakespeare*, p. 214.

24. Ibid. p. 214, p. 228.

25. Fisch, *The Biblical Presence in Shakespeare, Milton, and Blake*, p. 62 n33.

26. For an analogous reading of *Antony and Cleopatra*, see Cantor, *Shakespeare's Roman Trilogy*.

27. Quint ('The Tragedy of Nobility on the Seventeenth-Century Stage'), Davies ('Jacobean *Antony and Cleopatra*') and Yachnin ('"Courtiers of Beauteous Freedom"') all have suggested that the play refers to the context of the seventeenth-century crisis of the aristocracy and the corruption and excess of the Jacobean court in particular. This kind of local historical contextualisation of the tragedy holds much merit, and Quint is certainly correct when he argues that 'beneath its fall-of-princes plot [the play] suggests that the larger-than-life Antony personifies the last vestiges of noble generosity, chivalry, and risk-taking, while Octavius Caesar represents the modern Machiavellian monarch, a calculating and far less glamorous figure ruling over a world of reduced possibility' (p. 15). In fact, the play's topical allusions to the decline of the old aristocratic political class and the diminishment of its power serve to reinforce the deeper, more radical presentation of the demise of the ancient pagan system, and the rise of Octavius as sole emperor ushering in the Pax Romana and the Christian era.

28. Quoted in Gregory, 'Julian and the Last Oracle at Delphi', p. 356.

29. Plutarch, *The Philosophie*, trans. Holland, p. 1342.

30. Ibid. p. 1321.

31. Ibid. p. 1327.

32. Ibid. p. 1318.

33. *Shakespeare's Montaigne*, trans. Florio, ed. Greenblatt and Platt, pp. 193–4.

34. Ibid. p. 197.

35. Jeanneret, *Perpetual Motion*, p. 1.

Chapter 13

Montaigne, Shakespeare and the Metamorphosis of Comedy and Tragedy

Richard Hillman

The present chapter does not aim at adding to the list of Shakespeare's 'borrowings' from Montaigne/Florio (not all of which, of course, are unanimously accepted as such). I will, in fact, be proposing several more which have not, to my knowledge, hitherto been signalled. But I am more interested in pursuing the intertextual implications of certain points of contact that bear particularly on genre. The gist of the argument is that the playwright's presumptive 'discovery' of the *Essays* around 1600, on the evidence, especially, of *Hamlet* – a discovery reasonably attributed to reading Florio's translation in manuscript – had a transformative impact on the conceptual relationship between comic and tragic elements in his subsequent work, including the generic dynamic of the last plays. Implicit in this approach is a mild corrective of the increasingly dominant view of the final generic turn in Shakespeare's dramatic practice as a more or less direct (even exclusive) function of Italian models and theories.

In adopting this generic focus I diverge from the more familiar emphasis on intellectual affinity between two authors, particularly when it comes to what is now commonly regarded as the invention of (pre-)modern subjectivity.[1] Instead, I take a view of the playwright as reacting selectively and unsystematically (not to say casually) to diverse elements – including expressions, images, names and passing thoughts – that appealed to his sense of theatrical possibility. Arguably, of course, to do so is to recuperate affinity on another level, especially given the theatrical qualities and referentiality of the *Essais* themselves, which William M. Hamlin has valuably highlighted and shown to be considerably enhanced and inflected in an English direction by Florio's translation.[2] On the other hand, paradoxically, the movement I perceive in Shakespeare's post-1600 work leads away from what Hamlin identifies as Florio's own adherence to 'neoclassical literary principles and sharply-etched genre distinctions'.[3]

Nevertheless, it is well to recall that such principles were in place from the early Elizabethan period, if far from universally applied, as part of the theatrical culture shared by playwrights and spectators. Regardless of the resilient English tradition of 'mingling kings and clowns' decried by Philip Sidney,[4] which never ceased to colour stage practice, the basic notion of comedy and tragedy as diametrically opposed genres with classical standing, calculated to convey joy and sorrow, respectively, was a point of reference and capable of intruding even on heterogeneous and unsophisticated productions. Thus an allegorised Comedy and Envy (representing tragedy) dispute the outcome of that perennially popular romanesque ramble, the anonymous *Mucedorus* (*c.* 1590), with Envy threatening to 'make thee mourn where most thou joyest, / Turning thy mirth into a deadly dole'.[5] And while the title page of Thomas Preston's *Cambyses* (published 1569), which presents the piece as *A lamentable tragedy mixed full of pleasant mirth*,[6] may simply be casting the net wide for buyers, two parodies by Shakespeare assume an audience alert to absurd incompatibility: the first stems from the label of 'very tragical mirth' (*MND* V, i, 57)[7] attached to the Mechanicals' pageant in *A Midsummer Night's Dream*; the second is initiated by Falstaff in *Henry IV, Part 1*, who declaims histrionically 'in King Cambyses' vein' (II, iv, 387).

It is notable that, in both these cases, the impact on the spectator is measured by tears, which may be either of sorrow or laughter – but certainly not both:

> PHILOSTRATE: . . . And tragical, my noble lord, it is;
> For Pyramus therein doth kill himself;
> Which when I saw rehears'd, I must confess,
> Made mine eyes water; but more merry tears
> The passion of loud laughter never shed.
>
> (*MND* V, i, 66–70)

> FALSTAFF: Weep not, sweet queen, for trickling tears are vain.
> HOSTESS: O, the father, how he holds his countenance!
>
> (*1H4* II, iv, 391–2)

A Midsummer Night's Dream notoriously plays on a deeper level, too, with the opposition between comic and potentially tragic outcomes.

So does *Romeo and Juliet*, as its teasing reminders of romantic possibility, conventionally fulfilled in the consummation of marriage, are brutally negated by the interposition of funeral. Joy and sorrow, in short, are assumed to be contrasting, mutually exclusive experiences, as indeed seems perfectly natural (to use that expression advisedly).

Yet among the less often noted novelties that infiltrate Shakespeare's dramaturgy from *Hamlet* onwards is a complication of this assumption. This effect dovetails, no doubt, with the intrusions of melancholic elements into comedies of the late 1590s. Such intrusions are conspicuous in *The Merchant of Venice* (from Antonio – 'In sooth, I know not why I am so sad' [I, i, 1] – to Shylock, to the sombre evocations in Belmont: 'In such a night . . .' [V, i, 1, etc.]); in *Much Ado about Nothing* (witness Don John and the results of his actions); and in *As You Like It* (by way of Jaques, of course, but also Oliver and Duke Frederick). Still, such elements arguably remain distinct, in counterpoint to the comic. The more fundamental co-mingling that preoccupies me here may be specifically linked to Montaigne's relativism and scepticism concerning human nature, as numerous verbal echoes in *Hamlet* attest, especially of 'An Apologie of *Raymond Sebond* [Apologie de Raimond Sebond]' (II: 12).[8] And it is not surprising that there are generic implications, in keeping with Hamlet's insistence that the 'purpose of playing . . . is to hold as 'twere the mirror up to nature' (*Ham* III, ii, 20–2).

As is typical of Shakespeare, one vehicle of these implications is a secondary and comic figure. Polonius presents the versatility of the itinerant players as a capacity, not merely to switch between tragic and comic alternatives – the 'heavy' and 'light' extremes of Seneca and Plautus, respectively – but to exercise mimesis along a string of increasingly composite and overlapping genres. As that string discursively unravels, it calls into question generic distinctions as such, and implicitly the categories of lived experience they are supposed to reflect:

> The best actors in the world, either for tragedy, comedy, history, pastoral, pastoral-comical, historical-pastoral, tragical-historical, tragical-comical-historical pastoral, scene individable or poem unlimited; Seneca cannot be too heavy, nor Plautus too light. (*Ham* II, ii, 396–401)

In this context, the 'real' tears, so impressive to the laughable Polonius (519–20), which the Player produces in his speech on the tragic fall of Troy, may testify to more (or less) than the emotional power of tragedy, or rhetoric generally – an effect axiomatic from ancient times and duly remarked on by Montaigne.[9] As Hamlet's redeploys those tears in the soliloquy that closes the scene, and as he had anticipated from the outset of the play, they point more broadly to the inadequacy of all outward signs – 'actions that a man might play' (I, ii, 84) – to reflect inner truth, as opposed to 'fiction' (II, ii, 552):

> What's Hecuba to him, or he to Hecuba,
> That he should weep for her? What would he do
> Had he the motive and the cue for passion
> That I have? He would drown the stage with tears . . .
>
> (II, ii, 559–62)

Tragedy and comedy notably intertwine again thanks to Polonius, and at his expense. While they are waiting for the players to re-enact Hamlet's father's tragedy, Hamlet comically draws him out on his brief career as an actor in one of the classic tragic roles, Julius Caesar, killed by Brutus in the Capitol (III, ii, 98–106). (The joke would have been enhanced for audiences that had recently witnessed Shakespeare's version [1599] – perhaps with the same actors.[10]) This is almost the last time Hamlet makes a fool of 'so capital a calf' (105–6) before making the Queen's closet an abattoir for him. The final occasion, suggestively, will expose the possibility of infinite subjective readings of nature itself – a cloud '[v]ery like a whale' (382), among other animals – thus illustrating Hamlet's earlier claim to Rosencrantz and Guildenstern that 'there is nothing either good or bad, but thinking makes it so' (II, ii, 249–50).

Shortly after the latter affirmation, Hamlet effectively extends the principle by juxtaposing extreme interpretations of mankind as 'beauty of the world' and 'quintessence of dust' (II, ii, 307–8). He thereby thoroughly engages Montaigne's ironically oppositional thinking in the 'Apologie' – to the point where Ellrodt was induced by the resemblance to proclaim a 'kinship of spirit' between the playwright and the essayist.[11] On the less abstract level of genre, however, the implication is simply to posit comic and tragic readings of experience, not only as equally possible, but as emanating from the same human mind, hence as always coexisting within it.

We have an indication of this even in the introductory speech of Claudius, who intermingles the conventional generic symbolism to cover what is really on his mind: 'With mirth in funeral, and with dirge in marriage . . .' (I, ii, 12). And when Hamlet sardonically translates the images into comestible form – 'the funeral bak'd-meats / Did coldly furnish forth the marriage tables' (I, ii, 181) – he backhandedly acknowledges that the same dishes would do for both: they are the constant; the occasions are contingent, and will determine how things taste, the subjective prevailing over the objective.

I would suggest that an especially pertinent *essai* from the generic point of view – and de facto rich with implications for the representation of character and action – is another from Book II: 'We taste nothing purely [Nous ne goustons rien de pur]'. The contrast between the vast and sprawling explorations of the 'Apologie' and these few pages of concise observations is striking: the latter perhaps stand out more starkly as a result. Essentially, the impossibility of completely separating joy and sorrow is insisted on: 'Travell[12] and pleasure, most vnlike in nature, are notwithstanding followed together by a kind [of?] I wot not what natural conjunction [Le travail et le plaisir, tres-dissemblable de nature, s'associent pourtant de je ne sçay quelle joincture naturelle]' (Florio, II: 20, 389; Montaigne, 673C). And illustration comes in suggestive forms. The memory of departed[13] friends has the pleasingly bitter taste of over-aged wine or 'sweetely-sowre apples [pommes doucement aigres]' (ibid.). When applied artistically, the emotional mixture issues a challenge to interpretation:

> Nature discovereth this confusion unto vs: Painters are of opinion, that *the motions and wrinkles in the face, which serve to weepe, serve also to laugh*.[14] Verely, before one or other be determined to express which; behold the pictures successe, you are in doubt toward which one enclineth. And the extreamitie of laughing entermingles it selfe with teares.

> [Nature nous descouvre cette confusion; les peintres tiennent que les mouvements et plis du visage qui servent au pleurer, servent aussi au rire. De vray, avant que l'un ou l'autre soyent achevez d'exprimer, regardez à la conduict de la peinture: vous estes en doubte vers lequel c'est qu'on va. Et l'extremité du rire se mesle aux larmes.] (Florio, II: 20, 389; Montaigne, 674B)

This is not a matter of choosing between two kinds of tears, but rather of recognising their mutual imbrication and interdependence.

If an audience would never have doubted what formal category *Hamlet* belongs in – beginning, probably, with a stage draped in black and given the precursor tragedy usually assigned to Kyd – they might well have been disconcerted by the dislocation of familiar revenge play conventions. This effect has certainly been discussed – by myself, among many others[15] – usually in connection with the protagonist's ambivalence towards his task, which in turn has been linked with the conflict between human capacity and human futility developed by Montaigne. To focus narrowly on genre, by ironically problematising the relation between this revenger's ultimate success and his will to accomplish it, the play refuses to endorse the ending with the usual stamp of meaningful achievement (however bloody, mad or perverse) and therefore of closure. Instead, there is deferral even after the protagonist's death, with a strong final gesture towards action as play-acting, identity as constructed. First, Horatio offers himself as an interpreter of events, to be materialised by the bodies put on view '[h]igh on a stage' (V, ii, 378); then Fortinbras gives the order to do so, accompanied by a reminder that Hamlet was never 'put on' (397) the throne and the assertion that martial fanfare will '[s]peak loudly for him' (400).

The generic interest lurks in Horatio's anticipation of his own discourse:

> So shall you hear
> Of carnal, bloody, and unnatural acts,
> Of accidental judgments, casual slaughters,
> Of deaths put on by cunning and forc'd cause,
> And in this upshot, purposes mistook
> Fall'n on th' inventors' heads. (380–5)

With the visual support of the bodies, the matter is unmistakably coded as tragic, but also intermingled with mechanisms – 'accidental', 'casual', 'cunning', 'purposes mistook' – that strangely smack of comic convention, as does the anxiety about further 'plots and errors' (395). There is no hint of purpose realised or heroism displayed, so that Fortinbras's military praise seems all the more misplaced. Most centrally, there is no intimation that Horatio's explication will transcend bare narrative, much less attain the tearful exaltation exemplified by the Player. At the least, the tragic register has been infiltrated by a sense of blundering and finally jejune experiences that it cannot contain. And this is arguably to translate into generic terms the observation of Montaigne in his last essay of all, 'Of Experience [De l'experience]' (III: 13):

> *Reason hath so many shapes, that wee knowe not which to take hold of: Experience hath as many.* The consequence we seeke to draw from the conference of events, is vnsure, because they are ever dissemblable. No qualitie is so vniversall in this surface of things, as varietie and diversitie.

[La raison a tant de formes, que nous ne sçavons à laquelle nous prendre; l'experience n'en a pas moins. La consequence que nous voulons tirer de la ressemblance des evenemens est mal seure, d'autant qu'ils sont tousjours dissemblables: il n'est aucune qualité si universelle en cette image des choses que la diversité et varieté.] (Florio, III: 13, 633–4; Montaigne, 1065B)

There is no space to go into detail here, but before turning to the generic implications for the late plays, I would like briefly to suggest that several of Shakespeare's formally presented tragedies and comedies subsequent to *Hamlet* show a similar tendency to destabilise the neoclassical inheritance. It is especially telling that the three works most often labelled 'problem plays' make their appearance early in the seventeenth century.[16] *Troilus and Cressida*, *All's Well That Ends Well* and *Measure for Measure* have long seemed to many, not merely to mingle comic and tragic elements, but to bind them together so as to suggest that human experience itself necessarily partakes of both. In all three plays, the pleasures and pains of love – that comic subject par excellence – are shown to be inextricable in ways that put disruptive living flesh on the bare bones of Petrarchan paradox. We have moved beyond two alternative visions of human experience to one matching the pithy résumé served up in 'We taste nothing purely': '*Man all in all, is but a botching and party-coloured worke* [L'homme en tout et par tout, n'est que rapiessement et bigarrure]' (Florio, II: 20, 389; Montaigne, 675B). Montaigne's next sentence, moreover, extends his point to the sphere of social organisation in a way that strikingly intersects with *Measure for Measure*, in particular: '*The very Lawes of Iustice, can not subsist without some commixture of Iniustice* [Les loix mesmes de la justice ne peuvent subsister sans quelque meslange d'injustice]' (Florio, II: 20, 389; Montaigne, 675A).

More broadly to the point, as much for the later tragedies as for the problem plays, is the moral 'confession' Montaigne appends to the inevitable imbrication of contraries: 'When I religiously confesse my selfe vnto my selfe, I finde, the best good I have, hath some vicious tainte [Quand je me confesse à moy religieusement, je trouve que la meilleure bonté que j'aye, a de la teinture vicieuse]' (Florio, II: 20,389; Montaigne, 674B). This is to extend Hamlet's 'vicious mole of nature' (I, iii, 24) – which that character, by contrast, does not confess to – across the full spectrum of human qualities and truisms, and it arguably opens a further perspective on the complex psychological and moral mixtures characteristic of both tragic protagonists and antagonists, and affecting the relations between them. It may also bear on the evolution of soliloquy as a quasi-confessional practice.[17] One consequence for generically focused criticism, arguably, is that relativism on this scale tends to obviate the Aristotelian notion of *hamartia* (never securely in place anyway for Shakespearean tragedy), as well as extensions of that notion, whether in terms of early modern faculty psychology ('passion versus reason') or nineteenth-century moralism ('tragic flaw').

Finally, the virtual rapprochement, under Montaigne's auspices, of comedy and tragedy, with their respective markers of love and death, may help to account for the concentration of seemingly inevitable fatal love relations – between men and women, of course (Othello and Desdemona, Macbeth and Lady Macbeth, Antony and Cleopatra), but also between parents and children (Lear and his daughters, Gloucester and his sons, Volumnia and Coriolanus). In this light, too, the superficially contrasting extremes of the compulsively social, then hyper-solitary Timon appear more clearly in an interdependent reciprocal relation. Even the ultimate 'mingling' of a king and a clown on the English stage – Lear and his Fool – can thereby be authorised on its own generic terms, rather than as a defiant wrenching of the rules. So can the catalytic intervention of the comic but aspic-bearing countryman to make possible the tragic climax of *Antony and Cleopatra*. With that play's passage from love to death and back to love-in-death, however, we enter some way into the tragicomic territory of the final plays, and on this generic evolution Montaigne can again shed light, as appears most clearly, I believe, from *The Tempest* and *The Winter's Tale*.

To begin with a conveniently blatant case of Montaigne's intertextual presence, it is worth taking up the generic aspect of Gonzalo's wobbly utopian vision of a commonwealth in *The Tempest* (II, i, 148–69), which has long been recognised as substantially derived from 'Of the Caniballes [Des cannibales]' (I: 30, in Florio's translation).[18] The fact that the borrowing calls attention to itself – some spectators would certainly have identified it, and it is set off by the mocking interventions of Antonio and Sebastian – lends it a metadramatic, not just a thematic function, in a way that recycles Montaigne's rhetorical method in theatrical terms. For what finally emerges from the essayist's radical use of New World 'natural' humanity to subvert the unnatural inhumanity of the Old ('I think there is more barbarisme in eating men alive, then to feede vpon them being dead . . . [Je pense qu'il y a plus de barbarie à manger un homme vivant qu'à le manger mort . . .]' (Florio, I: 30, 104; Montaigne 209A) is the interdependence of the two perspectives, their contingency on interpretation. Each mode of seeing, as of being, lies within human capacity, and when Montaigne exposes the atrocious cruelty of 'our neighbours and fellow-citizens [des voisins et concitoyens]' (ibid.), he evokes the darkness within us all. So, effectively, does Prospero when he presents his anagrammatised cannibal, along with the hapless would-be murderers, Stephano and Trinculo, to the supposed elite of European 'civilisation': 'Two of these fellows you / Must know and own, this thing of darkness I / Acknowledge mine' (V, i, 274–6). This comes, of course, at the moment when the comic light shines most brightly. It is, then, the play's conclusion that fulfils the implicit promise made in the scene of Gonzalo's utopian speech to mobilise, by way of Montaigne, a tragicomic dynamic.

Even before that scene shows the good old counsellor's speech counterpointed by the mockery of Antonio and Sebastian, the notion of choice between comic and tragic visions of nature has been thrown into relief. Gonzalo's optimism ('How lush and lusty the grass looks! How green!' [II, i, 54]) clashes with the cynicism of the villains: '*Antonio.* The grass indeed is tawny. / *Sebastian.* 'With an eye of green in't' (55–6). But the issue would be highlighted by a stage presenting no grass of any kind: dramaturgically, if hardly in tone, we are not far from the perspective on tragedy and comedy as absurdly amalgamated that is afforded by the blind Gloucester on his supposed cliff-top. Moreover, Gonzalo's vision is indeed conspicuously partial and incoherent, inviting mockery as its supplement. That genre is at issue is confirmed by the immediate sequel, in which the two would-be usurpers try literally to highjack in a tragic direction a play destined to end comically, as Ariel's timely intervention, on Prospero's behalf, assures will be the case.

This point leads to another consequence of the intertextual intervention of Montaigne. The virtual flaunting of the borrowing ironically shows up Gonzalo as, in his naïveté, reciting someone else's script. The effect is thoroughly to destabilise the similar role he will finally play as a spokesman for eternal romance wonder ('set it down / With gold on lasting pillars' [V, i, 207–8]) and self-realisation ('all of us ourselves, / When no one was his own' [212–13]). His generic inflation here is arguably ventriloquised in service to a political and materialist agenda that again devalues the island: 'Prospero, his dukedom / in a poor isle' (211–12). The earlier debate over the grass is echoed by the exchange between the magician and his daughter: 'O brave new world . . . 'Tis new to thee' (183–4). To what extent the metadramatic structure enlists Prospero's self-styled comedy in a tragic cause is itself a question of interpretation, but it unquestionably entails renunciation of natural magic, well-founded scepticism about sincere penitence

('At this time / I will tell no tales' [128–9]), and a reminder that time and mortality have in no sense been transcended: 'Every third thought shall be my grave' (V, i, 312).[19] This makes an especially ironic ending for the only one of the final tragicomedies that formally excludes death from its fictional world, as Montaigne never did from his imaginative field of vision.

Despite the slight swerving from chronological order, I have reserved *The Winter's Tale* for final consideration because Montaigne's intertextual presence within it, while not generally recognised, seems to me highly influential in terms of genre. I am particularly concerned with the device of the statue apparently coming to life under Paulina's quasi-magical management. It is most blatantly that Shakespearean invention, seamlessly uniting possibility and impossibility, which reopens the generic closure abruptly imposed by Robert Greene on the infinite horizons of romance in the 'official' source-text, the very well-known *Pandosto: The Triumph of Time* (first published 1588, reed. 1607).[20] In Greene's pastoral novel, not only does the dead wife remain so, so that the seal of tragedy is decisively applied in her case, but a theatrical metaphor signals a last-minute reassertion of tragedy that cancels the otherwise happy ending: despite the joyous reunion with his lost daughter, the eponymous central character kills himself, 'To close up the comedy with a tragical stratagem'.[21]

Given contemporary audiences' familiarity with Ovid, the living-statue motif would virtually have announced its immediate source as the awakening of Pygmalion's statue under the influence of his love, as recounted in the *Metamorphoses*. And criticism has by and large been content to follow suit, although with a long-standing tendency – telling in itself, and encouraged by a parallel with the reunion in Euripides' play – to seek a deeper mythical basis in the recovery from death of Alcestis.[22] Nevertheless, the Ovidian landmark may also signal an intertextual link to a further neglected analogue: a brief but memorable narrative recounted by Montaigne in his essay 'Of Three Good Women [De trois bonnes femmes]', whose cornerstone is the essayist's recurrent ideal of companionate marriage, couched in terms that certainly resonate with *The Winter's Tale*:

> The touchstone and perfect triall of a good mariage, respects the time that the societie continueth; whether it have constantly beene milde, loyall and commodious.
>
> [La touche d'un bon mariage, et sa vraye preuve, regarde le temps que la societé dure: si elle a esté constamment douce, loyalle et commode.] (Florio, II: 35, 426; Montaigne, 744B)

The story in question lays claim to historical truth and to instructive value in specifically Stoic terms, according to Montaigne's well-known preference for edifying fact over diverting fiction. Yet the essayist concludes by recommending Ovid's compositional practice as a literary model. The authors of his time, he opines, might use such matter to create harmonious wholes out of different parts, 'And very neere, as *Ovid* hath sowen and contrived his Metamorphosis, with that strange number of diverse fables [à peu pres comme Ovide a cousu et r'apiecé sa Metamorphose, de ce grand nombre de fables diverses]' (Florio, II: 35, 430; Montaigne, 749A). No doubt, the ultimate classical fabulist of transformation serves all the more effectively to authorise the argument because he is evoked ironically. For the argument itself is that the three 'true' stories just recounted, at once 'pleasant' and 'tragicall', would make superior material for writers who currently invent 'fabulous tales':

> Loe heere my three true Stories, which in my conceite are as pleasant and as tragicall, as any wee devise at our pleasures, to please the vulgare sort withall: and I wonder, that those who invent so many fabulous tales, do not rather make choise of infinite excellent, and quaint Stories, that are found in Books, wherein they should have lesse trouble to write them, and might doubtlesse proove more pleasing to the hearer, and profitable to the Reader.

> [Voylà mes trois contes tres-veritables, que je trouve aussi plaisans et tragiques que ceux que nous forgeons à notre poste pour donner plaisir au commun; et m'estonne que ceux qui s'adonnent à cela, ne s'avisent de choisir plutost dix mille tres-belles histoires qui se rencontrent dans les livres, où ils auroient moins de peine et apporteroient plus de plaisir et profit.] (ibid.)

Whether or not Shakespeare thought of *The Winter's Tale* as a tale of three good women – as, from one angle, it surely is – he may have been particularly struck by Montaigne's tribute to the last in his series: Pompeia Paulina, the loving and learned wife of Seneca, who shared his Stoic philosophy. Out of devotion and conviction, she attempted to commit suicide when the tyrant Nero ordered her husband to do so, but

> *Nero* being advertized of all this, fearing lest *Paulinaes* death (who was one of the best alied Ladies in *Rome*, and to whome he bare no particular grudge) might cause him some reproach, sent in all poste haste to have her incisions closed vp againe, and if possibly it could be, to save

her life;[23] which hir servantes, vnwitting to her, performed, she being more then halfe dead and voyde of any sence.

[Neron, adverty de tout cecy, craignant que la mort de Paulina, qui estoit des mieux apparentées dames Romaines et envers laquelle il n'avoit nulles particulieres inimitiez, luy vint à reproche, renvoya en toute diligence luy faire r'atacher ses playes: ce que ses gens d'elle firent sans son sçeu, estant des-jà demy morte et sans aucun sentiment.] (Florio, II: 35, 429–30; Montaigne, 749A)

The apparent death of Hermione during her trial, newly vindicated by the Oracle but overwhelmed by Mamillius's demise, provokes a similar about-face on the part of Leontes. When the play's Paulina enjoins him to 'Look down / And see what death is doing' (III, ii, 148–9), he seeks, stricken with remorse and fear, to undo what he had sought to provoke: 'I have too much believ'd my own suspicion. / Beseech you tenderly apply to her / Some remedies for life' (151–3). And when Paulina reports that death has triumphed irrevocably over life – in effect, that comedy cannot be brought out of tragedy – she insistently and bitterly confronts him with his 'tyranny' (174, 179, 207).

The irony, as Leontes will discover sixteen years later, is that the 'remedies for life' do succeed in Hermione's case, as they did with Seneca's Paulina, who was revived despite herself and lived on, indelibly marked by the suffering she had nobly undergone:

And that afterward, contrary to her intent, she lived,[24] it was very honourable, and as befitted her vertue, shewing by the pale hew and wanne colour of her face, how much of her life she had wasted by her incisions.

[Et ce que, contre son dessein, elle vesquit dépuis, ce fut tres-honorablement et comme il appartenoit à sa vertu, montrant par la couleur blesme de son visage combien elle avoit escoulé de vie par ses blessures.] (Florio, II: 35, 430; Montaigne 749A)

The theatrical magic contrived by Shakespeare's Paulina reveals and re-enacts Hermione's concealed prior restoration – and identifies the essential 'remedy for life' as faith in the Oracle. Hermione's wrinkles are there, like the physical changes to Seneca's wife, to show 'how much of her life she had wasted', the verb 'waste' slipping easily from one heroine to another in its sense of destruction and its common Shakespearean application to time.[25] Made doubly visible is the impossibility of effacing sufferings endured, given that time moves in one direction only, if more quickly within the theatre than outside it.

But wrinkles are also generically pivotal, according to Montaigne's observation in 'We taste nothing purely' ('wrinkles', it should be noted, being Florio's translation of 'plis'). Besides the natural passage of time, they may express either weeping or laughing to the point of tears, and when this lesson of 'Nature' is captured in a work of art – taken out of time – onlookers are plunged into an aporia. The play shows this aporia both resolved, as the statue comes to life, returning to the world of time, and unresolvable, because 'joy and sorrow' are no longer a subject of 'combat' (V, ii, 73), as in the account of the discovery of Perdita:

> There might you have beheld one joy crown another, so and in such manner than it seem'd sorrow wept to take leave of them, for their joy waded in tears . . . Our king, being ready to leap out of himself for joy of his found daughter, as if that joy were now become a loss, cries, 'O, thy mother, thy mother!' (43–52)

Instead, the statue scene shows what Montaigne presents as the ever-present 'confusion' of the two emotions carried to a new level of intensity. And if it is still 'Nature' that 'discovereth' this effect, it conspicuously gives life also to Polixenes' earlier affirmation of an 'art' that 'itself is Nature' (IV, iv, 97).

It is essential to the complete experience of the ending, bitter-sweet like 'sweetly-sower apples' – 'For this affliction has a taste as sweet / As any cordial comfort' (V, i, 76–7) – to recognise that Leontes, too, has his wrinkles. No doubt there are outward ones, after sixteen years, but also inward, worn by his 'tears shed' (III, ii, 239) daily on the tombs of the victims of his tyrannical delusion. That delusion conspicuously rode roughshod over both reason and experience – the two possible means of attaining knowledge, according to Montaigne, however fallible and variable they both are. In 'On Experience', the essayist proves the unreliability of the closest apparent resemblances by the fact that, flying in the face of the common proverb,[26] men have been found whose experience enables them to make fine distinctions between eggs (Florio, III: 13, 634; Montaigne 1065B). Leontes implausibly lays claim to such ability, in effect, when he doubts his son's paternity: 'they say we are / Almost as like as eggs; women say so — / That will say anything' (I, ii, 129–31). This anticipates his furious denial when Paulina demonstrates his baby daughter's likeness to him at II, iii, 96–103. His obsession with specious similarity is hinted at ironically even when he teases his son – 'Mine honest friend, / Will you take eggs for money?' (I, ii, 160–1) – and it informs his effective repudiation of Polixenes' image of 'twinn'd lambs' (66): 'You have mistook, my lady, / Polixenes for Leontes' (II, i, 81–2). In a sense, he fell into the nightmare grip of Montaigne's radically desta-bilising insistence that '[d]issimilitude doth of it selfe insinuate into our workes [La dissimilitude s'ingere d'elle mesme en nos ouvrages]' (Florio, III: 13, 634; Montaigne, 1065B), while the impossibly life-like statue ('What fine chisel / Could ever yet cut breath?' [V, i, 78–9]) will restore belief in similitude, proving the essayist at once right and wrong: 'no arte can come neere vnto similitude [nul art peut arriver à la similitude]' (ibid.)

The fideistic trajectory of the 'Apologie' moves (if only, notori-ously, in the author's latest revision) from the inadequacy of human faculties and virtues to an injunction to rely on 'faith [foy]' (Florio, II: 12, 351; Montaigne, 604C). Leontes, too, is ready now, in the face of impossibility, to 'awake' his 'faith', when Paulina gives him his cue. The play thereby carries beyond the passive endurance exemplified by Montaigne's female epitome of Stoic virtue towards a symbolic spiri-tual redemption of which Shakespeare's Paulina is the instrument. But then Montaigne himself explicitly rejected the Stoic prescription for transcending humanity at the close of the 'Apologie', and he did so in terms that again might seem to prepare for the Ovidian graft that Shakespeare effected upon Greene's generic binarism: 'It is for our Christian faith, not for his Stoicke vertue, to pretend or aspire to this divine Metamorphosis, or miraculous transformation [C'est à nostre foy Chrestienne, non à sa vertu Stoique, de pretendre à cette divine et miraculeuse metamorphosis'] (Florio, p. 351; Montaigne, p. 604C). We are brought full circle by the fact that the 'he' in question here is Seneca himself.[27]

If, to return to 'We taste nothing purely', '*Man all in all, is but a botching and party-coloured worke*', all are effectively born 'Nature's bastards', contrary to what Perdita maintains in rejecting 'streak'd gillyvors' (IV, iv, 82–3) on the grounds of an 'art which in their piedness shares / With great creating Nature' (87–8). The play's version of the 'divine et miraculeuse metamorphosis' devoutly wished for by Montaigne – and an evocation of Ovid resounds willy-nilly within his piety – is Paulina's exercise of natural art, which transforms 'the fairest flow'rs o' th' season' (81) by at once transcending and accepting seasonality and all that goes with it: ''Tis time; descend; be stone no more; approach; / Strike all that look upon with marvel' (V, iii, 99–100).

Paulina's name has often, of course, been taken to evoke the redemptive message of the Apostle. Yet it cannot be ignored that, in this pagan universe, the Oracle of Apollo is vindicated and fulfilled, not silenced, or that, in a way not necessarily congenial to Saint Paul – even if Faith itself is traditionally figured as female – the injunction to its awakening comes from a spokeswoman for a virtuous feminine harmony with natural creation: a tale of 'Three Good Women' indeed. In the place of the 'sad' winter's 'tale' of Mamillius, with its 'ghosts and goblins' (II, i, 25–6), which heralds Leontes' misogynist violence, Paulina affirms this 'conte' as 'tres-veritable' beyond Montaigne's conception: 'That she is living, / Were it but told you, should be hooted at / Like an old tale, but it appears she lives' (115–17). If Montaigne thus unwittingly presented Shakespeare with a figure named Paulina to mediate between tragic loss and miraculous recovery, the dramatist effectively pursued the intertextual dialogue by recuperating Montaigne's fideism for the paganism the essayist rejected.

Another analogous intertextual manoeuvre sheds light on *The Winter's Tale*. The Shakespearean device of echoing serious themes on the comic level is exploited to impressive effect when the Clown, Perdita's supposed brother, is caught up in the transformative mechanisms of the conclusion. Between the two principal instances of joyful redemption from death to life, he too is miraculously re-'born' as a 'gentleman', enacting his own parodic triumph over reality and time itself. His new state enables him to confront Autolycus, who had once threatened him with a caricature of death by tyrannical torment:

> CLOWN: You denied to fight with me this other day, because I was no gentleman born. See you these clothes? Say you see them not and think me still no gentleman born . . . try whether I am not now a gentleman born.
> AUTOLYCUS: I know you are now, sir, a gentleman born.
> CLOWN: Ay, and have been so any time these four hours. (V, ii, 128–37)

The miracle extends, as the Clown recounts, to a sudden discovery, recovery and expansion of family that blends laughing and weeping in a fine tragicomic balance:

> the King's son took me by the hand, and call'd me brother; and then the two kings call'd my father brother; and then the Prince, my brother, and the Princess, my sister, call'd my father father; and so we wept; and there was the first gentleman-like tears that ever we shed. (140–5)

Nor does Shakespeare neglect a reminder of tragic sorrow as a function of time, when the Shepherd adds, with richly comic sagacity, 'We may live, son, to shed many more' (146).

It seems likely that Shakespeare remembered, even as he pointedly revived the slain bear from the eminently familiar *Mucedorus*, the 'clown' (Mouse) who in that play provides a more strictly farcical counterpoint to the wondrous revelations of the conclusion, and who needs to be reassured, 'the King means to make thee a gentleman'.[28] But also engaged intertextually, at first glance surprisingly, is Montaigne's exposition of the rigid caste system in India: '*No continuance of time, no fau[ou]r of Prince, no office, no vertue, nor any wealth can make a clowne to become a gentleman* [Nulle durée de temps, nulle faveur de prince, nul office ou vertu ou richesse peut faire qu'un roturier devienne noble'] (Florio, III: 5, 511; Montaigne, 851C). The linguistic specificity of the echo ('clowne'–'gentleman') is evidence that, as with Gonzalo's utopian speech in *The Tempest*, Florio's translation is the version the playwright had in mind. It is to the point that the prohibition of marriage across class boundaries is specified, and also that, just a few lines before, Montaigne had cited the contrary opinion of the Macedonian general Antigonus in favour of inward worth as outweighing noble birth (Florio, III: 5, 510–11; Montaigne, 851A). (Otherwise, no reason has been suggested for Shakespeare's use of that name for Paulina's husband.) These references are found, moreover, in the essay 'Upon some Verses of *Virgil* [Sur des vers de Virgile]', whose central subject is the requirements of companionate marriage and the potentially disruptive place of sexuality – treated at length in a way that acknowledges both women's desire and their vulnerability to men. Shortly after his mention of Antigonus and the Indian prohibitions, Montaigne evokes a good marriage (if, he stipulates, such may exist) in terms that resonate with 'Of Three Good Women' – and with *The Winter's Tale*'s multiple evocations of unions lost (including that of Paulina and Antigonus) and found: 'a sweete society of life, full of constancie, of trust, and an infinite number of profitable and solid offices, and mutuall obligations [une douce societé de vie, pleine de constance, de fiance et d'un nombre infiny d'utiles et solides offfices et obligations mutuelles]' (Florio, 3: 5, 511; Montaigne, 851B).

Such resonances would suggest that, if Shakespeare's gestures towards Montaigne in *The Winter's Tale*, as in *The Tempest*, ironically hint at confines and limits – finally, the limits of mortal understanding and of mortality itself – they also exploit an openness exposed by the essayist's very renunciation of certitude and accommodation of ambiguity. Montaigne chose as his motto, after all, 'Que sçay-je?' (II: 12, 527B), which Florio intriguingly translated so as implicitly to question the very capacity of language to capture experience, as in a tale: 'What can I tell?' (Florio, 305). From their radically different points of view, the intensively reflective inventor of the *essai* and the practically minded professional dramatist converge on a conceptual stretching of traditional categories of human suffering and happiness to allow for their reciprocal co-presence. True experience, Montaigne insists, like its fictional imitation, is inherently 'plaisans' and 'tragique'. To move beyond that condition of humanity requires the gift of divine grace, as he maintains at the conclusion of the 'Apologie'. In *The Winter's Tale*, Shakespeare deploys a dramatic form that encodes such transcendence, but attaches it to non-existent gods, to outrageous improbabilities and, as in *The Tempest*, to magic dependent on the human, to artifice frankly ephemeral. He stakes out a meeting-ground, perhaps, for the audience's deepest desires and the power of theatrical illusion, but only for the time of the play.

Notes

1. This history-of-ideas perspective, given special prominence by Ellrodt in an influential essay, 'Self-Consciousness in Montaigne and Shakespeare', was extensively developed, along with its philosophical ramifications, in the same author's magisterial monograph, *Montaigne et Shakespeare*, of which an English version, with revisions, was published in 2015 by Manchester University Press. Much in such interpretations naturally depends on the idea of the 'self' attributed to Montaigne. For a cultural materialist view, see Dollimore, *Radical Tragedy*, pp. 173–4; a stimulating analysis in Lacanian terms is offered by Desan, 'The Book, the Friend, the Woman'. Cf. Hillman, *Self-Speaking in Medieval and Early Modern English Drama*, pp. 138–9 and 161, n. 42.
2. Hamlin, *Montaigne's English Journey*, pp. 35–49. More broadly to the point is the production across the *Essais'* structures, expression and thought of an aesthetic dynamic which moves beyond classicism; cf. Buffum, *Studies in the Baroque Form from Montaigne to Rotrou*, pp. 1–76.
3. William M. Hamlin, *Montaigne's English Journey*, p. 44.
4. Sidney, *Apology for Poetry*, p. 135.
5. *Mucedorus*, in *Drama of the English Renaissance, I: The Tudor Period*, ed. Fraser and Rapkin, Induction, ll. 56–7. The anonymous domestic tragedy *A Warning for Fair Women* (pub. 1599) features a similar induction, adding the figure of History. As a genre, the English history play carried no classical heritage, of course, and, while often modulating

into tragedy (*Richard III*, *Richard II*), was technically not bound by the joy/sorrow binary – a freedom that playwrights can often be seen to exploit.

6. In both its first extant edition (London: John Allde, 1570?) and its reissue some twenty-five years later (London: Edward Allde, 1595).

7. Shakespeare's works are cited from *The Riverside Shakespeare*, 2nd edn, ed. Evans and Tobin.

8. I give priority in citing to Florio's translation, as is true to Shakespeare's own usage, and provide the original in square brackets. Florio is cited by book, chapter and page numbers from the first edition of 1603 (STC 18041), Montaigne's *Essais* from *Les Essais de Michel de Montaigne*, ed. Villey and rev. Saulnier, in which the letters A, B and C, here placed after the page reference, denote successive states of the text. For a view of the 'Apologie' as particularly informing Shakespeare's 'philosophical Hamlet', see Hillman, *French Reflections in the Shakespearean Tragic*, pp. 14–22.

9. In III: 4 (Florio, 504; Montaigne, 838C).

10. This is the plausible suggestion in *Hamlet*, ed. Jenkins, n. to III, ii, 103.

11. Ellrodt, 'Self-Consciousness', p. 40.

12. 'Travell', like French 'travail', from which it is derived, carries here the sense of 'Bodily or mental labour or toil, especially of a painful or oppressive nature; exertion; trouble; hardship; suffering' (*OED*, def. 1).

13. The 1603 folio and subsequent editions of Florio have 'last', which looks like an error for 'lost'. Montaigne speaks of friends 'perdus' (674).

14. It is notable that a number of the passages in Florio's translation that seem to connect closely with Shakespeare's plays, verbally or otherwise, were emphasised in the 1603 folio using italics, which I have retained.

15. See my *French Reflections*, pp. 16–17.

16. For a sustained effort to approach these plays as destabilising genre (among other things), although without reference to Montaigne, see Hillman, *William Shakespeare: The Problem Plays*. With respect to *Troilus*, a largely compatible chapter may be found in Hamlin, *Tragedy and Scepticism in Shakespeare's England*, pp. 167–83, where Montaigne is indeed evoked. More recently, I have returned to the tragical dimension of *All's Well That Ends Well* (*French Reflections*, pp. 150–201).

17. See Hillman, *Self-Speaking*, *passim*.

18. In *Essais*, ed. Villey and rev. Saulnier, the essay figures as I: 31. Gonzalo's effusion is a pastiche based on part of Florio, 102 (Montaigne, 206–7A). Despite the speech's frank dependence on Montaigne, it has been assimilated to 'modal dialogues' deriving from Italian pastoral tragicomedy. See Henke, *Pastoral Transformations*, p. 165.

19. On Prospero's manipulations and their generic implications, see Hillman, *Shakespearean Subversions*, pp. 230–50.

20. On *Pandosto*'s remarkable popularity, see Newcomb, *Reading Popular Romance in Early Modern England*, pp. 77–129.

21. Greene, *Pandosto: The Triumph of Time*, in *The Winter's Tale*, ed. Pafford, pp. 234–74, here at p. 274.

22. The most extensive exploration of the Pygmalion motif in Renaissance culture, with attention to its philosophical implications and emphasis on its Italian affiliation, is probably Barkan, 'Living Sculptures'. Modern applications of the Alcestis analogue range from Mueller, 'Hermione's Wrinkles' to Dewar-Watson, *Shakespeare's Poetics*, pp. 63–7.

23. Florio's addition at this point highlights her return to life.

24. The passing verbal parallel with Shakespeare's Paulina after the awakening is nonetheless striking: 'That she is living, / Were it but told you, should be hooted at / Like an old tale' (V, iii, 115–17). One may also compare Leontes' address to her at the beginning of the scene – 'O grave and good Paulina, the great comfort / That I have had of thee!' (1–2) – with Seneca's exclamation when his wife's resolution to die with him so moves him: 'Oh my deare *Paulina*!' (Florio, 429). This is Florio's addition; cf. Montaigne, 748A.

25. See *OED*, s.v., and cf. Richard II's ultimate tragic realisation: 'I wasted time, and now doth time waste me' (*R2* V, v, 49).

26. In English, 'As like as one egg to another' (Dent, *Shakespeare's Proverbial Language*, p. 99, E6). Montaigne states that the proverb exists in Greek and Latin, as well as French.

27. *Essais*, ed. Villey and rev. Saulnier, p. 604 n. 4; p. 1295, n. 1 to p. 604.

28. *Mucedorus*, ed. Fraser and Rabkin, sc. xviii, ll. 27–8. Mouse notably mistakes the promise to make him a 'knight' (23) for a threat to make him a 'sprite': 'How, a sprite? No, by Lady, I will not be a sprite. Masters, get you away; if I be a sprite, I shall be so lean I shall make you all afraid' (24–6). The exorcising of 'sprites', such as Mamillius inadvertently conjures in playfully seeking to 'fright' Hermione (*WT* II, i, 25ff.), thereby joins the neutralising of bears in reinforcing tragicomic transformation.

Chapter 14

Montaigne's *Essais,* Shakespeare's Trials and Other Experiments of Moment

Richard Scholar

Colin Burrow has said, rather teasingly, in a recent essay on Shakespeare and the *Essays*:

> It may or may not be the case that there was a 'Montaignian moment' in England around 1600, in which a shared body of rhetorical principles and texts, a growing interest in the difficulty of connecting individual experiences with general precepts, and a desire among many readers to read texts which appeared to enact thought and display personal experience all issued in a deep change in the collective mentality.[1]

I call Burrow's statement a tease, because he is careful to suspend the question as to whether or not such a moment took place in England around 1600, saying that 'it may or may not be the case'. He does so because he is above all concerned to explore what might be called (if we grant that it was the case) Shakespeare's idiosyncratic response to this broader cultural moment. That response, Burrow argues, is to be found in Shakespeare's creation, in plays written after 1599, of episodic 'moments' on the margins of the main action.

I want in what follows to suggest that when the moment is viewed in this way, as a conversational encounter rounded with a pause, then it may provide one useful way of thinking more flexibly than has sometimes been the case about questions of influence as these recur in the reception history of Montaigne in England. What I want to argue, first, is that the connection between Montaigne and his English readers – and specifically, here, Shakespeare – is not necessarily always best seen in terms of the specific influence of one author on another, but as an intertextual connection, a moment of virtual conversation between

them about the manner as well as the matter of their shared preoccupations. So – of the canonical example of Gonzalo's description of an
ideal commonwealth in *The Tempest* – I will be proposing that the virtual conversation between Shakespeare and Montaigne in that moment
concerns as much the rhetorical manner of Gonzalo's description, and
the reactions it provokes, as its verbal and conceptual matter. Close
analysis of an example such as this starts the work of dissolving the
putative monolithic Montaignian moment into a whole congeries of
mini-moments, all ready to be reassembled in the form of a broader
moment, but each requiring further specification in the first place.
I plan to do some of this closer work of specification, in the second
part of this chapter, by exploring some examples – taken from *The
Merchant of Venice* and *Julius Caesar* before I turn to *The Tempest* –
when I will suggest that a Shakespearean moment is best understood
as an encounter with, and a response to, Montaigne. What sorts of
Montaignian moments are these? And what do they reveal about the
connections that Montaigne's text affords its readers? My focus –
which is methodological in character – will be on how best to 'finesse
the question of direct influence' (in Lars Engle's 2006 phrase) if we wish
to understand connections between Montaigne and Shakespeare where
thinking, as well as or rather than direct verbal borrowing, is involved.[2]
Montaigne and Shakespeare belonged to an age that tested the limits of
what could be thought. Montaigne responds to this experimental intellectual culture by writing *essais* that implicate the reader in the freedom
and the challenge of thinking in the moment. Shakespeare found in
Montaigne's essays a precursor, an inspiration and a text to think with.

Ways of Finessing the Question of Direct Influence

First, let us return to the question of that broader 'Montaignian
moment' in England around 1600, observing briefly in its favour
that work on manuscript responses by William Hamlin (in copies of
Florio's English Montaigne) supports and extends the claim, already
made by some in respect of the printed responses (including Shakespeare's), that the early seventeenth-century English tend to approach
Montaigne with the same freedom of thought that Montaigne adopts
in respect of the authors he most prizes.[3] That is to say that they read
Montaigne and borrow from him in order to think with him about
the question in hand, and indeed to think against him, if need be.
Hamlin argues that the manuscript response exhibits the qualities
of eclecticism and wide-ranging autonomy that he finds in printed

responses, and that it thus adopts the Montaignian style of transformative readerly reaction, indeed entrenches that style.

These arguments have succeeded in making the seventeenth-century English Montaigne moment at once seem socially broader, emotionally more varied, and culturally more diffuse in its consequences than many might previously have allowed. I say diffuse, because Montaigne's text offered the English not only matter to borrow – in the guise of words, concepts and themes – but also a manner: the style of transformative, appropriative, readerly reaction. This is an argument with profound implications for the study of Montaigne's influence in England. It suggests that, when we are considering direct borrowings of Montaigne by English authors, we ought to expect to understand these better if we are prepared to explore whether or not the direct borrowing is accompanied by an imitation of Montaigne's signature style. It also suggests that, if we wish to capture the Montaignian moment in its totality, we will need in general to look beyond verbal or conceptual borrowings to other forms of encounter.

The study of Shakespeare's relationship with Montaigne has arguably been limited in its ambitions by the single piece of incontrovertible evidence yet found of a direct intertextual connection between the two authors. Even that direct connection is long known to have been mediated by a third party, since after Edward Capell in 1780 first observed Gonzalo's description of an ideal commonwealth in *The Tempest* (II, i) to be based upon Montaigne's chapter 'Des Cannibales' (I: 31), it was later established that Shakespeare's source for the passage was Montaigne in John Florio's 1603 translation of the *Essays*.[4] I will turn to that example later. I would like, first, to review two examples of more remote connection between the authors. My argument will be that the best way to approach Shakespeare's response to Montaigne is to see it as composed of moments that reward a flexible comparative exploration able to deal with a wide spectrum of intertextual connection ranging from direct influence, via triangulated encounter, to cases of apparent 'action at a distance'.

That spectrum of intertextual connection requires a broader understanding of what constitutes a 'source'. Burrow points out that this restrictive understanding has been the combined result of two tendencies. The first has been to impose on any putative source the test of the 'exact verbal parallel', and this has left Shakespeare criticism ill equipped 'with a vocabulary or method for writing about relationships between two authors where thinking, rather than direct verbal borrowing, is involved'. The second tendency has been to privilege those of Shakespeare's sources, as first Charlotte Lennox and then Geoffrey Bullough did, which offered the playwright material for the composition of his plots – fictional texts such as plays, poems and *novelle* – and to neglect discursive texts that lie behind passages of argumentation in Shakespeare. That neglect is in part explained by the first tendency I mentioned – to impose on putative sources the 'exact verbal parallel' test – since Shakespeare, like many other readers of discursive texts of his day, does not tend to respond to such texts by reproducing them verbatim but by thinking with them.[5]

If we are looking to establish a relationship between Shakespeare and Montaigne in which a manner of thinking as much as its subject-matter might be involved, then, we will have to approach the notion of the source altogether more flexibly. While the empirical search for the exact verbal parallel can and must remain, it must not be allowed to operate as a litmus test, but instead be reconceived as one part of a broader enquiry. Part of the breadth of that enquiry comes, as it were, from the outside: the external context in which Shakespeare encountered Montaigne and put Montaigne to use is now better understood, thanks to – to cite just three important studies – Hamlin's study of manuscript response to Montaigne in the age of Shakespeare, Peter Mack's cultural-historical work on the rhetorical and intellectual training that Montaigne and Shakespeare had in common,[6] and Warren Boutcher's social-historical work on the importance of Montaigne's work to the formation of the elite in Jacobean England. '[Montaigne] was used by scholars and advisers to furnish the real aristocracy and by playwrights to furnish the staged aristocracy with matter for topical philosophical discussion – as Gonzalo does Alonso,' says Boutcher, effortlessly connecting the external context of aristocratic Jacobean England to the internal context, in this case, of the displaced Neapolitan court in *The Tempest*.[7]

How, though, to deepen that connection so as to understand how, at particular moments in the plays, the connection with Montaigne is put to dramatic use? The approach I would like to recommend involves comparing and contrasting the matter that connects our authors – words, concepts, themes, other texts, literary forms – but also the manner – transformative, appropriative, readerly reaction – in asking, in essence, what happens to a Montaignian essay when it finds its way on to the Shakespearean stage.

Work done in this vein by Terence Cave and Colin Burrow has taken us into contrasting kinds of Shakespearean moment. Returning from a different perspective to the topic explored by Robert Ellrodt in 1975, the marked self-consciousness of Montaigne and Shakespeare,[8] Cave argues in a 2007 essay that this serves both authors as an instrument of experimental thought. He groups moments of theatrical self-dramatisation in Shakespeare together with quasi-theatrical situations. These examples, Cave says, are not to be understood as the dramatist's self-congratulatory asides, but as his experiments, second-level strategies by means of which the characters are induced to reflect on their situations and capacities, and we, to think with them. In this, they resemble key passages in the work of Montaigne, who consistently foregrounds the unfolding process of reflection over the matter ostensibly in hand. The term that Montaigne uses for this process is *essai*, meaning literally a 'trial', and referring here not to a genre of writing – this is a later development – but to an intellectual and literary experiment. This etymology allows Cave to encapsulate his literary parallel thus: 'Shakespeare's trials, and the other procedures that operate in the same way, are his *essais*.'[9] Note that the comparative approach here is no longer designed to establish 'influence' or even necessarily historical connection: some of the plays Cave mentions, such as *A Midsummer Night's Dream* (c. 1595), precede the earliest conjectured date upon which Shakespeare is thought to have read Florio's Montaigne. The encounter between the two writers is not located in history so much as in a quasi-allegorical critical fiction. The comparison is designed to do other work: it sets out, as A. D. Nuttall did in his work on Shakespeare and the ancient Greek playwrights, to account for a case of apparent literary 'action at a distance'; it chronicles in Montaigne and Shakespeare, as Laurie Maguire has put it, 'not the specific influence of one author over another, but the air that both breathed', thus recasting 'source-study as literal inspiration, from the Latin *inspirare*, to breathe in'.[10] Cave sees trials and false trials as moments of active Montaignian experimentation at the level of the plot. By contrast, Burrow focuses on moments of inaction at the level of plot, where experimental thinking aloud comes centre stage because there is at once no possibility of action and 'a huge weight of affect'. The encounter between the two writers is here relocated in history, since Burrow looks only at plays that postdate Shakespeare's reading of Florio's Montaigne, but the encounter is then subject less to 'an exercise in empirical discovery' than to 'an act of critical exploration'.[11]

Moments of Inspiration in *The Merchant of Venice* and *Julius Caesar*

I have so far pointed to studies focusing on either end of the wide spectrum of intertextual connection that, I have argued, relates Shakespearean moments to Montaigne, ranging from direct influence, via triangulated encounter, to apparent 'action at a distance'. What I want to do in the rest of this chapter is to focus on three Shakespearean moments, reflecting the same range, that have particularly interested me. Two of these, on which I have previously published essays, are otherwise not much discussed. The third, while endlessly discussed, looks perhaps a little different in the light of the two previous moments.

The first of my moments is a case of apparent 'action at distance' operating, at the level of the plot, in the trial scene of *The Merchant of Venice*.[12] Shakespeare there seems for all the world to borrow directly from Florio's Montaigne's account of occult sympathies and antipathies in nature when Shylock uses the language of occult antipathy to explain why he prefers to claim his pound of flesh from Antonio rather than receive the three thousand ducats owed to him. The passages differ above all in their contexts. They are similar, however, not just in their conceptual content but even in their phrasing.

Here is Florio's Montaigne, in 'Of the Institution and Education of Children', describing phobias he has seen develop in people who, as children, were not taught to control them:

> I have seene some to startle at the smell of an apple, more than at the shot of a peece; . . . and others to be scared with seeing a fetherbed shaken: as *Germanicus*, who could not abide to see a cocke, or heare his crowing.[13]

Here he is in 'An Apologie for *Raymond Sebond*' listing tricks that the senses play upon the judgement:

> I have seene some, who without infringing their patience, could not well heare a bone gnawne under their table: . . . others will be offended, if they but heare one chew his meat somwhat aloude; nay, some will be angrie with, or hate a man, that either speaks in the nose, or rattles in the throat.[14]

Here is Shakespeare, or rather Shylock in the trial scene of *The Merchant of Venice*, on being pressed to explain why he prefers to claim his pound of flesh from Antonio than to receive the three thousand ducats owed to him:

> I'll not answer that –
> But say it is my humour: is it answered?
> What if my house be troubled with a rat,

And I be pleased to give ten thousand ducats
To have it baned? What, are you answered yet?
Some men there are love not a gaping pig;
Some that are mad if they behold a cat;
And others when the bagpipe sings i'the nose
Cannot contain their urine: for affection
Masters oft passion, sways it to the mood
Of what it likes or loathes. Now for your answer:
As there is no firm reason to be rendered
Why he cannot abide a gaping pig,
Why he a harmless necessary cat,
Why he a wollen bagpipe, but of force
Must yield to such inevitable shame
As to offend, himself being offended:
So can I give no reason, nor will I not,
More than a lodged hate and a certain loathing
I bear Antonio, that I follow thus
A losing suit against him. Are you answered?

(IV, i, 42–62)[15]

The most striking parallels between these passages – their listing
of powerful antipathies towards harmless animals, their anaphoric
sequences starting 'some . . .' and finishing 'and others . . .', and their
use of phrases such as 'in the nose' and 'cannot abide' – led George
Coffin Taylor, an enthusiastic pioneer in the 1920s in the search for
'exact verbal parallels' between our two authors, to conclude that,
'except for the early date of *The Merchant of Venice*, one would naturally conclude the Shakespeare passage had been influenced by the
Montaigne passage'.[16] Since Taylor considers influence in this case to
be impossible, the passages appear as a dead-end in his study, a wrong
turning narrowly avoided. Despite more recent conjectures about the
earlier circulation of Florio's manuscript,[17] direct influence still seems
highly unlikely here, but the discussion of sympathies and antipathies
is repeated in enough late sixteenth-century European texts, learned
and popular, to suggest that there may be a network of sources common to both Montaigne and Shakespeare.[18] What is striking is how
differently the authors use the concept of occult sympathies and
antipathies, Montaigne to claim (in his chapter 'Of Friendship') that
occult sympathy was the indispensable and yet philosophically elusive 'certain something' that drew him into perfect friendship with
La Boëtie, Shakespeare to name the secret bond that links the Jewish
usurer Shylock to his arch-enemy, the Christian merchant Antonio.
Action at a distance produces a reversal of perspective whereby the

occult quality at work in Montaigne's friendship reappears in Shakespeare, maddened, at the inexplicable root of an intimate hatred.

The second of my moments, another trial scene of a sort, is probably a case of triangulated encounter. I have in mind Caesar's funeral in *Julius Caesar*.[19] Both Montaigne and Shakespeare look back to ancient writers on Rome – Cicero, Seneca and Plutarch – and explore Roman history and sensibility in dialogue with them. An ardent admirer of Plutarch, Montaigne was fascinated by Rome's philosophical traditions, not least the anti-authoritarian freethinking sensibility that he found allied with republican political thought. Montaigne highlights that sensibility in contrasting pronouncements on Roman Stoicism by Cicero and Seneca. What matters to Montaigne is that, despite their differences of perspective, Cicero and Seneca agree that Roman thinking is and must always be freethinking. Montaigne gives freethinking a new lease of life in the anti-authoritarian and experimental form of the *Essays*.

What Shakespeare does in parallel with Montaigne, but to quite different effect, is to depict in *Julius Caesar* the death of Roman freethinking as Rome lurches from its republican past towards an imperial future under the authoritarian rule of the Caesars. Shakespeare knew his Plutarch, studied Cicero at school, and may well have encountered Seneca directly or indirectly. Brutus, as Shakespeare dramatises his story in *Julius Caesar*, is the Roman freethinker who walked into a faction. Shakespeare takes from Plutarch (in the 1579 English translation by Thomas North) the main events of his drama – Brutus's speeches justifying the assassination and Antony's oration at Caesar's funeral – but these events, which days separate in Plutarch, Shakespeare compresses to form a single scene in which Brutus and Antony address, in turn, the same crowd of people. This scene resembles nothing more closely than a trial, containing speeches for the defence and prosecution, with the people acting as judge and jury. Brutus speaks first, and from a position of power, as the head of the faction that has just assassinated Caesar. He urges the crowd to exercise its judgement with the old Roman freedom: 'Censure me in your wisdom, and awake your senses, so that you may the better judge' (III, ii, 16–18).[20] He explains that he slew his friend Julius Caesar to save Rome from Caesar's ambition. He puts his case with compelling force. The people, who had first demanded satisfaction, now acclaim Brutus as Rome's saviour. In a chilling moment, and, as many have observed, the play's single most politically telling line, a member of the crowd shouts, of Brutus, 'Let him be Caesar!' That shout from the crowd suggests that Brutus has misjudged a political mood that is turning away from republican and intellectual freedoms towards voluntary servitude to authoritarian rule. Then Mark Antony steps forward and seizes the initiative. Closely associated with the dead 'tyrant', as people are now calling Caesar, and permitted to speak only on the whim of the new darling of the crowd, Brutus, Antony starts from a dangerously weak position. He does not take long triumphantly to transform it. The words he utters over Caesar's corpse amount to, in A. D. Nuttall's words, 'the greatest oration in the English language'.[21] That oration turns the tables on Brutus and his associates with breath-taking speed. Only some 130 lines into this most powerful and ruthless of political speeches, Antony has the entire crowd screaming to his tune, as one: 'Revenge! – About! – Seek! – Burn! – Fire! – Kill! – Slay! – Let not a traitor live' (III, ii, 206–7). He has transformed a funeral into a trial scene. This has issued in a death sentence for the embodied ideal of Roman freethinking.

Both of the examples discussed so far have presented cases of remote intertextual connection, and perhaps for that very reason have encouraged a critical exploration that ranges beyond questions of direct influence, comparing and contrasting instead not only the matter that connects our authors but also the shared manner – transformative, appropriative, experimental – that accounts for their divergences. My third and final example – Gonzalo's description of an ideal commonwealth in *The Tempest* (II, i) – will tend to suggest that such an approach will also enlarge our understanding of moments of encounter between the two writers to include an influence of manner that is, as it were, hiding in plain sight.

A Moment of Encounter in *The Tempest*

This much-studied episode – to return to the perspectives that I have tried to open up in this essay – may be said to expand Cave's suggestion, that Shakespeare translates the essaying of Montaigne into drama in the form of trials and quasi-trials, by connecting it with Burrow's suggestion that Montaigne offers Shakespeare material for interpersonal drama during lulls in the plot. For Gonzalo does both: he turns to Montaigne when trialling a kind of argument, about the perfect commonwealth he imagines for the island, and he does so in an episode of interpersonal drama.

Gonzalo's depiction of an ideal commonwealth is offered to his master, Alonso, as Alonso and his shipwrecked companions feel their way around the desert island on which a storm at sea has cast them on their journey home from the African wedding of Alonso's daughter Claribel to the King of Tunis (II, i, 139–70).[22] Gonzalo is explicitly the experimental thinker, here, starting his monologue as he does in the following terms: 'Had I plantation of this isle, my lord, ... / And were the King on't, what would I do?' What Burrow suggests, with reference to this episode, is that experimental thinking, while initially plotless, swiftly generates action in the form of 'interpersonal drama' as one character responds to another's thinking aloud in the light of their preoccupations. There is for Burrow, in particular, 'a direct comment on Montaigne's utopianism in the way that Sebastian and Antonio immediately after hearing about the golden world of Gonzalo's commonwealth set about attempting to kill their king'. At such moments, a non-narrative source 'feeds back in complex ways into the action of the play' and reflects back on its own composition as an essay, with component elements of the source assigned to different voices in the dialogue. Burrow comments:

> That makes Shakespeare a particularly valuable reader of Montaigne, since there are times when his drama can appear to pick apart the contexture of commonplaces, abstract principles, and personal experiences from which so many of the essays are so delicately woven. It is almost as though Shakespeare can sometimes allow one to see behind the *Essays*, and, as it were, allow his audience to glimpse their genesis.[23]

I would like to return to this observation from a different angle by identifying the form that Gonzalo's speech adopts and then suggesting that this form may be an inheritance from Montaigne as much as the words Gonzalo uses. This will cause me to challenge an assumption found in many readings of this episode, including those (already cited) of Burrow and Warren Boutcher, that the Montaignian material that Shakespeare puts to use in this scene is philosophical in character. My contention, in essence, is that what Montaigne provides Shakespeare here is not philosophical but rhetorical in character. Burrow and Hamlin hint at this when they point out, quite rightly, that, in launching on his speech, Gonzalo is (to quote Hamlin) 'attempting to relieve Alonso's misery' and that Gonzalo does so by, in Burrow's terms, playing the (courtly) 'fool'.[24] Only Frank Lestringant, to my knowledge, has connected the rhetorical choice that Gonzalo makes – as well as the material he uses – with Montaigne.[25]

Gonzalo launches into a set-piece speech in praise of a perfect commonwealth on the island because his master views the island not only as uncharted territory, but as his son's watery grave writ large,

and – like a good courtier – Gonzalo is trying to distract his master
from his woes. The rhetorical choice he makes is to attempt a declamation. This is the exercise in oratory in which a speaker exercises
or displays his or her talent by arguing with ingenuity a cause at one
remove from the pressing causes that would receive orations in the
tribunal and the assembly: the setting for a declamation is, then, not
so much a trial as a mock-trial; the aim ranges from admiration,
through consolation, to sheer pleasure.[26] A definition of the *declamatio* is to be found in Quintilian. Erasmus explores its possibilities
in several texts. These include a *Declamatio de morte*, containing
arguments in praise of death offered by way of consolation for the
death of a loved one, an aim that Gonzalo shares (since Alonso is in
despair at the loss of his son). Erasmus went on to write a famous
Renaissance declamation, *The Praise of Folly*, in which he pushes
the declamation to a virtuoso limit by making Folly speak in praise
of herself. Thomas More replied, in *Utopia*, with a similarly ironic
praise of the better political life to be found in the New World, on
Nowhere Island, where all things are held in common.

Montaigne provides the link in so far as he practises the mode of
declamation at times in his essay on the Cannibals. This essay is no
more direct a contribution than *Utopia* is to the debate in political
philosophy about the best state. It is a text in which Montaigne sets
out to unsettle his European readers' unthinking superiority complex
by praising – at least initially – the so-called barbarians of the New
World: by offering, in other words, a declamation in paradoxical
praise of communistic, polygamous, man-eating folly. This is the part
of the essay that Shakespeare recycles in *The Tempest*. Montaigne
goes on to judge the Tupinambá practice of cannibalism to be indeed
cruel, but less so than the atrocities of the Europeans who condemn
them, blind to their own faults. The argument is not relativistic, then,
but comparative and contrarian: it suggests that the very people we
unthinkingly despise may actually be living much better than we are.
While Montaigne seeks to unsettle his implied reader, Gonzalo imitates Montaigne in an unsuccessful attempt to distract his master, but
the genre of the declamation accommodates both of these aims and
provides them with a rhetorical structure. That rhetorical structure is
made available to Shakespeare by Montaigne's essay along with the
description of a better New World political life.

Montaigne's text may in fact form part of a longer sequence
of declamations connecting Shakespeare back to Erasmus. José de
Pina Martins and Frank Lestringant have suggested, as a possible
source for Montaigne's 'Des Cannibales', the anonymous short Italian

declamatory text on folly, *La Pazzia* (Venice, c. 1541), which appeared in a French translation by Jean du Thier in Paris in 1566. They point out how much *La Pazzia* owes to Erasmus's *Praise of Folly*.[27] Extending this intertextual chain to Shakespeare via Montaigne, as Lestringant does, gives us a sequence of declamations in which the New World emerges as praiseworthy folly in contrast with the morally bankrupt wisdom of Europe.

The passage from *The Tempest* subjects the foregoing sequence to a further sea-change. No longer the American reality that Montaigne depicts it to be, that better society has become the momentary projection of an Italian courtier on an island that is part-Mediterranean, part-American in its geography. There is a similar scattered transformation of other elements. It does indeed seem, on the one hand, that, in being turned into interpersonal drama in the way Burrow describes, the fabric of Montaigne's text has been unpicked: two strands, for example, that are interwoven in Montaigne – his praise of a better society in which all things are held in common and the self-ironising extravagance with which he offers that praise – are separated out and allocated, the one to the declamatory Gonzalo and the other to the carping Sebastian and Antonio, this allocation serving to animate the drama.

Many critics have treated Gonzalo's praise of a better society as the Montaignian borrowing in this scene, because it is the most easily identified in verbal terms, and they have seen that praise as having the character of a philosophical proposition in Montaigne's work. This has led some to conclude that Shakespeare is rather aggressively making a fool of Montaigne's proposition.[28] My suggestion has been all along that it is neither an act of aggression nor indeed of homage, but an appropriative borrowing of a kind that is quintessentially Montaignian, and therefore the borrowing of a manner – in this case, the rhetoric of declamation – along with the matter of Golden Age utopianism. His appropriation of declamatory rhetoric enables Shakespeare to do different theatrical work with it: to show what a trial in the rhetorical art of declamatory consolation looks like when it fails to achieve its aim of distraction, for example, even as that trial's praise of holding all things in common then throws into high relief the privatarian colonising impulses of character after character in the play; and to reveal the level of mental unreadiness among the Neapolitans for the political culture of the island they are about to encounter. Meanwhile, the connection between Montaigne and Shakespeare on the level of the rhetoric of declamation in this scene casts a certain light back on the Montaignian source, revealing its genesis to be its own kind of experiment with the praise of utopian folly.

Notes

1. Burrow, 'Montaignian Moments', p. 242.
2. Engle, 'Sovereign Cruelty in Montaigne and *King Lear*', p. 119.
3. William M. Hamlin, *Montaigne's English Journey*, pp. 91–2.
4. See Boutcher, 'Marginal Commentaries', p. 15.
5. Burrow, 'Montaignian Moments', p. 240.
6. Mack, *Reading and Rhetoric in Montaigne and Shakespeare*; see also, by the same author, 'Montaigne and Shakespeare: Source, Parallel or Comparison?'.
7. Boutcher, 'Marginal Commentaries', p. 25.
8. Ellrodt, 'Self-Consciousness in Montaigne and Shakespeare'.
9. Cave, 'When Shakespeare Met Montaigne', p. 117.
10. Nuttall, 'Action at a Distance'; Maguire, 'Part I: Editor's Introduction', p. 8.
11. Burrow, 'Montaignian Moments', p. 242, p. 249.
12. I recapitulate here the reading of *The Merchant of Venice* in my essay 'French Connections'.
13. *Montaigne's Essays*, trans. Florio, I: 25, p. 176; *Essais*, ed. Villey and Saulnier, I: 26, p. 166 (the chapter numberings in this part of Book I differ in these two editions).
14. *Montaigne's Essays*, II: 12, p. 316; Montaigne, *Essais*, II.12, p. 595.
15. *The Merchant of Venice*, ed. Mahood.
16. Taylor, *Shakspere's Debt to Montaigne*, p. 7.
17. See, e.g., Desan, '"Translata Proficit"'.
18. In my 2008 article 'French Connections', pp. 31–2 (n. 2), I cited the following potential instances of that network of sources: Girolamo Cardano, *De subtilitate* (On Subtlety) (1550), bk 18; Giovanni Battista Della Porta, *Magia naturalis* (On Natural Magic) (1558); Reginald Scot, *The Discovery of Witchcraft* (1584), bk 13; and Zachary Jones, in his English translation of Pierre Le Loyer's 1586 French study of ghosts, *A Treatise of Spectres* (1605). I now add that Sextus Empiricus argues, in his second mode of doubt, that 'there are many differences in our choice and avoidance of external things' (*Outlines*, p. 22), a passage on which Montaigne draws in 'Of the Institution and Education of Children', and which reappears in a partial English translation of Sextus's *Outlines* dating from around 1590 (Hamlin, 'A Lost Translation Found?', p. 48). I am grateful to Will Hamlin for suggesting to me this addition to the network.
19. I return here to arguments presented in my essay 'Trial by Theatre, or Free-Thinking in *Julius Caesar*'.
20. *Julius Caesar*, ed. Dorsch. Further references are to this edition.
21. Nuttall, *Shakespeare the Thinker*, p. 186.
22. *The Tempest*, ed. Orgel.
23. Burrow, 'Montaignian Moments', p. 243, p. 245.

24. Hamlin, *Montaigne's English Journey*, p. 86; Burrow, 'Montaignian Moments', p. 243.
25. Lestringant, 'Gonzalo's Books'.
26. See Chomarat, *Grammaire et rhetorque chez Érasme*, vol. 1, pp. 931–1001.
27. Martins, 'Modèles portugais et italiens de Montaigne'; Lestringant, 'Gonzalo's Books', pp. 180–5.
28. A recent example is Stephen Greenblatt's reading of this episode in his introduction to *Shakespeare's Montaigne*, ed. Greenblatt and Platt.

Chapter 15

Montaigne's Shakespeare: The Tempest as Test-case

Lars Engle

This chapter makes two related arguments, one large-scale and one local. In the first, it suggests that Shakespeareans have in general used references to Montaigne to make a Shakespeare full of modern attitudes more plausible. Setting up a Humean *Is/Ought* spectrum and comparing how Shakespeare and Montaigne position themselves on such a spectrum, the first part also suggests that, while both Shakespeare and Montaigne inhabit the *Is* end, a close juxtaposition suggests a Shakespeare sceptical about how tenable many Montaignean *Is* attitudes are. The second part of the chapter argues that one can read *The Tempest* plausibly as Shakespeare's dramatic meditation not only on theatre's power and limits, but also on the powers and limits of Montaignean reflection. I explore the possibility that Prospero and Gonzalo together (like Lafew and Parolles together in *All's Well That Ends Well*) show Shakespeare understanding, evaluating and registering ambivalence towards key aspects of Montaigne as Montaigne presents his life in the *Essays*, or in those essays that Shakespeare read.

Montaigne's Shakespeare

Montaigne's Shakespeare, the larger project of which this chapter is a part, claims that the Shakespeare modern readers and theatregoers feel close to is often a Shakespeare whose implicit core attitudes have been reconstructed to a surprising degree alongside attitudes articulated explicitly by his near-contemporary the French essayist Michel de Montaigne. To confirm the plausibility of a Shakespeare who is rather like many of his modern readers, a Shakespeare proto-modern and proto-liberal, eager to give voice to the other, anti-dogmatic, sceptical about knowledge and authority, exploratory about sexuality and gender, committed to exposing the horrors of human cruelty, whether it is familial or erotic or religious or political, we need to find someone else in Shakespeare's time who articulates that constellation of mental positions. We should be able to do this, given that we scholars often call Shakespeare's time 'early modernity'. Attempts to locate other early moderns who actually say the things we would like Shakespeare's plays to be implying end with remarkable frequency in extensive citation of Montaigne.

But despite fine modern translations by Donald Frame and M. A. Screech, and despite the recent success of Sarah Bakewell's excellent *How to Live: A Life of Montaigne in One Question and Twenty Attempts at an Answer*, most English-speaking readers do not know Montaigne well. Nor have most Shakespeare scholars pinpointed the ways Montaigne serves them in appropriating Shakespeare for contemporary socio-political ends. Some have noticed ways that Shakespeare, if he responds to Montaigne, does so in partial dissent from precisely those aspects of Montaigne that most appeal to modern readers, but very few have explored how this dissent casts light on why they are comparing Montaigne to Shakespeare in the first place.

Montaigne's *Essays* circulated in London in both French and English in the late 1590s. John Florio worked on a complete translation starting sometime in the late 1590s:[1] the *Essayes* were entered in the Stationer's Register in 1600 and eventually published in 1603. Two excellent recent books, William Hamlin's *Montaigne's English Journey* and Warren Boutcher's *The School of Montaigne in Early Modern Europe*, have improved our knowledge of how Montaigne was received, mostly but not entirely via Florio, in sixteenth- and seventeenth-century England. While we cannot be certain when Shakespeare began reading Montaigne (almost certainly by the time of *King Lear*, certainly by the time of *The Winter's Tale* and *The Tempest*, possibly as early as the writing of *As You Like It* and *Hamlet*), we can learn a good deal about Shakespeare's relations to the modern by thinking about plays where he might be responding to particularly striking proto-modern features of Montaigne's essays. Thus one might imagine Shakespeare feeling a kinship or validation in Montaigne's approach to questions concerning prescriptive morality: telling people how to live their lives.

Sarah Bakewell comments early in *How to Live* that 'how to live?' 'is not the same as the ethical question, "How *should* one live?" ' . . . [Montaigne] was less interested in what people ought to do than in what they actually did.'[2] Lurking behind this comment of Bakewell's, though she does not mention it, is David Hume's famous observation about how moralists leap without argument from is to ought.

> In every system of morality . . . of a sudden I am surpriz'd to find, that instead of the usual copulations of propositions, *is*, and *is not*, I meet with no proposition that is not connected with an *ought*, or an *ought not*. This change is . . . of the last consequence . . . 'tis necessary . . . that a reason should be given, for what seems altogether inconceivable, how this relation can be a deduction from others, which are entirely different from it. But as authors do not commonly use this precaution, I shall presume to recommend it to the readers; and am persuaded, that this small attention wou'd subvert all the vulgar systems of morality, and let us see, that the distinction of vice and virtue is not founded merely on the relations of objects, nor is perceiv'd by reason.[3]

Bakewell's way of putting things raises the question of whether 'ethics' itself is, as Bakewell herself seems to think, a matter of having made Hume's leap, a matter of should and ought, or whether 'ethics' should be opposed to 'morality' (as a number of recent philosophers, notably Bernard Williams, suggest), where morality articulates a system of oughts and ethics relies more on does and is. Williams, to put a complex position simply, thinks that 'morality' is the domain of systematic shoulds and 'ethics' the guiding residue of one's habits and commitments, of the particular ises of one's own life experience.[4] Thus Bakewell calls 'ethics' what I would call 'morality', but I think she is generally right about this aspect of Montaigne. Montaigne's essays juxtapose a diffuse and not-very-prescriptive ethics of is against the morality ethics of ought. Montaigne is an ethical thinker, but an anti-systematic one. He offers an ethics of the habitual, the embodied, the pagan and the immanent to oppose to a Christian morality of ought that requires self-transformation, self-denial and reliance on the transcendent (faith, grace, scripture). Montaigne, a Catholic with Jewish ancestors and three Protestant siblings, lived during the French civil wars of the Reformation. Disputes about liturgy and theology – about beliefs that eventuate in systematic oughts for adherents – were pursued with fire and blood all around him, and he himself barely escaped violent death on several occasions related to dogmatic conflict. As Montaigne often remarks, dogmatism in these particular cases went hand in hand with human greed, opportunism and bloody-mindedness. Because of this experience of brutal violence in the name of religion, which he himself links to imperial conquest in the name of Christ in the New World, his commitment to an ethics of *is* suggests political critique as well as reflective detachment. A powerful survey of human behaviour relying on an ethics of *is* will, rather in the manner of the Kinsey report on human sexuality, suggest that the natural or normal can best be approached by looking at what people actually do, rather than on a strong sense of what they ought or ought not to do. Exalting such an is-focus underlines ways Montaigne and Shakespeare resemble one another, since both seem more intent on subjecting or interrogating *ought* by comparison to *is* than in changing *is* in the direction of some super-salient *ought*. Exploring an ethics of the immanent involves revering the complexity and oddity of human subjectivity as well as human sociability, whence Shakespeare and Montaigne's well-earned joint reputation as pioneering surveyors of human inner space.

Shakespeare and Montaigne differ as much as they resemble each other, however. To lay out what I see as the general stake for students of Shakespeare in Montaigne/Shakespeare comparisons, I believe that Montaigne has, at least since the Second World War, been on the whole used in Shakespeare studies as a way to bring Shakespeare closer to us: to make Shakespearean anticipations of modern attitudes more plausible. To cite some strong examples, Jonathan Dollimore's 1984 *Radical Tragedy* quotes Montaigne frequently (and tendentiously) to show that Renaissance intellectuals held radical, secularising, anti-authoritarian positions on a variety of topics as part of Dollimore's effort to present English Renaissance tragedy in a modern Brechtian light. Hugh Grady's 2003 *Shakespeare, Machiavelli, and Montaigne* mobilises Montaigne as a Renaissance Habermas, to set against Machiavelli as a Renaissance Foucault committed to structural determination, so that Montaigne exemplifies early modern subjectivity speaking back to power. Peter Holbrook's 2010 *Shakespeare's Individualism* uses Montaigne powerfully in a similar way, and Stephen Greenblatt's prize-winning 2011 bestseller *The Swerve* also uses Montaigne as a vital bridge between Lucretius and Shakespeare – and, via Shakespeare, between Lucretius and us. All of these critics use Montaigne as a champion in discrediting *ought* by reference to *is*, and all imagine a Shakespeare similarly inclined who recognises Montaigne as a fellow. William Hamlin's account of Montaigne's reception via Florio in seventeenth-century Britain, and Warren Boutcher's discussion of appropriations of Montaigne by successive generations of readers from his own time to the twentieth century in *The School of Montaigne*, have enabled scholars to be more precise about these processes, though both Hamlin and Boutcher caution against exaggerating or sentimentalising Montaigne's particular impact on Shakespeare, as does Greenblatt in his introduction to the selection from Florio edited by Peter Platt.[5]

In philosophically inflected discussions of Shakespeare, critics also use Montaigne as a way to patch the hole in Shakespeare's collected works where an informed interest in classical philosophy might manifest itself.[6]

My own strategy in this project, then, while corrective of some modernisers, does not aim to de-modernise Shakespeare. Shakespeare shows an uncanny apprehension of issues around which Montaigne displays attitudes attractive to moderns. This apprehension might, or might not, derive from early reading of Montaigne in Florio's or other translations, or in French. It might also derive from the non-prescriptive tendencies, *is* rather than *ought* orientations, of writing for a public theatre under orders (often evaded but rarely ignored) to avoid religious and political tendentiousness.

I agree with Grady and Dollimore and Holbrook and Greenblatt and any number of other readers that Montaigne provides a fabulous index of the breadth of what was thinkable by a near-contemporary of Shakespeare's. But when, as happens very often in my view, we find Shakespeare treating issues on which Montaigne presents a somewhat distinctive position that anticipates common modern progressive ethical attitudes, I think Shakespeare displays fascinating resistance to what I and others find so congenial in Montaigne.

To treat two related topics briefly, Montaigne pioneers modern left-liberal ethical stances towards ethnocentrism and towards shame. Montaigne presents anti-ethnocentrism – curiosity about other cultures, active imaginative identification with their views, dismay at attempts to subjugate or erase their differences, dislike of narrow-mindedness, insularity and arrogance as manifested by members of his own culture – both as an ethical good and as a contribution to pleasure in living. 'Of the Cannibals' and 'Of Coaches' offer well-known examples. In these essays and many others Montaigne pioneers the way twenty-first-century anti-ethnocentric attitudes arise in horrified reaction to both twentieth and twenty-first-century genocides. Montaigne does not, I should add, see anti-ethnocentrism as a tenable intellectual foundation in itself. That is, anti-ethnocentrism does not remove one from a primary commitment to one's own ethnos.[7] Montaigne is a rooted cosmopolitan. But he exalts the aspects of his own culture that make learning from the other a goal, and he eloquently deplores those aspects of his culture that make silencing or enslaving or deracinating the other a programme. Montaigne thus anticipates, perhaps not consistently but strikingly, a number of modern or postmodern ethical attitudes that go along with anti-ethnocentrism: anti-dogmatism, categorical opposition to cruelty, distaste for and amusement at sexual repression, and adherence to the idea that many different kinds of lives should be liveable in a state of self-approval.

All of these, especially the last three, are related to Montaigne's generally liberatory attitude towards individual shame. Montaigne thinks that much personal shame (especially sexual and status shame) is unnecessary and that much shaming of others is cruel. If the *is* of sexual pleasure could replace the many *oughts* that haunt it, Montaigne suggests, we would all be better off. As Ann Hartle puts it, Montaigne 'makes his mind ashamed of itself for its attempt to be divine, and by bringing the body and its everyday needs into the public, he overcomes the shame of the human'.[8] Like later anti-ethnocentrists, Montaigne mobilises a kind of shame against bad forms of ethnocentrism, often by looking at things from the other's viewpoint. Montaigne, then, pioneers casting off personal shame and taking on collective shame. In particular, he shames the cruelty enabled by categorical contempt based on ethnic or religious difference. Judith Shklar comments that he innovates in 'putting cruelty first' among vices:[9] again, there are well-known examples in 'Of the Cannibals' and 'Of Coaches'. Stupid categorical contempt among his fellow-Europeans, or fellow-gentlepersons, or fellow-Christians, or fellow-Catholics, is a major target for Montaigne; he indeed tries to make Europeans ashamed of contempt.

If (as I think he does) Shakespeare models a more typical sensitive person's susceptibility to individual shame (for instance in the Sonnets), while at the same time putting provocative repudiations of individual shame into the mouths of morally eccentric characters like Falstaff and Parolles, we can trace in Shakespeare a coherent contrast, a potential reaction, to Montaigne's treatment of personal shame, particularly Montaigne's treatment of sexual shame in 'On Some Verses of Virgil', an essay that seems to influence *Othello*, *All's Well* and other late plays. And given that Shakespeare marks the difficulties and dangers of inter-cultural communication throughout his career in such plays as *Titus Andronicus*, *The Merchant of Venice*, *Othello* and *The Tempest* – plays which highlight the dangers more than the pleasures of cultural diversity – we can see Shakespeare differing substantially from Montaigne over the anti-ethnocentric ethical stance Montaigne presents so richly throughout his work and specifically in

'Of the Cannibals', to cite an essay we know Shakespeare did read. *The Tempest* offers the clearest as well as the culminating case.

Highlighting shame and ethnocentrism brings out not only interesting contrastive features of these important writers but also the potential contemporary utility of their works. Shaming others as ethnocentric or anti-ethnocentric is a dismaying feature of Left–Right disagreement in contemporary public life: dismaying because shaming someone is a way of interrupting civil communication, and because recurrent angry shame can easily settle into categorical contempt, which ends civil communication. Modern conservatives see anti-ethnocentrism as a sentimental betrayal of one's own culture on behalf of other cultures one cannot possibly know very well. Modern progressives see the ethnocentrism of modern conservatives as a self-serving denial of the validity of other viewpoints and of the reality of a history of domination. This significant divide involves shame: the cultivation of certain kinds of shame and the repudiation of others. Both sides of the divide see their opponents as wrong in their views of *is* and (either consequently or causally) very wrong in their constellation of *oughts*. In a more general way, however, there are commonalities between Left and Right here. Each sees the other as shameless on matters where shame is appropriate, and full of unnecessary shame in areas where shame is inappropriate.

I may mildly innovate in emphasising liberation from personal shame and recruitment to collective shame as a prime consequence of reading Montaigne, but Montaigne's anticipation of modern anti-ethnocentrism was recognised long before the term 'anti-ethnocentrism' became current. That anticipation plays a big part in making even historicising commentators remark on Montaigne's modernity. M. A. Screech, at the beginning of *Montaigne and Melancholy*, a book that in general situates Montaigne's self-understanding firmly in terms of Renaissance medicine, comments that Montaigne 'stands astride the gap separating Rabelais and Shakespeare, but, while Rabelais and Shakespeare partly share a common view of the universe now long discarded, [Montaigne] seems to inhabit a world whose intellectual assumptions are close to our own'.[10] If Montaigne's *is/ought* ratios or relations resemble our own, and if Shakespeare reacts to Montaigne's, then we may be able to use Montaigne to discuss how Shakespeare challenges us. Montaigne may offer us a way to historicise our presentism: this chapter joins a number of other recent commentaries in using Montaigne to situate Shakespeare with relation to intellectual modernity rather than simply to assert Shakespeare's modernity by way of Montaigne.[11]

Given this approach, it is important both to establish that anti-ethnocentrism is a distinctively modern mind set and that Montaigne exhibits it strongly. The word 'anti-ethnocentrism' is a neologism not yet in the *Oxford English Dictionary*. *OED* defines 'ethnocentric' as 'regarding one's own race or ethnic group as of supreme importance', and while that word, which dates roughly to the beginning of the twentieth century, may have emerged from psychology and anthropology as a value-neutral description, its post-Second World War use has been on the whole as a pejorative, even in social science. The *OED* illustrates the word with the anthropologist E. E. Evans-Pritchard's anti-ethnocentric comment that the 'ethnocentric attitude has to be abandoned if we are to appreciate the rich variety of human culture and social life'.[12] Certainly the word 'ethnocentric' is seen as marking dangerous social territory in T. W. Adorno et al., *The Authoritarian Personality*, published in 1950 under the auspices of the American Jewish Committee. That book develops what its authors call an 'e-scale', a sociological measure of ethnocentricity, in an attempt to study scientifically the 'potentially fascistic individual'.[13] Their attempts to measure Americans on the 'e-scale' included questions about attitudes towards a variety of groups facing social obloquy, including (alongside Jews and African Americans) non-racial others like 'zootsuiters' and 'Okies'.[14] For Adorno and his collaborators, ethnocentrism is a scaleable relative attitude, not an absolute. ('Anti-ethnocentrists' would presumably be, and would necessarily attempt to be, at the low end of the e-scale.) Putting Evans-Pritchard and Adorno together, we can see how modern anti-ethnocentrism both promises multicultural enjoyment and hopes to inoculate against further racist holocausts.

In somewhat the same way, Montaigne's anti-ethnocentrism seems to have been in part a cultivation of pleasure in difference, in part a defensive reaction to the cruelty of his times. However it is derived, Montaigne models modern anti-ethnocentrism in his writings, including some of the essays that Shakespeare makes direct use of. Indeed, as I will argue, some puzzling aspects of Shakespeare's *The Tempest* may be understood as Shakespeare's response to the anti-ethnocentrism of Montaigne in 'Of the Cannibals' and 'Of Cruelty', two essays that Shakespeare quotes in that play.

Moreover, commentators present Montaigne, and in particular Montaigne's anti-ethnocentrism and celebrations of difference, as points of origin for modern liberal individualism. Charles Taylor remarks in *Sources of the Self* that 'Montaigne is an originator of the search for each person's originality', a search that aims 'to identify the individual in his or her unrepeatable difference'.[15] Judith Shklar takes the title of her book *Ordinary Vices* from a sentence in 'Of the Cannibals', and, as noted above, credits Montaigne with originating a moral habit of 'putting cruelty first' among vices. She finds this habit characteristic of 'liberal and humane people' in the late twentieth century: 'Intuitively they would choose cruelty as the worst thing we do. They would then quickly find themselves faced with all the paradoxes and puzzles that Montaigne encountered.'[16] One consequence or corollary of this opposition to cruelty is Montaigne's widely distributed sympathy for various others, but, as Jean Starobinski remarks, Montaigne combines sympathy with a willingness to reverse the patterns of subordination that mark out objects suitable for sympathy: 'Montaigne does not stop simply at feeling compassion [for 'animals . . . cannibals . . . peasants . . . children . . . the oppressed']; . . . he is prepared to recognise the moral and intellectual superiority of the alleged inferiors'.[17] As Hugo Friedrich points out, with specific reference to Montaigne's 'Des caniballes', 'Montaigne assembles everything that can be said in favour of these "cannibals."' And, setting Montaigne's treatment of ethnographic material in the context of other treatments contemporary with Montaigne, Friedrich adds that what distinguishes Montaigne is precisely what we now call anti-ethnocentrism:

> Montaigne was not the only one who . . . reevaluated the concepts of 'culture' and 'barbarism.' But he merged what was a contemporary commonplace thought into his own vivid consciousness of the problems of European arrogance about their education and culture, which he contrasted with the breadth of all non-European possibilities of being human, which are called 'barbaric' only because of prejudice.[18]

One might supplement these observations by pointing out that Montaigne's omnipresent scepticism about the social imposition of new abstract principles on the bodies of human beings, when brought to bear on emergent colonial situations, amounts not merely to anti-ethnocentrism but to questions about whether any regime change forced from outside or above can possibly be good. To each her own *is*, to each his own *ought*, seems a Montaignean belief: as he says in I: 22, 'Of customs, and how a received law should not easily be changed', 'There riseth a great doubt, whether any so evident profit may be found in the change of a received law of what nature soever, as there is hurt in removing the same.'[19]

As all these commentators suggest, Montaigne consistently casts doubt on European accounts of the barbarism of the regimes of others.

At the same time, Montaigne notes that our notions of truth and reason must be the products of our culture. Given this, we cannot escape a certain kind of ethnic determination – the inability to know what our historical situation does not permit us to know, for instance. Montaigne implies, without exactly defining, a central paradox of an anti-ethnocentric position: that one is unlikely to hold such a position unless it is somehow part of one's ethnos, one's inherited, habituated system of *is*es and *oughts*.[20] Living amid the traumas of the Reformation, and using many of the intellectual tools of Reformers, Montaigne quite consistently prefers habituation combined with self-acceptance to radical conversion as a mode of forming minds.[21] A writer like Montaigne in fact makes an anti-ethnocentric position more available to others in his own culture by putting it in discursive circulation, thus making it part of a Western European's intellectual heritage.

To take a particular example, in 'Of the Cannibals', Montaigne moves immediately to ground respect for the New World other in what looks like Golden Age (or proto-Romantic) primitivism, but is actually something considerably more complicated.[22] Montaigne notes that we can complicate a culturally blinkered response to the other as 'barbarous' by reference to a theory of historical evolution away from a state of natural living towards social complexity and decadence – a way of looking at the 'savage' that would allow one to reverse the evaluation normally involved in use of the term. He comments, in a passage that Perdita and Polixenes appear to paraphrase in a discussion of hybridisation in *The Winter's Tale*:

> They [the Tupinambá, the Brazilian natives Montaigne discusses with an ethnographically inclined servant and then meets] are even savage, as we call those fruits wilde, which nature of her selfe, and of her ordinarie progresse hath produced: whereas indeed they are those which our selves have altered by our artificiall devices, and diverted from their common order, we should rather terme savage. (163)

Montaigne then invokes ancient philosophers and legislators as people who would have profited intellectually had the New World been available as an example to them, anti-ethnocentrically proposing that his own teachers and models from the distant non-Christian past might have profited from the model these savages provide. In doing this, however, Montaigne also demonstrates where his own '*Idea* of the customes and opinions of his own country' and of the possibility of a speculative life lived according to nature and reason partly comes from. He thus partly addresses the paradox of an anti-ethnocentric ethnos by showing that outsourcing one's ideas may be an ethnic characteristic:

> I am sometimes grieved the knowledge of [New World culture] came no sooner to light, at what time there were men, that better than we could have judged of it. I am sorie *Lycurgus* and *Plato* had it not: for me seemeth that what in those nations we see by experience, doth not only exceed all the pictures wherewith licentious Poesie hath proudly imbellished the golden age ... but also the conception and desire of Philosophy. They could not imagine a genuitie so pure and simple, as we see it by experience; nor ever beleeve our societie might be maintained with so little art and humane combination. It is a nation, would I answer *Plato*, that hath no kind of traffike, no knowledge of Letters, no intelligence of numbers, no name of magistrate, nor of politike superioritie; no use of service, or riches or of povertie; no contracts, no successions, no partitions, no occupation but idle; no respect of kinred, but common, no apparell but naturall, no manuring of lands, no use of wine, corne, or mettle. The very words that import lying, falshood, treason, dissimulations, covetousnes, envie, detraction, and pardon, were never heard of amongst them. How dissonant would hee finde his imaginarie commonwealth from this perfection! (163–4)

So, Montaigne shows, the New World natives (whose wars and cannibal customs have not yet been discussed in the essay) resonate as natural and perfect in the context of historical experience enlarged by an imaginary conversation with Plato. History and philosophy, as well as encounters with the other, allow one to get beyond the confines of one's own limiting customs and ideas, and Montaigne clearly wants to use the New World in much the same way that he uses the classical world: as a resource for gaining ironic or helpful perspective on himself and his own moment. As the essay develops, of course, the Tupinambá offer a more complex perspective from which to view sixteenth-century France and early imperial Europe. David Quint has, for instance, taken the last term, 'pardon', in the list of words not known to the Tupinambá as a starting point for a description of the cannibals as a model for a mercilessly honour-driven aristocracy who create 'a society at war with itself', incapable of mercy.[23] George Hoffman reads Montaigne's description of the cannibalism of the Tupinambá as a parody of the Mass and thus as a reflection on the disagreements about Real Presence that underlay the French religious wars.[24] In the brilliant ending of the essay – 'Tout cela ne va pas trop mal: mais quoy? ils ne portent point de haut de chausses' [All this is not bad, but what's the use? They wear no trousers][25] – Montaigne concedes with ironic flippancy that French ethnocentricity will doubtless govern the reception of his essay whatever he himself says or intends.[26]

Montaigne's ways of handling shame and ethnocentricity thus have real traction in our own time, and if we find Shakespeare somehow responding to them we may be glimpsing how Shakespeare might feel about us – an intoxicating possibility, though one that can never be more than a possibility.

The Tempest

Suppose, then, a thought-experiment involving the clearest instance of Shakespeare reading Montaigne: the appearance in *The Tempest* of the passage just quoted (and others) from Florio's 'Of the Cannibales' in the mouth of Gonzalo in a moment of apparent digression, and the use of a shorter passage from Florio's 'Of Crueltie' in the mouth of Prospero at a moment of maximal importance in the play's action.[27]

How did Shakespeare come to these particular essays? One might begin, taking Warren Boutcher and William Hamlin as guides, with paratexts, notably Florio's prefaces to *The Essayes* of 1603, supplemented by Samuel Daniel's commendatory poem. Boutcher has argued persuasively that the set of paratexts locates Florio's Montaigne less as a philosopher bringing sceptical Lucretian experientialism – a version of *is* that threatens a panoply of Elizabethan-Jacobean *oughts* — than as a 'knight-adventurer' who will help aristocratic ladies sort through an impossible flood of print:

> The twentieth-century literature on Tudor and Jacobean intellectual history is almost unanimous on the question of what Montaigne did for his early readers in England. He subversively undermined their traditional pieties. He broke up their traditional world picture. He was of that moment – just before the emergence of new philosophies in the seventeenth century – when all coherence was gone. He cleared the way for modernity.
>
> Maybe. But this preliminary look . . . suggests that those who introduced him . . . saw him and his book rather differently. Montaigne's was a healthy book . . . The author was inserted into an informal hierarchy of intellectual and scholarly figures whose collective office it was to mediate the information explosion . . . introduc[ing] a specific noble *persona* into social relations that mingle learning with nobility.[28]

If Boutcher is right, the paratexts position Florio's Montaigne for a readership shaped by the same desires to sort out the intellectual realm in order to promote good life and noble behaviour that Montaigne promotes in 1.25, 'Of the Institution and Education of Children', which, like Florio's Preface, addresses an aristocratic female friend.

How did Shakespeare, not aristocratic, and a reader whose purposes were in general appropriative rather than scholarly, read Florio's prefaces and Samuel Daniel's poem? As Boutcher remarks, 'the printed *persona* of Montaigne somehow sits at the crossroads of early modern elite identity and has something to say to all comers',[29] including new-minted gentleman like Shakespeare knocking at the boundaries of the elite. Knowing Daniel and probably Florio personally, Shakespeare could have used their comments on Montaigne as a guide to what to read in the large book in front of him. In his preface to the entire volume Florio mentions by book and chapter number III: 9 ('Of Vanitie'), II: 8 ('Of the Affections of Fathers to their Children'), I: 28 ('Nine and twentie Sonnets of *Steven de la Boétie*'), III: 1 ('Of Profit and Honesty'), III: 6 ('Of Coaches'), II: 23 ('Of Bad Meanes emploied to a Good End'), I: 41 ('That a Man should not communicate his Glorie'), mentions 'a captive Canniball fattend against my death' – thus alluding to I: 30 ('Of the Caniballes') – cites II: 16 ('Of Glory'), both cites and paraphrases II: 11 ('Of Crueltie'), cites I: 27 ('Of Friendship'), mentions III: 9 ('Of Vanitie') for a second time and then, in 'To the curteous Reader', adds yet another reference (xxii) to III: 9. While Florio's later paratexts do not put themselves forward at the opening of the big Folio, the 'Epistle' that precedes Book II, addressed to the Countess of Rutland and Lady Penelope Riche, adds another reference to I: 27, apologises for Montaigne's comments on women in II: 35 ('Of Three Good Women'), mentions Indian women who virtuously immolate themselves in II: 29 ('Of Vertue'), adds reference to courageous women in II: 27 ('Cowardize, the Mother of Cruelty') and in II: 3 ('A Custome of the Ile of *Cea*') cites I: 24 ('Of Pedantisme'), returns to II: 3 and mentions II: 36 ('Of the Worthiest and Most Excellent Men') (287–9). The 'Epistle' to Lady Elizabeth Grey and Lady Marie Nevill that precedes Book III apologises for Montaigne's representation of women in III: 3 ('Of Three Commerces or Societies') (710). Those interested in Shakespeare–Montaigne comparisons will note how many of these essays are regularly discussed by Shakespeareans. Daniel's poem says of Montaigne '*This Prince . . . / . . . hath made such bolde sallies out upon /* CUSTOME, *the mighty tyrant of the earth*' (xxv), thus drawing the reader's attention to I: 22, 'Of customs'. So, among others, the particular essays that Shakespeare has most clearly read are alluded to and cited by Florio in the Preface: 'Of the Affections of Fathers for their Children', used in *Lear*; 'Of Vanitie', source of what Colin Burrow terms 'Montaignian moments' in both *Lear* and *Measure for Measure*;[30] and, of course, 'Of the Caniballes' and 'Of Crueltie', quoted in *The Tempest*. Oddly, the essay that Boutcher rightly sees as most thoroughly implicated in the version of Montaigne conveyed by the paratexts, I: 25 ('Of the Institution and Education of Children'), is never cited in them.

Particular phrases in Florio's paratexts at the opening of 1603 seem to have caught Shakespeare's eye. In 'To the curteous Reader' (xxii), Florio refers 'any dog-tooth'de Criticke, or adder-tongu'd Satirist' to III: 9. 'Critic' is a relatively new word in English, listed by the *OED* as first appearing in Florio's *Worlde of Wordes* and in Shakespeare's *Love's Labour's Lost* in 1598. Shakespeare in Sonnet 112 (published 1609) writes: 'In so profound *Abisme* I throw all care / Of others voyces, that my Adders sence, / To cryttick and to flatterer stopped are.' Of course, if Florio reads Shakespeare's sonnets in manuscript, it is possible that the ever-plausible link between critics and adders passes the other way, but 112 is one of a group of sonnets that on stylistic grounds and in terms of the internal three-year period referred to in 106 seem to be among the latest, thus as likely to be influenced by a 1603 paratext as to influence it.

More verbal hints that Shakespeare read the initial paratexts come in Florio's phrasing while describing how his noble patronesses supported him in his labours:

> I must needs say while this [the translation of Montaigne] was in doing, to put and keepe mee in hart like a captive Canniball fattend against my death, you often cryed *Coraggio*, and called *çà çà*, and applauded as I passt, and if not fet mee in, yet set mee on . . . As for mee, I onely say as this mans embossed Hart out of hart (*Lib*. ii *c*. 11), I sweat, I wept, and I went-on, till now I stand at bay. (xvii)[31]

Not only does this passage mention both essays Shakespeare borrows from, it includes 'Coraggio', a word that occurs only twice in Shakespeare, both times after 1603 and both in Montaignean contexts – when Stephano says 'Coraggio, bully monster, coraggio!' to Caliban in *The Tempest* (V, i, 258)[32] and when the parodically Montaignean Parolles encourages Bertram to flee French marriage for Italian war in *All's Well*.[33] Even the encouraging '*çà çà*' may be echoed by mad Lear when he runs away from Cordelia's French troops who are trying gently to capture him: 'Come, and you get it, you shall get it by running. Sa, sa, sa, sa' (*KL* IV, vi, 173–4). It just might also feature visually rather than aurally in Caliban's improvised song, 'Ban, ban, Ca-Caliban / Has a new master, get a new man' (*Tem* II, ii, 179).

So it seems plausible that, faced with Florio's large book, Shakespeare read the paratexts retentively and, possibly, used them as a set of hints as to which chapters to read, at least two of which he definitely returned to in writing *The Tempest*. More speculatively, a focus on Montaigne might gloss some of the generic peculiarities of *The Tempest*. The play's action is, to an unusual degree, action remembered or proposed rather than action performed. Moreover, the accounts of past action and proposed future action are intensely coloured by moral judgements: what ought not to have been, what should be. Prospero's commentaries, full of angry intensity and, later, of self-altering auto-therapy, provide most of this material, but the narratives (again often past-tense self-justification or future subjunctive expressions of hopes or fears) of Ariel and Caliban and Miranda and Stephano and Gonzalo and Antonio and Sebastian and Alonso also take this dominant form. As Stephen Orgel puts one side of this, '[t]he rethinking of old issues is mirrored in the play's action: there is a profoundly retrospective quality to the drama, which is deeply involved in recounting and re-enacting past action, in evoking and educating the memory'.[34] Both Fred Parker and Alan de Gooyer see *The Tempest* as distinctive among Shakespeare's works in being a rather essay-like play.[35] I agree. In its capacity to suspend the present to bring the past and future together, *The Tempest* resembles an essay more than any other Shakespeare play.

But does *The Tempest* respond to Montaigne in more than quotation? I would like, following Colin Burrow, to enlist Montaigne as 'one of the ways Shakespeare broadened the range of his drama and differentiated it from that of the immediately preceding generation'. Burrow concludes (in a passage I also quote in the introduction to this collection):

> Montaigne was by no means the sole driver of this process; but Montaigne and the wide range of deliberative authors on whom he drew, from Plutarch to Seneca and Cicero, comprised a core of texts from which Shakespeare also drew, with which he argued, and with which he played (catlike), in order to fashion drama that both provoked and represented thinking in his own Montaignian moments.[36]

As a dramatist, Shakespeare embodies perspectives in characters, and thus embodies thinking in thoughtful characters. This banal observation points to a particular characteristic of *The Tempest*, which goes beyond any play before it in using otherworldly or new-worldly characters to express or explore new ontological and social perspectives. Ariel's peculiar status as an airy spirit, indentured after capture and eager for manumission, and Caliban's as an enslaved earthy dispossessed native wild child eager for release, revenge and a new master to serve, have relatively little precedent in Shakespeare (Puck in *Dream* in some ways anticipates Ariel). Caliban's subject-position has proved fertile and prophetic for colonial subjects seeking to turn the resources of colonising culture against the colonisers. Ariel, long held to exhibit the mysterious multidimensional powers of theatre, has through the line 'Mine would, sir, were I human' gained new life in fictions that explore the emancipatory and emotive aspirations of artificial intelligences (for example, Data's insertion of an emotion-chip in *Star Trek: The Next Generation*, and spaceships that achieve emotive consciousness and social citizenship in recent novels by Kim Stanley Robinson and Ann Leckie). Each of these subject-positions articulates itself as part of a partly fortuitous, partly providential, partly purposeful history, never fully revealed, of multiple relations involving Sycorax and Miranda (and perhaps Satan or Setebos) as well as Prospero, Ariel and Caliban. One of Shakespeare's distinguishing features as a dramatist is his capacity, which at times seems almost a need, to take characters with a function role in a plot and imagine their perspective as a multidimensional one full of choices and feelings. Examples (among many) include Lavatch from *All's Well That Ends Well* and Abhorson and Barnardine from *Measure for Measure* and Aguecheek from *Twelfth Night* ('I was adored once too' [II, iii, 165]). This bringing-to-life of function characters applies strongly to characters who are cultural or racial others: consider Shylock, Morocco, Aaron, Caliban. Shakespeare's getting inside others thus resembles Montaigne's anti-ethnocentrism in some ways. But in important ways it differs from Montaigne, because one cannot put Shakespeare securely at the low end of an e-scale. Shakespeare's others frequently do terrible things that make working with them dangerous and identification with them difficult. He may show categorical subordination from both sides, giving his others voice, but in *Othello* and *The Merchant of Venice* and *Titus Andronicus* as in *The Tempest*, Shakespeare seems to see categorical subjugation as semi-inevitable.

The Tempest may seem Montaignean in being essay-like. But at least in its present action (as opposed to its sketched-in futures and pasts) it reacts to, rather than follows, the Montaigne modern readers like in its treatment of subordination, authority and cruelty.

From the opening lines of the play to its final scene, *The Tempest* embodies a contest between subordination and insubordination. The Master orders the Boatswain to give orders to the Mariners; the Boatswain reproves the King and his court for getting in the way of this appropriate local subordinate hierarchy; and Gonzalo, establishing from the start his penchant for reflective asides, takes an odd form of consolation from the Boatswain's insubordination: 'Methinks he hath no drowning mark upon him – his complexion is perfect gallows' (I, i, 28–30).[37]

From his first appearance in Act I, scene ii, Prospero insists on re-subordinating the mostly compliant Ariel and forcing subordination on the only resentfully compliant Caliban. He hectors his almost entirely compliant daughter, Miranda, and he browbeats the lovestruck Ferdinand and forces him into manual labour. Later Prospero produces a disciplinary masque to subordinate the sexual feelings of Miranda and Ferdinand to Prospero's views of proper marriage. In Alonso's marooned court, Antonio and Sebastian ponder murderous usurpation to render themselves less subordinate, while Gonzalo quotes from Florio an Arcadian reflection on the possibility of a social order without subordination, instituted by a ruler who fosters freedom rather than obedience. Stephano and Trinculo seek empire in a new colony, subordinating a willing Caliban in a project to replace Prospero. Will-to-subordinate, paired with concomitant impulses to self-liberation, drives *The Tempest*. And in its central action Prospero, out of a mixture of vengeance and virtue, seeks to subordinate his enemies, announcing the possibility of driving them to suicide. To gratify Antonio's insubordinate ambition to usurp his brother, Alonso and Antonio attempted to use the sea to bloodlessly eliminate Prospero and Miranda. Ariel as harpy invokes the sea's agency, and indeed that of all natural agents, in return: 'The powers delaying, not forgetting, have / Incensed the seas and shores, yea all the creatures / Against your peace' (III, iii, 73–5). Having bound Alonso, Antonio and Sebastian in a trance of guilt, Ariel declares that 'I have made you mad; / And even with such-like valour men hang and drown / Their proper selves' (III, iii, 58–60). Here Ariel enacts a fantasy of the power of drama Shakespeare has long entertained, most explicitly in Hamlet's claim that theatre can 'make mad the guilty and appall the free' (II, ii, 484).[38] One might wish to connect Ariel's odd phrase 'such-like valour' not only contrastively with Hamlet's assertion that it is only the absence of valour that keeps us from suicide, 'conscience doth make cowards of us all' (III, I, 82), but also with Montaigne's oft-repeated reflections on suicide as a rational and at times admirable and courageous choice, centrally in I:19, 'That to Philosophise is to learn how to die', and II: 3, 'A Custome of the Ile of *Cea*', but also in the discussions of the elective deaths of Cato and Socrates in 'Of Crueltie'.

Given Shakespeare's method of embodying social attitudes in characters, we look for a character in *The Tempest* who either embodies Montaigne to register Shakespearean recognition of Montaigne's kinship and greatness, or caricatures Montaigne to register Shakespeare's rejection or mockery of Montaignean positions.[39] Given that dramatic portraits and caricatures blur, the same character might at different moments be either, especially given Shakespeare's lifelong self-protective avoidance of explicit satiric portraiture.

Both Ariel and Caliban, in the ways they find it necessary to adjust to Prospero's moral expectations and economic needs, remind us of Montaigne's constant anti-ethnocentric use of ethnography (and pseudo-ethnography) to suggest that what Europeans take to be natural in human behaviour may merely be customary. But neither Ariel nor Caliban offers a plausible dramatic embodiment of Montaigne. Both Prospero and Gonzalo do, however, and do so in ways salient even to someone whose acquaintance with Montaigne's project is quite limited, perhaps even confined to the prefatory materials in Florio and some of the essays pointed to in those metatexts, including the two essays quoted in *The Tempest*.

Prospero is a noble who has renounced the arts of rule to retire to a library, 'dukedom large enough', containing volumes that he 'prize[s] above [his] dukedom' (I, ii, 110, 168). This Montaignean strategy has not worked well for him, and both his experience of brotherly betrayal and usurpation, and his angry and agitated states of mind, mark contrasts to Montaigne's general tone of easy-going detachment and his policy of, as it were, limited or reluctant emotional engagement with the exercise of authority, evident in Montaigne's discussion of himself as a judge in 'Of Crueltie'. For most of *The Tempest*, Prospero models irritable authoritarian engagement rather than reflective detachment, managing a complex action that worries him as he attempts it and seems almost to surprise him when it eventually succeeds. But he did retire to a library before the play began, and he intends a life of contemplation 'where / Every third thought shall be my grave' when he gets back to Milan (V, i, 310–11). Prospero, then, remembers and aspires to return to a Montaignean life, but in the action we see devotes himself to anxious crisis-management of a theatrical kind – creating appearances, evoking feelings, browbeating reluctant performers and punishing rebellious ones, exposing rivals, all with the goal of returning to a place of stable high-status leisured identity and looking after his daughter. Thus, without undue exercise of interpretive force, one can easily turn the aspects of *The Tempest* that make readers imagine it as Shakespearean autobiography into aspects of a Shakespearean reflection on Montaigne. Such a reflection could focus on how Montaigne might find reflective serenity impossible were he stuck with Shakespeare's professional life, or on how Shakespeare would behave if, within the confines of his own temperament and powers, he imagined himself adopting Montaigne's life choices. For Prospero resembles Montaigne's distinctive life not only in his bookish Milanese past and reflective death-meditating Milanese future, but also to some extent on the island where, in conversation with his books and the alien voices he finds in the natural world, he conducts solitary experiments with the education of children and the proper civilisation of natives.[40]

Gonzalo plays even better as an embodiment of Montaigne, particularly the version of Montaigne as a courtly counsellor presented by Florio's prefaces and Daniel's poem. A learned noble courtier rather than a ruler, Gonzalo recommends to his prince (as Warren Boutcher has argued) alternatives to violence and despair in comparative contemplation of literary alternatives. In his Arcadian fantasia, Gonzalo suggests that rulers should aim to enfranchise subjects and create lives for them free of degrading subservience and degrading work.[41] He is highly compassionate, and he weeps freely, a characteristic readers of Florio's 'Of Crueltie' might attribute to Montaigne.[42] Moreover, he has been both an obedient agent of a Machiavellian prince[43] and something very close to a disobedient servant who prevents the complete execution of a cruel royal command.[44] Figuring out Gonzalo's moral past involves us in paradoxes about mental and moral independence within service relations which preoccupy Shakespeare in late plays (*King Lear, The Winter's Tale, Cymbeline, The Tempest*),[45] but which also exercise Montaigne, perhaps most extensively in III: 1, 'Of Profit and Honesty', an essay mentioned in Florio's preface.

If Prospero and Gonzalo both count as candidates for Shakespearean portraits of Montaigne, the relations between them deserve close scrutiny. And they reward it. In Prospero's initial account of him to Miranda, Gonzalo seems morally incoherent (or Prospero seems angrily inconsistent). Prospero naturally enough regards his usurpation as wicked, and while the wickedness may reside most intensely in his brother Antonio, it extends to the agents who kidnapped Prospero and Miranda and then set them on the sea out of sight of land in an unrigged leaky boat:

A treacherous army levied, one midnight
Fated to th' purpose did Antonio open
The gates of Milan, and i'th' dead of darkness
The ministers for th' purpose hurried thence
Me and thy crying self.   (I, ii, 128–31)

Miranda, perhaps acquainted with Machiavelli's recommendations concerning secure usurpation in *The Prince*, asks 'Wherefore did they not / That hour destroy us?' (I, ii, 138–9). Prospero replies: 'Dear, they durst not, / So dear the love my people bore me, nor set / A mark so bloody on the business; but / With colours fairer painted their foul ends' (I, ii, 140–4). Thus far, Prospero casts the entire process, attributed to 'the ministers for the purpose', as 'foul'. It is important to note that these 'ministers' answer to Alonso, not Antonio. The usurpation results from Antonio's 'suit' to which 'The King of Naples, being an enemy to me inveterate / Hearkens' (I, ii, 121–2). Antonio's suit requests, in exchange for future 'homage and I know not how much tribute' (I, ii, 124) from hitherto independent Milan to the Kingdom of Naples, that 'he' (i.e. Alonso) 'Should presently extirpate me and mine / Out of the dukedom, and confer fair Milan, / With all the honours, on my brother' (I, ii, 125–7). Thus Antonio, rather like Lear after the first scene of *King Lear*, becomes a ruler who is not quite a ruler but has all the 'honours' of one. (Antonio seems to find this ambiguity chafing, since his later murderous intrigue with Sebastian would, if completed, restore Antonio to less qualified sovereignty. Sebastian, preparing to murder the sleeping Gonzalo, tells Antonio, standing over the sleeping Alonso, 'Draw thy sword — one stroke / Shall free thee from the tribute that thou payest, / And I the King shall love thee' [II, i, 290–2].) In any case, the 'ministers' Prospero regards as 'foul' are Alonso's agents in fulfilling Antonio's suit.

And, as it turns out, Gonzalo leads as chief agent of Alonso and Antonio's plan. Only a bit later in this retrospective account, Prospero explains to Miranda how they survived:

By providence divine;
Some food we had, and some fresh water, that
A noble Neapolitan, Gonzalo,
Out of his charity, who being then appointed
Master of this design, did give us, with
Rich garments, linens, stuffs, and necessaries,
Which since have steaded much; so of his gentleness,
Knowing I loved my books, he furnished me
From mine own library with volumes that
I prize above my dukedom.   (I, ii, 159–69)

Suddenly the execution of 'this design' becomes 'noble' instead of 'foul'. Gonzalo has performed it with 'charity', and Prospero implicitly separates him from its violence by locating Gonzalo's actions within the zone of necessary obedience to authority. Gonzalo's subordination, his 'being then appointed / Master of this design', apparently separates him from moral responsibility for the design itself, and in Prospero's and Miranda's moral imaginations Gonzalo's intentional action becomes the gentle mitigation of the 'foul end' Gonzalo has necessarily served. Prospero celebrates Gonzalo for the exercise of clemency within duteous subordination.

But is Gonzalo an obedient subordinate? Should he have done things that helped Prospero and Miranda survive? Antonio's 'suit' called on Antonio 'to extirpate' Prospero and his heir. 'Extirpate' is a complex word, but given the way that Prospero describes the 'design' it seems to intend bloodless assassination rather than survival on an island from which restoration to ducal power is possible. Of course, in plays and folktales bloodless assassinations – entrusting subordinates to abandon stigmatised infants on mountainsides or seashores, for instance – have a high failure rate. But does Gonzalo's clemency, particularly in regard to Prospero's books and to the supplies he offers, confine itself to soft-hearted obedience? Or does he actually undermine the project with which Alonso charged him? If the latter, he might more closely resemble Camillo, the virtuously disobedient counsellor in *The Winter's Tale* who hustles Polixenes on board a ship rather than poisoning him as Leontes has commanded, than he does Antigonus, who exits pursued by a bear after obediently depositing Perdita on the Bohemian seacoast.[46] Successful extirpation of a dynasty rules out the kind of vengeful comeuppance Prospero has in mind for his enemies.

If we think of Gonzalo as *consigliere* to Alonso's scheme, undertaken at Antonio's suit, then Gonzalo rather than Sebastian would naturally be the third of the 'three men of sin' in Ariel's spell-casting harpy speech: 'you three / From Milan did supplant good Prospero, / Exposed unto the sea, which hath requit it, / Him and his innocent child' (III, iii, 69–72). Though Shakespeare tidies this later (see V, i, 74–5), at this point an attentive reader or listener has no idea that Sebastian was involved in supplanting Prospero and has detailed testimony that Gonzalo planned the operation. So we are encouraged to ask ourselves how Gonzalo gets away with it, earning Prospero's gratitude rather than his vengeance. We know that Shakespeare read 'Of Crueltie': a great deal of Gonzalo's past behaviour tracks Montaigne's account of himself as a reluctant and compassionate enforcer of authority, and of Montaigne's distaste for the infliction of pain on humans or animals, even when hunting (generally justified as both aristocratic preparation for war and the extirpation of animal vermin) or torturing condemned criminals (sometimes justified as the deterrence and extirpation of human vermin). So Gonzalo's extended quotation from 'Of the Caniballes' to describe the institution of a commonwealth where the cruelties associated with subordination do not exist fits into an attentive Shakespearean reading of Montaigne's larger purposes, even as it floats unanchored over the invisible currents shaping the fates of the Neapolitan castaways who first hear it. Stephen Orgel's pithy comment that 'Shakespeare has taken everything from Montaigne except the point' registers the unanchored flotation.[47] But if Shakespeare thinks globally about Montaigne's writing in *The Tempest* as well as borrowing locally from 'Of the Caniballes' and 'Of Crueltie', precisely this unmoored quality of Montaigne's, to pursue a speculative, other-exalting mental course in deliberate counterpoint to pressing local circumstances, would be something Shakespeare might notice and choose to dramatise through Gonzalo's digression. Gonzalo, after all, has evidently been prone to digressive sympathy with victims amid enforcement-crises in the past: his provision of Prospero's books attests to it. Moreover, Gonzalo amply demonstrates optimism with respect to new places and new kinds of being, notably in his anti-ethnocentric commentary on the spirits who set a banquet before the lost Neapolitans prior to Ariel's harpy-speech:

> If in Naples
> I should report this now, would they believe me?
> If I should say I saw such islanders—
> For certes these are people of the island—
> Who though they are of monstrous shape, yet note
> Their manners are more gentle-kind than of
> Our human generation you shall find
> Many, nay almost any.   (III, iii, 27–34)

Montaigne's extended reflection, in 'Of Crueltie', on the difference between habituation, strenuous imposition of virtue, and innate good nature, seems at play in the characterisations of Prospero and Gonzalo, and shapes the mockery of Gonzalo exhibited by some critics as well as by Antonio and Sebastian.[48] This thought begins the essay, in the passage on rarer action Shakespeare puts in Prospero's mouth, but Montaigne returns to it (as Richard Strier points out in his forthcoming book *Fine Issues*) during his discussion of Cato and Socrates in 'Of Crueltie' (II: 11):

> A man shall plainly perceive in the minds of these two men, and of such as imitate them (for I make a question whether ever they could be matched) so perfect a habitude unto vertue, that it was even converted into their complexion . . . It is her [the soul's] naturall and ordinarie habit . . . Now that it be not more glorious, by an undaunted and divine resolution, to hinder the growth of temptations, and for a man to frame himselfe to vertue, so that the verie seeds of vice be cleane rooted out; than by mayne force to hinder their progresse; and having suffred himselfe to be surprised by the first assaults of passions, to arme and bandie himselfe, to stay their course and to suppresse them: And that this second effect be not also much fairer, than to be simply stored with a facile and gentle nature, and of it selfe distasted and in dislike with licentiousnesse and vice, I am persuaded there is no doubt. For, this third and last manner, seemeth in some sort, to make a man innocent, but not vertuous, free from doing ill, but not sufficiently apt to doe well . . . The verie names of Goodnesse and innocencie, are for this respect in some sort names of contempt. (375–6)

Montaigne then goes on 'to speake a word of my selfe' (376), and he himself turns out to be one of these good innocents of a facile and gentle nature whom some may regard with affectionate contempt, a person who, as he comments, is more virtuous in his passions than in his opinions. (This anticipates the extended critique of human rationality and rationalisation in II: 12, the 'Apologie', that makes Montaigne philosophically anticipate not only Hume on *is* and *ought* but also anticipate Hume's claim that reason is the slave of the passions.) But, as 'On Crueltie' proceeds further, Montaigne makes clear that he does not, in fact, dishonour his own temperament, but finds in it the arbitrary source of that hatred of cruelty that shapes his views of society, education, justice, colonialism, and religion.[49] Gonzalo's virtuous disobedience, or limited participation in a cruel act required as part of service, closely resembles how Montaigne describes his own diplomatic service in III: 1, 'Of Profit and Honesty'. Some rare-word evidence suggests that III: 1 was on Shakespeare's mind around the time of *The Tempest*: Florio writes of 'so tender or cheverall a conscience', and the phrase 'soft cheveril conscience' appears at *Henry VIII* II, iii, 32, in a scene attributed to Shakespeare rather than Fletcher.[50]

As noted above, III: 1. appears in Florio's preface, during the self-dramatising segment concerning Florio's extended labour of translation. Florio in fact cites not Montaigne himself, but Lucretius as quoted by Montaigne.[51] Florio addresses Lucy, Countess of Bedford, and Lady Anne Harrington with reference to their overseeing his work: 'I say not you tooke pleasure at shore (as those in this Author) to see me sea-tosst, wether-beaten, shippe-wrackt, almost drowned' (xvii).[52] Situated like Miranda witnessing the shipwreck at the opening of *The Tempest*, watching others suffer (and unlike the observers postulated by Lucretius), they feel compassion and seek to help. The lines from Lucretius to which Florio alludes occur in a passage of Montaignean generalisation near the opening of III: 1:

> – *Our composition, both publike and private, is full of imperfection;* yet there is nothing in nature unserviceable, no not inutility it selfe; nothing thereof hath beene insinuated in this huge universe, but holdeth some fit place therein. Our essence is cymented with crased qualities; ambition, jealosie, envy, revenge, superstition, dispaire, lodge in us, with so natural a possession, as their image is also discerned in beasts: yea and cruelty, so unnaturall a vice: for in the middest of compassion, we inwardly feele a kinde of bitter-sweet-pricking of malicious delight, to see others suffer; and children feel it also:
>
> *Suave mari magno turbantibus aequora ventis,*
> *E terra magnum alterius spectare laborem.*
>   LUCR. ii. I.
> 'Tis sweet on graund seas, when windes waves turmoyle,
> From land to see an others grievous toyle. (713–14)

So, while apparently absolving his patronesses of schadenfreude, Florio alludes to Montaigne's assertion that 'bitter-sweet-pricking of malicious delight' seems present even amid compassion, thus hinting that his patronesses may have at some level enjoyed his pain. At the same time, Montaigne argues that this disturbing aspect of the *is*, which La Rochefoucauld later makes into a famous maxim, must have some natural utility given that anything that has been put in the universe has a place even if we cannot see it.[53] Montaigne's paragraph asserts that nature makes nothing unnecessarily, part of the point of Lucretius' Proem to Book Two of *On the Nature of Things* whose quoted opening lines describe how pleasant it is to look from a safe shore on those in danger at sea. But Montaigne also asserts that neither internal mental life nor the outer natural world seems orderly from an ordinary human perspective. The essay then turns to politics, describing Montaigne's own Gonzalo-like relation to the kings he has served and his successful efforts to retain selfhood, consistency and clear conscience while doing his duty, partly by trying not to know more as an ambassador than he is commissioned to say:

> I carry nothing to the one, which I may not (having opportunity) say unto the other . . . For my part, I am content one tell me no more of his business then he will have me know or deale in; nor desire I, that my knowledge exceede or straine my word. If I must needs be the instrument of cozinage, it shall at least be with safety of my conscience. I will not be esteemed a servant, nor so affectionate, nor yet so faithfull, that I be judged fit to betray any man. *Who is unfaithfull to himself, may be excused if hee be faithlesse to his Master.* But Princes entertaine not men by halfes, and despise bounded [and] conditionall sevice. What remedy? I freely tell them my limits; for, a slave I must not be but unto reason, which yet I cannot compasse: And they are to blame, to exact from a free man, the like subjection unto their service, and the same obligation, which they may from those they have made and bought; and whose fortune dependeth particularly and expressly on theirs. (717)

If Gonzalo evades Alonso's intents (as he certainly thwarts Antonio's desires) in helping Prospero and Miranda survive, he does so in roughly this way, by cheerfully following his own noble conscientious independence within service. Given Prospero's continuous focus on whether his servants do his bidding exactly, one should surely ask whether Gonzalo did so with respect to Alonso's bidding. Moreover, one object of Prospero's sovereign wrath, Caliban, shows an interest in precisely this issue of the freedom or lack of it in the instruments of that wrath:

> > His spirits hear me,
> And yet I needs must curse. But they'll nor pinch,
> Fright me with urchin shows, pitch me i'th' mire,
> Nor lead me like a firebrand in the dark
> Out of my way, unless he bid 'em . . .　　　　(II, ii, 4–7)

> Thou dost me yet but little hurt; thou wilt anon, I know it by thy trembling. Now Prosper works upon thee.　　　　(II, ii, 76–7)

> > Remember
> First to possess his books; for without them
> He's but a sot, as I am, nor hath not
> One spirit to command – they all do hate him
> As rootedly as I.　　　　(III, ii, 89–93)

Thus the dynamic of subordinates fulfilling cruel orders reluctantly, or against conscientious scruples, extends to the spirit-world. Ariel, carefully steering Prospero away from cruelty without disobeying or expressing overt will-to-disobey, brings up Gonzalo and Prospero's attitude towards Gonzalo as part of the argument:

> ARIEL: The King,
> His brother, and yours, abide all three distracted,
> And the remainder mourning over them,
> Brimful of sorrow and dismay; but chiefly
> Him that you termed, sir, the good old Lord Gonzalo,
> His tears runs down his beard like winter's drops
> From eaves of reeds. Your charm so strongly works 'em
> That if you now beheld them, your affections
> Would become tender.
> ·PROSPERO: Dost thou think so, spirit?
> ARIEL: Mine would, sir, were I human.
> PROSPERO: And mine shall. (V, i, 11–20)

Prospero, about to quote from 'Of Crueltie', is being handled by Ariel as though Prospero has the same vulnerability that Montaigne ascribes to himself in 'Of Crueltie':

> I have a verie feeling and tender compassion of other mens afflictions, and should more easily weep for companie sake, if possiblie for any occasion whatsoever, I could shed teares. There is nothing sooner moveth teares in me, than to see others weepe, not onely fainedly, but howsoever, whether truly or forcedly. I do not greatly waile for the dead, but rather envie them. Yet doe I much waile and moane the dying. The Canibales and savage people do not so much offend me with roasting and eating of dead bodies, as those which torment and persecute the living. (380)

Moreover, Ariel's description illustrates how closely Gonzalo in his tears of good-natured sympathy resembles Montaigne, even as Ariel manoeuvres Prospero towards a Montaigne-quoting renunciation of vengeance for virtue. And the exchange illustrates the power that a cheerful but conscientious form of service, attributed by Montaigne to himself in 'Of Profit and Honesty', moderates cruelty not only when Gonzalo oversees the exposure of Prospero and Miranda to the waves, but also when Ariel supervises the inducement of sui-cidal guilt, shame, grief and anger in Alonso, Antonio and Sebastian. Given this, it makes sense that both Gonzalo and Prospero should obliquely assert that Gonzalo's handling of the expulsion from

Milan shows both providential moral luck and enlightened loyalty. Gonzalo says, when Prospero reveals Miranda and Ferdinand,

> I have inly wept,
> Or should have spoke ere this: look down, you gods,
> And on this couple drop a blessed crown;
> For it is you that have chalked forth the way
> Which brought us hither.   (V, i, 200–4)

'The way' includes Gonzalo's initial clemency: without Prospero's books, none of this could happen. And Prospero, when revealing himself to the Neapolitans, both gives Gonzalo credit for this and absolves him of disobedience to Alonso. He also asserts that the commands Alonso gave Gonzalo were 'cruel':

> O good Gonzalo,
> My true preserver, and a loyal sir
> To him thou follow'st, I will pay thy graces
> Home in both word and deed! Most cruelly
> Didst thou, Alonso, use me and my daughter.   (V, i, 68–72)

Moreover, Prospero defers any detailed account of what Gonzalo did to be a 'true preserver', perhaps in order that calling him 'a loyal sir' to Alonso will not be cast in question.[54] When Alonso says 'there is in this business more than nature / Was ever conduct of', Prospero replies 'Sir, my liege / Do not infest your mind . . . / At picked leisure . . . I'll resolve you / . . . till when, be cheerful, / And think of each thing well' (V, i, 243 . . . 51). Prospero thus defers discussion of two awkward topics: Prospero's manipulative magic and Gonzalo's role as 'preserver' rather than extirpator of Prospero and Miranda.

Thus proponents of the view that *The Tempest* responds to Montaigne can summon evidence for several claims. These include the claim that Prospero and Gonzalo reflect Shakespeare's awareness of Montaigne's choices and Montaigne's nature, respectively, and that Gonzalo in particular seems to represent Montaigne's portrayal in 'Of Crueltie' and 'Of Profit and Honesty' of his own gentle and conscientious role in public life. In fact, if Gonzalo is a partial portrait of Montaigne, Gonzalo's odd combination of complicity in the operations of power, exemption for any sort of responsibility for them, and propensity to Arcadian fantasy and optimism fit together better than they do without reference to Montaigne. Evidence also exists for the claim (as far as I know a new one) that Shakespeare paid close attention to the paratexts to Florio, and, thus, the claim that Shakespeare's reading in Montaigne may to some extent follow Florio's implicit suggestions about which essays are important to read.

So one could read *The Tempest* as Shakespeare's meditation on whether Montaigne's strategies of detachment, both mental and professional, could work for a Shakespeare whose career, temperament and social status differ markedly from Montaigne's. If Prospero offers a self-portrait of Shakespeare at work, then it is an ambivalent one, showing a Shakespeare impatient, anxious, demanding towards subordinates, and ultimately pessimistic about what the creation of emotionally powerful representations can accomplish. The Prospero who breaks off the masque, and who also breaks the spell of self-condemnation he has cast over Alonso, Antonio and Sebastian, and who releases Stephano, Trinculo and Caliban from their pool of piss, certainly seems to aim at a future of Montaignean reflection that will focus on Prospero's inability to control the mutability of nature and culture, rather like the Montaigne who remarks, in III: 11, 'Of the Lame or Crippel', that 'miracles and strange events, are until this day hidden from me: I have seene no such monster, or more expresse wonder in this world, then my selfe' (931). 'This thing of darkness I acknowledge mine', says Prospero of Caliban, perhaps in a similar spirit.

To return to *is* and *ought*: *The Tempest* more clearly than any play before it marks Shakespeare's experiment with Montaigne's exploration of the mutability of *ought* by reference to the non-unity or diversity of *is*. It also marks Shakespeare's dramatisation of two Montaignean moralists. Prospero, reacting to failed privileged retirement, attempts to impose his *ought* on the *is*es of others, and on the next generation in his own dynasty, but breaks off this attempt when he accepts that such impositions usually fail and often contradict themselves. (I take Prospero's sending Miranda and Ferdinand to his cave without supervision while he and Ariel deal with Caliban, Stephano and Trinculo as an abandonment of the helicopter parenting around sex that the masque epitomises.) Gonzalo in his Montaignean speech seeks new forms of *is* where the painful force of *ought* will not be strongly felt, and in his past history of power-relations and present actions seeks to be as conscience-clear as he can be within a stance of limited subordination. Thus a strong argument can be made that *The Tempest* contains Shakespeare's attempt to sum up the powerful, yet hard-to-follow and hard-to-credit, example of Florio's Montaigne.

Notes

I gratefully acknowledge William Hamlin, Hugh Grady, Patrick Gray, Peter Holbrook, Richard Strier, and audiences in Brisbane, Adelaide, Tulsa, Lawrence, the MLA, the BSA, the SAA, Seoul, Yale, and the Newberry for helpful responses to earlier versions of this chapter.

1. Hamlin, 'Conscience and the God-Surrogate', p. 8.
2. Bakewell, *How to Live*, p. 4.
3. Hume, *A Treatise of Human Nature*, pp. 244–5.
4. Williams, *Ethics and the Limits of Philosophy*, pp. 174–96.
5. Greenblatt, 'Shakespeare's Montaigne', pp. xxvi–xxxi.
6. For examples, see Engle, 'Shame and Reflection in Montaigne and Shakespeare', pp. 251–2.
7. See Quint, *Montaigne and the Quality of Mercy*, pp. 89–92.
8. Hartle, *Montaigne and the Origins of Modern Philosophy*, pp. 88; see also p. 83.
9. Shklar, *Ordinary Vices*, p. 44.
10. Screech, *Montaigne and Melancholy*, p. 1.
11. E.g. Grady, ed., *Shakespeare and Modernity*.
12. Evans-Pritchard, *Social Anthropology*, p. 127.
13. Adorno et al., *The Authoritarian Personality*, p. 1.
14. Ibid p. 102.
15. G. C. Taylor, *Shakspere's Debt to Montaigne*, p. 182.
16. Shklar, *Ordinary Vices*, p. 44.
17. Starobinski, *Montaigne in Motion*, p. 249.
18. Friedrich, *Montaigne*, p. 205.
19. *The Essayes of Montaigne, John Florio's Translation*, p. 84. Hereafter, page references to this edition of Florio's translation are given in parentheses in the text.
20. For an account of why the ethnic anti-ethnocentrism of contemporary bourgeois liberals should not constitute a philosophic problem for them, see Rorty ('On Ethnocentrism'), for whom Montaigne would count as an anti-anti-ethnocentrist, one who excavates a principle of tolerance and exaltation of otherness from his own cultural formation.
21. See Strier, *The Unrepentant Renaissance*, pp. 208–29; for reservations about Montaigne's opposition to conversion, see pp. 228–9.
22. See Hamlin, *The Image of America*, p. 53.
23. Quint, *Montaigne and the Quality of Mercy*, p. 76.
24. Hoffmann, *Montaigne's Career*, pp. 213–14.
25. Montaigne, *Les Essais*, ed. Balsamo, p. 221.
26. Montaigne, *Les Essais*, ed. Villey, rev. Saulnier, p. 159. Florio has 'All that is not verie ill; but what of that? They weare no kinde of breeches nor hosen' (171).
27. Kenji Go has demonstrated that Shakespeare made extensive use of other parts of Florio's 'Of the Caniballes': see Go, 'Montaigne's "Cannibals" and *The Tempest* Revisited'.

28. Boutcher, *The School of Montaigne*, I: p. 142.
29. Ibid. II: p. 215.
30. Burrow, 'Montaignian Moments', pp. 241, 244.
31. See Engle, 'Shame and Reflection in Montaigne and Shakespeare', p. 256.
32. See Hamlin, *Montaigne's English Journey*, p. 280 n. 1.
33. See Engle, 'Shakespearean Normativity in *All's Well That Ends Well*', and for Montaigne in general in *All's Well*, Kirsch, 'Sexuality and Marriage in Montaigne and *All's Well That Ends Well*'.
34. Orgel, 'Shakespeare and the Cannibals', p. 5.
35. Parker, 'Shakespeare's Argument with Montaigne', p. 18; de Gooyer, 'Montaigne and *The Tempest* Reconsidered', pp. 514–15.
36. Burrow, 'Montaignian Moments', p. 250.
37. *The Tempest*, ed. Mason Vaughan and Vaughan. Further references are to this edition.
38. *Hamlet*, in *The Norton Shakespeare*, ed. Greenblatt et al. Further references are to this edition.
39. For an account of Hamlet as such a figure for Shakespearean ambivalence about Montaigne's Epicureanism, see Gray, 'Montaigne, Hamlet, and Epicurean Ethics'.
40. Go, 'Montaigne's "Cannibals" and *The Tempest* Revisited'.
41. See Strier, *Fine Issues*.
42. See Engle, 'Shame and Reflection in Montaigne and Shakespeare', pp. 255–6.
43. See Yachnin, 'Shakespeare and the Idea of Obedience'.
44. See Strier, 'Normal and Magical Politics in *The Tempest*', pp. 13–15, and the chapter 'Faithful Servants' in Strier, *Resistant Structures*.
45. See Schalkwyk, *Shakespeare, Love, and Service*.
46. See ibid. pp. 263–6 and, for an opposing view, Yachnin, 'Shakespeare and the Idea of Obedience', p. 11.
47. Orgel, 'Shakespeare and the Cannibals', p. 36.
48. See Maguin, *The Tempest* and Cultural Exchange', pp. 152–3; see also Burrow, 'Montaignian Moments', p. 243, noting astutely that Gonzalo here behaves rather like a Fool character.
49. See Engle, 'Sovereign Cruelty in Montaigne and *King Lear*', pp. 123–7.
50. See Taylor, *Shakspere's Debt to Montaigne*, p. 49, misattributing Montaigne's phrase from III: 1 to a non-existent III. 16, perhaps because the word 'cheverall' also appears in III: 11; Shakespeare also uses the word in *Twelfth Night* (III, i, 12).
51. See Hamlin, *Montaigne's English Journey*, p. 55 for the observation that Florio's Montaigne contains 'among the very first' English translations (by Florio's friend Matthew Gwinne) of about a sixth of Lucretius's *De Rerum*.
52. *Mon. lib.* iii *c.* 1.
53. 'Il y a quelque chose, dans les malheurs de nos meilleurs amis, qui ne nous deplait pas.'
54. Compare Yachnin, 'Shakespeare and the Idea of Obedience', pp. 13–15.

Chapter 16

Falstaff's Party: Shakespeare, Montaigne and Their Liberal Censors

Patrick Gray

We must be careful not to believe things simply because we want them to be true.

Richard Feynman

In his best-known work, *Process and Reality*, Alfred North White-head argues that the 'the final real things of which the world is made up' are neither Plato's forms nor Epicurus's atoms but instead subjective 'occasions of experience', connected to each other in patterns over time by a dynamic 'ultimate principle' he calls 'creativity'. Stability is an illusion; the world is nothing other than a 'process' of fleeting 'occasions' coming into being and passing away. Thus having turned Plato's distinction between 'being' and 'becoming' upside-down, Whitehead surprisingly insists nonetheless that his 'train of thought' is 'Platonic'. 'It falls within the European tradition', he explains, and 'the safest general characterization of the European philosophical tradition is that it consists of a series of footnotes to Plato'.[1] Turning to Shakespeare's *1* and *2 Henry IV*, William Empson sees moral assessment of Falstaff as a similar point of origin. 'The question whether Falstaff is a coward may be said to have started the whole snowball of modern Shakespeare criticism; it was the chief topic of Morgann's essay nearly two hundred years ago, the first time a psychological paradox was dug out of a Shakespeare text.'[2]

Like William Blake's *Marriage of Heaven and Hell* (1790–3), Maurice Morgann's *Essay on the Dramatic Character of Sir John Falstaff* (1777) is an early manifestation of the upheaval of moral and aesthetic assumptions now known as Romanticism. Morgann's place within Shakespeare studies resembles in this sense Blake's within

Milton studies, summed up in Blake's notorious claim that Milton was 'of the Devil's Party without knowing it'.[3] As Stanley Fish observes in *Surprised by Sin*, by the late 1960s the problem Fish calls simply 'the Milton Controversy' had become well established, even definitive. 'The world of Milton studies was divided into two armed camps: one proclaiming (in the tradition of Blake and Shelley) that Milton was of the devil's party with or without knowing it, the other proclaiming (in the tradition of Addison and C. S. Lewis) that the poet's sympathies are obviously with God and the angels loyal to him.'[4]

'I know how universally the contrary opinion prevails,' Morgann begins.[5] His 'vindication of Falstaff's courage' is 'attended with all the difficulties and dangers of Novelty'.[6] Since then, times have changed; many have rallied to Morgann's side. Nowadays it is more unusual to find a critic praising Henry V than a critic praising Falstaff. The first-order question, therefore, as regards Shakespeare's Falstaff as well as Milton's Satan is which of two rival positions is correct: the new or the old. But a second-order question is also in play. Why did it take so long, more than a hundred years, for a defence of these characters to emerge? If they are indeed so sympathetic, the secret protagonists of the works in which they appear, why did we have to wait for the Romantics before anyone said so?

'Falstaff, how shall I describe thee!' Writing not long before Morgann (1764), Samuel Johnson acknowledges that Falstaff is a complex character, but only in the sense that his 'vice' is camouflaged by his 'gaiety' and his 'power of exciting laughter'. 'The moral to be drawn from this representation is that no man is more danger-ous than he that, with a will to corrupt, hath the power to please; and that neither wit nor honesty ought to think themselves safe with such a companion, when they see Henry seduced by Falstaff.' As is revealing of the assumptions underpinning Shakespeare studies at the time, Johnson does not give a moment's thought to the possibil-ity Falstaff's moral 'faults' might be reimagined as virtues. 'He is a thief and a glutton, a coward and a boaster, always ready to cheat the weak, and prey upon the poor.'[7]

In later years, Boswell reports that Johnson dismissed Morgann's revisionist account of Falstaff as a rhetorical stunt, akin to the soph-ist Gorgias's *Encomium of Helen*, defending Helen of Troy's inno-cence and praising her virtue. 'Johnson being asked his opinion of this Essay, answered, "Why, Sir, we shall have the man come forth again; and as he has proved Falstaff to be no coward, he may prove Iago to be a very good character".'[8] Johnson's notes on Iago recall at first his notes on Falstaff: 'There is always danger, lest wickedness, conjoined with abilities, should steal upon esteem, though it misses of approbation.' 'The character of Iago', however, he maintains, 'is so conducted that he is from the first scene to the last hated and despised.'[9] One can only imagine, then, the dismay, maybe even incredulity, with which Johnson would have greeted the legacy Falstaff shares with Milton's Satan, as well as Iago: the Byronic antihero.

As Peter Cochran points out, 'a doomed, Byronic version of Falstaff can be sensed subtextually beneath much of *Don Juan*'.[10] 'I have rarely met with a person more conversant with the works of Shakespeare than was Byron,' one of his contemporaries, the Countess of Blessington, records. 'I have heard him quote passages from them repeatedly.'[11] Reading through his correspondence, G. Wilson Knight notes how frequently Byron quotes Falstaff in particular: 'he feels himself and Falstaff as akin, almost one'.[12] Cochran, too, observes that, although Byron 'often identifies with the heroic, tragic figures of Macbeth and Coriolanus', it is nonetheless 'the comic, overweight, almost-over-the-hill Sir John Falstaff who, from the Shakespearean gallery, means most to him in terms of his private self-image'.[13] For Harold Bloom, 'Iago's progeny begins with Milton's Satan and passes on to such High Romantic heroes as Shelley's Prometheus and Byron's Cain.'[14] By way of comic parallel, one might add here Byron's Don Juan, who recreates Iago's less successful and less obviously suspect analogue, Falstaff. The influence of this Romantic reimagining of ethics on our present culture would be difficult to overstate, recasting what was once considered sin as sublime.[15] Surveying nineteenth- and twentieth-century English and European literature, Jacques Barzun marvels at the sway of Byronism. 'From Goethe, Pushkin, Stendhal, Heine, Balzac, Scott, Carlyle, Mazzini, Leopardi, Berlioz, George Sand, and Delacroix down to Flaubert, Tennyson, Ruskin, the Brontës, Baudelaire, Becque, Nietzsche, Wilde, and Strindberg, one can scarcely name a writer who did not come under the spell of Byronism and turn it to some use in his own life or work.'[16]

Many aspects of Shakespeare's plays today can give us pause, especially their endings, including not only the newly crowned Henry V's rebuke of Falstaff's presumption at the end of *2 Henry IV*, but also Portia's sentencing of Shylock in *The Merchant of Venice*, Kate's speech on the authority of husbands over their wives at the end of *The Taming of the Shrew*, Helena's recapture of Bertram in *All's Well that Ends Well*, and the Duke's offer of marriage at the end of *Measure for Measure*. Were these conclusions designed to be troubling, or is our discomfort the result instead of new preoccupations that have arisen in the several centuries that have intervened between Shakespeare's historical moment and our own? As J. Dover Wilson observes, 'Shakespeare lived in the world of Plato and St Augustine; since the French Revolution we have been living in the world of Rousseau; this fact lays many traps of misunderstanding for unsuspecting readers.'[17] Even if we suppose that Shakespeare was unusually broad-minded, many opinions that are commonplace today would have shocked great swathes of his contemporaries. And we might readily imagine that the reverse is also true. Moral perspectives Shakespeare's original audience took for granted may today seem scandalous.

Does Shakespeare agree with us? Is he on our side? For many critics, this entire line of inquiry may seem wrong-headed. For Empson, author of *Seven Types of Ambiguity*, Falstaff's moral character not surprisingly proves an example of an irreducible 'Dramatic Ambiguity'. 'The text is so arranged that the uncertainty can still not be dispelled even after the most careful study.'[18] This cutting of the Gordian Knot of Shakespeare's meaning is not exactly novel; the claim that Shakespeare is 'undecidable' is by now a critical commonplace, dating back to Keats's singling out Shakespeare as a paragon of 'Negative Capability'. Empson gives us a reprise of this approach to Falstaff in his treatment that same year, 1953, of what is by now the most notorious critical chestnut of them all: 'the Hamlet Problem'. Hamlet's 'weirdly baffling' delay, he maintains, is the result of nothing more than a 'purely technical' decision on Shakespeare's part to introduce a 'hole' or 'blank' in the middle of play. Empson recognises his proposed solution, to wit, that there is no solution, may be disappointing: 'The bafflement thrown in here was not the tedious one of making a psychological problem or a detective story insoluble.' But he sticks to his guns nonetheless. Hamlet's motivation is an 'ambiguity' that cannot be resolved.[19]

Looking back on Empson's treatment of Hamlet's hesitation, A. D. Nuttall finds it 'too clear', 'too neat' and 'finally somehow dispiriting'. 'You are all puzzled because you were meant to be puzzled; Hamlet is constructed as a mystery, and there's an end on't.' On the contrary, Nuttall points out, 'trails of suggestion are laid down, so that we can sense at once that certain interpretations, though they may indeed be irremediably speculative and insusceptible of a final determination, are manifestly more reasonable than others.'[20] In his essay on *Hamlet*, Empson ignores such hints in favour of his distinctive thesis. But Empson was nothing if not a man of strong opinions: an outspoken atheist and lifelong polyamorist, sent down from Cambridge for the indiscretion of keeping condoms in his room.[21] In the end, with regards to Falstaff, as well as Milton's God, Empson cannot resist taking a side. 'Of course there must be a basic theme which the basic contradictions of the play are dramatizing, which some interpretations handle better than others; after planting my citadel on the high ground of the Absolute Void, I still feel at liberty to fight in the plains.'[22]

Empson's move here is by no means sui generis. As I have noted elsewhere, unargued assertions about Shakespeare's essential 'ambivalence' or 'undecidability' tend to prove in practice disingenuous or at least misleading opening gambits.[23] What follows turns out not to be the balanced counterpoint of *sic et non* one might expect from such a principled non-partisan preamble but instead a series of subtle, complex and tendentious efforts to align Shakespeare with Romanticism and its legacy, modernism. In the Middle Ages, an all-but-unassailable inner stone tower ('motte') would often stand at the centre of an outer area of land ('bailey') full of houses, stores and gardens but protected only by a ditch and a wooden palisade. In the essay which first introduced the concept of 'motte-and-bailey doctrines', 'The Vacuity of Postmodernist Methodology', philosopher Nicholas Shackel draws an analogy between this medieval practice of fortification and a duplicitous form of argumentation which he sees as characteristic of anti-foundationalists such as Foucault.

> Being dark and dank, the Motte is not a habitation of choice. The only reason for its existence is the desirability of the Bailey, which the combination of the Motte and ditch makes relatively easy to retain despite attack by marauders. When only lightly pressed, the ditch makes small numbers of attackers easy to defeat as they struggle across it: when heavily pressed the ditch is not defensible and so neither is the Bailey. Rather one retreats to the insalubrious but defensible, perhaps impregnable, Motte.[24]

For postmodernists, for example, the 'motte' tends to be the claim that morality is socially constructed, and the 'bailey' the much more contentious claim that traditional concepts of right and wrong should be dismissed or, if possible, reversed.

Within Shakespeare studies, familiar claims about Shakespeare's open-endedness often serve in like fashion as an axiomatic 'motte', from which the critic can then sally forth to defend the 'bailey': the desired but more doubtful conclusion that, despite a historical context that by our standards today, at least, was deeply conservative, devoutly Christian and unapologetically nationalistic, despite having been, in other words, an early modern Englishman, Shakespeare is anti-establishmentarian, secular and cosmopolitan;

proto-Romantic; proto-modern; a fellow liberal; perhaps even politically progressive. What the critic says up front is that Shakespeare, of course, as we all know, has no discernible fixed opinions about anything controversial. But what the critic wants to say, and what gradually comes across, is a very different position: Shakespeare is 'our contemporary'.

Jan Kott tackles this question more directly in his influential book *Shakespeare, Our Contemporary*. Such is the weight of critical tradition that even here, however, in a revisionist account written as a deliberate provocation, Kott feels compelled to begin by conceding that Shakespeare is, of course, as we all know, nothing more than a kind of Rorschach blot. 'Shakespeare is like the world, or life itself. Every historical period finds in him what it is looking for and what it wants to see.'[25] As is often the case, the reading of Shakespeare Kott advances afterwards is the furthest thing imaginable from such po-faced relativism. Kott's 1964 reimagining of Shakespeare as a nihilist akin to Samuel Beckett would go on to animate Peter Brooks's *King Lear* (1971) and Roman Polanski's *Macbeth* (1971), as well as Jonathan Dollimore's more scholarly monograph *Radical Tragedy* (1984), an anti-humanist take on Jacobean tragedy which exploded within Shakespeare studies in the 1980s and 1990s like a barrel of dynamite underneath a bridge.[26]

Despite continuing interest in Kott's claims now more than fifty years later, one word in his title nonetheless has not attracted the scrutiny it deserves. Who is the 'we' that lies behind Kott's 'our'? To put the question another way, who among us would choose Kott as our spokesman? He does not command any obvious personal moral authority. He was not a hero; not a martyr; not a daring leader of a principled Resistance like, say, Camus. In fact, if anything, Kott was the opposite: a propagandist for a ruthless police state. After the Soviet takeover of Poland, Kott served for seven years as a zealous proponent of Stalinism and a leading advocate for the subordination of Polish culture to communist ideology.[27]

Recalling when he first heard the news of Stalin's death, Kott later wrote, 'I was terrified. I thought the world had collapsed.'[28] Eventually, Kott renounced the Party, but only several years after Stalin had passed away, by which point the political tide in Poland had begun to turn. Kott's description of 'history' in *Shakespeare, Our Contemporary* not as the dialectic of class conflict and the triumph of the proletariat Marx had once predicted but instead as 'no more than a gigantic slaughter' can be seen by this light as a harbinger of the disillusionment that later beset France: the rejection of Althusser's

Stalinist Marxism and the beginnings of postmodernism in the writings of Foucault and Lyotard.[29]

Having abandoned his own former professions of Marxism, in *Shakespeare, Our Contemporary*, Kott flatly and emphatically rejects the possibility that Shakespeare suggests at any point anywhere in his oeuvre that either Marxism or any other more traditional narrative of history might perhaps be true. For Shakespeare, he maintains, events have no 'definite direction': history 'stands still' or else 'constantly repeats its cruel cycle', 'not only in the period when he was writing *Hamlet* and *King Lear*, but in all his writings, from the early Histories up to *The Tempest*'.[30] Maybe yes, maybe no; one might argue instead as Empson does that the Roman plays as well as the English history plays are a series of cautionary tales: 'How to Avoid Civil War'.[31]

More immediately, however, what Kott fails to recognise is that the cyclical sense of history he describes is not at all incompatible with Christianity. In his *City of God*, Saint Augustine takes pains to note that what he calls 'the City of Man', meaning, human society in its broadest possible sense, cannot be relied on to make stable, incremental progress towards establishing any kind of earthly paradise, not at least until the Second Coming of Christ, but instead alternates between fragile, fleeting moments of peace and the internecine conflict characteristic of mankind in its present, fallen state.[32] The 'tragic farce' Kott labels 'the Grand Mechanism' is the same cycle that authors and artists in the Middle Ages illustrated as 'Fortune's wheel'.[33] The point of showing beggars become kings and kings become beggars, as in Chaucer's *Monk's Tale*, was not to sow doubts about God's providence but instead to reinforce the Christian message that wealth, power and social status are at best ephemeral; one might even say irrelevant; what matters is instead the state of each man's immortal soul as he prepares to encounter God in the afterlife.

Kott's aim, by contrast, is to separate Shakespeare from this theological context, which he dismisses as 'medieval awe' and 'the illusions of the early Renaissance'. 'There are no gods in Shakespeare,' he insists. 'There are no gods, and there is no fate.' The nihilism Kott ascribes to Shakespeare, 'the conviction that history has no meaning', foreshadows in this sense the opposition to any and all grand narratives of history (*métarécits*), Marxist as well as Christian, Hegelian and Whig, that we now more typically associate with Foucault, Lyotard and French postmodernism.[34] Citing Nietzsche's *Dawn*, Foucault insists on 'effective history' as the only way of grasping 'the singular randomness of events', meaning, history explained solely in terms of what Aristotle calls 'effective' or 'efficient' causation, without reference to essences or teleology. Unlike 'the Christian world' and 'the world of the Greeks', 'the world of effective history knows only one kingdom, without providence or final cause, where there is only "the iron hand of necessity shaking the dice-box of chance"'.[35] Like Rhodri Lewis in his recent study of *Hamlet*, Kott for his part turns to Hobbes: 'Shakespeare's view of history, pessimistic and cruel', he concludes, 'is already very near to the materialistic philosophy of Hobbes, as expressed in his *Leviathan*.'[36] That is to say, for Shakespeare, or so Kott insists, 'the world is vile'; 'the world is as Iago sees it'.[37]

Despite Kott's self-assurance, as well as Lewis's, comparing Shakespeare to Hobbes remains a tall order. Shakespeare as 'materialistic'? Shakespeare with his fairies, his witches and his ghosts? His portents, his soothsayers and their prophecies repeatedly fulfilled? His felicitous coincidences, as if directed by divine providence? One struggles to square the circle. Is Shakespeare really our English Euripides, challenging the traditional beliefs of his day? Marlowe would be better cast in this role, although even he is not without some tortured doubts of his own: the repressed misgivings of the atheist who, despite himself, fears God might exist. Ford, Webster and Middleton, sure: gleeful neo-pagans all. But Shakespeare?

Bracketing Shakespeare and his contemporaries, we might also ask how many people even now, here in our own much more secular age, could be said to agree wholeheartedly with Hobbes or Nietzsche, especially if we take into account what has come to be known as 'the Global Majority', as opposed to the more limited sub-population known to social psychologists as W.E.I.R.D.: 'Western, Educated, Industrialised, Rich, and Democratic'.[38] Even here, moreover, within this narrow band, professional scholars in the humanities are an outlier. We are a social class unto ourselves, a coterie, with distinctive, homogenous and unusual opinions, historically and globally considered; it would be remarkable indeed if our tribal credo turned out to be the same as that of a sixteenth-century Englishman, howsoever prescient, influential or extraordinary.

Lest I seem to exaggerate our homogeneity, some statistics may be helpful. It is no surprise to find that the academy leans left, especially in the humanities. The uniformity of our beliefs, however, can be startling. In a 1999 survey of 1,643 American professors across 183 institutions, 69 per cent of English professors identified themselves as Democrats, as opposed to 2 per cent as Republicans.[39] In a 2006 survey of 1,471 American professors across 927 institutions, again only

2 per cent of English professors identified themselves as in any sense 'conservative'.[40] In 2018, among tenure-track professors in English departments at fifty top-ranked colleges and universities, registered Democrats outnumbered registered Republicans 48 to 1.[41]

In the United Kingdom, Conservative Party affiliation among academics in all disciplines has dwindled from 35 per cent in 1964 to 18 per cent in 1989 and 15 per cent in 2014–16.[42] In the United States, for forty years, 1974 to 2014, the American electorate as a whole remained remarkably stable (+/- ~ 5 points): an average of 35 per cent conservative, 38 per cent moderate and 27 per cent liberal. Within the academy, however, over less than half that time, a fifteen-year span from 1995 and 2010, as the Greatest Generation (Second World War era) left the stage and Baby Boomers (Vietnam era) consolidated their hold on teaching posts, faculty across all disciplines, including business, law and the sciences, went from leaning left (19 per cent conservative, 40 per cent liberal) to a clear majority on the left (11 per cent conservative, 60 per cent liberal).[43]

Why did this change occur? Why are almost all English professors (not to mention our colleagues in French) now on the left? The grandiose reply with which some of us, perhaps, may be inclined to flatter ourselves is intelligence: 'great minds think alike'. The distribution of political affiliation is the same, however, for the top 5 per cent of the population by IQ as it is for the population as a whole.[44] So, the answer probably lies elsewhere. One contributing factor, for example, might be that tenure-track faculty at top institutions are thirty times more likely than the general public to have at least one parent with a PhD. Recipients of a PhD who have at least one parent with a PhD are twice as likely to secure a tenure-track job and four times as likely to work at an institution ranked in the top 20 per cent nationally for their discipline.[45]

What this data suggests, not to mince words, is that since the expansion of higher education after the Second World War, as an unintended consequence of pervasive, self-selecting patterns, the professoriate at elite liberal arts colleges and research institutions is increasingly beginning to resemble a privileged hereditary caste.[46] Oliver Wendell Holmes Sr. once coined the phrase 'Boston Brahmins'; Noam Chomsky, 'the New Mandarins'; geographer Joel Kotkin calls us in like vein simply 'the Clerisy'.[47] Our beliefs are increasingly uniform, Kotkin observes, because we are becoming a tribe, a cohesive, exclusive, high-status, endogamous tribe, with all the conformity, taboos and peculiar norms any such tight-knit network by its very nature will entail.[48] Professions of political allegiance are our equivalent of flashing gang signs, making small talk about local sports, or the more elaborate pleasantries expected of aristocrats at the court of the Sun King. Intelligence and education not only do not prevent such tribalism but, if anything, seem to exacerbate it. As sociologist Musa al-Gharbi explains, summarising several recent studies, 'compared to the general public, cognitively sophisticated voters are much more likely to form their positions based on partisan cues as to what they are "supposed" to think by virtue of their identity as Democrats, Republicans, etc.'[49]

Whether its origins lie in social pressure, however, or in more independent inquiry, the ideological schism in question is profound. And it has a single fault-line at its base, which over the centuries has opened up into a chasm. From the perspective of intellectual history, our synchronic divide in the present day between right and left very precisely corresponds to a diachronic divide between medieval and modern. To understand the parallels between these seemingly disparate conflicts, we have to focus, however, on their essential underlying bone of contention: the question whether the world has any *logos* ('intrinsic structure') and, by extension, whether this 'natural law' imposes immutable moral as well as physical constraints on what it means to be human.

In a science-fiction novel now considered a classic of the genre, *A Canticle for Leibowitz*, Walter M. Miller Jr. imagines an America destroyed by a global nuclear war ('the Flame Deluge'), followed by a backlash against learning ('the Simplification'), including mass book burning and data destruction. When the story opens centuries later, books are a great rarity, and science and the Catholic Church have become inextricably confused. The protagonist, Brother Francis Gerard, spends much of his life illuminating a 'relic' which he does not understand: a fragment of a blueprint of an electrical circuit.

At the beginning of his influential 'study in moral theory', *After Virtue*, Alasdair MacIntyre sees an analogy between this hypothetical post-apocalyptic world and the present state of academic thought about ethics. 'Imagine that the natural sciences were to suffer the effects of a catastrophe,' he proposes. Generations later, 'enlightened people seek to revive science', but 'all that they possess are fragments': 'instruments whose use has been forgotten; half-chapters from books, single pages from articles, not always fully legible because torn and charred'. 'Nonetheless all these fragments are reembodied in a set of practices which go under the revived names of physics, chemistry and biology.'

Under such conditions, MacIntyre imagines, many people might not realise 'that what they are doing is not natural science in any proper sense at all'. 'Everything that they do or say' might well conform to new 'canons of consistency and coherence'. For example, 'if in this imaginary world analytical philosophy were to flourish', it would never on its own be able to diagnose 'a grave state of disorder', 'for the techniques of analytical philosophy are essentially descriptive and descriptive of the language of the present at that'. Likewise in our time, MacIntyre proposes, 'we have – very largely, if not entirely – lost our comprehension, both theoretical and practical, of morality'. What we 'possess' is not the thing itself, ethics, but instead 'fragments of a conceptual scheme, parts of which now lack the contexts from which their significance derived'.[50]

A bold claim, to say the least! What could we possibly have lost 'that roars so loud and thunders in the index'? According to MacIntyre (among others), what is missing now from our general consciousness is, in short, the concept of 'natural law'. Nietzsche captures the enormity of this intellectual vacuum in his parable of a 'madman' shouting in a marketplace, 'God is dead.' 'Is there still any up or down?' he asks. 'Are we not straying, as through an infinite nothing? Do we not feel the breath of empty space?'[51] MacIntyre's argument, however, can be separated from the question whether God exists. By 'natural law', what is meant is more precisely a moral order of whatever origin, possibly divine, possibly not, that is woven into the fabric of the universe and that exists independent of our perception of it: a set of rules about right and wrong that is not socially constructed. Man-made or 'positive' law can reflect this underlying ethical framework, but it can also distort it, just as portrait artist can either adhere to or depart from the appearance of his model, depending on his skill and intent.

In his *Rhetoric*, for example, Aristotle distinguishes between 'particular law', 'which each community lays down and applies to its own members', and 'universal law', 'which is the law of nature'. 'Particular law' is 'partly written and partly unwritten' and corresponds to what Montaigne (and Hume) call 'custom'. 'Universal law', by contrast, is 'a natural justice and injustice that is binding on all men, even on those who have no association or covenant with each other'.[52] According to Aristotle, 'everyone to some extent divines' – that is, everyone has some sense, some awareness of – this 'universal' law. The same observation can be found in Saint Paul's Epistle to the Romans: 'when the Gentiles, which have not the law, do by nature the things contained in the law, these, having not the law, are a law unto themselves: Which shew the work of the law written in their hearts, their conscience also bearing witness, and their thoughts meanwhile accusing or else excusing one another.'[53]

This concept of natural law is not unique to Western culture but instead can be better understood as a defining feature of, if not all, at least the vast majority of all known intellectual traditions worldwide that date back to the centuries before colonialism, the European Enlightenment and the Industrial Revolution, in the form of analogues such as the Tao in Taoism and Confucianism and *dharma* in Hinduism and Buddhism. Not to believe in natural law is deeply strange, globally as well as historically, even if to us academics here in the West at present it may seem obvious.

How, then, did we happen to depart from the norm? In brief, one might say that controversies within theology eventually reshaped philosophy. Most immediately, the divide between Catholic and Protestant in Western Europe, culminating in decades of brutal warfare, undermined belief in traditional intellectual authorities. Historian Richard Popkin describes this ebbing of what Matthew Arnold calls 'the sea of faith' as the 'sceptical crisis' of the sixteenth and seventeenth century. Troubled by divisions within Christianity, Montaigne and others after him, including most notably Francis Bacon, as well as David Hume, rediscovered classical scepticism in the works of authors such as Sextus Empiricus and Cicero.

The side of this theological conflict that won out in early modern England added further fuel to the fire. Given the depths of our supposed depravity, Protestant authors such as Fulke Greville, taking their cues from Calvin, not only railed against the belief, shared by traditional Catholics as well as most classical philosophers, that we human beings have some capacity to choose what is morally good of our own volition, but also, and arguably to more damaging effect, laid siege to the more basic assumption that we have some capacity to know what it is true on our own, independent of God's grace.[54] If this line of attack seems to anticipate Nietzsche, that is no accident; Nietzsche's cynical perspective on human nature was in part a product of his Lutheran upbringing.

Turning back to seventeenth-century England, the more proximate nemesis of natural law is typically held to be Hobbes, whose *Leviathan* proved a *succès de scandale*. Hobbes does not so much slay the concept of natural law outright, however, as heighten and secularise contemporary doubts about epistemology. Hobbes channels, in effect, a distinctive Protestant pessimism about our capacity for knowledge that, by the time he wrote *Leviathan*, had become pervasive. Yes, Hobbes concedes, natural law exists – but we cannot know it; all we have in practice is positive law.[55] The total eclipse of natural law in the English common law tradition cannot be said, therefore, to be entirely Hobbes' doing. But it did follow not long afterwards: as the historian Robert Pasnau observes, 'the human mind tends to suppose that what it does not know about does not exist'.[56]

Meanwhile, with regards to metaphysics, over the course of the seventeenth century in England, the Netherlands and France, the problem Popkin calls 'the sceptical crisis' exacerbated an ongoing loss of interest among philosophers in what Aristotle calls 'formal' and 'final' causation in favour of an increasingly exclusive focus on what he calls 'material' and 'effective' causation. Here, too, theology prepared the ground. Much as al-Ghazali overturned Avicenna's synthesis of Islam, Aristotle and Neoplatonism, so, too, Duns Scotus and William of Ockham undermined Aquinas's compromise between Christianity and classical philosophy. Whereas in the Muslim world, however, it was science that ultimately yielded to revelation, in the Christian West, it was metaphysics that began to crumble. According to what is now known as nominalism, essences or forms are categories of the human mind, rather than the bedrock of reality. According to what is now known as voluntarism, God's intellect is not as important as his will, which by its very nature as illimitably free is less perspicuous to our human understanding. This late medieval sense of both God and the world as less tractable to human reason than had been assumed theretofore set the stage for early modern pessimism regarding our capacity as human beings to discern the truth about 'natural law'.

The story of the rise of a new 'mechanistic' worldview in the seventeenth century is familiar from intellectual history, although on close examination gradual, complex and hesitant.[57] In an exasperated letter to a Dutch philosopher, Hendrik de Roy ('Regius'), after the Rector of the University of Utrecht tried to have him removed from his chair, Descartes, for example, reprimands the self-proclaimed 'Cartesian' for too publicly and too explicitly rejecting the reality of essences. 'What need was there for you to openly reject substantial forms . . .?' he asks.

> Don't you remember that in my *Meteorology* I said explicitly that I didn't reject or deny them, but simply found them unnecessary in setting out my explanations? If you had taken this course, all your audience would have rejected them when they saw they were useless, and in the meantime you wouldn't have been so unpopular with your colleagues.[58]

In his *New Organon*, Francis Bacon is bolder. He not only dismisses 'Discovery of Form' as 'hopeless' but also flat-out rejects

Aristotle's sense of the world as purpose-driven. Aristotle conceives of each and every physical entity, including but not limited to human beings, not only in terms of its actual existence but also in terms of its potential, which it is led to realise over time by an intrinsic impetus: its end (Greek, *telos*) in the sense of aim or purpose, which Aristotle calls its 'final' cause.[59] Bacon, by contrast, sees all such talk of teleology as a frustrating distraction. 'Final causes', he maintains, 'are plainly derived from the nature of man rather than of the universe, and from this origin have wonderfully corrupted philosophy.'[60]

It is not far from here to the moment in the history of 'moral theory' Alasdair MacIntyre singles out as most closely akin to a post-apocalyptic nomad baffled by a fragment of an ancient blueprint.[61] Writing more than a century after Bacon's break with Aristotle, in his *Treatise of Human Nature*, Hume protests that he can see 'no foundation for that distinction, which we sometimes make . . . betwixt efficient causes, and formal, and material, and exemplary, and final causes'. For him, 'all causes are of the same kind', 'efficient', as in the case of flint striking steel and a spark being produced. No other kind of 'cause', he insists, can be said to exist. [62]

Hume's reductive definition of causality is not entirely surprising, given the direction of travel of early modern philosophy in the previous century.[63] The effect of his blithe disdain for formal and final causes, however, is to leave Hume at an apparent loss when it comes to understanding moral reasoning.

> In every system of morality, which I have hitherto met with, I have always remark'd, that the author proceeds for some time in the ordinary way of reasoning, and establishes the being of a God, or makes observations concerning human affairs; when of a sudden I am surpriz'd to find, that instead of the usual copulations of propositions, *is*, and *is not*, I meet with no proposition that is not connected with an *ought*, or an *ought not*. This change is imperceptible; but is, however, of the last consequence. For as this *ought*, or *ought not*, expresses some new relation or affirmation, 'tis necessary that it shou'd be observ'd and explain'd; and at the same time that a reason should be given, for what seems altogether inconceivable, how this new relation can be a deduction from others, which are entirely different from it.[64]

Hume is confused here (or, more likely, pretending to be) because he does not see (or, more likely, is not willing to concede) that '*ought*' is a statement of fact about purpose, an observation as regards an end-goal that we have the potential to attain, just as '*is*' is a statement of fact about our actual present.[65]

Alfred North Whitehead's 'process philosophy' helps illuminate the problem, despite his wholesale reversal of most aspects of classical metaphysics. Precisely because he places such a premium on 'becoming' as opposed to 'being', Whitehead sees the so-called 'is/ought' or 'fact/value' gap Hume introduces here as an artificial separation, arising from a failure to take due account of patterns of development over time. More conventionally, as MacIntyre explains, in the traditional perspective on morality Aristotle usefully articulates, 'The precepts which enjoin the various virtues and prohibit the vices instruct us how to move from potentiality to act, how to realize our true nature, and to reach our true end. To defy them will be to be frustrated and incomplete, to fail to achieve that good of rational happiness which it is peculiarly ours as a species to pursue.'[66]

Hume is unwilling, by contrast, to allow for any such intrinsic connection between past, present and potential future. He doubts that we can justify moving from 'is' to 'ought' much as he also doubts that we can justify moving from 'cause' to 'effect'. As he observes in his *Enquiry Concerning Human Understanding*, 'we never can, by our utmost scrutiny, discover anything but one event following another; without being able to comprehend any force or power by which the cause operates, or any connexion between it and its supposed effect'.[67] In his 'Apology for Raymond Sebond', Montaigne describes such thoroughgoing scepticism as the 'final fencer's trick': 'a desperate stroke, in which you must abandon your weapons to make your adversary lose his'. Because this 'secret trick' can so easily go awry, he warns, it should be used only 'rarely and reservedly'.[68]

In this case, for example, as Stephen Riker points out, 'the denial of necessary causality', although 'a powerful philosophical argument', is 'a two-edged sword', which 'can be used against religion by leading to further scepticism or against philosophy in leaving room for faith in the omnipotence of God'.[69] Seven centuries before Hume, in his treatise *The Incoherence of the Philosophers*, the Persian philosopher al-Ghazali anticipates Hume's doubts about causation: 'the connexion between what is usually believed to be a cause and what is believed to be an effect is not a necessary connexion', he maintains, but instead 'based on a prior power of God to create them in a successive order'.[70] Hume's next move is to criticise belief in miracles; in keeping with later Western voluntarism, however, as well as his own Ash'arite school of Islamic theology, al-Ghazali finds in the same insight confirmation of their possibility. God is not constrained by a natural order that may seem to be self-perpetuating but upon reflection can be better understood as wholly contingent on his will.

Meanwhile, in the wake of Kant and what is sometimes called his 'Copernican Revolution' in epistemology, recentring the question of what we can know on the structure of our minds as opposed to the structure of the cosmos itself, Bacon's claim that final causes are 'derived from the nature of man' turns out not to be as devastating a charge as he intended. Thinking in terms of essences and purposes, like thinking in terms of time and space, is inevitable, and for precisely the same reason Bacon singles out: 'the nature of man'. Formal and final causation are built in to our cognition, part of how we think, like the operating system in a computer.[71] Whether or not such abstractions really do exist 'out there' independent of us is beyond our capacity to know.[72]

For example, in his short story 'Funes the Memorious', Borges imagines a man, Ireneo Funes, who after falling off his horse and injuring his head, finds himself paralysed but now able to remember absolutely everything he encounters in each and every particular detail: the forms of clouds, the foam raised by an oar, the changing shapes of a flickering fire. This gift proves a curse; as Borges explains, Funes becomes over time 'almost incapable of ideas of a general, Platonic sort'. 'His own face in the mirror, his own hands, surprised him every time he saw them.' 'I suspect he was not very capable of thought,' Borges concludes. 'To think is to forget differences, generalize, make abstractions. In the teeming world of Funes, there were only details, almost immediate in their presence.'[73] Borges' story corroborates the account of a Russian stage memory-artist ('mnemonist') Solomon Shereshevsky, active in the 1920s, who reported similar difficulties. As a contemporary neuropsychologist, Alexander Luria, explains, Shereshevsky's memory, although prodigious, was 'lacking in one important feature': 'the capacity to convert encounters with the particular into instances of the general, enabling one to form general concepts'.[74]

Similar incapacitation would beset anyone who tried to free themselves altogether from thinking in terms of 'final causes'. A case in point here is the difficulty biologists encounter trying to explain evolution without introducing any suggestion of purpose. As even, for example, Daniel Dennett concedes, 'treating parts of the world as intentional systems' is 'virtually unavoidable'. Since we cannot escape this element of what he calls 'folk psychology', Dennett proposes that we might as well accept it. 'The answer lies in seeing that the process of natural selection is the source of all functional design, and hence, when considered from the intentional stance, the ultimate source of meaning.' But why should we assume this source ('natural selection') and not another: God, for example? On what grounds are we making this decision?

Dennett himself makes no apology for his leap of faith. 'One must start from somewhere,' he admits, 'and my choice is to begin with the objective, materialistic, third-person world of the physical sciences.'[75] Even if we grant, however, as Dennett seems willing to do, that this 'choice' is unjustified, another question still remains. Is such a step possible? Can we somehow see the world from outside ourselves? For Thomas Nagel, it is not so easy to leave out the subjective, the immaterial and the first person:

> One limit encountered by the pursuit of objectivity appears when it turns back on the self and tries to encompass subjectivity in its conception of the real. The recalcitrance of this material to objective understanding requires both a modification of the form of objectivity and a recognition that it cannot by itself provide a complete picture of the world, or a complete stance toward it.[76]

'There is no combat so violent among philosophers', Montaigne observes, 'and so bitter, as that which arises over the question of the sovereign good of man.'[77] Nonetheless, it is not a combat that we can escape. I speculate elsewhere that Shakespeare's Hamlet may be a critique (among other things!) of Montaigne's disengaged persona in his *Essays*: 'The Anglo-Saxon legend of Amleth provides Shakespeare, perhaps, with a vehicle for putting Montaigne's charming nonchalance under greater circumstantial pressure.'[78] As Hamlet discovers, no matter how desperately we may want to avoid committing ourselves to any one particular course of action, the human condition forces us to draw conclusions; to make choices ('To be or not to be'); to do one thing and not another. Even inaction is a kind of action: an implicit decision.

Whether or not Shakespeare had Montaigne in mind, for critics such as Ivan Turgenev and A. C. Bradley, *Hamlet* is Shakespeare's illustration of the hidden dangers that can arise from scepticism, if it precludes commitment to a fixed and deliberate sense of purpose.[79] Montaigne cites a Tuscan proverb to the same effect: '*he who grows too keen cuts himself*'.[80] Students, like professors, enjoy the luxury of giving equal weight to both sides of a question. When Hamlet is called away from private speculation, however, to the public world of politics, his dialectical cast of mind proves to have produced a paralysing habit of irresolution, which then breaks down under pressure into rash, misdirected violence. According to a story Montaigne recounts in his essay 'Of Virtue', after the sceptic Pyrrho was seen climbing a tree to escape a dog, as opposed to doubting its existence and, *ipso facto*, letting himself be savaged, the philosopher admitted, 'It is very difficult entirely to strip off the man.'[81] One can imagine Hamlet saying the same, after he realises he has stabbed Polonius.

Much as Montaigne may have inspired Hamlet, so, too, Hamlet may have inspired Hume. In his *Treatise of Human Nature*, in several long passages that, probably not by mere coincidence, call to mind Hamlet's soliloquies, Hume explains that he finds himself prey from time to time to vacillation, self-condemnation and existential fears. 'Affrighted and confounded with that forlorn solitude, in which I am plac'd in my philosophy', 'every step I take is with hesitation, and every new reflection makes me dread an error and absurdity in my reasonings'. 'Where am I, or what? From what causes do I derive my existence, and to what condition shall I return? . . . I am confounded with all these questions, and begin to fancy myself in the most deplorable condition imaginable, inviron'd with the deepest darkness.' 'Most fortunately', however, Hume observes, 'it happens that since reason is incapable of dispelling these clouds, nature herself suffices to that purpose, and cures me of this philosophical melancholy and delirium.' After a 'game of backgammon' and 'three or four hours' amusement', 'these speculations appear so cold, and strain'd, and ridiculous, that I cannot find in heart to enter into them any further'.[82]

What emerges from these thought-experiments (Pyrrho's, Montaigne's, Shakespeare's, Hume's . . .) is, in short, that our flirtations with the most rigorous forms of scepticism can only ever be flirtations. Unwarranted conclusions about what is popularly called 'the meaning of life' are simply part of what it means to be human. Such conclusions will not and cannot ever be entirely justified. But they will be drawn, willy-nilly, one way or another. The real question, then, is not whether we can somehow remove final causes from our processes of cognition but instead which stories we decide to tell ourselves about their origins. Are purposes (our own, other people's, those of things in general) something we invent and assign? Or are end-goals something that we sense and discern? Is teleology, that is, the 'law' of how things 'ought' to develop over time, 'positive' or 'natural'?

In practice, no individual or culture answers this question entirely one way or the other. Conceptually, however, this insoluble mystery, the ontology of teleology, is what lies at the heart of the divide between medieval and modern ethics, as well as the divide today between conservative and progressive politics. Isaiah Berlin attributes this change to Romanticism, which he sees, not without reason, as 'a great revolution in consciousness'. 'The general proposition of the eighteenth century', he explains, 'indeed of all previous centuries', is 'that there is a nature of things, there is a *rerum natura*, there is a structure of things'. For the Romantics, by contrast, 'there is no structure of things'; 'there is no pattern to which you must adapt yourself'. 'You create values, you create goals, you create ends, and in the end you create your own vision of the universe, exactly as artists create works of art.'[83]

As MacIntyre concedes, what he himself sees as a tragic 'loss of traditional structure and content' can also be recast and even celebrated as 'the achievement by the self of its proper autonomy', 'liberated from all those outmoded forms of social organization which had imprisoned it simultaneously within a belief in a theistic and teleological world order and within those hierarchical structures which attempted to legitimate themselves as part of such a world order'.[84] Transgender rights, for instance, are a flashpoint at the moment precisely because they serve as a synecdoche and litmus test for this point of view. And it is intriguing that, even though advocates for transgender rights seek to overturn one aspect of 'natural law', at least as it has been traditionally understood, they nonetheless remain tenaciously attached to teleology. In the case of what they describe as 'gender confirmation' surgery, for example, they argue that the biology of 'is' not only can but should be allowed to give way to what 'ought to be'.[85] Efforts to require other people to use preferred pronouns reveal still further what Charles Taylor calls 'the politics of recognition'.[86] As Taylor points out, human beings not only want to have a formal and a final cause, that is, an identity to fulfil, but also for other people to acknowledge that identity as in some sense valid; legitimate; true. Howsoever unreasonably, by Hume's exigent standards, we as human beings nonetheless want our narratives of value to be treated as fact.

Looking back not simply to the nineteenth century, but much further still, Isaiah Berlin is right that there has been 'a great revolution in consciousness'. What he misses, however, are the many crucial early modern precursors, some theological, of the philosophers such as Fichte whom he describes as 'the roots of Romanticism'.[87] In his *New Organon*, Francis Bacon dismisses ambition for 'personal power' and national 'empire' as relatively petty. 'But if anyone attempts to renew and extend the power and empire of the human race itself over the universe of things, his ambition (if it should be so called) is without a doubt both more sensible and more majestic.' 'The task and purpose of human power', he maintains, 'is to generate and superinduce on a given body a new nature or new natures.'[88] In his *Discourse on Method*, Descartes, too, dreams of replacing 'that speculative philosophy taught in the schools' with 'a practical philosophy' that would allow us to 'render ourselves, as it were, masters and possessors of nature'.[89] We see here in early, less radical form important precedents for the more sweeping 'proposition' Berlin finds at the core of Fichte's thought: 'things are as they are, not because they are so independent of me, but because I make them so; things depend on the way I treat them, what I need them for.'[90] 'I am not determined by ends,' Fichte proclaims; 'ends are determined by me.'[91]

We thus arrive at a crucial corollary question. Can we achieve such a conquest? If so, to what extent? Does human nature impose any limits on what Bacon calls 'the kingdom of man'?[92] In his work in 2004 as a speechwriter for an unsuccessful Democratic candidate for president, John Kerry, social psychologist Jonathan Haidt found himself frustrated with what he diagnoses as 'psychological naïveté'. 'The conservative advantage', he argues, is that 'Republicans understand moral psychology'; 'Democrats don't'.[93] Republicans, in other words, respect what Haidt sees as the constants of human nature, whereas Democrats tend to think in terms of the more enlightened creatures that they hope we human beings might someday become.

As French Thomist philosopher Jacques Maritain observes, an idealising impulse leads the left, like Tennyson's Ulysses, always ever onward, past the horizon of possibility: 'The pure man of the left detests being, always preferring, in principle in the words of Rousseau, *what is not* to *what is*.' Thus Sartre: 'The real is never beautiful.' But the other side is no better: 'The pure man of the right', by contrast, 'detests justice and charity, always preferring . . . *injustice to disorder*.' The left, for Maritain, may be as insufferable as Tolstoy, but the right is as frightening as Nietzsche.[94] Economist Thomas Sowell, too, describes the difference as 'a conflict of visions'. The conservative vision of our human nature and potential is 'constrained' and 'tragic', whereas the progressive is 'unconstrained' and 'utopian'.[95]

Sociologically speaking, it is not difficult to imagine why different social classes today, and by extension, different sets of voters, may be attracted to one of these visions as opposed to the other. For managers, lawyers, consultants, marketing directors, student affairs administrators, and other well-educated, office-bound professionals, as well as professors, journalists, actors, artists and other members of the cultural elite, people whose work revolves around words, pictures, and intangible ideas, who command attention and are listened to, the world can indeed seem infinitely malleable. We are like Doctor

Faustus, able to whiz about at will; to make things happen with a single email or a viral tweet.[96]

For those, however, who have to go out and actually deal with refractory physical objects; farmers, builders, dentists, pilots and so on; those who work with their hands, rather than in cyberspace; who are subject to the whims of the weather; who police the streets, put out fires, and actually do the fighting in the wars abroad that politicians talk about; those who are told what to do, rather than doing the telling; to this half, or more than half, of our population, the progressive message that the world is ours to make of what we will tends to come across instead as a dangerous delusion, or perhaps at best the resented luxury of a privileged few. And the same contrast holds true historically. In the wake of the wonders that science has brought forth, it is much easier now to believe that human nature might be limitless than it was in the Middle Ages or even the sixteenth century.

Where do Montaigne and Shakespeare stand with respect to this 'conflict of visions'? This question is what animates some of the most thoughtful and illuminating studies of both authors. Too often, however, we as critics have been unwilling to concede that the side of the great divide these towering figures of the past are standing on, the perspective that they ultimately choose, may not be our own. We are in this respect the 'liberal censors' of my title; or, at least, we are in danger of becoming so. Our censorship is all the more subtle, moreover, in so far as it is typically a sin (so to speak) of omission rather than commission: a result of what we overlook, rather than what we focus on.

For example, with regards to Shakespeare, in his seminal monograph *Radical Tragedy*, Jonathan Dollimore is indebted to the precedent set by Kott but much more judicious in his selection of the evidence he chooses to foreground. He does not say as Kott does that all of Shakespeare's plays are nihilistic but instead focuses, without ever explicitly acknowledging that he does so, on plays, still more specifically, tragedies, that Shakespeare sets in a world before the advent of Christianity: *Troilus and Cressida*, *King Lear*, *Antony and Cleopatra* and *Coriolanus*. To suggest that these plays are representative of Shakespeare's oeuvre as a whole would be a gross distortion. And to his credit, Dollimore never does, at least not explicitly. But he also takes no precautions to dispel that possible inference. As a result, it is all too easy to mistake the world as the characters in these plays perceive it, the world as it appears from the pagan point of view, for the world as Shakespeare himself perceives it, that is, the world reframed by Christian revelation.

As I argue elsewhere, in a book on Shakespeare's Roman plays, the tragedy of these plays is not so much the missteps of a particular individual as of a society which, in the absence of Christianity, does not provide otherwise sympathetic protagonists with the cultural resources and framework of social support necessary to make better sense of their ethical dilemmas and to find more satisfying forms of consolation when confronted by heartbreak or political defeat.[97] In such plays, precisely as Dollimore says, 'sensitive people brutalise themselves in order to survive in a brutal world', and 'the irony, or rather the tragedy, lies in the fact that, in so doing, they earn the esteem of their society'. Characters such as Troilus 'internalise rather than transcend the violence of their society, being incapable of surviving its alienating effects except by re-engaging with it'.[98] What Dollimore misses, however, and what is much clearer now in the wake of new work within Shakespeare studies such as Hannibal Hamlin, *The Bible in Shakespeare*, is that the 'irony' he discerns in plays such as *Julius Caesar*, *Coriolanus* and *Antony and Cleopatra* is not nihilistic, not the 'womp womp' sad trombone of Beckett's theatre of the absurd, but instead a deliberate double vision that arises from a myriad of subtle allusions to Scripture, Christian doctrine and biblical drama, belying the perspective of the characters themselves.[99]

Dollimore's touchstone, meanwhile, for the dissolution of belief in natural law that he ascribes to Shakespeare, as well as Jacobean tragedy more generally, is Montaigne's *Essays*. 'Machiavelli, Montaigne, and Hobbes', he maintains, as well as Bacon, 'testify unambiguously' to the 'recognition' that 'ethical truth' is 'relative to custom and social practice'. Montaigne is the obvious outlier in this line-up, yet he also receives the greater part of Dollimore's attention, perhaps for that very reason. Dollimore knows that the well-informed reader is likely to raise an eyebrow here, at the appropriation of Montaigne, more so than elsewhere. Does Montaigne really believe that 'law and morality' – that is, not just positive 'law', but also 'ethical truth' – 'have their origins in custom rather than with an eternal order of things (God or nature or both)'? Does he 'reject the belief that we possess some given, unalterable essence or nature in virtue of which we are human'?

Dollimore's insistent refrain that Montaigne is a fellow 'anti-essentialist' is out of keeping with Montaigne's pointed mockery of the counterintuitive claims of various classical philosophers, especially Stoics, throughout his *Essays*. Again and again, Montaigne shows their high-minded aspirations to transcend the human condition brought down to earth by its humbling constants: physical embodiment, emotional inconstancy and intellectual ignorance. Does Montaigne see these perennial stumbling blocks as nothing more than products of 'custom'? As Dollimore admits, Montaigne 'confidently declares that there are at least "inclinations" and "passions" which are given'.[100]

In *Radical Tragedy*, Dollimore's term of choice for what he argues Jacobean tragedy undermines is 'Christian humanism', meaning, in his own formulation, 'Christian-stoic accounts of identity', as well as an associated 'providentialist orthodoxy'.[101] This broad-brush hypothetical construct, 'Christian humanism', is so fraught with internal self-contradiction, however, that its value as a framework for interpretation is debatable at best. Conflating Christianity with humanism overlooks substantive points of contrast not only between Christian and classical thought but also internally between rival forms of Christian theology, as well as between rival schools within the larger canon of classical philosophy Renaissance humanism sought to revive. At the core of this fractious jumble lie opposing claims about our human capacity for autonomy. Do we need God's help in order to be wise, virtuous and content? What about what Bernard Williams calls 'moral luck'? Many external factors can help us to be or at least to seem virtuous, including mundane material goods such as health, wealth and superior force of arms, as well as education and the help of friends and family.[102]

In his magisterial essay 'The Two Faces of Humanism', historian William Bouswma presents the nature and extent of human self-sufficiency as the defining intellectual battleground of early modern Europe. More specifically, Bouwsma identifies 'two ideological poles': 'Stoicism and Augustinianism'. 'The notion of the compatibility and even the affinity between Stoicism and Christianity goes back to the yearning of early Christian converts for some bridge between the old world of thought and the new.' Nevertheless, 'at a deeper level Stoicism and Augustinian Christianity were in radical opposition'.

> The issue between them, in its most direct terms, was the difference between the biblical understanding of creation, which makes both man and the physical universe separate from and utterly dependent on God, and the Hellenistic principle of immanence, which makes the universe eternal, by one means or another deifies the natural order, and by seeing a spark of divinity in man tends to make him something more than a creature of God.

For Bouwsma, 'this fundamental difference has massive implications'. From the perspective of 'Augustinian anthropology', Bouwsma explains, as opposed to 'Stoic anthropology', 'reason (howsoever wonderful)' is not 'naturally capable of knowing the will of God'; 'such knowledge' is 'available to man only in the Scriptures'. 'Human wickedness', too, 'presents a much more serious problem than Stoics can dream of': 'the notion that man in his fallen condition can rely on his own powers to achieve virtue is utterly implausible'.[103]

Much of the novelty and appeal of Plato's ethics, as well as of inheritors such as Stoicism, arises from his strenuous insistence that happiness is entirely dependent on virtue, which he believes we can control, as opposed to circumstance, which he concedes that we cannot. Such a claim may seem implausible, and Plato acknowledges that his conclusions are counterintuitive. At the beginning of his *Republic*, Glaucon asks Socrates to imagine the contrast between a criminal mastermind who enjoys the greatest possible reputation for virtue and an innocent man thought to be the worst possible kind of criminal. The vicious man would enjoy 'money', 'friends' and public acclaim, whereas the virtuous man would be 'scourged, racked, bound' and finally 'impaled'. 'Knowing all this,' Glaucon asks, 'how can a man who has any superiority of mind or person or rank or wealth be willing to honour justice; or indeed to refrain from laughing when he hears justice praised?'[104]

Socrates' answer, which takes Plato the entirety of the *Republic* to explain, is that the tyrant who seems to have everything is nonetheless made miserable by his own insatiable desires. 'His soul is full of meanness and vulgarity; the best elements in him are enslaved.' As we see in Shakespeare's *Macbeth*, a man who falls prey to vice finds himself a prisoner of regret, remorse and relentless fears, unable to escape the stinging 'gadfly' of dissatisfaction.[105]

This 'transvaluation of all values', to borrow a phrase from Nietzsche, served as the starting point for all of the various Hellenistic schools of thought about ethics, as well as Nietzsche's own irritated, reactionary revival of Socrates' opponents, the Sophists.[106] The Church Fathers of late antiquity, too, found in Plato and his legacy a useful toolkit for articulating Christian theology.[107] St Clement of Alexandria, for instance, finds in Plato's thought-experiment an anticipation of Christ's Passion: 'Plato all but predicts the economy [*oikonomia*] of salvation.'[108] Unlike the pagans before them, however, Christians see internal freedom from turmoil (*ataraxia*) as impossible to attain without God's help.

Before setting out for Cyprus, Othello scoffs at the suggestion that he might be distracted by the company of his wife. If 'light-wing'd toys / Of feather'd Cupid' should 'seal' his 'speculative and officed instruments', he proclaims, or 'taint and corrupt' his 'business', 'Let housewives make a skillet of my helm . . .!' His 'young affects' are 'defunct' – or so he thinks. By the end of the play, the dangerous folly of Othello's self-assurance has become all too painfully apparent. As Lodovico asks, aghast, after he sees Othello strike Desdemona,

> Is this the noble Moor whom our full senate
> Call all in all sufficient? Is this the nature
> Whom passion could not shake? whose solid virtue
> The shot of accident, nor dart of chance,
> Could neither graze nor pierce?   (I, iii, 262–71)

In *Love's Labour's Lost*, Berowne wisely dismisses his companions' unwarranted confidence that they will be able to resist the charms of female company. 'For every man with his affects is born / Not by might master'd but by special grace' (I, i, 149–50).[109] At the end of his 'Apology for Raymond Sebond', Montaigne comes to a similar conclusion: man cannot 'raise himself above himself and humanity'. 'He will rise, if God by exception lends him a hand; he will rise by abandoning and renouncing his own means, and letting himself be raised and uplifted by purely celestial means.'[110]

Reflecting on accounts of martyrs and philosophers defying their torturers, Montaigne comes down on the side of Aristotle as opposed to the Stoics. 'Enough for the sage [*Luy suffise*] to curb and moderate his inclinations; for to do away with them is not in him.' Montaigne concedes that it is possible to ignore physical suffering in short bursts, much as soldiers find themselves capable of fearless forays in the heat of battle, which afterwards they can only marvel at. 'Howsoever holy it may be', the 'frenzy' that allows such feats, however, is at best short-lived. Nor is it necessarily divine inspiration so much as human pride: a martial spirit or, in Plato's terms, *thymos* (cp. Fr. *courage*, from *cœur*, 'heart') that has overstepped its bounds. 'Who does not judge that these are the sallies of a runaway courage?'[111]

To put these observations in different terms, the general trajectory of Montaigne's *Essays* is away from what William Bouwsma calls 'Stoic' anthropology towards what he calls 'Augustinian'. As Montaigne himself explains emphatically and at considerable length in the opening pages of his 'Apology for Raymond Sebond', the target of his ire is not the first-order premise that the world has some sort of intrinsic structure: 'natural law' in the objective sense of *logos* or deep truth. What he aims to dispel instead is a second-order 'presumption' that we as human beings have any kind of trustworthy, straightforward capacity to discern that *logos* on our own, independent of God's grace and supernatural revelation: 'natural law' in the subjective sense of unaided, efficacious human reason; private conscience unprompted by God himself; or universally acknowledged, uniformly practised 'custom'. 'If it does not enter into us by an extraordinary infusion, if it enters, I will not say only by reason, but by human means of any sort, it is not in us in its dignity or its splendor.'[112]

Montaigne's doubts about human judgement are not absolute; compared to other sceptics, as William Hamlin notes, Montaigne's 'truly original move' is to argue that 'accurate judgment is possible', albeit 'extremely difficult'.[113] Montaigne's aim in his *Apology*, however, is, as he says from the beginning, 'to crush and trample underfoot human arrogance and pride'.[114] To this end, his argument is not about metaphysics, much though Dollimore makes it out to be, but instead about epistemology. That is to say, Montaigne is not arguing that natural law does not exist, in the sense of what Dollimore variously calls 'ethical truth', 'an in-forming absolute' and 'teleological design', but instead that we ourselves cannot know it without 'faith and divine grace'.[115] 'Our human reasons and arguments are as it were the heavy and barren matter; the grace of God is their form; it is that which gives them shape and value.'[116]

Understanding Montaigne's Augustinian purposes in his *Apology* may help to make sense of a crucial moment elsewhere in his *Essays* that modern commentators tend to find a non sequitur, if not an outright, baffling self-contradiction. In 'Of Custom, and Not Easily Changing an Accepted Law', Montaigne recounts a myriad of startling and contradictory customs he has heard of worldwide in order to demonstrate that, as he puts it, 'there is nothing that custom will not or cannot do'. Even 'the laws of conscience', he maintains, 'which we say are born of nature, are born of custom'. One might expect from this preamble the conclusions of a libertine. But, instead, Montaigne insists that 'these considerations' should not 'deter a man of understanding from following the common style'. In closing, Montaigne professes himself 'disgusted with innovation, in whatever guise', and in particular with the ongoing Protestant Reformation, which he describes as ruinous.[117]

For twentieth-century critics Freida Brown and Francis Heck, Montaigne presents the 'seeming paradox' of an author 'liberal in thought' but 'conservative in action'.[118] Philosopher and outspoken progressive atheist Julian Baggini finds a similar 'paradox' in the works of David Hume. How did Hume's 'admirable scepticism in the world of ideas', Baggini asks, dismayed, translate into his 'reactionary stance in the world of practical affairs'?[119] The answer, however, is not hard to find. Like Montaigne, as well as Montaigne's own model, Sextus Empiricus, when it comes time to act as opposed to speculate, Hume defers to past precedent and established institutions.[120] He does not challenge 'custom' but instead embraces it as what he calls 'the great guide of human life'.[121]

If I may venture an analogy, for Hume as well as Montaigne, human society is like a country of the blind in which everyone relies on guide dogs: 'custom'. These dogs seem to be blind themselves, and they are as many and as various as there are towns and people in them. Nonetheless, they have kept us alive and well so far, relatively speaking. So, it seems unwise to try to replace them with anything new and untested: drones, for example, or androids of our own invention. Why would we take such a risk? As Thomas Mann points out, 'all experiments here are dangerous, because one is dealing with the most unmanageable material, the human race, which is almost as dangerous to deal with as high explosives.'[122] 'Whoever meddles with choosing and changing usurps the authority to judge,' Montaigne warns, 'and he must be very sure that he sees the weakness of what he is casting out and the goodness of what he is bringing in.'[123] The principle Montaigne advances here is now sometimes known as Chesterton's Fence, after the novelist and Christian apologist G. K. Chesterton: 'Do not remove a fence until you know why it was put up in the first place.'[124]

More specifically, Montaigne decries 'the innovations of Luther' because he sees them as the first step down a slippery slope to the condition we now celebrate as 'modernity', in which, as he complains of his own age, people 'accept nothing to which they have not applied their judgment and granted their personal consent'. In the opening of his 'Apology', Montaigne notes that a learned contemporary of his father, Pierre Bunel, 'rightly' foresaw that the Reformation, 'this incipient malady', would 'degenerate into an execrable atheism', at least among 'the common herd'. 'When some articles of their religion have been set into doubt and upon the balance, they will soon after cast easily into like uncertainty all the other parts of their belief', until they at last 'shake off' and finally trample underfoot 'the authority of ancient laws' and 'the reverence of ancient usage'.[125]

If Montaigne is a radical, he is hiding it well here! In the end, in order to align Montaigne with Machiavelli, Bacon and Hobbes, Dollimore finds himself obliged to explain away Montaigne's manifest 'conservatism', which he presents as a failure of nerve, as well as

Montaigne's professions of faith, which he speculates might be disingenuous. Montaigne's scepticism leads 'perilously close to nihilism', Dollimore observes, but Montaigne himself 'avoids it by embracing a form of fideism'. 'Are to take this "straight",' he asks, 'or are we to read behind it a political discretion laced with irony, a scepticism being officially allayed but in language which actually alerts it?'[126]

Dollimore is not the first to raise this question but instead can be better understood as one of a number of readers who, perplexed by these apparent tensions in Montaigne's thought, have sought to resolve them by concluding that Montaigne's repeated attestations to his Christian faith and conservative politics must be insincere. Donald Frame finds such claims dubious: 'His irony everywhere else is perfectly clear, and here no irony is clear.'[127] Nonetheless, the belief that Montaigne paid no more than lip-service to the pieties of his day has had many enthusiasts over time, including most notably in the early decades of the twentieth century the editor and scholar Arthur Armaingaud, as well as the novelist André Gide.[128]

Montaigne's reputation as indifferent or even hostile to Christianity dates back not to his contemporaries but instead to his reception by later Jansenists such as Pascal and Malebranche. Papal censors during Montaigne's own lifetime let him off lightly; his *Essays* were not placed on the Index for Forbidden Books until almost a century later (1676).[129] And coming from Jansenists, accusations of *libertinage* should be taken with a grain of salt. For them to accuse a fellow Catholic of irreligion is like Ben Jonson sniping at Shakespeare for having only 'small Latin' or Milton describing him as an untutored outsider artist, 'Fancy's child', warbling his 'native wood-notes wild'. Compared to them, yes; compared to the rest of us, maybe not. Nonetheless, by the eighteenth century, Montaigne's supposed anti-establishmentarianism was so well established that Voltaire could describe him as a fellow traveller: 'un philosophe complet'.[130]

Is Montaigne a scoffing *philosophe* in disguise? We might call this conclusion the 'esoteric' reading of Montaigne, after Leo Strauss, were it not that the secret Strauss believes 'esoteric' thinkers such as Maimonides and al-Farabi aim to hide is its polar opposite: a recognition of the limits of philosophy and theology vis-à-vis each other, such that each theoretical approach, one proceeding by reason, the other by faith, depends on the other for its practical success.[131] This synthesis is exactly what Dollimore finds so disappointing in Montaigne's *Essays* and suggests that Montaigne surely, if we read between the lines, cannot possibly believe; a compromise position that Montaigne would reject, if he only had the courage to follow through on the promptings of his inner firebrand; that is, his inner Dollimore. Why does Montaigne not 'cry "Havoc!", and let slip the dogs of war?' Dollimore's frustration is almost palpable.

Writing in the early 1960s, Roland Mushat Frye notes 'considerable disagreement' regarding 'the relevance of theology to Shakespeare's plays'. 'Some, who may for convenience be epitomized in A. C. Bradley, hold that Christian theology is irrelevant to Shakespeare's writing, while others, who may be conveniently placed in the train of G. Wilson Knight, hold that Shakespeare's plays are essentially and pervasively – even blatantly – Christian.'[132] By the end of the twentieth century, it had become a critical commonplace to speak of Shakespeare as a paradigmatic example of a secular sensibility: G. G. Gervinus, one might say, won out over his fellow nineteenth-century German critic Hermann Ulrici, who presents Shakespeare as a Christian moralist.

Yet this consensus has not held. In recent years, what Donald Frame describes as 'the perennial debate over Montaigne's Christianity' has been replaced by a debate about his relation to liberalism.[133] Shakespeare studies, however, has experienced a 'religious turn'.[134] As Brian Cummings observes, 'for almost all of the twentieth century', Shakespeare was 'idolized as a secular author, so that attempts to place him within a religious framework were marginalized and often seen as maverick or bizarre'. Since the turn of the twenty-first century, however, 'there has been a volte-face': a myriad of critics have begun to reaffirm and explore Shakespeare's sympathetic, thoroughgoing engagement with Christian theology, as well as Christian Scripture and medieval biblical drama.[135] 'If it is not plausible to read Shakespeare's plays as Christian allegories,' Debora Shuger suggests, 'neither is it likely that the popular drama of a religiously saturated culture could, by a secular miracle, have extricated itself from the theocentric orientation informing the discourses of politics, gender, social order, and history.'[136]

Much in contrast to Montaigne studies, as well as the New Historicism of the late 1980s and 1990s, what is now almost never contested within Shakespeare studies is no longer his supposed secularism but instead his relation to liberalism. In his essay 'Invisible Bullets' (1981, 1985, 1988), Stephen Greenblatt makes a case for Shakespeare's conservatism which became a touchstone as well as a provocation for a generation of critics: a Foucauldian argument that Shakespeare's representations of rebellion ultimately reinforce the established political order.[137] Now more than thirty years on, carried forward by the screw of dialectic, Shakespeare studies as a field is all but defined by its opposition to this claim, to the point that the time is ripe, perhaps, for a synthesis of thesis and antithesis.[138] 'More than any other pre-Romantic writer', Peter Holbrook argues, 'Shakespeare is committed to fundamentally modern values: individuality, self-realization, authenticity.'[139] For Ewan Fernie, 'Shakespeare means freedom'. 'That is why the plays matter, and not just aesthetically but also in terms of the impact they historically have had and continue to have on personal and political life in the world.'[140]

'Why Shakespeare?' Jeffrey Wilson asks. 'What is it about him – as opposed to Chaucer or Spenser or Milton – that led modernity to say, He's the one for us, given his methods and concerns and given our values and commitments?' Shakespeare 'is celebrated today', he concludes, 'because he signifies liberty'. More specifically, nineteenth-century liberal canon-makers such as Hazlitt and Keats elevated Shakespeare above Milton because his plays are 'liberal in form'. Milton's poetry may be 'liberal in content', but it is 'authoritarian in method', whereas Shakespeare's plays 'have the feeling of freedom'. Wilson notes the long line of successors to Keats's concept of 'negative capability', amounting to 'a critical consensus':

> William Empson's (1930) 'ambiguity' (Empson 1966), A. P. Rossiter's (1961) 'essential ambivalence,' Fredson Bowers's (1963) 'dramatic vagueness,' Norman Rabkin's (1967) 'complementarity,' Terence Hawkes's (1992: 147) 'meaning by Shakespeare' (the plays 'don't, in themselves, "mean." It is we who mean by them'), Jonathan Bate's (1997: 327) 'first law' (that 'truth is not singular'), Stephen Greenblatt's (2004) 'strategic opacity,' Julia Reinhard Lupton's (2014) 'affordances,' Emma Smith's (2019) 'permissive gappiness,' and a host of other commentators, including Tzachi Zamir (2007) and Peter G. Platt (2009), showing Shakespeare putting his audience in uncertainties, mysteries, and doubts.[141]

Similar observations about Montaigne's *Essays* have likewise become a critical commonplace. 'What Montaigne teaches us especially', André Gide proclaims, writing just after the Second World War, 'is what was called at a much later date "liberalism"': 'this rare and extraordinary propensity, of which he often speaks, to listen to, and even espouse, other people's opinions, to the point of letting them prevail over his own'.[142] Writing just after the Second World War, Hugo Friedrich praises Montaigne for his 'amazing readiness for the contradictory in himself and in all things'. 'There is no desire to impose his opinions on others, or to be seen knowing it all. There is no lecturing'. Instead, the *Essays* 'grant every person the same right to the freedom of being himself that the author claims for himself'.[143]

What prompted what Philippe Desan decries as 'this liberal appropriation of Montaigne'? For Desan, 'this self-sufficiency of the subject, removed from his historical reality, is the trap par excellence of many contemporary commentaries on the *Essais*', leaving Montaigne 'emptied of his political dimension'. 'We like to see in him the moment of introspection, of withdrawal.'[144] In his dazzling account of the *Essays*' reception, Warren Boutcher explains how an appealing but perhaps misleading vision of Montaigne as a model for an ideal self, 'the authentically free-minded, private reader-writer', 'retired from society into repose amongst books', rose to the fore 'between the 1880s and the 1940s': 'the period of global crisis in which the twentieth-century humanities were founded'. Scholars such as Friedrich 'cemented the place of Montaigne's work' in 'the history of the secular, liberal West' as a testimony to the possibility of 'autonomous selfhood'. Now almost a hundred years later, Boutcher observes, this 'distinctively modern biographical picture of Montaigne himself' as 'the happy existentialist without metaphysical supports of any kind, the knight of non-possession', is 'no longer so secure or clear'.[145]

The most prominent exponents at present of the liberal reading of Montaigne's *Essays* that Boutcher flags up as under duress are Felicity Green and Richard Scholar, each of whom brings to bear a different emphasis. Green finds in the *Essays* a 'project of voluntary disengagement', 'indebted to ancient thought, and in particular to Stoic conceptions of independence as a state of inner tranquillity and detachment'; Montaigne in her account seeks the kind of 'personal liberty', 'freedom as nondomination', Quentin Skinner classifies as 'neo-Roman' or 'republican' rather than 'liberal'.[146] The distinction Skinner posits between republicanism and liberalism is tendentious, however, and to my mind, at least, does not correspond to how either Montaigne or Shakespeare understands possible alternatives in practice to the traditional social hierarchy Shakespeare's Ulysses calls 'degree'.[147] What we have here, in more straightforward terms, is Montaigne as a defender of the enabling fiction, or more charitably, premise, of liberalism, as well as Hellenistic ethics: the belief that it is possible to enjoy some measure of what Boutcher calls 'autonomous selfhood'. It is Epicureanism, moreover, rather than classical Stoicism, as mediated through Seneca more immediately than Lucretius, which is the chief source for this ideal of withdrawn 'self-possession'. Overlooking or misinterpreting key moments of irony and self-deprecation, Green misses Montaigne's profound ambivalence towards such 'disengagement', culminating in what amounts to reluctant disapproval.[148]

Richard Scholar's animating interest, by contrast, is the question of the coherence of Montaigne's *Essays* more generally considered, in relation to any form of fixed or particular ideological commitment. In keeping with Jean Starobinski's emphasis on Montaigne's thought as 'in motion', Scholar objects to what he describes as 'the still widespread tendency to reduce Montaigne's thought to the expression of an "-ism"'. The 'value' of following Montaigne's 'train of thought', he argues, lies instead 'in its volatility, its refusal to submit to the crystallizations of doctrine, its determination to remain on the move in the search for an elusive truth'. 'In his last book, *Shakespeare the Thinker*,' Scholar explains, 'A. D. Nuttall says of his subject that "the fiery track of his thinking" can never be followed to a settled terminus because Shakespeare was "simply too intelligent to be able to persuade himself that the problems were completely solved". I would say the same of Montaigne.'[149]

This vision of the author as uncatchable Teumessian fox is certainly beguiling. In Golding's translation of Ovid, Cephalus recounts, 'Net ne toyle was none so hie that could his wightnesse stop, / He mounted over at his ease the highest of the top.'[150] But even the Teumessian fox met his match in the inescapable hound Laelaps. Towering genius though he was, Montaigne, like Shakespeare, eventually fell prey to death; his train of thought in that sense, bluntly speaking, came to end, even though it may continue in a different sense in his afterlife. Montaigne might well have moved on from where he ended up, had he lived longer. But he did not; we have before us a finite work, the *Essays*, which although voluminous does have a beginning and an end.

Likewise, the possibility that Montaigne's thought might be singled out as an exception to the logical principle of non-contradiction is attractive, or, at least, convenient, not least because it allows us as critics to avoid taking a stand. Why trouble ourselves with a divisive 'either/or' when we can go for a 'both/and'? For Scholar, Montaigne is 'neither the irreligious *libertin* nor the pious Catholic humanist, neither the sceptic nor the Stoic, neither the revolutionary nor the conservative, neither the modern writer nor the Renaissance sage that he has been portrayed to be at various moments in his various – and continuing – afterlife'. Instead, 'he is, in each case, both – and therefore neither'.[151] An eirenic conclusion, and one I wish I could accept more easily! I find myself haunted, however, by one of Carl Schmitt's objections to liberalism, which he argues is an unsustainable fiction. 'The essence of liberalism is negotiation, a cautious half measure, in the hope that the definitive dispute, the decisive bloody battle, can be transformed into a parliamentary debate and permit the decision to be suspended forever in an everlasting discussion.'[152]

Schmitt's warning that 'liberal-neutralist' concepts of politics cannot be reconciled to human nature strikes home because, unmistakeably by now, even within the well-insulated confines of our college campuses, we critics find ourselves swept up in an alarming and occasionally violent upheaval; a polarisation and a hardening of positions wholly in keeping with the conflict between 'friend' and 'enemy' Schmitt portrays as inescapable.[153] Neo-liberalism on the left and libertarianism on the right were two sides of the same coin, a liberal centre that is disappearing rapidly. What is emerging instead, to the dismay of those who would prefer quieter, less committed lives, is a ferocious rivalry between a less compromising, activist strain of progressivism and a 'post-liberal', populist reimagining of conservatism.[154]

We return, then, with more urgency than before to the question with which we began. Whose side are Shakespeare and Montaigne on? Is it possible to see these authors as in some meaningful sense either conservative or progressive without either transforming their works into partisan propaganda or dismissing them, in effect, as no more than formal play, the inconsequential *aporia* of Derridean Deconstruction? In the terms first proposed by the pioneering postmodernist Jean-Yves Pouilloux, is it possible to discern these authors' *penser* without reducing them to static systems of *pensée*?[155]

Since the 1970s, critics such as Andre Tournon as well as Terence Cave have drawn our attention to the *Essays'* 'dispersion': 'distortions that regenerate concepts, enigmatic or aporetic configurations, emphatic silences, multiple perspectives, discordances'.[156] As Felicity Green points out, however, as well as Richard Scholar, this 'almost exclusive focus' on the apparent self-contradictions of the text 'leaves important questions unanswered'. 'Might it be possible', Green asks, to combine such 'exemplary attention to the *Essais*' *manière* with a deeper consideration of its *matière*', 'not in the justly discredited sense of definite answers or single points of view, but in the more dialogical and polyphonic sense of Montaigne's "convictions" and "problèmes"?'[157]

As a starting point for solving this problem, it is helpful to recognise that, in practice, almost all literary criticism performs the same basic operation, even if we call it by different names and propose various different justifications. The critic identifies two opposing voices within a work of literature, one of which (X) is dominant, and the other (not-X) recessive but also in play. New Critics, for example, reimagine the narration of a lyric as a debate, only to show that the apparent contrariety they have teased out in the end resolves itself into coherence. Deconstructionists, by contrast, see irreconcilable division. But they still think in terms of two opposing voices. In his analysis of Rousseau's *Essay on the Origin of Language*, for instance, in *Of Grammatology*, Derrida begins by setting out what Rousseau 'affirms . . . unambiguously', 'says . . . clearly', and so on, then identifies 'strands' in the same *Essay* which contradict these claims: a contrast between what Rousseau 'wishes to say' and what 'he says without wishing to say it'.[158]

As J. Hillis Miller explains, 'deconstructive criticism' is not a 'free-for-all' but instead 'a very precise identifiable movement back and forth among possibilities'.[159] Derrida first 'construes' a text then 'disseminates' it. M. H. Abrams calls these 'possibilities' reading1 and reading2; I call them here more simply X and not-X. New Historicists align one with 'containment' and the other with 'subversion'. Psychoanalytic critics describe one as 'conscious' and the other as 'unconscious', 'subconscious' or 'repressed'. What all these different types of criticism have in common, however, is that they see a definite set of voices, a particular debate: X versus not-X. Several such oppositions might conceivably be found in the same text: not only X versus not-X but also Y versus not-Y and Z versus not-Z. But there are not an endless number of such controversies to be found in a single work.

For example, Spenser might be Protestant. Or he might be 'of the Catholic party without knowing it'. We can rest assured, however, that he is not deeply invested in the outcome of the next US presidential election. His *Faerie Queene* is not an investigation of competing claims to be the Mahdi. Some possibilities we can rule out as neither here nor there: 'not even wrong', as physicist Wolfgang Pauli was wont to say when attempts at proofs proved especially lacklustre. Even Deconstruction in this sense is not entirely nihilistic. As critics, we can see which particular impasse we are in, even if in the end we cannot find our way out. Moreover, the two sides of the *abyme* are distinct. One emerges readily before us; the other is elusive, slipping away even as we try to discern it. One, it seems, is the thing itself; the other, something like its shadow.

As I propose elsewhere, these two voices can be best understood as expressions of an author's simultaneous faith and doubt.[160] To borrow terms from Deconstruction, doubt is the trace of the other in the self-same; the sense of uncertainty that accompanies bold assertion. Authors write texts not merely as a form of propaganda or manipulation, that is, as a means to persuade others of their own settled opinions, but also a form of more private cognitive catharsis, airing and, if possible, exorcising internal misgivings about their own assumptions. The doubt that shadows a contested belief drives an author to create a work of literature much as a grain of sand in an oyster might lead it to form a pearl – or a question might prompt a philosopher to engage in a thought-experiment.

Great authors such as Shakespeare and Montaigne are willing to concede, moreover, that doubts can never be entirely overcome. Misgivings can be eased but not eradicated altogether. Like Archimago in Spenser's *Faerie Queene,* Satan in Milton's *Paradise Lost* remains in the end still at large, still a threat. Shakespeare's Henry V banishes Falstaff, but not very far; 'ten mile'; close enough to be called back, if Henry V should change his ways (*2H4* V, v, 65).[161] No belief can wholly dominate the mind because its opposite is always already there, whispering; soliciting attention; exerting a contrarian cognitive pressure. Great literature acknowledges this fundamental human ambivalence. No official dogma can entirely overwhelm us because its opposite, a counterpoint of dissidence or heresy, is always there, as well, waiting to be chosen in its place. Propaganda attempts to deceive its own author, as well as its audience, by presenting such possibilities as foreclosed. Literature, by contrast, accepts the impossibility of its own set task. The doubt it sets out from the beginning to explore and, if possible, dispel persists to some extent, albeit diminished, to the very end of its own elaboration.

In the case of Montaigne and Shakespeare more specifically, what they believe about the most important underlying controversies of their time as well as ours tends to be what we as a social class, we professional scholars, I mean, in the humanities today, fear might be true, and what we believe tends to be likewise what they fear might be true. Their not-X has become our X; the substance of their doubts has become the substance of our faith. This chiasmus continues to cause all manner of confusion, and it can be untangled only if, first, we allow these authors to disagree with us, that is, if we do not force them against the grain of their own conclusions to grant our beliefs their supposed imprimatur, and, second, if we take into account the nature of literature, including not only stage-plays such as Shakespeare's but also essays such as Montaigne's, as, like music, an experience that unfolds over time. It is no good plucking out one static moment, the equivalent of a single note or chord, and holding it forth as evidence. Instead, the only way to understand what is at stake in any given work, as well as its resolution, is to think in terms of process and sequence. A great work of literature is an attempt at a cognitive catharsis which by its very nature can never be completely successful. And the same is true in a larger sense for an author's oeuvre as a whole.

For example, the best two readings of Falstaff remain to this day A. C. Bradley, 'The Rejection of Falstaff' (1909), and J. Dover Wilson, *The Fortunes of Falstaff* (1943).[162] Taken together, these two rival perspectives do wonders to illuminate the character, not only because they are so precisely opposed, but also because they both take pains to consider how and why Shakespeare's representation of Falstaff changes over time. Both critics muster considerable evidence to show that Shakespeare aims at disenchantment. The difference is that Bradley thinks Shakespeare fails, whereas Wilson thinks he succeeds. Working his way through various particular scenes, Bradley concedes that 'Shakespeare's purpose' is 'to work a gradual change in our feelings towards Falstaff', so that we move from 'sympathy into repulsion'. But all of Shakespeare's 'excellent devices', he insists, 'fail to change our attitude'. 'Our pain and resentment, if we feel them, are wrong, in the sense that they do not answer to the dramatist's intention. But it does not follow that they are wrong in a further sense. They may be right, because the dramatist has missed what he aimed at.'[163]

Bradley's unshakeable Romantic admiration for Falstaff continues to enjoy many sympathisers still today. For Ewan Fernie, writing more than a hundred years later, the 'freedom' that 'Shakespeare means' is most immediately 'freedom *to do what you like*', as in Rabelais' Abbaye de Thélème. And the first example of this licentious spirit Fernie calls to mind is Falstaff. 'In Falstaff, we touch something essential: the unrestrained subversive freedom of Shakespeare's own imagination. Falstaff not only nails the freedom to be yourself; he magnificently exemplifies its value.'[164] For Fernie, as for Bradley, as well as Harold Bloom, Falstaff is an antinomian ideal. 'We praise him, we laud him', Bradley explains, 'for he offends none but the virtuous, and denies that life is real or life is earnest, and delivers us from the oppression of such nightmares, and lifts us into the atmosphere of perfect freedom.' 'He is the enemy of everything that would interfere with his ease, and therefore of anything serious, and especially of everything respectable and moral. For these things impose limits and obligations, and make us the subjects of old father antic the law.'[165]

Would Shakespeare agree that Falstaff warrants Bradley's praise? For my own part, I must confess, I can never in the end look past his taking bribes to allow the rich, who would have been healthier and better trained, to escape military service, and instead leading hapless, unprepared peasants to their death. When other commanders raise concerns, Falstaff brushes them aside, showing no sign of remorse: 'Tut, tut; good enough to toss; food for powder, food for powder; they'll fill a pit as well as better' (*1H4* IV, iii, 64–6). Hard words to hear, for a man from a military family! Confronted by Michael Williams, at least Henry V seems to care. I suppose, as well, that Falstaff to me does not seem altogether extraordinary. There are a thousand Falstaffs in every major city; maybe more; he is a representation of a familiar type. Some background may help to explain: when I was younger, to improve my French, I worked for a time in Marseille as a live-in counsellor at a charity run by a family friend, a free rehab clinic for homeless men, most of whom were addicted to heroin. I continued some of the same work in New Haven at an American branch of the same charity after I got to Yale. So, by the time I was studying Shakespeare's Falstaff, I had already met him many times over: charming, witty, callous, self-aggrandising, entertaining, opportunistic, unapologetic, calculating, gone to seed and destructive. A victim, yes, in some cases. But also a victimiser. The experience proved a shock, to put it mildly, to my progressive pieties.[166]

In any case, for Dover Wilson, our modern discomfort with 'the rejection of Falstaff' is in the eye of the beholder. 'Falstaff', he writes, 'for all his descent from a medieval devil, has become a kind of god in the mythology of modern man, a god who does for our imaginations very much what Bacchus or Silenus did for those of the ancients.' 'We find it extraordinarily exhilarating to contemplate a being free of all the conventions, codes, and moral ties that control us as members of human society, a being without shame, without principles, without even a sense of decency, and yet one who manages to win our admiration by his superb wit, his moral effrontery, his intellectual agility, and his boundless physical vitality.'[167]

This perspective, Wilson maintains, is very much our own, as opposed to Shakespeare's. Taken on its own terms, *Henry IV* can be better understood as 'Shakespeare's great morality play': 'Hal associates Falstaff in turn with the Devil of the miracle play, the Vice of the morality, and the Riot of the interlude.' Falstaff is, in a word, the doubt that Shakespeare aims to dispel, not the faith that he seeks to embrace. Bradley complains that the newly crowned Henry V talks 'like a clergyman'. As Wilson urges us to remember, however, Shakespeare and his contemporaries were accustomed to sermons; saw them as 'fine and appropriate'; even sought them out as salutary spectacles with an eagerness that today can seem bewildering – unless we look outside our own secular academic echo-chamber; that is, venture over to the world of conservatives, where preaching can still draw a crowd and function as a form of entertainment.

Wilson's more basic point is that we should not take Falstaff as he appears at the beginning of the first part of *Henry IV,* Falstaff at his most attractive, as indicative of Shakespeare's settled belief, but instead reckon with 'the fundamental fact of dramatic structure, its serial character'.[168] The same is true on a grander scale for Montaigne's *Essays* or Shakespeare's oeuvre taken as a whole. Both authors come to conclusions over time that, although not entirely consistent or explicit, do have a discernible 'form and pressure'. Starting with *Titus Andronicus*, Shakespeare engages repeatedly with the precedent set by Senecan tragedy, which itself is much indebted to Euripides. He worries that Seneca's challenge to theodicy might be justified and explores that possibility. As Gordon Braden and I both point out, however, Shakespeare never goes as far as Seneca himself.[169] Even in the tragedies of his middle period, the wicked are punished and order is restored, as is not the case in, for example, Seneca's *Thyestes* or *Medea*. In his late plays, Shakespeare departs from Seneca (and Euripides) still further. Drawing on the rival conventions of medieval romance, he rewrites his own tragedies with happy endings made possible by what seems to be divine providence: *Othello* as *The Winter's Tale*, *King Lear* as *Pericles*, Ophelia as the Jailor's Daughter in *The Two Noble Kinsmen*.

William Hamlin sees a similar kind of rough trajectory in Montaigne's *Essays*, as regards what Felicity Green calls his 'project of voluntary disengagement'. Montaigne is certainly attracted to the Epicurean ideal of withdrawing into comfortable, self-sufficient isolation: a fantasy of rustic *otium* ('idleness') familiar from poets such as Horace. 'As we move deep into the *Essays*', however, Hamlin observes, 'reading the chapters of Book Three and attending to post-1588 additions throughout, it's hard not to feel that Montaigne's confidence in freedom-through-retreat undergoes a final diminishment.' 'On the whole,' Hamlin concludes, 'we're left with a rueful sense that while liberty may be both a natural endowment and a powerful desire, the human will is nonetheless constantly constrained by external and internal forces.'

Late in the *Essays*, Montaigne's pronouncements about liberty sound distinctly more circumscribed than those earlier on: a man lives 'not so much as he would himselfe, but as others will: not according to that he proposeth to himselfe, but to that which is proposed to him: according to times, to men and to affaires.'

Nor is this conclusion entirely out of the blue: 'even in earlier chapters,' Hamlin notes, 'we find hints of this circumscription'.[170] As regards the possibility of self-sufficiency, Montaigne is engaged throughout his *Essays* in what Hugo Friedrich calls 'an inner dialogue'.[171] By the time we get to the end, he has come to a conclusion.

Among other motives, Shakespeare and Montaigne as authors want relief from private cognitive dissonance. We are observers, bystanders, looking in on their internal thought-experiments. At the same time, we, too, as readers have our own motivations; our own doubts that we hope to explore at one remove and perhaps to exorcise. Much of the attraction of these authors, I believe, as well as their value as objects of study, lies in their articulation, not of what we already believe, though that tends to be what we officially emphasize, but instead of an opposing credo, a set of beliefs that despite ourselves we sometimes start to think might be better grounded than our own: the medieval as opposed to the modern; the conservative as opposed to the progressive.

That is to say, Shakespeare and Montaigne intrigue us, at least in part, because immersing ourselves in their thought is an opportunity to entertain heresies in private that it would be scandalous for us to profess in public, not least to ourselves. They are similar enough to us to allow us to see ourselves in them but also different enough to allow us to imagine what it would be like to be otherwise. By their very strangeness, their belonging to the past, they allow us to escape an intellectual echo-chamber which can often feel cosy and comfortable but at other times claustrophobic, even oppressive.[172] What lurks out there beyond our respectable Overton window, out 'where the wild things are'?[173] For us, the W.E.I.R.D, the educated elite, the peculiar slice of present-day society that is the humanities professoriate, Shakespeare and Montaigne are 'transgressive', 'subversive', 'anti-establishmentarian', precisely because, in the ordinary sense of those terms, they are not.

To admit as much, however, we would have to stop censoring not only these authors but also ourselves. We would have to acknowledge that some part of us, some still, small voice within, thinks despite our efforts our opponents might be right. Emotionally as well as intellectually, that breach of our taboos, not to mention that unwinding of our own self-satisfaction, what Montaigne might call our 'presumption', is no small task.[174] Are we liberal enough not only to admit we might be wrong but also to allow and even encourage genuine viewpoint diversity? Or will education in the humanities become, as it already often is, something else altogether?

As Jonathan Haidt observes, many of us in the humanities today are trying to pursue two goals at once: 'social justice' as well as 'truth'. 'What happens if they conflict?' he asks. 'Can any institution or profession have two *teloi*?'[175] Speaking of 'God and mammon', Jesus says in the Gospels, 'no man can serve two masters; for either he will hate the one and love the other; or else he will hold to one, and despise the other.'[176] So, too, Haidt warns, sooner or later, as individuals, as well as members of corporate entities such as departments, disciplines,and universities, we each will find ourselves forced to choose. Which in the end is more important to us? Social justice? Or truth?

Perhaps I am more optimistic than Haidt, even Polyanna-ish; for my own part, however, I do not see the two goals he identifies, truth and social justice, as necessarily incompatible. Social justice can be pursued most effectively when it is grounded in a clear-eyed grasp of the reality it seeks to change. To get to 'ought', one might say, we have to start with 'is'. Then again, much depends on how we define 'social justice'. Dangers arise when the pursuit of social justice refuses to take into account the conditions of the world 'as is', especially human fallibility, and instead operates 'as if' the world already were or ever could be some other, simpler moral universe. As Thomas Mann warns, 'Complete justice, with no injustice remaining, is simply an ideal goal that can only be approximated. If, for example, injustice is thrown out from one side, it slips in again from the other, for injustice is deeply embedded in the human character.'[177] We enable injustice one way or another, either by being too severe or by being too lax, if we strip human nature of inherent complications such as personal responsibility, choice, and the possibility of repentance.[178]

In the present case, we fool ourselves and, much worse, place the vulnerable in danger, if we talk and write as if Falstaff were a victim rather than a perpetrator: 'a man more sinned against than sinning', as Lear says of himself (III, ii, 59). What are we teaching our students when we praise Falstaff for his unrepentant licence? Is taking advantage of the Mistress Quicklys of this world, for instance, to be laughed off as a joke? In the second part of *Henry IV*, we learn Falstaff has sworn to marry Mistress Quickly and make her a 'lady'; she recounts every detail of the proposal with painful precision. Citing his 'word as a gentleman', he convinces this 'poor widow' to pawn, not just a tapestry, but the dishes themselves that she uses to serve her customers, even her own gown, if need be, in order to cover his debts and preserve his affection. She herself is distraught, but Falstaff takes it all in stride. And as he does, the comedy starts to wear thin; a certain sadness and unease creeps in, at least for those of us who have encountered such behaviour in real life. 'You'll pay me all together?' Mistress Quickly asks plaintively, just before he leaves. But we know he will not.

Are we so indifferent to Falstaff's sense of class privilege? Male entitlement? Are we not able to see past entertaining malapropisms to the human being underneath? 'I have borne, and borne, and borne, and have been fubbed off, and fubbed off, and fubbed off, from this day to that day, that it is a shame to be thought on. There is no honesty in such dealing; unless a woman should be made an ass and a beast, to bear every knave's wrong' (2H4 II, i, 38–41). Mistress Quickly aside, what about the 'pitiful rascals', 'exceeding poor and bare', whom Falstaff forces into military service? 'I have misused the King's press damnably', he admits. 'There's not three of my hundred and fifty left alive, and they are for the town's end, to beg during life' (1H4 IV, iii, 63; V, iii, 36–8). How a critic or theatre-maker committed to progressive politics can continue to celebrate Falstaff after such abuses of power come to light, I find difficult to understand. It is easy enough for us to conclude, from the relative safety of our ivory tower, that Falstaff's 'freedom' is to be glorified, even imitated, rather than a selfish, unsustainable attempt at moral autonomy. But there are real-world consequences to our perpetuation of this Romantic myth.[179]

The lesson to be learned from Falstaff is not simply that criminals and conmen can be glamourous but also that they are harmful and, in the end, self-destructive. Nor is that self-destruction the sublime apodiabolosis, that is, inverse apotheosis, of the Byronic antihero. In Shakespeare's plays, the unrepentant antinomian, including here Iago and Richard III, as well as Falstaff, ends up not only defeated but also diminished; disenchanted; unmasked as less than he imagines himself to be, in his earlier delusions of grandeur. Part of social justice is protecting potential victims from such wilful victimisers, which is only possible if we recognise that individuals can make ethical mistakes. People can choose evil and, like Falstaff, refuse to change their ways; in which case, at some point, they need to be constrained to prevent them from doing further harm. Proclaiming that the vices such characters indulge are somehow praiseworthy virtues, albeit of a different sort, will not help the cause of social justice. On the contrary, this Romantic delusion will only make social justice all the more difficult to discern, much less secure through any kind of effective public policy. Like Byronism, Falstaff's parasitic 'freedom' is not in the end compatible with any kind of lasting, cooperative good.

Notes

1. Whitehead, *Process*, pp. 18, 21, 39.
2. Empson, 'Falstaff', p. 135. Cp. Bradley, 'Rejection', pp. 274–5; Carver, 'Influence', and Shakespeare, *2 Henry IV*, ed. Johnson, p. 522: 'None of Shakespeare's plays are more read than *The First and Second Parts of Henry the Fourth*.'
3. Blake, 'Marriage', p. 182.
4. Fish, *Surprised*, p. x.
5. Morgann, *Essay*, p. 2.
6. Morgann, 'Preface', pp. 3, 8.
7. Shakespeare, *2 Henry IV*, ed. Johnson, pp. 523–4.
8. Boswell, *Life*, 4:192 n. 1.
9. Shakespeare, *Othello*, ed. Johnson, 1047. For an example of Iago 'stealing upon esteem', see Greenblatt, *Renaissance Self-Fashioning*, pp. 233–52.
10. Cochran, 'Byron and Shakespeare', p. 203.
11. Blessington, *Conversations*, pp. 203–4; cited in Levao, 'Byron's Falstaff', p. 127.
12. Knight, *Byron and Shakespeare*, pp. 132–3.
13. Cochran, 'Byron's Legacy, and Byron's Inheritance', p. 176.
14. Bloom, *Iago*, 4; cp. Bloom, *Visionary Company*, pp. 245–6.
15. See, for example, Burton, 'Dark History'.
16. Barzun, 'Byron and the Byronic', p. 50.
17. J. Dover Wilson, *Fortunes*, p. 7.
18. Empson, 'Falstaff', pp. 135, 138.
19. Empson, '*Hamlet*', pp. 17, 21, 37–8, 31.
20. Nuttall, '*Hamlet*', p. 57.
21. On Empson's turbulent life and idiosyncratic criticism, with a focus on his essays on Shakespeare, see Engle, 'William Empson'.
22. Empson, 'Falstaff', p. 136.
23. Patrick Gray, 'Reply', pp. 198–9.
24. Shackel, 'Vacuity', pp. 298–9.
25. Kott, *Shakespeare*, p. 3.
26. Dollimore, *Radical Tragedy*. See also McAlindon, 'Cultural Materialism'.
27. Wilniewczyc, 'Two Directions', pp. 26–7; cp. Kott, 'Theatre', p. 3.
28. 'Byłem przerażony. Myślałem, że zawalił się świat', in Kott, *Contributions*, p. 111.
29. Kott, *Shakespeare*, p. 37.
30. Ibid. pp. 30–1.
31. Empson, '*Hamlet*', p. 20.
32. On similarities between Montaigne's view of history and Saint Augustine's, see, esp., Starobinski, '"To Preserve"'.
33. Kott, *Shakespeare*, p. 33.
34. Ibid. pp. 40, 16, 62, 31.

35. Foucault, 'Nietzsche', pp. 154–5.
36. Kott, *Shakespeare*, p. 267; cp. Rhodri Lewis, *Hamlet*, pp. 26, 41, on Falstaff as a symbol of 'opportunistic nominalism', as well as the relation between Shakespeare and Hobbes.
37. Kott, *Shakespeare*, pp. 87, 99.
38. Henrich, 'Weirdest'; cp. Haidt, *Righteous*, and Henrich, *WEIRDest*.
39. Rothman and Lichter, 'Vanishing'.
40. Gross and Simmons, 'Views'.
41. Langbert, 'Homogenous'. The author draws his sample from the fifty institutions in the top sixty-six in the *U.S. News and World Report* which are located in states that disclose voter registration.
42. Halsey, *Donnish*; cp. Adekoya, Kaufmann, and Simpson, *Academic*, p. 47.
43. Samuel J. Abrams, 'Professors Moved Left'.
44. Carl, 'Intelligence'.
45. Morgan et al., 'Socioeconomic'.
46. On other forms of self-selection, see Gross and Fosse, 'Why', as well as Neil Gross, *Why are Professors Liberal?* But note the critique of their methods and conclusions in Langbert, 'Neil Gross'. Like Kaufmann, 'Academic Freedom', Langbert sees reason to suspect viewpoint discrimination as a contributing factor, in addition to more benign forms of self-selection.
47. Chomsky, *American Power*; Kotkin, *New Class Conflict*. On 'Boston Brahmins', cp. Samuel J. Abrams much more recently on the unusually 'pronounced' liberalism of 'the New England professoriate' in Abrams, 'Not in These States'.
48. Cp. Chua, *Political Tribes*.
49. Al-Gharbi, 'Elitism'; cp. Joslyn and Haider-Markel, 'Who Knows Best?', as well as Stanovitch, *Bias*.
50. MacIntyre, *After Virtue*, pp. 1–2.
51. Nietzsche, *Gay Science*, §125. On this passage as an allusion to Lady Macbeth's madness ('Who will wipe this blood off of us?'), see Cummings, *Mortal Thoughts*, pp. 5–6.
52. Aristotle, *Rhetoric* 1373b.
53. Rom. 2:14–15.
54. See, esp., Greville, *Treatie of Humane Learning*.
55. On this aspect of Hobbes' thought, see R. S. White, *Natural Law*, pp. 12–16, and Rommen, *Natural Law*, pp. 72–7.
56. Pasnau, *Metaphysical Themes*, p. 3.
57. See, esp., the work of Stephen Gaukroger, as well as Pasnau, *Metaphysical Themes*.
58. Descartes, *Correspondence*, p. 148 (To Regius, 1642).
59. For a controversial but nonetheless intriguing recent analogue of Aristotle's thought on teleology, see also Nagel, *Mind and Cosmos*.
60. Bacon, *New Organon*, pp. 44–5.

61. For an earlier, longer and more sympathetic treatment of this passage, sensitive to Hume's characteristic irony, see also MacIntyre, 'Hume'.

62. Hume, *Human Nature*, p. 171.

63. See, esp., Carraud, *Causa sive ratio*.

64. Hume, *Human Nature*, p. 469.

65. On 'normative facts' within the context of contemporary moral realism, see Parfit, *On What Matters*; Larmore's review essay on Parfit, 'Morals and Metaphysics'; Larmore, *Autonomy of Morality*; and, esp., Larmore, *Morality and Metaphysics*.

66. MacIntyre, *After Virtue*, p. 51.

67. Hume, *Human Understanding*, p. 113.

68. Montaigne, *Essays*, II: 12, 418–19.

69. Riker, 'Al-Ghazali', p. 323.

70. Al-Ghazali, *Tahāfut al-falāsifah* ('The Incoherence of the Philosophers'), cited in Averroes, *Tahāfut al-tahāfut* ('The Incoherence of the Incoherence'), 1: 316. Together with Sextus Empiricus, al-Ghazali seems to have been one of Hume's sources, albeit indirectly; see Groarke and Solomon, 'Some Sources', pp. 659–62.

71. On Bacon's reimagining of formal causation, see Ott, '*Leges sive Natura*'. On the persistence of formal causation in Descartes' thought despite his efforts to discard it, see Flage and Bonnen, 'Descartes'. Cp. Hübner, 'Significance', on Spinoza.

72. On analogous premises within American pragmatism, as well as their application to Shakespeare studies, see Engle, 'Pragmatism'.

73. Borges, 'Funes', p. 94.

74. Luria, *Mnemonist*, p. 9; cited in Verberne, 'Hypermnesia', p. 254.

75. Dennett, 'Précis', pp. 503, 495.

76. Nagel, *View from Nowhere*, p. 6. See also Nagel, *Mind and Cosmos*.

77. Montaigne, *Essays*, II: 12, 435.

78. Patrick Gray, '"HIDE THY SELFE"', p. 232.

79. For nineteenth- and early twentieth-century critics on Hamlet as sceptic, including but not limited to Turgenev and Bradley, see Cefalu, '"Damnèd Custom"', esp. pp. 401–2 and 412.

80. Montaigne, *Essays*, II: 12, 419.

81. Montaigne, *Essays*, II: 29, 533.

82. Hume, *Human Nature*, pp. 264–5, 268–9. For further discussion of these passages, as well as the more general question of the 'durability' of scepticism, see Ribiero, 'Hume's Changing Views'.

83. Berlin, *Roots of Romanticism*, pp. 20, 114, 119.

84. MacIntyre, *After Virtue*, p. 60.

85. For the intellectual history in the *longue durée* leading up to present-day controversies over legal recognition of transgender identity, with reference to Rousseau, Freud, Marx, Marcuse and 'expressive individualism', see, esp., Trueman, *Modern Self*.

86. Charles Taylor, 'Politics'.

87. See, esp., Brague, *Kingdom of Man.*
88. Bacon, *New Organon*, pp. 100, 102.
89. Descartes, *Discourse*, p. 35.
90. Berlin, *Roots of Romanticism*, p. 89.
91. Fichte, *Sämmtliche Werke*, 2: 264–5; cited in Berlin, *Roots of Romanticism*, p. 89.
92. Bacon, *New Organon*, p. 102; cp. Brague, *Kingdom of Man.*
93. Haidt, *Righteous Mind*, p. 180.
94. Maritain, *Peasant*, pp. 21–2.
95. Sowell, *Conflict of Visions*; cp. Sowell, *Vision of the Anointed.*
96. On the ongoing 'gentrification of the left', see, esp.y, al-Gharbi, *Woke*, as well as Kotkin, *Neo-Feudalism.*
97. Patrick Gray, *Shakespeare and the Fall*; see also Patrick Gray, 'Reply' and 'Shakespeare and the Other Virgil'.
98. Dollimore, *Radical Tragedy*, pp. 41, 49.
99. Hannibal Hamlin, *Bible*. On *King Lear*, see also Jason Crawford, 'Shakespeare's Liturgy'.
100. Dollimore, *Radical Tragedy*, pp. 11, 16, 18, 173.
101. Ibid. pp. 19, 50, 39; cp. Rhodri Lewis, *Hamlet*, p. 307.
102. Bernard Williams, *Moral Luck*. Cp. Nussbaum, *Fragility*, as well as Cummings, *Mortal Thoughts*, pp. 228–35.
103. Bouwsma, 'Two Faces', pp. 24–6
104. Plato, *Republic* 360e–367e.
105. Ibid. 571–80; cp. Bristol, 'Macbeth the Philosopher', pp. 658–9.
106. See, for example, Long on the 'Socratic legacy of self-mastery', pp. 142–53, in Long, 'Hellenistic Ethics'.
107. See, esp., Sorabji, *Emotion.*
108. Saint Clement of Alexandria, *Stromata* ('Miscellanies') 5.14, comparing Plato, *Republic* 361e to Wis. 2:12.
109. For analogous passages in *Hamlet* and *Measure for Measure*, as well as their theological context, see Gillies, 'Original Sin'.
110. Montaigne, *Essays*, II: 12, 458. This conclusion is slightly different in the versions of Montaigne's *Essays* published during Montaigne's own lifetime. 'He will rise, if God lends him his hand; he will rise by abandoning and renouncing his own means, and letting himself be raised and uplifted by divine grace; but not otherwise' (Frame translation, 458 n. 66).
111. Montaigne, *Essays*, II: 2, 250–1.
112. Montaigne, *Essays*, II: 12, 327, 321.
113. William M. Hamlin, *Montaigne's English Journey*, pp. 72–3. Cp. Wee, 'Montaigne'.
114. Montaigne, *Essays*, II: 12, 327.
115. Dollimore, *Radical Tragedy*, pp. 39–40; Montaigne, *Essays*, II:12, 327.
116. Montaigne, *Essays*, II: 12, 326. Cp. Saint Cyril of Alexandria, *Thesaurus* 34 and *In Joannem* 11; quoted in Burghardt, *Image of God,*

p. 72. In his *De anima*, 412b, Aristotle presents the soul as the form of the body. So, too, for Saint Cyril, God is the form of the soul.

117. Montaigne, *Essays*, I: 23, 83, 86.
118. Brown, *Religious*, p. 96; cited in Heck, 'Montaigne's Conservatism', p. 165.
119. Baggini, 'Hume Paradox'.
120. On the relation between scepticism and social quietism, including further details on Sextus Empiricus, see Laursen, *Politics of Skepticism*, as well as William M. Hamlin, *Montaigne's English Journey*, 87–8. Cp. Hartle on 'the limits of politics' in Hartle, *Accidental Philosopher*, pp. 220–2.
121. Hume, *Human Understanding*, p. 44. Cp. Rorty on 'solidarity' in Rorty, *Contingency*, as well as Larmore, *Autonomy of Morality*, p. 30.
122. Mann, 'Reflections', p. 105.
123. Montaigne, *Essays*, I:23, 88.
124. Chesterton, *Thing*, p. 157.
125. Montaigne, *Essays*, II:12, 320.
126. Dollimore, *Radical Tragedy*, pp. 173, 21.
127. Frame, 'Did Montaigne Betray Sebond?', p. 297.
128. On Armaingaud, see Schaefer, 'Arthur Armaingaud'. On Gide and Montaigne, see Guggenheim and Strawn, 'Gide and Montaigne'. The most prolific exponent of this point of view in more recent decades is David Lewis Schaefer; see Schaefer, *Political Philosophy*; James Supple's essay-length review, 'Armaingaud Rides Again'; and Schaefer's response to Supple, 'Montaigne'.
129. Desan, *Montaigne*, pp. 387–91, 621–7; cp. Boutcher, *School of Montaigne*, 1: 284–93.
130. Dréano, *Renommée*, p. 321.
131. See esp. Strauss, 'Some Remarks'; cp. Strauss, *Maimonides*. Kenneth Hart Green sums up what he takes to be Strauss's conclusion in Green, *Leo Strauss*, pp. 158–9: 'Reason needs revelation precisely in order to remain reasonable.' As Green notes, however, '*the* essential conflict in interpreting Straus himself among students of his thought centers on what one camp contends is Strauss's atheism and another camp maintains is his piety and patriotism', otherwise known as the clash between the so-called East Coast and West Coast Straussians. For an opposing perspective, see Schaefer, 'Montaigne and Leo Strauss'.
132. Frye, *Shakespeare and Christian Doctrine*, p. 4.
133. Frame, 'Did Montaigne Betray Sebond?', p. 297.
134. For an early account of this change, see Jackson and Marotti, 'Turn to Religion'.
135. Brian Cummings, *Mortal Thoughts*, p. 14.
136. Shuger, 'Subversive Fathers', p. 46.
137. Greenblatt, 'Invisible Bullets'. See also McAlindon, 'Testing'.

138. Greenblatt explores the possibility of such a synthesis in Greenblatt, *Shakespeare's Freedom*. See also Fernie, *Shakespeare for Freedom*, pp. 57–8.
139. Holbrook, *Shakespeare's Individualism*, p. 23.
140. Fernie, *Shakespeare for Freedom*, p. 1.
141. Jeffrey R. Wilson, 'Why Shakespeare?', pp. 36, 38, 53.
142. Gide, 'Montaigne', p. 69.
143. Friedrich, *Montaigne*, p. 2.
144. Desan, *Montaigne*, p. 630.
145. Boutcher, *School of Montaigne*, pp. lxiv, 375, 379, lxv. Boutcher cites work by George Hoffman, Jean Balsamo and Katherine Almquist; see also Desan, *Montaigne*.
146. Felicity Green, *Life of Freedom*. Cp. Skinner, *Liberty before Liberalism*.
147. For opposition to the strong distinction in kind between liberalism and republicanism Skinner posits in *Liberty before Liberalism*, see discussion and related bibliography in Patrick Gray, 'Reply', p. 196. On Shakespeare and 'degree', see also Gray and Samely, 'Shakespeare and Henri Lefebvre'. On Montaigne as supposed 'proto-democrat', see Williamson, 'Liberalizing'.
148. Patrick Gray, '"HIDE THY SELFE"', pp. 220–1. On misinterpreting this aspect of Seneca's thought as Stoic rather than Epicurean, see Patrick Gray, *Shakespeare and the Fall of the Roman Republic*, pp. 57–8.
149. Scholar, *Art of Free-Thinking*, pp. 7, 6, 17; cp. Nuttall, *Shakespeare the Thinker*.
150. Ovid, *Metamorphosis*, trans. Golding, p. 185.
151. Scholar, *Art of Free-Thinking*, p. 16. Cp. Sayce on Montaigne as 'conservative and revolutionary' in Sayce, *Essays*, pp. 233–59.
152. Carl Schmitt, 'Counterrevolutionary', p. 63.
153. Carl Schmitt, *Concept of the Political*.
154. See, esp., Hochuli, 'Brazilianization', for a compelling global overview. For specific countries, in addition to Kotkin, *New Class Conflict*, Lind, *New Class War*, Deneen, *Why Liberalism Failed*, and al-Gharbi, *Woke* (United States), see also Goodhart, *Road to Somewhere* (United Kingdom), and Guilluy, *Twilight* (France).
155. Pouilloux, *Montaigne*.
156. 'Distortions régénératrices de concepts, configurations énigmatiques ou aporetiques, silences marqués, multiplication des perspectives, discordances.' Tournon, '"*Route par ailleurs*"', p. 310; cited in Felicity Green, 'Reading Montaigne', pp. 1092–3. Cp. the chapter on Montaigne in Cave, *Cornucopian Text*, as well as Cave, 'Problems of Reading'.
157. Felicity Green, 'Reading Montaigne', p. 1093.
158. Derrida, *Of Grammatology*; cp. M. H. Abrams, 'Construing and Deconstructing'.
159. J. Hillis Miller, 'On Edge', pp. 195–6.

160. Patrick Gray, 'Faith and Doubt'; see also Patrick Gray, 'Seduced by Romanticism'. Cp. Larmore on Montaigne in Larmore, 'Scepticisme sans tranquillité'; Empson's interest in 'an author's struggle to live well' in Engle, 'William Empson'; and J. Hillis Miller, 'George Poulet'.

161. All citations of Shakespeare's plays are from the Samuel Johnson edition: *Johnson on Shakespeare*, ed. Sherbo.

162. Bradley, 'Rejection', and J. Dover Wilson, *Fortunes*.

163. Bradley, 'Rejection', pp. 272–3, 260.

164. Fernie, *Shakespeare for Freedom*, pp. 2–3. Cp. Bloom, *Falstaff*. On Shakespeare and Rabelais' Abbaye de Thélème, see Gray and Samely, 'Shakespeare and Henri Lefebvre', pp. 79ff.

165. Bradley, 'Rejection', p. 263.

166. See, e.g., Samenow, *Criminal Mind*, as well as Yochelson and Samenow, *Criminal Personality*. For a more sympathetic take on what Falstaff represents, in terms of male 'anti-social behaviour' in the present, see Bayley, *No Boys Play Here*.

167. J. Dover Wilson, *Fortunes*, p. 128. Cp. Auden, 'The Prince's Dog'.

168. J. Dover Wilson, *Fortunes*, pp. 20, 122, 3.

169. Braden, 'Senecan Tragedy'; cp. Patrick Gray, 'Shakespeare vs. Seneca'.

170. William M. Hamlin, '"Repentance"', pp. 551–2. In like vein but with different emphases, cp. Patrick Gray, '"HIDE THY SELFE"'.

171. Friedrich, *Montaigne*, p. 2.

172. Kaufmann, 'Academic Freedom'. See also Chamlee-Wright, 'Self-Censorship'.

173. Sendak, *Wild Things*.

174. Montaigne, *Essays*, II: 12, 328.

175. Haidt, 'Why'; cp. Friedersdorf, 'Truth vs. Social Justice'.

176. Matt. 6:24.

177. Mann, 'Reflections', p. 105.

178. See, e.g., Dalrymple, 'Sex and the Shakespeare Reader'. On personal responsibility, choice and repentance in Shakespeare's thought about ethics, see Patrick Gray, 'Shakespeare versus Aristotle'.

179. See Dalrymple, *Life at the Bottom* and *Our Culture*, esp. the first chapter, 'The Frivolity of Evil'; cp. Rob Henderson, '"Luxury Beliefs"' and 'Thorstein Veblen's Theory of the Leisure Class'.

Afterword: A Philosophical Shakespeare or a Dramatic Montaigne?

George Hoffmann

Facile celebration nips at the heels of Montaigne and Shakespeare ready-framed and laden with admiration. Placing the two together multiplies the temptation to project on to them qualities one wishes to possess today. A particular tradition of reading Montaigne as proto-liberal freethinker, born out of the politics of France's Third Republic and refracted through a willing Anglo-American context by Donald Frame has wreathed the Renaissance author in modern attitudes.[1] His anachronistic moral portrait risks in turn enabling related projects regarding Shakespeare, as Lars Engle argues. Compassion, sympathy, toleration, non-violence and relativism appeared as virtues to neither of their worlds and yet are routinely 'recognised' in their works.[2]

Beyond authorising discussion of modern values in the sixteenth century, Montaigne's presence serves to license philosophical readings of Shakespeare. But philosophy at the time meant something starkly different from abstract reflection, as Alison Calhoun reminds us in drawing attention to the central importance that biographical sketches of philosophers held for their early modern audience.[3] The way that Shakespeare embodied viewpoints in characters proves not so removed from how Montaigne understood schools of thought to be embodied in their founders' lives – something that a generation of French philosophers newly reinvested in rehabilitating Montaigne's philosophical profile would do well to remember.

A number of essays in this collection compare Montaigne's and Shakespeare's attitudes towards scepticism, such as Richard Dillane's tonic rereading of Hamlet's 'To be' soliloquy. After more than a century of easy celebration of Montaigne the sceptic, it is refreshing to read here demurring voices that nuance this received wisdom. To search in the sixteenth century's rediscovery of Sextus Empiricus a recipe for questioning established political and religious orders is to indulge in an anachronistic exercise, as William M. Hamlin makes clear in exploring the qualified appreciation of belief one finds in both authors.[4] Moreover, Montaigne's method of thought fit only imperfectly into sceptical schools, as David Schalkwyk discusses. Montaigne emphasised inquisitiveness over Pyrrhonism's *ataraxia*, or tranquility, and engagement over *epochē*, or suspension of judgement – what Charles Larmore calls an unconventional and 'dynamic' scepticism.[5] Perhaps most surprisingly, Cassie Miura beautifully exhumes the rich diversity of attitudes that the sceptical tradition entailed, including elaborate therapeutic and comic uses far removed from rigid institutional definitions of philosophy.[6]

Maria Devlin McNair posits instead a stoic Montaigne, a view that runs counter to the bulk of current Montaigne scholarship. Returning to stoicism after more than a century of discredit holds great interest: if Montaigne breaks with the Neostoical emphasis on constancy, he often does so through mobilising the more capacious resources of classical stoicism.[7] Yet, even here, Montaigne's position proves highly unorthodox: in an essay discussing possible responses to the threat of assassination, Montaigne cites Caesar who, 'entrusting himself to the protection of the gods and of fortune', 'trusted himself and his fortune'. Montaigne adapts the attitude to his own nonchalance in which, rather than affirming stoic invulnerability to fortune, he throws himself onto its mercy.[8] Episodes such as these acquire a strange allure from the way in which Montaigne presents an abdication of agency as heroic and in which he fashions the gracious acceptance of 'moral luck' into a kind of virtue of serendipity.

The French did not read Montaigne as a philosopher but as an informal noble advisor.[9] The offhand name-dropping that placed him among high nobility at various political junctures, his early and thereafter frequent reference to France's Italian campaigns and his father's participation in them, and the ostentatious discretion with which he referred either to confidences from, or rumours about, high figures at court would perhaps have been hard to parse for an English audience. But it is difficult not to think that they would quickly have grasped his distinctly unscholarly treatment of classical materials, as Richard Hillman illustrates regarding Montaigne's unconventional handling of Ovid. Montaigne presented his Latin learning in an idiosyncratic and flamboyantly amateur light; at times his cavalier attitude towards the classics could prove shocking, at others, beguilingly recreative and playful. But nothing could be further from the French reception of the *Essays* than the picture of an erudite Montaigne: nowhere does a 'university' smell emanate from the *Essays*.

The skilled profile that did suit Montaigne was that of a legal professional. True, he seemed eager to hide his legal training in the *Essays*, nowhere alluding to nearly the decade he served as judge in Bordeaux's regional sovereign Parlement. Yet, while the challenging technical analyses of the late and deeply regretted André Tournon have not encouraged many to delve into the labyrinth of renaissance jurisprudence, a legal perspective everywhere informs Montaigne's outlook.[10] This becomes particularly salient in Montaigne's response to political cruxes, specifically those that seek to articulate the individual's relation to the body politic, which William McKenzie studies, and thus proves relevant to questions of liberalism, which Patrick Gray explores. Richard Scholar's intriguing suggestion that one needs to study Shakespeare's legal moments, particularly in trial scenes, fittingly offers rich grounds for comparison with Montaigne.

If laying down the law and designating exceptions to it define sovereignty, jurisdiction defines the law. Jurisdiction establishes the scope of when and where the law applies, who falls under its enforcement, and who judges its infraction. Jurisdiction draws the boundaries that lend law (and hence sovereignty) its force: law comes into being only through jurisdiction.[11] Yet, jurisdiction proved hardly a simple matter in pre-modern Europe. Nowhere did the problem of determining jurisdiction prove more acute than in sixteenth-century France, riven by parallel royal, seigneurial, municipal and ecclesiastical court systems each with competing hierarchies and all exerting claims of authority. Occasionally, these conflicts proved so intractable that a particular locality switched annually between tribunals: on the eve of the French Revolution nearly two thousand parishes followed this arrangement.[12] Since most judges earned wages by the case, they naturally vied for the right to hear appeals. A typical suit could see at least four separate appeals to different courts.[13] As judgment of last resort, Parlements sorted out the various judgments of lower courts; their officers thus stood as the recognised experts on thorny questions of jurisdiction.

It comes as no surprise, then, that in the *Essays* Montaigne invokes jurisdiction as both a diagnostic and a solution regarding a wide array of issues. One's health amounts to respecting one's internal organic jurisdiction, or: 'If we did not disturb within our members the jurisdiction that belongs to them in this matter, it is probable that we should be better off.'[14] Moral life depends as well on an internal jurisdiction: 'our judgment, laying upon another the blame which is then in question, should not spare us from judging ourselves [*d'une interne jurisdiction*]'.[15] Grave political and social matters of his time lent themselves to the same analysis: the Reformation essentially boiled down to the desire to 'subject public and immutable institutions and observances to the instability of a private fantasy (private reason has only private jurisdiction)'.[16] Montaigne circumscribes the *Essays* as a whole within the purview of personal jurisdiction: 'I speak my mind freely on all things, even on those which perhaps exceed my capacity and which I by no means hold to be within my jurisdiction.'[17] Elsewhere, he defines the private individual as a 'magistrate without jurisdiction'.[18] Jurisdiction rested on the principle of *suum cuique*, 'to each one's own', foundation of the law since Cicero (*On the Nature of the Gods*, III, 38) and Justinian (*Institutes*, 1, 1, 4) and a famous definition of justice dating to Plato (*Republic*, IV, 433b).[19] It thus allowed Montaigne to envision a resolution to the Wars of Religion, a reconciliation between private liberty and political obligation, and the proper course of moral action.

Many of this volume's essays contrast Montaigne and Shakespeare according to the genre of their works; the distinction between essay and play in turn authorises further oppositions between the rhetorical and the dramatic, between thinker and writer, philosopher and playwright. What gets left out of these contrasts is the properly dramaturgical mode of the *Essays* themselves, their 'latent theatricality' as Hamlin has remarked in studying John Florio's keen response to the dramatic potential of the *Essays*.[20] In the latter half of this Afterword, I will argue that a sceptical attitude involved for Montaigne an exercise in acting.

The essay on assassination mentioned above allows one to examine the theatrical dimension if the *Essays* with particular precision.[21] 'Various Events from the Same Counsel' (I: 23) proves notable for how it breaks from what had preoccupied Montaigne up until then, a narrow engagement with stoic valour dressed with appropriate historical allusions to adapt it to suit the French nobility.[22] This essay inaugurates a more idiosyncratic form of heroism rooted in a sceptical demeanour by foregrounding the question of what bearing one should adopt towards risk in the absence of foresight, or *phronesis*.[23]

After relating an anecdote told to him by Jacques Amyot, the famous French translator of Plutarch, Montaigne proceeds to imitate Plutarch in the freewheeling manner similar to that described by N. Amos Rothchild, fielding a series of comparisons between a classical paragon and a modern-day exemplar: Augustus with François de Guise, Alexander with Henri de Navarre, and Caesar with Tristan de Moneins. Alone among the moderns, Montaigne maintains his composure during an episode occurring during his mayoralty, in which he matches Caesar's serenity in the face of rumours of assassination. Against generally critical views of the Roman general in the essayist's milieu, Montaigne implicitly compares himself to the 'generous' Caesar found in the late 1540s proto-tragedy by Jean-Antoine Muret, *Julius Caesar*, the first tragedy to devote itself to the emperor's assassination and one that may have inspired the more overtly heroic postures of Shakespeare's Caesar.[24]

Muret's play debuted in Montaigne's *collège* at a time when Montaigne himself often played leading roles. Shorter in stature and three years junior to his peers at school, he must have begun with the roles of youths in school plays and very likely those of maidens. But lingering on as an *artiens* student after he graduated from the *collège* in 1547,[25] Montaigne now fell among the oldest students and was almost certainly the school's most experienced actor. More to the point, when he considers in 'Various events' the advice to accept death 'a better one, I think, than to remain in continual fever over an accident that has no remedy,' he seems to be translating from memory a line spoken by Muret's Caesar, 'but better by far to die at once than to be oppressed by continual fear'.[26]

Muret's Caesar constitutes the most likely 'leading part' Montaigne remembers having played in the *Essays*. Like Polonius, who 'did enact Julius Caesar' (*Ham* III, ii, 109), Montaigne betrays no small pride in his youthful theatrical prowess. But, unlike Polonius, he modelled the role into a personal attitude of knowing detachment in face of threat. The word Montaigne associates most closely with his theatrical apprenticeship is 'assurance', the quality that earned him top roles. [27] Seemingly taken from Muret's depiction of Caesar's sangfroid as *securus* (183 and 322), 'assurance' returns in the *Essays* like clockwork in situations where one confronts danger with considered fearlessness. Montaigne thus projected his boyhood memory of Caesar on to Henry of Navarre whose conflict with Henri de Guise begins to resemble, in Jean Balsamo's words, a 'modern avatar of the battle between Caesar and Pompey'[28]:

> In those [accidents] that have no remedy he at once makes up his mind to bear them . . . he composedly awaits what may ensue. In truth, I have seen him at work, maintaining a great nonchalance and freedom in his actions and countenance throughout very great and thorny affairs.

But he also attributed Caesar's 'assured' demeanour to ordinary folk: 'How many low-born people do we see led to death – and not a simple death, but mingled with shame and sometimes with grievous torments – bringing to it such assurance.' And to cannibal prisoners, 'He who relaxes none of his assurance, no matter how great the danger of imminent death; who, giving up his soul, still looks firmly and scornfully at his enemy.' Or to the woman of Céa who ends her own life in taking 'the cup that held the poison with a steady [assured] hand'.[29]

But, most importantly, Montaigne claimed this standard of heroic conduct for himself. At the end of a chapter that Anita Gilman Sherman studies in detail, Montaigne recounts the story of a band of armed soldiers invading his chateau. Feigning fear for their lives, these assailants gained entry to Montaigne's chateau where they quickly outnumbered him and his servants. Once Montaigne realises the danger, he 'commits himself to Fortune and abandons himself bodily into her arms' and continues to extend courtesy to the visitors, ultimately disarming them with his openness.[30] In Montaigne's copy of Caesar's *Commentarii de Bello Civili*, he annotated a passage portraying Caesar as *confisus*, confident or assured: 'Caesar trusting in his good fortune more than in the number of his men' (III, 106.3).[31]

Muret's stroke of brilliance lay in taking the 'confident' Caesar of historical record and recasting the portrait as an explicit role. Muret's Caesar steps on to the stage expounding on his name and stature, costume and character (ll. 8, 11, 36, 48–51), before anticipating his imminent apotheosis (l. 31). Once he attains divinity, Caesar dispassionately regards his former human nature as mere *simulacra* or *umbra* (ll. 537–8). Few places in the *Essays* show Montaigne's adaption of this idea of social role as character part to better effect than does the one of his home invasion. In it, theatrical training affords poise akin to the aplomb that Shakespeare awarded his heroes.

Montaigne would extend the worth of thespian practice to all areas of life. The essay 'That Our Happiness Must Not be Judged until after Our Death' quotes Laberius lamenting that Caesar has forced him to play a role in a play ('I have lived one day longer than I should have'). Rather than posing an antithesis to the stage, however, the moment of death itself proves a 'role' one must play, for the 'assurance of a well-ordered soul, should never be attributed to a man until he has been seen to play the last act of his comedy'.[32] Death comes as each person's assassin, a killer that one must meet with either confidence or cowardice. Montaigne hopes to face his own end as did Caesar striding towards Brutus:

> Of all the wonders that I yet have heard,
> It seems to me most strange that men should fear;
> Seeing that death, a necessary end,
> Will come when it will come. (II, ii, 36–9)

Thus do great philosophical questions of fate, freedom and foreknowledge become in the *Essays* fundamentally theatrical questions. In this, Montaigne only followed classical precedent. According to Sextus, the sceptic 'shall attempt to fit in with the people around' and 'say what is not going to be laughed at'.[33] No matter the local dialect, the sceptic alters his speech, so that 'deftly responding to each occasion with just the right word, [h]e shall seem to speak faultless Greek' (*Against the Grammarians*, 235). Given the preschool Latin charade enacted for Montaigne's benefit back at the family's chateau, it is not hard to see why he should have identified later in life with this model of a philosopher who proved a linguistic parrot: 'I have an aping and imitative nature,' he confides. 'In Paris I speak a language somewhat different that at Montaigne.'[34] Skeptics played their part as if it merited conviction and certitude even while granting it neither in their hearts. This is exactly what Montaigne has just concluded in the preceding essay devoted to custom, or: 'the wise man should withdraw his soul within, out of the crowd . . . but as for externals, he should wholly follow the accepted fashions and forms.'[35] This is a point to which he will return two chapters later in 'Of the Education of Children', when he recommends his ideal pupil become 'fit for all nations and companies', following Alcibiades' ability to 'change so easily to suit such different fashions . . . So I would make my pupil.'[36]

The sceptic's versatility in adapting to the environment at hand arose from more than simple prudence; for Montaigne, it proved fully heroic. For, like Muret's Caesar, Sextus's sceptic 'is aware both of the instability of the world and the insecurity of events'.[3] Diogenes Laertius painted Pyrrho in an even more explicitly courageous stance, 'taking no precaution, but facing all risks as they come'.[38] These figures of the dispassionate philosopher and the fearless general merged in Montaigne's mind to produce serene self-assurance thanks to distancing from oneself as from a role. Read in context, the *Essays'* discussion of philosophical scepticism thus fashions a heroic posture for Montaigne that, at times, could serve rather unsceptical ends within the apologetic enterprise of his book.[39]

Shakespeare's relationship to Montaigne cannot fully be grasped until one appreciates the extent to which Montaigne's thinking manifested itself in intrinsically theatrical performance shot through with the postures and demeanour of colourful lives of philosophers like Pyrrho. This must have facilitated the embodiment of Montaignian attitudes in Shakespeare's characters that Engle argues regarding *The Tempest* or Miura regarding *Othello*. Montaigne did not serve as an empirical exemplar that Shakespeare seized upon and refashioned into, say, Hamlet; instead, Montaigne had already developed a complex persona in the essays that contrasted alert lucidity with sanguine acceptance to create an impression of deep character. Both Shakespeare and Montaigne, then, gravitated in their mature years towards studying how the mind can both inhibit and enable, using the tension between action and reflection to portray the kind of self-conflicted and divided subjectivity that Daniel Vitkus and Zorica Bečanović-Nikolić examine or the bitter-sweet mixture of affect discussed by Peter Platt. The hesitations and contradictions, discordances and vacillations, that they examine imply not only the split between knowledge and behaviour in Muret's Caesar but, more generally, the actor's double nature as both a character in a scene and a professional playing a part.

Even if Shakespeare had enjoyed no access to the *Essays*, Montaigne would have emerged as one of his major continental counterparts. Few authors from the time have acquired a comparable institutional stature and generated so considerable a critical infrastructure. Yet, the inevitability of their comparison does not guarantee its pertinence as Hamlin examines in this study's introduction. If the two authors' combined stature towers such that Engle can dwell on a *New Yorker* piece linking the two by resident pundit on all things French, Adam Gopnik, those links remain no less elusive and, at times, misleading thanks in no small part to the ways in which Montaigne has been cast as a liberal paragon before his time, a learned reader rather than playful one, and a philosopher who serves to lead one to Descartes.

Notes

1. Boutcher, 'Schooling America' and 'Awakening the Inner Man'; Keffer, *Publication History*.
2. The following studies suggest how little disposed Montaigne could prove towards a straightforward endorsement of these values: Ibbett, *Compassion's Edge*; Nazarian, 'Montaigne against Sympathy' and 'Montaigne

on Violence'; Dionne, *Montaigne, écrivain de la conciliation*, especially pp. 23–4, pp. 149–61; Fontana, 'Lâcher la bride'; Curley, 'Skepticism and Toleration'; and Shannon Connolly, 'Equity and Amerindians in Montaigne's "Des cannibales" (I, 31)'.

3. In addition to Calhoun, *Montaigne and the Lives of the Philosophers*, see Balsamo, 'La critique des dispositions testamentaires' and Desan, *Montaigne*.
4. Thorne, *Dialectic of Counter-Enlightenment*.
5. Larmore, 'Montaigne, Michel Eyquem de, 1533–1592', especially p. 982, and Larmore, 'Un scepticisme sans tranquillité'.
6. See, further, her PhD thesis, *Humor of Skepticism: Therapeutic Laughter from Montaigne to Milton*.
7. See Sebastian Prat's excellent *Constance et inconstance chez Montaigne*.
8. 'se fioit tant à soy et à sa fortune', 'se remettant à la garde des dieux et de la fortune' (I: 24, 130b, 131a; 95, 96). The first page number refers to *Les Essais*, ed. Villey, rev. Saulnier. The second number refers to *The Complete Works*, trans. Frame.
9. Boutcher, '"Le pauvre patient"'; Legros, 'Montaigne, son livre et son roi'.
10. *Montaigne: la glose et l'essai*; *Montaigne en toutes lettres*; *'Route par ailleurs.' Le 'Nouveau langage' des* Essais.
11. Cormack, *A Power to Do Justice*.
12. Mousnier, *Les Institutions de la France sous la monarchie absolue*, 2: 250, trans. Arthur Goldhammer, *The Institutions of France under the Absolute Monarchy*, 2: 252.
13. Doucet, *Les Institutions de la France au XVIe siècle*, 2: 516.
14. 'Si nous ne troublions pas en noz membres la jurisdiction qui leur appartient en cela, il est à croire que nous en serions mieux' (I: 14, 58c; 39 [cf. II: 17, 650a; 493]).
15. 'Mais j'entens que nostre jugement, chargeant sur un autre duquel pour lors il est question, ne nous espargne pas d'une interne jurisdiction' (III: 8, 930c; 710).
16. 'sousmettre les constitutions et observances publiques et immobiles à l'instabilité d'une privée fantasie (la raison privée n'a qu'une jurisdiction privée)' (I: 23, 121c; 88).
17. 'Je dy librement mon advis de toutes choses, voire et de celles qui surpassent à l'adventure ma suffisance, et que je ne tiens aucunement estre de ma jurisdiction' (II: 10, 410a; 298).
18. 'magistrat sans jurisdiction' (III: 9, 1001b; 766).
19. Cicero, *On the Nature of the Gods* III, 38; Justinian, *Institutes* 1, 1, 4; Plato, *Republic* IV, 433b.
20. Hamlin, *Montaigne's English Journey*, pp. 35–49, especially p. 38.
21. Hoffmann, 'Self-Assurance and Acting in the *Essais*'.
22. Quint, *Montaigne and the Quality of Mercy*; Posner, *The Performance of Nobility in Early Modern European Literature*, pp. 22–79.
23. On *phronesis* in the *Essays*, see Goyet, *Les Audaces de la prudence*.

24. Ayres, 'Shakespeare's *Julius Cæsar* in the Light of Some Other Versions'.
25. Trinquet, 'Recherches chronologiques sur la jeunesse de Marc-Antoine Muret', especially p. 278.
26. 'vaudroit-il mieux le prendre que de demeurer en la fievre continuelle d'un accident' (I: 24, 132a) is usually believed to derive from Suetonius's *insidias undique imminentis subire semel quam cavere semper sollicitum maluisse*, 'he elected to expose himself once for all to the plots that threatened him on every hand, rather than to be always anxious and on his guard' (p. 86), but lies closer to Muret's *sed tamen quando semel / Vel cadere praestat, quam metu longo premi* (pp. 385–6).
27. 'Une asseurance de visage, et souplesse de voix et de geste, à m'appliquer aux rolles que j'entreprenois' (I: 26, 176b; 131).
28. 'avatar moderne du combat entre César et Pompée,' in Balsamo, 'Montaigne et les grands hommes de son temps', p. 149.
29. 'elle print d'une main asseurée la coupe où estoit le venin' (II: 3, 361a; 261); 'Qui pour quelque dangier de la mort voisine ne relasche aucun point de son asseurance, qui regarde, encores, en rendant l'ame, son ennemy d'une veue ferme et desdaigneuse' (I: 31, 211a; 157); 'Combien voit-on de personnes populaires, conduictes à la mort, et non à une mort simple, mais meslée de honte et quelque fois de griefs tourmens, y apporter une telle asseurance' (I: 14, 51a; 34); '[aux accidents] qui n'ont point de remede, il se resout soudain à la souffrance ... il attend en repos ce qui s'en peut suyvre. De vray, je l'ay veu à mesme: maintenant une grande nonchalance et liberté d'actions et de visage, au travers de bien grands affaires et espineux' (III: 10, 1008b; 771).
30. 'suis homme en outre qui me commets volontiers à la fortune et me laisse aller à corps perdu entre ses bras' (III: 12, 1059–1060bc; 812–13).
31. 'Cesar se fiant en sa bone fortune plus qu'au nombre de ses homes', Alain Legros, 'Notes de lecture', in Montaigne, *Essais*, ed. Balsamo, Magnien, Magnien-Simonin and Legros, 1294, n. 700.
32. 'asseurance d'un'ame reglée, ne se doive jamais attribuer à l'homme qu'on ne luy aye veu jouer le dernier acte de sa comédie' (I: 19,79a; 55).
33. Sextus, *Against the Grammarians*, 234; cf. *Outlines of Pyrrhonism*, I, 17.
34. 'Or j'ay une condition singeresse et imitatrice', 'A Paris, je parle un langage aucunement autre qu'à Montaigne' (III: 5, 875bc; 667).
35. 'le sage doit au dedans retirer son ame de la presse ... mais, quant au dehors, qu'il doit suivre entierement les façons et formes receues' (I.23.118a; 86).
36. 'commode à toutes nations et compaignies ... se transformer si aisément à façons si diverses ... Tel voudrois-je former mon disciple' (I.26.166–7a; 123–4).
37. Sextus Empiricus, *Against the Ethicists*, p. 208.
38. Diogenes Laertius, *Lives of the Philosophers*, 9, 62.
39. Balsamo, 'Montaigne et les grands hommes de son temps'.

Afterword: A Philosophical Montaigne and a Dramatic Shakespeare?

Katharine Eisaman Maus

When I was a child, one of my favourite books was *Van Loon's Lives*, by Hendrik Willem Van Loon. Each chapter imagines a dinner party in which two or three famous artists, or queens, or philosophers, or conquerors, or spiritual leaders, or murderous fanatics, are welcomed from their different historical eras and parts of the globe to Van Loon's summer home in Zealand for a convivial evening. Van Loon's fellow Dutchman Desiderius Erasmus is invited to all the parties, both to serve as a translator and because Van Loon envisions him as socially omni-competent (although even Erasmus finds the Torquemada/Robespierre get-together unnerving and declines to attend). Van Loon's book captures what for many of us is an enduring fantasy: not merely, in Stephen Greenblatt's phrase, to 'speak with the dead', but to induce them into conversation with one another, and with us.[1]

The question of what William Shakespeare and Michel de Montaigne would have had to say to one another is an especially tantalising one. The textual evidence, summarised by William Hamlin in his introduction to this volume, is scanty but unmistakable: Shakespeare certainly encountered Montaigne in Florio's 1603 translation, possibly reading it several years earlier in manuscript. Yet Montaigne's presence in Shakespeare seems to exceed an occasional textual borrowing: it is more properly what Peter Platt calls a 'hovering and haunting',[2] a set of provocative resemblances, suggesting a convergence of sensibility between these two great writers. They are both remarkably independently minded: their lack of dogmatism permits an unusual openness to an imaginative apprehension of the classical past, and a marked capacity for empathy with marginal or stigmatised perspectives. Both gravitate to experimental, hybrid genres and emotionally complex psychological dilemmas. And both develop unprecedented, highly detailed ways to convey subjective experience: Bečanović-Nikolić, reading them through Ricœur, sees them as attempting to portray a fluctuating self that creates itself through narrative. As Lars Engle points out, all of these similarities seem especially pertinent because they put Shakespeare and Montaigne on the leading edge of what would eventually develop as a new way of being in the world: 'proto-modern and proto-liberal, eager to give voice to the other, anti-dogmatic, exploratory about sexuality and gender, committed to exposing the horrors of human cruelty, whether it is familial or erotic or religious or political'.[3] Or, in another formulation:

> Montaigne may have nudged Shakespeare after 1600 not merely to be more thoughtful, but also more self-indulgent, more moody, more appropriative, more content to delve into simply the thing he was. If Montaigne helped make that happen, he helped with something all Shakespeareans deem important.[4]

Because the resemblances between Montaigne and Shakespeare suggest a temperamental overlap, as much as 'influence' per se, many of the chapters in this volume are understandably more concerned with delineating the terms of that overlap than with describing a history of derivation. Gilman Sherman associates the outlaw scenes in *Two Gentlemen of Verona* with Montaigne's reflections upon suffering a home invasion and a kidnapping. Amos Rothschild compares Montaigne's ideas about imitation, pedagogy and pedantry to Shakespeare's in *Love's Labour's Lost*: both these are early plays that presumably predate Shakespeare's acquaintance with Montaigne. Likewise William McKenzie's chapter discusses similarities in Shakespeare's and Montaigne's use of the Narcissus myth, similarities which do not imply appropriation (*Richard II*, the subject of McKenzie's chapter, is another early play). Alison Calhoun compares ways the two authors imagine flayed skin and the endurance of suffering. Exploring other areas of affinity, Richard Hillman and Peter Platt discuss Montaigne's and Shakespeare's interest in mixed literary forms – an interest often, in Shakespeare's case, tied to Italian tragicomic models – and Daniel Vitkus suggests that both writers are drawn to a 'discontinuous' model of subjectivity more in debt to paganism than to Christianity. Vitkus speculates that the paradigm provided by Montaigne helped Shakespeare 'slow down' and make more detailed the representation of thought-processes. Yet this

process of elaboration emerges in Shakespeare before his likely exposure to Montaigne, in (Kenneth Gross argues) *Merchant of Venice*, in
(I argue) *Julius Caesar* and (Rachel Eldendrath argues) in *Hamlet*.[5]
Of course, the existence of multiple lines of influence hardly inval-
idates the point of these chapters. If Shakespeare was trending in
a particular direction anyway – experimenting with tragicomedy,
deepening and elaborating the complexity of his characters – then he
could well have found Montaigne a natural fit for his interests, read
him with special attention and appreciation, and borrowed some
of his ideas and techniques.

As a number of the essayists take care to point out, the contrasts
are as telling as the similarities. Shakespeare is famously the master
of negative capability, disappearing behind his creations, whereas
Montaigne, with unprecedented frankness and detail, takes himself
as his subject. As a result, as William M. Hamlin notes, we tend to
know 'Shakespeare' by implication, through his characters, whereas
'Montaigne', though, of course, also a literary creation, seems more
immediately related to the author.

> The Shakespearean entity we call 'Kent', after all, is essentially finite
> inasmuch as it is comprised of words spoken by Kent, the actions attrib-
> uted to Kent, and the ways in which Kent is perceived and discussed by
> other similar entities within the same verbal object. We can therefore
> speak with considerable confidence about beliefs that Kent holds with
> respect to monarchical authority, social subordination, loyalty, service,
> and so forth . . . This is not the case with Montaigne. Not only did he
> exist for almost sixty years in more or less the same ways that we exist,
> but the vast majority of what he perceived, thought, said, knew, and
> believed during that existence has vanished from the possibility of our
> apprehension.[6]

Yet, in this apples-to-oranges comparison, even our incomplete
knowledge of Montaigne is fuller than our knowledge of Shakespeare:
although Montaigne-on-the-page is not necessarily Montaigne-the-
whole-person, we know a lot more about his personal experiences
and reactions than we know about Shakespeare's. Moreover, despite
Montaigne's exploratory, anti-dogmatic stance, it is much easier to
detect an agenda in his works than it is in Shakespeare's – even if that
agenda is to counsel humility, scepticism and ironic detachment.

Some of the most interesting chapters in the volume, for me, are
those that, in the context of the two authors' likemindedness, analyse
the significance of their differences. McNair compares the two authors'
attitudes towards 'moral luck': Montaigne wants to evaluate people's

actions purely on the basis of their motives – a Neostoic maxim—whereas Shakespeare factors in results and unforeseen, sometimes unforeseeable consequences. Will Hamlin argues that Shakespeare is more receptive to belief than is Montaigne, a committed sceptic, even though Shakespeare's actual faith commitments are more obscure than Montaigne's. David Schalkwyck contrasts Montaigne's often cynical and exclusionary attitudes towards women with Shakespeare's more expansive, less misogynist attitudes towards women in the romantic comedies. Lars Engle discusses Shakespeare's undoubted borrowings from Montaigne in *The Tempest*; his chapter suggests Shakespeare deliberately coming to terms with a Montaignian exemplum and, in some respects, demurring from it.

Yet the differences between Montaigne and Shakespeare often seem not matters of 'personality', howsoever that might be ascertained, but matters of literary genre – though, of course, it is possible that the generic difference may reflect, or stem from, fundamental disparities in the way the two authors imagine the world and their place in it. Montaigne typically leapfrogs from self-observation to philosophical claims about universal human nature. For instance in 'We Taste Nothing' – an essay which several authors in this collection highlight in relation to Shakespeare's output – Montaigne presents himself as an individual incapable of unmixed pleasure or suffering, and as ethically adulterated: 'When I religiously confess myself unto myself, I find the best good I have hath some vicious taint.' Yet even while he glories in his own idiosyncrasies, he uses them as the basis for a general claim, arguing that everybody is similarly adulterated: 'Man all in all is but a botching and parti-coloured work.' Introspection, supplemented by a variety of anecdotes drawn from wide experience and even wider reading, helps Montaigne realise what is true not only for him but all human beings. He expects his readers to appreciate that introspection because it helps them understand what is true of them as well.

Shakespeare's plays almost never work this way. Plays require plots, plots require conflict, and those conflicts are generated by a clash of cathexes and affiliations. Because drama concerns itself with emotionally fraught social arrays, Shakespeare is much more interested than Montaigne in what we might call the intermediate terms mediating between the particular and the universal. His characters must negotiate a spectrum of various allegiances which are, to some extent, mutually delimiting, We see this difference most clearly, perhaps, in the way the two writers represent same-sex friendship. For Montaigne, perfect friendship manifests its perfection in so far as two participants merge into one – 'in the amity I speak of, they intermix and confound themselves one in the other, with so universal a commixture that they wear out and no more find the seam that hath conjoined them together'.[7] Other relationships, even other friendships, are precluded: 'each one gives himself so entirely to his friend, that he has nothing left to distribute to others . . . all things being by effect common between them — wills, thoughts, judgments, goods, wives, children, honour and life.'[8] This conception of a complete amalgamation of interests is foreign to Shakespeare, for whom the relationship with the friend always competes with other attachments. Again and again, the plays ask us to consider what is appropriate deference or service to friends: what Bassanio owes Antonio in *Merchant*, what Romeo owes Mercutio in *Romeo and Juliet*, what Prince Harry owes Falstaff in *2 Henry IV*, how Timon's friends ought to repay his generosity in *Timon of Athens*. But none of the plays provide clear answers, except that there are clearly more limits than Montaigne would acknowledge: in plays from the very early *Two Gentlemen of Verona* through *Midsummer Night's Dream* to the very late *Two Noble Kinsmen*, sharing seems impossible between sexual rivals. The beloved must end up with one or the other but not both. Other relationships besides friendship are similarly bounded by competing affiliations, as Cordelia recognises when she points out to Lear that marriage partially displaces the attachment between parent and child: 'I love your majesty / According to my bond, no more nor less . . . Haply when I shall wed / That lord whose hand must take my plight shall carry / Half my love with him, half my care and duty' (*KL* I, i, 93–4, 100–2). The repressed or deflected hint of incestuous possibility in *Lear* and in the romances suggest a limit beyond which even the closest parent–child relationship should not proceed.

Although in Shakespeare plays, no single relationship provides the total conflation of interests that Montaigne envisages in perfect friendship, plot nonetheless compels the characters of Shakespearean drama into passionate networks of association: individuals need to be sustained by relationships and wreck them at their peril. In *Lear*, Albany warns Goneril: 'She that herself will sliver and disbranch / From her material sap perforce must wither' (*KL* IV, ii, 35–6). As Cassie Miura notes, a routine dramatic situation, for Shakespeare as for many other early modern playwrights, is the dilemma of the sexually jealous man, which has shattering consequences, even though, in most of Shakespeare's plays, male suspicion is unfounded. Claudio's, Othello's, Leontes', Posthumus' distrust of innocent women do not merely wreck their relationships with the targets of their jealousy but ruin their respective worlds, at least (in the comedies and romances) temporarily. And that is because the supposed cuckold is willy-nilly sustained by a network of connections to others, even when he refuses to acknowledge, and does his best to destroy, those connections.

The passionate possessiveness of many of Shakespeare's characters seems foreign to Montaigne, who lampoons sexual jealousy as an especially pointless waste of energy. Lars Engle suggests that Shakespeare may have seen Montaigne's philosophic detachment as an indication of the privilege from which Shakespeare was, for most of his life, excluded: Shakespeare cannot afford the leisure that Montaigne, as a gentleman with an inherited status and income, could opt to enjoy (although possibly he was attempting to enact some version of it in his last years, when he retired from the theatre and moved home to Stratford). Yet detachment is less a matter of privilege than a matter of plot positioning in Shakespeare plays. In Shakespeare it is generally the minor and marginal characters who are able to philosophise convincingly. Thus Peter Platt aptly comments, of *All's Well That Ends Well*, that the play's 'true Montaignists' are the Dumaine brothers.[9] Observing Bertram's behaviour, they attempt to draw conclusions about human frailty and inconsistency: 'our virtues would be proud if our faults whipped them not, and our crimes would despair if they were not cherished by our virtues' (IV, iii,). But the Dumaines play a kind of choric role: mere observers of the action, not themselves caught up in it. When characters with a greater investment in a play's action try to philosophise, as Hamlet, Lear, Gloucester and others do, their comments seem driven by their particular circumstances, and therefore rarely seem valid as truth-claims. So when Lear, for instance, fumes of women that 'Down from the waist they are centaurs' (*KL* IV, vi, 121–2) we evaluate this statement in the context of his fury at Goneril and Regan, not as a dogma of Shakespeare's, or even as a fixed opinion of Lear's.

The need, in drama, to present a complex social situation with a variety of differentiated characters also means that while, as Daniel Vitkus argues, both writers share an interest in 'discontinuous' and inconsistent subjectivities, the effect is quite different in Montaigne and in Shakespeare's *Antony and Cleopatra*. While Montaigne closely examines himself, and then, as is typical of him, generalises to the human race in general, Shakespeare's play presents a heterogeneous cast of characters, of various ethnicities, social classes, occupations, cultural backgrounds. Antony's military comrades see him as having fallen away from a heroic Roman ideal of masculine hardihood and constancy to which Cleopatra simply does not aspire. Cleopatra's 'infinite variety', on the other hand, flirts with but transcends the stereotypes of female fickleness normally conflated with whorishness. While Antony and Cleopatra are both internally inconsistent, they are different flavours of discontinuity.

It may also not be surprising that an essayist and a dramatist would differ on the issue that McNair highlights, the question of moral luck. Intentions, in the wildly eventful world of the Shakespeare play, often seem to have little to do with outcomes. Some characters, particularly those in the comedies, reap benefits entirely out of proportion to their merits, while others, particularly those in the tragedies, suffer undeservedly or disproportionately. Shakespeare's Brutus, as McNair points out, fails calamitously despite his rigorous purity of motive – in fact, most of his mistakes come from his efforts to maintain that purity. The exemplary Christian piety and forbearance of Henry VI, rather similarly, renders him a calamitously weak king. In the case of military and political leaders especially – a category of human with which Shakespeare is much preoccupied – the success or failure of their endeavours is never entirely their own doing, not only because they perforce rely on others to execute their plans, but because in many plays Shakespeare emphasises the working in the world of ineluctable and mysterious forces beyond human agency: the arm of God in *Henry V*, the fates hinted at by omens and portents in *Julius Caesar* and *Antony and Cleopatra*, and witchcraft in *Macbeth*. But the questions raised by Shakespeare's plots, or the plots he adapts from others, often seem less ethical than ontological: in what kind of world are rewards and punishments distributed so apparently arbitrarily?

In the end, I think that the most useful way for us to think about Montaigne's influence upon Shakespeare is as heuristic, as effectively highlighting a set of specific issues, ably addressed by the contributors to this volume. The Venn diagram of Montaigne-circle and Shakespeare-circle converges on an interesting slice of shared territory that deserves our attention. Still, the fantasy of an overheard conversation between geniuses endures. Montaigne does not make an appearance In *Van Loon's Lives*, but Shakespeare is invited to a dinner party with Cervantes and Molière. The first part of the evening is disrupted by the attempted intrusion their characters, Quixote, Hamlet and Argan, who, rather irritatingly, turn out to be just as 'alive' as their now long-dead creators.

> 'As for me,' Molière added, 'I could live most happily without ever being reminded of my relationship to that old fraud whom I bestowed upon the world.'

Then Erasmus spoke, addressing himself to all three of our guests at the same time. 'I am very much afraid, my illustrious friends,' he observed with a great deal of dignity, 'I am afraid that that that can never happen.'

'Why not?' they asked.

'Because, most unfortunately, you gave them life everlasting.'[10]

In *Van Loon's Lives*, despite their durability, the troublesome characters are firmly dismissed, as not having been invited to the dinner party, and then the real exchange can finally begin.

What did they talk about? What do artists do when they meet? They do what engineers do and polar explorers and lion-tamers or any other group of men or women sincerely and deeply interested in their own kind of work. They talk shop! These three writers discussed different kinds of plots. They quarreled about how long a play or a book should be (Erasmus was in the thick of the fray when that point was reached and was enjoying himself right heartily.) They compared the honesty of their respective publishers, the generosity of their erstwhile patrons, and the fickleness of the public . . . what they had to say upon these subjects sounded exactly as if a group of modern composers and playwrights had been drinking tea in one of the Russian *trakteers* along West Fifty-seventh Street, indulging in the same pastime.[11]

Notes

1. Greenblatt, *Shakespearean Negotiations*, p. 1.
2. Platt, p. 242 in this volume.
3. Engle, p. 296–7 in this volume.
4. Ibid. p. 38.
5. Gross, *Shylock is Shakespeare*; Maus, 'The Will of Caesar'; Eisendrath, 'The Long Night-Watch'.
6. William M. Hamlin, p. 200 in this volume.
7. *Essayes*, trans. Florio, p. 149.
8. Ibid., p. 150–1.
9. Platt, p. 240 in this volume.
10. Van Loon, *Van Loon's Lives*, p. 211.
11. Ibid. pp. 212–13.

Bibliography

Abrams, M. H. 'Construing and Deconstructing', in Abrams, *Doing Things with Texts: Essays in Criticism and Critical Theory*, 297–332. New York: W. W. Norton, 1989.

Abrams, Samuel J. 'Professors Moved Left Since 1990s, Rest of Country Did Not', *Heterodox Academy*, 9 January 2016.

——. 'There are Conservative Professors. Just Not in These States', *New York Times* (3 July 2016), SR: 10.

Adekoya, Remi, Eric Kaufmann and Thomas Simpson, *Academic Freedom in the UK: Protecting Viewpoint Diversity*. London: Policy Exchange, 2020.

Adelman, Janet. *The Common Liar: An Essay on* Antony and Cleopatra. New Haven, CT: Yale University Press, 1973.

——. *Suffocating Mothers: Fantasies of Maternal Origin in Shakespeare's Plays,* Hamlet *to* The Tempest. New York: Routledge, 1992.

Adorno, Theodor. *Minima Moralia: Reflections from Damaged Life*, trans. E. F. N. Jephcott. London: Verso, 1978.

Aggeler, Geoffrey. '"Good Pity" in *King Lear*: The Progress of Edgar', *Neophilologus* 77 (1993): 321–31.

Alciato, Andrea. *Andreae Alciati emblemata, elucidate doctissimis Claudii Minois commenatariis*, trans. Claude Mignault. n.p. [Lyon?] G. Rouille?, 1614 [1571].

——. *Emblemes d'Alciat: de nouveau translatez en francois, vers pour vers, jouxte les latins, ordonnez en lieux communs avec briefves expositions et figures nouvelles appropriées aux derniers emblems*, trans. B. Aneau. Lyon: G. Rouille, 1549.

al-Gharbi, Musa. 'Academic and Political Elitism', 27 August 2019. https://www.insidehighered.com/views/2019/08/27/academe-should-avoid-politicizing-educational-attainment-opinion

——. *We Have Never Been Woke: Social Justice Discourse, Inequality, and the Rise of a New Elite*. Princeton, NJ: Princeton University Press, in press.

Alexander, Nigel. *Poison, Play, and Duel*. London: Routledge & Kegan Paul, 1971.

Allen, Don Cameron. *Doubt's Boundless Sea: Skepticism and Faith in the Renaissance*. Baltimore: Johns Hopkins University Press, 1964.

——. 'The Rehabilitation of Epicurus and His Theory of Pleasure in the Early Renaissance', *Studies in Philology* 41.1 (1944): 1–15.

Altman, Joel B. *The Improbability of Othello: Rhetorical Anthropology and Shakespearean Selfhood*. Chicago: University of Chicago Press, 2010.

Anselm. *Proslogion*, trans. M. J. Charlesworth. Notre Dame, IN: Notre Dame University Press, 1979.

Anzai, Tetsuo. *Shakespeare and Montaigne Reconsidered*. Tokyo: Renaissance Institute of Sophia University, 1986.

Aquinas, Thomas, *Summa Contra Gentiles*, trans. the English Dominican Fathers. London: Burns, Oates, and Washbourne, 1993 [1265–74].

——. *Summa Theologiæ*, trans. The English Dominican Fathers. London: Burns, Oates, and Washbourne, 1981 [1265–74].

Arber, Edward, ed. *A Transcript of the Registers of the Company of Stationers of London, 1554–1640*, 5 vols. London, 1876.

Arendt, Hannah. *Essays in Understanding, 1930–1954*, ed. Jerome Kohn. New York: Harcourt Brace, 1994.

——. *The Life of the Mind*. San Diego, New York and London: Harcourt, 1978.

——. *The Human Condition*. Chicago: University of Chicago Press, 1958.

Aristotle. *The Nicomachean Ethics*, trans. Martin Ostwald. Indianapolis: Bobbs-Merrill, 1962.

——. *Rhetoric*, trans. W. Rhys Roberts. New York: Modern Library, 1984.

Armstrong, Edward. *A Ciceronian Sunburn: A Tudor Dialogue on Humanistic Rhetoric and Civic Poetics*. Columbia, SC: University of South Carolina Press, 2006.

Ascham, Roger. *The Schoolmaster (1570)*, ed. Edward Arber. Birmingham: English Reprints, 1870.

Auden, W. H. 'The Prince's Dog', in Auden, *The Dyer's Hand and Other Essays*, 182–208. London: Faber & Faber, 1948.

Auerbach, Erich. *Mimesis: The Representation of Reality in Western Literature* [1946], trans. Willard R. Trask. Princeton: Princeton University Press, 2003.

Augustine. *City of God*, ed. Philip Schaff, trans. Marcus Dods. Buffalo: Christian Literature Publishing, 1887.

——. *Confessions*, trans. Henry Chadwick. Oxford: Oxford University Press, 2008.

Aulotte, Robert. *Amyot et Plutarque: la tradition des moralia au XVIe siècle*. Geneva: Librairie Droz, 1965.

Averroes, *Tahāfut al-tahāfut (The Incoherence of the Incoherence)*, 2 vols, trans. Simon Van den Burgh. Oxford: Oxbow Books for the E. J. W. Gibb Memorial Trust, 1954.

Ayres, Harry Morgan. 'Shakespeare's *Julius Cæsar* in the Light of Some Other Versions', *PMLA* 25.2 (1910): 183–227.

Bacon, Sir Francis. *The New Organon and Related Writings*, ed. Fulton H. Anderson. Indianapolis: Bobbs-Merrill, 1960.

——. *The New Organon*, trans. Michael Silverthorne, ed. Lisa Jardine and Michael Silverthorne. Cambridge: Cambridge University Press, 2000.

Baggini, Julian. 'The Hume Paradox: How Great Philosophy Leads to Dismal Politics', *Prospect* (June 2021). https://www.prospectmagazine.co.uk/philosophy/david-hume-paradox-philosophy-politics-mistakes

Bakewell, Sarah. *How to Live: A Life of Montaigne in One Question and Twenty Attempts at an Answer*. London: Chatto & Windus, 2010.

Bakhtin, Mikhail Mikhailovic. *The Dialogic Imagination: Four Essays*, ed. Michael Holquist, trans. Caryl Emerson. Austin, TX: University of Texas Press, 1982.

Baldwin, William et al. *The Mirror for Magistrates*, ed. Lily B. Campbell. New York: Barnes and Noble, 1960 [1559].

Balsamo, Jean. 'La critique des dispositions testamentaires: un scepticisme peu philosophique', in Marie-Luce Demonet and Alain Legros, eds, *L'Écriture du scepticisme chez Montaigne*, 275–87. Geneva: Droz, 2004.

——. '"Ma fortune ne m'en a fait voir nul": Montaigne et les grands hommes de son temps', *Travaux de littérature* 18 (2005): 139–55.

Baltzly, Dirk, 'Stoicism', *The Stanford Encyclopedia of Philosophy* (Spring 2018 Edition), ed. Edward N. Zalta. https://plato.stanford.edu/archives/spr2018/entries/stoicism/

Barbour, Reid. *English Epicures and Stoics: Ancient Legacies in Early Stuart Culture*. Amherst, MA: University of Massachusetts Press, 1998.

Barkan, Leonard. 'Living Sculptures: Ovid, Michelangelo and *The Winter's Tale*', *ELH* 48.4 (1981): 639–67.

——. 'What Did Shakespeare Read?', in ed. Margreta de Grazia and Stanley Wells, eds, *The Cambridge Companion to Shakespeare*, 31–48. Cambridge: Cambridge University Press, 2001.

Barker, Francis. *The Tremulous Private Body: Essays in Subjection*. London: Methuen, 1984.

Barnes, Bernadine. 'Skin, Bones, and Dust: Self-Portraits in Michelangelo's *Last Judgment*', *Sixteenth Century Journal* 35.4 (2004): 969–86.

Barthes, Roland. 'The Death of the Author', trans. Richard Howard, *Aspen Magazine* 5–6 (1968): n.p.

Barton, John. *Playing Shakespeare*. London: Methuen, 1984.

Barzun, Jacques. 'Byron and the Byronic', *Atlantic Monthly* (August 1953), 47–52.

Bassnet, Susan. *Translation*. New York: Routledge, 2014.

Bate, Jonathan. 'Introduction', *All's Well That Ends Well*, ed. Jonathan Bate and Eric Rasmussen. New York: Modern Library, 2011.

——. 'Montaigne and Shakespeare: Two Great Writers of One Mind', *New Statesman*, 10 July 2014. http://www.newstatesman.com/culture/2014/07.

——. 'Shakespeare's Foolosophy', in Grace Ioppolo, ed., *Shakespeare Performed: Essays in Honor of R. A. Foakes*, 17–32. Newark: University of Delaware Press, 2000.

Battenhouse, Roy. *Shakespearean Tragedy: Its Art and Its Christian Premises*. Bloomington, IN: Indiana University Press.

Bayley, Sally. *No Boys Play Here: A Story of Shakespeare and My Family's Missing Men*. London: William Collins, 2021.

Bečanović-Nikolić, Zorica. *Hermeneutika i poetika. Teorija pripovedanja Pola Rikera*. [Hermeneutics and Poetics: Paul Ricœur's Theory of Narrative]. Belgrade: Geopoetika, 1998.

Beckwith, Christopher I. *Greek Buddha*. Princeton: Princeton University Press, 2015.

Beckwith, Sarah. *Shakespeare and the Grammar of Forgiveness*. Ithaca: Cornell University Press, 2011.

Bell, Millicent. *Shakespeare's Tragic Skepticism*. New Haven, CT: Yale University Press, 2002.

Belsey, Catherine. 'Iago the Essayist: Florio between Montaigne and Shakespeare', in Andreas Hofele and Werner von Koppenfels, eds, *Renaissance Go-Betweens: Cultural Exchange in Early Modern Europe*, 262–78. Berlin and New York: Walter de Gruyter, 2005.

——. *The Subject of Tragedy*. London and New York: Methuen, 1985.

Bender, John. 'The Day of *The Tempest*', *ELH* 47 (1980): 235–58.

Benfell, V. Stanley. 'Disowning Certainty: Tragic and Comic Skepticism in Cavell, Montaigne, and Shakespeare', in Garry Hagberg, ed., *Stanley Cavell on Aesthetic Understanding*, 109–32. New York: Palgrave Macmillan, 2018.

Bennett, Roger E. 'Sir William Cornwallis's Use of Montaigne', *PMLA* 48 (1933): 1080–9.

Benveniste, Emile. *Problems in General Linguistics*. Miami Linguistics Series, no. 8. Coral Gables, FL: University of Miami Press, 1971.

Berggren, Paula S. '"*Imitari* Is Nothing": A Shakespearean Complex Word', *Texas Studies in Literature and Language* 26.1 (Spring 1984): 94–127.

Berlin, Isaiah. *The Roots of Romanticism*, ed. Henry Hardy. Princeton, NJ: Princeton University Press, 2001.

Bernard, John. 'Theatricality and Textuality: The Example of *Othello*', *New Literary History* 26.4 (1995): 931–49.

Bett, Richard. *Pyrrho: His Antecedents and His Legacy*. Oxford: Oxford University Press, 2000.

Blake, William. 'The Marriage of Heaven and Hell', in *Complete Poems*, ed. Alicia Ostriker, 180–95. New York: Penguin, 1977.

Blessington, Marguerite. *Lady Blessington's Conversations of Lord Byron*, ed. Ernest J. Lovell, Jr. Princeton, NJ: Princeton University Press, 1969.

Bloom, Harold. *Falstaff: Give Me Life*. New York: Simon & Schuster, 2017.
——. *Iago: The Strategies of Evil*. New York: Scribner, 2019.
——. *The Visionary Company: A Reading of English Romantic Poetry*. Garden City, NY: Doubleday, 1961.
Boas, Frederick S. *Shakspere and His Predecessors*. London: John Murray, 1947.
Boitani, Piero. *The Gospel According to Shakespeare*, trans. Vittorio Montemaggi and Rachel Jacoff. Notre Dame: University of Notre Dame Press, 2013.
Bono, Barbara. *Literary Transvaluation: From Vergilian Epic to Shakespearean Tragicomedy*. Berkeley and Los Angeles: University of California Press, 1984.
Bontea, Adriana. 'Montaigne's "On Physiognomy"', *Renaissance Studies* 22.1 (2007): 41–62.
Borges, Jorge Luis. 'Funes the Memorious', trans. James E. Irby, in Borges, *Labyrinths: Selected Stories and Other Writings*, 87–95, ed. Donald A. Yates and James E. Irby. London: Penguin, 1985.
Bossuet, Jacques Bénigne. *Méditations sur l'Évangile*, ed. Maturin Dréano. Paris: Vrin, 1966.
Boswell, James. *Boswell's Life of Johnson*, 6 vols, ed. George Birkbeck Hill and L. F. Powell. Oxford: Oxford University Press, 1971.
Bourland, Caroline. 'Gabriel Harvey and the Modern Languages', *Huntington Library Quarterly* 4 (1940–1): 85–106.
Boutcher, Warren. 'Awakening the Inner Man: Montaigne Framed for Modern Intellectual Life', *EMF: Studies in Early Modern France* 9 (2004): 30–57.
——. '"A French Dexteritie, & An Italian Confidence": New Documents on John Florio, Learned Strangers and Protestant Humanist Study of Modern Languages in Renaissance England from *c.* 1547 to *c.* 1625', *Reformation* 2 (1997): 39–109.
——. 'From Cultural Translation to Cultures of Translation? Early Modern Readers, Sellers and Patrons', in Tania Demetriou and Rowan Tomlinson, eds, *The Culture of Translation in Early Modern England and France, 1500–1660*, 22–40. Basingstoke: Palgrave Macmillan, 2015.
——. 'Humanism and Literature in Late Tudor England: Translation, the Continental Book and the Case of Montaigne's *Essais*', in Jonathan Woolfson, ed., *Reassessing Tudor Humanism*, 243–68. London and New York: Palgrave Macmillan, 2002.
——. '"Learning Mingled with Nobilitie": Directions for Reading Montaigne's *Essais* in their Institutional Context', in Keith Cameron and Laura Willett, eds, *Le Visage changeant de Montaigne / The Changing Face of Montaigne*, 337–62. Paris: Champion, 2003.
——. 'Marginal Commentaries: The Cultural Transmission of Montaigne's *Essais* in Shakespeare's England', in Pierre Kapitaniak and Jean-Marie

Maguin, eds, *Shakespeare et Montaigne: vers un nouvel humanisme.* Montpellier and Paris: Société Française Shakespeare, 2004. 13–27.

——. 'Montaigne et Anthony Bacon: la *familia* et la fonction des lettres', *Montaigne Studies* 13 (2001): 241–76.

——. 'Montaigne in England and America', in Philippe Desan, ed., *The Oxford Handbook to Montaigne*, 306–27. New York: Oxford University Press, 2016.

——. 'Montaigne's Legacy', in Ullrich Langer, ed., *The Cambridge Companion to Montaigne*, 27–52. New York: Cambridge University Press, 2005.

——. 'The Origins of Florio's Montaigne: "Of the Institution and Education of Children, To Madame Lucy Russell, Countess of Bedford"', *Montaigne Studies* 24 (2012): 7–32.

——. '"Le pauvre patient": Montaigne agent dans l'économie du savoir', in Philippe Desan, ed., *Montaigne Politique*, 243–61. Paris: Honoré Champion, 2006.

——. *The School of Montaigne in Early Modern Europe*, 2 vols. Oxford: Oxford University Press, 2017.

——. 'Schooling America: Donald Frame, Pierre Villey, and the Educational History of the *Essais*', *Montaigne Studies* 20 (2008): 117–28.

Bouwsma, William J. 'The Two Faces of Renaissance Humanism', in Heiko A. Oberman, ed., *Itinerarium Italicum: The Profile of the Italian Renaissance in the Mirror of its European Transformations*, 3–60. Leiden: Brill, 1975. Reprinted in William Bouwsma, *A Usable Past: Essays in European Cultural History*, 19–73. Berkeley, Los Angeles and Oxford: University of California Press, 1990.

Braden, Gordon. *Renaissance Tragedy and the Senecan Tradition: Anger's Privilege*. New Haven: Yale University Press, 1985.

——. 'Senecan Tragedy and the Renaissance', *Illinois Classical Studies* 9.2 (1984): 177–92.

Bradley, A. C. 'The Rejection of Falstaff', in Bradley, *Oxford Lectures on Poetry*, 247–78. London: Macmillan, 1909.

——. *Shakespearean Tragedy*, 2nd edn. London: Macmillan, 1905.

Bradshaw, Graham. *Shakespeare's Scepticism*. Ithaca, NY: Cornell University Press, 1987.

Brague, Rémi. *The Kingdom of Man: Genesis and Failure of the Modern Project*, trans. Paul Seaton. Notre Dame, IN: University of Notre Dame Press, 2021.

Brahami, Frédéric. *Le Scepticisme de Montaigne*. Paris: Presses universitaires de France, 1997.

Brandes, Georg. *William Shakespeare: A Critical Study*. London: Heinemann, 1899.

Bredvold, Louis I. *The Intellectual Milieu of John Dryden: Studies in Some Aspects of Seventeenth-Century Thought*. Ann Arbor: University of Michigan Press, 1934.

Breitenberg, Mark. 'The Anatomy of Masculine Desire in *Love's Labour's Lost*', *Shakespeare Quarterly* 43.4 (1992): 430–49.

Brenk, Frederick E. 'Antony-Osiris, Cleopatra-Isis: The End of Plutarch's *Antony*', in Philip A. Stadter, ed., *Plutarch and the Historical Tradition*, 159–82. New York: Routledge, 2011.

Bristol, Michael. 'Macbeth the Philosopher: Rethinking Context'. *New Literary History* 42.4 (2011): 641–62.

Bromwich, David. 'What Shakespeare's Heroes Learn', *Raritan* 29 (2010): 132–48.

Brown, Frieda S. *Religious and Political Conservatism in the* Essais *of Montaigne*. Geneva: Droz, 1963.

Bruster, Douglas. *To Be or Not to Be*. London: Continuum, 2007.

Buffum, Imbrie. *Studies in the Baroque Form from Montaigne to Rotrou*. New Haven, CT: Yale University Press; Paris: Presses universitaires de France, 1957.

Burghardt, Walter J. *The Image of God in Man according to St. Cyril of Alexandria*. Washington, DC: Catholic University of America Press, 1957.

Burrow, Colin. 'Montaignian Moments: Shakespeare and the *Essays*', in Neil Kenny, Richard Scholar and Wes Williams, eds, *Montaigne in Transit: Essays in Honour of Ian Maclean*, 239–52. Cambridge: Legenda, 2016.

——. *Shakespeare and Classical Antiquity*. Oxford: Oxford University Press, 2013.

Burton, Tara Isabella. 'The Dark History of Letting Male "Geniuses" Get Away with Bad Behavior', *Vox* (26 October 2017). https://www.vox.com/identities/2017/10/26/16504856/art-men-sexual-harassment-film-morality

Butler, F. G. 'Who Are King Lear's Philosophers? An Answer, with Some Help from Erasmus', *English Studies* 67.6 (1986): 511–24.

Calhoun, Alison. *Montaigne and the Lives of the Philosophers: Life-Writing and Transversality in the* Essais. Newark, DE: University of Delaware Press, 2015.

Campbell, W. K., and J. D. Miller, eds. *The Handbook of Narcissism and Narcissistic Personality Disorder*. Hoboken, NJ: Wiley & Sons, 2011.

Cantor, Paul A. *Shakespeare's Roman Trilogy: The Twilight of the Ancient World*. Chicago: University of Chicago Press, 2017.

Capell, Edward. *Notes and Various Readings to Shakespeare*. London: Henry Hughs, 1780.

Cardano, Girolamo. *Cardanus Comforte*, trans. Thomas Bedingfield. London, 1576.

Carl, Noah. 'Can Intelligence Explain the Overrepresentation of Liberals and Leftists in American Academia?' *Intelligence* 53 (2015): 181–93.

Carraud, Vincent. *Causa sive ratio: la raison de la cause de Suarez à Leibniz*. Paris: Presses universitaires de France, 2002.

Carroll, William C. *The Great Feast of Language in* Love's Labour's Lost. Princeton, NJ: Princeton University Press, 1976.

Carson, Rob. 'Hearing Voices in *Coriolanus* and Early Modern Skepticism', *Shakespearean International Yearbook 6: Special Section, Shakespeare and Montaigne Revisited*, ed. Graham Bradshaw, T. G. Bishop and Peter Holbrook, 140–69. Burlington, VT: Ashgate, 2006.

Carver, P. L. 'The Influence of Maurice Morgann', *Review of English Studies* 6.23 (1930): 320–22.

Cathcart, Charles. 'Marston, Montaigne, and Lady Politic Would-Be', *English Language Notes* 36.4 (1999): 4–8.

Cave, Terence. *The Cornucopian Text: Problems of Writing in the French Renaissance*. Oxford: Clarendon, 1979.

——. *How to Read Montaigne*. London: Granta, 2007.

——. 'Problems of Reading in the *Essais*', in I. D. McFarlane and Ian Maclean, eds, *Montaigne: Essays in Memory of Richard Sayce*, 133–66. Oxford: Clarendon Press, 1982.

——. 'When Shakespeare Met Montaigne', in William Poole and Richard Scholar, eds, *Thinking with Shakespeare: Comparative and Interdisciplinary Essays for A. D. Nuttall*, 115–19. London: Legenda, 2007.

Cavell, Stanley. *The Claim of Reason: Wittgenstein, Skepticism, Morality, and Tragedy*. Oxford: Oxford University Press, 1979.

——. 'A Cover Letter to Molière's *Misanthrope*', in Cavell, *Themes Out of School: Effects and Causes*, 97–105. San Francisco: North Point Press, 1984.

——. *Disowning Knowledge in Seven Plays of Shakespeare*. Cambridge: Cambridge University Press, 2003.

——. *Disowning Knowledge in Six Plays of Shakespeare*. Cambridge: Cambridge University Press, 1988.

——. *Pursuits of Happiness: The Hollywood Comedy of Remarriage*. Cambridge, MA: Harvard University Press, 1984.

Cefalu, Paul. '"Damnèd Custom . . . Habits Devil": Shakespeare's *Hamlet*, Anti-Dualism, and the Early Modern Philosophy of Mind', *English Literary History* 67.2 (2000): 399–431.

Chambers, E. K. *The Elizabethan Stage*, 4 vols. Oxford: Clarendon Press, 1923.

——. *Shakespeare: A Survey*. London: Sidgwick & Jackson Ltd, 1925.

Chamlee-Wright, Emily. 'Self-Censorship and Associational Life in the Liberal Academy', *Society* 56 (2019): 538–49.

Chappuit, Jean-François. '"I must be cruel only to be kind": le concept de dignité humaine chez Montaigne et Shakespeare', in Pierre Kapitaniak and Jean-Marie Maguin, eds, *Shakespeare et Montaigne: vers un nouvel humanisme*. Montpellier and Paris: Société Française Shakespeare, 2004. 53–78.

Charron, Pierre. *Of Wisdome*, trans. Samson Lennard. London, 1608.

Chasles, Philarète. *Études sur W. Shakespeare, Marie Stuart, et l'Arétin: Le Drame, les mœurs et la religion au XVIe siècle*. Paris: Amyot, 1851.

Chaudhuri, Sukanta. *Infirm Glory: Shakespeare and the Renaissance Image of Man*. Oxford: Clarendon, 1981.

Chesterton, G. K. 'The Thing: Why I am a Catholic', in *The Collected Works of G. K. Chesterton*, 37 vols, ed. James J. Thompson Jr, 3:133–6. San Francisco: Ignatius Press, 1990.

Chomarat, Jacques. *Grammaire et rhétorique chez Érasme*, 2 vols. Paris: Les Belles Lettres, 1981.

Chomsky, Noam. *American Power and the New Mandarins: Historical and Political Essays*. New York: Pantheon, 1969.

Chua, Amy. *Political Tribes: Group Instinct and the Fate of Nations*. New York: Penguin Books, 2018.

Cicero, Marcus Tullius. *De Natura Deorum* and *Academica*, trans. Harris Rackham. Cambridge, MA: Harvard University Press, 1951.

——. *The Nature of the Gods*, trans. P. G. Walsh. Oxford: Oxford University Press, 1998.

——. *On Oratory and Orators*, trans. J. S. Watson. Carbondale, IL: Southern Illinois University Press, 1970.

Clayton, Tom, Susan Brock and Vincente Forés, eds. *Shakespeare and the Mediterranean: Selected Proceedings of the International Shakespeare Association World Congress, Valencia, 2001*. Newark, DE: University of Delaware Press, 2004.

Clemen, Wolfgang. *Shakespeare's Soliloquies*, trans. Charity Scott Stokes. London: Methuen, 1987.

Clifford, W. K. 'The Ethics of Belief', in A. J. Burger, ed., *The Ethics of Belief*. NP: A. J. Burger, 2008.

Cochran, Peter. 'Byron and Shakespeare', in Cochran, *The Burning of Byron's Memoirs: New and Unpublished Essays and Papers*, 197–219. Newcastle upon Tyne: Cambridge Scholars Publishing, 2014.

——. 'Byron's Legacy, and Byron's Inheritance', in Cochran, *The Burning of Byron's Memoirs: New and Unpublished Essays and Papers*, 169–81. Newcastle upon Tyne: Cambridge Scholars Publishing, 2014.

Collington, Philip D. 'Self-Discovery in Montaigne's "Of Solitarinesse" and *King Lear*', *Comparative Drama* 35.3–4 (2001–2): 247–69.

Collins, John Churton. *Studies in Shakspere*. Westminster: Archibald Constable & Co., Ltd., 1904.

Conley, Tom. 'Institutionalizing Translation: On Florio's Montaigne', in Samuel Weber, ed., *Demarcating the Disciplines: Philosophy, Literature, Art*, 45–58. Minneapolis: University of Minnesota Press, 1986.

Connolly, Shannon R. 'Equity and Amerindians in Montaigne's "Des cannibals" (I, 31)', *Renaissance and Reformation / Renaissance et Réforme* 43.3 (Summer 2019): 195–228.

Copenhaver, Brian, and Charles Schmitt. *Renaissance Philosophy*. Oxford: Oxford University Press, 1992.

Cormack, Braden. *A Power to Do Justice: Jurisdiction, English Literature, and the Rise of Common Law*. Chicago: University of Chicago Press, 2007.

Cormack, Braden, and Carla Mazzio, eds. *Book Use, Book Theory: 1500–1700*. Chicago: University of Chicago Libraries, 2005.

Cornwallis, William. *Essayes*, ed. Don Cameron Allen. Baltimore, MD: Johns Hopkins University Press, 1946, 1st edn. London, 1600–1.

Cosman, Bard C. 'All's Well That Ends Well: Shakespeare's Treatment of Anal Fistula', *Diseases of Colon and Rectum* 41.7 (1998): 914–24.

Cotgrave, Randle. *A Dictionarie of the French and English Tongues*. London, 1611.

Cox, John D. *Seeming Knowledge: Shakespeare and Skeptical Faith*. Waco, TX: Baylor University Press, 2007.

——. 'Suspicion and Belief in Shakespeare's Early Comedies', *Shakespearean International Yearbook 6: Special Section, Shakespeare and Montaigne Revisited*, ed. Graham Bradshaw, T. G. Bishop and Peter Holbrook, 56–76. Burlington, VT: Ashgate, 2006.

Craig, Hardin. 'Hamlet's Book', *Huntington Library Bulletin* 6 (1934): 17–37.

Crawford, Charles. 'Montaigne, Webster, and Marston: Donne and Webster', *Collectanea*, 2nd series, 1–63. Stratford-upon-Avon: Shakespeare Head Press, 1907.

Crawford, Jason. 'Shakespeare's Liturgy of Assumption', *Journal of Medieval and Early Modern Studies* 49.1 (2019): 57–84.

Cross, Gustav. 'Marston, Montaigne, and Morality: *The Dutch Courtezan* Reconsidered', *ELH* 27 (1960): 30–43.

Cruz, L. and S. Buser, eds. *Clear and Present Danger: Narcissism in the Era of President Trump*. Asheville, NC: Chiron Publications, 2016.

Cummings, Brian. *Mortal Thoughts: Religion, Secularity, & Identity in Shakespeare and Early Modern Culture*. Oxford: Oxford University Press, 2013.

Cummings, Robert. 'Modern Philosophical and Moral Writing', in Gordon Braden, Robert Cummings and Stuart Gillespie, eds, *The Oxford History of Literary Translation in English: Volume 2, 1550–1660*, 390–407. Oxford: Oxford University Press, 2010.

Curley, Edwin M. 'Skepticism and Toleration: The Case of Montaigne', *Oxford Studies in Early Modern Philosophy* 2 (2005): 1–33.

Curtius, Ernst Robert. *European Literature and the Latin Middle Ages*. Princeton, NJ: Princeton University Press, 1953.

Cushman, Fiery, and Joshua D. Greene. 'Finding Faults: How Moral Dilemmas Illuminate Cognitive Structure'. *Social Neuroscience* 7 (2012): 269–79.

Cushman, Fiery, and Liane Young. 'The Psychology of Dilemmas and the Philosophy of Morality', *Ethical Theory and Moral Practice* 12 (2009): 9–24.

Dalrymple, Theodore. 'The Frivolity of Evil'. *City Journal* (Autumn 2004). Reprinted in Dalrymple, *Our Culture*. https://www.city-journal.org/html/frivolity-evil-12835.html

——. *Life at the Bottom: The Worldview that Makes the Underclass.* Chicago: Ivan R. Dee, 2001.

——. *Our Culture, What's Left of It: The Mandarins and the Masses.* Chicago: Ivan R. Dee, 2005.

——. 'Sex and the Shakespeare Reader', *City Journal* (Autumn 2003). Reprinted in Dalrymple, *Our Culture.* https://www.city-journal.org/html/sex-and-shakespeare-reader-12478.html

Davies, H. N. 'Jacobean *Antony and Cleopatra*', *Shakespeare Studies* 17 (1985): 123–58.

Davis, J. C. *Utopia and the Ideal Society: A Study of English Utopian Writing, 1500–1700.* Cambridge: Cambridge University Press, 1981.

Davis, Philip. *Sudden Shakespeare.* London: Athlone, 1996.

De Gooyer, Alan. '"Their senses I'll restore": Montaigne and *The Tempest* Reconsidered', in Patrick M. Murphy, ed., *The Tempest: Critical Essays*, 509–31. New York and London: Routledge, 2001.

De Rocher, Gregory. 'Montaigne and *Mollities*: Problems with the Essayist's Public "Filthie frigging"', *Montaigne Studies* 9 (1997): 121–34.

Deitch, Judith A. 'Love's Hologram: Shakespeare, Ricœur, and the Equivocations of Erotic Identity', *Poetics Today* 29 (2008): 525–64.

Deneen, Patrick J. *Why Liberalism Failed.* New Haven, CT: Yale University Press, 2018.

Denis, Lara and Eric Wilson. 'Kant and Hume on Morality', *The Stanford Encyclopedia of Philosophy* (Fall 2016 Edition), ed. Edward N. Zalta. https://plato.stanford.edu/archives/fall2016/entries/kant-hume-morality/.

Dennett, Daniel C. 'Précis of *The Intentional Stance*', *Behavioral and Brain Sciences* 11 (1998): 465–546.

Dent, R. W. *Shakespeare's Proverbial Language: An Index.* Berkeley and Los Angeles: University of California Press, 1981.

Derrida, Jacques. *Of Grammatology*, trans. Gayatri Chakravorty Spivack. Baltimore, MD: Johns Hopkins University Press, 1976.

Desan, Philippe. *Bibliotheca Desaniana: Catalogue Montaigne.* Paris: Classiques Garnier, 2011.

——. 'The Book, the Friend, and the Woman: Montaigne's Circular Exchanges', trans. Brad Bassler, in Marie-Rose Logan and Peter L. Rudnytsky, eds, *Contending Kingdoms: Historical, Psychological and Feminist Approaches to the Literature of Sixteenth-Century England and France*, 225–62. Detroit: Wayne State University Press, 1991.

——. *Montaigne: A Life* [Paris, 2014], trans. Steven Rendall and Lisa Neal. Princeton: Princeton University Press, 2017.

——. *Montaigne: Les Formes du monde et de l'esprit.* Paris: Presses de l'Université Paris-Sorbonne, 2008.

——. '"Translata Proficit": John Florio, sa réécriture des *Essais* et l'influence de la langue de Montaigne-Florio sur Shakespeare', in Pierre Kapitaniak and Jean-Marie Maguin, eds, *Shakespeare et Montaigne: vers un nouvel humanism*, 79–93. Montpellier and Paris: Société Française Shakespeare, 2004.

Desan, Philippe, ed. *Dictionnaire de Michel de Montaigne*, 2nd edn. Paris: Honoré Champion, 2007.

——. *The Oxford Handbook of Montaigne*. New York: Oxford University Press, 2016.

Descartes, René. *Discourse on the Method for Conducting One's Reason Well and for Seeking Truth in the Sciences*, trans. Donald A. Cress (Indianapolis: Hackett, 1998).

——. *Philosophical Writings*, trans. and ed. Elizabeth Anscombe and Peter Geach. Indianapolis: Bobbs-Merrill, 1971

——. *Selected Correspondence of René Descartes*, 148, trans. and ed. Jonathan Bennett. Early Modern Texts, 2017. https://www.earlymoderntexts.com/assets/pdfs/descartes1619_3.pdf

Deutschbein, Max. 'Shakespeares Hamlet und Montaigne', *Shakespeare-Jahrbuch* 80–1 (1944–5): 70–107.

——. 'Shakespeares Kritik an Montaigne in *As You Like It*', *Neuphilologische Monatsschrift* 5 (1934): 369–85.

Dewar-Wilson, Sarah. 'Othello, Virgil, and Montaigne', *Notes and Queries* 255.3 (September, 2010): 384–5.

——. *Shakespeare's Poetics: Aristotle and Anglo-Italian Renaissance Genres*, Anglo-Italian Renaissance Studies, 17. London: Routledge, 2018.

Diogenes Laertius. *Lives of Eminent Philosophers*. Loeb Classical Library, trans. R. D. Hicks. London: Heinemann, 1925.

Dionne, Valérie. *Montaigne, écrivain de la conciliation*. Paris: Garnier, 2014.

DiSanto, Michael John. 'Nothing if Not Critical: Stanley Cavell's Skepticism and Shakespeare's *Othello*', *The Dalhousie Review* 81.3 (2012): 359–82.

Dollimore, Jonathan. *Radical Tragedy: Religion, Ideology and Power in the Drama of Shakespeare and His Contemporaries*. Chicago: University of Chicago Press, 1984. 2nd edn, Durham, NC: Duke University Press, 1993. 3rd edn, Durham, NC: Duke University Press, 2003.

Doloff, Steven. '"Let me talk with this philosopher": The Alexander/Diogenes Paradigm in *King Lear*.' *Huntington Library Quarterly* 54.3 (1991): 253–5.

Donaldson, Ian. '*All's Well That Ends Well*: Shakespeare's Play of Endings', *Essays in Criticism* 27.1 (1977): 34–55.

Donawerth, Jane. 'Diogenes the Cynic and Lear's Definition of Man, *King Lear* 3.4.101–9', *English Language Notes* 15.1 (1977): 10–14.

Doucet, Roger. *Les Institutions de la France au XVIe siècle*, 2 vols. Paris: Picard, 1948.

Dowling, William C. *Ricoeur on Time and Narrative: An Introduction to Temps et récit*. South Bend, IN: University of Notre Dame Press, 2011.

Dréano, Maturin. *La Renommée de Montaigne en France au XVIIIe siècle, 1677–1802*. Angers: Éditions de l'Ouest, 1952.

Dusinberre, Juliet. 'Virginia Woolf and Montaigne.' *Textual Practice* 5 (1991): 291–41.

Eagleton, Terry. *William Shakespeare*. Oxford and New York: Basil Blackwell, 1986.

Eisendrath, Rachel. 'The Long Night-Watch: Augustine, *Hamlet*, and the Aesthetic', *ELH* 87.3 (Fall 2020): 581–606.

Eliot, T. S. 'Shakespeare and Montaigne', *Times Literary Supplement* (24 December 1925).

——. 'Shakespeare and the Stoicism of Seneca', in Eliot, *Selected Essays*, 107–20. New York: Harcourt Brace, 1960.

Ellrodt, Robert. 'Constance des valeurs humanistes chez Montaigne et chez Shakespeare', in Pierre Kapitaniak and Jean-Marie Maguin, eds, *Shakespeare et Montaigne: vers un nouvel humanisme*. Montpellier and Paris: Société Française Shakespeare, 2004. 95–116.

——. 'Genèse et dilemme de la conscience moderne'. *Revue de la Méditerranée* 49–50–51 (1952): 293–306; 387–403; 543–60.

——. *Montaigne and Shakespeare: The Emergence of Modern Self-Consciousness*. Manchester: Manchester University Press, 2015.

——. *Montaigne et Shakespeare: l'émergence de la conscience moderne*. Paris: José Corti, 2011.

——. 'Self-Consciousness in Montaigne and Shakespeare', *Shakespeare Survey* 28 (1975): 37–50.

——. 'Self-Consistency in Montaigne and Shakespeare', in Tom Clayton, Susan Brock and Vincente Forés, eds, *Shakespeare and the Mediterranean: Selected Proceedings of the International Shakespeare Association World Congress, Valencia, 2001*, 135–55. Newark, DE: University of Delaware Press, 2004.

Emerson, Ralph Waldo. 'Montaigne; Or, the Skeptic', in *Selections from Ralph Waldo Emerson*, ed. Stephen E. Whicher, 284–301. Boston, MA: Houghton Mifflin, 1957.

Empson, William. 'Falstaff and Mr Dover Wilson', in G. K. Hunter, ed., *Henry IV: Parts I and II: A Casebook*, 135–54. London: Macmillan, 1970.

——. 'Hamlet When New', *The Sewanee Review* 61.1 (1953): 15–42.

Engel, William E. 'Aphorism, Anecdote, and Anamnesis in Montaigne and Bacon', *Montaigne Studies* 1 (1989): 158–76.

——. 'Cites and Stones: Montaigne's Patrimony', *Montaigne Studies* 4 (1992): 180–99.

Engle, Lars. '*Measure for Measure* and Modernity: The Problem of the Sceptic's Authority', in Hugh Grady, ed., *Shakespeare and Modernity: Early Modern to Millennium*, 85–104. London: Routledge, 2000.

——. 'Moral Agency in *Hamlet*', *Shakespeare Studies* 40 (2012): 87–97.

——. 'Pragmatism', in Arthur F. Kinney, ed., *The Oxford Handbook of Shakespeare*, 641–62. Oxford: Oxford University Press, 2012.

——. 'Shakespearean Normativity in *All's Well That Ends Well*', *Shakespearean International Yearbook* 4 (2004): 264–78.

——. 'Shame and Reflection in Montaigne and Shakespeare', *Shakespeare Survey* 63 (2010): 249–61.

——. 'Sovereign Cruelty in Montaigne and *King Lear*', *Shakespearean International Yearbook 6: Special Section, Shakespeare and Montaigne Revisited*, ed. Graham Bradshaw, T. G. Bishop,and Peter Holbrook, 119–39. Burlington, VT: Ashgate, 2006.

Erasmus, Desiderius. *De duplici copia verborum ac rerum commentarii duo*, trans. Betty I. Knott, in *The Collected Works of Erasmus*, ed. Craig R. Thompson, vol. 24, 279–659. Toronto: University of Toronto Press, 1978.

——. *The Praise of Folly and Other Writings*, trans. Robert M. Adams. New York: Norton, 1989.

Erickson, Peter. 'The Failure of Relationship between Men and Women in *Love's Labour's Lost*', *Women's Studies* 9.1 (1981): 65–81.

Escobedo, Andrew. '"Unlucky Deeds" and the Shame of Othello', in Michael D. Bristol, ed., *Shakespeare and Moral Agency*, 159–70. London and New York: Continuum, 2010.

Esolen, Anthony. 'Spenserian Chaos: Lucretius in *The Faerie Queene*', *Spenser Studies* 11 (1994): 31–51.

——. 'Spenser's 'Alma Venus': Energy and Economics in the Bower of Bliss', *English Literary Renaissance* 23 (1993): 267–86.

Evett, David. *Discourses of Service in Shakespeare's England*. New York: Palgrave Macmillan, 2005.

Federico, Silvia. 'Queer Times: Richard II in the Poems and Chronicles of Late Fourteenth-Century England', *Medium Ævum* 79:1 (2010): 25–46.

Feis, Jacob. *Shakspere and Montaigne: An Endeavour to Explain the Tendency of 'Hamlet' from Allusions in Contemporary Works*. London: Kegan Paul, Trench, 1884; rpt. Geneva: Slatkine, 1970.

Fernie, Ewan. *Shakespeare for Freedom: Why the Plays Matter*. Cambridge: Cambridge University Press, 2017.

——. *Shame in Shakespeare*. London and New York: Routledge, 2002.

Fichte, Johann Gottlieb. *Sämmtliche Werke*, 11 vols, ed. Imanuel Hermann Fichte. Berlin: Verlag von Veit, 1845–46.

Fisch, Harold. *The Biblical Presence in Shakespeare, Milton, and Blake: A Comparative Study*. Oxford: Clarendon Press, 1999.

Fischer, Michael. *Stanley Cavell and Literary Skepticism*. Chicago: University of Chicago Press, 1989.

Fish, Stanley. *Surprised by Sin*. Cambridge, MA: Harvard University Press, 1998.

Flage, Daniel E. and Clarence A. Bonnen. 'Descartes on Causation'. *Review of Metaphysics* 50.4 (1997): 841–72l.

Florio, John. *A Worlde of* Wordes, *Or Most copious, and exact* Dictionarie *in Italian and* English, collected by *Iohn Florio*. London, 1598.

Floyd-Wilson, Mary. *Occult Knowledge, Science, and Gender in the Shakespearean Stage*. Cambridge: Cambridge University Press, 2013.

Flygare, William. *Montaigne–Shakspere: 1780–1980*. Montaigne–Shakspere–Studies, Study A. Kyoto: Apollon Press, 1983.

Fontana, Biancamaria. 'Lâcher la bride: tolérance religieuse et liberté de conscience dans les Essais de Michel de Montaigne', *Cahiers philosophiques* 114.2 (2008): 27–39.

Ford, Philip. 'George Buchanan et Montaigne', *Montaigne Studies* 13 (2001): 45–64.

——. 'Montaigne in England', *Montaigne Studies* 24 (2012): 3–6.

Foucault, Michel. *Discipline and Punish: The Birth of the Prison*, trans. Alan Sheridan. New York: Vintage, 1995.

——. 'Nietzsche, Genealogy, History', in *Language, Counter-Memory, Practice: Selected Essays and Interviews*, trans. Donald F. Bouchard and Sherry Simon, ed. Donald F. Bouchard, 139–64. Ithaca: Cornell University Press, 1977.

Frame, Donald M. 'Did Montaigne Betray Sebond?' *Romanic Review* 38.4 (1947): 297–329.

——. *Montaigne: A Biography*. New York: Harcourt Brace, 1965.

Frampton, Saul. '"To Be, or Not To Be": *Hamlet* Q1, Q2 and Montaigne', *Critical Survey* 31:1/2 (2019): 101–12.

——. 'Who Edited Shakespeare?' *The Guardian*, 12 July 2013.

Friedersdorf, Conor. 'Truth vs. Social Justice', *The Atlantic* (1 November 2018). https://www.theatlantic.com/ideas/archive/2018/11/academics-truth-justice/574165/

Friedman, Michael D. *'The World Must Be Peopled': Shakespeare's Comedies of Forgiveness*. Madison: Fairleigh Dickinson University Press; London: Associated University Presses, 2002.

Friedrich, Hugo. *Montaigne* [Bern: Francke, 1949], trans. Dawn Eng, ed. Philippe Desan. Berkeley: University of California Press, 1991.

Frye, Roland Mushat. *Shakespeare and Christian Doctrine*. Princeton, NJ: Princeton University Press, 1963.

Fulkerson, Laurel. *No Regrets: Remorse in Classical Antiquity*. Oxford: Oxford University Press, 2013.

German, Christopher St. *Salem and Bizance* [1533], in *The Yale Edition of the Complete Works of St. Thomas More*, ed. John Guy, Ralph Keen, Clarence H. Miller and Ruth McGugan, 325–92. New Haven and London: Yale University Press, 1987.

Gide, André. 'Montaigne', *The Yale Review* (March 1939): 53–71.

Gilbert, Allan H. 'Montaigne and *The Tempest*', *Romanic Review* 5 (1914): 357–63.

Gillespie, Stuart. *Shakespeare's Books: A Dictionary of Shakespeare's Sources*. London: Continuum, 2004.

Gillies, John. 'The Question of Original Sin in Hamlet', *Shakespeare Quarterly* 64.4 (2013): 396–424.

——. 'Shakespeare's Virginian Masque', *ELH* 53 (1986): 673–707.

Gless, Darryl J. *Measure for Measure, the Law, and the Convent*. Princeton: Princeton University Press, 1979.

Glidden, Hope H. 'The Face in the Text: Montaigne's Emblematic Self-Portrait (*Essais* III:12)', *Renaissance Quarterly* 46.1 (1993): 71–97.

Go, Kenji. 'Montaigne's "Cannibals" and *The Tempest* Revisited', *Studies in Philology* 109.4 (2012): 455–73.

Goffman, Erving. 'On Face-Work: An Analysis of Ritual Elements in Social Interaction', in Goffman, *Interaction Ritual*, 5–45. New York: Doubleday, 1967.

Goldberg, Jonathan. *Desiring Women Writing: English Renaissance Examples*. Stanford: Stanford University Press, 1997.

Golec de Zavala, J. et al. 'The Relationship between the Brexit Vote and Individual Predictors of Prejudice: Collective Narcissism, Right Wing Authoritarianism, Social Dominance Orientation', *Frontiers in Psychology* 8 (2017): 20–3.

Goodhart, David. *The Road to Somewhere: The Populist Revolt and the Future of Politics*. London: Hurst Publishers, 2017.

Gopnik, Adam. 'Montaigne on Trial', *The New Yorker*, 16 January 2017.

Gordon, D. J. 'Name and Fame: Shakespeare's *Coriolanus*', in Stephen Orgel, ed., *The Renaissance Imagination: Essays and Lectures by D. J. Gordon*, 203–19. Berkeley: University of California Press, 1975.

Gottlieb, Derek. *Skepticism and Belonging in Shakespeare's Comedy*. New York: Routledge, 2015.

Gournay, Marie de. *Preface to the Essays of Michel de Montaigne, by his Adoptive Daughter, Marie le Jars de Gournay*, trans. with supplementary annotation by Richard Hillman and Colette Quesnel, from the edition prepared by François Rigolot. Tempe, AZ: Medieval & Renaissance Texts & Studies, 1998.

Goyet, Francis. *Les Audaces de la prudence. Littérature et politique aux XVIe et XVIIe siècles*. Paris: Classiques Garnier, 2009.

Grady, Hugh. 'Afterword: Montaigne and Shakespeare in Changing Cultural Paradigms', *Shakespearean International Yearbook 6: Special Section, Shakespeare and Montaigne Revisited*, ed. Graham Bradshaw, T. G. Bishop, and Peter Holbrook, 170–81. Burlington, VT: Ashgate, 2006.

——. *Shakespeare and Impure Aesthetics*. Cambridge: Cambridge University Press, 2009.

——. *Shakespeare, Machiavelli, and Montaigne: Power and Subjectivity from* Richard II *to* Hamlet. Oxford: Oxford University Press, 2002.

——. 'Shakespeare's Links to Machiavelli and Montaigne: Constructing Intellectual Modernity in Early Modern Europe', *Comparative Literature* 52.2 (2000): 119–42.

Grady, Hugh, ed. *Shakespeare and Modernity: Early Modern to Millennium*. London and New York: Routledge, 2000.

Grafton, Anthony, and Lisa Jardine. *From Humanism to the Humanities: Education and the Liberal Arts in Fifteenth- and Sixteenth-Century Europe*. Cambridge, MA: Harvard University Press, 1986.

Gray, Floyd. 'The Women in Montaigne's Life: Autobiography and the Rhetoric of Misogyny', *Montaigne Studies* 8 (1996): 9–22.

Gray, Patrick. 'Faith and Doubt: An Alternative Dialectic', in Gillian Beer, Malcolm Bowie and Beate Perrey, eds., *In(ter)discipline: New Languages for Criticism*, 174–87. Oxford: Legenda, 2007.

——. "HIDE THY SELFE": Montaigne, Hamlet, and Epicurean Ethics', In Gray and John D. Cox, eds, *Shakespeare and Renaissance Ethics*, 213–36. Cambridge: Cambridge University Press, 2014.

——. 'Shakespeare and the Fall of the Roman Republic: A Reply to Paul A. Cantor', *Skenè. Journal of Theatre and Drama Studies* 6.2 (2020): 189–204.

——. *Shakespeare and the Fall of the Roman Republic: Selfhood, Stoicism, and Civil War*. Edinburgh: Edinburgh University Press, 2019.

——. 'Shakespeare and the Other Virgil: Pity and Imperium in *Titus Andronicus*', *Shakespeare Survey* 69 (2016): 46–57.

——. 'Shakespeare vs. Seneca: Competing Visions of Human Dignity', in Eric Dodson-Robinson, ed., *Brill's Companion to the Reception of Senecan Tragedy: Scholarly, Theatrical, and Literary Receptions*, 203–32. Brill Companions to Classical Reception, ed. Kyriakos Demetriou, vol. 5. Leiden and Boston, MA: Brill, 2016.

——. 'Shakespeare versus Aristotle: *Anagnorisis*, Repentance, and Acknowledgment', *Journal of Medieval and Early Modern Studies* 49 (2019): 85–111.

Gray, Patrick, and Helen Clifford. 'Shakespeare, William', in *The Encyclopedia of Renaissance Philosophy*, ed. Marco Sgarbi. Cham: Springer, 2021.

Gray, Patrick, and John D. Cox, eds. *Shakespeare and Renaissance Ethics*. Cambridge: Cambridge University Press, 2014.

Gray, Patrick, and Maurice Samely. 'Shakespeare and Henri Lefebvre's "Right to the City": Subjective Alienation and Mob Violence in *Coriolanus, Julius Caesar*, and *2 Henry VI*', *Textual Practice* 33 (2019): 73–98.

Green, Felicity. *Montaigne and the Life of Freedom*. Cambridge: Cambridge University Press, 2012.

——. 'Reading Montaigne in the Twenty-First Century', *The Historical Journal* 52.4 (2009): 1085–109.

Green, Kenneth Hart. *Leo Strauss and the Rediscovery of Maimonides*. Chicago: University of Chicago, 2013.

Greenblatt, Stephen. *Hamlet in Purgatory*. Princeton: Princeton University Press, 2013.

——. 'Invisible Bullets', in Greenblatt, *Shakespearean Negotiations: The Circulation of Social Energy in Renaissance England*, 21–65. Berkeley, CA, and Los Angeles: University of California Press, 1988. First published in *Glyph* 8 (1981): 40–61, then in Jonathan Dollimore and Alan Sinfield, eds, *Political Shakespeare: New Essays in Cultural Materialism*, 18–47. Manchester: Manchester University Press, 1985; then in Peter Erickson and Coppelia Kahn, eds, *Shakespeare's 'Rough Magic': Renaissance Essays in Honor of C. L. Barber*, 276–302. Newark, DE: University of Delaware Press, 1985.

——. *Shakespearean Negotiations*. Berkeley: University of California Press, 1988.

——. *Shakespeare's Freedom*. Chicago: University of Chicago Press, 2007.

——. 'Shakespeare's Montaigne', in Stephen Greenblatt and Peter G. Platt, eds, *Shakespeare's Montaigne: The Florio Translation of the* Essays. *A Selection*, ix–xxxiii. New York: New York Review Books, 2014.

——. *The Swerve: How the World Became Modern*. New York: Norton, 2011.

Greene, Robert. *The Life and Complete Works in Prose and Verse of Robert Greene*, vol. 12, ed. A. B. Grosart. London: Hazell, Watson, & Viney, 1881–6.

——. *Pandosto: The Triumph of Time*, in William Shakespeare, *The Winter's Tale*, ed. J. H. Pafford, 234–74. London: Methuen, 1963.

Greene, Thomas M. *The Light in Troy: Imitation and Discovery in Renaissance Poetry*. New Haven, CT: Yale University Press, 1982.

Greenlaw, Edwin. 'Spenser and Lucretius', *Studies in Philology* 17 (1920): 455–84.

——. 'Spenser's Mutabilitie', *PMLA* 45.3 (1930): 684–703.

Gregory, Timothy E. 'Julian and the Last Oracle at Delphi', *Greek, Roman, and Byzantine Studies* 24.4 (1983): 355–66.

Greville, Fulke. *A Treatie of Humane Learning. In Greville, Certaine learned and elegant vvorkes of the Right Honorable Fulke Lord Brooke written in his youth, and familiar exercise with Sir Philip Sidney*, 23–52. London: E[lizabeth] P[urslowe] for Henry Seyle, 1633.

Groarke, Leo, and Graham Solomon, 'Some Sources for Hume's Account of Cause', *Journal of the History of Ideas* 52.4 (1991): 645–63.

Gross, Kenneth. *Shylock Is Shakespeare*. Chicago: University of Chicago Press, 2006.

——. 'Slander and Skepticism in *Othello*', *ELH* 56 (1989): 819–52.

Gross, Neil. *Why are Professors Liberal and Why do Conservatives Care?* Cambridge, MA: Harvard University Press, 2013.

Gross, Neil, and Ethan Fosse. 'Why are Professors Liberal?' *Theory and Society* 41.2 (2012): 127–68.

Gross, Neil, and Solon Simmons. 'The Social and Political Views of American College and University Professors', in *Professors and Their Politics*, ed. Neil Gross and Solon Simmons, 19–52. Baltimore: Johns Hopkins Press, 2014.

Gauna, Max. *Montaigne and the Ethics of Compassion*. Lewiston, NY: Edwin Mellen, 2000.

Guest, Claire Lapraik. *The Understanding of Ornament in the Italian Renaissance*. Leiden: Brill, 2015.

Guggenheim, Michael, and Richard Strawn, 'Gide and Montaigne', *Yale French Studies* 7 (1951): 107–14.

Guild, Elizabeth. *Unsettling Montaigne: Poetics, Ethics and Affect in the* Essais *and Other Writings*. Cambridge: D. S. Brewer, 2014.

Guillory, John. *Cultural Capital*. Chicago: University of Chicago Press, 1993.

Guilluy, Christophe. *Twilight of the Elites: Prosperity, the Periphery, and the Future of France*, trans, Malcolm Debevoise. New Haven, CT: Yale University Press, 2019.

Gurr, Andrew. 'Industrious Ariel and Idle Caliban', in *Travel and Drama in Shakespeare's Time*, ed. Jean-Pierre Maquerlot and Michèle Williams, 193–208. Cambridge: Cambridge University Press, 1996.

Haidt, Jonathan, *The Righteous Mind: Why Good People are Divided by Politics and Religion*. New York: Pantheon, 2012.

——. 'Why Universities Must Choose One Telos: Truth or Social Justice'. https://heterodoxacademy.org/blog/one-telos-truth-or-social-justice-2/

Hall, Joan Lord. '"To play the man well and duely": Role-Playing in Montaigne and Jacobean Drama', *Comparative Literature Studies* 22.2 (1985): 173–86.

Halsey, A. H. *The Decline of Donnish Dominion: The British Academic Professions in the Twentieth Century*. Oxford: Oxford University Press, 1992.

Hamlin, Hannibal. *The Bible in Shakespeare*. Oxford: Oxford University Press, 2013.

Hamlin, William M. 'Conscience and the God-Surrogate in Montaigne and *Measure for Measure*', in Patrick Gray and John D. Cox, eds, *Shakespeare and Renaissance Ethics*, 237–60. Cambridge: Cambridge University Press, 2014.

——. 'Florio's Montaigne and the Tyranny of "Custome": Appropriation, Ideology, and Early English Readership of the *Essayes*', *Renaissance Quarterly* 63.2 (2010): 491–544.

——. *The Image of America in Montaigne, Spenser, and Shakespeare: Renaissance Ethnography and Literary Reflection*. New York: St. Martin's Press, 1995.

——. 'A Lost Translation Found? An Edition of *The Sceptick* (*ca.* 1590) Based on Extant Manuscripts', *English Literary Renaissance* 31.1 (2001): 34–51.

——. '*Montagnes Moral Maxims*: A Collection of Seventeenth-Century English Aphorisms Derived from the *Essays* of Montaigne', *Montaigne Studies* 21 (2009): 209–24.

——. *Montaigne: A Very Short Introduction*. New York: Oxford University Press, 2020.

——. 'Montaigne and Shakespeare', in Philippe Desan, ed., *The Oxford Handbook of Montaigne*. New York: Oxford University Press, 2016. 328–46.

——. *Montaigne's English Journey: Reading the* Essays *in Shakespeare's Day*. Oxford: Oxford University Press, 2013.

——. 'On Continuities between Skepticism and Early Ethnography; Or, Montaigne's Providential Diversity', *Sixteenth Century Journal* 31.2 (2000): 361–79.

——. 'On Florio's "Repentance"', in Jean Balsalmo and Amy Graves, eds, *Global Montaigne: Mélanges en l'honneur de Philippe Desan*, 549–59. Paris: Classiques Garnier, 2021.

——. 'Sexuality and Censorship in Florio's Montaigne', *Montaigne Studies* 23 (2011): 17–38.

——. 'The Shakespeare–Montaigne–Sextus Nexus: A Case Study in Early Modern Reading', *Shakespearean International Yearbook 6: Special Section, Shakespeare and Montaigne Revisited*, ed. Graham Bradshaw, T. G. Bishop and Peter Holbrook, 21–36. Burlington, VT: Ashgate, 2006.

——. *Tragedy and Scepticism in Shakespeare's England*. Basingstoke and Basingstoke and New York: Palgrave Macmillan, 2005.

——. 'What Did Montaigne's Skepticism Mean to Shakespeare and His Contemporaries?' *Montaigne Studies* 17 (2005): 195–210.

Hankinson, R. J. *The Sceptics*, 2nd edn. London: Routledge, 1998.

Hardin, Richard F. *Plautus and the English Renaissance of Comedy*. Lanham, MD: Fairleigh Dickinson University Press, 2018.

Harmon, Alice. 'How Great Was Shakespeare's Debt to Montaigne?' *PMLA* 57.4 (1942): 988–1008.

Hartle, Ann. *Michel de Montaigne: Accidental Philosopher*. Cambridge: Cambridge University Press, 2003.

——. *Montaigne and the Origins of Modern Philosophy*. Evanston, IL: Northwestern University Press, 2013.

——. '"Sociable Wisdom": Montaigne's Transformation of Philosophy', *Philosophy and Literature* 39.2 (2015): 285–304.

Haydn, Hiram. *The Counter-Renaissance*. New York: Scribner, 1950.

Hazlitt, William. 'On the Periodical Essayists', in Hazlitt, *Lectures on the English Comic Writers*. London: Taylor and Hessey, 1819.

Heck, Francis S. 'Montaigne's Conservatism and Liberalism: A Paradox?', *Romanic Review* 66.3 (1975): 165–71.

Henderson, Rob. '"Luxury beliefs" are the Latest Status Symbol for Rich Americans', *New York Post* (17 August 2019).

——. 'Thorstein Veblen's Theory of the Leisure Class – A Status Update'. *Quillette* (16 November 2019).

Henderson, W. B. Drayton. 'Montaigne's *Apologie of Raymond Sebond* and *King Lear*', *Shakespeare Association Bulletin* 14 (1939): 209–25, and 15 (1940): 40–56.

Hendrick, Philip. 'Montaigne, Florio and Shakespeare: The Mediation of Colonial Discourse', in Pierre Kapitaniak and Jean-Marie Maguin, eds, *Shakespeare et Montaigne: vers un nouvel humanisme*. Montpellier and Paris: Société française Shakespeare, 2004. 117–33.

Henke, Robert. *Pastoral Transformations: Italian Tragicomedy and Shakespeare's Late Plays*. Newark, DE: University of Delaware Press, 1997.

Henrich, Joseph. *The WEIRDest People in the World: How the West Became Psychologically Peculiar and Particularly Prosperous*. London: Farrar, Straus, and Giroux, 2020.

Henrich, Joseph, et al. 'The Weirdest People in the World?', *Behavioral and Brain Sciences* 33.2–3 (2010): 61–135.

Henry, Patrick. 'The Rise of the Essay: Montaigne and the Novel', *Montaigne Studies* 6 (1994): 113–34.

Herrick, Robert. *The Complete Poetry of Robert Herrick*, ed. J. Max Patrick. New York: Norton, 1968.

Herrup, Cynthia B. 'Law and Morality in Seventeenth-Century England', *Past and Present* 106 (1985): 102–23.

Hershinow, David. 'Diogenes the Cynic and Shakespeare's Bitter Fool', *Criticism* 56.4 (2014): 807–35.

Hillier, Russell M. 'Hamlet the Rough-Hewer: Moral Agency and the Consolations of Reformation Thought', in Patrick Gray and John D. Cox, eds, *Shakespeare and Renaissance Ethics*. Cambridge: Cambridge University Press, 2014. 159–85.

Hillman, Richard. 'Entre Shakespeare et Montaigne: quelques nouveaux tours d'escrime', in Pierre Kapitaniak and Jean-Marie Maguin, eds, *Shakespeare et Montaigne: vers un nouvel humanisme*. Montpellier and Paris: Société française Shakespeare, 2004. 135–53.

——. *French Reflections in the Shakespearean Tragic: Three Case Studies*. Manchester: Manchester University Press, 2012.

——. *Self-Speaking in Medieval and Early Modern English Drama: Subjectivity, Discourse and the Stage*. Basingstoke, Hampshire: Macmillan, 1997.

——. *Shakespearean Subversions: The Trickster and the Play-Text*. London: Routledge, 1992.

——. *The Shakespearean Comic and Tragicomic: French Inflections*. Manchester: Manchester University Press, 2020.

——. *William Shakespeare: The Problem Plays*. Twayne's English Author Series. New York: Twayne Publishers, 1993.

Hirst, Derek, and Richard Strier, eds. *Writing and Political Engagement in Seventeenth-Century England*. Cambridge: Cambridge University Press, 1999.

Hobbes, Thomas. *Leviathan*, ed. Herbert W. Schneider. Indianapolis: Bobbs-Merrill, 1958.

Hochuli, Alex. 'The Brazilianization of the World'. *American Affairs* 5.2 (2021): 93–115.

Hodgen, Margaret T. 'Montaigne and Shakespeare Again', *Huntington Library Quarterly* 16.1 (1952): 23–42.

Hoffmann, George. *Montaigne's Career*. Oxford: Clarendon Press, 1998.

——. 'Montaigne, Lear, and the Question of Afterlife', in Pierre Kapitaniak and Jean-Marie Maguin, eds, *Shakespeare et Montaigne: vers un nouvel humanisme*, 157–73. Montpellier and Paris: Société Française Shakespeare, 2004.

——. 'Self-Assurance and Acting in the *Essais*', in Jean Balsamo, ed., *Montaigne écrivain*, special issue of *Montaigne Studies* 26:1–2 (2014): 55–78.

Holbrook, Peter. *English Renaissance Tragedy: Ideas of Freedom*. London: Bloomsbury, 2015.

——. 'Introduction: Shakespeare and Montaigne Revisited', *Shakespearean International Yearbook* 6 (2006): 5–20.

——. 'Shakespeare, Montaigne, and Classical Reason', in Patrick Gray and John D. Cox, eds, *Shakespeare and Renaissance Ethics*, 261–83. Cambridge: Cambridge University Press, 2014.

——. *Shakespeare's Individualism*. Cambridge: Cambridge University Press, 2010.

Honigmann, E. A. J., and D. A. West. 'With a Bare Bodkin', *Notes and Queries* 28.2 (1981): 129–30.

Hooker, Elizabeth Robbins. 'The Relation of Shakespeare to Montaigne', *PMLA* 17.3 (1902): 312–66.

Horkheimer, Max, and Theodore Adorno. *Dialectics of Enlightenment: Philosophical Fragments* [1944/1947], ed. Gunzelin Schmid Noerr and trans. Edmund Jephcott. Stanford: Stanford University Press, 2002.

Hovey, Kenneth Alan. '"*Mountaigny* Saith Prettily": Bacon's French and the Essay', *PMLA* 106.1 (1991): 71–82.

H[owell], T[homas]. *The fable of Ouid treting of Narcissus, tra[n]slated out of Latin into Englysh mytre, with a moral there vnto, very pleasante to rede. M.D.LX.* ('Imprynted at London: By [J. Tisdale for] Thomas Hackette, and are to be sold at hys shop in Cannynge strete, ouer agaynste the thre Cranes'), 1560.

Hübner, Karolina. 'On the Significance of Formal Causes in Spinoza's Metaphysics', *Archiv für Geschichte der Philosophie* 97.1 (2015): 196–233.

Hume, David. *An Enquiry Concerning Human Understanding*. La Salle, IL: Open Court, 1988.

——. *A Treatise of Human Nature*. Oxford: Clarendon Press, 1896.

——. *A Treatise of Human Nature*, ed. David Fate Norton and Mary J. Norton. Oxford: Oxford University Press, 2000.

——. *A Treatise of Human Nature*, ed. L. A. Selby-Bigge and P. H. Niddith. Oxford: Clarendon Press, 1978.

Hunter, R. G. *Shakespeare and the Comedy of Forgiveness*. New York: Columbia University Press, 1965.

Hutson, Lorna. *The Invention of Suspicion: Law and Mimesis in Shakespeare and Renaissance Drama*. Oxford: Oxford University Press, 2007.

——. 'Imagining Justice: Kantorowicz and Shakespeare', *Representations* 106 (2009): 118–43.

Hutton, James. *The Greek Anthology in France and in the Latin Writers of the Netherlands to the Year 1800*, vol. 28. Ithaca, NY: Cornell University Press, 1946.

Hyman, Wendy. 'Seizing Flowers in Spenser's Bower and Garden', *English Literary Renaissance* 37 (2007): 193–214.

Ibbett, Katherine. *Compassion's Edge: Fellow-Feeling and Its Limits in Early Modern France*. Philadelphia: University of Pennsylvania Press, 2018.

Jackson, Ken, and Arther F. Marotti. 'The Turn to Religion in Early Modern English Studies'. *Criticism* 46.1 (2004): 167–90.

James, William. 'The Will to Believe', in A. J. Burger, ed., *The Ethics of Belief*. np: A. J. Burger, 2008.

Jameson, Fredric. *The Ancients and the Postmoderns: On the Historicity of Forms*. New York: Verso, 2015.

Jeanneret, Michel. *A Feast of Words: Banquets and Table Talk in the Renaissance*, trans. Jeremy Whitely and Emma Hughes. Chicago: University of Chicago Press, 1991.

——. *Perpetual Motion: Transforming Shapes in the Renaissance from Da Vinci to Montaigne*. Baltimore: Johns Hopkins University Press, 2000.

Johnson, Christopher. 'Florio's 'Conversion' of Montaigne, Sidney and Six Patronesses', *Cahiers Elisabéthains* 64 (2003): 9–18.

Jonson, Ben. *The Poems, The Prose Works*, vol. 8, ed. C. H. Herford, P. Simpson and E. Simpson. Oxford: Oxford University Press, 1947.

Joslyn, Mark R., and Donald P. Haider-Markel, 'Who Knows Best? Education, Partisanship, and Contested Facts'. *Politics and Policy* 42.6 (2014): 919–47.

Jourdan, Serena. *The Sparrow and the Flea: The Sense of Providence in Shakespeare and Montaigne*. Salzburg: Institut für Anglistik und Amerikanistik, Universität Salzburg, 1983.

Kant, Immanuel. *Groundwork for the Metaphysics of Morals*, ed. Allen W. Wood and J. B. Schneewind. New Haven: Yale University Press, 2002.

Kantorowicz, Ernst. *The King's Two Bodies: A Study in Mediaeval Political Theology*. Princeton: Princeton University Press, 1957.

Kapitaniak, Pierre, and Jean-Marie Maguin, eds. *Shakespeare et Montaigne: vers un nouvel humanisme*. Montpellier and Paris: Société française Shakespeare, 2004.

Kaufmann, Eric. 'Academic Freedom in Crisis: Punishment, Political Discrimination, and Self-Censorship'. San Gabriel, CA: Center for the Study of Partisanship and Ideology (CPSI), 2021. https://cspicenter.org/reports/academicfreedom/

Kechagia, Eleni. *Plutarch against Colotes: A Lesson in History of Philosophy*. Oxford: Oxford University Press, 2011.

Keener, Andrew S. 'Prefatory Friendships: Florio's Montaigne and Material Technologies of the Self', *Renaissance Papers* (2013): 83–100.

Keffer, Ken. *A Publication History of the Rival Transcriptions of Montaigne's Essays*. Lewiston, NY: Edwin Mellen, 2001.

Keilen, Sean. *Vulgar Eloquence: On the Renaissance Invention of English Literature*. New Haven, CT: Yale University Press, 2006.

Kellenberger, Hunter. '"Consummation" or "Consumation" in Shakespeare', *Modern Philology* 65.3 (1968): 228–30.

Kellermann, Frederick. 'The *Essais* and Socrates', in Dikka Berven, ed., *Montaigne: A Collection of Essays*, 1:58–70. New York and London: Garland, 1995.

Kellogg, Amanda Ogden. 'Pyrrhonist Uncertainty in Shakespeare's Sonnets', *Shakespeare* 11.4 (2015): 408–24.

Kenny, Neil. 'Making Sense of Intertextuality', in John O'Brien, ed., *The Cambridge Companion to Rabelais*. Cambridge: Cambridge University Press, 2010. 57–72.

Kenny, Neil, Richard Scholar and Wes Williams, eds. *Montaigne in Transit: Essays in Honour of Ian Maclean*. Cambridge: Legenda, 2016.

Kinney, Arthur F., ed. *The Oxford Handbook of Shakespeare*. Oxford: Oxford University Press, 2012.

Kirsch, Arthur. 'The Bitter and the Sweet of Tragicomedy: Shakespeare's *All's Well That Ends Well* and Montaigne', *Yale Review* 102.2 (2014): 63–84.

——. 'The Integrity of *Measure for Measure*'. *Shakespeare Survey* 28 (1975): 89–105.

——. 'Sexuality and Marriage in Montaigne and *All's Well That Ends Well*', *Montaigne Studies* 9 (1997): 187–202.

——. *Shakespeare and the Experience of Love*. Cambridge: Cambridge University Press, 1981.

——. 'Virtue, Vice, and Compassion in Montaigne and *The Tempest*', *SEL* 3.2 (1997): 337–52.

Knapp, James A., ed. *Shakespeare and the Power of the Face*. Abingdon and New York: Routledge, 2016.

Knapp, Jeffrey. *An Empire Nowhere: England, America, and Literature from* Utopia *to* The Tempest. Berkeley and Los Angeles: University of California Press, 1992.

Knight, G. Wilson. *Byron and Shakespeare*. New York and London: Routledge, 2002.

——. 'The Third Eye: An Essay on *All's Well That Ends Well*', in *The Sovereign Flower: On Shakespeare as the Poet of Royalism together with Related Essays and Indexes to Earlier Volumes*, 93–160. New York: Macmillan, 1958.

——. *The Wheel of Fire*. Oxford: Oxford University Press, 1930.

Knight, Jeffrey Todd. *Bound to Read: Compilations, Collections, and the Making of Renaissance Literature*. Philadelphia: University of Pennsylvania Press, 2013.

Knights, L. C. *An Approach to Hamlet*. London: Chatto & Windus, 1960.

Knoespel, K. *Narcissus and the Invention of Personal History*. New York: Garland Publishing, 1985.

Knowles, Ronald. '*Hamlet* and Counter-Humanism', *Renaissance Quarterly* 52.4 (1999): 1046–69.

Konstantinovic, Isabelle. *Montaigne et Plutarque*. Geneva: Librairie Droz, 1989.

Kotkin, Joel. *The Coming of Neo-Feudalism: A Warning to the Global Middle Class*. New York: Encounter Books, 2020.

——. *The New Class Conflict*. Candor, NY: Telos Press, 2014.

Kott, Jan. *Shakespeare, Our Contemporary*, trans. Bolesław Taborski. London: Methuen, 1965.

——. 'O Teatr Godny Naszej Epoki' [For Theatre Worthy of Our Epoch], *Sprawy i Ludzie* 12.3 (1951): 3.

——. *Przyczynk do biografii* [Contributions to a Biography]. Kraków: Aneks, 1990.

Kramer, Jane. 'Me, Myself, and I', *The New Yorker*, 9 September 2009.

Kritzman, Lawrence D. *The Fabulous Imagination: On Montaigne's Essays*. New York: Columbia University Press, 2009.

Kuzner, James. *Shakespeare as a Way of Life*. New York: Fordham University Press, 2016.

Kuzminski, Adrian. *Pyrrhonism*. Plymouth, UK: Lexington, 2008.

Lacan, Jacques, and Jacques-Alain Miller. *My Teaching*, trans. David Macey. London and New York: Verso, 2009.

Langbert, Mitchell. 'Homogenous: The Political Affiliations of Elite Liberal Arts College Faculty', *Academic Questions* 31 (2018): 186–97.

——. 'Neil Gross's Plantation Model of the Academic Labor Market', *Academic Questions* 29 (2016): 49–58.

Langer, Ullrich, ed. *The Cambridge Companion to Montaigne*. Cambridge: Cambridge University Press, 2005.

Larmore, Charles. *The Autonomy of Morality*. Cambridge: Cambridge University Press, 2008.

——. 'Montaigne, Michel Eyquem de, 1533–1592', *Dictionnaire d'éthique et de philosophie morale*, ed. Monique Canto-Sperber, 981–7. Paris: Presses universitaires de France, 1996.

——. *Morality and Metaphysics*. Cambridge: Cambridge University Press, 2021.

——. 'Morals and Metaphysics', *European Journal of Philosophy* 21.4 (2013): 665–75.

——. 'Scepticism', *The Cambridge History of Seventeenth-Century Philosophy*, 2 vols, ed. Daniel Garber and Michael Ayers, 2:1145–92. Cambridge: Cambridge University Press, 1998.

——. 'Un scepticisme sans tranquillité: Montaigne et ses modèles antiques', in Vincent Carraud and Jean-Luc Marion, eds, *Montaigne: scepticisme, métaphysique, théologie*, 15–31. Paris: Presses universitaires de France, 2004.

Laursen, John Christian. *The Politics of Skepticism in the Ancients, Montaigne, Hume, and Kant*. Leiden: E. J. Brill, 1992.

Lawrence, Sean. *Forgiving the Gift: The Philosophy of Generosity in Shakespeare and Marlowe*. Pittsburgh: Duquesne University Press, 2012.

Leckie, Ann. *The Imperial Radch Trilogy: Ancillary Sword, Ancillary Justice, Ancillary Mercy*. New York: Orbit, 2017.

Lee, John. 'The English Renaissance Essay: Churchyard, Cornwallis, Florio's Montaigne and Bacon,', in Michael Hattaway, ed., *A Companion to English Renaissance Literature and Cultures*, 600–8. Oxford: Blackwell, 2000.

——. '"A judge that were no man": Montaigne, Shakespeare, and Imagination', *Shakespearean International Yearbook 6: Special Section, Shakespeare and Montaigne Revisited*, ed. Graham Bradshaw, T. G. Bishop and Peter Holbrook. Burlington, VT: Ashgate, 2006. 37–55.

——. *Shakespeare's* Hamlet *and the Controversies of Self*. New York and Oxford: Oxford University Press, 2000.

——. 'Unreasonable Men? Categories and Metaphor in Shakespeare and Montaigne', *Shakespearean International Yearbook* 3 (2003): 268–81.

Lee, Sidney. *The French Renaissance in England: An Account of the Literary Relations of England and France in the Sixteenth Century*. New York: Charles Scribner's Sons, 1910.

Legros, Alain. 'Montaigne, son livre et son roi', *Studi Francesi* 122:2 (1997): 259–74.

Lestringant, Frank. 'Gonzalo's Books: La République des Cannibales, de Montaigne à Shakespeare', in Pierre Kapitaniak and Jean-Marie Maguin, eds, *Shakespeare et Montaigne: vers un nouvel humanism*, 175–93. Montpellier and Paris: Société française Shakespeare, 2004.

Levao, Ronald. '"They Hate Us Youth": Byron's Falstaff', *Literary Imagination* 11.2 (2009): 127–35.

Levin, Harry. *The Question of Hamlet*. New York: Oxford University Press, 1959.

Lewis, C. S. *Mere Christianity*. New York: HarperCollins, 2001.

——. 'On Obstinacy in Belief', In *Essay Collection and Other Short Pieces*, ed. Lesley Walmsley, 206–15. New York: HarperCollins, 2000.

Lewis, Rhodri. *Hamlet and the Vision of Darkness*. Princeton, NJ: Princeton University Press, 2017.

Leys, Ruth. 'The Turn to Affect: A Critique', *Critical Inquiry* 37.2 (2011): 434–72.

Lind, Michael. *The New Class War: Saving Democracy from the Metropolitan Elite*. New York: Portfolio for Penguin Random House, 2020.

Lloyd, Michael. 'Cleopatra as Isis', *Shakespeare Survey* 12 (1959): 88–94.

Long, A. A. 'Hellenistic Ethics and Philosophical Power', in Peter Green, ed., *Hellenistic History and Culture*, 138–56. Berkeley: University of California Press, 1993.

Longworth-Chambrun, Clara. 'Influences françaises dan la "Tempête" de Shakespeare', *Revue de la littérature comparée* 5 (1925): 37–59.

Lucretius (Titus Lucretius Carus). *On the Nature of the Universe*, trans. R. E. Latham. New York: Penguin, 1994.

——. *On the Nature of Things*, trans. Martin Ferguson Smith. Indianapolis: Hackett, 2001.

Lupton, Julia Reinhard. *Citizen-Saints: Shakespeare and Political Theology*. Chicago: University of Chicago Press, 2005.

——. *Thinking with Shakespeare: Essays on Politics and Life*. Chicago: University of Chicago Press, 2010.

Luria, A. R. *The Mind of a Mnemonist: A Little Book about a Vast Memory*, trans. L. Solotaroff. Ringwood, Victoria: Penguin, 1975.

Lutaud, Olivier. 'Montaigne chez les niveleurs anglais: Walwyn et les *Essais*', *Rivista di Letterature Moderne e Comparate* 12 (1959): 53–8.

McAlindon, Tom. 'Cultural Materialism and the Ethics of Reading: or, the Radicalizing of Jacobean Tragedy'. *Modern Language Review* 90.4 (1995): 411–38. Reprinted in McAlindon, Shakespeare Minus 'Theory'.

——. *Shakespeare Minus 'Theory'*. Burlington, VT: Ashgate, 2004.

——. 'Testing the New Historicism: "Invisible Bullets" Reconsidered', *Studies in Philology* 92.4 (1995): 411–38. Reprinted in McAlindon, *Shakespeare Minus 'Theory'*. Burlington, VT: Ashgate, 2004.

McEachern, Claire. *Believing in Shakespeare: Studies in Longing*. Cambridge: Cambridge University Press, 2018.

McFarlane, I. D., and Ian Maclean, eds. *Montaigne: Essays in Memory of Richard Sayce*. Oxford: Clarendon Press, 1982.

McGinn, Colin. *Shakespeare's Philosophy: Discovering the Meaning Behind the Plays*. New York: HarperCollins, 2006.

Machacek, Gregory. 'Allusion', *PMLA* 122.2 (2007): 522–36.

Machielson, J. 'Thinking with Montaigne: Evidence, Skepticism, and Meaning in Early French Demonology', *French History* 25.4 (2011): 427–52.

MacIntyre, Alasdair. *After Virtue: A Study in Moral Theory*, 3rd edn. Notre Dame, IN: University of Notre Dame Press, 2007.

——. 'Hume on "Is" and "Ought"', *Philosophical Review* 68.4 (1959): 451–68.

Mack, Peter. 'Madness, Proverbial Wisdom, and Philosophy in *King Lear*', in Patrick Gray and John D. Cox, eds, *Shakespeare and Renaissance Ethics*, 284–303. Cambridge: Cambridge University Press, 2014.

——. 'Marston and Webster's Use of Florio's Montaigne', *Montaigne Studies* 24 (2012): 67–82.

——. 'Montaigne and Florio', in Andrew Hadfield, ed., *The Oxford Handbook of English Prose, 1500–1640*, 77–90. Oxford: Oxford University Press, 2013.

——. 'Montaigne and Shakespeare: Source, Parallel or Comparison?' *Montaigne Studies* 23 (2011): 151–80.

——. *Reading and Rhetoric in Montaigne and Shakespeare*. London: Bloomsbury, 2010.

McKinley, Mary. 'Montaigne on Women', in Philippe Desan, ed., *The Oxford Handbook of Montaigne*, 581–99. New York: Oxford University Press, 2016.

Maclean, Ian. 'Montaigne and the Truth of the Schools', in Ullrich Langer, ed., *The Cambridge Companion to Montaigne*, 142–62. New York: Cambridge University Press, 2005.

Magnien, Michel. 'La Boétie and Montaigne', in Philippe Desan, ed., *The Oxford Handbook of Montaigne*, 97–116. New York: Oxford University Press, 2016.

Maguin, Jean-Marie. '*The Tempest* and Cultural Exchange', *Shakespeare Survey* 48 (1995): 147–54.

Maguire, Laurie, 'Part I: Editor's Introduction', in Maguire, ed., *How to Do Things with Shakespeare: New Approaches, New Essays*, pp. 7–10. Oxford: Wiley-Blackwell, 2008.

Malone, Edmond, ed. *The Plays and Poems of William Shakspeare*, 10 vols. London, 1790.

Mann, Thomas. *Reflections of a Nonpolitical Man*, trans. Walter D. Morris, in Mann, *Reflections of a Nonpolitical Man*, ed. Mark Lilla, 5–490. New York: New York Review of Books, 2021.

Maritain, Jacques. *The Peasant of the Garonne: An Old Layman Questions Himself about the Present Time*, trans. Michael Cuddihy and Elizabeth Hughes. Eugene, OR: Wipf & Stock, 1968.

Marlowe, Christopher. *Doctor Faustus*, ed. John D. Jump. London: Methuen, 1962.

Martindale, Charles, and Michelle Martindale. *Shakespeare and the Uses of Antiquity*. New York: Routledge, 1990.

Masten, Jeffrey. *Textual Intercourse: Collaboration, Authorship, and Sexualities in Renaissance Drama*. Cambridge: Cambridge University Press, 1997.

Mates, Benson. *The Skeptic Way: Sextus Empiricus's Outlines of Pyrrhonism*. Oxford: Oxford University Press, 1996.

Mathieu-Castellani, Gisèle. 'Plutarque chez Montaigne et chez Shakespeare', in Pierre Kapitaniak and Jean-Marie Maguin, eds, *Shakespeare et Montaigne: vers un nouvel humanisme*, 195–208. Montpellier and Paris: Société française Shakespeare, 2004.

Mathieu-Castellani, Gisèle, and François Cornilliat. 'Intertexte phénix', *Littérature* 55 (1985): 5–9.

Matthiessen, F. O. *Translation, an Elizabethan Art*. Cambridge, MA: Harvard University Press, 1931.

Maus, Katharine Eisaman. 'The Will of Caesar: Choice-Making, the Death of the Roman Republic, and the Development of Shakespearean Character', *Shakespeare Survey* 70 (2017): 249–58.

Mercer, Peter. *Hamlet and the Acting of Revenge*. London: Macmillan, 1987.

Miernowski, Jan. 'Le "beaujeu" de la philosophie', *Montaigne Studies* 12 (2000): 25–44.

Miles, Geoffrey. *Shakespeare and the Constant Romans*. Oxford: Clarendon Press, 1996.

Miller, Jr., Walter M. *A Canticle for Leibovitz*. Philadelphia: J. B. Lippincott, 1959.

Miller, J. Hillis. 'On Edge: Crossways of Contemporary Criticism', in Miller, *Theory Now and Then*, 171–200. London: Harvester Wheatsheaf, 1991.

———. 'The Literary Criticism of Georges Poulet', *Modern Language Notes* 78.5 (1963): 471–88.

Milton, John. *The Complete Poems and Major Prose*, ed. Merritt Y. Hughes. New York: Odyssey Press, 1957.

Miola, Robert S. *Shakespeare and Classical Comedy: The Influence of Plautus and Terence*. Oxford: Clarendon Press, 1994.

——. *Shakespeare's Reading*. Oxford: Oxford University Press, 2000.

Montaigne, Michel de. *The Complete Essays*, trans. M. A. Screech. London and New York: Penguin, 1987.

——. *The Complete Works of Montaigne*, trans. Donald M. Frame. Stanford: Stanford University Press, 1958; rpt. New York: Everyman Library, 2003.

——. *Essais*, 3 vols, ed. Micha Alexandre. Paris: Garnier-Flammarion, 1969.

——. *Les Essais*, ed. Jean Balsamo, Michel Magnien and Catherine Magnien-Simonin. Bibliothèque de la Pléiade. Paris: Gallimard, 2007.

——. *Les Essais. Édition conforme au texte de l'exemplaire de Bordeaux avec les additions de l'édition posthume, etc.*, 3 vols, ed. Pierre Villey, rev. V.-L. Saulnier. Paris: Presses universitaires de France, 1965; rpt. 1978; rpt. 1992.

——. *Les Essais, Publiés d'après l'Exemplaire de Bordeaux par Fortunat Strowski*, 5 vols in 3 vols. Hildesheim and New York: Georg Olms Verlag, 1981.

——. *The Essayes of Michael, Lord of Montaigne*, 3 vols, trans. John Florio, London: J. M. Dent, 1928.

——. *The Essayes or Morall, Politike and Millitarie Discourses of Lo[rd]: Michaell de Montaigne*, trans. John Florio. London: Valentine Sims for Edward Blount, 1603.

——. *The Essayes of Montaigne, John Florio's Translation*. New York: Modern Library, 1933.

——. *The Essays of Michel de Montaigne*, 3 vols, trans. and ed. Jacob Zeitlin. New York: Alfred A. Knopf, 1934–6.

——. *Montaigne's Essays*, 3 vols, trans. John Florio. London and New York, NY: Dent and Dutton, 1965.

——. *Œuvres complètes*, ed. Albert Thibaudet and Maurice Rat. Paris: Gallimard, 1962.

——. *Selected Essays of Montaigne*, trans. John Florio; ed. Walter Kaiser. Boston, MA: Houghton Mifflin, 1964.

——. *Shakespeare's Montaigne: The Florio Translation of the Essays*, ed. Stephen Greenblatt and Peter G. Platt. New York: New York Review Books, 2014.

Montini, Donatella. 'John Florio and Shakespeare: Life and Language', *Memoria di Shakespeare: A Journal of Shakespearean Studies* 2 (2015): 109–29.

More, Sir Thomas. *The Complete Works of Thomas More*, ed. Edward Surtz, S. J. and J. H. Hexter, 4 vols. New Haven, CT: Yale University Press, 1964.

Morgan, Allison, Aaron Clauset, Daniel Larremore, Nicholas LaBerge and Mirta Galesic, 'Socioeconomic Roots of Academic Faculty', *SocArXiv*, 24 March 2021 (pre-print). https://doi.org/10.31235/osf.io/6wjxc

Moss, Ann. *Ovid in Renaissance France: A Survey of the Latin Editions of Ovid and Commentaries Printed in France before 1600*. London: Warburg Institute Surveys and Texts, 1982.

——. 'Montaigne et Shakespeare: rencontres au féminin', in Pierre Kapitaniak and Jean-Marie Maguin, eds, *Shakespeare et Montaigne: vers un nouvel humanisme*, 209–19. Montpellier and Paris: Société française Shakespeare, 2004.

Mousnier, Roland. *Les Institutions de la France sous la monarchie absolue: 1598–1789*, 2 vols. Paris: Presses universitaires de France, 1974; trans. Arthur Goldhammer, *The Institutions of France under the Absolute Monarchy, 1598–1789*. Chicago: University of Chicago Press, 1984.

Mucedorus, in Russell A. Fraser and Norman Rabkin, eds, *Drama of the English Renaissance, I: The Tudor Period*, 463–80. New York: Macmillan, 1976.

Muir, Kenneth. *Shakespeare: Hamlet*. London: Edward Arnold, 1963.

——. *Shakespeare's Tragic Sequence*. London: Hutchinson, 1972.

——. *The Sources of Shakespeare's Plays*. London: Methuen, 1977.

Mueller, Martin. 'Hermione's Wrinkles, or, Ovid Transformed: An Essay on *The Winter's Tale*', *Comparative Drama* 5 (1971): 226–39.

Murphy, Patrick M., ed. *The Tempest: Critical Essays*. New York and London: Routledge, 2001.

Murry, John Middleton. *Things to Come*. London: Cape, 1928.

Nagel, Thomas. *Mind and Cosmos: Why the Materialist Neo-Darwinist Conception of Nature is Almost Certainly False*. Oxford: Oxford University Press, 2012.

——. *Mortal Questions*, ed. John Rawls. Cambridge: Cambridge University Press, 1979.

——. *The View from Nowhere*. Oxford: Oxford University Press, 1986.

Nakam, Géralde. *Les Essais de Montaigne: Miroir et procès de leur temps*. Paris: Honoré Champion, 2001.

——. 'La Mélancolie de la "Vanitas": Des *Essais* à *Hamlet*, de Montaigne au Prince Hamlet', in *Shakespeare et Montaigne*, ed. Pierre Kapitaniak and Jean-Marie Maguin, 221–43. Montpellier: Société française Shakespeare, 2003.

Nazarian, Cynthia. 'Montaigne against Sympathy: On Affect and Ethics in the *Essais*', *Montaigne Studies* 30 (2018): 125–38.

——. 'Montaigne on Violence', in *The Oxford Handbook of Montaigne*, ed. Philippe Desan, 493–507. New York: Oxford University Press, 2016.

Nelson, Nicolas H. 'Montaigne with a Restoration Voice: Charles Cotton's Translation of the *Essais*', *Language and Style* 24.2 (1991): 131–44.

Newcombe, Lori Humphrey. *Reading Popular Romance in Early Modern England*. New York: Columbia University Press, 2002.

Newell, Anthony. *The Soliloquies in Hamlet*. Rutherford, NJ: Fairleigh Dickinson University Press, 1991.

Nietzsche, Friedrich. *The Gay Science*, trans. and ed. Walter Kaufmann. New York: Vintage, 1984.

Nordlund, Marcus. 'Pride and Self-Love in Shakespeare and Montaigne', *Shakespearean International Yearbook 6: Special Section, Shakespeare and Montaigne Revisited*, ed. Graham Bradshaw, T. G. Bishop and Peter Holbrook, 77–98. Burlington, VT: Ashgate, 2006.

Nosworthy, J. M. *Shakespeare's Occasional Plays*. London: Edward Arnold, 1965.

Nussbaum, Martha Craven. *The Fragility of Goodness: Luck and Ethics in Greek Tragedy and Philosophy*. Cambridge: Cambridge University Press, 1986.

——. *The Therapy of Desire*. Princeton, NJ: Princeton University Press, 1994.

Nuttall, A. D. 'Action at a Distance: Shakespeare and the Greeks', in *Shakespeare and the Classics*, ed. Charles Martindale and A. B. Taylor, 209–22. Cambridge: Cambridge University Press, 2004.

——. '*Hamlet*: Conversations with the Dead', *Proceedings of the British Academy* 74 (1988): 53–69.

——. 'Ovid's Narcissus and Shakespeare's Richard II: The Reflected Self', in Charles Martindale, ed., *Ovid Renewed: Ovidian Influences on Literature and Art from the Middle Ages to the Twentieth Century*, 137–50. Cambridge: Cambridge University Press, 1988.

——. *Shakespeare the Thinker*. New Haven, CT, and London: Yale University Press, 2007.

O'Brien, John. 'A Fantasy of Justice', in Pierre Kapitaniak and Jean-Marie Maguin, eds, *Shakespeare et Montaigne: vers un nouvel humanism*, 245–58. Montpellier and Paris: Société française Shakespeare, 2004.

——. 'Introduction: The Time of Theory', In John O'Brien and Malcolm Quainton, eds, *Distant Voices Still Heard: Contemporary Readings of French Renaissance Literature*, 1–52. Liverpool: Liverpool University Press, 2000.

——. 'Montaigne in Some London Libraries', *Montaigne Studies* 24 (2012): 141–62.

——. 'Montaigne, Sir Ralph Bankes and other English Readers of the *Essais*', *Renaissance Studies* 28.3 (2013): 377–91.

——. 'Translating Scepticism and Transferring Knowledge in Montaigne's House', in Tania Demetriou and Rowan Tomlinson, eds, *The Culture of Translation in Early Modern England and France, 1500–1660*, 162–74. Basingstoke: Palgrave Macmillan, 2015.

O'Connor, Brian. *Idleness: A Philosophical Essay*. Princeton, NJ: Princeton University Press, 2018.

O'Connor, Desmond. 'John Florio', *Oxford Dictionary of National Biography*. Oxford: Oxford University Press, 2004.

Olivier, T. 'Shakespeare and Montaigne: A Tendency of Thought', *Theoria: A Journal of Social and Political Theory* 54 (May 1980): 43–59.

O'Malley, Susan Gushee, ed. *'Custome is an Idiot': Jacobean Pamphlet Literature on Women*. Urbana: University of Illinois Press, 2004.

Orgel, Stephen. 'Shakespeare and the Cannibals', in Marjorie Garber, ed., *Cannibals, Witches, and Divorce: Estranging the Renaissance*, 40–66. Baltimore: Johns Hopkins University Press, 1987.

Ott, Walter. 'Leges Sive Natura: Bacon, Spinoza, and a Forgotten Concept of Law', in Walter Ott and Lydia Patton, eds, *Laws of Nature*, 62–79. Oxford: Oxford University Press, 2018.

Ovid (Publius Ovidius Naso). *Ovid's Metamorphosis: Englished, Mythologiz'd, and Represented in Figures*, trans. George Sandys. Oxford, 1632.

Ovid. *The xv. Booke of P. Ouidius Naso, entytuled Metamorphosis, translated oute of Latin into English meeter, by Arthur Golding Gentleman*. London: Willyam Seres, 1567.

L'Ovide moralisé, ed. C. de Boer. Amsterdam: Johannes Müller, 1915 [c. 1316–28].

Page, Frederick. 'Shakespeare and Florio', *Notes and Queries* 184 (1943): 283–5; *Notes and Queries* 185 (1943): 42–4, 107–8.

Panichi, Nicola. 'Montaigne and Plutarch: A Scepticism that Conquers the Mind', in Gianni Paganini and José R. Maia Neto, eds, *Renaissance Scepticisms*, 183–211. Dordrecht: Springer Verlag, 2009.

Parfit, Derek. *On What Matters*. Oxford: Oxford University Press, 2011.

Parker, Fred. *Scepticism and Literature: An Essay on Pope, Hume, Sterne, and Johnson*. Oxford: Oxford University Press, 2003.

——. 'Shakespeare's Argument with Montaigne', *Cambridge Quarterly* 28.1 (1999): 1–18.

Partridge, Eric. *Shakespeare's Bawdy*, 3rd edn. London: Routledge, 1990.

Parvini, Neema. *Shakespeare's Moral Compass*. Edinburgh: Edinburgh University Press, 2018.

Pascal, Blaise. *Pensées* and *Discussion with Monsieur de Sacy*, in Pascal, *Pensées and Other Writings*, trans. Honor Levi and ed. Anthony Levi. Oxford: Oxford University Press, 1999.

Pascoe, David. '*The Dutch Courtesan* and the Profits of Translation', in T. F. Wharton, ed., *The Drama of John Marston: Critical Re-Visions*, 162–80. Cambridge: Cambridge University Press, 2000.

Pasnau, Robert. *Metaphysical Themes, 1274–1671*. Oxford: Oxford University Press, 2011.

Paster, Gail Kern. 'Montaigne, Dido, and *The Tempest*: "How came that widow in?"' *Shakespeare Quarterly* 35.1 (1984): 91–4.

Perkins, David, ed. *English Romantic Writers*. New York: Harcourt, Brace & World, 1967.

Petronella, Vincent F. 'Hamlet's "To Be or Not to Be" Soliloquy: Once More unto the Breach', *Studies in Philology* 71.1 (1974): 72–88.

Pfister, Manfred. 'Inglese Italianato – Italiano Anglizzato: John Florio', in Andreas Höfele and Werner von Koppenfels, eds, *Renaissance*

Go-Betweens: Cultural Exchange in Early Modern Europe, 32–54. Berlin: Walter de Gruyter, 2005..

Phillips, Joshua. '"Th'Intertraffique of the Minde"': Publishing John Florio's Translation of the *Essais*', *Montaigne Studies* 11 (1999): 209–32.

Pigman III, G. W. 'Versions of Imitation in the Renaissance', *Renaissance Quarterly* 33.1 (1980): 1–32.

Pina Martins, José V. de. 'Modèles portugais et italiens de Montaigne', in *Montaigne et l'Europe: Actes du colloque international de Bordeaux*, ed. Claude-Gilbert Dubois, 139–52. Mont-de-Marsan: Editions Inter-Universitaires, 1992.

Plato. *The Republic*, trans. Benjamin Jowett. Oxford: Oxford University Press, 1888.

Platt, Peter G. '"I am an Englishman in Italian"': John Florio and the Translation of Montaigne', in Stephen Greenblatt and Peter G. Platt, eds, *Shakespeare's Montaigne: The Florio Translation of the* Essays, *A Selection*, xxxiv–xlv. New York: New York Review Books, 2014.

——. *Shakespeare's Essays: Sampling Montaigne from* Hamlet *to* The Tempest. Edinburgh: Edinburgh University Press, 2020.

Prat, Sebastian. *Constance et inconstance chez Montaigne*. Paris: Garnier, 2011.

Plutarch (Lucius Mestrius Plutarchus). *The Philosophie, commonlie called, the Morals, written by the learned Philosopher Plutarch of Chaeronea*, trans. Philemon Holland. London, 1603.

Pooley, Roger. *English Prose of the Seventeenth Century, 1590–1700*, 173–90. London and New York: Longman, 1992.

Popkin, Richard H. *The History of Scepticism from Savonarola to Bayle*. Oxford and New York: Oxford University Press, 2003.

Posner, David. *The Performance of Nobility in Early Modern European Literature*. Cambridge: Cambridge University Press, 1999.

Post, Jerrold M. *Dreams of Glory: Narcissism and Politics*. Cambridge: Cambridge University Press, 2014.

Pouilloux, Jean-Yves. *Montaigne: l'éveil de la pensée*. Paris: Honoré Champion, 1995. Revised and expanded edition of Pouilloux, *Lire les Essais de Montaigne*. Paris: F. Maspero, 1969.

Pranger, M. B. *Eternity's Ennui: Temporality, Perseverance and Voice in Augustine and Western Literature*. Brill's Studies in Intellectual History. Leiden: Brill, 2010.

——. 'Time and Narrative in Augustine's *Confessions*', *The Journal of Religion* 81 (2001): 377–93.

Prosser, Eleanor. *Hamlet and Revenge*. Stanford: Stanford University Press, 1967.

——. 'Shakespeare, Montaigne, and the Rarer Action', *Shakespeare Studies* 1 (1965): 261–4.

Quint, David. *Montaigne and the Quality of Mercy: Ethical and Political Themes in the Essais*. Princeton: Princeton University Press, 1998.

——. 'Montaigne and the Suicide Bombers: A Discussion of "De la Vertu"', *The Yale Review* 97.4 (2009): 73–84.

——. 'The Tragedy of Nobility on the Seventeenth-Century Stage', *Modern Language Quarterly* 67.1 (2006): 7–29.

Quintilian, Marcus Fabius. *The Institutio Oratoria of Quintilian*, vol. 4, trans. H. E. Butler. New York: Putnam, 1922.

Rawls, John. *A Theory of Justice*. Oxford: Oxford University Press, 1972.

Rettig, John W., ed. *The Fathers of the Church, Volume 88: Tractates on the Gospel of John 28–54*. New York: Catholic University Press of America, 2010.

Rhodes, Neil. 'Status anxiety and English Renaissance Translations', in Helen Smith and Louise Wilson, eds, *Renaissance Paratexts*, 107–20. Cambridge: Cambridge University Press, 2011.

Ribiero, Brian. 'Hume's Changing Views on the "Durability" of Scepticism', *The Journal of Scottish Philosophy* 7.2 (2009): 215–36.

Richards, Irving T. 'The Meaning of Hamlet's Soliloquy', *PMLA* 48.3 (1933): 741–66.

Rigolot, François. 'Les "visages" de Montaigne', in Marguerite Soulié, ed., *La Littérature de la Renaissance: Mélanges offerts à Henri Weber*, 357–70. Geneva: Slatkine, 1984.

Ricœur, Paul. *The Course of Recognition*. Cambridge, MA: Harvard University Press, 2005.

——. 'Life: A Story in Search of a Narrator', in M. C. Doeser and J. N. Kraay, *Facts and Values: Philosophical Reflections from Western and Non-Western Perspectives*, 121–32. Martinus Nijhoff Philosophy Library 19. Springer, Dordrecht, 1986.

——. *Oneself as Another*, trans. Kathleen Blamey. Chicago and London: The University of Chicago Press, 1992.

——. *Time and Narrative. Volume 1*, trans. Kathleen McLaughlin and David Pellauer. Chicago and London: The University of Chicago Press, 1984.

——. *Time and Narrative. Volume 2*, trans. Kathleen McLaughlin and David Pellauer. Chicago and London: The University of Chicago Press, 1985.

——. *Time and Narrative. Volume 3*, trans., Kathleen McLaughlin and David Pellauer. Chicago and London: The University of Chicago Press, 1988.

Riker, Stephen. 'Al-Ghazali on Necessary Causality in The Incoherence of the Philosophers', *The Monist* 79.3 (1996): 315–24.

Rimbaud, Arthur. *Œuvres*. Paris: Éditions Garnier Frères, 1960.

Robertson, John M. *Montaigne and Shakespeare, and Other Essays on Cognate Questions*. London: The University Press, 1897; rev. edn, 1909; rpt. New York: Burt Franklin, 1969.

Robinson, Kim Stanley. *Aurora*. New York: Orbit, 2015.

Rockett, William. 'Labor and Virtue in *The Tempest*', *Shakespeare Quarterly* 24 (1973): 77–84.

Rogers, Stephen. '*Othello*: Comedy in Reverse', *Shakespeare Quarterly* 24.2 (1973): 210–20.

Romão, Rui Bertrand. 'From the Theatre in Montaigne to the Philosophy in Shakespeare: The Many-Sided Skepsis', in Pierre Kapitaniak and Jean-Marie Maguin, eds, *Shakespeare et Montaigne: vers un nouvel humanisme*, 259–76. Montpellier and Paris: Société française Shakespeare, 2004.

Rommen, Heinrich A. *The Natural Law: A Study in Legal and Social History and Philosophy*, trans. Thomas Hanley. St Louis, MO: B. Herder, 1947.

Rorty, Richard. *Contingency, Irony, and Solidarity*. Cambridge: Cambridge University Press, 1989.

———. 'On Ethnocentrism: A Reply to Clifford Geertz', *Objectivity, Relativism, and Truth: Philosophical Papers, Volume I*. Cambridge: Cambridge University Press, 1991. 203–10.

Rossiter, A. P. *Angel with Horns, and Other Shakespearean Lectures*, ed. Graham Storey. London: Longmans, Green, & Co., 1961.

———. 'The Problem Plays', in *Angel with Horns: Fifteen Lectures on Shakespeare*, ed. Graham Storey, 108–28. London: Longman, 1989.

Rothman, Stanley, and S. Robert Lichter. 'The Vanishing Conservative – Is There a Glass Ceiling?', in Robert Maranto, Richard E. Redding, and Frederick M. Hess, eds, *The Politically Correct University: Problems, Scope, and Reforms*, 60–76. Washington, DC: American Enterprise Institute Press, 2009.

Rothschild, N. Amos. 'Learning to Doubt: *The Tempest, imitatio*, and Montaigne's "Of the Institution and Education of Children"', *REAL: Yearbook of Research in English and American Literature* 29 (2013): 17–36.

Rowe, Dorothy. *What Should I Believe?* Hove: Routledge, 2009.

Russell, Bertrand. *The Problems of Philosophy*. Oxford: Oxford University Press, 1967.

Salingar, Leo. *Dramatic Form in Shakespeare and the Jacobeans*. Cambridge: Cambridge University Press, 1986.

———. '*King Lear*, Montaigne and Harsnett;, *Aligarh Journal of English Studies* 8.2 (1983): 124–66.

———. '*King Lear*, Montaigne and Harsnett', *Anglo-American Studies* III:2 (November 1983): 145–74.

———. *Shakespeare and the Traditions of Comedy*, ed. William Empson. Cambridge: Cambridge University Press, 1974.

Sayce, R. A. *The Essays of Montaigne: A Critical Exploration*. London: Weidenfeld & Nicolson, 1972.

Schaefer, David Lewis. 'Arthur Armaingaud (1842–1935): Montaigne as Liberal Rationalist', *Montaigne Studies* 20.1–2 (2008): 91–104.

———. 'Montaigne: Founder of Modern Liberalism', *Perspectives on Political Science* 48.1 (2019): 33–45.

———. 'Montaigne and Leo Strauss', *Montaigne Studies* 2.2 (1990): 34–57.

———. *The Political Philosophy of Montaigne*. Ithaca, NY: Cornell University Press, 1990.

Schalkwyk, David. 'Cavell, Wittgenstein, Shakespeare, and Skepticism: *Othello* vs. *Cymbeline*', *Modern Philology* 114.3 (2017): 601–29.

——. 'The Discourses of Friendship and the Structural Imagination of Shakespeare's Theater: Montaigne, *Twelfth Night*, De Gournay', *Renaissance Drama* 38.1 (2010): 141–71.

——. *Shakespeare, Love, and Service*. Cambridge: Cambridge University Press, 2008.

Schmid, E. E. 'Shakespeare, Montaigne und die schauspielerische Formel', *Shakespeare Jahrbuch* 82–3 (1945–6).

Schmitt, Carl. *The Concept of the Political*, trans. George Schwab. Chicago: University of Chicago Press, 1996.

——. 'On the Counterrevolutionary Philosophy of the State (de Maistre, Bonald, Donoso Cortes)', in *Political Theology: Four Chapters on the Concept of Sovereignty*, trans. George Schwab, 53–66. Chicago: University of Chicago Press, 2005.

Schmitt, Charles. *Cicero Scepticus: A Study of the Influence of the* Academica *in the Renaissance*. The Hague: Martinus Nijhoff, 1972.

Schneewind, J. B. *The Invention of Autonomy: A History of Modern Moral Philosophy*. Cambridge: Cambridge University Press, 1998.

——. *Moral Philosophy from Montaigne to Kant*, 2 vols. Cambridge: Cambridge University Press, 1990.

Scholar, Richard. 'French Connections: The *Je-Ne-Sais-Quoi* in Montaigne and Shakespeare', in Laurie Maguire, ed., *How to Do Things with Shakespeare*, 11–33. Oxford: Blackwell, 2008.

——. *Montaigne and the Art of Free-Thinking*. Oxford: Peter Lang, 2010.

——. 'Trial by Theatre, or Free-Thinking in *Julius Caesar*', in *Living with Shakespeare: Essays by Writers, Actors, and Directors*, ed. Susannah Carson, 228–50. New York: Vintage Books, 2013.

Schopenhauer, Arthur. 'On Suicide', *Essays*, trans. S. H. Dircks, 219–24. London: Scott, 1897.

——. *The World as Will and Representation*, trans. E. F. J. Payne. New York: Dover, 1966.

Schücking, L. L. *The Meaning of Hamlet*, trans. G. Rawson. London: Allen & Unwin, 1966.

Scodel, Joshua. 'The Affirmation of Paradox: A Reading of Montaigne's "De la phisionomie" (III:12)', *Yale French Studies* 64 (1983): 209–37.

Scott-Warren, Jason. 'Was Elizabeth I Richard II? The Authenticity of Lambarde's "Conversation"', *Review of English Studies* 64.2 (2013): 208–30.

Screech, M. A. *Montaigne and Melancholy: The Wisdom of the* Essays. Selinsgrove, PA: Susquehanna University Press, 1983.

Sedley, David L. 'Sublimity and Skepticism in Montaigne', *PMLA* 113 (1998): 1079–92.

Sellars, John, ed. *The Routledge Handbook of the Stoic Tradition*. London and New York: Routledge, 2016.

Sellevold, Kirsti. "Peradventure' in Florio's Montaigne', in Tania Demetriou and Rowan Tomlinson, eds, *The Culture of Translation in Early Modern England and France, 1500–1660*, 145–61. Basingstoke: Palgrave Macmillan, 2015.

Sendak, Maurice. *Where the Wild Things Are*. New York: Harper and Row, 1963.

Seneca, Lucius Annaeus. *Moral Letters to Lucilius*, trans. Richard M. Gummere. Loeb Classical Library. London: Heinemann, 1920.

——. *The Works of Lucius Annaeus Seneca, Both Morall and Naturall*, trans. Thomas Lodge. London: William Stansby, 1614.

Sextus Empiricus. *Outlines of Pyrrhonism*, trans. Benson Mates, in Mates, *The Skeptic Way*, 88–217. Oxford: Oxford University Press, 1996.

——. *Outlines of Scepticism*, trans. and ed. Julia Annas and Jonathan Barnes, 2nd edn. Cambridge: Cambridge University Press, 2000.

Shaheen, Naseeb. *Biblical References in Shakespeare's Plays*. Newark, DE: University of Delaware Press, 1999.

Shackel, Nicholas. 'The Vacuity of Postmodernist Methodology', *Metaphilosophy* 36.3 (2005): 295–320.

Shakespeare, William. *All's Well That Ends Well*, ed. Arthur Quiller-Couch and John Dover Wilson. Cambridge: Cambridge University Press, 1929.

——. *All's Well That Ends Well*, ed. G. K. Hunter. London and New York: Routledge, 1991.

——. *All's Well That Ends Well*, ed. Jonathan Bate and Eric Rasmusen. New York: Modern Library, 2011.

——. *As You Like It*, ed. Richard Knowles, with a survey of criticism by Evelyn Joseph Mattern. New Variorum Edition. New York: Modern Language Association of America, 1977.

——. *The First Quarto of Hamlet*, ed. Kathleen O. Irace. Cambridge: Cambridge University Press, 1998.

——. *Hamlet*, ed. Harold Jenkins. London: Methuen, 1982.

——. *Hamlet*, ed. G. R. Hibbard. Oxford: Oxford University Press, 1987.

——. *Hamlet*, ed. Samuel Johnson, in *The Plays of William Shakespeare*, vol. 8. London, 1765.

——. *Hamlet*, ed. T. J. B. Spencer. Harmondsworth: Penguin, 1980.

——. *Hamlet*, ed. Ann Thompson and Neil Taylor. London: Bloomsbury, 2006; rev. edn 2016.

——. *Hamlet, Prince of Denmark*, ed. Philip Edwards. Cambridge: Cambridge University Press, 1985.

——. *2 Henry IV*, ed. Samuel Johnson, in *Johnson on Shakespeare*, ed. Arthur Sherbo, 1:490–524. New Haven, CT: Yale University Press, 1968.

——. *Julius Caesar*, ed. T. S. Dorsch. London: Methuen, 1994.

——. *King Lear*, ed. Mark Eccles. New York: Modern Language Association of America, 1980.

——. *King Lear*, ed. R. A. Foakes. Walton-on-Thames: Thomas Nelson, 1997.

——. *King Lear*, ed. Kenneth Muir. The Arden Shakespeare. London: Methuen, 1952; rev. edn, London: Methuen, 1972.

——. *Love's Labour's Lost*, ed. William C. Carroll. New York: Cambridge University Press, 2009.

——. *Macbeth*, ed. Kenneth Muir. London: Methuen, 1984.

——. *The Merchant of Venice*, ed. M. M. Mahood. Cambridge: Cambridge University Press, 2003.

——. *The Norton Shakespeare*, ed. Stephen Greenblatt, Walter Cohen, Jean E. Howard and Katharine Eisaman Maus. New York: Norton, 1997.

——. *The Norton Shakespeare*, 2nd edn, ed. Stephen Greenblatt, Walter Cohen, Jean E. Howard and Katharine Eisaman Maus. New York: Norton, 2008.

——. *The Norton Shakespeare*, 3rd edn, ed. Stephen Greenblatt, Walter Cohen, Suzanne Gossett, Jean E. Howard, Katharine Eisaman Maus and Gordon McMullan. New York: Norton, 2016.

——. *Othello*, ed. E. A. J. Honigmann, rev. Edn. London: Bloomsbury, 2016.

——. *Othello,* ed. Samuel Johnson, in *Johnson on Shakespeare*, ed. Arthur Sherbo, 2:1012–47. New Haven, CT: Yale University Press, 1968.

——. *The Riverside Shakespeare*, 2nd edn, ed. G. Blakemore Evans and J. J. M. Tobin. Boston, MA: Houghton Mifflin, 1997.

——. *Richard II*, ed. Anthony B. Dawson and Paul Yachnin. Oxford: Oxford University Press, 2012.

——. *The Tempest*, ed. Frank Kermode. London: Routledge, 1954.

——. *The Tempest*, ed. Stephen Orgel. Oxford and New York: Oxford University Press, 1987.

——. *The Tempest*, ed. Alden Vaughan and Virginia Mason Vaughan. London: Thomson Learning, 1999.

——. *The Tragedy of Antony and Cleopatra*, ed. Michael Neill. Oxford: Oxford University Press, 1994.

——. *The Tragedy of Hamlet*, ed. Edward Dowden. London: Methuen, 1899.

——. *The Winter's Tale*, ed. J. H. Pafford. London: Methuen, 1963.

Shannon, Laurie. *The Accommodated Animal: Cosmopolity in Shakespearean Locales*. Chicago: University of Chicago Press, 2013.

——. 'Poor, Bare, Forked: Animal Sovereignty, Human Negative Exceptionarlism, and the Natural History of *King Lear*', *Shakespeare Quarterly* 60.2 (2009): 168–96.

Shapiro, James. *1599: A Year in the Life of William Shakespeare*. New York: HarperCollins, 2005; London: Faber, 2005.

Shell, Alison. *Shakespeare and Religion*. Oxford: Oxford University Press, 2010.

Sherman, Anita Gilman. 'The Aesthetic Strategies of Skepticism: Mixing Memory and Desire in Montaigne and Shakespeare', *Shakespearean International Yearbook 6: Special Section, Shakespeare and Montaigne*

Revisited, ed. Graham Bradshaw, T. G. Bishop and Peter Holbrook, 99–118. Burlington, VT: Ashgate, 2006.

———. *Skepticism in Early Modern English Literature: The Problems and Pleasures of Doubt*. Cambridge: Cambridge University Press, 2021.

———. *Skepticism and Memory in Shakespeare and Donne*. New York: Palgrave Macmillan, 2007.

Shklar, Judith N. *Ordinary Vices*. Cambridge, MA: Belknap Press of Harvard University Press, 1984.

Shuger, Debora K. 'Subversive Fathers and Su ering Subjects: Shakespeare and Christianity', in Donna B. Hamilton and Richard Strier, eds, *Religion, Politics, and Literature in Post-Reformation England, 1540–1688*, 46–69. Cambridge: Cambridge University Press, 1996.

Sidney, Sir Philip. *An Apology for Poetry*, ed. Geoffrey Shepherd. Manchester: Manchester University Press, 1973.

Sipahigil, Teoman. 'Montaigne's *Essays* and *Othello* (IV.i.260–64)', *Notes and Queries* 21 (1974): 130.

Simon, David Carroll. *Light without Heat: The Observational Mood from Bacon to Milton*. Ithaca, NY, and London: Cornell University Press, 2018.

Skinner, Quentin. *Liberty before Liberalism*. Cambridge: Cambridge University Press, 2012.

Skulsky, Harold. 'Revenge, Honor, and Conscience in *Hamlet*', *PMLA* 85.1 (1970): 78–87.

Skura, Meredith Anne. 'Dragon Fathers and Unnatural Children: Warring Generations in *King Lear* and Its Sources', *Comparative Drama* 42.2 (2008): 121–48.

———. *Shakespeare the Actor and the Purposes of Playing*. Chicago: University of Chicago Press, 1993.

Smith, Matthew James and Julia Reinhard Lupton, eds. *Face-to-Face in Shakespearean Drama: Ethics, Performance, Philosophy*. Edinburgh: Edinburgh University Press, 2019.

Sorabji, Richard. *Emotion and Peace of Mind: From Stoic Agitation to Christian Temptation*. Oxford: Oxford University Press, 2003.

———. *Time, Creation, and the Continuum*. London: Duckworth, 1983.

Sowell, Thomas. *A Conflict of Visions: Ideological Origins of Political Struggles*. New York: William Morrow, 1987.

———. *The Vision of the Anointed: Self-Congratulation as a Basis for Social Policy*. New York: Basic Books, 1995.

Spencer, Theodore. *Shakespeare and the Nature of Man*. 2nd edn. Cambridge, MA: Harvard University Press, 1949.

Stanovitch, Keith E. *The Bias that Divides Us: The Science and Politics of Myside Thinking*. Cambridge, MA: MIT Press, 2021.

Starobinski, Jean. *Montaigne in Motion*, trans. Arthur Goldhammer. Chicago: University of Chicago Press, 1985.

———. '"To Preserve and to Continue": Remarks on Montaigne's Conservatism', trans. R. Scott Walker, *Diogenes* 30.118 (1982): 103–20.

Starnes, Dewitt T. 'John Florio Reconsidered', *Texas Studies in Literature and Language* 6 (1965): 407–22.

Statman, Daniel, ed. *Moral Luck*. Albany: State University of New York, 1993.

Starobinksi, Jean. *Montaigne in Motion*, trans. Arthur Goldhammer. Chicago: University of Chicago Press, 1985.

Stedefeld, G. F. *Hamlet: ein Tendenzdrama Shakespeares gegen die skeptische und kosmopolitische Weltanschauung des Michael de Montaigne*. Berlin: Gebriider Paetel, 1871.

Sterling, John. 'Montaigne and His Writings', *London and Westminster Review* 31.2 (July 1838): 321–52.

Strachey, William. *A True Repertory of the Wreck and Redemption of Sir Thomas Gates, Night upon and from the Islands of the Bermudas: His Coming to Virginia and the Estate of that Colony then and after*, in Louis B. Wright, ed., *A Voyage to Virginia*. Charlottesville, VA: University of Virginia Press, 1964.

Strauss, Leo. *Leo Strauss on Maimonides: The Complete Writings*, ed. Kenneth Hart Green. Chicago: Universiy of Chicago, 2013.

——. 'Some Remarks on the Political Science of Maimonides and Farabi', trans. Robert Bartlett, *Interpretation* 18.1 (1990): 3–30.

Strier, Richard. *Fine Issues: Agency, Skepticism, and Other Shakespearean Puzzle*s. Philadelpha: University of Pennsylvania Press, forthcoming.

——. 'Happiness: *Othello, I Henry IV, Antony and Cleopatra*', in Katharine A. Craik, ed., *Shakespeare and Emotion*, 275–87. Cambridge: Cambridge University Press, 2020.

——. '"I am Power": Normal and Magical Politics in *The Tempest*', in Derek Hirst and Richard Strier, eds, *Writing and Political Engagement in Seventeenth-Century England*, 10–30. Cambridge: Cambridge University Press, 1999.

——. *Resistant Structures*. Berkeley: University of California Press, 1996.

——. 'Shakespeare and the Skeptics', *Religion and Literature* 32.2 (2000): 171–96.

——. 'Taking *Utopia* Seriously – and Positively', *Moreana* 54 (2017): 141–8.

——. *The Unrepentant Renaissance: From Petrarch to Shakespeare to Milton*. Chicago: University of Chicago Press, 2011.

Stump, Eleonore. *Wandering in Darkness: Narrative and the Problem of Suffering*. Oxford: Oxford University Press, 2010.

Supple, James. 'Armaingaud Rides Again', in *Le Visage changeant de Montaigne – The Changing Face of Montaigne*, ed. Keith Cameron and Laura Willett, 259–75. Paris: Honoré Champion, 2003.

Swift, Daniel. *Shakespeare's Common Prayers: The Book of Common Prayer and the Elizabethan Age*. Oxford: Oxford University Press, 2013.

Tartamella, Suzanne M. *Rethinking Shakespeare's Skepticism: The Aesthetics of Doubt in the Sonnets and Plays*. Pittsburgh: Duquesne University Press, 2013.

Taylor, Charles. 'The Politics of Recognition', in Amy Gutmann, ed. *Multiculturalism: Examining the Politics of Recognition*, 25–73. Princeton, NJ: Princeton University Press, 1994.

——. *Sources of the Self: The Making of the Modern Identity*. Cambridge, MA: Harvard University Press, 2001 [1989].

Taylor, E. M. M. 'Lear's Philosopher.' *Shakespeare Quarterly* 6.3 (1955): 364–5.

Taylor, Gary, and Gabriel Egan, eds. *The New Oxford Shakespeare Authorship Companion*. Oxford: Oxford University Press, 2017.

Taylor, George Coffin. 'Montaigne–Shakespeare and the Deadly Parallel', *Philological Quarterly* 22.4 (1943): 330–7.

——. *Shakspere's Debt to Montaigne*. Cambridge, MA: Harvard University Press, 1925.

Tetel, Marcel. 'Idéologie et traductions de Girolamo Naselli à John Florio', *Montaigne Studies* 7 (1995): 169–82.

Thomson, Judith Jarvis. 'Morality and Bad Luck' *Metaphilosophy* 20 (1989): 214–15.

Thorne, Christian. *The Dialectic of Counter-Enlightenment*. Cambridge, MA: Harvard University Press, 2009.

Tournon, André. *Montaigne en toutes lettres*. Paris: Bordas, 1989.

——. *Montaigne: la glose et l'essai*. Lyon: Presses universitaires de Lyon, 1983.

——. *'Route par ailleurs.' Le 'Nouveau Langage' des* Essais. Paris: Honoré Champion, 2006.

Tracy, Larissa, ed. *Flaying in the Pre-Modern World: Practice and Representation*. Cambridge: D. S. Brewer, 2017.

Traversi, Derek. *An Approach to Shakespeare*, 2 vols. London: Paladin, 1938.

Trevor, Douglas. 'Love, Anger, and Cruelty in "De l'affection des peres aux enfans" and *King Lear*', *Montaigne Studies* 24 (2012): 51–66.

Trillini, Regula Hohl. *Casual Shakespeare: Three Centuries of Verbal Echoes*. New York: Routledge, 2018.

Trinquet, Roger. 'Recherches chronologiques sur la jeunesse de Marc-Antoine Muret', *Bibliothèque d'humanisme et renaissance* 27:1 (1965): 272–85.

Trueman, Carl R. *The Rise and Triumph of the Modern Self: Cultural Amnesia, Expressive Individualism, and the Road to Sexual Revolution*. Wheaton, IL: Crossway, 2020.

Türck, Susanne. *Shakespeare und Montaigne: Ein Beitrag zur Hamlet-Frage*. Berlin: Junker und Dünnhaupt, 1930.

Upham, Alfred Horatio. *The French Influence in English Literature from the Accession of Elizabeth to the Restoration*. New York: Columbia University Press, 1908.

Van Loon, Hendrick Willem. *Van Loon's Lives: Being a True and Faithful Account of a Number of Highly Interesting Meetings With Certain Historical Personages, From Confucius and Plato to Voltaire and Thomas Jefferson, About Whom We Had Always Felt a Great Deal of Curiosity and Who Came to Us as Dinner Guests in a Bygone Year.* New York: Simon & Schuster, 1942.

Verberne, Tom. 'Borges, Luria, and Hypermnesia – A Note', *Australian and New Zealand Journal of Psychiatry* 10 (1976): 253–5.

Villey, Pierre. *Les Sources et l'évolution des* Essais *de Montaigne.* Paris: Hachette, 1933.

——. 'Montaigne en Angleterre', *Revue des deux mondes* 17 (1913): 115–50.

——. 'Montaigne et François Bacon', *Revue de la Renaissance* 11 (1911): 122–58.

——. *Montaigne et François Bacon.* Paris, 1913; rpt. Geneva: Slatkine, 1973.

——. 'Montaigne et les poètes dramatiques anglais du temps de Shakespeare', *Revue d'histoire littéraire de la France* 24 (1917): 357–93.

——. 'Notes relatives à l'influence et à la fortune des *Essais* en France et en Angleterre', in Montaigne, *Les Essais*, ed. Pierre Villey and V.-L. Saulnier, 3:1117–200.

Vinge, Louise. *The Narcissus Theme in Western European Literature up to the Early Nineteenth Century*, trans. R. Dewsnap L. Grönlund, N. Reeves and I. Söderburgh-Reeves. Gleerups: Skänska Centraltry-cheriet, Lund, 1967.

Walker, Margaret Urban. 'Moral Luck and the Virtues of Impure Agency', *Metaphilosophy* 22 (1991): 14–27.

Weber, Max. *From Max Weber: Essays in Sociology*, ed. H. Gerth and C. Mills. Oxford: Oxford University Press, 1991 [1946].

——. *The Protestant Ethic and the Spirit of Capitalism*, trans. Talcott Parsons. New York: Scribner's, 1958.

Wee, Cecilia. 'Montaigne on Reason, Morality, and Faith', *History of Philosophy Quarterly* 28.3 (2011): 209–26.

Weid, Herman von. *A simple, and religious consultation of . . . Herman by the grace of God Archebishop of Colone.* London: John Day, 1547.

Welch, Marcel Maistre. 'John Florio's Montaigne: From "Fine French" to "True English"', *Style* 12 (1978): 286–96.

Westling, Louise. 'Montaigne in English Dress from Florio to Cotton', *Pacific Coast Philology* 13 (1978): 117–24.

White, Harold Ogden. *Plagiarism and Imitation during the English Renaissance: A Study in Critical Distinctions.* London: Frank Cass, 1935.

White, R. S. *Natural Law in English Renaissance Literature.* Cambridge: Cambridge University Press, 1996.

Whittington, Leah. 'Shakespeare's Virgil: Empathy and *The Tempest*', in Patrick Gray and John D. Cox, eds, *Shakespeare and Renaissance Ethics*, 98–120. Cambridge: Cambridge University Press, 2014.

Wiley, Margaret L. *Creative Sceptics.* London: Allen & Unwin, 1966.

——. *The Subtle Knot: Creative Skepticism in Seventeenth-Century England.* Cambridge, MA: Harvard University Press, 1952.

Williams, Bernard. 'Deciding to Believe', in *Problems of the Self: Philosophical Papers, 1956–1972.* Cambridge: Cambridge University Press, 1973.

——. *Ethics and the Limits of Philosophy*. Cambridge, MA: Harvard University Press, 1985.

——. *Moral Luck: Philosophical Papers, 1973–1980*, ed. John Rawls. Cambridge: Cambridge University Press, 1981.

Williams, Travis D. 'The *Bourn* Identity: *Hamlet* and the French of Montaigne's *Essais*', *Notes and Queries* 58.2 (2011): 254–8.

Williamson, Edward. 'On the Liberalizing of Montaigne: A Remonstrance', *The French Review* 23.2 (1949): 92–100.

Wilniewczyc, Teresa. 'Dwa Kierunki Uderzenia' [Two Directions of Impact], *Notatnik Teatralny* 27 (2003): 26–7.

Wilson, J. Dover. *The Fortunes of Falstaff*. Cambridge: Cambridge University Press, 1943.

Wilson, Jeffrey R. 'Why Shakespeare? Irony and Liberalism in Canonization', *Modern Language Quarterly* 81.1 (2020): 33–64.

Wittgenstein, Ludwig. *On Certainty*, ed. G. E. M. Anscombe and G. H. von Wright. New York: Harper & Row, 1969.

——. *Philosophical Investigations*, trans. G. E. M. Anscombe. Oxford: Blackwell, 1973.

Wootton, David. *The Invention of Science: A New History of the Scientific Revolution*. New York: HarperCollins, 2015.

Yachnin, Paul. '"Courtiers of Beauteous Freedom": *Antony and Cleopatra* in Its Time.' *Renaissance and Reformation / Renaissance et Réforme* 15.1 (1991): 1–20.

——. 'Eating Montaigne', in Marshall Grossman, ed., *Reading Renaissance Ethics*, 157–72. New York: Routledge, 2007.

——. 'Shakespeare and the Idea of Obedience: Gonzalo in *The Tempest*', *Mosaic* 24.2 (1991): 1–18.

Yates, Frances A. *John Florio: The Life of an Italian in Shakespeare's England*. Cambridge: Cambridge University Press, 1934.

Yochelson, Samuel, and Stanton E. Samenow. *The Criminal Personality*, 3 vols. New York: Jason Aronson, 1976–86.

Zeitlin, Jacob. 'The Development of Bacon's *Essays* – with Special Reference to the Question of Montaigne's Influence upon Them', *Journal of English and Germanic Philology* 27 (1928): 496–519.

Ziegler, Georgianna. 'En-Gendering the Subject: Florio's Feminization of Montaigne's "Moy-mesmes"', *Montaigne Studies* 8 (1996): 125–44.

Index

Page numbers followed by n are notes. Titles of Essays are given according to Florio's translation.

Abrams, M. H., 359
An Acte for the punishment of Vacabondes and for Releif of the Poore & Impotent, 245n
Adelman, Janet, 9, 24n, 252, 257
  The Common Liar, 247
Adorno, Theodor, 102, 244n, 303
  The Authoritarian Personality, 303
Alciato, Andrea, 93
al-Gharbi, Musa, 335
al-Ghazali, 338, 340
Allen, Don Cameron, 23n
All's Well That Ends Well
  confession, 154, 207–8
  Engle, Lars, 16, 25n
  function characters, 311
  gentlemanly valour, 83–4
  Helen (character), 207–8
  Kirsch, Arthur, 9
  mixed worlds, 233–45
  Paroles (character), 16, 83–4, 88n, 89n
  problem plays, 269
  'On Some Lines of Virgil', 301
  uncertainty, 244n
  'We taste nothing purely', xix
Althusser, Louis, 12
American Jewish Committee, 303
Amyot, Jacques, 248, 261n, 377
Anselm, Saint, 212n
anti-essentialism, 347–8

anti-ethnocentrism, 300–6, 311–14, 324n
Antigonus, 181–2, 189, 191, 193
anti-humanism, 331
anti-materialism, 252–3
Antony and Cleopatra, 12, 14, 118–19, 232n, 270
  Antony (character), 255–6
  Cleopatra (character), 247, 252, 254
  discontinuous identity, 246–62
Aquinas, Thomas, 45, 93, 142, 154, 159, 161n
Arendt, Hannah, 105, 112
Aristocles, 182, 191–2
Aristotle, 36, 105, 107, 116, 164n, 333, 338–40, 350
  Nicomachean Ethics, 116
  Poetics, 106
  Rhetoric, 336
Armaingaud, Arthur, 353
Arminianism, 45
Armitage, David, 41
Arnold, Matthew, 337
As You Like It, 30–1, 33, 153, 163n, 265
  Jacques (character), 30–1, 33
  Rosalind (character), 131
Ascham, Roger, *The Scholemaster*, 62
'Assassins', 183–4, 191
Auerbach, Erich, *Mimesis*, 43, 111

Augustine, Saint, Bishop of Hippo, 45, 92, 115–17, 142, 153, 159, 199, 348–9, 350
   City of God, 163n, 332
   Confessions, 106–7, 113
Aulotte, Robert, 186
Avicenna, 338
Ayres, Harry Morgan, 383n

Bacon, Sir Francis, 204–6, 210, 211n, 244n, 337, 341, 347
   Idols of the Tribe, 204–5
   New Organon, 48, 204–5, 214n, 338–9, 344–5
   Preface to 'The Great Instauration', 205
Baggini, Julian, 351–2
Bakewell, Sarah, *How to Live: A Life of Montaigne in One Question and Twenty Attempts at an Answer*, 297–8, 324n
Bakhtin, Mikhail, 126
Balsamo, Jean, 20n, 324n, 378, 382n, 383n
Barkan, Leonard, 21n
Barker, Francis, 43, 109–10
Barthes, Roland, 62, 65, 106, 125
Bartholomew, Saint, 186–7
Barton, John, 216
Barzun, Jacques, 328
Bassnett, Susan, 76n
Bate, Jonathan, 11, 12, 17, 25n, 27n
Bečanović-Nikolić, Zorica, 42–3, 51, 381, 385
Beckwith, Sarah, 57
Bedouins, 183
bees, 59–77
Behn, Aphra, 33
belief, 198–215
Belsey, Catherine, 43, 110
Benveniste, Émile, 125–6
Berlin, Isaiah, 343–5
Bett, Richard, 181, 182
Bible, 15, 199, 201, 211n, 212n, 214n, 215n, 254–5
birds, 59–77, 75n, 117

Blake, William, *Marriage of Heaven and Hell*, 326–7
Bloom, Harold, 57, 328, 361
Boas, F. S., 233–4, 243n
'body politic', 90–6, 101
Bono, Barbara, 261n
Bontea, Adriana, 84
Borges, Jorge Luis, 'Funes the Memorious', 341
Boutcher, Warren, 10–11, 25n, 28, 54–5, 76n, 285, 307–8, 356, 381n, 382n
   The School of Montaigne in Early Modern Europe, 297, 299–300
Bouwsma, William J., 156, 350
   'The Two Faces of Humanism', 348–9
Braden, Gordon, 37, 58n, 363
Bradley, A. C., 354
   'The Rejection of Falstaff', 361–3
Brahami, Frédéric, 214n
Bromwich, David, 113
Brook, Peter, *King Lear* (1971), 331
Brown, Freida, 351
Bullough, Geoffrey, 285
   Narrative and Dramatic Sources, 35
Bunel, Pierre, 352
Burckhardt, Jacob, 57
Burrow, Colin, 3, 20n, 21n, 26n, 34–7, 54, 57–8, 282–6, 291, 293, 309, 310, 325n
Byron, *Don Juan*, 328
Byronic antihero, 328, 366

Caesar, *Commentarii de Bello Civili*, 379
Calhoun, Alison, 47–8, 374, 385
Calvin, John, 45, 142, 154, 155–6, 337
Capell, Edward, 2, 4, 6, 8, 21n, 284
Carson, Rob, 12–13, 26n
Catholicism, 164n, 251, 336–7
Cato, 48, 144–5, 184, 313, 318
causation, 338–42
Cave, Terence, 13–14, 26n, 54, 60, 285–6, 290, 358

Cavell, Stanley, 14, 27n, 46–7, 58n,
117, 120, 166–79, 188, 192
*Disowning Knowledge in Seven
Plays of Shakespeare*, 167
'Othello and the Stake of the Other',
166
Pursuits of Happiness, 173
Cervantes, 390–1
Chambers, E. K., *Shakespeare: A Survey*,
243n
Chasles, Philarète, 7, 23n
Chaucer, Geoffrey, 33
Chesterton's Fence, 352
Christianity
Antony and Cleopatra, 254–5,
257, 260
'Christian Pyrrhonism', 205–6
effective history, 332–3
ethics and morality, 298–9
and failure, 158–9
flaying, 184–6
Hamlet, 217–19, 222, 224
intentionalism and virtue, 155–7
King Lear, 191, 195
and learning, 150–1
and miracles, 340
Papal censors, 353
Plato, 349
Reformation, 151–2, 337
Roman plays, 346–8
and scepticism, 201–2, 203–4
Shakespeare and, 354
and Stoicism, 140–3, 348–9
temptation, 164n
virtue, 183
Cicero, xvii, 36–7, 61, 202, 209, 211n,
230n, 236, 289, 337, 377
Academica, 48, 203, 214n
The Nature of the Gods, 48, 202–3,
211n, 213n, 214n
Tusculan Disputations, 203
Clifford, Helen, 152
Clifford, W. K., 209, 214n
Cochran, Peter, 328
cogito, 118
Collington, Philip, 11, 25n

comedy
of the cuckold, 166–79
and tragedy, 263–81
Condren, Conal, 41
Connolly, Shannon, 382n
conscience, 15–16
'consummation', 227–8, 231n
Cooper, Helen, 57
Coriolanus, 7, 12–13, 184
Coriolanus (character), 191
Cormack, Bradin, 382n
Cornillat, François, 74n
Cornwallis, Sir William, 7–8, 23n
Cosell, Howard, 29
Cotton, Charles, 20n
Cox, John, 15, 27n, 57
cruelty, 25–6n, 25n, 30–2, 301
in *King Lear*, 11, 199–200
see also Essays: 'Of Crueltie'
Cummings, Brian, 57, 143, 354
Curley, Edwin M., 382n
Cymbeline, 155
cynicism, 187, 189–90

d'Agrate, Marco, *St Bartholomew
Flayed*, 186
Damiens, 194
Daniel, Samuel, 307–8, 314
The Queen's Arcadia, 179n
Data, character in *Star Trek: The Next
Generation*, 311
Davies, H. N., 262n
De Gooyer, Alan, 310
deconstructionism, 359–60
Dennett, Daniel, 341–2
Derrida, Jacques, *Of Grammatology*,
359
'Des Cannibales', 2, 5–6, 10–11, 16,
17–18, 20n, 22n, 270–1, 284,
292–3; *see also Essays*: 'Of the
Caniballes'
Desan, Philippe, 20n, 29–33, 56, 58n,
87n, 88n, 120, 356, 382n
'The Book, the Friend, and the
Woman: Montaigne's Circular
Exchanges', 133

Descartes, René, 118, 169, 199, 211n,
    230n, 338
    Discourse on Method, 345
    Meditations on First Philosophy, 167
desire, 128–38, 138n
digestion, 64, 68, 71
Digital Humanities, 60
Dillane, Richard, 49–50, 374
Diogenes Laertius, 185, 187, 188,
    189–90, 193, 380
    'Life of Pyrrho', 181, 182–3
    Lives of Eminent Philosophers,
        181–2, 221
Diogenes of Sinope, 189
Dionne, Valérie, 382n
distinguo, 110
Dollimore, Jonathan, 11–12, 25n, 51,
    351, 353–4
    Radical Tragedy, 11–12, 246, 299,
        331, 346–8
Donaldson, Ian, 245n
Doucet, Roger, 382n
Dowling, William C., 106
Dryden, John, 33
Du Bellay, Martin, *Memoires*, xvii

Eagleton, Terry, 43, 109
Eden, Kathy, xxii
'effective history', 332–3
Egypt, 251–8
Eldendrath, Rachel, 386
Eliot, T. S., 4, 21n, 120
Elizabeth I, 100, 102
Ellrodt, Robert, 6, 8, 22n, 25–6n,
    25n, 35, 266, 285
    Montaigne and Shakespeare, 22n,
        58n, 105
    'Self-Consciousness in Montaigne
        and Shakespeare', 279n
Emerson, Ralph Waldo, 211n, 213n
emplotment, 106–7, 112–17, 120
Empson, William, 326, 332
    Seven Types of Ambiguity, 329–30
Engle, Lars, 11, 16, 20n, 25n, 27n, 34,
    55–7, 58n, 199–200, 234, 325n,
    374, 381, 385, 387, 389

enlightenment, 202, 244n
Epicharmus, 248
Epicureanism, 16–17, 36, 160n, 202,
    253, 356, 363
Epicurus, 63
epochal change, 90–104
Erasmus, Desiderius, 210, 215n, 384,
    390–1
    Apothegmes, 190
    De Copia, 70
    Praise of Folly, 210, 215n, 292–3
Essays, xxiii–xxiv n, 1–19
    'Of Affectionate Relationships', 128
    'Of the Affections of Fathers to their
        Children', 6–7, 11, 17, 18, 23n,
        308–9
    'An Apologie of *Raymond Sebond*',
        11, 13, 22n, 30, 151, 198, 201–4,
        210, 213n, 221–2, 246–53, 258,
        259, 261n, 265–7, 276, 287, 318,
        340, 350–2
    'Of the Art of Conferring', xx–xxi
    'Of Bookes', xvi–xviii, xxi–xxii, 143
    'Of the Caniballes', 2, 5, 10, 16, 17,
        20n, 22n, 25n, 130, 177, 179n,
        270–1, 292–3, 300–9, 317
    'Of *Cato* the younger', 144
    'Of Coaches', 300, 301
    'Of Cripples', 178
    'Of Crueltie', xviii, 5–6, 10, 11,
        30–1, 144, 156, 303, 307, 309,
        313, 314, 316–18, 321–3
    'To the curteous Reader', 65–6, 309
    'Of customs and how a received law
        should not be easily changed',
        90–104, 214n, 351–2
    'A Defence of *Seneca and Plutarch*',
        143
    'Divers Events from one selfsame
        counsell', 145, 147–8, 377–8
    'Of Diverting and Diversions', 10, 18
    'Of Drunkennesse', 163n
    'Of Exercise or Practice', 86
    'Of Experience', 110–11, 163n,
        180–97, 185, 243n, 268–9, 275–6
    'On the force of Imagination', 10

'Of Friendship', 288

'Of the inconstancie of our Actions', 110, 258–9

'Of the Institution and Education of Children', 60, 66–9, 194–5, 287, 294n, 308, 309, 380

'Of Names', 35

'Of Pedantisme', 60, 66–7

'Of Physiognomy', 79–80, 86, 224

'Of Presumption', 37–8, 170–1

'Of Profit and Honesty', 314, 318, 321–3

'Of Repenting', 86, 110, 111, 145, 146–7, 253

'Of Solitarinesse', 11

'That our Intention judgeth our Actions', 144

'That we should not judge our Happinesse untill after our Death', 379–80

'Of Three Good Women', 143, 272–5, 277, 278

'Upon some Verses of *Virgil*', 9, 26n, 128–38, 144, 166, 169, 175–6, 214n, 278, 301–2

'Of Vanitie', 8, 309

'Of Vertue', 180–97, 343

'We taste nothing purely', xix, 233–45, 387

Estienne, Henri, 181

'ethics', 298, 300–1

ethical blendedness, 235–6

ethnocentrism, 132

anti-ethnocentrism, 300–6, 311–14, 317, 324n

Euripides, 363

Eusebius of Caesarea, 191–2

Evans-Pritchard, E. E., 303

exceptionality, 29–30, 33

exhibitionism, 32

experientialism, 307–8

experiments of moment, 282–95

Federico, Silvia, 102

feeling indifference, 180–97

Feis, Jacob, 4, 7

female sexual intemperance, 128–9, 169–79

Fernie, Ewan, 355, 361

Feynman, Richard, 326

Fichte, Johann Gottlieb, 345

Fischer, Michael, 170

Fitzmaurice, Andrew, 41

flaying, 180–97

Fletcher, John, 318

Florio, John, *Worlde of Wordes*, 309–10

Florio's translation, xv–xxiii, xxiii–xxiv n, 2, 3–4, 5, 8, 10, 17, 19, 23n, 87n, 88n, 297, 300

Antony and Cleopatra, 246–7

'An Apologie of *Raymond Sebond*', 248

'consummation', 224–5

'Des Cannibales', 2, 284

education, 76n

Hamlet, 24n

immitatio, 60, 65–9

'Of the inconstancie of our Actions', 258–9

paratexts as guides to Shakespeare's reading, 307–10, 314

Pyrrho, 181

Shakespeare and, 2, 3–4, 7–8, 17–19, 20n, 30, 242n, 263, 280n, 384

The Tempest, 307–14, 318–19, 323

theatrical performance, 377

Foakes, R. A., 21n

Fontana, Biancamaria, 382n

forgiveness, 152, 157–9

forme maistresse, 43, 111–12, 145–6, 162n

Foucault, Michel, 12, 299, 330, 332–3, 354

Discipline and Punish, 194

Frame, Donald, 261n, 297, 353, 354

translation, 211n

Frampton, Saul, 8, 20n

French civil wars, 79–82, 88n

Friedrich, Hugo, 22n, 304, 355–6, 364

friendship, 123–8, 138n, 288–9, 387–9

Frye, Roland Mushat, 354

Fulkerson, Laurel, 146, 148, 150, 158

gender, 123–39
genre, 123–39
Gide, André, 353, 355
Glidden, Hope, 88n, 89n
'the Global Majority', 333–5
Go, Kenji, 10, 25n, 324n
Goffman, Erving, 120
Gopnik, Adam, 381
    'Montaigne on Trial', 29–33,
      56, 58n
Gottlieb, Derek, 174
Gournay, Marie de, 128, 138n, 213n
Goyet, Francis, 382n
Grady, Hugh, 8, 12, 20n, 25–6n,
    51, 113, 243n, 247, 260n,
    324, 324n
    Shakespeare, Machiavelli, and
      Montaigne, 299
Grafton, Anthony, 67
Grantley, Darryll, 72
Gray, Patrick, 8, 16–17, 27n, 56–8,
    58n, 116, 118–19, 150, 151, 152,
    162n, 324, 376
Green, Felicity, 356, 358, 363
Green, Kenneth Hart, 371n
Greenblatt, Stephen, 7, 17, 18, 20n,
    24n, 27n, 30, 33, 354, 384
    Shakespeare's Montaigne, 17, 18,
      324n
    The Swerve, 299–300
Greene, Robert, 73
    Pandosto: The Triumph of Time,
      272
Greene, Thomas M., 59, 60, 89n
    The Light in Troy, 61–3
Greville, Fulke, 337
Gross, Kenneth, 386
Guana, Max, 146
Guazzo, Stefano, *Civile Conversation*,
    23n
Guicciardini, xvii–xviii
Guild, Elizabeth, *Unsettling*
    Montaigne, 87n
Guillory, John, 58n
Gwinne, Matthew, 325n
gymnosophists, 183

Habermas, Jürgen, 299
Hadot, Pierre, 192
Haidt, Jonathan, 345, 365
Hamlet
    attestation of individual self, 119–20
    'To be or not to be', 49–50, 216–32
    Claudius (character), 117–18
    Cornwallis, Sir William, 8
    'Of Diverting and Diversions', 18
    Ellrodt, Robert, 6
    Epicureanism, 16–17
    Florio's translation, 24n, 263
    Hamlet (character), 17, 30, 108–12,
      115–16, 119–20, 197n, 207, 329,
      342–3
    Hobbes, Thomas, 333
    Horatio (character), 119–20
    Lee, John, 14
    Ophelia (character), 207
    Polonius (character), 37, 378
    Pyrrhonism, 3
    scepticism, 21n, 342–3
    tragedy and comedy, 265–9
Hamlin, Hannibal, *The Bible in*
    Shakespeare, 57, 254–5, 347
Hamlin, William M., 47–8, 54, 324,
    375, 377, 384, 386, 387
    conscience, 15–16, 154, 163–4n,
      324n
    education, 69
    Florio's preface, 307
    The Image of America, 324n
    judgement, 351
    'Montaignian moments' in
      Shakespeare, 283–5
    Montaigne's English Journey, 26n,
      27n, 58n, 297
    scepticism, 76n, 174–5
    self-sufficiency, 363–4
    Shakespeare and Montaigne, 28,
      299–300
    theatrical performance, 263
Harmon, Alice, 4–6, 22n
Hartle, Ann, 215n, 301, 324n
Hazlitt, William, 110, 355
Heck, Francis, 351

Hegel, Georg Wilhelm Friedrich, 108, 116
Henderson, W. B. Drayton, 23n
Hendrick, Philip, 10, 25n
Henry IV Part 1 and *Part 2*, 83, 85–6, 264
  Falstaff (character), 41, 83, 85–6, 264, 326–9, 360–6
Henry V, 208–9
  Henry V (character), 208–9, 214n, 360, 362
  Williams, Michael (character), 208–9, 214n, 362
Henry VI Part 2, 37
Henry VIII, 318
Herrup, Cynthia, 158, 165n
Hershinow, David, 189, 190
Hesiod, 5
Hillman, Richard, 3, 7, 8, 21n, 52–3, 213n, 375, 385
Hobbes, Thomas, 214n, 347
  Leviathan, 214n, 333, 337–8
Hodgen, Margaret, 5, 22n
Hoffmann, George, 57–8, 306, 382n
  Montaigne's Career, 20n, 324n
Holbrook, Peter, 12, 16, 26n, 102, 324, 355
  Shakespeare's Individualism, 299
Holinshed, Raphael, 37
Holland, Philemon, 261n
Homer, 33
Hooker, Elizabeth, 3, 4, 19, 21n
Horace, 36, 63, 73, 75n, 363
Horkheimer, Max, 244n
Howell, Thomas, 96
  Fable treting of Narcissus, 97–8
'human condition', 86, 151, 218, 342, 347–8
humanism, 227, 250–1, 348–9
  idealism, 7, 18
  pragmatic, 67
Hume, David, 55, 199, 211n, 212n, 214n, 298, 318, 324n, 337, 344, 351–2
  Enquiry Concerning Human Understanding, 340

The Incoherence of the Philosophers, 340
Treatise of Human Nature, 199, 339–40, 343

Ibbett, Katherine, 381n
idem-identity, 108, 110, 112, 115–16
identity
  discontinuous, 246–62
  moral, 43, 117–18, 120
  as narrative, 105–22
Idols of the Tribe, 204–5
imitation, 59–77
imitatio, 59–62, 66–7, 69–73, 76n
impurity, 236–42, 243n, 245n
influence, direct, 283–6
'The Instruments of a States-man', 8
intentionalism, 144–6, 148, 150, 152–5, 161n
  Stoic, 151
ipse-identity, 108, 112, 115–16

James I, 239
James, William, 211n
Jameson, Frederic, 102
Jansenism, 353
Jardine, Lisa, 67
Jenkins, Harold, 8, 24n
Johnson, Samuel, 216, 232n, 327–8
Jonson, Ben, 33, 37
Jourdan, Serena, 26n
Julius Caesar, xxii, 37, 147–51
  Brutus (character), 147–51, 158, 162n
  moments of inspiration in, 286–90
jurisdiction, 376–7
Justinian, 377

Kant, Immanuel, 105, 106, 141–2, 160n, 341
Kantorowicz, Ernst, 91, 95
Keats, John, 329, 355
Keffer, Ken, 381n
Kellenberger, Hunter, 227
Kelly, George E., 115
Kenny, Neil, 74n

King Lear
  'Of the Affections of Fathers to their
    Children', xx, 18, 23n
  compassion, 15
  Cordelia (character), 191–4, 195
  cruelty in, 11, 199–200
  disallows transcendence, 12
  Ellrodt, Robert, 22n
  flaying, 180–97
  Florio's translation, 17
  Gloucester (character), 188–94
  'humanist idealism', 6–7
  Kent (character), 200
  Lear (character), 113, 114–15,
    188–94, 196n
  'Montaignian moments' in, 3, 309
  Muir, Kenneth, 4, 21n
  Parker, Fred, 16
  Tom (character), 190
Kirsch, Arthur, 9–10, 24n, 88n,
  89n, 325n
Knight, G. Wilson, 244n, 328, 354
Kott, Jan, 346
  Shakespeare, Our Contemporary,
  331–2
Kramer, Jane, 58n
Krier, Isabelle, 132
Kritzman, Lawrence, 82, 88n
Kuzner, James, 188, 192
Kyd, Thomas, 267

La Boétie, Étienne de, 14, 115–16,
  123–4, 138n, 213n, 288
La Pazzia, 293
Lacan, Jacques, 124–5, 133
Lacedaemonians, 95
Lambard, William, 100
Langbert, Mitchell, 368n
Larmore, Charles, 213n, 375, 382n
La Rochefoucauld, François de, 325n
Leckie, Ann, 311
Lee, John, 8, 14, 43, 110, 115, 174,
  260n
Legros, Alain, 20n, 382n, 383n
Lennox, Charlotte, 285
Lestringant, Frank, 291, 292–3

Levin, Harry, 23n
Lévinas, 87n, 108, 119–20
Lewis, C. S., 154, 211n, 212n
Lewis, Rhodri, 333
liberal censorship, 326–73
liberalism, 29, 29–33, 56, 91, 354,
  355–8, 376
Livy, 236
Lodge, Thomas, translation of Seneca,
  62–9
Loughnane, Rory, 23n
Love's Labour's Lost, 60, 69–73, 77n,
  309, 350
  Berowne (character), 69–72
  Costard (character), 72
  Holofernes (character), 60, 69–72
  Nathaniel (character), 71
Lucretius, 36, 51–2, 63–4, 130–1, 299,
  307, 319, 325n, 356
  On the Nature of Things, 134,
  252–3, 319
Lupton, Julia Reinhard, 58n
Luria, Alexander, 341
Lycurgus, 306

Macbeth, 37, 89n, 349
  Macbeth (character), 113
McEachern, Claire, 171–2, 215n
Machiavelli, Niccolò, 299, 347
  The Prince, 314–15
Machielson, J., 58n
MacIntyre, Alastair, 110, 339–40, 344
  After Virtue, 335–6
Mack, Peter, 7, 13–14, 15, 21n, 26n,
  76n, 244n, 285
McKenzie, William, 38, 41–2, 376, 385
McKinley, Mary, 130
Maclean, Ian, 212n
McNair, Maria Devlin, 45–6, 375,
  386–7, 390
Magnien, Michel, 20n
Magnien-Simonin, Catherine, 20n
Maguin, Jean-Marie, 16, 27n, 325n
Maguire, Laurie, 286
Malone, Edmond, 2, 4, 20n
Mann, Thomas, 352, 365

Maritain, Jacques, 345
Marlowe, Christopher, 33, 37
marriage, 133–8
Marston, John, *Antonio's Revenge*, 246
Marsyas, 186
Martindale, Charles, 74n
Martindale, Michelle, 74n
Marxism, 331–2
materialism, 260, 333
Mathieu-Castellani, Gisèle, 14–15,
    27n, 74n
Maus, Katharine Eisaman, 58
Measure for Measure, 3, 15–16, 35,
    84–5, 152–5, 157, 233–4, 269,
    309, 311
    Pompey Bum (character), 35
Melanchton, 156
The Merchant of Venice, 265, 286–90
    Portia (character), 131–2
    Shylock (character), 131–2
The Merry Wives of Windsor,
    xxiii–xxiv n
Metrodorus, 235
Michelangelo, *The Last Judgment*, 186
A Midsummer Night's Dream, 264, 286
Mignault, Claude, 93
Miles, Geoffrey, 12, 13, 14, 26n, 147,
    149
Miller, J. Hillis, 359
Miller, Walter M., Jr., *A Canticle for
    Leibowitz*, 335
Milton, John, 327, 329–30, 355
    Paradise Lost, 360
Miola, Robert, 21n
Mirandolla, Giovanni Pico della,
    185, 206
The Mirror for Magistrates, 96–8,
    100, 102
misogyny, 126–38, 214n
Miura, Cassie, 46–7, 375, 381, 382n,
    388
mixed worlds, 233–45
Molière, 390–1
monks, 183
'Montaignian moments' in
    Shakespeare, 3, 35, 283–6, 309

Montaigne Project, xv–xix
moral identity, 43, 117–18, 120
moral luck, 45–6, 140–65
More, Thomas, *Utopia*, 292
Morgann, Maurice, *Essay on the
    Dramatic Character of Sir John
    Falstaff*, 326–7
Mousnier, Roland, 382n
Mucedorus, 264, 278, 279–80n, 281n
Much Ado about Nothing, 111–12,
    158–9, 174–5, 265
    Benedick (character), 111–12
Muir, Kenneth, 4, 6, 21n, 23n
Muret, Jean-Antoine, *Julius Caesar*,
    378–9

Nagel, Thomas, 149, 342
Nakam, Géralde, 8, 83
narcissism, 41, 90–104
'natural law', 336–8, 350–1
nature of presence, 78–89
Nazarian, Cynthia, 381n
Neill, Michael, 26n, 51, 247, 252
neo-paganism, 246–62
Neoplatonism, 98–9
Neostoicism, 140–1, 143–4
New Historicism, 6, 354
New World, 177
The New Yorker, 29–33, 381
Nietzsche, Friedrich, 336, 337, 349
    Dawn, 332–3
nominalism, 338
Nordlund, Marcus, 89n
North, Sir Thomas, 251, 261n, 289
Nuttall, A. D., 13, 26n, 42, 54, 91,
    286, 290, 329
    Shakespeare the Thinker, 357

O'Brien, John, 60, 74n
'occasions of experience', 326
occult, 288
Orgel, Stephen, 22n, 310, 317
Othello
    comedy of the cuckold, 166–79
    Desdemona (character), 135–7,
    166–79

Othello (cont.)
  female sexual voracity, 134–7
  Iago (character), 327–8
  Othello (character), 113, 120, 134–5,
    166–79, 349–50
  Parker, Fred, 16
  sexual shame, 301
  tragic scepticism, 166–79
otherness, 43, 105, 108, 115–16, 133
Ovid, 37, 41–2, 90, 92, 112, 357, 375
  Metamorphoses, 96–8, 252, 272–6
Ovide Moralisé, 93

paganism, 251–2
  neo-paganism, 246–62
Page, Frederick, 4
paradoxes
  All's Well That Ends Well, 9, 50,
    236–7, 245n
  Antony and Cleopatra, 247, 252
  'Of the Caniballes', 304–6
  cruelty, 188
  Falstaff (character), 326
  Montaigne's liberalism, 351–2
  'moral luck', 140
  problem plays, 269
  Saint Augustine, 107
  'shiftingness', 242–3n
  The Tempest, 314
Parker, Fred, 16, 17, 27n, 58n, 310
Pascal, Blaise, 211n, 212n
Pasnau, Robert, 338
Paster, Gail Kern, 10, 25n
Paul, Saint, 45, 112, 180, 184–5, 187,
  190, 195, 196n, 211n, 336
Pericles, 95
Petrarch, 269
phenomenology, 109–10
physiognomy, 84
Pico della Mirandola, Gianfrancesco,
  206
Pigman, G. W. III, 62, 74–5n, 74n
Pina Martins, José, 292–3
Plato, 36, 129, 190, 236, 306, 326, 377
  Apology, 109, 224–5
  The Republic, 224, 349

Platt, Peter, 8, 17–18, 24n, 27n, 50–1,
  58n, 300, 381, 384, 385, 389
Plautus, 37, 265
pleasure, 234–5, 242
Pléiade, 36
Pliny the Elder, 214n
Plutarch
  Antony and Cleopatra, 12, 26n
  'Of Bookes', xvi–xvii
  discontinuous identity, 246–62
  'Divers Events from one selfsame
    counsell', 377–8
  education, 150
  'The EI at Delphi', 248, 253, 258,
    261n
  humanism, 249–50
  'Of Isis and Osiris', 254, 258
  Julius Caesar, 289
  Life of Brutus, xxi–xxii
  Lives, 149, 251
  Moralia, 246, 253, 256–7, 261n
  'Of the Oracles that Have Ceased to
    Give Answer', 256–7
  Pyrrhonism, 220–1
  Shakespeare and Montaigne, 14–15,
    36–7
  syncrisis, xxi
Polanski, Roman, *Macbeth* (1971), 331
Popkin, Richard, 205, 213n, 337–8
Posner, David, 382n
Pouilloux, Jean-Yves, 358
Pranger, M. B., 107
Prat, Sebastian, 382n
Preston, Thomas, *Cambyses*, 264
problem plays, 233–4, 242–3n,
  243n, 244n
'process philosophy', 340
pronouns, 125–7, 135–7, 138n
Prosser, Eleanor, 5–6, 8, 9–10
Protestantism, 93, 96, 101, 351–2;
  see also Reformation
Proust, Marcel, *Remembrance of
  Things Past*, 112–13
providential plays, 151–7, 363
psychoanalysis, 132–3
psychology, personal construct, 115

'public necessity', 90–104
Purchas, Samuel, 5
Pyrrho, 180–97, 221, 223, 225, 231n, 343, 380–1
Pyrrhonism, 3, 47–8, 198, 201–4, 205–6, 209, 214n, 219–26, 230n
  'An Apologie of *Raymond Sebond*', 13, 201–2
  belief, 201–6, 209, 214n
  Cavell, Stanley, 167–8
  Christian, 205–6
  comedy, 176
  deliberative authors, 36
  flaying, 180–97
  Hamlet, 3
  radical, 251
  suspension of judgement, 15
  tragedy, 173
  see also scepticism

Quint, David, 58n, 82, 185, 187, 262n, 306, 324n, 382n
Quintilian, Marcus Fabius, 61, 292

Rabelais, François, 302, 361
Rawls, John, 146
Reformation
  forgiveness, 158
  Montaigne and, 298, 305, 351–2, 377
  repentance, 164n
  Saint Augustine, 142
  see also Protestantism
Richard II, 41, 90–104
  Bolingbroke (character), 97–100
  John of Gaunt (character), 96–7, 100, 101
  Richard II (character), 96–100, 101–2, 113–15
Richard III, 113
Ricœur, Paul, 42–3, 105–22
  Oneself as Another, 108–10, 115–16, 118
  Time and Narrative, 105–7, 112
Riker, Stephen, 340
Robertson, John, 3
  Montaigne and Shakespeare, 21n

Robespierre, 384
Robinson, Kim Stanley, 311
Roman Empire, 251–2, 255–8, 289
Roman plays, 12, 147–51, 346–7
Romanticism, 326–7, 344, 361, 366
Romeo and Juliet, 265
Rorty, Richard, 324n
Rossiter, A. P., 242–3n
Rothschild, N. Amos, 38–9, 377–8, 385
Rousseau, Jean-Jacques, 345
  Essay on the Origin of Language, 359
Russell, Bertrand, 211n, 215n

Saint German, Christopher, 157
Salingar, Leo, 6–7, 11, 16, 17, 18, 22–3n
Sandys, George, 252
Sartre, Jean-Paul, 345
Saussure, Ferdinand de, 125
scepticism
  All's Well That Ends Well, 238–40
  'An Apologie of *Raymond Sebond*', 201–3, 350–2
  as versatility in adapting to environments, 379
  Christianity, 205–6, 224
  Descartes, René, 230n
  Epicureanism, 17
  flaying, 180–97
  'flexible', 13
  Hamlet, 21n, 197n, 342–3
  Measure for Measure, 15–16
  and memory, 14
  Montaigne and, 374–5
  Renaissance, 12
  Sextus Empiricus, 202, 380
  suspension of judgement, 76n
  tragic, 166–79
  see also Pyrrhonism
Schalkwyk, David, 43–4, 56, 174–5, 325n, 375, 387
Schmitt, Carl, 357–8
Schmitt, Charles, 213n
Scholar, Richard, 13–14, 26n, 54–5, 356–7, 358, 376
Schopenhauer, Arthur, 227

Screech, M. A., 297
  Montaigne and Melancholy,
    302, 324n
Seneca
  autonomy, 105
  'Of Bookes', xvi–xvii
  constancy, 147
  deliberative authors, 36–7
  digestion, 68
  Epicureanism, 356
  Epistulae Morales, 62–9
  Hamlet, 265
  identity, 111–12
  Julius Caesar, 289
  neo-stoicism, 143, 159–60n
  pleasure and pain, 235
  Stoicism, 162n
  suicide, 218, 229n, 231n
  tragedy, 363
  women, 130–1
Sextus Empiricus, 48, 191–2, 202–3,
    205–6, 211n, 213n, 337, 352,
    375, 380
  Outlines of Pyrrhonism, 180–2,
    205–6, 214n, 219–21, 294n
sexual love, 125–6, 128–38, 234–5
Shackel, Nicholas, 'The Vacuity of
    Postmodernist Methodology', 330
shadow and substance, 98–100, 101
Shagan, Ethan, 213n
shame, 300–2
Shannon, Laurie, The Accommodated
    Animal, 22n
Shapiro, James, 8, 24n
Shaw, George Bernard, 33
  Plays Pleasant and Unpleasant, 243n
Shell, Alison, 151
Shereshevsky, Solomon, 341
Sherman, Anita Gilman, 14, 26n, 38,
    40–1, 379, 385
'shiftingness', 242–3n
Shklar, Judith, 301
  Ordinary Vices, 30–1, 58n, 303–4
Shuger, Debora, 354
Sidney, Philip, 33, 264

Skinner, Quentin, 356
Skulsky, Harold, 217
Skura, Meredith Anne, 87n
Socrates, 36, 79–82, 86, 88n, 109,
    224–5, 231n, 313, 318
Sonnets, 12, 16, 98, 175, 199, 309
Sorabji, Richard, 107
source study, xix–xx, 2–3, 35
Sowell, Thomas, 345
Spenser, Edmund, 33, 260–1n
  Faerie Queene, 359–60
Starobinski, Jean, 304, 357
Stedefeld, G. F., 4, 7, 21n
Sterling, John, 7, 23n
Stoicism
  'An Apologie of Raymond Sebond',
    11, 350
  Christianity, 348–9
  Cicero, 202
  constancy, 375
  deliberative authors, 36
  intentionalism, 151
  Julius Caesar, 162n
  and liberalism, 356
  moral luck, 140–4, 160n
  passions, 163n
  Roman, 289
  Roman plays, 12–13
  Seneca, 159–60n
  Socrates, 80
  suicide, 149–50
Strabo, 5
Straus, Leo, 353, 371n
Strier, Richard, 20n, 317–18, 324,
    324n, 325n
structural imagination, 123–8
suicide, 149–50, 157, 183–4, 217–18,
    249, 254, 257, 312–13

Tacitus, 214n
The Taming of the Shrew, 179n
Taylor, Charles, 43, 344
  Sources of the Self, 111, 303
Taylor, Gary, 23n
Taylor, George Coffin, 3–4, 288

Shakspere's Debt to Montaigne, xxii–xxiii, xxiii–xxiv n, 3–4, 21n, 325n
The Tempest, 296–325
  'Of the Caniballes', xxi, 2, 5, 10, 16, 17, 22n, 25n
  'Of Crueltie', xviii, 5–6
  Daniel, Samuel, 179n
  'Des Cannibales', 2, 16–18, 20n, 284
  Go, Kenji, 10–11
  Gonzalo (character), xxi, 2, 5, 10–11, 16–18, 20n, 22n, 25n
  Jacobean England, 285
  Kirsch, Arthur, 9–10
  'Montaignian moments' in, 3
  narrative, 113
  Prospero (character), xviii, 5–6, 113
  source study, 35
  tragedy and comedy, 270–2, 278–9
theatrical performance, 379–81
  actors and audience, 87n
Thevet, André, 5
Thier, Jean du, 293
Thomson, Judith Jarvis, 154–5
Thorne, Christian, 382n
Titus Andronicus, 37, 363
Torquemada, 384
Tournon, André, 358, 376
tragedy and comedy, 263–81
translation, 62, 66, 76n
Trevor, Douglas, 11, 25n
trials, 282–95
Trinquet, Roger, 383n
Troilus and Cressida, 233–4, 258, 269
  Troilus (character), 223
Twelfth Night, 123–8, 311
  Feste (character), 243n
  Orsino (character), 125–6
  Viola (character), 127–8, 131
The Two Gentlemen of Verona, 82

'universal law', 336–7
utopianism, 291, 365

Van Loon, Hendrik Willem, *Van Loon's Lives*, 384, 390–1
Venus and Adonis, 214n
verbal parallels, xxii–xxiii, xxiii–xxiv n, 3–7
Vesalius, Andreas, *De humani corporis*, 186
Villey, Pierre, 4, 21n, 36, 143
Villey-Saulnier edition of Montaigne, 36, 324n
violence, 78–89
Virgil, 37
virtue, 141–2, 151, 156, 161n, 349
Vitkus, Daniel, 51–2, 381, 385, 389
Voltaire, 353
voluntarism, 338, 340

Weber, Max, 103
Whitehead, Alfred North, 340
  Process and Reality, 326
Wilde, Oscar, 33
Williams, Bernard, 45–6, 150, 159, 211n, 298, 324n, 348
Williams, Travis, 23n
Wilson, J. Dover, 329
  The Fortunes of Falstaff, 361–3
Wilson, Jeffrey, 355
The Winter's Tale, 35, 154, 206–7, 270, 272–9, 281n, 305, 316
  Hermione (character), 206–7
Wittgenstein, Ludwig, *Philosophical Investigations*, 12–13, 133, 138–9n, 211n, 215n
Wootton, David, 211n

Yachnin, Paul, 2–3, 10, 21n, 262n, 325n
Yates, Frances A., 76n